International Productivity and Competitiveness

International Productivity and Competitiveness

Edited by

BERT G. HICKMAN

New York • Oxford
OXFORD UNIVERSITY PRESS
1992

Oxford University Press

Oxford   New York   Toronto
Delhi   Bombay   Calcutta   Madras   Karachi
Petaling Jaya   Singapore   Hong Kong   Tokyo
Nairobi   Dar es Salaam   Cape Town
Melbourne   Auckland
and associated companies in
Berlin   Ibadan

Published by Oxford University Press, Inc.,
200 Madison Avenue, New York, New York 10016

Oxford is a registered trademark of Oxford University Press

Library of Congress Cataloging-in-Publication Data
International productivity and competitiveness /
edited by Bert G. Hickman.
p. cm. Includes bibliographical references and index.
ISBN 0-19-506515-8
1. Industrial productivity—Congresses. 2. Competition,
International—Congresses. I. Hickman, Bert G., 1924–
HC79.I52I6   1992
338.6'048—dc20   90-39134

9 8 7 6 5 4 3 2 1

Printed in the United States of America
on acid-free paper

Acknowledgments

Each chapter in this volume is a revised version of a paper originally presented at the Conference on International Productivity and Competitiveness held in Palo Alto, California, October 28–30, 1988. The conference was sponsored by the Social Science Research Council Committee on Economic Stability and Growth. Members of the organizing committee were Hidekazu Eguchi (Hitotsubashi University), Herbert Giersch (Kiel Institute for World Economics), Bert G. Hickman (Stanford University), Lawrence R. Klein (University of Pennsylvania), and William D. Nordhaus (Yale University). The generous financial support of the Ford and Sloan foundations and the Japan-United States Friendship Fund is gratefully acknowledged.

Thanks are due to our colleagues who contributed their time and expertise as invited discussants and whose comments on the papers served to sharpen and enhance the final versions: Orazio Attanasio (Stanford University), Robert M. Coen (Northwestern University), Paul A. David (Stanford University), Hidekazu Eguchi, Robert Eisner (Northwestern University), Harry Huizinga (Stanford University), Pierre Lasserre (University of Montreal and MIT), John M. Litwack (Stanford University), Ronald I. McKinnon (Stanford University), William D. Nordhaus, J. R. Norsworthy (Rensselaer Polytechnic Institute), Daniel L. Okimoto (Stanford University), Peter Pauly (University of Pennsylvania), Peter A. Petri (Brandeis University), Margaret Slade (University of British Columbia), and T. N. Srinivasan (Yale University).

Contents

1. International Productivity and Competitiveness:
   An Overview   3
   Bert G. Hickman

   I GLOBAL PERSPECTIVES

2. Restructuring of the World Economy   33
   Lawrence R. Klein

3. Aggregate Productivity and Growth
   in an International Comparative Setting   49
   John F. Helliwell and Alan Chung

4. Productivity, Competitiveness, and
   Export Growth in Developing Countries   80
   F. Gerard Adams, Jere R. Behrman, and Michael Boldin

5. Productivity, Competitiveness, and
   the Socialist System   97
   Gur Ofer

   II COMPARATIVE STUDIES OF MARKET ECONOMIES

6. An International Comparison of Manufacturing
   Productivity and Unit Labor Cost Trends   137
   Arthur Neef

7. Intercountry Changes in Productivity in the
   Manufacturing Sector of Five OECD Countries, 1963–86   158
   Klaus Conrad

8. An International Comparison of the
   Multisectoral Production Structure of the United States,
   West Germany, and Japan   177
   Mitsuo Saito and Ichiro Tokutsu

9. Productivity and International Competitiveness in Japan
   and the United States, 1960–85   203
   Dale W. Jorgenson and Masahiro Kuroda

10. International Competitiveness of U.S.
    and Japanese Manufacturing Industries   230
    Toshiko Tange

III   U.S. INTERNATIONAL COMPETITIVENESS

11. Macroeconomic Policies, Competitiveness, and
    U.S. External Adjustment   255
    Peter Hooper

12. U.S. Competitiveness and the Exchange Rate: A General
    Equilibrium Analysis of the U.S. Economy, 1982–86   276
    Irma Adelman and Sherman Robinson

13. Technology, Capital Formation, and
    U.S. Competitiveness   299
    Ralph Landau

IV   COUNTRY STUDIES

14. Price and Output Adjustment in
    Japanese Manufacturing   329
    William H. Branson and Richard C. Marston

15. The Trade and Industrial Policies of Postwar Japan:
    A Theoretical Perspective   345
    Motoshige Itoh and Kazuharu Kiyono

16. Protection and International Competitiveness: A View from
    West Germany   362
    Gernot Klepper and Frank D. Weiss

Index   393

Contributors

F. Gerard Adams
University of Pennsylvania

Irma Adelman
University of California, Berkeley

Michael Boldin
University of Pennsylvania

William H. Branson
Princeton University

Alan Chung
University of British Columbia

Klaus Conrad
University of Mannheim

John F. Helliwell
University of British Columbia

Bert G. Hickman
Stanford University

Peter Hooper
Federal Reserve Board

Motoshige Itoh
University of Tokyo

Dale W. Jorgenson
Harvard University

Kazuharu Kiyono
Gakushuin University

Lawrence R. Klein
University of Pennsylvania

Gernot Klepper
Kiel Institute for World Economics

Masahiro Kuroda
Keio University

Ralph Landau
Listowel Inc. and
Stanford University

Richard C. Marston
University of Pennsylvania

Arthur Neef
United States Bureau of Labor
Statistics

Gur Ofer
Hebrew University and the
Brookings Institution

Sherman Robinson
University of California, Berkeley

Mitsuo Saito
Kobe University

Toshiko Tange
Kanto Gakuin University

Ichiro Tokutsu
Kobe University

Frank D. Weiss
Kiel Institute for World Economics

International Productivity and Competitiveness: An Overview

BERT G. HICKMAN

This book is about the determinants of productivity growth and competitiveness on an international scale. It deals with arguably the most important problems facing contemporary economies. In the United States, the rapid increase in our current-account deficit during the 1980s and our slow rate of productivity growth in comparison to other advanced economies raised the specter of declining competitiveness. From a less parochial viewpoint, the changing structure of the global economy is a matter of worldwide interest in an age of increasing international interdependence of trade and finance. One index of this worldwide interest is the multinational authorship of the chapters in this volume, which includes economists from Canada, Israel, Germany, and Japan in addition to the United States.

The volume attempts to convey the "state of the art" of contemporary research on international competitiveness through papers covering a number of complementary topics, tools, and approaches. The authors were given wide latitude as to the specific concepts of productivity measurement and competitiveness to be employed and the particular subjects to be emphasized within their general area. Several papers endeavor to clarify thinking about "competitiveness" by developing formal definitions of the concept and relating it to more conventional concepts such as productivity. Some of the papers provide a macroeconomic perspective, whereas others deal with microeconomic aspects of individual industries, sectors, and policies. Some make use of econometric or general equilibrium models, others of quantitative-historical analyses of indexes of productivity and costs, and still others of verbal analyses emphasizing theoretical or institutional aspects of competitiveness.

This chapter provides an overview of the contents of the volume. The first section describes the concepts and measures of productivity and competitiveness used and discusses price and output conversion in international comparisons. The contents of the individual chapters are summarized in the second section, and the chapter concludes with some comments on key findings and issues cutting across the individual papers.

BASIC CONCEPTS

Productivity Concepts and Measures

Productivity measurement is best considered in relation to the concept of the production function as a description of technology. In the two-factor case appropriate for value-added measures of output, for example, the production function may be written as

$$Q = F(K,L,t) \qquad (1\text{-}1)$$

Thus output Q is a function of the inputs of capital K and labor L. The variable t indexes time and allows for *technical change,* defined as a shift in the production function holding factor inputs fixed. In the special case of *Hicks-neutral* technical change, which simply increases the output attainable from given inputs without altering their marginal rate of substitution, the function may be written in the form

$$Q = A(t) f(K,L) \qquad (1\text{-}2)$$

where the multiplicative factor $A(t)$ measures the cumulative effect of technical change or progress over time.

One way to provide an empirical estimate of $A(t)$ is to estimate the parameters of the production function. For example, one common approach is to assume a Cobb–Douglas function and exponential progress

$$Q = A\, e^{\Gamma t}\, K^\alpha\, L^\beta \qquad (1\text{-}3)$$

where Γ is the rate of technical progress and α and β are the output elasticities of capital and labor inputs, respectively.

Technical progress and *labor productivity,* or output per unit of labor input, may be related through the production function:

$$Q/L = A\, e^{\Gamma t} K^\alpha L^{\beta-1} \qquad (1\text{-}4)$$

In the case of constant returns to scale, $\alpha + \beta = 1$, and Equation 1-4 can be rewritten as

$$Q/L = A\, e^{\Gamma t}\, (K/L)^\alpha \qquad (1\text{-}5)$$

Viewed over time, this expression factors the growth of labor productivity between technical progress at the rate Γ and the rate of change of the capital–labor ratio, or the rate of *capital deepening.* Even without technical change, capital formation may increase labor productivity by increasing the ratio of capital and labor inputs.

Equation 1-3 can be rearranged to yield an expression for *total factor pro-*

ductivity, TFP, defined as output per unit of total factor input, where the combined inputs are weighted by their output elasticities:

$$TFP = Q / (K^\alpha L^\beta) = A\ e^{\Gamma t} \tag{1-6}$$

Thus Hicks-neutral technical progress is a synonym for TFP growth and is frequently estimated as a separable expotential time trend in the production function.

An alternative approach to the measurement of technical change does not require the specification and estimation of the production function. As shown in the classic article of Solow (1957),[1] logarithmic differentiation of Equation 1-2 leads to

$$\dot{Q}/\dot{Q} = \dot{A}/A + w_K\ \dot{K}/K + w_L\ \dot{L}/L \tag{1-7}$$

where w_K and w_L are the proportional marginal products or output elasticities of capital and labor, respectively. Given the output elasticities, Equation 1-7 is easily solved for the rate of technical change from data on the rates of change of output and factor inputs. Under constant returns to scale, the elasticities sum to unity, so that

$$\dot{Q}/Q - \dot{L}/L = \dot{A}/A + w_K\ (\dot{K}/K - \dot{L}/L) \tag{1-8}$$

Thus the rate of change of labor productivity depends on the rate of technical progress and the rate of capital deepening.

Equations 1-7 and 1-8 form the theoretical basis of growth accounting. On the assumption of constant returns to scale and perfectly competitive markets for products and factors, the latter are paid their marginal products and the output elasticities in production, which are equal to the factor shares in the value of output, may be estimated from data on the latter. An index of the rate of TFP growth may then be computed from data on the changes in output and inputs, and the relative contributions of the inputs and of technical change to the change in either total output or labor productivity are readily calculated.

Many of the chapters in this volume utilize empirical measures of labor or total factor productivity or both. The simplest concept is labor productivity, which requires data only on output and hours of employment for direct computation. The U.S. Bureau of Labor Statistics regularly publishes estimates of labor productivity, as measured by output per hour, in manufacturing for twelve industrial economies. These time series form the basis for the analysis of international productivity trends during 1960–87 in Neef and are also used by Klein. Chapter 5 by Ofer compares estimated annual rates of growth of GDP per employed person (for lack of data with which to calculate TFP) during 1950–85 for the socialist, OECD, and developing economies. Table 4-1 of Adams, Behrman, and Boldin shows the average and standard deviation from 1974 to 1986 of the growth rate of GDP per worker for two groups of developing countries and one of industrialized countries. The *level* of aggregate manufacturing output per hour in the United States is compared with that for an aggregate of ten OECD countries at selected intervals from 1960 to 1988 by Hooper.

The concept of technical progress or TFP figures prominently in several

other chapters. In Chapter 10, Tange estimates three-factor Cobb–Douglas production functions with Hicks-neutral progress for gross output in nine matched
manufacturing industries for Japan and the United States. A more elaborate
formulation is provided by Saito and Tokutsu, who estimate two-level constant
elasticity of substitution (CES), four-factor (KLEM) production functions incorporating Hicks-neutral progress and capital, labor, energy, and materials
inputs for individual manufacturing industries in Germany, Japan, and the
United States. A conceptually different approach is used by Helliwell and
Chung, who estimate two-factor CES production functions for aggregate output
in nineteen industrial countries, but with technical progress specified to be
purely labor-augmenting, or Harrod-neutral, in form. Hence they interpret
their estimated rate of technical progress as a measure of the trend rate of
growth of labor productivity or efficiency rather than total factor productivity.
    Variations on the growth-accounting approach to direct computation of in-
dexes of productivity change are also featured in several chapters. Thus Saito
and Tokutsu compute TFP indexes using Denison's (1962) method, based on
Equation 1-7, for comparison with their production-function estimates of
Hicks-neutral technical progress.
    A similar growth-accounting approach is used by Jorgenson and Kuroda,
except that their TFP indexes for Japan and the United States are based on the
price dual to the (translog) production function and hence are computed as the
difference between the change in output price and the weighted average of
changes in input prices, with weights given by the value shares of the inputs.
Finally, Conrad combines the two approaches, using index methods to compute
annual productivity gaps among five countries and an econometric model of
the cost dual to explain the sources of change in the gaps. It should be noted
that the theoretical specification used in these two studies does *not* assume the
technical progress or productivity increase is Hicks-neutral, allowing instead
for biased technical change along with a neutral component of progress (Jorgenson, Gollop, and Fraumeni, 1987, Chapter 2).

Concepts and Measures of Competitiveness

The concept of international competitiveness has many dimensions among the
various authors in this volume. The broadcast definition is offered by Landau:
"What we should mean by competitiveness, and thus the principal goal of our
economic policy, is the ability to sustain, in a global economy, an acceptable
growth in the real standard of living of the population with an acceptably fair
distribution, while efficiently providing employment for substantially all who
can and wish to work, and doing so without reducing the growth potential in
the standard of living of future generations." Thus he is basically concerned
with the determinants of productivity growth in an open economy where
growth in living standards cannot be independent of international competitiveness.
    Another broad view of competitiveness is taken in the chapter by Ofer on
the socialist economies. He judges the level of competitiveness of a country by
four criteria: performance in catching up to the leading countries, as reflected

in faster productivity gains; the effect of trade policies on growth and comparative advantage; choice of growth strategy as affecting industrial structure and technical change; and particular characteristics involving history, natural endowments, and location of a country.

Other chapters deal with particular aspects of competitiveness. Thus Adelman and Robinson focus on changes in the structure and volume of U.S. trade arising from changes in relative prices, especially as resulting from short-run macroeconomic forces affecting the real exchange rate. In Chapter 16 Klepper and Weiss associate "international competitiveness" with "comparative advantage" and thus are concerned with the long-term consequences of protectionist policies in Germany for its trade volume and structure. Similarly, Itoh and Kiyono offer a theoretical analysis of the long-run effects of early postwar protection for infant industries on the subsequent penetration of world markets by Japan.

The most pervasive concept, however, is *price* competitiveness, although this again has many dimensions and indexes. One widely used decomposition underlies the Bureau of Labor Statistics (BLS) measures of manufacturing productivity and unit labor cost in twelve countries. The published tables include output per hour (Q/L) and hourly compensation (W) in national currency units, and unit labor cost in national currency units ($ULCN$) and dollars (ULC), all of which are related in the identity

$$ULC \equiv E * ULCN \equiv E * W * (Q/L) \tag{1-9}$$

where E is the exchange rate in dollars per national currency unit. Provided prices track costs closely, one may use these dollar-denominated measures of unit labor cost to compare relative prices and competitiveness among the various countries in a common currency and to decompose changes in competitiveness between changes in relative productivity, relative wage inflation, and the exchange rate. See, for example, the chapters by Klein, Neef, and Hooper in this volume, which examine relative trends in unit labor costs in their discussions of productivity and competitiveness.

In another application of cost comparisons, Tange presents an econometric model of the export competitiveness of Japan and the United States with constant markups over average *total* cost, so that (unmeasured) relative export prices are assumed to be proportional to (measured) relative unit costs. Changes in unit cost in turn are estimated from a weighted average of changes in the prices of labor, capital, and materials; changes in output (to reflect scale economies); and the rate of TFP growth, bypassing direct measurement of average total costs by industry and facilitating a decomposition of the sources of changes in relative costs over time. Saito and Tokutsu also assume constant markups in their cost-based concept of the rate of change of competitive power due to technical change, which accounts for the cost-reducing influence of TFP growth but abstracts from the effects of changes in relative factor prices or markups.

One problem with cost comparisons is that price markups may vary to drive a wedge between changes in relative costs and relative prices. Moreover, when exchange rates change, domestic prices may be adjusted to stabilize the foreign-currency prices of exports. Branson and Marston, for instance, conclude from their econometric model of markup pricing that Japanese manufacturers systematically vary their profit margins to absorb the impact of exchange-rate fluctuations on their competitive positions in overseas markets. As a result, when the yen appreciates, only a portion of the gain is "passed through" into prices of Japanese exports expressed in dollars and other foreign currencies, mitigating the effects of the appreciation on current-account positions at home and abroad.

In theories of markup pricing behavior, firms are assumed to be price set-ters on imperfect markets, no matter whether the markups are assumed to be variable or fixed, or whether they are applied to unit costs for all inputs or for labor alone, or to marginal cost. Another important approach assumes that markets are perfectly competitive and always in long-term equilibrium, so that the observed price always equals average total cost, as measured by the cost dual to the production function. This is the assumption used by Jorgenson and Kuroda in their computation of relative competitiveness and productivity gaps between the United States and Japan and in their decomposition of the relative price movements between changes in relative input prices and changes in rel-ative productivity levels. A modified measure of price competitiveness, also assuming perfect competition but postulating Marshallian short-run equilib-rium rather than immediate adjustment of capital input to optimal levels, is derived by Conrad, who compares the resulting productivity gaps with those based on long-run equilibrium.

Price and Output Conversion in International Comparisons

In international comparisons, *growth rates* of output or productivity are cus-tomarily calculated on the basis of quantities measured in constant national-currency prices.[2] The international comparison of output or productivity *levels*, however, requires conversion of the output and input measures to a common currency unit. This may be done using either market exchange rates or *pur-chasing-power parity rates*, where PPP is defined as the number of units of a given currency required to purchase the same amount of goods as a unit of the numeraire currency and is measured by careful sampling of prices of matching categories of goods in the various countries. The two methods would be equiv-alent if the market exchange rate always equaled PPP, that is, if the PPP theory of exchange-rate determination always held in absolute form, so that the mar-ket rate always adjusted to offset incipient changes in relative price levels in national currency units. It is well known, however, that large deviations be-tween the two rates are persistent and that exchange-rate conversions system-atically understate per capita real GDP for lower income countries relative to richer countries, by as much as two or three times for the poorest countries (Kravis, 1984). The biases from exchange-rate conversion are much smaller for comparisons among high-income countries, but even here swings in market rates substantially affect real exchange rates over the short run, as shown by Hooper in Chapter 11.

Several of the conference papers employ PPP rates to convert quantities, prices, or both, for their analyses of the patterns and convergence of productivity levels among groups of countries. Thus Helliwell and Chung use recent estimates of PPPs from the OECD to convert the constant-price measures of GDP in national currencies for nineteen industrial countries into common units of "international dollars." Similarly, Adams, Behrman, and Boldin utilize PPP data on per capita incomes drawn from the International Comparison Project (ICP) for their study of ninety-five developing and industrial market economies. Conrad employs PPPs for total manufacturing outputs and inputs in his estimates of the trends in absolute productivity gaps between four European countries and the United States. Jorgenson and Kuroda calculate yen/dollar PPPs for total industrial output (value added) and for gross output in twenty-nine individual industries, together with the associated PPPs for the relevant inputs, as data for their analysis of trends in price competitiveness and productivity gaps between the United States and Japan.[3] Finally, Hooper uses PPPs to compute comparative levels of manufacturing productivity in the United States and a grouping of eleven industrial countries.

In all of these studies, the underlying PPP levels are estimated from direct price comparisons only in a single base year. The base-year PPP provides the conversion factor to shift the level of an entire national-currency constant-price income or output series to a dollar (or international dollar) basis. Similarly, the base-year PPP may be used to adjust the ratio of the national-currency price index to the numeraire price level in the base year. The base-year PPP is then extrapolated to earlier and later years in the sample by the ratio of the national-currency price indexes for the comparison and numeraire countries. Thus the benchmark PPPs serve to adjust the levels of the price and quantity series in relation to the numeraire country while preserving the original time paths and variances of prices and quantities in each country's social accounts for estimating behavioral parameters.

Intercountry comparisons of prices as well as incomes must be made in a common currency unit, and yet the estimated PPPs are ratios of prices in national-currency units to prices in the numeraire currency (e.g., the number of yen required in Japan to purchase an amount of output costing one dollar in the United States). For comparisons of international competitiveness, the PPPs are therefore converted to a relative price R, denominated in, say, dollars, through division by the national currency/dollar market exchange rate, $1/E$, the reciprocal of the dollar/national currency rate defined earlier, so that

$$R = E\,(PC/P) \tag{1-10}$$

where PC/P is the ratio of the national-currency price level (PC) in the comparison country to the U.S. price level (P) in dollars. Thus R shows the number of dollars required in country C to buy an amount of output costing one dollar in the United States. When applied to an individual industry, R is simply a relative price; when applied to aggregate price levels, it is an expression for the *real exchange rate* between the two countries, defined as the nominal exchange rate adjusted for changes in purchasing power in the two countries. The con-

cept of the real exchange rate is independent of the precise measurement of
PC/P, of course, so that it applies equally to price variables taken directly from
the social accounts of each country and not to the PPP-based price indexes,
but the latter are generally preferred for international comparisons involving
real quantities as well as prices.

In Chapter 9 Jorgenson and Kuroda plot the relative prices for twenty-nine
manufacturing industries in Japan and the United States from 1960 to 1985 and
account for their principal fluctuations in terms of the relative movements of
factor prices and productivity in the two countries. On the aggregative level,
Helliwell and Chung present estimates of the PPP-based real exchange rates
for their sample of nineteen industrial countries in 1980 and 1985 and explore
the relationship between the relative price and GDP levels, finding that countries with higher GDPs tend to have higher price levels.

TOPICAL SURVEY

Global Perspectives

Part I provides a global perspective on productivity and growth among the developed and developing economies and the planned and market economies.

In "Restructuring of the World Economy," Lawrence R. Klein offers a per-
ceptive discussion of the ongoing process of structural change, providing a historical perspective and commentary on many of the topics that receive more
detailed analysis in subsequent chapters. These include the slowdown of productivity growth in the world economy after the energy shock of 1973, the
perceived relative decline in manufacturing activity in the industrialized economies, shifts in the composition of international production and trade, the U.S.
trade deficit and its implications for U.S. competitiveness, and the emergence
of newly industrialized economies (NIEs) on world markets.

The identity relating price (local foreign currency, LFC) to the product of
the wage rate (in dollars), unit labor requirements (reciprocal of labor productivity), the profit margin, and the exchange rate (LFC/dollar), provides the
framework for a descriptive quantitative analysis of the contributions of the
various factors to changes in competitiveness since 1960. The large role of exchange depreciation in the recent improvements of U.S. competitiveness is
noted, and the need for greater reliance on policies to improve technical progress and productivity growth as essential ingredients in the fundamental restructuring process is stressed. In this connection, the preferred concept is
total factor productivity. To establish the importance of energy and its role in
the productivity slowdown after 1973, production functions and productivity
indexes should be defined for gross output and should include energy and other
intermediate inputs.

With regard to U.S. policy, Klein's recommendations include raising the
saving and investment ratios and easing interest rates as stimuli to capital formation; increased investment in education and research and development
(R&D) activities is also suggested. The need for a better balance of fiscal and

monetary policies domestically and better international policy coordination is also stressed. Selective industrial policies may enhance competitiveness, and direct intervention in the energy field is endorsed, since the market solution has not been satisfactory.

In "Aggregate Productivity and Growth in an International Comparative Setting," John F. Helliwell and Alan Chung investigate several aspects of the interaction among productivity, competitiveness, and economic growth. They begin by using national income data from the World Bank and the International Monetary Fund for twenty industrialized and sixty-nine developing countries to explore the linkages among investment, domestic and foreign saving, and growth rates of income per capita. Their correlations and regressions covering 1973–83 show strong linkages between investment shares and growth rates but no evidence that countries with higher growth rates made greater use of foreign savings to finance their domestic investment outlays. The positive correlation between investment and growth rates, they stress, does not necessarily mean that high investment produces high growth, since causation may run from growth to investment via an accelerator or capital stock adjustment mechanism. Another finding, suggesting that for many countries growth is primarily export-led, is that countries with stronger net exports, for given levels of investment, also tend to have higher average growth rates of real GNP.

The same data for eighty-nine countries are also used to test the hypothesis that the international transferability of knowledge and goods entails a process of convergence of the levels of income among countries, so that from any given starting point, countries with lower initial income levels will have higher growth rates than richer countries. The cross-section regressions support the hypothesis, although the effect is rather weak.

Next, Helliwell and Chung turn to a sample of nineteen industrial countries for which comparable data are available on output, capital stocks, and employment annually from 1960 to 1985. The data are converted to common dollar units using purchasing-power parity (PPP) exchange rates as the most appropriate means of obtaining internationally comparable measures of real outputs and inputs. A two-factor CES production function framework assuming the same substitution and scale parameters for each country permits the estimation of comparable indexes of Harrod-neutral technical progress or productivity for the nineteen countries.

These productivity indexes are then used to test two versions of the convergence hypothesis. In the first, it is assumed that each country experiences constant technical progress over time at a rate which varies inversely with its initial income level. The regression results provide fairly strong evidence of convergence of productivity levels among the nineteen industrialized countries since 1960.

A specific model of convergence is tested in the second version, in which it is assumed that each of the other countries was gradually converging toward the productivity growth rate, and possibly the productivity level, of the United States from 1960 to 1985. This hypothesis is also supported by the data, with the results showing general convergence, albeit at differing rates across countries and to levels differing from that of the United States in most countries.

Additional evidence is adduced in support of the hypothesis that the process of convergence was augmented by the increasing internationalization of markets for goods and services during the period. According to the Helliwell–Chung tests, moreover, this convergence model dominates an alternative explanation of the observed narrowing of productivity growth differentials over time, namely, that a general slowdown of technical progress occurred beginning in 1974 because of energy shocks or for other reasons.

In their concluding section, Helliwell and Chung investigate the reverse linkage between productivity increases and competitiveness. Although productivity increases necessarily translate into lower unit costs in individual firms and industries, given factor prices and exchange rates, aggregate productivity increases may actually reduce foreign competitiveness overall by inducing higher real exchange rates, both because of induced increases in real wages and because growing current-account surpluses must eventually be equilibrated by the real exchange rate to maintain macroeconomic balance of savings, investment, and portfolio preferences. Their empirical evidence shows that countries with higher real incomes per capita tend to have higher real exchange rates as measured by the ratio of the PPP and market exchange rates against the dollar, so that when income-improving productivity advancements become important at the aggregate level, they tend to increase the real exchange rate and reduce the international competitiveness of the richer countries.

Whereas Helliwell and Chung concentrate on the industrialized countries in their cross-sectional international comparisons, a complementary paper by F. Gerard Adams, Jere R. Behrman, and Michael Boldin focuses on "Productivity, Competitiveness, and Export Growth in Developing Countries." Their basic sample comprises annual data for 1974–86 and is taken from the International Comparison Project (ICP) based on careful PPP comparisons. The sample of ninety-five countries is divided between thirty-five low-income countries, forty-one middle-income countries, and nineteen industrial countries. An introductory section of their chapter compares the historical experience of the three country groupings with regard to export performance and the growth rates of GDP and labor productivity, discusses alternative estimates of technical progress and their imprecision in this data set, and stresses that the correlation between export performance and income growth—the primary focus of the chapter—does not resolve the question of causation, which could run in either or both directions.

They begin the econometric analysis by estimating pooled Cobb–Douglas (CD) production functions for each of the three country groups and for all countries combined. No allowance is made for technical progress in this initial specification. The marginal product of capital in both the middle- and low-income groups is substantially higher than in the industrialized countries, because capital is less plentiful, capital markets are imperfect, or investment risks are greater in the developing countries. Adult literacy rates and school enrollment rates are insignificant when added to the specification as indicators of human capital accumulation.

The authors turn next to an investigation of the impact of export growth on overall output growth, using a two-sector model developed by Gershon Feder and modified by the authors to take explicit account of capital depreciation in the measurement of net capital formation. The results are unsatisfactory for the low-income countries, with insignificant coefficients for most of the variables, perhaps owing to the poor quality of the data or even to an inability of these economies to properly utilize their resources.

Better results are obtained for the middle-income developing economies, however, where there is significant statistical evidence that the export industries are more productive, reflecting the substantial duality between the traditional and advanced sectors in such economies and the positive externalities exhibited by exports with respect to production in the rest of the economy.

Finally, the authors add an initial-conditions variable in the form of GDP per capita in 1974 to the Feder model to test for convergence of growth rates among the middle-income group, with similar results to those of Helliwell and Chung, namely, that growth rates are slower, other factors constant, for countries with initially higher incomes per capita. The convergence hypothesis is not tested for the high-income sample of countries, however, since the data rejected the basic Feder model of export-led growth in these industrialized economies, which lack the sectoral production duality of the LDCs.

In a concluding section the authors estimate several reduced-form equations for the middle-income group to explain GDP growth and two of its important determinants, investment shares and export growth, with generally disappointing results. They find that investment is determined principally by GDP growth through the accelerator effect, plus lagged investment, and that other variables, including export growth, do not have statistically significant effects. Export growth is significantly related only to its own past level, and it appears to be uncorrelated with real exchange rates. The reduced forms for GDP show no significant association of growth rates with literacy, capital inflows, or openness to international trade, appearing to depend only on past export and investment performance and initial per capita income. They conclude accordingly that disentanglement of structure and causation must be left to additional research, perhaps using a richer data set in a time-series setting rather than the cross-sectional approach of their chapter.

In "Productivity, Competitiveness, and the Socialist System," Gur Ofer compares the productivity growth and trade performance of the Soviet Union, East Germany, Czechoslovakia, Poland, Hungary, Bulgaria, and Romania with the advanced market economies and the middle- and low-income developing economies, and he concludes that the centrally planned economies (CPEs) did not advance relative to most industrialized economies in their last thirty years but instead may have deteriorated. To account for these developments, he poses the question in a general growth-theoretic framework which predicts convergence of follower economies to leaders because of technological diffusion, and then he explains the failure of the CPEs to achieve convergence by their autarkic trade policies emphasizing import substitution, their extensive growth strategy concentrating on expansion of heavy industry, and their comparative disadvantage in the production and diffusion of technological change.

Professor Ofer's empirical evidence on comparative productivity growth consists primarily of data on GDP per employed worker for 1950–85 and covers the CPEs in detail, the United States, the OECD as a whole, and aggregates for the upper and lower middle-income countries. Consideration of the data on labor productivity, together with an appraisal of investment and education trends in the CPEs, lead to the conclusion that those limited advances that have been achieved by the CPEs since 1950 have been due to human and physical capital formation more than any increase in total factor productivity or technical progress. Direct estimates of total factor productivity for the Soviet Union show an average improvement of 0.7 percent per year from 1950 to 1980, with a drop from 1.6 percent in 1950–60 to negative figures in recent years.

The focus of the second part of the paper is on the lasting adverse consequences for competitiveness of the import-substitution growth strategy adopted in the late 1920s and early 1930s in the Soviet Union and imposed or emulated by its Eastern European satellites after World War II. With its emphasis on rapid development of heavy industry as a basis for large domestic investment and military programs, the strategy emphasized economic self-sufficiency rather than competitiveness on world markets as the primary goal. For this and other reasons discussed by Ofer, including the conduct of foreign trade through state monopolies that insulated the domestic sector from foreign competition, it appears that most of the CPEs missed trade opportunities in sectors with potential comparative advantage, such as agriculture, food products, and consumer manufactures, and were unable to develop a compensating advantage in metals and machinery.

In his section on trade structure and trade direction, Ofer presents and evaluates data on exports and market shares for the CPEs and several groupings of market economies, including the OECD and NIEs. He concludes that over the twenty years or so that preceded the failure of the CPEs, these economies did not attain the role in the world market that was to be expected from their stage of economic development but instead lost their "natural" place to the NIEs.

The concluding section of the chapter concerns the economic reforms in the CPEs, including efforts to overcome the protectionist and isolationist policies of the past and eventually to reach a long-term goal of full convertibility of the ruble. However, these initiatives in the international sector cannot succeed without supporting domestic reforms. There is a need for a much more flexible system of price determination, in addition to more correct prices. It is also necessary to create a favorable environment for a fast development of financial, commercial, and business services to handle the new foreign economic activities. According to a 1986 estimate of Abram Bergson, the socialist economic system is less efficient than market economies at a similar stage of development by a margin of 25–30 percent, implying that there is a substantial potential for productivity gains under a reformed system. However, owing to the scope and time-consuming nature of the needed reforms, Ofer concludes that it does not take a hopeless pessimist to foresee no such developments taking place in the very near future.

Market Economies

The chapters in Part II involve comparative studies of market economies. The most comprehensive in terms of country coverage is "An International Comparison of Manufacturing Productivity and Unit Labor Cost Trends," by Arthur Neef of the Bureau of Labor Statistics. For many years the BLS has prepared annual measures of output per hour, hourly compensation costs, and unit labor costs for the United States, Canada, Japan, and nine European economies. Neef presents a descriptive analysis of productivity and cost trends since 1960, comments on various issues of measurement and interpretation of the data, and introduces new measures for component manufacturing industries covering the United States, Germany, and Japan. These new measures are used to analyze the contribution of relative shifts in labor inputs among the component industries to each country's manufacturing productivity gains and to compare the pace of productivity growth in industry detail among the three countries.

The chapter also documents the general slowdown of productivity growth after 1973 in the manufacturing sectors of these twelve countries and also the strong rebounds that occurred in the United States and the United Kingdom from 1979 to 1987. The U.S. rebound was primarily a reflection of the sharp increase in productivity growth in computers. Productivity growth in nonelectrical machinery, which includes the computer industry in the U.S. classification system, jumped from 0.8 percent in 1973–79 to 10.6 percent in 1979–85. For manufacturing as a whole, the corresponding gain is from 1.4 to 3.4 percent, but the rise was from 1.5 to only 2.2 percent if nonelectrical machinery is excluded from the total index.

Over the entire period from 1960 to 1987, the United States had the lowest and Japan the highest growth rate of labor productivity. Hourly compensation increased the least in the United States over the same period, however, so that unit labor costs in the United States showed the smallest average annual increase on a national-currency basis over the entire period, although it ran ahead of Japan and Germany after 1973. When unit costs are measured in U.S. dollars to allow for exchange-rate movements, however, it is found that unit labor costs in the United States rose less than in Japan and Europe in 1973–79, continued to rise as dollar appreciation actually decreased unit costs elsewhere in 1979–85, and then fell slightly as unit costs skyrocketed abroad with dollar depreciation in 1985–87.

Next Klaus Conrad writes about "Intercountry Changes in Productivity in the Manufacturing Sector of Five OECD Countries, 1963–1986." This is a technical study applying production and cost theory to the quantitative analysis of productivity gaps between the United States and the United Kingdom, Italy, France, and West Germany. Conrad's methodology attributes the difference in manufacturing output levels among countries, for given common quantities of factor inputs (labor, capital, electricity, and nonelectric fuel), to short-run differences in the utilization of capital, on the one hand, and to differences in technology, or relative levels of the production function in the various countries, on the other. Thus his measure of the purely technological gap refers to a state of long-term equilibrium and is purged of any element occurring from short-term or cyclical disequilibrium and resulting in an efficiency gap from being off the production surface. Inputs and outputs for all countries are measured in U.S. dollars utilizing PPP exchange rates.

The empirical analysis proceeds in two steps. First, annual (Tornqvist) indexes of the productivity gaps are computed and compared for the period 1963–86. In 1963, the temporary disequilibrium gaps in the European countries ranged from 35 to 57 percent below the United States, whereas the technological shortfalls were between 26 and 58 percent. The disequilibrium shortfalls had been eliminated by 1980 in France and Germany but remained at 30 percent in the United Kingdom and 10 percent in Italy. Germany had no technological gap in 1980, but in France a small technological shortfall was offset by a positive efficiency gap, and the overall shortfall in Italy was due to relative inefficiency rather than a technological gap vis-à-vis the United States. Large efficiency and technological gaps both contributed to the continuing large productivity gap for the United Kingdom. Thus Conrad's results show substantial convergence to the United States in productivity *levels* for France, Germany, and Italy, but not for the United Kingdom, by 1980. The productivity gaps enlarged again in the European countries during the early eighties, however, and by 1986 measured respectively 8, 4, 16, and 31 percent below the United States for France, Germany, Italy, and the United Kingdom on the disequilibrium basis.

In the second step of the empirical analysis, Conrad offers an econometric analysis of the productivity gaps, using a translog specification of the cost dual to the joint production function for the five countries. The estimated parameters indicate that faster rates of total factor productivity growth account for much of the reduction in the productivity gaps of the European countries in the catching-up process, but that changes in relative factor prices also affected convergence by affecting the relative input shares of labor, capital, and energy in the various countries. Hence the relatively favorable performance of the United States since 1982 is a result of worldwide moderation of wage increases rather than a change in the relative rates of technical progress in Conrad's model. However, as factor intensities and marginal productivities show a strong tendency to equalize, only changes in TFP will affect the differences in productivity over the medium run.

In "An International Comparison of the Multisectoral Production Structures of the United States, West Germany, and Japan," Mitsuo Saito and Ichiro Tokutsu estimate four-factor KLEM production functions incorporating capital, labor, energy, and materials inputs for individual manufacturing industries in the three countries. Technical progress is Hicks-neutral and the technology is defined by a two-level constant elasticity of substitution (CES) production function. Allowance is made for changes in the estimated rate of technical progress after the energy shocks of 1973 and 1979.

According to their estimates, in the United States the average rate of technical progress for manufacturing as a whole rose slightly in 1974–79 compared with 1949–73, whereas the reverse was true for Germany. In the case of Japan, the average rate of progress declined in 1974–79 and recovered some, but not all, of the loss in 1980–86. In an appendix these econometric estimates of Hicks-neutral technical progress are compared with corresponding indexes of TFP growth, calculated by the authors for the same industries and data by the Denison method. There is a striking disparity. For all three countries, the Denison-type estimates are much lower than the production-function results for the entire sample period, and after 1973 they show large decreases in the rate of productivity growth for the United States and Japan and a substantial increase for Germany.

Their econometric estimates of the elasticities of substitution and the own-price elasticities of demand for the four productive factors indicate that, among the three countries, the greatest sensitivity of labor and materials inputs to price changes is found in Japan, whereas Germany shows the highest flexibility in the demand for capital and energy inputs. Such greater flexibility leads to a larger cost reduction or increase in productive efficiency in the case of a fall in factor prices, although the authors note that the differences among the countries are not very significant in this respect.

With regard to the implications of their findings for other aspects of competitiveness, the authors point out the rate of cost reduction due to technical progress was higher in Japan than in either the United States or Germany in 1960–79 but that the margin over both countries narrowed somewhat after 1973. Similarly, Germany had a substantially higher rate of technical change than the United States throughout the period, but again the margin narrowed after the energy shock. After allowing for exchange-rate trends after 1970, however, Saito and Tokutsu conclude that the United States gained in competitiveness relative to Germany and Japan both before and after the first energy crisis, and that Japan also lost competitiveness relative to Germany in both periods. Finally, they conclude from the combined trends in technical progress and dollar depreciation that the United States had not achieved parity with Japan in the *level* of competitiveness by 1985, before the most recent round of dollar depreciation, whereas the United States had expanded its competitive advantage over Germany in the same period.

"Productivity and International Competitiveness in Japan and the United States, 1960–85," by Dale W. Jorgenson and Masahiro Kuroda, analyzes the relative performance of twenty-nine individual industries and aggregate output as a whole in Japan and the United States. Particularly noteworthy is its explicit treatment of the trends in the competitiveness, as measured by relative prices denominated in U.S. dollars, of the various industries in the two countries. The roles of the relative growth of productivity in Japanese and U.S. industries, changes in relative input prices, and changes in the market exchange rate are analyzed in explaining the trends in competitiveness of Japanese industries relative to their U.S. counterparts.

The authors prepare annual PPP (yen/dollar) indexes for inputs and outputs of the individual industries in Japan and then convert them to dollar prices by division by the market exchange rate for comparison with the corresponding price indexes for U.S. industries. For industrial output as a whole they provide a comparison of the value-added prices and associated input prices for capital

and labor; for individual industries they shift to relative gross output prices and
add input prices for energy and intermediate materials. On the aggregative
level, the price comparisons indicate that except in 1973 and 1978–79, the Japanese economy was more competitive than the U.S. economy throughout the
period 1960–85.

Using similar techniques to those employed by Conrad, Jorgenson and Kuroda also analyze the behavior over time in the relative productivity levels of
Japan and the United States, building on their earlier study for 1960–79 by
revising and extending the estimates through 1985. They conclude that average
productivity growth in both Japan and the United States has revived somewhat
since 1980, though at appreciably lower rates than prevailed before the energy
shock of 1973. According to their analysis, the convergence of Japanese and
U.S. productivity levels during the 1960s gave way to sharply divergent trends
in relative productivity during the 1970s and especially the 1980s, as the energy
crisis had a substantial impact on patterns of productivity growth by industry.
The competitiveness of U.S. industries declined in 1980–85, however, owing to
more rapidly rising input prices and to dollar appreciation during that period.

"International Competitiveness of U.S. and Japanese Manufacturing Industries," by Toshiko Tange, completes the set of comparative productivity and
cost studies. Tange focuses on cost competitiveness between the two countries,
since a continuous increase in relative unit costs must eventually be reflected
in higher relative export prices. Instead of direct measures of unit costs in the
nine manufacturing industries in her sample, however, she infers the average
annual rate of change of unit cost for gross output over discrete periods from
data on the rates of change of input prices, output, and technical progress. The
theoretical framework assumes a multifactor Cobb–Douglas production function in capital, labor, and materials inputs and incorporates unconstrained returns to scale and Hicks-neutral technical progress. Firms are assumed to minimize cost, given factor prices and the production function constraint, and the
estimated parameters of the production function provide the weights for the
unit cost expression. This expression also facilitates an explicit decomposition
of the proximate sources of the changes in unit cost.

Tange's empirical results show a slowdown of TFP growth in both countries
after 1973, but with a substantial recovery of the pace of growth in the United
States after 1980. On balance, technical progress in this sample of industries
was faster in Japan before 1973 and in the United States thereafter. When it
comes to cost trends measured in local currency units, however, Japan had a
decided advantage over the United States both before and after the energy
shocks. After 1973, energy conservation reduced materials costs rapidly in Japan and was the major source of the reduction in local-currency unit costs
relative to the United States. The appreciation of the yen more than offset the
relative downtrend in domestic Japanese costs in all the covered industries in
1973–79, however, and it negated the domestic cost advantage in three Japanese industries in 1980–86. As Tange observes, the recovery of productivity
growth in the United States in the 1980s and the recent trend toward dollar
depreciation have improved the prospects for competitive gains in U.S. manufacturing industries.

U.S. Competitiveness

The contributions in Part III concern important factors affecting the competitiveness of the U.S. economy. In "Macroeconomic Policies, Competitiveness, and U.S. External Adjustment," Peter Hooper presents an empirical analysis of the relationships among the U.S. external balance, exchange rates, macroeconomic policies, and longer term trends in relative labor productivity. Trends and fluctuations in key variables and relationships are explored graphically from the 1960s through the 1980s and interpreted through theoretical principles and empirical findings in the literature concerning macroeconomic policy, balance-of-payments adjustment, exchange-rate determination, and the sources of relative productivity growth. His charts offer a notably compact and succinct presentation of the data on America's competitiveness and its consequences.

At first Hooper is concerned primarily with the shorter run effects of macroeconomic policies on external adjustment through their impacts on real interest rates, competitiveness, and relative domestic demand. In his opening section, he shows that movements in the international price and cost competitiveness of the U.S. economy have heavily influenced the observed swings in the external balance since 1970. Next he demonstrates that the fluctuations in U.S. competitiveness, as measured by unit labor costs in manufacturing, have been dominated by swings in nominal exchange rates, with movements in relative labor productivity among the United States and other countries having only minor impacts in the aggregate. Hooper then concludes the short-run analysis by exploring the links among macroeconomic policies and exchange rates, using the real interest parity condition as the basic model of real exchange-rate determination, and linking the historical changes in real interest and exchange rates to the fiscal and monetary actions of the period by citing evidence from simulation studies using multicountry econometric models.

In the final section of the chapter, Hooper explores the longer run consequences of large and sustained shifts in exchanges rates on relative productivity at home and abroad. His basic insight is that the exchange-rate and productivity effects on cost competitiveness are interdependent. This is because a relative reduction in U.S. unit labor costs from dollar depreciation will tend to induce a rise in real U.S. capital formation, and hence a subsequent rise in U.S. labor productivity, relative to investment and productivity abroad. Moreover, the same real interest decline that depresses the dollar will also reduce the relative cost of capital in the United States, further augmenting the relative attractiveness of real capital formation in the U.S. economy. Hooper concludes that the recent labor cost differential in favor of the United States, if sustained, could induce an upshift in relative capital stocks that would result in significant relative gains in labor productivity in U.S. manufacturing industries, thereby reducing the amount of dollar depreciation needed to restore balance in the external accounts.

In "U.S. Competitiveness and the Exchange Rate: A General Equilibrium Analysis of the U.S. Economy, 1982–86," Irma Adelman and Sherman Robinson use their computable general equilibrium model of the U.S. economy in counterfactual simulations to assess the short-term impacts of the twin deficits—fiscal and international—on the real exchange rate, relative prices, and the structure of output, employment, demand, and trade. The model is Walrasian, focuses on flow equilibria, and excludes the asset and money markets. Their comparative-static experiments assume full employment, sectorally fixed capital stocks, exogenous price levels at home and in world markets, and exogenous fiscal and trade balances. In the simulation exercises, the real exchange rate adjusts to maintain full employment by reallocating resources between tradable and nontradable goods and services. The model permits an analysis of the impacts of exchange revaluation on output, employment, relative prices, exports, and imports in ten producing sectors spanning agricultural, industrial, and service activities.

In the first simulation Adelman and Robinson answer the question "What would the effects have been if the economy had achieved the same balance-of-payments surplus in 1986 as actually achieved in 1980?"—that is, if no reliance had been placed on foreign borrowing to finance the fiscal deficit. Comparison with the baseline historical solution incorporating the actual flow of foreign borrowing indicates that the latter went mostly into investment, thereby avoiding a crowding-out effect from the fiscal deficit. As a result of the foreign borrowing, however, the real exchange rate appreciated by 15 percent and had a major adverse impact on U.S. competitiveness, decreasing both agricultural and nonagricultural exports by substantial percentages. Indeed, the revaluation of the dollar more than accounts for the loss of international competitiveness on the export side. With regard to the import side, however, the revaluation accounts only partially for the decrease in competitiveness of import substitutes, so that room is left for other explanatory factors affecting the relative productivity of the U.S. economy.

A similar experiment holding constant the 1986 government deficit at the 1980 level by assuming tax increases sufficient to offset the observed increase in public expenditures leads to the conclusion that the real exchange rate would have appreciated nearly as much under such a balanced-budget expansionary policy, with proportionately small effects on the actual reduction of competitiveness in the short run. The experiment makes it clear that the major effect of the budget deficit per se is on crowding out of total investment. As a result, the impacts of the budget deficit on capital formation and long-run competitiveness are likely to be significant despite the deficit's small effect on the exchange rate and short-run competitiveness.

In "Technology, Capital Formation, and U.S. Competitiveness," Ralph Landau evaluates the performance of the U.S. economy from the perspective of an engineer and technologist. Drawing on both the technical and popular literature and his own industrial experience, Landau offers an interpretation of recent U.S. developments in terms of growth theory and the production-function approach to sources of growth. His view embraces a broad definition of competitiveness as the ability to sustain, in a global economy, an acceptable growth rate of real consumption per capita under conditions of full employment with an acceptably fair income distribution and without sacrificing the growth potential of future generations.

On the role of technological change, Landau emphasizes the view that it is not exogenous as usually assumed in the neoclassical growth model, but rather it is endogenously related to real capital formation as well as to investment in R&D activities. The natural growth rate is not independent of the investment ratio. Embodiment and learning by doing interact with capital investment to improve growth rates, and capital investment is critical both in reaching a higher equilibrium path and in approaching the technological frontier at a faster rate. Citing new findings by Jorgenson and others, which impute to capital a much higher contribution to growth than did earlier studies, he concludes that there is a priority list for improving growth rates over the next twenty to thirty years: physical capital investment, R&D and technology, and improvement in labor quality.

Landau's basic policy recommendation is accordingly to stimulate saving by reducing the federal deficit and to ease monetary policy to promote lower interest rates and stimulate investment demand. Corporate tax reduction for direct stimulation of cash flow and investment should also be studied, as should a change in the taxation of capital gains to encourage longer term investment. Apart from these policies to stimulate reinvestment in the medium and long term, Laundau also presents a comprehensive menu of policies to deal with possible recessionary tendencies in the interim, including a recommendation that the federal deficit be reduced gradually to avoid acute deflationary pressures at home and abroad.

Country Studies

Part IV deals with various aspects of competitiveness in Japan and Germany. In "Price and Output Adjustment in Japanese Manufacturing," William H. Branson and Richard C. Marston suggest that one reason for the slow adjustment of U.S. imports from Japan to yen appreciation in recent years may be an attempt by Japanese manufacturers to defend their export markets by reducing profit margins. Since the mid-1970s, Japanese manufacturers are said to have varied the yen price of exports to limit the effects of fluctuations in the real exchange rate on Japanese output and employment. The authors specify a formal model of markup pricing to investigate this question and apply it to monthly data for nine Japanese manufacturing industries with significant reliance on exports. The sample covers the period starting with generalized floating in January 1974 and ends in December 1986.

Individual industry demand is assumed to depend negatively on the yen price of the domestic good relative to the yen price of a competing good, converted from the foreign currency price by the market exchange rate, and positively on total domestic output and total foreign output. Marginal cost is increasing in output, wages, and raw material prices. The markup is defined as the ratio of price to marginal cost. The reduced-form equation for industry price is derived from the first-order condition for profit maximization, and the response of domestic price to a change in the real exchange rate is found to depend on the elasticity of demand with respect to price and on the elasticity of the markup with respect to price.

With a variable markup, if yen appreciation raises the foreign currency price of exports, the exporting firm reduces the markup to limit the rise in that price, so the firm's price in domestic currency falls. If the firm "prices to market," it may reduce the domestic currency price of its exports more than the price of its domestic goods. The authors find from their estimated price equations that export price is universally more sensitive than domestic price to changes in the foreign price, providing strong evidence of pricing-to-market behavior. This evidence is confirmed when the authors estimate structural demand functions for each industry and find that the equations exhibit little sensitivity to foreign prices, since this implies that the reduced-form coefficients in the price equations reflect variable markups rather than high demand elasticities.

The role of industrial policies in postwar Japanese growth is the subject of "The Trade and Industrial Policies of Postwar Japan: A Theoretical Perspective," by Motoshige Itoh and Kazuhara Kiyono. The authors take a middle position between the extreme views that Japan's industrial policies were primarily responsible for its rapid postwar growth and that the growth occurred despite the perverse effects of the industrial policies. Their theoretical analysis supports the efficacy of Japan's policy of protection for infant industries, but they do not advocate the policy or provide an overall evaluation of its effects, since the effects fall unevenly on various economic agents in the society and are more complicated than indicated by the static and partial equilibrium theory of infant-industry protection.

Itoh and Kiyono begin with a brief historical overview of Japanese protectionist policies after World War II. They conclude that the establishment of Japan's major industries during the fifties and sixties relied on the crucial role played by the protection of the domestic market against foreign competition by import quotas, tariffs, and restrictions on direct investment by foreign competitors, whereas the Japanese government provided little direct support to indigenous manufacturing industries through export, production, or investment subsidies. The remainder of the chapter is devoted to a theoretical analysis of the economic mechanisms behind the industrial policies.

The remarkable worldwide growth of capital- or technology-intensive industries is attributed to the presence of large economies of scale, both static and dynamic. Three types are distinguished: industry-wide Marshallian externalities yielding technological benefits to each firm; dynamic sources of scale economies from learning by doing; and information externalities enabling the coordination of mutually beneficial expansion among interrelated industries. All three types have the property that the average cost of the industries or industry groups is decreasing in total output.

For a late-developing country to obtain these advantages, however, it is necessary to protect the fledgling domestic industries until their successful entry into domestic and world markets is ensured. The policy of selective industrial targeting is credited with much of the success of Japanese protectionist policies, since it permitted the establishment and expansion of industries producing borderline technology goods in which the international competitiveness of late-developing countries was close to the advanced countries. They argue that protection was viewed as temporary by the affected industries, owing to external pressures from international institutions and trading partners, and therefore that protection encouraged large-scale investment to secure scale economies and market shares before it could expire. Finally, they invoke Stackelberg-leadership theory to rationalize the presumed effectiveness of import quotas in preventing foreign companies from undertaking entry-limiting price strategies against Japanese firms.

In "Protection and International Competitiveness: A View from West Germany," Gernot Klepper and Frank D. Weiss take a different approach to the subject. They associate international competitiveness with comparative advantage and ask how protection in West Germany has affected the realization of its comparative advantages in various industries and hence its long-run international competitiveness.

In the first section, they present data measuring the effective rates of assistance (ERA) to forty-six industries comprising both traded and nontraded goods. The effective rates take into account border restrictions and subsidies and are available for the 1970s and 1980s. These data demonstrate that the pattern of industrial assistance is biased toward old industries lacking competitiveness.

They turn next to the interindustry structure of competitiveness as defined by revealed comparative advantage (RCA), that is, by a measure of net exports in each industry adjusted for overall trade imbalances for thirty industries. The commodity patterns cannot be explained by relative factor endowments along the lines of Heckscher–Ohlin theory, since regressions of RCA on measures of human and physical capital intensities have low explanatory power, although they show statistically significant effects for human capital. In another application of the data, the changes between 1978 and 1985 in average firm size and in labor productivity growth are separately regressed on the change in ERA, which is significantly negative in both instances, confirming the authors' hypothesis that increases in protection have led to an inefficient scale of production in Germany.

Finally, Klepper and Weiss undertake a painstaking computation of the factor content of German trade in order to take account of the lack of theoretical justification for applying Heckscher–Ohlin concepts to the prediction of the commodity composition of trade in a multidimensional world in which there are more goods than factors of production. They compare the predicted factor content of free trade with the realized content under protection and find that protection substantially reduces the amount of implicit trade in factors of production. Since protection impinges heavily on those industries that use intensively some of the resources which are scarcest in Germany—land, minerals, and labor—Klepper and Weiss conclude that protection reduces the exploitation of Germany's comparative advantage and reduces its international competitiveness.

FINDINGS AND ISSUES

The purpose of this section is to comment on some key findings and issues that cut across chapters.

The Productivity Slowdown

The growth rate of output per hour in manufacturing decelerated substantially between 1960–73 and 1973–79 in each of the twelve industrial countries covered by the BLS data (Neef). From 1979 to 1987 labor productivity growth recovered sharply in the United States and the United Kingdom, while remaining little changed or declining in the other countries. Despite the recoveries in the eighties in some countries, the average productivity growth rate for 1973–87 as a whole was lower than for 1960–73 in all countries.

Estimated rates of technical progress or TFP growth rates, given in several chapters, present a mixed picture insofar as breaks in trends after 1973 are concerned. Helliwell and Chung assume no trend breaks in their econometric estimates of the rate of Harrod-neutral technical progress in the various countries in their sample. Saito and Tokutsu allow for a trend break in the rate of technical progress in 1974–79 in their econometric models of manufacturing industries in the United States, Japan, and West Germany. According to their econometric estimates, the growth rate of TFP for manufacturing as a whole actually increased slightly after 1973 in the United States, although decreasing slightly in Germany and Japan. When they measure TFP on the same data set using standard growth-accounting methods, however, they find a sharp deceleration in 1974–79 in the simple average of annual rates of change of TFP for the United States and Japan, and a moderate acceleration for Germany. When they subsequently compute a cumulative chain index from the annual rates of change and fit trends before and after 1973, the estimated slowdowns for the United States and Japan are considerably moderated and the smoothed growth rate for Germany is virtually the same before and after 1973. Tange's production function estimates show TFP growth declining sharply in her sample of eight manufacturing industries after 1973 in Japan and recovering slightly on average after 1979. For the United States, the estimates indicate that five of the eight industries experienced a slowdown in 1973–79 and that total manufacturing recovered strongly in 1980–85 compared with 1973–79. Finally, Jorgenson and Kuroda conclude that after slowing sharply in 1973–80, the average productivity growth rates in Japanese and U.S. industries revived somewhat in 1980–85 but remained well below those for 1960–73, especially in Japan.

On balance, there is a preponderance of evidence that a widespread slowdown occurred in both labor and total factor productivity after the first energy shock in 1973, so that the deceleration of the former was not due simply to a decrease in investment rates and capital deepening. The relative importance of the energy shocks in the slowdown of TFP growth is problematical. It is hard to see how the energy shocks could have altered the underlying component of neutral technical progress, but the sharp increase in energy costs could adversely affect value-added labor productivity by rendering existing capital obsolete, as argued, for example, by Baily (1981).

As for gross industrial output, according to Jorgenson and Kuroda, the 1973–79 period was dominated by the energy crisis, which slowed U.S. growth significantly and Japanese growth substantially. They do not specifically address, however, the extent to which the slowdowns in total growth were attributable to energy-induced slowdowns in productivity, as opposed to the substitution effects of higher energy prices on relative factor inputs. Conrad refers to the impact of higher energy prices on input proportions, particularly in the four European countries in his sample, but he appears to attribute more overall significance to changes in relative wages and capital prices in his explanation of the effects of induced changes in input proportions on relative productivity gaps.

Productivity Convergence Among Countries

Several chapters provide evidence in support of the hypothesis that growth rates of at least the industrialized countries of the West have converged during the postwar period because of the international transferability of knowledge and goods, the basic idea being that countries with initially lower levels of income and productivity should tend to catch up over time with the richer countries by adopting the best-practice techniques of the leaders. Thus Helliwell and Chung find a highly significant negative association between initial per capita GDP levels and the 1960–85 growth rates of both GDP per capita and Harrod-neutral technical progress in cross-sectional regressions for nineteen industrial countries. The same association is much weaker, however, in their data on per capita growth rates for eighty-nine countries for 1973–83. Whether this is because of weaker data, a shorter sample, the fact that energy-importing and exporting countries fared differently during this particular historical period, or the possibility that the poorest countries were unprepared to take advantage of newer technologies cannot be ascertained from the available information, although a rough test of the last possibility led to its rejection by Helliwell and Chung. Finally, some support for the hypothesis of convergence among growth rates of middle-income developing countries is found by Adams, Behrman, and Boldin for the period 1974–86.

The aforementioned findings of Helliwell and Chung about convergence among the industrial countries were from regressions using *constant* Harrod-neutral rates of technical progress over the entire sample period as the dependent variable, and without specifying any productivity leader. These authors also test a more explicit model of the convergence hypothesis, labeled the "catch-up case," in which it is postulated that the other industrialized countries were gradually approaching the growth rate, and perhaps the level, of aggregate productivity in the United States, which had the highest level throughout the 1961–85 sample period. These are log-linear time-series regressions relating the annual index of productivity growth in each country to its own lagged value, the U.S. index of trended productivity growth, and a constant term. The regressions fit well and confirm the catch-up process for virtually all countries. Note that this model provides an explanation of the productivity slowdown in the follower countries as resulting from the convergence process, but none for the United States, where a constant rate of growth is assumed in the catch-up regressions, after testing against the alternative hypothesis of a trend break after 1973.

The productivity-gap study of Conrad deals with convergence explicitly of productivity levels, whereas Jorgenson and Kuroda report growth rates as well as gaps. Thus the indexes developed by Jorgenson and Kuroda for Japan and the United States indicate that productivity growth in Japan exceeded that in the United States in almost all industries in 1960–73, but that after the energy crisis in 1973, there were few significant differences in productivity growth rates between the two countries. Insofar as productivity levels are concerned, their gap measures indicate that Japan had overtaken the United States in twelve of twenty-eight industries by 1980, but no further gains occurred on balance between 1980 and 1985. Similarly, Conrad's results show substantial convergence to the United States of the total manufacturing productivity levels of France, West Germany, and Italy, but not the United Kingdom, by 1980, followed by a renewed widening of the U.S. lead through 1986.

Exchange Rates, Productivity, and Competitiveness

Exchange-rate fluctuations must be assigned an important role as a source of short-run movements of U.S. price competitiveness since the regime of floating rates began in the early seventies. More recently, for example, dollar appreciation in 1979–85 far more than offset relatively favorable movements in hourly compensation and labor productivity in the U.S. economy, whereas the subsequent depreciation has greatly augmented the gains in U.S. cost competitiveness from wage restraint and productivity improvements (Neef, Klein). The empirical findings of Tange and of Jorgenson and Kuroda also document the importance of changes in the yen–dollar exchange rate on relative costs of individual industries in the two countries.

The key role of U.S. macroeconomic policies as causes of the recent fluctuations in real interest rates, and hence in exchange rates, is documented by Hooper, who observes that the rise in real interest rates in the early 1980s has been attributed to a combination of monetary tightening and fiscal expansion, whereas the subsequent decline in 1984–86 has been linked to both the adoption of a more accommodative monetary policy stance and improved prospects for a significant reduction of the federal budget deficit owing to the Gramm–Rudman–Hollings Act of 1985. His own quantitative estimates, based on econometric model simulations, suggest that taken separately neither the shift of monetary policy nor that of fiscal policy can adequately explain the changes in the external sector during the first half of the 1980s, but that together they accounted for two-thirds of the increases in both the dollar and the external deficit.

Finally, as noted earlier, two chapters call attention to significant longer term interactions between productivity and exchange rates. First, Hooper views a relative reduction in U.S. labor costs from dollar depreciation and the associated reduction in the real interest rate as factors inducing a relative rise in U.S. investment and labor productivity. Second, Helliwell and Chung emphasize the opposite reverse linkage from productivity to competitiveness, since aggregate productivity improvements in a given country may induce a higher real exchange rate in order to equilibrate the resulting current-account surplus.

Competitiveness of the U.S. Economy

A principal cause of the widespread concern about U.S. competitiveness is the sharp decline in the U.S. external balance during the 1980s. One school of thought attributes the increase in the current-account deficit during the early eighties primarily to dollar appreciation induced by tight monetary and easy fiscal policies, whereas the other posits an underlying secular decline of competitiveness from a shortfall in U.S. productivity growth. If the former view is correct, what is basically needed to correct the external imbalance is a shift in macroeconomic policy in the direction of internal deficit reduction and easier money, as occurred to some extent during the late eighties, whereas the latter view may call for measures directed more toward an enhancement of the climate for individual decisions concerning investments, inventions, innovations, and educational opportunities. The difference between the views is often a matter of emphasis, and many observers recommend policies on each front.

Apart from the external deficit, much concern has been expressed in recent years about the pace of productivity increase and position of the United States in the world economy. The BLS data indeed show that the U.S. average growth rate of manufacturing labor productivity was lowest among twelve industrial countries in 1960–73 and among all but Canada and Denmark in 1973–87 (Neef). With the exception of New Zealand, the estimates of Harrod-neutral technical progress presented by Helliwell and Chung also show the United States with the smallest average rate of increase among nineteen industrial countries in 1960–85. Two important points must be kept in mind for a proper perspective on such comparisons, however.

First, the faster growth observed abroad is largely the result of the process of postwar convergence toward U.S. productivity levels, and to that extent reflects an endogenous diffusion of best-practice techniques rather than any inherent deficiencies in U.S. policies or industrial practices. That is not to say that the United States cannot do better insofar as domestic productivity growth is concerned, but it is unlikely to attain an above-average long-term growth rate in future years because of superior international competitiveness, given the approximate parity today among leading industrial countries.

Second, the evidence in this volume indicates that the United States remains ahead of the pack in its attained level of productivity, with the inevitable degree of uncertainty attaching to such PPP comparisons. Thus in support of their choice of the United States as the leader in their catch-up model of convergence, Helliwell and Chung point out that throughout 1960–85 the United States had the highest level of income per capita and the highest measured index of aggregate productivity in their sample of nineteen industrial countries. Similarly, Conrad's estimates of productivity gaps with respect to France, West Germany, and Italy indicate that the United States lead narrowed drastically during the sixties and seventies but enlarged again to moderately positive levels in the early eighties, whereas a sizable lead over the United Kingdom persisted throughout the period 1963–86. Finally, the industry-level technology gaps estimated by Jorgenson and Kuroda show the United States ahead of Japan in sixteen of twenty-four industries in 1980–85.

As we have seen, Hooper sees some room for optimism concerning the prospects for U.S. external adjustment and the dollar, based on his analysis of past movements in the external balance, competitiveness, labor productivity, and macroeconomic policies. Exchange rates in the late 1980s were at levels that could contribute to an upturn in U.S. relative investment, productivity, and competitiveness and an associated improvement in the external balance during the 1990s. These developments would tend to lessen further deprecia- tion that would be needed to close the external deficit. As Hooper points out, however, the scope for external adjustment through such shifts in relative out- put capacity to the United States would be limited in the absence of macroeco- nomic policies to increase U.S. government and private saving rates and facil- itate capital deepening.

A similar but somewhat broader view is offered by Klein, who emphasizes that in recent years the United States has relied too heavily on exchange de- preciation in order to become more competitive. True, there have been relative gains in output per hour, but they were less important for competitiveness than changes in the value of the dollar. The United States should do more techni- cally to improve productivity and rely less on major swings in macroeconomic policy, because such swings have powerful destabilizing effects on the rest of the world. To gain competitiveness through improved economic efficiency in the longer term, the United States should look to increased capital forma- tion, the development of a stable noninflationary economic environment, a strong work ethic, an emphasis on quality as well as price competition, and vigorous scientific and technical progress. Klein's specific recommendations include an appropriate balance between monetary and fiscal policy in each country and international policy coordination to avoid extreme swings in trade and payment balances among the participating countries. Industrial policies could be used to target particular sectors for support of investment, work train- ing, and R&D outlays. If industrial policy is unacceptable to a wide range of economists, completely general support for investment, training, and R&D is less controversial and should be pursued. Interventionist energy policy is also recommended to develop synthetic substitutes, provide ample storage stocks, and augment energy conservation.

If one turns for guidance on the efficacy of industrial policy to our chapters on German and Japanese experience, one finds conflicting viewpoints. Thus Itoh and Kiyono support the view that infant-industry protection fostered the Japanese takeoff in the 1960s by allowing borderline technology industries to take advantage of scale economies they would otherwise have been denied, whereas Klepper and Weiss conclude that protection has reduced the exploi- tation of West Germany's comparative advantage in particular industries and thereby reduced its international competitiveness.

In keeping with his broad view of U.S. competitiveness as the ability to sustain healthy long-term growth, Landau provides a wide-ranging program of actions affecting federal spending, taxation and the budget deficit, interest rates, the external deficit, international policy coordination, domestic saving, and capital formation, while rejecting protectionism or industrial policies. The basic thrust of his recommendations, however, is to augment investment in physical capital as a first priority. This is based on Landau's rejection of the concept of exogenous technical change, so that the natural growth rate is not independent of the investment ratio as it is in the neoclassical growth model, and his acceptance of the proposition that the economy is continuously in a stage of dynamic transition between steady-state growth paths. Also cited is evidence of a positive cross-country correlation between gross saving ratios and growth rates of output per person employed, and Jorgenson's finding that real capital formation accounted for the largest share of real GNP growth in 1948–79.

The desirability of stimulating real investment probably commands a wide consensus among contemporary economists, although not necessarily in preference to encouraging R&D and human capital formation. The precise role of real investment in economic growth is still a controversial subject, however. For example, Helliwell and Chung also confirm a positive correlation between investment ratios and growth rates among eighty-nine economies in various stages of development, but they emphasize that this cannot simply be taken to mean that high investment produces high growth, since the acceleration principle reverses the causation by explaining high investment rates in terms of high rates of output growth. Note also that the large contribution attributed by Jorgenson and his colleagues to investment as an independent source of U.S. growth is in contrast to the much lower estimates provided by Denison, and the differences are due primarily to conceptual issues, involving the measurement of capital input and its weight in aggregate output, on which opinions differ (Abramowitz, 1989, pp. 18–20).

Interesting recent work by Romer (1987) provides a growth model in which endogenous technological change is an increasing function of aggregate investment because of knowledge externalities. As noted by his discussants, however, it is difficult to obtain empirical evidence on a causal link between investment and externalities or to discriminate econometrically between Romer's model and a Solow model with exogenous technical change. Moreover, the parameterized Romer model generates the same large residuals (i.e., unexplained shifts in the production function or changes in technology) as do conventional growth-accounting models when applied to postwar U.S. data. In view of the great importance of these issues for economic welfare and public policy, contemporary research on the determinants of growth, with the goal of providing definitive evidence for the choice among models, should be accorded the highest priority.

NOTES

1. Citations to works published elsewhere carry numbers referring to the year of publication as listed in the References. References cited by authors' names only refer to the papers published in this volume.

2. The advantages and disadvantages of this practice, compared with calculations using real quantities based on the "international prices" underlying multilateral PPP indexes, are discussed in Kravis and Lipsey (1989).

3. The PPP estimates of Jorgenson and Kuroda are used subsequently by Tokutso and Saito in their discussion of productivity gaps between Japan and the United States and between the United States and Germany.

REFERENCES

Abramowitz, M. 1989. *Thinking About Growth*. Cambridge: Cambridge University Press.

Baily, M. N. 1981. "Productivity and the Services of Capital and Labor." *Brookings Papers on Economic Activity* 1, 1–50.

Denison, E. F. 1962. *The Sources of Economic Growth in the United States*. New York: Committee for Economic Development.

Jorgenson, D. W., F. M. Gollop, and B. M. Fraumeni. 1987. *Productivity and U.S. Economic Growth*. Cambridge, Mass.: Harvard University Press.

Kravis, I. B. 1984. "Comparative Studies of National Incomes and Prices." *Journal of Economic Literature* (March), 1–39.

Kravis, I. B. and R. E. Lipsey. 1989. "The International Comparison Program: Current Status and Problems." *Conference on International Economic Relations: Issues in Measurement and Empirical Research*. Conference on Research in Income and Wealth, National Bureau of Economic Research, Cambridge, Mass., November 3–4.

Romer, P. M. 1987. "Crazy Explanations for the Productivity Slowdown." In *NBER Macroeconomics Annual 1987*. Cambridge, Mass.: MIT Press, pp. 163–202.

Solow, R. M. 1957. "Technical Change and the Aggregate Production Function." *Review of Economics and Statistics* (August), 312–20.

I

GLOBAL PERSPECTIVES

2

Restructuring of the World Economy

LAWRENCE R. KLEIN

SCOPE AND MEANING OF RESTRUCTURING

There is a great deal of economic change taking place now in the world economy. New kinds of jobs are becoming available; new industries are being created; the combination of production, consumption, and trade is changing; markets are unsettled; and economic policies are shifting. There is no doubt that economic change has always occurred. It would be difficult to say that today's changes are more significant, for example, than the changes associated with the industrial revolution, the fall of the gold standard, or many other momentous economic events in history, but today's changes are here—upon us—and we must appreciate them and understand why they are occurring in order to deal with them.

In short historical perspective, it is convenient to start with the end of World War II. In the late 1940s and the 1950s, the main problem was reconstruction of the damage. There followed a period of great expansion, together with a reentry of Germany and Japan into the mainstream (eventually shared leadership) of the world economy. The United States had to play the key leadership role for several years. Now it is shared, a development that, in itself, has created imbalances requiring an adjustment process in which restructuring takes place on a large scale.

The Third World has seen enormous but very uneven development in this period. If Japan may be taken as an example of a country that moved from less to fully developed status (starting with admission to the Organization for European Cooperation and Development [OECD] membership in 1964), then we may note that other developing countries want to emulate Japan. This requires a great deal of restructuring, both in the internal economic makeup of the countries concerned and in the composition of world trade. A fundamental aspect of the immediate postreconstruction stage was the liberalization and rapid expansion of world trade volume after the 1960s.

The World Bank estimates the growth rate of trade volume (exports) in two phases, 1965–73 and 1973–85 (see Table 2-1). The very rapid pace of expansion

Table 2-1 Annual Growth Rate of World Exports[a]

1965–73	10.7%
1973–85	5.3%

[a]Industrial market economies and developing countries (including high-income oil exporters).

in the late 1960s came to a slowdown phase after the change in terms of trade for energy products. World trade expansion is still a very important basis of the world economy, but it is considerably slower in this transition period of restructuring.

There are many ways to look at restructuring, for it has many dimensions. First, consider employment opportunities. American data are readily available, and they will be used, to a great extent, as indicators of the general process, but similar developments are occurring in many countries. From 1965, employment in the United States has declined significantly in manufacturing. The share has also declined in primary sectors but grown in services. In longer perspective, covering more than a hundred years, we have had no basic trend in the manufacturing share but offsetting gains and losses in the service and primary sectors, respectively.

On a world scale, agriculture has experienced a declining share between 1965 and 1980 in developing countries, but the *level* is very high, and the decline is modest. There is a sharp fall in the agricultural share in the industrial countries and also in the socialist countries (excluding China). The industrial share (including mining, construction, and utilities) went up in both the Third World and among socialist countries. The service share rose in all areas, not always through similar declines in the other sectors, but to a certain extent from a decline in the agricultural shares (see Table 2-2).

Jobs are shifting, and it is significant that the service category is gaining generally in relative importance. It is worthwhile to probe further into the nature and composition of job gains, especially in the service sector. This route is relatively easy to pursue with U.S. data, and since job expansion has recently been unusually large in the United States, it provides a very good base for looking at some important issues. Job expansion has been much more rapid in the United States than in Japan and major European countries since the late sixties. A great deal of this employment expansion in the United States has been in "service" as opposed to "goods" production. It is hard to make a clear separation because there is much service work in the goods sectors of the economy. Some of the reverse may take place as well, but the share of employment in the goods-producing sector now is about 25 percent, whereas at the end of

Table 2-2 Percentage Distribution of Labor Force

	Agriculture		Industry		Services	
	1965	1980	1956	1980	1965	1980
Developing countries	70	62	12	16	18	22
High-income oil exporters	58	35	15	21	28	44
Industrial market economies	14	7	38	35	48	58
Socialist economies	34	22	34	39	32	39

World War II, it was more than 40 percent. The decline over four decades has been steady, with some cyclical variation, and has not accelerated during the present expansion. In the present expansion, beginning in late 1982, the rate of growth of services-producing jobs has been about 3.7 percent per annum. The corresponding figure of goods-producing jobs is only 1.8 percent.

An important issue is whether the strong expansion of jobs in services is mainly in undesirable or relatively attractive jobs. There is a false impression that the expansion is taking place in low-quality, low-paying service jobs that offer little future potential, especially for young employees. But services comprise a mixed group of activities. Zoltan Kenessey of the Federal Reserve Board makes the interesting distinction between tertiary and quaternary sectors. The former consists of transport, wholesale trade, and retail trade. The latter consists of finance, insurance, and real estate (services per se) along with government. Finance, insurance, and real estate offer some very attractive employment opportunities—perhaps carried to excess in 1987, but nevertheless still attractive. Government service should not be looked down upon. The services per se grouping contains both low-wage, dead-end jobs and technical jobs requiring high degrees of skill and education.

Looking at the matter from the point of view of median weekly wage, one report finds that the "high-wage" ($479/week) group accounted for almost 50 percent of employment growth during the expansion of 1983–87. The "middle-wage" ($322/week) group accounted for 42 percent of job growth, while the "low-wage" ($214/week) group accounted for only 8.2 percent (Leisenring, 1988). The important high-wage group included managerial, professional, technical, and highly skilled workers.

Immediately following the stock market crash of 1987, financial service jobs and production fell, but there is evidence that there will be some recovery in this area, and other service jobs were essentially unaffected.

In an interesting comment at a meeting of Project LINK (March 1988, United Nations, New York), N. Garganas of the Bank of Greece noted that U.S. job performance had been better than Europe's because of the degree of expansion that occurred in the service sector. He conjectured that Europe would eventually follow the American path, and that this would be a sensible way to bring down the persistently high unemployment rate in most European countries.

The concept of restructuring can also be examined from the production as well as the employment side. There are some interesting trends in the American data, and they have raised important technical issues (see Figures 2-1 and 2-2). In *real* terms, the share of U.S. GNP that originates in the manufacturing sector has been remarkably steady. In 1982 prices, this share is about 20–22 percent, and it has been in this range for most of the period since the end of World War II. There is no apparent trend in the time series of official data whether for manufacturing as a whole or for durables and nondurables separately. In *current* prices, the share of total manufacturing has fallen from roughly 30 to 20 percent over four decades.

According to the data, which show approximately constant real shares, the

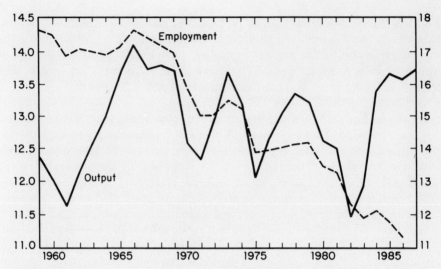

Figure 2-1 Percent share of manufacturing durable goods in real GNP and total employment. *Source:* Bureau of Labor Statistics and Department of Commerce, Bureau of Economic Analysis.

falling employment shares imply that productivity is rising. In a sense, these data also suggest that the United States is not becoming deindustrialized; we are simply restructuring. Of course, the data can simply be interpreted as an interesting statistical constant showing a productivity gain that is not strong enough to overcome countertendencies toward lack of competitiveness. It will be noted in the next section that there is, indeed, evidence of declining competitiveness, even within the framework of these data on the constancy of the manufacturing shares.

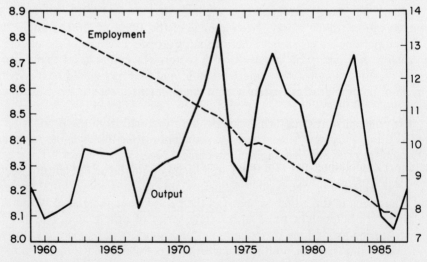

Figure 2-2 Percent share of manufacturing nondurable goods in real GNP and total employment. *Source:* Bureau of Labor Statistics and Department of Commerce, Bureau of Economic Analysis.

If we enlarge the scope of the share statistics to encompass total goods production and not simply manufacturing production, we find that the real share of goods in GNP has fallen since 1950 by about 2–3 percentage points, but that the share has been very steady at about 43 percent since 1970 (Leisenring, 1988).

Value added is measured by the following formula:

$$VA \quad = \quad GR \quad - \quad I$$

| value added | gross output | intermediate input |

The controversy concerning measurement of the manufacturing share of real value added is based on several issues, the principal one being that real *intermediate* inputs that are subtracted from gross output to get value added are understated; therefore, value added is overstated (Mishel, 1988). Domestic price indexes are used to deflate I, but these make real I estimates lower than if actual price indexes reflecting foreign sourcing are used. These prices are lower and would make estimates of real I higher. Foreign sourcing grew rapidly in the period when the share statistics estimated by other methods were falling, suggesting that the official data on real shares should be lower during the past few years.

Statistics of gross output, rather than value added, and statistics of current dollar shares for value added both indicate that the manufacturing share has been falling.

The controversy has not been resolved, but there may have been a slight decline of up to 3–5 percentage points in the manufacturing share of real output. In studying productivity trends and the laws of production in general, I would argue strongly for using gross output rather than value added, together with intermediate inputs as explanatory production factors. In proceeding this way, we do find a slight decline in the manufacturing share statistics. From 1979 to 1985 the drop is estimated to be about 2 percent (from 35.6 to 33.5 percent) (Mishel, 1988, p. 13).

Even if the manufacturing share is not absolutely constant, its decline is slight and may be in the process of changing direction. A more interesting avenue of investigation is the changing composition among types of manufacturing making up the total sector share estimate (see Table 2-3). In independent compilations, the Federal Reserve Board shows changing weights between 1977 and 1984 in the makeup of the index of industrial production, using value-added data. The FRB figures show large increases in shares for nonelectrical machinery (including the computer group) and electrical machinery. Rubber and plastic products and instruments are two other gaining groups. Declining in relative importance during this period were primary metals, fabricated metal products, transportation equipment, textiles, and apparel. These five declining cases are often cited in arguments that the United States is in industrial decline. Inadequate attention is paid to the impressive gains in sectors with rising shares. A comprehensive listing, using official data on shares in real value added, brings out the same kind of statistical picture.

Some high-technology sectors, but not chemicals and allied products, show

Table 2-3 Change in Manufacturing Share of GNP, 1979–86

Industry	Percentage Points
Machinery except electrical	1.44
Electric and electronic equipment	0.40
Instruments and related products	0.10
Other transportation equipment	0.14
Rubber and miscellaneous plastic products	0.07
Miscellaneous manufacturing	0.01
Paper and allied products	−0.01
Food and kindred products	−0.03
Printing and publishing	−0.04
Chemicals and allied products	−0.14
Furniture and fixtures	−0.03
Textile mill products	−0.04
Lumber and wood products	−0.08
Fabricated metal products	−0.24
Apparel and other textile products	−0.08
Stone, clay, and glass products	−0.13
Motor vehicles and equipment	−0.30
Petroleum and coal products	−0.20
Tobacco manufactures	−0.12
Primary metal products	−0.62
Leather and leather products	−0.05

Source: Paying the Bill: Manufacturing and America's Trade Deficit. Washington, D.C.: Office of Technology Assessment, 1988, p. 39.

gains in importance. Aerospace, included in other transportation equipment, is a gainer, whereas motor vehicles are losers. Petroleum and coal declines reflect enormous swings in the terms of trade. Many traditional sectors are losing ground, but they may revive in restructured form. Socially undesirable sectors, such as tobacco, show a decline, although their export continues on a fair scale. There are no surprises in this listing, but it does clearly show the significant restructuring that is taking place.

Another way of looking at the sector distribution of growth and decline within manufacturing is in the growth of capital stock, as a main factor of production, in the individual manufacturing categories (see Table 2-4). Investment in fixed capital was not impressive during the 1980s, but some sectors exhibited notable gains. As seen in Table 2-4, we find electrical and nonelectrical machinery to be areas of strong and continuing expansion. Instruments and other transportation equipment (especially aircraft) are also expanding capital. Printing and publishing have invested in capital but do not show an increasing share of output. The same is true of tobacco. Primary metals, fabricated metals, textiles, and apparel are all seen to be retreating sectors. They may regain world competitiveness, but probably not at their earlier size and structure.

In the United States, some traditional sectors have trimmed facilities, laid off employees, and produced a different range or volume of output. In this process there has been a great deal of retraining, early retirement, and opening of new positions in other sectors—on balance, the service-producing sectors. There has also been a restructuring in the United Kingdom. Many workers were released, as "redundant," at British Steel, for example. The British result, however, has not been as favorable as in the United States with respect to

Table 2-4 Growth of Real Capital Stock in U.S. Manufacturing

Industry	1970s	1980s
Manufacturing, total	3.3%	1.5%
Lumber and wood	4.9	−1.9
Furniture and fixtures	4.0	2.4
Stone, clay, and glass	2.7	−1.6
Primary metals	1.6	−1.6
Fabricated metals	4.0	1.4
Nonelectrical machinery	4.5	4.1
Electrical machinery	4.6	7.5
Motor vehicles and parts	2.8	0.5
Other transportation equipment	2.4	4.4
Instruments	4.4	5.3
Other	4.4	−0.2
Food	2.7	0.9
Tobacco	5.2	8.3
Textiles	1.6	−1.6
Apparel	4.3	−1.6
Paper	3.2	2.1
Printing and publishing	3.1	4.8
Chemicals	4.2	−0.3
Petroleum	3.3	1.1
Rubber	4.6	0.4
Leather	0.7	−1.3

Source: Stephen S. Roach, "Beyond Restructuring: America's Investment Challenge," *Economic Perspectives* (Morgan Stanley, New York), July 14, 1988. (Reprinted by permission from the author.)

unemployment. The rate of growth of the labor force, for one thing, slowed down much more between the 1970s and 1980s in the United States than in the United Kingdom. In both cases, though, national productivity growth responded positively in manufacturing as a result of the restructuring.

Another dimension of restructuring deals with international trade flows. In the next section I consider the market-adjustment process; in this section I focus on the changes in trade relationships. Technical change, which accounts for much of national restructuring, shows up in international trade flows. The leading industrial countries compete with one another in discovery, economic innovation, and the capturing of world markets in the new technologies, such as microelectronics, software, bioengineering, and new materials. The leaders among the newly industrialized economies (NIEs) also vie for a niche in this market as well as for growing shares of more conventional manufacturing— some of it sophisticated but not necessarily involving advanced technology. The United States maintained a trade surplus in "high-tech" manufactures until 1986, when the figure went into deficit by $2.6 billion, and recovered to near balance by 1987. In non–high-tech manufactures, the United States has experienced a steadily worsening deficit since 1980. The main losses at the high-tech end of the scale are to Japan and East Asian NIEs.

Another force driving a restructuring of world trade has been the existence of severe debt burdens for many developing countries. The main less developed country (LDC) debtors, apart from South Korea, have been forced to restrict imports. They try to export on a scale that would enable them to service debt comfortably, but they are unable to do so because of the modest growth performance of the world economy. It was indicated previously that in the expansive period, world trade grew at a rate in excess of 10 percent. Both developing and developed economies participated in this rapid expansion, and the United States and Western Europe looked to the developing world as customers for their manufactured goods on a scale that would allow both parties to grow well. In the slowdown period after the Organization of Petroleum Exporting Countries (OPEC) forced a drastic change in terms of trade for energy products, the patterns changed, especially after the OPEC surplus had been recycled into unbearable debts for many developing countries.

In today's economy of modest growth in GDP and trade volume, there is much restructuring at the international level. Developing countries have maintained their established growth rate of exports, but much of their earnings goes to debt service. On the other hand, they have drastically reduced their import growth. With fewer capital purchases from abroad, they are forced to cut back the rate of expansion of domestic production. Industrial countries, on the other hand, have experienced a sharp drop in export growth (related to LDC import restraint) and have also reduced their import expansion. There is, however, a major exception in the industrial world, with respect to import performance. That exception is the United States, where import growth expanded as export growth fell. Herein lies much of the restructuring problem, in the international trade area, for the world economy.

The figures in Table 2-5 are striking. They present a picture of the creation of serious world imbalance that calls for restructuring guided by market adjustment. The figures indicate much of the restructuring that has already taken place. The countries that have emerged economically strong at the international level are the surplus industrial countries—Japan and West Germany—and the surplus NIEs—Taiwan and South Korea. The weakened countries are the LDC debtors and the United States. The countries with large oil export surpluses are, for the moment, living well by virtue of their past accumulation of reserves. It remains to be seen how strong they will remain.

The United States has emerged from this series of developments as the world's largest debtor, having once been the world's largest creditor. As the statistics in Table 2-5 show, the United States has not had to restrain imports as other debtors have, because people throughout the world are willing to take dollar-denominated debt instruments (securities) and supply funds to the United States in return. Other debtors cannot generally market securities in their own currencies. Obviously, this process cannot continue indefinitely; that is one reason why restructuring is taking place in the United States.

Table 2-5   Growth of Merchandise Trade (percent per year)

	Exports		Imports	
	1965–80	1980–85	1965–80	1980–85
Developing countries	3.1	3.9	5.3	0.4
Highly indebted countries	0.5	1.1	6.3	−8.6
Industrial market economies	7.5	3.7	6.7	3.9
United States	6.7	−2.8	6.6	8.4

Source: World Development Report, 1987. World Bank, Washington, D.C., 1987.

Both high-tech and other manufactures in trade have contributed to the large American external deficit, but agriculture remains as a major surplus area where the United States has a competitive edge. U.S. agriculture exports exceeded imports by $25 billion in 1981, making a very significant contribution toward offsetting deficits in other goods. The surplus is now between $5 billion and $10 billion, but it was as low as $3.4 billion in 1986. Improvements are occurring, but there will be declines, for example, related to drought, as in 1988, and it is unlikely that agriculture can be as important as it formerly was because other countries have become competitive in grain and food products that are crucial to the U.S. surplus. It is now considered essential that restructuring enable the United States to make significant improvements in net exports of manufactures.

Another field of trade preeminence for the United States has been in services (so-called invisibles). The main net earnings for the United States have come from investment and financial income. The shift to net debtor status has seriously impaired the ability of the United States to rely on net factor earnings abroad to offset the merchandise deficit. Formerly, this offset was possible, but interest service on the foreign debt has changed the pattern. This, indeed, is a form of (adverse) restructuring.

As far as receipts and payments of returns on existing international investment are concerned, the United States will have a long wait until it can improve the net balance by a significant amount, but it can compete with other countries now for international earnings in financial markets. The twenty-four–hour global market is a reality, and the export or import of financial services is a growing base of international economic activity. A large pool of international financial capital has developed, and it is this pool that uses the twenty-four–hour global market facilities.

The large financial centers (London, New York, Frankfurt, Zurich, Paris, Montreal, Sydney, Hong Kong, Tokyo, Singapore, Rome, and others) are all participating in these new activities. The source of the activity may be called *financial innovation*. This concept consists of new hardware facilities of telecommunication and computation—at amazing speed with capability of handling mass transactions—associated software, new securities instruments, and new activities, such as mergers and acquisitions. Traditional commodity markets for primary products have been made much more efficient, flexible, and available. Commodity trade has been integrated into financial markets.

At least two developing countries have been able to enter this area of international economic activity at the highest level of sophistication, Singapore and Hong Kong. Others are preparing to compete too, and the business of offshore international banking has taken hold in a few centers of the developing world. The main centers, however, are in the leading industrial countries and, in a sense, a new type of international trade has been created—trade in financial services. The major economic powers have all built up this area of activity, as a natural extension of domestic banking and finance. This area will be important for the United States and is a part of the restructuring taking place, and it is also happening in other large OECD countries in addition to Switzerland, Australia, Benelux, and Scandinavia. International finance will also prove to be more important in the future for the Soviet Union and China, as part of their restructuring. China will soon become a major player in this market through the acquisition of control over Hong Kong in 1997.

THE ADJUSTMENT PROCESS

The coexistence of unusually large international surpluses and deficits indicates that the present situation is not in equilibrium, and that change must take place on a large scale. Restructuring is a part of this change process.

There are many imbalances, but the major cases are the American current-account deficit and the surpluses of Japan, Germany, Taiwan, and South Korea. Other LDC imbalances are related to hyperinflation, debt servicing, and commodity market fluctuations. These require more specialized adjustments. For the major imbalances, however, a primary adjustment process takes place through exchange-rate fluctuations. Apart from the changes that are taking place in shifting employment and output distributions, described in the previous section, there is a short-run adjustment in foreign exchange markets. Many of the structural adjustments have been taking place over decades, whereas the exchange-rate movements in one direction or another may last only a few years at a time.

There are very short-run rallies or plunges but by and large the U.S. dollar has been falling since February 1985. As a result, American goods are more price competitive on world markets, exports are enhanced, and imports are restrained. The surplus countries experience currency appreciation and the opposite effects on trade flows. After a long delay, U.S. trade figures have finally started to respond in the usual way, but the adjustment process will have to continue for several years to restore equilibrium. The German and Japanese accounts show corresponding changes, but not of a magnitude that wipes out their large surpluses. As for Taiwan and South Korea, their currencies have appreciated by smaller amounts and the resulting adjustments to trade accounts are barely visible, although they do seem to be taking place at the present time.

A useful decomposition of the factors of price competitiveness can be demonstrated by the following identity:

Price (local foreign currency) = unit cost × reciprocal of productivity × profit margin × exchange rate

where

unit cost = average wage rate ($)
productivity = output per worker-hour (labor productivity)
exchange rate = local currency units per dollar ($L/\$$)

as first approximations, determined by data availability. The yearly tabulations of these results for manufacturing without profit margins, by the Bureau of Labor Statistics, are an invaluable reference for international comparisons. They are presented in detail by the principal investigator in Chapter 6. For purposes of this discussion, it is useful to point out that among twelve industrial

countries, the United States showed the slowest rate of growth in labor productivity in 1960–73 and second slowest in 1973–79. The United Kingdom was
the slowest in the latter period and second slowest in the first period. It is also
important to note that all twelve major industrial countries showed very substantial slowdowns in labor productivity growth in 1973–79 compared with
1960–73. After the change in terms of trade for energy products, there was a
worldwide productivity slowdown. This is more than coincidental, but it is not
meant to imply that energy alone accounts for the productivity retardation.

In the most recent period, since 1979, several countries showed weaker
productivity growth than the United States or United Kingdom, and Japan was
usually high in the ranking. By 1986, the United States and United Kingdom
ranked just below Belgium in productivity improvement. In 1987, the United
Kingdom was second best (behind Norway), and the United States was in the
middle of the world distribution. It appears, however, that restructuring has
helped in the recuperation of efficiency in the two countries that had slipped
the most.

Unit costs, measured by hourly wage rates, did not rise rapidly in the
United States from 1960 to 1973. They were the slowest, and those in the
United Kingdom were the second slowest. In the next phase, 1973–79, the U.S.
rates rose fairly slowly, but not as slowly as those of Japan, Germany, and the
Netherlands. But in 1986 and 1987, the United States held wages to a growth
rate slower than that in any other major country except the Netherlands.

When the wage series are converted from local currency to U.S. dollar
units, American wage rates generally rose most slowly, except for Canadian
rates, up to 1979. During the period of the unusual rise in the value of the U.S.
dollar, American rates rose faster than those of others in dollar units, but by
1986 and 1987 wage rates, in dollar terms, rose least in the United States, except for Canadian rates in 1986.

When productivity, wage rates, and exchange rates are combined into unit
labor costs, measured in U.S. dollars, we find that the United States was cost
competitive in 1960–73 and 1973–79 (only Canada was more cost effective) but
was extremely noncompetitive during the period of the rising dollar, 1979–85.
When the dollar fell in 1986 and 1987, U.S. costs were again rising the least
(actually falling).

The Bureau of Labor Statistics recently included South Korea in the country comparisons, and this NIE was formerly cost ineffective in 1973–79 but
became very effective in 1986 and 1987. South Korea remained competitive by
preventing the won from appreciating very much until recent months.

These tabulations tell an interesting story, even though they do not include
the fourth factor, namely, profit margin. They show how macroeconomic policy adjustments can influence exchange rates and wage rates in becoming cost
competitive. They also show the fundamental contribution of technical factors,
subsumed in productivity growth. In the big adjustment that is presently ongoing, the United States relies heavily on exchange depreciation, almost like
an "economic crutch," to promote competitiveness. There are some productivity gains, but they are not as striking in a comparative quantitative sense as the
exchange-rate changes. This situation gives rise to the feeling that the United

States should do more, in a technical way, to become more efficient and rely less on major swings in macroeconomic policy, because such swings have destabilizing side effects for the rest of the world, particularly for the heavily indebted developing countries. Another way of looking at the matter is to argue that restructuring can be extremely important, in a sense necessary, but that it is a long-run process. In the present phase, large-scale depreciation has not brought quick restoration of equilibrium. There are many reasons for this, one being the net debtor status, so the search for means of achieving more technical efficiency must continue.

Reliable measures of the appropriate statistics on the profit margin factor are not generally available, but the end result enabling one to compare countries for competitiveness is shown in the final price, figured in a common currency unit. Price indexes for exports and imports are reported for Japan, Germany, and a few other countries. For a limited period such indexes are available for the United States. More common statistics, which are widely available, are the estimates of *unit value*. Flawed though such measures are, they do show the most important movements. In particular, they show that the United States became seriously noncompetitive after 1980, during the periods of both dollar appreciation and dollar depreciation. The United States costs, shown by the first three factors mentioned previously, were moving in an extremely noncompetitive direction during the period of the rising dollar, 1979–85. If they have been moving in a very competitive direction since 1986, as the published data show, then changes in profit margins may have prevented our becoming competitive. General opinion prevails that some countries whose currencies have appreciated very much since 1985 have been willing to accept lower-than-usual profit margins in order to retain as much market share as possible in the U.S. economy. Profit margins are quite flexible and cyclical. Countries with appreciating currencies or rising costs due to other factors can manipulate profit margins in order to remain competitive, but such policies rarely can be maintained for long periods of time. Eventually margins must approach normal values, and the forces making for competitiveness such as exchange depreciation, restrained unit costs, and higher productivity growth will eventually prevail.

Cyclical fluctuations in profits, exchange rates, and unit costs (wage rates) will always be taking place and will affect competitiveness, sometimes benefiting one economy and sometimes another, but the underlying factors are those associated with economic efficiency—productivity in the simple formula. To improve economic efficiency, a country should look to capital formation, a stable noninflationary economic environment, attitudes supporting a strong work ethic, and vigorous scientific and technical progress.

Investment in fixed capital is very important. An economy that is able to devote abundant resources to high rates of capital formation of the most advanced vintage will realize productivity gains. The progress that people all over the world admire in Japan and other East Asian economies has been driven by strong capital formation. Macroeconomic policy should be supportive of capital formation. Such instruments as special tax concessions, favorable borrowing costs, and strong fiscal demand can all enhance the rate of capital expansion.

Favorable borrowing costs will be affected partly by public policy, partly by saving decisions. Saving at all levels—personal, business, government, and foreign—is equally important, but countries that have had great success in realizing strong capital formation have also had significant portions of personal income devoted to saving. Without going into accounting and other institutional differences, the low American rates, near 3–5 percent, are not supportive of high rates of capital formation at low rates of interest, whereas Japanese, some European, and some other Asian rates in excess of 15 percent have supported high rates of capital formation. Competitiveness has usually been effective following periods of sustained capital expansion. Achievement of a high-savings–high-investment economy is the objective. If the savings rate is high and if funds are channeled into productive investment, it is possible to limit inflation. This has been demonstrated in many of the cases cited in Japan, other East Asian economies, and some European economies. Inflation can be highly distractive and moderate interest rates can be very accommodating. Low inflation with low interest rates, both well under 5 percent, are good targets.

The analysis has been quantitative thus far, but qualitative aspects are also important. A parsimonious attitude among people helps maintain a supportive saving rate. A strong work ethic helps to promote strong productivity. Another qualitative dimension is job satisfaction, that is, interest in one's job sufficient to ensure high-quality work. Japanese and East Asian products are not competitive in price alone, but also in quality of product. Goods from this part of the world formerly were cheap and of poor quality. From the 1960s, Japan concentrated on delivering high-quality products—first in traditional lines such as textiles; then in optics, electronics, chemicals, foodstuffs; later in cars; and now in virtually any good that is significant in international trade. Some of the most recent goods are extremely sophisticated and of excellent quality. Computers, scientific instruments, and pharmaceuticals are all of world-class quality. Many NIEs have been able to follow in Japan's footsteps. They are still behind Japan at the top level but have gradually reached high quality standards in textiles, apparel, shoes, food, optics, electronics, and most recently in cars. They too will move into the latest sophisticated lines.

Scientific and technical progress are exhibited in the products now available and in their quantitative rates of increase, but the basis for strength at this level comes from the educational and scientific research establishments. While North American and Western European institutions remain preeminent, it is apparent that significant gains are being made elsewhere. Also, the established institutions educate and train scholarly workers from everywhere. In my professional lifetime, I have seen American educational and research establishments grow to staffing ratios of more than one-half foreign-born. It is evident that competition will remain keen in the production of new ideas that ultimately show up in improved economic efficiency. Every competing economy will have to give high priority to the provision of resources for teaching and research. The outcome will be important for both quantity and quality in dimensions of competitiveness.

Two other developments are taking place in the world economy that can have profound effects on competitiveness. The socialist countries, which have lagged behind, are now taking major steps to compete in the world economy, led by economic reforms in China and perestroika in the Soviet Union. These countries obviously want to deliver better living conditions to their own citizens, but they fully realize that it will be necessary for them to open their economies and participate more fully in the international trading/financing system in order to be successful.

China is much further along than is the Soviet Union in these developments. Inflation is becoming an obstacle to China's progress, but the chances of success are still overwhelmingly favorable. As for the Soviet Union, the restructuring is just beginning, and it remains to be seen how it will succeed. Both countries are competitive in some primary commodities and in selected manufactures. Both are advanced militarily and trade in weaponry. They have a long distance to travel, however, before they can become competitive in the world economy in a general sense.

The Soviet Union is involved in another major development, the possibility of large-scale disarmament. The situation has never looked better for progress along this line. If the Soviet Union is to free resources for delivering a better living standard to its citizens, it will probably be necessary to lower the priority of the military. Both the United States and the Soviet Union would stand to gain in world competitiveness if they devoted fewer resources to national defense. It is no mere coincidence that Japan and Germany are strongly competitive and bear light defense burdens.

There are technological side effects from military research and development (R&D), but this is hardly a good or efficient way to realize benefits from technical progress. It remains to be seen if large-scale mutual disarmament can be realized and how released resources from such a development might be used, but there is a sizable potential to be used for civilian economic advantage, not only for domestic production but for economic efficiency.

POLICIES FOR ACHIEVING COMPETITIVENESS

The discussion thus far has indicated where some policy priorities might be placed, but an overall strategy for improving competitiveness in individual economies needs to be outlined. Establishment of a good balance between fiscal and monetary policy is of primary importance. All the instruments should be used together to try to achieve steadiness in exchange rates, interest rates, inflation, growth, and employment. This means that both fiscal and monetary authorities should act jointly. Through macro model simulation, rough equivalence can be established between effectiveness of the two types of policies. Within fiscal policy and within monetary policy there should also be balance. In the former case, both spending and tax changes should be used together; in the latter case, both domestic and foreign-oriented instruments should be used.

In the United States during the early part of the 1980s there was great imbalance between fiscal and monetary policies. This imbalance resulted in extremely high interest rates, which affected competitiveness in many ways. The extremely high rates that resulted from the imbalance increased unit (capital) costs, contributed to increases in the value of the dollar, and made it necessary for heavily indebted developing countries to curtail imports. These all were strongly adverse for American competitiveness. Had the same targets for the economy been reached in a balanced way, American competitiveness would not have suffered as much as it did.

International policy coordination can work in many ways to avoid extreme swings in trade and payments balances among countries participating in the coordination effort. International coordination makes use of the same instruments for fiscal and monetary policy that are used nationally; the only difference is that national choices are subordinated to the group decision about what is appropriate for each nation. Coordination does not imply complete similarity, only that policies be appropriate for world performance. Commercial policy, dealing with trade relations among countries, should be liberal, in support of free trade.

Competitiveness may be furthered by resort to industrial policy. Such policy directions are not generally accepted by economists, but they can be important in enlarging capital facilities in promising new areas, training workers in selective skills, and supporting R&D in promising industrial sectors. Educational and research support, particularly in scientific and engineering fields, can be aligned with industrial policy.

Support for capital formation, education, and R&D can, of course, be completely general and not targeted, as with industrial policy. This kind of policy emphasis gains wider acceptance among economists. Knowledge, training, and facilities expansion generally can be supported on the assumption that the results will diffuse, undirected, through the economy in a perfectly satisfactory way. That, too, is an appropriate policy line. The movement of an economy toward a system of high savings and high investment (typical of Japan now and not typical of the United States, for example) is perfectly consistent with the general, and weaker form of policy support for capital formation, education, and R&D.

For economies that have drifted toward a series of public controls, supervision, and regulation, a policy of deregulation may be pursued in the hopes of improving economic efficiency, which is very important for competitiveness. Such policies currently are quite popular. Some gains have been realized as a result of lessening regulatory policies, but there have been many excesses. It is often claimed that a loose attitude toward regulation encouraged financial activities that pulled corporate attention from the business of achieving greater efficiency in goods production and also contributed to such disturbing excesses as the stock market crash of 1987. Since deregulation, safety factors and operational efficiency in the airline industry appear to have deteriorated. There are many overall statistics to show improvement of airline production of service since deregulation, but the quality of service has definitely deteriorated, and there are many anecdotal reports indicating the deregulated drive for profits has been detrimental to safety and to the general quality of the transport services offered. Deregulation remains a controversial policy for improving competitiveness.

In this chapter, an underlying point has been that one of the most important steps that a country can take to become or remain competitive is to achieve economic efficiency. In this respect, strong productivity growth is crucial. For simplicity, I have referred to figures of labor productivity, but the proper concept is total factor productivity. In general, policy should be directed toward achieving such overall productivity growth; to be specific, energy policy should receive a great deal of attention. In the United States, inefficient use of energy over long periods of time made the country ill prepared to deal with the oil embargo and change in terms of trade for energy products after 1973. To quantify and establish the importance of energy, it is essential to estimate production functions that determine gross output as functions of such traditional inputs as labor and capital, but also to consider intermediate inputs. In other words, the KLEM production function (or one that is more disaggregated by input category) is essential to the analysis. Value-added production functions depending on capital and labor inputs are not adequate. The importance of energy variables (including their price) in contributing to the productivity slowdown is not always appreciated.[1] From this point of view, direct interventionist energy policy is called for. The market solution has not been satisfactory. As energy prices declined, the United States retreated from conservationist tendencies, used energy wastefully, and generated significant balance-of-payments deterioration. Oil is readily available now, as it was deceptively in the 1950s and 1960s, but will the supply be as available in the 1990s and later? There is enough doubt to suggest that policies to develop synthetic substitutes, ample storage stocks, and conservation need to be reintroduced and strengthened.

NOTE

1. Two University of Pennsylvania dissertation studies that approach the problem both from time-series and cross-section (for different industry groups) samples are Y. Kumasaka, *A Comparison of the Slowdown in Productivity Growth After the First Oil Crisis and Productivity Experiences from the Two Oil Crises between Japan and the USA*, 1984, and M. Prywes, *Three Essays on the Econometrics of Production, Productivity, and Capacity Utilization*, 1981. Both attribute a great deal of significance to energy changes in the productivity slowdown.

REFERENCES

Leisenring, C. A. 1988. "Job Growth in the 1980s: McJobs and Related McIssues." In *Comments on the Economy and Financial Markets*. Philadelphia: Core States Financial Corp.

Mishel, L. 1988. *Manufacturing Numbers: How Inaccurate Statistics Conceal US Industrial Decline*. Washington, D.C.: Economic Policy Institute.

3

Aggregate Productivity and Growth in an International Comparative Setting

JOHN F. HELLIWELL AND ALAN CHUNG

Aggregate productivity, competitiveness, and economic growth are linked in complex ways, both within and among countries. Countries or industries that have, from whatever source, higher rates of growth of output per unit of factor input are usually considered, when viewed in a microeconomic perspective, to be increasing in competitiveness, since their costs, in terms of real factor inputs, are rising less fast than are those of their competitors. Yet in the macroeconomic context the reverse is likely to be the case, as countries with more rapidly growing levels of productivity will generally require continuing increases in their real exchange rates to keep their current accounts in balance with any desired pattern of international investment. This will generally mean that their relative wage rates, which are a frequently used measure of international competitiveness, will rise in response to the faster technical progress.[1] In this chapter we use aggregate comparative data for national economies to unravel some of these complex relationships.

We start by exploring in a tentative way the evolution of real output per capita in eighty-nine economies and of more precisely defined measures of aggregate labor productivity in a smaller sample of nineteen industrial economies which have comparable data for output, employment, and capital stock. We shall proceed in four separate stages. In the second section, using a large sample of countries, we make international comparisons of per capita real income growth over the 1973–83 period. We are restricted to this fairly short and unrepresentative data period in order to cover a large number of countries. This large sample of data is used to consider in a preliminary way some simple hypotheses explaining international differences in growth rates. We are particularly interested in whether there is any evidence of convergence in growth rates, which is one of the key ideas we investigate in subsequent sections, using a longer sample of more complete data for the industrial countries.

In the third section, we use an explicit production function, based on aggregate data for a group of nineteen industrial countries, to measure the average rates of growth of labor efficiency or Harrod-neutral technical progress over a longer time period, running from 1960 to 1985. We use these data to assess the strength of the evidence for international convergence in the levels and rates of growth of aggregate productivity in industrial countries over this period and to provide some rough measures of comparative productivity levels to use in our subsequent analysis.

Next we assess whether globalization, spurred by more open trading rules and by declining relative costs of transportation and communications and evidenced by growth rates for trade well in excess of those for output, may have increased average rates of growth of income and productivity in those countries that were or became more open to foreign trade.

Finally, we consider some reverse linkages from aggregate productivity to competitiveness, where competitiveness is measured by gaps between market and purchasing-power parity (PPP) exchange rates.

SAVINGS, INVESTMENT, AND GROWTH

In this section we explore some of the macroeconomic linkages among investment, savings, both domestic and foreign, and the rates of growth of per capita income. We find strong linkages between investment rates and growth rates, but little evidence that countries with relatively high rates of investment and growth have financed their investment by net inflows of foreign capital.

How essential have net international transfers of resources been to the growth of industrial and developing countries? To what extent have the countries with high growth rates been able to achieve that growth by importing foreign capital to finance their investment? Put the other way around, to what extent have capital-importing countries tended to have higher rates of economic growth?

The statistics in Appendix 3-1 shed some light on this question by showing, for the sample of eighty-nine countries for which comparable data are available, the correlation between average current-account balances and average rates of growth of real GNP per capita from 1973 to 1983.[2] When all countries are considered together, the cross-sectional correlation between current-account balances and real growth rates is slightly positive. The correlation is also positive if the developing countries are examined as a group by excluding the industrial countries. There is thus little evidence that countries with higher growth rates also, on average, made greater use of net foreign savings.[3]

This is an intriguing result. If the additional use of net foreign capital is not generally associated with higher rates of economic growth, is this because (a) economic growth has not required additional investment, and hence saving, or (b) because the necessary investment was matched by domestic savings? If the latter, was this because foreign capital was not available, or because the sources of economic growth automatically generated enough domestic saving to finance the needed investment?

Looking at these possibilities in order, we first consider whether there is a close correlation between investment rates and growth rates. Columns 1 and 2 in Table 3-1 show the results of regressions testing the linkage between international differences in growth rates and differences in investment rates, along with some other factors that have been found in earlier studies to help explain the comparative growth performance of large samples of diverse economies.[4] The first result to note is that there is a fairly strong relationship between investment and growth, with a 1 percent faster rate of growth being associated with investment being higher by just over 0.2 percent of GDP.

The same linkage is also evident in the correlations seen in Appendix 3-1, which show that for all groups of countries, growth rates are positively correlated with investment rates. This cannot be taken to mean simply that high investment produces high growth, as the reverse relationship, long known as the accelerator model of investment, explains high investment rates in terms of the high rates of growth of output. The important point, for our present purposes, is not whether investment is driving growth, or vice versa, but that countries with high average growth rate do tend, for whichever reason, to have high investment rates as well.

Regression 2 also shows that once the effects of investment on growth are accounted for, the partial effect of the current account on growth is significantly positive. What this suggests is that for many countries growth is primarily export-led. Thus countries with stronger net exports, and hence current

Table 3-1 Factors Influencing per Capita GNP Growth and the Effects of Domestic Savings on Investment[a]

Explanatory Variables	Estimated Coefficients				
	(1) All	(2) All	(3) Developed	(4) Developing	(5) All
LCU	−0.29813	−0.49081			
	(1.59)	(2.61)			
I	0.21008	0.22377			
	(5.08)	(5.66)			
CA		0.13624			
		(3.20)			
SAVE			0.79491	0.52281	0.52794
			(6.04)	(8.35)	(9.60)
CONSTANT	−3.1926	−3.0841	5.8341	12.7620	12.4360
	(3.29)	(3.34)	(2.01)	(10.18)	(11.04)
$\bar{R}^2$	0.2140	0.2904	0.6511	0.5026	0.5089
SEE	2.1702	2.0619	2.3133	4.3780	4.0389

[a]The variables in the regressions are derived from the data described in Appendix 3-1. The full eighty-nine–country sample is denoted by "All." The developed countries are the industrial country group specified in the *IMF International Financial Statistics Yearbook*. The developing countries are defined as the remaining countries. The dependent variable for equations 1 and 2 is the average annual percentage growth of real GNP per capita 1973–83. LCU is the logarithm of 1973 GDP per capita in thousands of nominal U.S. dollars. I is the average annual nominal investment to GDP ratio (percent) for 1973–83. CA is the average annual current account to GDP ratio (percent) for 1973–83. The dependent variable for equations 3, 4, and 5 is the average annual nominal investment to GDP ratio (percent) for 1973–83. SAVE is the average annual total nominal domestic saving to GDP ratio (percent) for 1973–83.

accounts, for given levels of investment, also tend to have higher average growth rates of real GNP.

Another important hypothesis about international differences in growth rates, tested principally by the experience of the industrial countries (e.g., Baumol, 1986; Helliwell, Sturm, and Salou, 1985; and Maddison, 1982), is that the international transferability of knowledge and goods, with or without the net transfer of resources by means of capital flows, entails a process of convergence of the levels of income among countries.

Thus from any given starting point, countries with lower initial levels of income will have higher rates of growth than will richer countries. This should mean that if the initial level of per capita income is included in the equation explaining international differences in growth rates, it should reveal that countries with higher levels of income have lower average growth rates, for given rates of investment spending. This is what the results in columns 1 and 2 of Table 3-1 show, although the effect is rather weak.[5]

There is also the possibility that the poorest countries may be, for one reason or another, unprepared or ill-equipped for the process of convergence. To provide a rough test of this possibility, we followed Chenery's (1986, p. 29) suggestion of adding a quadratic term in initial income. If on average the poorest countries were in some form of poverty trap, and unable to take part in the process of convergence, then the initial level of income would attract a positive coefficient while income squared would take a negative coefficient, as reported by Chenery. We found, for our sample, that both the linear and quadratic terms took negative signs, implying higher average rates of growth for the poorest countries, after accounting for the effects of investment. Of course it is important to remember that the average income levels in the poorest countries are so far below those in the rest of the world that these countries would have to have higher rates of growth for many years before their absolute income levels were increasing as much from year to year as those in the richer countries.[6]

In supplementary experiments, we included separate constant terms for each of the regions of the developing world, to test whether their average rates of growth have been above or below those in the industrial countries, after allowing for the effects of growth convergence and for different investment rates. The coefficients on these variables show that growth rates in Africa and Latin America have been below those in the industrial countries, whereas those of developing countries in Europe and Asia have been above those in industrial countries. These differences were not statistically significant.

The evidence we have assessed so far seems to suggest that higher growth has generally been associated with higher investment, so that the lack of correlation between growth and inflows of foreign savings does not mean that growth does not require investment. Since by definition domestic investment equals the sum of domestic and foreign savings, if high investment is not financed by foreign savings, there must be a rise in domestic savings. In almost all regions, as shown by the correlations reported in Appendix 3-1, there is a significant positive association between domestic investment and domestic savings rates. There is an exception posed by the Middle Eastern countries, where there is a negative correlation between domestic savings and investment rates.

This arises because the countries in the Middle East with the highest savings rates (Oman and Saudi Arabia) had those high rates because of the dramatic increase in oil revenues, which far exceeded any feasible plans for domestic spending, and hence were recycled abroad. The highest investment rates, on the other hand, were in countries like Jordan and Yemen, with much smaller GDP per capita and little by way of oil revenues.

Equations 3 to 5 of Table 3-1 show regressions of the type used by Feldstein and Horioka (1980) and Felstein (1983), to explain international differences in investment rates in terms of international differences in savings rates. Feldstein and Horioka argue that if capital mobility, and hence the ease of international transfer of resources to the nations with the highest rates of return on investment, were perfect, then there would be no significant effect of domestic savings rates on domestic investment rates. The coefficients reported in Table 3-1 are estimated for all countries as well as for the industrial and developing countries as separate groups.

Our results show, as do those of Frankel, Dooley, and Mathieson (1986), that the link between national savings and domestic investment is slightly closer for the developed than for most of the groups of developing countries. This result is thought to cast doubt on the idea that the high correlation between domestic investment and savings rates is an index of the extent to which there are impediments to international transfer of resources, since by most measures capital appears to move more easily to and from individual industrial countries than to and from developing countries. The result may be due to the fact that for some developing countries, especially the smaller ones, major investment projects (e.g., the Bougainville copper mine in Papua New Guinea) tend to be directly financed by foreign savings, thus loosening the link between domestic investment and national savings.

It must be true that in some circumstances a larger and more accessible pool of international resources would increase economic growth possibilities for developing countries. The average aggregate experience, as shown by the international data for the last twenty years, is either that there have not been great international differences in the marginal returns on investment or that savings have not been directed to where the resulting growth prospects were systematically better. It is also possible, of course, that there were such differences, and that the resources transferred were on average of net benefit, but that the other reasons for international differences in growth rates were so much larger in total importance that the effect of the transfer of resources is obscured in the overall data.

PRODUCTIVITY GROWTH IN THE INDUSTRIAL COUNTRIES

For the industrial countries, there are comparably defined output data for a longer period and reasonably comparable data for employment and capital stocks (see Appendix 3-2). Thus it is possible to use a production function approach, adjusting for international differences in the growth rates of employment and capital stock and for abnormal rates of capacity utilization, to develop a more precise measure of aggregate productivity, and to test some alternative hypotheses about the determinants of productivity growth. We shall do this by applying a "factor utilization" approach (Helliwell and Chung 1986), which combines a production function to define normal output with an explicit production decision modeling the choice by firms of the rate of utilization of the stocks of employed labor and capital. This model was applied by Helliwell, Sturm, and Salou (1985), in the context of a three-factor nested CES production function (labor, combining with a bundle of capital and energy), to compare the 1973–85 productivity slowdown in the seven major industrial countries, and by Helliwell (1989), using a two-factor CES production function for normal output, to compare the levels and growth rates of Harrod-neutral technical progress or productivity in the United States, Japan, and Canada.

In this chapter, we apply the same two-factor CES framework to 1960–85 data for nineteen OECD countries. The details of the specification and estimation are reported in Appendix 3-2. The larger sample of countries permits stronger tests of some competing hypotheses about the reasons for international differences in the levels and rates of growth of aggregate productivity. To permit international comparisons of productivity levels, the constant-price output and capital stock data for the different countries are converted into common units, referred to as international dollars,[7] using the most recently available estimates for purchasing-power parity (PPP) exchange rates (OECD, 1987). We leave until the final section of the chapter our discussion of the linkages between real exchange rates (as represented by differences between actual and PPP exchange rates), productivity, income levels, and competitiveness. For the purposes of this section, we ignore actual exchange rates and use the PPP rates as the most appropriate means of obtaining internationally comparable measures of real output.

To simplify our comparisons, and to avoid straining the quality of our data, which require a number of arbitrary approximations, especially in the estimation of real capital stocks, we assume the same substitution and scale parameters in the CES production functions for each country, thus permitting the definition and comparison of Harrod-neutral productivity indexes for each of the nineteen countries for which PPP exchange rates are available. Following the factor utilization approach, the trends, but not the cyclical variations, of these series can be examined to cast light on the longer term levels and changes in aggregate productivity.[8]

In this section, we consider two alternative models of the determination of technical progress. The first, which we refer to as the constant case, assumes that there is for each country a rate of Harrod-neutral technical progress that is constant over time, but which may differ among countries. International variations in this rate of technical progress are examined in Table 3-2 to search for evidence for or against the hypothesis of convergence.

The second model of technical progress applies and tests a particular model of convergence, in which productivity growth rates, and possibly levels, converge to those of the United States, which throughout the sample period had the highest level of income per capita and the highest measured level of the aggregate productivity index among the major industrial countries.[9] This we

Table 3-2   Cross-Country Evidence of Convergence[a]

Explanatory	Estimated Coefficients		
Variables	(1)	(2)	(3)
LCUGDP	− 2.0551	− 2.8714	
	(5.03)	(7.05)	
ln π_m			− 2.7218
			(7.59)
CONSTANT	5.9070	6.8502	92.2580
	(9.52)	(11.08)	(7.81)
$\bar{R}^2$	0.5742	0.7301	0.7589
SEE	0.5884	0.5864	0.5542

[a]The dependent variable of Equation 1 is the average annual percentage growth of gross domestic product per capita in international dollars between 1960 and 1985. The dependent variable of equations 2 and 3 is the constant annual percentage growth rate of the productivity index for Harrod-neutral technical progress (see Appendix 3-2). The independent variable LCUGDP is the logarithm of the initial 1960 level of GDP per capita for each country in thousands of international dollars. The variable ln π_m is the logarithm of the measured Harrod-neutral productivity index in each country in 1960. The sample includes the G-7 and twelve smaller OECD countries. Estimation by ordinary least squares.

refer to as the catch-up case, because convergence implies that the countries starting with lower levels of productivity will, by dint of higher rates of productivity increase during the convergence process, eventually catch up to the technology and productivity levels of the leading countries. This terminology is strictly appropriate only in the case where productivity levels and rates of growth both converge as time progresses. In the case where growth rates converge but levels do not, the countries with initially lower levels of productivity may never catch up, or they may catch up and then pass the countries with initially higher levels.

Starting with the constant case, Appendix 3-2 reports the average growth rates of the Harrod-neutral productivity index Π, and columns 2 and 3 in Table 3-2 list the results of regressions attempting to test the convergence hypothesis by regressing the international differences in these productivity growth rates on the initial (1960) levels of per capita real income (in column 2 of Table 3-2) and on the measured productivity index (in column 3).

According to the convergence hypothesis, advanced for the European countries by Gerschenkron (1962) and supported by some earlier empirical results,[10] the average rate of growth of productivity should be higher for those countries that were relatively "backward" (i.e., with low levels of income or productivity) at the beginning of the period of history under review.[11] Thus there should be a negative correlation between international differences in growth rates and initial levels of income or productivity. In principle, this relation should be stronger when the growth rates and productivity levels are adjusted for differences in levels and rates of growth of investment, and when PPPs rather than market exchange rates are used to make international comparisons of productivity levels. The data analyzed in Appendix 3-1, and discussed in the previous section, show for industrial countries only a weak negative correlation (− 0.09) between 1973 real GNP per capita (valued at market exchange rates) and the growth rates of real per capita GNP over the subsequent decade. In this section we consider the effects of using a longer sample period, using PPPs for international conversions, and using productivity indexes adjusted for labor force and capital stock growth, for changes in the unemployment rate, and for cyclical variations in factor utilization.

The first changes we consider are to extend the sample period to twenty-five years and to use PPP exchange rates published by the OECD (1987) to place the initial measures of real output (we use real GDP, as published by the OECD in their standardized national accounts, SNAs) on a comparable basis. These changes substantially support the convergence hypothesis, as shown by column 1 in Table 3-2. The simple correlation between the growth rates and the initial income levels is −0.77, and the regression explains more than half of the international variance in growth rates of real GDP.[12]

The next adjustment is to move from total output growth to the growth of the Harrod-neutral productivity index Π to represent the relevant measure of productivity, thus abstracting from changes in labor force participation, changes in unemployment, and different rates of capital stock growth. This is done in column 2 of Table 3-2, which changes the dependent variable but still uses initial differences in per capita GDP as the measure of relative backwardness. The new dependent variable has substantially more variance, and a higher proportion of this variance is explained by the regression.

The final conceptual improvement is to use the initial level of the measured productivity variable, rather than of real GDP per capita, as the measure of the amount of "backwardness," or of catch-up remaining to be done. This provides still further improvement, as shown by column 3, which now explains more than 75 percent of the international variance in productivity growth rates. This is much stronger evidence in favor of convergence than was available from the shorter and cruder comparisons possible in the preceding section, and yet the sample of countries is large enough, and the sample period still short enough, to avoid the sample selection and measurement error problems suggested by De Long (1988).

Given the fairly strong evidence favoring convergence of productivity levels among the industrial countries, at least over the period since 1960, it would seem desirable to model the growth of productivity indexes in a way that embodies the central notion of convergence, which is that productivity indexes will tend toward common rates, and perhaps toward common levels.[13] Table 3-3 shows the results of the application to each of the industrial countries (excluding the United States) of the catch-up model described here and detailed in Appendix 3-2. The coefficients on the calculated U.S. productivity index (which has a constant rate of growth)[14] and the lagged national measured productivity index are constrained to sum to 1.0, which forces the productivity growth rates to converge eventually to a common value, equal to that of the United States. If the constant terms are zero, then the levels will also eventually be the same.[15]

The results in Table 3-3 reveal significant evidence in favor of the catch-up hypothesis for all countries except New Zealand and Norway, whose results are still supportive but less so because of the lower levels of significance of the catch-up coefficients. Although these results are strikingly strong in their support of the catch-up hypothesis, there is also evidence that the rate of conver-

Table 3-3   The Catch-Up Model of Technical Progress[a]

	ln π_{m-1}	ln $\hat{\pi}_{us}$	Constant	See	R^2	Durbin–Watson
Japan	0.8619 (46.00)	0.1381 (7.37)	−0.0612 (3.96)	0.0300	0.9896	1.7107
West Germany	0.9127 (43.54)	0.0873 (4.16)	−0.0267 (1.93)	0.0216	0.9899	1.7821
France	0.9157 (87.86)	0.0843 (8.09)	−0.0174 (2.45)	0.0138	0.9974	1.1117
United Kingdom	0.8698 (14.83)	0.1302 (2.22)	−0.0765 (1.80)	0.0266	0.9563	1.9199
Italy	0.8749 (44.08)	0.1251 (6.30)	−0.0500 (3.46)	0.0255	0.9900	1.5916
Canada	0.8806 (27.57)	0.1194 (3.74)	−0.0150 (1.52)	0.0191	0.9818	1.4768
Australia	0.7963 (13.53)	0.2037 (3.46)	−0.0753 (2.74)	0.0274	0.9487	2.0571
Austria	0.9351 (55.26)	0.0649 (3.84)	−0.0199 (1.43)	0.0199	0.9936	1.7143
Belgium	0.9293 (51.43)	0.0707 (3.91)	−0.0076 (0.73)	0.0209	0.9917	2.1764
Denmark	0.8842 (28.02)	0.1158 (3.67)	−0.0584 (2.47)	0.0231	0.9812	2.4685
Finland	0.9396 (43.06)	0.0604 (2.77)	−0.0243 (1.15)	0.0263	0.9877	1.7463
Ireland	0.9326 (33.45)	0.0674 (2.42)	−0.0325 (1.13)	0.0369	0.9811	1.7472
Netherlands	0.9393 (39.41)	0.0607 (2.55)	0.0058 (0.59)	0.0249	0.9870	1.8457
New Zealand	0.9226 (13.76)	0.0774 (1.15)	−0.0242 (0.97)	0.0366	0.5289	1.7647
Norway	0.9524 (29.73)	0.0476 (1.49)	−0.0056 (0.25)	0.0231	0.9833	2.0154
Spain	0.9084 (65.61)	0.0916 (6.61)	−0.0197 (1.86)	0.0204	0.9953	1.8117
Sweden	0.7988 (20.21)	0.2012 (5.09)	−0.1103 (4.27)	0.0228	0.9670	2.0747
Switzerland	0.8313 (20.72)	0.1687 (4.20)	−0.0445 (2.86)	0.0208	0.9712	1.5212

[a]The dependent variable is ln π_m, the measured Harrod-neutral productivity index. ln π_{m-1} is the lagged value and ln $\hat{\pi}_{us}$ the calculated U.S. values from the U.S. constant-case regression. The coefficients of these two variables are restricted to sum to one. See the section on specification in Appendix 3-2 for a more complete description. Estimation was by seemingly unrelated regressions (SUR) using a 1961–85 sample.

gence differs from country to country and that the equilibrium productivity levels vary from country to country, as indicated by constant terms that in many cases differ significantly from zero. We turn in the next section to consider some of the possible reasons for these international differences.

GLOBALIZATION AND PRODUCTIVITY

What are the linkages between productivity growth and international trade and competitiveness? In the next section we consider the links between productivity and competitiveness, but here we present some preliminary findings on the extent to which the globalization of economic activity since 1960 may have facilitated the convergence of productivity growth documented earlier. Over that period, the relative costs of transportation and communications have dropped dramatically, and markets for trade in goods and services, especially capital services, have become much more international. It is almost inevitable that this globalization of production and investment has played a part in the productivity convergence that has taken place among the industrial countries.

In this section, we look for measures of the extent to which national economies have become more open and markets more globalized, with the aim of seeing whether differences in the degree of openness among countries and over time play a role in explaining differences in the rate of productivity increase. We saw earlier, perhaps surprisingly, that growth of incomes was not correlated with net inflows of capital from abroad. This does not necessarily mean that the general opening up of world capital markets has not played an important role in the transfer of technology, since these transfers can easily take place without net flows of financial capital. In the absence of easily available quantitative measures of the extent of the openness of national capital markets, we restrict our current empirical investigations to the markets for goods and services, without making any special allowance for capital services.

The primary measure we employ for the opening up to trade is the increase in the ratio of total trade to GNP. Table 3-4 reports the results of cross-sectional regressions, similar to those in columns (2) and (3) of Table 3-2, with a variable measuring the growth of trade[16] added to see if it contributes to the explanation of international differences in average growth rates for real income and productivity. The results show significant evidence that countries that increased

Table 3-4 Cross-Country Evidence of the Effects of Globalization on the Growth of the Labor Productivity Index[a]

Explanatory	Estimated Coefficients	
Variables	(1)	(2)
LCUGDP	−2.3797	
	(5.13)	
ln π_m		−2.2465
		(6.84)
OPEN	1.2260	1.5689
	(1.86)	(3.12)
CONSTANT	5.3663	75.6320
	(5.44)	(6.89)
$\bar{R}^2$	0.7641	0.8408
SEE	0.5483	0.4503

[a]The dependent variable is the constant annual percentage growth rate of the productivity index for Harrod-neutral technical progress (see Appendix 3-2). The independent variable LCUGDP is the logarithm of the initial 1960 level of gross domestic product per capita for each country in thousands of international dollars. The independent variable ln π_m is the logarithm of the measured Harrod-neutral productivity index in each country in 1960. The independent variable OPEN measures the change in "openness" in each country, where the degree of openness is measured by the sum of exports and imports over gross national product. The change is for the period 1960–85, and the variable is defined as the logarithm of the 1985 value over the 1960 value. The sample includes the G-7 and twelve smaller OECD countries. Estimation by ordinary least squares.

their trade shares most between 1960 and 1985 also had faster rates of growth of productivity, even after accounting for differences caused by initial productivity levels. The addition of the trade growth variable (called OPEN in the table) raises from 0.76 to 0.84 the portion of the international differences in average productivity growth rates that is explained by the convergence hypothesis. If it is reasonable, as we would suppose, to treat the growth of trade shares as a proxy for the increasing internationalization of markets, and to view this as a major channel by which convergence takes place, then Table 3-4 supports the convergence hypothesis even more strongly than Table 3-2.

The results of adding a five-year moving average of changes in trade shares to the time-series catch-up equations of Table 3-3 are shown in Table 3-5. The change in each country's openness is included as an additional variable, with all coefficients (except the constant terms) constrained to be the same for each country,[17] and with the U.S. rate of productivity growth assumed to be constant, as in the earlier equations. The hypothesis is that the change in openness will influence the rate of convergence toward the attainable productivity frontier. The results support the hypothesis.[18]

Although the results presented thus far may seem to support the convergence hypothesis strongly, they do not discriminate between convergence and the most prevalent alternative view of recent productivity history—that there was for some reason a general reduction in the underlying rate of productivity growth starting in 1974, linked originally to the consequences of the first OPEC oil price increases. If there had been a general slowdown of productivity increase starting in 1974, for reasons unrelated to convergence, then the regressions fitted in Table 3-3 would nonetheless indicate significant support for the convergence hypothesis, which also implies productivity slowdown. To distinguish the two possibilities, we need sharper tests. Such tests are possible within the context of the factor utilization model of production and within any set of

Table 3-5 Effects of Globalization on the Rate of Technical Progress[a]

RTIME	CONSTANT	SEE	$\bar{R}^2$	Durbin–Watson
United States				
0.007248	33.402	0.04307	0.6178	0.3284
(5.32)	(406.87)			

Non U.S. restricted coefficients

$\ln \pi_{m-1}$	$\ln \hat{\pi}_{us}$	DOPENA
0.91913	0.080868	0.14084
(183.28)	(16.13)	(3.74)

[a]The dependent variable is $\ln \pi_m$, the logarithm of the measured Harrod-neutral productivity index. The U.S. equation has RTIME as an independent variable, and is estimated by ordinary least squares (sample 1960–85). RTIME is a time index (= 1 in 1960). The non-U.S. equations are estimated using the SUR estimator (sample 1963–85) with all coefficients (except the constant) constrained to be the same for each country. $\ln \pi_{m-1}$ is the lagged value of $\ln \pi_m$ and $\ln \hat{\pi}_{us}$ is the calculated U.S. value of the measured Harrod-neutral productivity index (obtained from the predicted values of the U.S. equation). The coefficients of these two variables are restricted to sum to one. DOPENA is the annual change in "openness" defined as the log difference of current and lagged values of the five-year moving average of exports plus imports divided by GNP.

derived investment and labor demand equations that are consistently derived from an explicit production function that embodies a specific model of technical progress. The structure of the output and derived factor demand equations is described briefly in Appendix 3-2.

For each of several alternative models of technical progress, we derive and estimate the corresponding equations for output, investment, and employment, to see whether the resulting equations allow us to choose among the competing models of technical progress. The U.S. output equation is tested first with the results reported in Appendix 3-2, Table 3-6.[19] The three competing models of technical progress tested for the United States are the constant-productivity growth model, the constant growth model adjusted for a post-1974 productivity break, and the constant growth model adjusted for the effects of increased openness. Overall, the tests reject the break model, shown by the significant additional information provided by the competing convergence and constant models in the P test and by the lower C-test coefficients for the break model when it is compared directly with each alternative model. The C test indicates weak preference for the constant growth model over the model including the effects of increased openness. The Godfrey tests do not support one particular model. We therefore choose the constant model for the United States in the subsequent models of convergence.

Tests of alternative models of technical progress applied to the remaining eighteen industrial countries are reported in the remaining tables of Appendix 3-2 (Tables 3-7 to 3-9).[20] The output tests in Table 3-7 indicate strong preference for the convergence models, both alone and with openness. The P tests in Table 3-7 show that the additional information provided by the constant and break models, given the convergence models, is not significant, while the convergence models add significant additional information at the 95 percent level to the constant and break models. The C tests indicate that the convergence models are uniformly more important than either constant or break models. The investment and employment tests, in Tables 3-8 and 3-9, appear to have less power to discriminate between models[21] and to provide less clear-cut evidence of preference for the convergence models. The tests, especially for employment, rank the constant growth model above the convergence models, which in turn are preferred to the productivity break model. These test results should be regarded as provisional, especially since they are based on a particular model of output determination, and given that the derived factor demand equations provide less supportive evidence relative to the output equation tests in favor of the convergence hypothesis.

PRODUCTIVITY AND COMPETITIVENESS

We have thus far seen evidence of international convergence in rates of growth, and to some extent of levels, of income, output, and aggregate productivity. We have also seen some evidence that this convergence is faster, and eventual productivity levels higher, for countries that have done most to increase their openness, as measured by ratios of trade to GDP. What are the likely consequences of this for international competitiveness? Seen from the viewpoint of the individual firm or industry, which can treat wage rates, prices, and exchange rates as determined by larger forces, any increase in productivity translates into lower costs per unit of output, thus increasing the firm's or industry's ability to compete successfully in domestic and international markets. At the aggregate level, matters are very different, for two key reasons. First, if aggregate productivity is higher, by dint of the labor-augmenting technical progress modeled in this chapter, then real wages will also tend to rise. Second, even if the productivity increases were concentrated in the production of tradable goods, the resulting current-account surpluses (assuming elastic world demand) would eventually have to be sufficiently choked off, by an appreciating real exchange rate, to maintain macroeconomic balance of savings, investment, and portfolio preferences. For both reasons, countries with rapidly growing productivity will tend to have rising real exchange rates that will, to an extent that differs by industry and that depends on the industrial pattern of technical progress, reduce the foreign competitiveness of their domestic output. Whether this effect will, for a specific industry or firm, more than offset the cost-reducing effects of their own technical progress will depend on the relation between their own productivity increases and those in the economy as a whole, in competing industries abroad, and at the aggregate level in other countries. What is there by way of evidence?

Since we are dealing here with aggregate data, we cannot report on relative productivity growth in different industries, let alone compare these interindustry differences among countries. At the aggregate level, however, some important regularities appear. Most generally, when PPPs are calculated for GDP, using either bilateral or multilateral expenditure weights, they show that for any pair of countries with differing real GDP per capita, the exchange rate of the richer country will tend to exceed the PPP value. If PPPs are calculated for different categories of final expenditure, then divergences from PPP, between pairs of countries with different levels of real per capita GDP, are larger for services than for goods.[22] This is to be expected, given the generally lower transport costs for goods and the fact that many service prices move closely with wage rates, which in turn depend on per capita GDP.

Figure 3-1 shows the influence of per capita GDP levels on international differences in price levels. For two example years, 1980 and 1985, Figure 3-1 shows the price levels and the values that are predicted by log-linear equations. The dependent variable, which we follow Hill (1986) in calling the international price level, is for each country the PPP exchange rate in that year divided by the market exchange rate, where in each case the exchange rate is defined in terms of the amount of domestic currency required to purchase one U.S. dollar. Values above 100.0 thus indicate countries where the average price of GDP, taken from OECD (1987) and using OECD average expenditure weights, is higher than in the United States, when compared at current exchange rates. The regression lines are from pooled log-linear equations with separate intercepts for each year and a common slope parameter equal to 0.413.[23] The interpretation of the equation is that a 10 percent higher real GDP, relative to

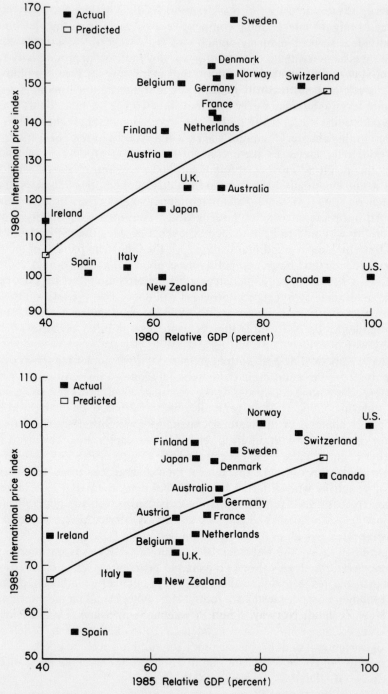

Figure 3-1   International Price indices and real GNP per capita relative to the United States. *Source:* OECD (1987).

the international average, will be associated with a 4 percent higher real value of the domestic currency.

In 1980, price levels were lower in North America than almost anywhere else, even before allowing for the effects of income differences, so that the United States and Canada lie furthest from the regression plane for that year. Chief among the countries with high real exchange rates in 1980 were the countries of northern Europe, excluding only the United Kingdom.

By 1985, real exchange rates had moved substantially, and the regression line in general fits the data more closely than in 1980. The United States ties with Norway in having the highest price level, although the U.S. price level is almost exactly what would be expected given its high level of real GDP per capita.

The fact that the United States was right on the regression line in 1985 should provide adequate warning that PPP calculations, whether adjusted or not for income differences, are not a guide to the exchange rates that are needed to maintain a sustainable current-account balance. Our reason for presenting the data and for emphasizing the relationship between per capita income and the real exchange rate is to expose one of the reverse linkages between productivity increases and competitiveness. When income-increasing productivity improvements become important at the aggregate level, they tend to lead to increases in the real exchange rate. The partial effect of these higher real exchange rates for the richer countries is to reduce their international competitiveness relative to countries with lower levels of income. The higher exchange rate then promotes reallocation of resources to accommodate the changing pattern of comparative advantage implied by the higher domestic levels of income.[24]

APPENDIX 3-1   CORRELATION MATRICES OF VARIABLES

This appendix reports correlation matrices for a sample of eighty-nine countries and six variables. The underlying data are available upon request to the authors.

Country Classifications

- *Industrial Countries:* Australia, Austria, Belgium, Canada, Denmark, Finland, France, Germany, Iceland, Ireland, Italy, Japan, Netherlands, New Zealand, Norway, Spain, Sweden, Switzerland, United Kingdom, United States
- *Developing Asian Countries:* Fiji, India, Indonesia, Korea, Malaysia, Myanmar, Pakistan, Papua New Guinea, Philippines, Singapore, Sri Lanka, Thailand
- *Developing African Countries:* Algeria, Burkina Faso, Cameroon, Congo, Ethiopia, Gana, Ivory Coast, Kenya, Malawi, Mauritius, Morocco, Niger, Nigeria, Rwanda, Senegal, Sierra Leone, South Africa, Togo, Tunisia, Zaire, Zambia

- *Developing European Countries:* Greece, Hungary, Malta, Portugal, Yugoslavia
- *Developing Middle Eastern Countries:* Egypt, Israel, Jordan, Libya, Oman, Saudi Arabia, Syrian Arab Republic, Yemen Arab Republic
- *Developing Western Hemisphere Countries:* Bahamas, Barbados, Bolivia, Brazil, Chile, Columbia, Costa Rica, Dominican Republic, Ecuador, El Salvador, Guatemala, Guyana, Haiti, Honduras, Jamaica, Mexico, Nicaragua, Panama, Paraguay, Peru, Trinidad and Tobago, Uruguay, Venezuela

Variables

GNP, real GNP per capita, annual percentage growth rate, 1973–83
CU, 1973 GDP per capita, U.S. dollars
CA, average 1973–83 current account surplus as percent of GDP
I, average 1973–83 investment as percent of GDP
SAVE, average 1973–83 domestic saving as percent of GDP
OIL, dummy variable set equal to 1 for oil-producing countries

All Countries

(1) GNP	1.00000					
(2) CU	−0.05127	1.00000				
(3) CA	0.21212	0.29603	1.00000			
(4) I	0.45745	0.10115	−0.02698	1.00000		
(5) SAVE	0.48457	0.28080	0.67721	0.71725	1.00000	
(6) OIL	0.12530	−0.02237	0.19861	0.21326	0.29542	1.00000
	GNP	CU	CA	I	SAVE	OIL

All Developing Countries

(1) GNP	1.00000					
(2) CU	−0.02778	1.00000				
(3) CA	0.22924	0.26621	1.00000			
(4) I	0.46272	0.21016	−0.02583	1.00000		
(5) SAVE	0.49933	0.34029	0.68140	0.71407	1.00000	
(6) OIL	0.15158	0.10893	0.26643	0.22673	0.35259	1.00000
	GNP	CU	CA	I	SAVE	OIL

Industrial Countries

(1) GNP	1.00000					
(2) CU	−0.09583	1.00000				
(3) CA	0.14411	0.39576	1.00000			
(4) I	0.54950	−0.18927	−0.25769	1.00000		
(5) SAVE	0.61960	0.05161	0.34468	0.81820	1.00000	
(6) OIL	−0.10504	−0.25321	−0.24874	0.16491	0.01221	1.00000
	GNP	CU	CA	I	SAVE	OIL

Developing Asian Countries

	GNP	CU	CA	I	SAVE	OIL
(1) GNP	1.00000					
(2) CU	0.38974	1.00000				
(3) CA	−0.39820	−0.73892	1.00000			
(4) I	0.56981	0.85340	−0.54985	1.00000		
(5) SAVE	0.48820	0.66578	−0.19041	0.92468	1.00000	
(6) OIL	0.27490	−0.04363	0.38004	0.15357	0.35373	1.00000

Developing African Countries

	GNP	CU	CA	I	SAVE	OIL
(1) GNP	1.00000					
(2) CU	0.01179	1.00000				
(3) CA	−0.20384	0.09487	1.00000			
(4) I	0.33051	0.49041	−0.32850	1.00000		
(5) SAVE	0.19852	0.55335	0.32205	0.78839	1.00000	
(6) OIL	0.33986	−0.11649	0.26304	−0.14538	−0.02560	1.00000

Europe

	GNP	CU	CA	I	SAVE	OIL
(1) GNP	1.00000					
(2) CU	−0.55760	1.00000				
(3) CA	0.91016	−0.36460	1.00000			
(4) I	0.03824	−0.75871	−0.14423	1.00000		
(5) SAVE	0.79162	−0.81908	0.74401	0.55388	1.00000	
(6) OIL	0.00000	0.00000	0.00000	0.00000	0.00000	1.00000

Developing Middle Eastern Countries

	GNP	CU	CA	I	SAVE	OIL
(1) GNP	1.00000					
(2) CU	−0.92537	1.00000				
(3) CA	−0.14328	0.21742	1.00000			
(4) I	0.30255	−0.39044	−0.43343	1.00000		
(5) SAVE	−0.01524	0.05576	0.90370	−0.00584	1.00000	
(6) OIL	−0.04187	−0.00949	0.57849	0.38747	0.82600	1.00000

Developing Western Hemisphere Countries

	GNP	CU	CA	I	SAVE	OIL
(1) GNP	1.00000					
(2) CU	0.04329	1.00000				
(3) CA	0.29532	0.26394	1.00000			
(4) I	0.31604	−0.01531	−0.08040	1.00000		
(5) SAVE	0.44982	0.19109	0.70810	0.64689	1.00000	
(6) OIL	−0.03373	0.10098	−0.28084	0.55732	0.17994	1.00000

Note: The following countries were omitted from the sample because of missing observations in the period 1973–83: Maldives, Botswana, Benin, Liberia, Madagascar, Mauritania, Zimbabwe, Seychelles, Sudan, Swaziland, Tanzania, Turkey, Kuwait, Argentina, Antigua and Barbuda, Dominica, Belize, St. Lucia, St. Vincent, and Suriname.

Sources: Real GNP per capita growth data, 1973–83, were obtained from *The World Bank Atlas, 1986.* Current-account, nominal GDP, investment (gross fixed capital formation), consumption, and population data were obtained from *International Financial Statistics, Yearbook, 1986.* (Washington, D.C.: International Monetary Fund).

APPENDIX 3-2

This appendix briefly describes the specification and estimation of the CES production function and related output and factor demand equations which underlie our statistical analyses of productivity growth and convergence for nineteen industrial countries. The data are drawn primarily from OECD sources and are comparably defined across the sample of nineteen countries. A data appendix citing all variables and sources is available on request from the authors.

Variables and Parameters

Variable	Description
k	Real total gross fixed capital stock, billions, 1980 currency
p_a	Implicit price of absorption, 1980 = 1.0
p_k	Price of capital services
p_q	Implicit price for gross domestic output, 1980 = 1.0
q	Real gross output (at factor cost), billions, 1980 currency
q_s	Real synthetic supply, billions, 1980 currency
W	Wage rate, thousands of dollars per year per employed person
δ_2	Scrapping rate for capital stock (including housing)
μ	Distribution parameter in the CES function (estimated parameter)
ν	Distribution parameter in the CES function (estimated parameter)
Π	Harrod-neutral productivity index, in CES function for q
ρ_r	Real supply price of capital (estimated parameter)
τ	Elasticity of substitution between labor and capital in the CES function (estimated parameter)

Specification and Estimation

The Production Function and Harrod-neutral Productivity Index

The CES two-factor production function which defines normal output q_s is

$$q_s = [\mu(\Pi N)^{(\tau-1)/\tau} + vk^{(\tau-1)/\tau}]^{\tau/(\tau-1)} \qquad (3A\text{-}1)$$

The procedure used to derive expressions for the country-specific parameters v, μ, and Π is discussed first. The final values of these parameters depend on the value of τ, the elasticity of substitution between labor and capital, which is determined iteratively. The iteration method used to calculate τ is examined last.

Equation 3A-1 can be rewritten by setting $q = q_s$ and by isolating the following expression for gP:

$$\Pi = [(q^{(\tau-1)/\tau} - vk^{(\tau-1)/\tau}) / (\mu N^{(\tau-1)/\tau}]^{\tau/(\tau-1)} \qquad (3A\text{-}2)$$

Equation 3A-2 is used to obtain an expression for the parameter v. First the optimum factor ratio is derived. The partial derivatives of Equation 3A-1 with respect to labor and capital are first calculated and set equal to the prices W and p_k. Assuming the factor ratio is optimal provides the following ratio:

$$\Pi N^*/k^* = (p_k\Pi/W)^\tau (\mu/v)^\tau \qquad (3A\text{-}3)$$

where the price of capital services is

$$p_k = (\langle\delta\rangle_2 + 0.01\rho_r)p_a$$

and where

$$\rho_r = \frac{100\langle 1 - (WN + \langle\delta_2\rangle \bar{k}p_a)/(qp_q)\rangle}{\langle(\bar{k}p_a)/(qp_q)\rangle}$$

so that the ratio of factor costs to revenues is unity, on average (as $\langle x\rangle$ denotes the sample average of x).

Equation 3A-2 is substituted into Equation 3A-3. The parameter μ drops out and can be determined empirically when Π is normalized, as shown below. The parameter v is isolated in the substituted equation and sample averages are taken to provide the following expression:

$$v = \frac{\langle(p_k/W)(q/N)^{(\tau-1)/\tau}\rangle}{\langle(N/k)^{1/\tau}\rangle + \langle(p_k/W)(k/N)^{(\tau-1)/\tau}\rangle} \qquad (3A\text{-}4)$$

Note that we normalize so that the sample average of the ratio of the factors raised to the $1/\tau$ power is equal to the average for optimum proportions.

The value of Π, the productivity index for Harrod-neutral technical progress, is derived by the following procedure. Output attributable to labor is defined by rewriting Equation 3A-2:

$$\mu\Pi^{(\tau-1)/\tau} = \frac{q^{(\tau-1)/\tau} - vk^{(\tau-1)/\tau}}{N^{(\tau-1)/\tau}} \qquad (3A\text{-}5)$$

In the constant model, the technical progress index is modeled to grow at a constant rate. It is estimated by ordinary least squares by regressing the logarithm of the measured efficiency level, which is the logarithm of the value provided by Equation 3A-5, referred to as $\ln \pi_m$, on an annual time index. Given the final value of τ, the fitted values $\ln \hat{\pi}$ can be estimated for each year. Using the latter, the value of μ is calculated by setting $\Pi = 1.0$ in 1980. Given that the value of μ is constant throughout the sample period, Π is defined simply as the exponent of $\ln \hat{\pi} - 1980 \ln \hat{\pi}$, which ensures it has a value of 1 in 1980.

In the second model, the growth of technical progress in the non-U.S. countries is assumed to catch-up to the U.S. rate of growth. This is modeled by regressing $\ln \pi_m$ on its lagged value and on the calculated U.S. values ($\ln \hat{\pi}_{us}$), with the coefficients restricted to sum to 1. Then $\ln \hat{\pi}_{us}$ is the predicted values from the U.S. constant case regression. In the third model, to allow for the effects of globalization on the model, we include the variable DOPENA along with the catch-up variables in the non-U.S. equations. DOPENA is the annual change in "openness" defined as the log difference of current and lagged values of the five-year moving average of exports plus imports divided by GNP. The values of the CES parameters are derived in a similar way to the constant case, using the fitted values of the catch-up case, $\ln \hat{\pi}$. The fourth model tests the break hypothesis. The technical progress index is modeled with a constant-time index but includes an additional index starting in 1974. If the latter index is negative, there is some evidence for the hypothesis that there was general reduction in the underlying rate of productivity growth starting in 1974.

Finally, an estimate of τ is needed to derive final values of the foregoing parameters. The iterative procedure uses the expression for the optimum factor ratio, Equation 3A-3. The log of this equation provides the following form, which can be estimated:

$$\ln (\Pi N^*/k^*) = \tau \ln(\mu/v) + \tau \ln(p_k\Pi/W) \qquad (3A\text{-}6)$$

τ is the coefficient of the inverse price ratio. An arbitrary value of τ is used to define μ, v, and Π. Equation 3A-6 is then estimated by ordinary least squares and the estimated coefficient provides a new value of τ, which is used to redefine the other parameters in the next round. The process is repeated until the value of τ in Equation 3A-6 converges. This value is used to obtain the final values of μ, v, Π and normal output q_s.

For our final estimates, a variant of Equation 3A-6 was used in which the lagged capital labor ratio was included along with cyclical demand and profitability variables (outlined in Helliwell and Chung, 1986) as right-hand-side variables. The latter were included since the factor share ratio has, in addition to its responsiveness to relative prices, a cyclical variance caused by the fact that labor adjusts more quickly than the capital stock to changes in desired output. The distributed lag response on the relative price term (which tends to produce a higher estimated equilibrium elasticity of substitution) also provides more reasonable elasticities across countries.

In the pooled estimation, we use an average of the country-specific τ and v (with value of 0.99 for τ), thus providing common production function parameters.

The average growth rate of the productivity index from the constant case is as follows:

Country	Percent	
	1960–85	1963–85
United States	0.72	0.43
Japan	4.08	3.43
Canada	1.93	1.71
France	3.71	3.40
Germany	2.95	2.77
Italy	3.50	3.01
United Kingdom	1.70	1.61
Australia	1.64	1.42
Austria	3.38	3.19
Belgium	3.16	3.00
Denmark	2.37	2.10
Finland	3.27	3.13
Ireland	3.67	3.67
Netherlands	2.96	2.79
New Zealand	0.18	0.05
Norway	2.51	2.37
Spain	4.23	3.81
Sweden	1.74	1.42
Switzerland	1.63	1.36

Output, Investment, and Employment

The following discussion briefly describes the specification of the equations used in the nonnested tests reported in Tables 3-6 to 3-9.

Table 3-6 Tests of U.S. Output Equations

The following models of labor productivity were estimated and tested using nonnested tests of the U.S. output equations. H_0 denotes the maintained hypothesis, which is tested against the competing models. The output equations were estimated by two-stage least squares over the sample 1963–85 for all models.

Case 1: H_0: Constant case:
$\ln \pi_m = \alpha * \text{RTIME} + c$
H_1: Break case:
$\ln \pi_m = \alpha * \text{RTIME} + \beta * T74 + c,$ $T74 = 1(1974), 2(1975), \ldots$
H_2: Open case:
$\ln \pi_m = \alpha * \text{RTIME} + \beta * \text{DOPENA} + c$

Case 2: H_0: Break   *Case 3: H_0:* Open
H_1: Constant H_1: Constant
H_2: Open H_2: Break

P Test[a]

	T statistics		
	Case 1	Case 2	Case 3
H_1	0.60306	2.5821[b]	0.84879
H_2	0.05363	2.3831[b]	0.60928

Table 3-6   (cont.)

	F statistics		
	Case 1	Case 2	Case 3
$H_1 = H_2 = 0.0$	0.18506		0.54468
(2,17) df			
$H_1 = 0.0$	0.36368	6.66713^c	0.83029
(1,17) df		(1,18) df	
$H_2 = 0.0$	0.00288	5.67904^c	0.37121
(1,17) df		(1,18) df	

C Tests

	Coefficient	T ratio
Model 1: Constant	0.75144	2.71
Model 2: Break	0.24856	0.90
Model 1: Constant	0.83329	1.42
Model 3: Open	0.16671	0.28
Model 2: Break	0.37684	1.61
Model 3: Open	0.62316	2.66

Godfrey Test

	Case 1	Case 2	Case 3
H_1	0.4383	1.5259	0.38028
H_2	1.5333	1.0676	0.44562

[a]Because of collinearity between H_1 and H_2, they were tested in separate regressions for case 2.

[b]Significant at the 95 percent level.

[c]Indicates rejection of the null hypothesis at 5 percent significance.

Test methods: For the *P* test, the following procedure was used (Davidson and MacKinnon, 1981). Given two alternative models:

$$H_0: Yt - ft(Xt, \beta) + e_0t$$
$$H_1: Yt = gt(Zt, \gamma) + e_1t$$

The following artificial regression can be estimated for the *P* test:

$$Yt - fht = \beta^*Xt + \lambda^*(ght - fht)$$

where *fht* and *ght* denote the fitted values based on H_0 and H_1. The *t* ratio for λ is the *P* test. If it is significant, H_0 is rejected; if it is insignificant, H_0 is not rejected. In cases 1 and 3 H_0 was tested against more than one alternative hypothesis at a time, with joint *F* statistics reported to test whether H_1 and H_2 are zero.

For the *C* test, again following Davidson and MacKinnon (1981), the *C* test involves estimating the following regression:

$$Yt = \alpha^*fht + (1 - \alpha)^*ght$$

where *fht* and *ght* are the fitted values of *yt* from the two competing models. For $\alpha > 1 - \alpha$ and significant, *fht* is the dominating model.

The statistics for the Godfrey test are derived using Godfrey's (1983) test of competing nonnested models estimated by an instrumental variable (IV) estimator (e.g., two-stage least squares). Let the two models be

$$H_0: Yt = ft(Xt, \beta) + e_0t$$
$$H_1: Yt = gt(Zt, \gamma) + e_1t$$

Let *W* be the set of exogenous variables included in the two-stage least-squares estimation. We first estimate H_0 and H_1 by two-stage least squares and obtain the sample values of *b* and *c* (the two-stage least-squares estimates of β and γ given *W*). We calculate the ordinary least-squares predicted values *Xht* and *Zht* from the regression of *X* and *Z* on *W*. We then obtain the residual vector from the ordinary least-squares regression of *Xht*b* on *Zht* and add it as an independent variable in the regression of the maintained hypothesis. The table reports the *t* statistic for the variable. If it is significant, it indicates that H_1 adds significant explanatory power to H_0 and it implies the rejection of the null hypothesis against H_1.

Table 3-7 Tests of Output Equations for the Industrial Countries

The following models of labor productivity were estimated and tested using nonnested tests of the output equations for the nineteen industrial countries. For all non–break models, the constant case is used for the United States, since it is the preferred case in Table 3-6. In the break case, the break model is used for U.S. and non-U.S. models, consistent with the hypothesis that the productivity slowdown was a feature of all the industrial countries. In the tests in this table, H_0 denotes the maintained hypothesis, which is tested against the competing models.

The output equations were estimated by the Zellner seemingly unrelated regression technique with instrumental variables, using the sample period 1963–85 for all models.

Case 1: H_0: Pure catch-up case:
$$\ln \pi_m = a_1 {}^* \ln \pi_{m-1} + a_2 {}^* \ln \hat{\pi}_{us} + a_3$$
H_1: Catch up with openness:
$$\ln \pi_m = a_1 {}^* \ln \pi_{m-1} + a_2 {}^* \ln \hat{\pi}_{us} + a_3 {}^* DOPENA + a_4$$
H_2: Constant case:
$$\ln \pi_m = a_1 {}^* RTIME + a_2$$
H_3: Break case:
$$\ln \pi_m = a_1 {}^* RTIME + a_2 {}^* T74 + a3, \qquad T74 = 1(1974), 2(1975), \ldots$$

Case 2: H_0: Catch up/open	Case 3: H_0: Constant	Case 4: H_0: Break
H_1: Pure catch up	H_1: Catch up	H_1: Catch up
H_2: Constant	H_2: Catch up/open	H_2: Catch up/open
H_3: Break	H_3: Break	H_3: Constant

P Test

	T statistics			
	Case 1	Case 2	Case 3	Case 4
H_1	2.42[a]	2.58[a]	2.99[a]	3.17[a]
H_2	1.54	1.48	2.10[a]	2.03[a]
H_3	1.38	1.49	1.72	1.54

	F statistics			
	Case 1	Case 2	Case 3	Case 4
$H_1 = H_2 = H_3 = 0$ (4,430) df	2.52	5.42[b]	68.03[b]	80.78[b]
$H_1 = 0.0$ (1,430) df	5.86[b]	6.66[b]	8.99[b]	10.02[b]
$H_2 = 0.0$ (1,430) df	2.39	2.18	4.44[b]	4.12[b]
$H_3 = 0.0$ (1,430) df	1.90	2.22	2.96	2.37

[a]Significant at the 95 percent level.

[b]Indicates rejection of the null hypothesis at 5 percent significance.

[c]Model 1 = pure catch up; model 2 = catch up with openness; model 3 = constant; model 4 = break.
Test methods: For the *P* test, the following procedure was used (Davidson and MacKinnon, 1981). Given two alternative models:

H_0: $Yit = fit(Xt, \beta) + e_0 it$, $\quad i (= 1, m)$ indexes equations
H_1: $Yit = git(Zt, \gamma) + e_1 it$, $\quad t (= 1, n)$ indexes observations

The following artificial regression can be estimated for the *P* test:

$$Yit - fhit = b {}^* Xit + \lambda {}^* (ghit - fhit)$$

where *fhit* and *ghit* denote the fitted values based on H_0 and H_1. The *t* ratio for λ is the *P* test. If it is significant, H_0 is rejected; if it is insignificant, H_0 is not rejected. In the results here H_0 was tested against more than one alternative hypothesis at a time, with *F* statistics reported to test whether H_1, H_2, and H_3 are zero.

For the *C* test, again following Davidson and MacKinnon (1981), the *C* test involves estimating the following regression:

$$Yit = \alpha {}^* fhit + (1 - \alpha) {}^* ghit$$

where *fhit* and *ghit* are the fitted values of *yt* from the two competing models. For $\alpha > 1 - \alpha$ and significant, *fit* is the dominating model.

Table 3-7 (cont.)

C Tests[c]

	Coefficient	T ratio
Model 1	0.55333	4.23
Model 2	0.44667	3.42
Model 1	0.97458	13.80
Model 3	0.02542	0.36
Model 1	1.03120	15.13
Model 4	−0.03125	0.46
Model 2	0.84014	13.84
Model 3	0.15986	2.63
Model 2	0.89692	14.96
Model 4	0.10308	1.72
Model 3	0.80523	5.33
Model 4	0.19477	1.29

Table 3-8 Tests of Investment Equations for the Industrial Countries

The investment equations were estimated by the Zellner seemingly unrelated regression technique with instrumental variables, using the sample period 1963–85 for all models. The models of labor productivity are identical to those outlined in Table 3-7.

P Test

	T statistics			
	Case 1	Case 2	Case 3	Case 4
H_1	2.96[a]	1.96[a]	1.96[a]	1.97[a]
H_2	3.90[a]	3.90[a]	2.96[a]	2.96[a]
H_3	1.24	1.24	1.24	3.91[a]

	F statistics			
	Case 1	Case 2	Case 3	Case 4
$H_1 = H_2 = H_3 = 0$ (4,430) df	6.83[b]	5.80[b]	3.20[b]	9.50[b]
$H_1 = 0.0$ (1,430) df	8.76[b]	3.83[b]	3.84[b]	3.91[b]
$H_2 = 0.0$ (1,430) df	15.24[b]	15.26[b]	8.76[b]	8.78[b]
$H_3 = 0.0$ (1,430) df	1.55	1.55	1.54	15.31[b]

C Tests[c]

	Coefficient	T ratio
Model 1	0.34281	1.19
Model 2	0.65719	2.29
Model 1	−0.09442	0.28
Model 3	1.09442	3.32
Model 1	0.79748	2.89
Model 4	0.20252	0.73
Model 2	0.35870	1.80
Model 3	0.64130	3.22
Model 2	0.74069	3.65

Table 3-8   (cont.)

Model 4	0.25931	1.28
Model 3	1.25870	4.45
Model 4	−0.25870	0.91

[a]Significant at the 95 percent level.

[b]Indicates rejection of the null hypothesis at 5 percent significance.

[c]Model 1 = pure catch up; model 2 = catch up with openness; model 3 = constant; model 4 = break. See notes accompanying Table 3-7 on the test method.

Table 3-9   Tests of Employment Equations for the Industrial Countries

The employment equations were estimated by the Zellner seemingly unrelated regression technique with instrumental variables, using the sample period 1963–85 for all models. The models of labor productivity are identical to those outlined in Table 3-7.

P Test

	T statistics			
	Case 1	Case 2	Case 3	Case 4
H_1	1.84	1.07	1.00	1.00
H_2	2.65[a]	2.66[a]	1.82	1.82
H_3	1.10	1.10	1.13	2.64[a]

	F statistics			
	Case 1	Case 2	Case 3	Case 4
$H_1 = H_2 = H_3 = 0$ (3,432) df	3.60[b]	2.85[b]	2.56	6.32[b]
$H_1 = 0.0$ (1,432) df	3.38	1.14	1.00	1.02
$H_2 = 0.0$ (1,432) df	7.05[b]	7.05[b]	3.31	3.32
$H_3 = 0.0$ (1,432) df	1.22	1.21	1.27	6.97[b]

C Tests[c]

	Coefficient	T ratio
Model 1	−0.26382	0.37
Model 2	1.26382	1.77
Model 1	0.33418	1.40
Model 3	0.66582	2.79
Model 1	0.63502	2.61
Model 4	0.36498	1.50
Model 2	0.43208	1.96
Model 3	0.56792	2.58
Model 2	0.69747	3.06
Model 4	0.30253	1.33
Model 3	1.0697	3.23
Model 4	−0.0697	0.21

[a]Significant at the 95 percent level.

[b]Indicates rejection of the null hypothesis at 5 percent significance.

[c]Model 1 = pure catch up; model 2 = catch up with openness; model 3 = constant; model 4 = break. See notes accompanying Table 3-7 on the test method.

The Output Equation. We follow the factor utilization approach outlined in Helliwell and Chung (1986). The rationale for explicitly modeling factor utilization rates lies in the observation that factors of production are quasi-fixed. That is, it is costly for firms to adjust the levels of inputs in response to short-term changes in demand and cost conditions. Consequently, temporary fluctuations in demand are met by varying the intensity of factor use—working the inputs harder or less hard—or, in other words, by changing the factor utilization rates.

One difficulty with this approach is that factor utilization rates are not directly observable. In particular, we have no idea what constitutes a "normal" factor utilization rate. A simple way around the problem is to define the utilization rate as the ratio of actual to normal output and to form suitable proxies for the demand and cost conditions. When the proxy variables are at their normal values—the sample averages—we have a normal rate of factor utilization.

The output equation thus has the following specification:

$$\ln q = \ln q_s + \beta^* \ln s_{\text{gap}} + \beta_1^* \ln cq + \beta_2^* \ln i_{\text{gap}} + e$$

where s_{gap} is the ratio of sales to normal sales, i_{gap} is the ratio of desired to lagged actual inventories, and cq is the ratio of current unit cost relative to output price (an inverse measure of profitability). Normal sales is defined as $\langle s/q_s \rangle {*} q_s$ and desired inventories is $\langle k_{\text{inv}} - 1/q_s \rangle {*} q_s$, where k_{inv} is inventory stock. The sample averages ensure that the means of s_{gap}, i_{gap}, and cq are 1, which ensures "normal" utilization rates on average.

Investment Equation. The equation explains fixed investment as a fraction of the corresponding capital stock, with the lagged ratio entering the equation to enrich the distributed lag response. Driving the investment equation is the gap between desired and the actual capital stock $(k^* - \bar{k})/\bar{k}$. The desired k^* is derived as follows. First, define a level of output q^* which is the expected desired output for firms. We define $q^* = q_a^*(q/q - 2)$, where q_a is aggregate demand (output minus unintended change in inventories). The time horizon implicit in q^* is thus two years. Given our CES production function, the level of desired output is used in the long-run production function to determine the levels of capital and labor that would minimize costs if future relative prices were the same as those currently prevailing. Analytic expressions for k^* and N^* are thus easily obtained:

$$k^* = [v + \mu^\tau (\Pi p_k/Wv)^{\tau-1}]^{\tau/(1-\tau)}q^*$$

and

$$N^* = (1/\Pi) [q^{*(\tau-1)/\tau} - vk^{*(\tau-1)/\tau)}/\mu]^{\tau/(\tau-1)}$$

Finally, we include cq. This attempts to capture financial market conditions by defining profitability as the ratio of current unit operating costs to the current output price, where the numerator includes a rental charge of capital, which varies with the long-term nominal interest rate.

Employment Equation. The employment equation describes a partial adjustment to the two-year forward-looking demand for labor N^*. The employment
equation follows a simple adaptive adjustment, with right-hand-side variables
and lagged and desired employment levels constrained to sum to one.

NOTES

We are grateful for research support from the Social Sciences and Humanities Research Council of Canada. In revising this paper for publication, we were greatly aided
by many helpful comments from Bob Coen and Bert Hickman and by suggestions from
Moses Abramovitz, Gerry Adams, Lawrence Klein, Ron McKinnon, Bill Nordhaus,
and Sherman Robinson.

1. There is an extensive literature, surveyed by Findlay (1984), that spells out the
conditions under which this presumption may be overturned. It is more likely to hold
when the foreign demand for the domestic products is elastic. If that demand is inelastic
enough, there arises the famous case of "immiserizing growth" (Bhagwati, 1985), where
the foreign demand for the domestic product is so inelastic that the domestic terms of
trade worsen by enough that domestic real incomes, measured in terms of the consumption bundle, fall in response to technical progress in the domestic industry.

2. Real gross national product (GNP) is better for this purpose than real gross domestic product (GDP), because GNP equals (approximately) GDP less net payments for
foreign capital. Thus GDP might show growth if foreign capital were brought in and
produced a low rate of return, whereas GNP would show growth only if the foreign
capital raised GDP by more than enough to pay for the interest and dividend costs
required to pay for its use.

3. Among the developing countries there are, however, some subgroups within
which there is a negative correlation coefficient between average current accounts and
GNP growth. These regions are Asia (-0.39), Africa (-0.20), and the Middle East
(-0.14). The correlations suggest that within these regions there was a tendency for the
faster growing countries to have made more net use of foreign capital. The correlation
is strongest for the developing countries of Asia, mainly because of the experiences of
Korea and Singapore, which had the two highest average growth rates, and among the
highest net inflows of foreign capital. The correlations are positive for the developing
countries in Europe (0.91) and the Western Hemisphere (0.29), where the faster growing
countries were not in general those with greater net inflows of capital.

4. A number of earlier studies are surveyed by Chenery (1986). He classifies the
main variables into "neoclassical" (growth of the capital stock, growth of the labor
force, and changes in the quality of labor) and "structural" (reallocation of labor and
capital, export growth, capital inflow, and the level of development). Due to data limitations, and in order to make the sample size as large as possible, we are able to account
explicitly only for the ratio of gross investment to GDP (as a proxy for the growth of
the capital stock), the current account (which is the negative of net capital inflow and
is positively affected by the level of exports), and the initial level of income (as a proxy
for the initial level of development).

5. Since our sample includes all countries, it avoids the sample-selection problem emphasized by De Long (1988). This problem may arise if a sample of currently rich countries is drawn from an initial population containing other countries that had been rich long ago but are poor now. The sample selection problem is largely obviated in this section by using all countries, and in the next section by looking at differences among all of the industrialized countries, covering a short enough period so that they were all relatively rich both at the beginning and the end of the sample period.

6. For example, the rate of growth of a country with an average level of annual income of $400 has to be ten times as high as in a country with an annual income of $4000 before the levels will start to converge. However, as long as the poorer countries have higher rates of growth and can sustain them for long enough, the process of convergence will eventually equalize real income levels.

7. See Hill (1986) for details. The units are "international" because the basket of final goods and services is defined using average expenditure weights for the set of industrial countries considered as a whole. The units are called "dollars" because they are normalized so that one international dollar would buy one dollar's worth of U.S. GNP in the 1985 base period.

8. Cyclical variations in output, and hence in the measured labor productivity index defined by inverting the production function, are explained by the determinants of the factor-utilization decision, as described in more detail in Helliwell and Chung (1986).

9. Since innovations arise in all countries, it would be more appropriate to define the achievable frontier on a global basis, and not on the data for a single country. In light of the arbitrariness of our estimates of the capital stocks in most of the smaller countries, and of the complexities in defining the global frontier based in part on the experience of countries which are themselves converging to that frontier, we still use the U.S. index as the basis of the convergence model, as was done in the earlier G-7 application by Helliwell, Sturm, and Salou (1985).

10. The results of Maddison (1982) and Baumol (1986) relate to the experience, over a century of data, of countries that are now among the richest, and show strong evidence of convergence. De Long (1988) argues that there may be a severe sample selection bias, since a random sample of countries in 1870 would include some that subsequently became rich and others that became relatively poor. By selecting only those countries that are now rich, De Long argues, the studies of Baumol and Maddison overstate the likely degree of convergence. De Long adds data for a number of countries that were rich in 1870 and adjusts for likely errors in the measurement of 1870 income levels, and he finds no evidence of convergence. The results reported here, as well as those of Helliwell, Sturm, and Salou (1985), should be free of this potential difficulty, since the use of a shorter sample period permits the sample selection problem to be avoided, as the chosen countries are among the richest at both the beginning and the end of the sample period.

11. This assumes that the countries under review all had the necessary conditions for a sustained growth process to "take off." Gerschenkron (1962) argues that there is no obviously nontautological way to define such conditions. In any event, countries rich enough to have been in the OECD in 1960 can be safely assumed to have met any such conditions.

12. Subsidiary tests show that extending the sample period raises the simple correlation between the initial level of GNP per capita and subsequent growth of GNP to -0.56, while the use of PPP exchange rates raises it further to -0.77.

13. The question of whether the levels should tend to equalize depends to a considerable extent on whether it is possible for the data to allow for international differences

in endowments of natural resources, climate, location, ease of access to transportation and markets, social structure, social values, political stability, education, and various other factors that have important bearing on production possibilities and efforts.

14. In addition, we considered alternative versions in which the U.S. rate of technical progress was also influenced by changes in openness. However, tests of the derived output equation showed that the constant model was preferred for the United States, so we used that simpler alternative in our subsequent work.

15. An alternative stochastic specification is used in Helliwell and Chung (1989) to help eliminate the effects of cyclical variance associated with the measured productivity index. This is done by defining the measured productivity index relative to that in the United States, thus eliminating the cyclical variance that is common to the United States and other countries. The dependent variable is respecified in logarithmic change form as $d \ln(\pi_{mi}/\pi_{mus})$, where π_{mi} is the measured productivity index for country i and π_{mus} the corresponding value for the United States. The output equations fit somewhat better when estimated using efficiency indexes derived under this alternative form. The estimated catch-up coefficients are generally lower than those reported in Table 3-3 of this chapter but are still significant for the majority of countries.

16. The variable used is the change in the logarithm of trade dependence between 1960 and 1985, where trade dependence is measured as the ratio of the sum of real imports and exports to real GNP.

17. The results of unconstrained reqressions were mixed, with the effects, especially the significant ones, generally being positive, but the range of coefficient values being great enough to suggest that for many countries there were important other omitted variables that were correlated with the changes in openness, even when a five-year moving average was used to reduce the effect of cyclical influences. More compact and usable results are obtained by constraining the effect of changes in openness to have the same effect in each country, as shown in Table 3-5.

18. We also considered an alternative version in which the level of the trade ratio is added to the equation. The hypothesis was that while the rate of change of openness will influence the rate of convergence, the level of openness may also influence the ultimate level of productivity attainable. The results showed no significant effect from adding the level to the equation that already included the change in openness.

19. The P and C nonnested test procedures, described in Davidson and MacKinnon (1981), and the Godfrey test, from Godfrey (1983), are used.

20. To provide broad tests of the competing models, the data for the eighteen countries are stacked and used to calculate test statistics for output, employment, and investment. For these remaining tests, only the P and C test procedures are done.

21. In the investment P tests, this is borne out by the F statistics rejecting, for each model, the joint hypothesis that the competing models provide no additional information to the model being tested at the 95 percent level of significance. In the employment case, the constant-growth model passes this hypothesis, as does the catch-up convergence case in the output tests.

22. See Hill (1986), Table 8.

23. The regression lines drawn in Figure 3-1 are from a sample of eighteen countries, excluding the United States. The t values on the slope parameter range from 12.24 in 1980 to 17.09 in 1985. If the data for the United States are included, the slope of the regression line drops to 0.364 (with t values ranging from 10.60 in 1980 to 16.79 in 1985), reflecting the fact that the U.S. price level was much below PPP at the end of the 1970s, as shown in Figure 3-1a. The common slope parameter restriction is accepted in both equations, while the data would have strongly rejected the imposition of a common

constant term. Thus there are systematic departures from PPP, even after allowing for the effect of international differences in income levels, and these departures vary significantly from year to year.

24. These processes have been most recently studied in the context of the so-called Dutch disease (e.g., Neary and Van Wijnbergen, 1986), where the increase in the real exchange rate comes from an increase in the price of resource exports rather than from an increase in the rate of growth of domestic productivity. In both cases, the analysis is similar, with the increase in the real exchange rate dampening the increase in competitiveness of the favored industry and putting increasing external pressure on other domestic producers of tradable goods.

REFERENCES

Baumol, W. M. 1986. "Productivity Growth, Convergence, and Welfare: What the Long-Run Data Show." *American Economic Review* 76, 1072–85.

Baumol, W. M., and E. N. Wolff. 1988. "Productivity Growth, Convergence, and Welfare: Reply." *American Economic Review* 78, 1155–59.

Bhagwati, J. 1958. "Immiserizing Growth: A Geometrical Note." *Review of Economic Studies* 25, 201–5.

Chenery, H. 1986. "Growth and Transformation." In H. Chenery, S. Robinson, and M. Syrquin, eds., *Industrialization and Growth: A Comparative Study*. Washington, D.C.: Oxford University Press for the World Bank, pp. 13–36.

Chenery, H., S. Robinson, and M. Syrquin, eds. 1986. *Industrialization and Growth: A Comparative Study*. Washington, D.C.: Oxford University Press for the World Bank.

Davidson, R., and J. G. MacKinnon. 1981. "Several Tests for Model Specification in the Presence of Alternative Hypotheses." *Econometrica* 49, 781–94.

De Long, J. B. 1988. "Productivity Growth, Convergence, and Welfare: Comment." *American Economic Review* 78, 1138–54.

Feldstein, M. S. 1983. "Domestic Saving and International Capital Movements in the Long Run and the Short Run." *European Economic Review* 21, 129–51.

Feldstein, M. S., and C. Horioka. 1980. "Domestic Saving and International Capital Flows." *Economic Journal* 90, 314–29.

Findlay, R. 1984. "Growth and Development in Trade Models." In R. W. Jones and P. B. Kenen, eds., *Handbook of International Economics,* Vol. 1. Amsterdam: North-Holland, pp. 185–236.

Frankel, J. A., Dooley, M., and D. Mathieson. 1986. "International Capital Mobility in Developing Countries vs. Industrial Countries: What Do Savings–Investment Correlations Tell Us?" NBER Working Paper, No. 2043. Cambridge, Mass.: National Bureau of Economic Research.

Gerschenkron, A. 1962. *Economic Backwardness in Historical Perspective*. Cambridge, Mass.: Harvard University Press.

Godfrey, L. G. 1983. "Testing Non-nested Models after Estimation by Instrumental Variables or Least Squares." *Econometrica* 51, 355–65.

Gordon, R. J., and M. Baily. 1989. "Measurement Issues and the Productivity Slowdown in Five Major Industrial Countries." Paper presented at International Seminar on Science, Technology and Economic Growth, Paris, June 6.

Helliwell, J. F. 1989. "Some Comparative Macroeconomics of the United States, Japan, and Canada." In R. M. Stern, ed., *United States and Canadian Trading Relations with Japan*. Chicago: University of Chicago Press.

Helliwell, J. F., and A. Chung. 1986. "Aggregate output with Variable Rates of Utilization of Employed Factors." *Journal of Econometrics* 33, 285–310.

Helliwell, J. F., and A. Chung. 1989. "Macroeconomic Convergence: International Transmission of Growth and Technical Progress." Paper prepared for the NBER Conference on Research on Income and Wealth meeting on International Economic Transactions: Issues in Measurement and Empirical Research, Washington, D.C., November 3–4, 1989. (Revised version available as NBER Working Paper No. 3264, *National Bureau of Economic Research*, February, 1990.)

Helliwell, J. F., P. Sturm, and G. Salou. 1985. "International Comparison of the Sources of Productivity Slowdown 1973–1982." *European Economic Review* 28, 157–91.

Hill, P. 1986. "International Price Levels and Purchasing Power Parities." *OECD Economic Studies* 6, 133–59.

Maddison, A. 1982. *Phases of Capitalist Development*. New York: Oxford University Press.

Neary, J. P., and S. Van Wijnbergen, eds. 1986. *Natural Resources and the Macroeconomy*. Oxford: Basil Blackwell.

OECD. 1987. *Purchasing Power Parities and Real Expenditures*. Paris: OECD.

4

Productivity, Competitiveness, and Export Growth in Developing Countries

F. GERARD ADAMS, JERE R. BEHRMAN, AND MICHAEL BOLDIN

In recent decades, the developing countries have undergone varied experiences with regard to growth, productivity, and exports. The theoretical and empirical materials on economic development are suggestive about the relation between exports and growth, but much remains to be learned from a careful analysis of the statistics.

From the perspective of growth, as measured by GDP growth rates, for the years from 1974 to 1986, the average annual growth rate for the middle-income countries was 3.3 percent (Table 4-1) based on data from the International Comparison Project (ICP), compared to an average annual growth of 2.4 percent for the industrial market economies and 1.9 percent for the low-income countries.[1] But the averages hide a remarkably diverse record among the individual countries. At the positive extreme, among the middle-income group, the countries of Southeast Asia have undergone stunning growth—6.8 percent for Korea, 7.5 percent for Taiwan, and 9.2 percent for Hong Kong, for example—sufficient to make optimists of many development economists. At the other extreme, there has been low growth performance among some of the middle-income countries—Argentina, −0.2 percent, Uruguay, 0.7 percent, and Mozambique, −0.2 percent—and some of the poorest countries, particularly in Africa, have shown little growth. Indeed some of them, like Uganda, Togo, Zaire, and Zambia, have shown continued decline in their already low incomes.[2]

The variation in growth rates reflects considerable variation in the underlying experience regarding productivity. The statistics measuring labor productivity show that output per worker on average rose 0.8 percent annually for the middle-income countries, compared to 1.4 percent for the industrial countries, a reversal of the difference compared to aggregate GDP growth, showing the impact of the less favorable population growth experience in the less developed world. Since population growth tends to be highest in the low-income countries, the low-income countries' growth rates translate into negative growth, −0.2 percent, in per worker terms. Again, the differences between countries

Table 4-1 Data Base Statistics, 1974–86

Variable	N	Mean	Standard Deviation	Minimum	Maximum
Low					
RGDP per capita (1974)	35	522.6	164.4	296.0	841.0
RGDP/labor	35	885.2	314.9	422.9	1,626.8
Capital/labor	35	923.4	589.6	209.7	3,195.3
Capital/output	35	1.0	0.4	0.5	2.6
RGDP growth rate	35	1.9%	3.3%	−8.7%	7.7%
RGDP/labor growth rate	35	−0.2%	3.2%	−10.7%	5.8%
Export growth rate	31	3.4%	5.1%	−9.0%	13.0%
Investment/RGDP	35	12.7%	5.5%	4.9%	27.7%
Export/RGDP	31	20.1%	12.0%	4.3%	53.6%
Adult literacy rate	34	29.4%	16.9%	5.0%	70.0%
Labor growth	35	2.2%	0.5%	1.2%	3.6%
Middle					
RGDP per capita (1974)	41	2,326.0	1,149.2	934.0	4,490.0
RGDP/labor	41	4,318.1	2,380.7	1,109.4	11,751.5
Capital/labor	41	6,189.5	4,598.1	808.3	19,109.6
Capital/output	41	1.3	0.4	0.7	2.4
RGDP growth rate	41	3.3%	2.9%	−1.6%	10.0%
RGDP/labor growth rate	41	0.8%	2.8%	−4.4%	7.3%
Export growth rate	35	5.3%	5.3%	−8.0%	17.0%
Investment/RGDP	41	19.0%	7.1%	5.5%	38.0%
Export/RGDP	33	28.6%	15.9%	7.4%	90.0%
Adult literacy rate	39	68.1%	22.1%	15.0%	98.0%
Labor growth	41	2.5%	0.8%	0.5%	3.9%
Industrial					
RGDP per capita (1974)	19	7,832.1	1,392.3	5,467.0	10,382.0
RGDP/labor	19	14,539.9	2,572.4	9,880.3	19,080.9
Capital/labor	19	28,439.4	7,031.6	12,907.0	40,360.6
Capital/output	19	1.9	0.3	1.3	2.7
RGDP growth rate	19	2.5%	0.8%	1.1%	4.5%
RGDP/labor growth rate	19	1.4%	0.9%	0.1%	3.5%
Export growth rate	19	4.7%	1.3%	2.7%	8.1%
Investment/RGDP	19	24.5%	5.2%	16.4%	37.2%
Export/RGDP	19	30.6%	13.3%	8.8%	60.2%
Adult literacy rate	19	97.8%	2.9%	88.0%	99.0%
Labor growth	19	1.1%	0.6%	0.4%	2.3%

are remarkable. Examples are the rapid growth of output per worker in Korea, at 4.1 percent per year, and the very much lower growth of productivity in Brazil, 0.8 percent, and the decline in output per worker in numerous countries like Argentina, Ivory Coast, and Guatemala, for example.

Productivity measures based on a single factor has long been seen as an incomplete indicator of underlying productivity trends which reflect the availability of capital as well as labor. The total factor productivity approach (Kendrick, 1961) is a simple and frequently used scheme. But the assumptions about competitive markets and correspondence between factor shares and marginal productivities which underlie these calculations are not likely to apply in many of the countries included in our sample. Moreover, the difficulty is that data on factor shares are not available from our primary data source, the ICP, and other sources of material are not likely to provide the comparability between different countries that we require.

The cross-sectional estimates (Feder-type equations)[3] presesnted later in this chapter suggest that neutral technological change is -0.02 percent per year for the low-income countries, 1.3 percent annually for the middle-income countries, and 2.6 percent annually for the industrial countries. We have also tried to estimate traditional total factor productivity on an individual-country time-series basis. These estimates, which are sensitive to the assumption about the factor shares, show that when the growth of capital is taken into account the evidence on "residual" productivity becomes more pessimistic. The assumption of labor shares of 0.33 or higher reduces the technical change effect in the low-income and middle-income countries into the negative range.[4]

Export performance also varies widely. Growth of exports is at annual rates of 3.4 percent for the low-income countries, 5.3 percent for the middle-income, and 4.7 percent for the industrial countries. Some of the countries in each group have done extremely well; others, unfortunately, have done badly. The association of economic growth with export growth is a critical consideration in view of the widespread acceptance of the hypothesis that export promotion has been a highly successful development strategy. The high correlations of economic growth and export performance are suggestive in this regard. The simple correlations between real GDP growth and export growth are 0.309, 0.698, and 0.578, respectively, in the low-income, middle-income, and industrial countries.

The measurement of competitiveness of less developed countries poses some special theoretical and empirical challenges. It is not sufficient, obviously, to argue that countries with good export growth performance are ipso facto highly competitive. The forces that lie behind export growth are, however, not easy to disentangle. Competitiveness is a relative cost phenomenon that depends on real exchange rates as well as improvements in underlying factor productivity.[5] In this regard the figures on the relationship between export growth and the growth of labor productivity are at least suggestive. We observe similar positive correlation between exports and aggregate economic growth and in particular note that high-productivity countries such as Korea and Hong Kong had high export growth rates of 12.7 and 11.9 percent, respectively. The difficulty with this relationship lies in the unresolved questions of causation: do exports cause growth or does improvement in productivity cause exports?

In this chapter we attempt to characterize the nature of these experiences on the basis of analysis of cross-country data for the "post–oil crisis" period (1974–86). For comparative purposes we include the low-income and the industrial market economies in the analysis, although we focus on the middle-income developing economies. We discuss two sets of estimates for these comparisons: production functions and a Feder (1982) two-sector model.

Our analysis of the data points to the importance of capital accumulation and export growth in the development process. The most striking conclusion is that the diverse patterns of economic growth seem to be well described by simple models in the middle-income group of countries but not so well in the others.

DATA

Our basic data are annual country data for 1960–86 from the International Comparison Project (ICP) based on careful purchasing-power parity (PPP) comparisons as described in Kravis, Heston, and Summers (1982). We also use data from the World Bank *Development Report* and 1987 World Bank Tables tape. We focus on the 1974–86 period for our estimates and on data for ninety-five developing and industrial market economies that we subdivide into the three groups listed in Appendix 4-1 on the basis of 1974 per capita ICP incomes in terms of 1980 international dollars: (1) thirty-five low-income countries, (2) forty-one middle-income countries, and (3) nineteen industrial countries.[6] Means and ranges of the data are summarized in Table 4-1. This table shows a mean per capita GDP in 1974 dollars of $522 for the low-income countries with a range from $296 for the lowest to $841 for the highest. For the middle-income group mean GDP per capita is $2326, ranging widely from $934 to $4490; for the industrial countries the mean is $7832, ranging from $5467 to $10,382.

For the production function estimates the critical data that we use are GDP, investment, and labor force. GDP statistics in constant international prices are provided directly by the ICP. Capital stock estimates are not provided, so we use the gross investment in constant prices that is provided to generate capital stock estimates based on an assumed depreciation rate of 10 percent per year and an assumed initial value in 1960 (1961 in some cases) equal to that necessary to generate the GDP observed in that year if the capital output ratio for that year were 1.25 in the developing countries and 2.0 in the industrial countries.[7] We recognize that a better approach would have been to use country-specific factors to depreciate capital stock and to compute initial capital values. But our efforts to estimate them from country time-series data were not robust. Labor force data are drawn from the *World Development Report*. For the Feder two-sector model, the export share and export growth rates were drawn from the World Bank data tape.

PRODUCTION FUNCTION ESTIMATES

Our basic concern in this section is to determine the extent to which production function estimates differ among the three country groups. Such differences may account for differences in growth and competitiveness. We have explored whether our estimates are robust to weighting each country by some function of their populations, more general production function specification, possible unobserved country-fixed effects, the use of ICP conversion factors versus official exchange rates, and changes between the late 1970s and the 1980s.[8]

We begin with ordinary least-squares Cobb–Douglas estimates for the three

country groups and for all of the countries combined. Results are given in Table
4-2. An F test rejects restricting the coefficients to be the same for the three
country groups ($F = 12.5$). The three-country group estimates suggest a larger
output elasticity with respect to capital for the middle-income group than for
the other two and the opposite pattern for the output elasticity with respect to
labor. Although the estimated elasticity of output with respect to the capital
stock is higher for the middle-income than for the low-income countries, at the
points of sample means the marginal products of capital are basically the same
for both of these developing country groups (about 0.49), but these values are
substantially higher than the estimated marginal productivity of capital of 0.26
at the point of sample means for the industrial group. Such results suggest that
capital is in relatively greater shortage in both groups of developing countries
and/or that there are much greater risks in such countries than in the high-
income countries and/or that costs of marginal capital investments are much
higher in the developing than in the high-income countries and/or that markets
for international physical capital investments are far from perfect. The estimated returns to scale are 5.1 percent for the low-income group, 0.8 percent
for the middle-income group, and 2.3 percent for the high-income group. Only
in the low-income countries can we reject a constant-returns-to-scale restriction, and this suggests that possibilities remain for exploiting scale economies
in these countries.

In these estimates, we weight each country equally, even though they differ
enormously (e.g., by 450 to 1 for India versus Mauritania) in population. It
might seem preferable to weight countries by some function of their populations.[9] Therefore, we reestimated the production relations with alternative
weights of log population and the square root of the population. The coefficient
estimates that we obtained with such weights (which we do not present in order
to conserve space) do not differ much from the unweighted estimates.

Human capital is thought by many to be an important determinant of eco-

Table 4-2 Cobb–Douglas Production Function Estimates
Dependent Variable = ln(RGDP),[a] 1974–86

	Low	Middle	Industrial	All
Intercept	2.850	2.703	3.867	1.393
	(4.67)	(5.46)	(3.50)	(4.66)
ln(capital)	0.474	0.643	0.517	0.735
	(8.09)	(17.11)	(5.22)	(45.34)
ln(labor)	0.577	0.365	0.506	0.303
	(9.27)	(7.58)	(5.15)	(11.25)
N	35	41	19	95
R^2	0.979	0.980	0.994	0.986
Adjusted R^2	0.977	0.979	0.993	0.985
Test that groups are the same				
F	12.510			
Pr	0.000			
Tests for constant returns to scale				
F	3.504	0.091	1.310	
Pr	0.070	0.764	0.268	

[a]ln(RGDP) = log of real GDP.

nomic productivity. Most emphasized in this regard is formal schooling, which, through literacy, is thought to improve productivity and the capacity to deal with the increasing change that is associated with development. If we add within-sample adult literacy rates or presample schooling enrollment rates (the two indicators of investment in schooling that are available to us for most of the sample countries) to the production functions in Table 4-2, however, in no country group do we obtain a significantly nonzero coefficient estimate. Of course, current adult literacy rates and previous schooling enrollment rates may be crude measures of the relevant human capital characteristics. But they are widely used indicators of such human capital, so it is noteworthy that neither has significantly nonzero effects in these estimates.

The Cobb–Douglas production function is widely used but very restrictive in its assumptions. Therefore, we explored the use of the much more general translog production function. Since the Cobb–Douglas production function is nested in the translog production function, the restrictions required for the Cobb–Douglas case can be tested with an F test. For all three country groups the F tests do not reject imposing such restrictions ($F = 0.66$, 0.09, and 0.16, respectively). Therefore, we continue to work with the Cobb–Douglas formulation.

Table 4-3 Cobb–Douglas Production Function Estimates

	Low	Middle	Industrial
Dependent variable = ln(RGDP), 1974–79			
Intercept	3.732	2.809	3.684
ln(capital)	0.410	0.625	0.528
ln(labor)	0.615	0.389	0.499
N	35	41	19
R^2	0.981	0.968	0.993
Adjusted R^2	0.980	0.966	0.992
Dependent variable = ln(RGDP), 1980–86			
Intercept	2.274	2.746	3.937
ln(capital)	0.522	0.642	0.515
ln(labor)	0.545	0.361	0.507
N	35	41	19
R^2	0.972	0.983	0.994
Adjusted R^2	0.970	0.982	0.994
Dependent variable − D ln(RGDP/labor), 1980–86 vs. 1974–79			
Intercept	−0.579	−0.110	−0.187
	(1.88)	(0.39)	(0.49)
D ln(capital/labor)	0.450	0.434	0.638
	(3.70)	(4.03)	(4.41)
ln(capital/labor)	0.079	0.009	0.022
	(1.73)	(0.26)	(0.58)
N	35	41	19
R^2	0.322	0.309	0.555
Adjusted R^2	0.279	0.272	0.500
Test that intercept and ln(capital/labor) parameters = 0			
F	2.735	0.736	2.783
$\Pr(> F)$	0.080	0.486	0.092

Given the economic turbulence in the sample period and the ongoing high rate of technological change, some may suspect that aggregate production structures changed between the 1970s and the 1980s. Therefore, we estimated the relations separately for 1974–79 and 1980–86. These estimates are summarized in the first panel of Table 4-3.

Basically the estimates are quite stable. The only change that is significant is an increase for the output elasticity with respect to capital for the low-income group, which increases from 0.41 to 0.52. Another way to test for the stability of the parameters, as well as to see if there are impacts of any unobserved fixed effects (e.g., cultural attitudes toward work), is to estimate the differenced relation between the two periods, allowing both the variables and the parameters to change between the periods. Panel 2 in Table 4-3 summarizes such estimates.[10] Note that an F test does not reject the hypothesis that there are no significant changes for the middle group while changes for the other groups are marginal. Much lower elasticities with respect to capital are found in the lower and middle groups, which may signify that the assumptions of a common Cobb–Douglas technology is too restrictive. We thus consider a more general model in the next section.

FEDER TWO-SECTOR MODEL

Feder (1983) presented a simple two-sector model that has been widely used and cited to explore the impact of export growth on overall product growth. The two sectors are exports X and nonexports N. For each sector there is a production function that indicates that output depends on the labor L_X or L_N) and the capital stock used in that sector (K_X or K_N). In addition, exports are assumed to have externalities that positively increase nonexport output; thus

$$N = N(K_N, L_N, X) \qquad (4\text{-}1)$$

$$X = X(K_X, L_X) \qquad (4\text{-}2)$$

Total differentiation of Y yields:

$$\dot{Y} = \dot{N} + \dot{X} = N_K \dot{K}_N + N_L \dot{L}_N + N_X \dot{X} + X_K \dot{K}_X + X_L \dot{L}_X \qquad (4\text{-}3)$$

Feder also assumes (1) that marginal productivities differ by the same amount for both capital and labor in the export sector from those in the nonexport sector:

$$X_K/N_K = X_L/N_L = 1 + \delta \qquad (4\text{-}4)$$

(2) that the marginal product of labor in the nonexport sector is proportional to the average product of labor in the whole economy:[11]

$$N_L = \beta \, Y/L \qquad (4\text{-}5)$$

and (3) that the marginal product of capital in the nonexport sector is constant:

$$N_K = \alpha \qquad (4\text{-}6)$$

Under these assumptions Equation 4-3 can be rewritten as

$$\dot{Y}/Y = \alpha(I/Y) + \beta(\dot{L}/L) + [\delta/(1 + \delta) + N_x]\,(\dot{X}/X)(X/Y) \qquad (4\text{-}7)$$

If there are no differences in marginal productivities between the sectors and if there are no intersectoral externalities, this expression reduces to the standard growth-rate expression often used in growth accounting.[12] Note that to apply this equation across countries, the assumption of a common production function is not necessary.

If, in addition, the marginal product of exports on nonexport production is assumed to be quasi–Cobb-Douglas,

$$N_X = \theta\,\frac{N}{X} \qquad (4\text{-}8)$$

the following relation can be used to separate the differential marginal productivity effect from the externality of exports on nonexport production effect:

$$\dot{Y}/Y = \alpha(I/Y) + \beta(\dot{L}/L) + (\delta/(1 + \delta) - \theta)(\dot{X}/X)(X/Y) + \theta\,\dot{X}/X \qquad (4\text{-}9)$$

Under the strong assumptions about functional forms noted, the Feder model permits some interesting deductions about the role of exports in economic growth.

The fact that investment is typically measured in gross terms (I_g) rather than net investment (I_n) is a complication in this equation, which has not been previously allowed for. Presumably this affects the work of Feder and of others along similar lines. Since

$$\frac{I_n}{Y} = \frac{I_g - \gamma K}{Y}$$

where γ is a depreciation factor, we can rewrite Equation 4-9 in the following form:

$$(4\text{-}10)$$
$$\dot{Y}/Y = \hat{\alpha}\,\gamma K/Y + \hat{\alpha}\,I_n/Y + \beta(\dot{L}/L) + (\delta/(1 + \delta) - \theta)(\dot{X}/X)(X/Y) + \theta\,\dot{X}/X$$

This allows us to separate the capital depreciation effect and produces a more reasonable elasticity with respect to investment. Also, in our estimations, an intercept term is added to allow for neutral technical change. In Table 4-4, we show the results of ordinary least-squares regressions for Equation 4-10 and discuss each of the three country groups in turn.

For the low-income countries, the results are decidedly unfavorable in all cases. As we noted earlier, the low-income countries represent problems with respect to obtaining anticipated or reliable statistical results. This may reflect problems with the data[13] or even problems faced by these economies in realizing the proper utilization of their limited resources. In any case, most of the coefficients are not statistically significant. (We note that the coefficients of export growth do not show statistically significant coefficients.)

The results for the middle-income countries are much more promising. Such a contrast between the low-income countries and the middle-income countries

Table 4-4   Feder-Type Models
Dependent Variable = RGDP Growth

	Low	Middle	Industrial
Intercept	− 0.002	0.013	0.026
	(0.06)	(1.03)	(2.23)
Capital/RGDP	− 0.040	− 0.036	− 0.038
	(1.64)	(3.47)	(3.14)
Investment/RGDP	0.366	0.263	0.314
	(1.73)	(3.14)	(3.80)
Labor growth	0.518	0.319	− 0.226
	(0.47)	(1.08)	(0.87)
Weighted export growth	0.057	0.385	− 0.004
	(0.05)	(2.72)	(0.02)
Export growth	0.102	0.094	− 0.047
	(0.47)	(1.50)	(0.32)
N	31	33	19
R^2	0.240	0.802	0.706
Adjusted R^2	0.088	0.766	0.593

Note: Figures in parentheses are t-ratios.

has been noted elsewhere.[14] The parameter estimates for Equation 4-10 are satisfactory even though some of the coefficients fall somewhat below the margin of statistical significance. There is a relatively high $\bar{R}^2$. The elasticity of output with respect to labor is on the low side (though not statistically significant), perhaps reflecting the labor surplus position of many of these economies. The coefficient of investment is reasonable and highly significant. The δ variable measuring the productivity differential is computed to have a value of 0.41, a consequence of the highly significant coefficient of weighted export growth. The elasticity associated with export growth shows an externality effect of 0.9 (at the margin of significance). It is noteworthy that the constant of the equation, which picks up technological change, represents growth of 1.3 percent per year.

We conclude that in the middle-income group the differential marginal productivity and externalities associated with exports appear to have some statistical support. This is not altogether surprising since this country group, consisting of the countries on the way to development, probably includes the countries with substantial duality between the traditional and the advanced sectors. It would appear from our estimates that the export sectors show higher marginal productivity than the nonexport sectors and have external effects on the rest of the economy.

In contrast, our results for the industrial countries do not support the export growth hypothesis in either of these variants. Export growth does not make a statistically significant contribution to output growth. It would appear that industrial countries, lacking the duality of the LDCs, do not show differential marginal products and spillover effects from the export sector to the nonexport parts of the economy. The coefficient of labor does not show good results, but this may represent a data problem since in these countries worker-hours of labor input may deviate greatly from the labor force.

A number of other questions have been investigated, but they do not greatly change the conclusion.[15] The results for the middle group, which encompasses a wide range of developing countries, are quite robust. Manufacturing exports could be considered distinct from traditional exports (Hess, 1988), but much of the rapid growth of exports is in manufactures. In any case, the results are not greatly affected by substituting data on exports of manufactures for total exports or by disaggregating exports into manufacturing, fuel, and primary products. There is undoubtedly simultaneity in the system, and the ordinary least-squares methods we used may introduce bias. To test for biases, we reestimated the equation for the middle-income developing countries using a two-stage least-square technique.[16] The results, shown in Table 4-5, are not qualitatively different from those obtained from the ordinary least-squares estimates, but the standard errors of the coefficients are naturally somewhat greater. The measure of neutral technological change is lower, the coefficient of labor is somewhat higher, but the impact of export growth remains about the same magnitude.

An important question is whether these effects change as countries move from low to higher income levels. We might assume, for example, that there is a tendency for growth to slow as countries reach higher levels of per capita income. This issue is closely related to recent investigations of whether there is a tendency for growth rates to converge. Such an effect could be independent of the elasticities of output with respect to capital or labor or it could be captured with interaction effects. We have investigated these phenomena. In particular, Table 4-6 shows the results of including an initial-conditions variable, GDP per capita in 1974, in the Feder equation (the equation presented here corresponds to the equation for the middle-income developing countries presented in Table 4-4). It is interesting to note that the initial conditions have a statistically significant and negative effect; the growth rate is slower by 0.5

Table 4-5 Feder-Type Models, Middle-Income Group
(Two-Stage Least Squares Estimate)

Dependent Variable = RGDP Growth	
Intercept	0.003
	(0.22)
Capital/RGDP	−0.032
	(2.22)
Investment/RGDP	0.255
	(1.87)
Labor growth	0.529
	(1.62)
Weighted export growth	0.337
	(2.14)
Export growth	0.100
	(0.63)
N	32
R^2	0.831
Adjusted R^2	0.792

Note: Figures in parentheses are t-ratios.

Table 4-6 Feder-Type Models, Middle-Income Group Only
Dependent Variable = RGDP Growth

Intercept	0.015
	(1.23)
RGDP/population, 1974	−0.000005
	(2.10)
Capital/RGDP	−0.025
	(2.27)
Investment/RGDP	0.234
	(2.92)
Labor growth	0.331
	(1.19)
Weighted export growth	0.484
	(3.42)
Export growth	0.082
	(1.38)
N	33
R^2	0.831
Adjusted R^2	0.792

Note: Figures in parentheses are t-ratios.

percent for every $1000 of additional per capita GDP. This effect appears to be largely neutral since the elasticities with respect to capital and labor are hardly affected. The presence of this variable does result in a somewhat higher coefficient associated with weighted export growth, so that there is some offset from export growth.

On the basis of the results of this equation, a "sources of growth" allocation for the middle-income countries (at the sample means) can be made as in Table 4-7. We also explored controlling for the effect of education level as both an additive term and an interaction effect with labor growth but did not find statistically significant coefficients, just as in the production function estimates.

The effects of government spending are investigated by Adams, Behrman, and Boldin (1989). They suggest that growth of government spending for military as well as nonmilitary purposes has a positive association with growth except in the "warring" countries, but this effect may reflect the direct inclusion of government production in the measurement of GDP.

Table 4-7 Source of Growth Allocation for Middle-Income Group

Variable	Percent of Growth
Neutral technical change	8.2%
Intercept	
RGDP/population, 1974	
Capital accumulation	33.9
Investment/RGDP	
Depreciation	
Labor growth	23.5
Labor force growth	
Export growth	34.3
Export productivity differential	
Export externality	
Total	100.0%

REDUCED-FORM APPROACHES

Whereas the Feder equation demonstrates the role of exports both as a high-productivity sector and as a contributor of externalities to the rest of the developing-country economy, such an equation leaves unexplained the causative origin of the growth process. The equation is not a reduced form. The right-hand-side variables should be seen as endogenous variables in a more complex dynamic structure.

We have taken advantage of our data set to run some two-stage least-squares equations to explain growth of exports and investment (Table 4-8), the central growth-determining variables in our analysis. This work is just for the middle-income group, since the results for the low-income and industrial country groups were not satisfactory. The equation for investment/GDP shows a significant accelerator effect, that is, a positive effect of GDP growth, and a lag effect on the past investment/GDP ratio. Other variables do not have statistically significant effects. It is noteworthy that there is no interaction between export growth and investment share.

The equation for export growth is more daunting since nothing comes even close to statistical significance except past export growth. We experimented at length with various definitions of competitiveness but found little support for the hypothesis that export growth can be associated with price competitiveness in the developing countries. Regressions of exports on real exchange rates showed little correlation. This may reflect the structure of developing-country exports, many of which are standardized goods to which the "law of one price" may apply. An alternate possibility was to compare actual real exchange rates with the corresponding PPP. But again we were not able to provide an expla-

Table 4-8 Regression for Growth-Determining Variables, Middle-Income Group Only (Two-Stage Least-Squares Estimates)

Dependent Variable =	RGDP Growth	Investment/RGDP	Weighted Export Growth
Intercept	0.010	0.017	−0.009
	(0.70)	(0.61)	(0.59)
RGDP/population, 1974	−0.000005	−0.000008	−0.000004
	(1.75)	(0.93)	(0.87)
RGDP growth	0.019[a]	1.405	0.006
	(0.20)	(2.10)	(0.01)
Capital/output	−0.025		
	(1.84)		
Investment/RGDP	0.268	0.584[a]	−0.011
	(2.67)	(6.20)	(0.13)
Labor growth	0.387		
	(1.19)		
Weighted export growth	0.460	−0.159	0.854[a]
	(2.56)	(0.25)	(2.33)
N	32	32	32
R^2	0.681	0.761	0.513
Adjusted R^2	0.604	0.726	0.441

[a]Lagged values from the period 1967–73 were used for these variables.

Note: Figures in parentheses are t-ratios.

nation for export growth with such a variable. We might have visualized an impact from investment to exports, a supply-side phenomenon, but this data set does not show evidence of such causation. One hesitates to leave export growth as an unexplained cultural phenomenon.

An alternative test of the factors influencing growth is through the computation of reduced-form equations. In Table 4-9 we report reduced-form equations for GDP growth. These incorporate only past or current exogenous variables. An extensive amount of data mining was carried out introducing variables to measure past economic performance, past investment, literacy, external capital inflows, and openness. These calculations showed little in the way of promising explanations for growth. Stage of economic growth and past performance appear to be the only significant variables. As we noted earlier, there is a negative effect from GDP per capita, and there are positive effects of past export growth and investment shares. Notice the much lower $\bar{R}^2$ values compared to those from the more structured two-stage least-squares equations. Additional variables that theory may suggest as possibly important have little additional explanatory value. Education level and stage of development, respectively, have the correct signs but are not significant. Foreign investment effects and openness measured by the last two variables have signs that are opposite what would be expected. None of these conclusions is changed if the other variables are not included in the equation.

The disentanglement of structure and causation consequently must be left to additional research, perhaps using a richer source of data in a time-series setting. What determines the level of investment in the high-growth economy? What determines the rapid growth of exports? What is the interaction between rapid growth of exports and high levels of investment? What are the interactions among investment, exports, and labor force growth?

Table 4-9   Reduced-Form Models, Middle-Income Group Only
Dependent Variable = RGDP Growth

Intercept	0.039	0.034	0.063
	(3.19)	(2.67)	(1.33)
RGDP/population, 1974	− 0.000007	− 0.00001	− 0.00002
	(1.68)	(2.15)	(2.06)
Weighted export growth, 1967–74	0.505	0.429	0.442
	(1.85)	(1.55)	(1.21)
Investment/RGDP, 1967–74	0.088	0.108	
	(1.31)	(1.36)	
Adult literacy, 1979			0.00003
			(0.11)
Agricultural labor share, 1974			− 0.0002
			(0.57)
Net capital inflow/ RGDP, 1974–86			− 0.00003
			(1.54)
(Imports + exports)/ RGDP, 1974–86			− 0.016
			(0.76)
N	31	31	31
R^2	0.243	0.288	0.370
Adjusted R^2	0.189	0.209	0.178

Note: Figures in parentheses are t-ratios.

CONCLUSION

The calculations reported in this study, as well as many which we did not report here, ranged widely using the available data sets to explore the production function and the Feder hypothesis in the three sets of countries. Robust results appear only for the middle group, which encompasses the countries in the midst of the development process. Here the ICP data point clearly to a much higher elasticity of output with respect to capital than in the other groups, and the computations support the Feder notion of differential productivity in the export and nonexport sectors and of the spillover from the export sector to the nonexport sectors.

APPENDIX 4-1
COUNTRY GROUPINGS BASED ON ICP RGDP PER CAPITA IN 1974

Low-Income Countries

Burundi	296	Somalia	427	Kenya	604
Tanzania	309	Chad	429	Madagascar	620
Burkina	311	Bangladesh	453	Sudan	666
Mali	326	Nepal	489	Afghanistan	672
Ethiopia	328	Central African Republic	495	Togo	707
Rwanda	331	Sierra Leone	510	Senegal	725
Uganda	349	Lesotho	525	Egypt	735
Niger	361	Mauritania	533	Cameroon	769
Zaire	379	India	554	Liberia	780
Malawi	383	Ghana	587	Pakistan	821
Mayanmar	388	Benin	592	Zambia	841
Guinea	405	Haiti	592		

Middle-Income Countries

Mozambique	934	Papua New Guinea	1569	Costa Rica	2642
Honduras	943	Dominican Republic	1607	Portugal	3352
Morocco	954	Republic of Korea	1713	Uruguay	3416
Sri Lanka	997	Guatemala	1725	Greece	3478
Zimbabwe	1024	Taiwan	1956	Mexico	3509
Ivory Coast	1030	Ecuador	2040	Iraq	3605
Angola	1086	Turkey	2084	Chile	3870
Thailand	1260	Colombia	2095	Singapore	4010
Philippines	1281	Malaysia	2339	South Africa	4083
Jordan	1286	Jamaica	2355	Ireland	4144
Paraguay	1341	Panama	2423	Argentina	4306
Bolivia	1420	Peru	2470	Iran	4456
Tunisia	1440	Brazil	2539	Hong Kong	4490
El Salvador	1463	Nicaragua	2631		

Industrial Countries

Spain	5467	New Zealand	7449	Norway	8337
Italy	5895	Australia	7646	France	8373
Israel	5954	Belgium	8058	Denmark	8498
Japan	6430	Netherlands	8177	Switzerland	10,010
Austria	7043	Sweden	8233	Canada	10,214
United Kingdom	7090	West Germany	8254	United States	10,382
Finland	7300				

NOTES

1. These growth rates and per capita incomes are based on purchasing-power parity (PPP) comparisons. See Kravis, Heston, and Summers (1982) for examples and discussion. In our estimates, which follow, we primarily use the ICP PPP data developed by Kravis, Heston, and Summers with updated data provided in Summers and Heston (1988). We classified countries into groups to match closely the system used in the World Bank *Development Report:* low-income developing countries, middle-income developing countries, and the industrial market economies.

2. It is worth noting that growth in the 1974–86 period considered here is significantly slower, at all levels of development, than in the preceding decade.

3. The seminal reference is Feder (1983). The details of these equations are discussed later. There is no constraint to constant returns to scale and there is recognition of the impact of export growth. We also consider later in more detail the sources of growth of the middle-income countries.

4. Various assumptions about factor shares yield the following results. The technical change effect, in percent is

Technical change = GDP growth − [α(labor growth) + (1 − α)(capital growth)]

With assumed labor shares (α) of 0, 0.33, and 0.66, country group averages (in percent per year) are -0.24, -0.57, and -0.92 for low-income countries, 0.74, -0.01, and -0.67 for middle-income countries, and 1.40, 0.95, and 0.50 for industrial countries.

5. For a discussion of the determinations of international competitiveness see Kravis and Lipsey (1971).

6. We exclude countries with 1974 population less than a million and countries with fuel exports that average greater than 60 percent of total exports. We lose some countries from the sample when we include additional variables because of lack of particular data values. The division among country groups is very similar, but not identical, to the World Bank division for the same year even though the relative levels of per capita product tend to be higher for the poorer countries with the ICP data than with the World Bank data based on official exchange rates.

7. These are consistent with the median of the estimates that we obtain for the 1974–86 averages. We explored other alternatives: a value of 1.7 and country-specific values equal to the marginal capital–output ratio for the 1960–86 period. Our capital stock estimates for the estimation period of 1974–86 do not differ substantially with these other assumptions. Alternatively, we considered using the capital stock estimates of Dadkhah and Zahedi (1986, 1988). However, these estimates assume a fixed-coefficient technology with capital stock being the binding constraint on production. Therefore, they are not useful for our purpose of estimating characteristics of the technology.

8. We discuss these explorations in a particular order for expositional convenience, but our conclusions do not depend on the particular sequence.

9. Heteroskedasticity tests suggest weighting.

10. To avoid unrealistic coefficients on labor, these equations have been formulated to assume constant returns to scale. Under the Cobb–Douglas assumptions, the intercept coefficient would correspond to neutral technological change, the coefficient for the change in the log of the capital–labor ratio would be the later period's elasticity of output with respect to capital, and the last term captures changes in the elasticity.

11. This prima facie may appear to be a quasi–Cobb-Douglas assumption for production in the nonexport sector. But the marginal product of labor in the nonexport sector is assumed to be proportional to the economy-wide average product of labor, *not* to the average product of labor in the nonexport sector alone. Therefore, this is consistent with a quasi–Cobb-Douglas assumption only if the two sectors have the same output–labor ratio.

12. Kendrick (1961). In this case α is interpreted as the marginal productivity of capital in the economy as a whole. We note that Summers and Heston (1988) rate much of the data for this group of countries in the poor range.

13. Michaely (1977) argues that there is a threshold income level under which the traditional approach does not work.

14. Similar regressions based on data from the World Bank converted to U.S. dollars on an exchange-rate basis, rather than the ICP basis we use, yield similar results except that the coefficients of investment in the data are considerably lower in the World Bank figures than in those provided by the ICP. This could reflect the fact that the ICP measures of investment are more appropriate to cross-country comparisons.

15. The Feder model can be extended to four sectors—domestic, manufacturing exports, fuel exports, and primary product exports—with separate externality effects calculated for each of the export sectors. An F test ($F = 0.01$) strongly rejects the hypothesis that the coefficients are different among these sectors.

16. The instruments used were the lagged values (1967–73) of all variables except labor growth, which was considered exogenous.

REFERENCES

Adams, F. G., J. R. Behrman, and M. Boldin. 1989. "Defense Expenditures and Economic Growth in the LDCs: A Revised Perspective." Center for Analysis for Developing Economies. Philadelphia: University of Pennsylvania. (unpublished)

Balassa, B. 1978. "Exports and Economic Growth: Further Evidence." *Journal of Development Economics* 5(2), 181–89.

Balassa, B. 1985. "Exports, Policy Choices, and Economic Growth in Developing Countries After the 1973 Oil Shock." *Journal of Development Economics* 18(1), 23–35.

Dadkhah, K. M., and F. Zahedi. 1986. "Simultaneous Estimation of Production Functions and Capital Stocks in Developing Countries." *Review of Economics and Statistics* 68, 443–51.

Dadkhah, K. M., and F. Zahedi. 1988. "Estimation of Cross-Country Comparison of Capital Stocks." (mimeographed)

Feder, G. 1983. "On Exports and Economic Growth." *Journal of Development Economics* 12(1/2), 59–73.

Heller, P., and R. Porter. 1978. "Exports and Growth: An Empirical Reinvestigation." *Journal of Development Economics* 5(2), 191–93.

Hess, P. N. 1988. "Openness, Export Composition, and Economic Growth in LDCs." Chapel Hill: University of North Carolina. (mimeographed)

Jung, W., and P. Marshall. 1985. "Exports, Growth, and Causality in Developing Countries." *Journal of Development Economics* 18(1), 1–12.

Kavoussi, R. 1984. "Export Expansion and Economic Growth: Further Empirical Evidence." *Journal of Development Economics* 14(1/2), 241–50.

Kendrik, J. 1961. *Productivity Trends in the United States*. Princeton, N.J.: Princeton University Press.

Kravis, I. B., A. Heston, and R. Summers. 1982. *World Product and Income: International Comparisons of Real Gross Product*. Baltimore, Md.: Johns Hopkins University Press.

Kravis, I. B., and R. Lipsey. 1971. *Price Competitiveness in World Trade*. New York: National Bureau of Economic Research.

Krueger, A. 1980. "Trade Policy as an Input to Development." *American Economic Review* 70(2), 288–92.

Michaely, M. 1977. "Exports and Growth: An Empirical Investigation." *Journal of Development Economics* 4(1), 141–43.

Ram, R. 1985. "Exports and Economic Growth: Some Additional Evidence." *Economic Development and Cultural Change* 33(2), 415–225.

Ram, R. 1987. "Exports and Economic Growth in Developing Countries: Evidence from Time-Series and Cross-Section Data." *Economic Development and Cultural Change* 36(1), 51–72.

Salvatore, D. 1983. "A Simultaneous Equations Model of Trade and Development with Dynamic Policy Simulations." *Kyklos* 36(1), 66–90.

Summers, R., and A. Heston. 1988. "A New Set of International Comparisons of Real Product and Price Levels: Estimates for 130 Countries, 1950–1985. *Review of Income and Wealth* 34(1), 1–25.

Tyler, W. 1981. "Growth and Export Expansion in Developing Countries: Some Empirical Evidence." *Journal of Development Economics* 9(1), 121–30.

World Bank. 1987. *World Development Report 1987*. New York: Oxford University Press.

5

Productivity, Competitiveness, and the Socialist System

GUR OFER

In the march of nations along the road of economic modernization and growth, the natural place of the countries of eastern and southern Europe is following their neighbors to the west and north. With the establishment of socialist regimes in Russia following World War I and in eight other eastern European countries in the aftermath of World War II, the general assumption in both the East and the West was that these countries would not only join the march but also move fast to catch up and possibly even surpass some of the leading market economies over a relatively short period. And indeed this assumption had been supported by the early record of growth of most of these countries. However, both the assumption and the record have been put into serious doubt for some time now as the pace of catching up has slowed down considerably since the 1960s and has been completely halted more recently. Moreover, a number of countries in Latin America and East Asia, apart from Japan, are now in a position to surpass the socialist countries. The halt in the trend of converging with the advanced market economies (MEs) came when the socialist countries reached levels of per capita GNP ranging only from less than one-third to one-half the U.S. level, that is, at a rather early stage of the modernization process. Two questions are raised in view of these developments. What are the explanations for the slowdown? And can the currently observed trends be altered or are they likely to become permanent? The question of whether and how these trends can be changed has been the subject of intense study by most socialist regimes in recent years. The analysis of the economic record and of the present situation offered by East bloc leaders and economists, and the reform measures initiated by them, reveal that at least they are convinced that some basic elements of the socialist system and past policies are responsible for the stagnation and therefore have to be radically changed before the trends can be reversed.

One very distinct policy common to all centrally planned economies (CPEs) is their relatively low participation in international trade with nonsocialist countries.[1] Up to the early 1960s such trade was very minimal, but even following a substantial expansion since then, their contribution to nonsocialist trade is still much lower than their share in world production. Their currencies are not convertible and their economies are virtually isolated and protected from outside competition. Most of their trade is conducted by state monopolies making bilateral barter deals. It is therefore claimed that despite their growing involvement in world trade, CPEs can still be considered autarkic. Such isolation from world market prices and the world's best quality goods and technological levels is no doubt one factor, some consider a major factor, responsible for the low level of productivity observed in these countries. It is certainly also one explanation for the generally assumed low competitive ability of these countries in the nonsocialist world market. One major aspect of the economic reforms being contemplated and partly implemented in the CPEs consists of opening up these economies to a much more intensive and genuine interaction with the world market. Some CPESs now permit foreign investments in the form of joint ventures. It is interesting to explore the nature of the mutual relationship between productivity growth and foreign economic relations under the traditional socialist system and how this relationship might evolve under currently planned reforms for their combined benefit.

This chapter outlines the three-way interrelationship between the level and development of productivity, the external trade behavior and capabilities, and the main elements of the socialist economic system and the socialist growth strategy as manifested in the economic history of the Soviet Union and of Eastern Europe during recent decades. The analysis is mostly long-term oriented, nested in the general theoretical framework of modern economic growth of follower countries as developed and articulated by Balassa (1981), Chenery and Syquin (1975), Gerschenkron (1962), Gomulka (1986), Kuznets (1966), Maddison (1982, 1987), and others. The foreign trade implications of such growth are incorporated in the main argument of the paper as follows.

The theoretical framework stipulates the patterns and speed of the convergence of follower countries toward the leading economies, the changes in their industrial structure and in the structure of their comparative advantage and trade patterns. A most naive benchmark model of "following" is one in which followers go in the footsteps of their predecessors, emulating their structural changes and encroaching on their comparative advantage from below. The speed of convergence is determined by the technological and income gap between the follower and the leader: the wider the gap, the easier is the process of technological diffusion and the faster the convergence.

Individual countries, or groups of countries, can and most likely will diverge from the uniform pattern due to their particular natural and historical endowments. They may do this by following different growth and trade policies from each other or by operating under completely different economic systems. As a result, catching up might be faster or slower, and the trade patterns might be different.

The level of competitiveness of a country is judged with respect to four criteria. First, the extent of catching up: the faster a country converges on the leaders or forerunners, the faster it bites into their exports and thus is considered more competitive. Under this criterion the level of competitiveness is directly related to the pace of productivity growth. According to the naive model, a country that catches up will also see its trade structure advance in both composition and direction of trade, whereas a country that falls behind will see its trade structure stagnate or even deteriorate. Second, past and present trade policies may affect the level of competitiveness. According to Balassa (1981) and others, growth strategies based on import substitution or autarky tend not only to retard growth but also to affect the normal pattern of comparative advantage. Isolation from world markets retards technological advance and limits the production range of qualified and advanced tradables. It also hampers competitiveness when a change toward a more open policy is sought, due to lack of export and trade experience. It should, however, be emphasized that different trade policies also produce different trade structures. Therefore, a trade structure different from normal is not necessarily by itself an indication of the level of competitiveness, but it may affect it. Third, a different economic system and a special growth strategy may influence the level of competitiveness *in addition* to affecting the general level of productivity or growth or the structure of trade. A different growth strategy may result in a different industrial structure and a different pattern of technological change. A different system may develop organizational forms that are more or less conducive to competition. Fourth, particular characteristics of individual countries, such as natural endowments, geographical location, and history, also affect competitiveness.

The main proposition of the paper is that the level of competitiveness of the European CPEs suffers because of each of the first three criteria just mentioned. Since 1960 they have not been catching up in relation to most of the industrial countries, even though their per capita GNP levels remained less than half those of the leaders. The autarkic trade policies of the EEs in the past made it very difficult to create a competing base now or in the near future. (Of special significance is the minimal use so far of foreign investment.) The price of autarkic policies falls more heavily on the EEs than on the Soviet Union due to their smaller size and fewer natural resources; the command economy of central planning has a systematic comparative disadvantage in technological change, so important for trade. The extensive growth strategy of CPEs weakens further their technological capabilities; their choice of industrial structure, of concentrating on heavy industry at the expense of agriculture, services, and consumer manufacturing, in conjunction with a weak technological capability, impairs their competitiveness in likely exportable products. The rigidities of the system of central planning, including a state monopoly on trade, deny these countries the flexibility and quick response so crucial in international trade. Finally, the combination of rigid economic systems with authoritarian political systems blocks these countries from taking full advantage of the electronic information revolution, which is already an important element in both the conducting and the substance of international trade.

Reforms directed at opening up the CPEs to all kinds of mutual international economic activities—ranging from trade to foreign investment and the free flow of scientific and technological exchanges; decentralizing price determination and bringing prices nearer to world levels; and making the decision-making mechanism much more independent from the center and thereby more flexible—may eventually improve the competitiveness level of the CPEs. Such radical reforms are making their way into the systems of the individual countries at a rather slow pace and the improvements in competitiveness are therefore expected to be equally slow.

Following a review and restatement of the theoretical conception of this chapter, we discuss and analyze the slowdown of productivity growth in the CPEs in a comparative setting. We then consider other factors affecting the low competitiveness of the CPEs in addition to the lag in productivity. We also examine the relationship between competitiveness and the trade structure of the CPEs, by goods and by destination. This section is followed by a comparative analysis of the development of the structure of trade of the CPEs and other country groups and of their respective revealed comparative advantages. Finally, by way of conclusion, the potential significance of the various reform measures in improving productivity and competitiveness is summarized.

THEORETICAL FRAMEWORK

The relationship between the overall productivity of an economy and its foreign trade performance and level of competitiveness in international markets can be described as follows: if the rate of productivity growth lags behind that of other economies, and assuming for the moment a uniform productivity movement across all sectors, then as the declining world market prices become less and less profitable for exporters and more attractive for importers, exports decline and imports rise. In a regime with a flexible exchange rate this would be followed by a decline of the exchange rate and a deficit would be avoided. In a regime with a fixed exchange rate, or when adjustments are slow, a deficit would show up and the country would keep on losing markets. Eventually it would be forced to devalue and/or reduce production costs and profit margins in order to restore a balanced account. The opposite would happen if a country was catching up in its productivity level relative to other countries.[2]

Before pursuing further the relationship between productivity and competitiveness we should reiterate the fact that foreign trade performance is affected by a large number of factors that have little or no relation to productivity. These factors include speculative capital movements and short-term changes in interest rates, temporary changes in international prices (like oil), an increase in a government's budget deficit, shifts in monetary policy, or a discovery of a new natural resource. With few exceptions (discussed later), this chapter concentrates on the longer term relationship between productivity and the ability to sell on international markets, not on changes in foreign trade performance that result from short-term factors. The problem we face is that actual or revealed trade performance of any country at any given time is a combined result of the long-term productivity factors as well as the others just mentioned.

An intrinsic characteristic of productivity is that it grows at different rates in different sectors and industries, thus creating, as it rises, a dynamic change of the industrial structure, accompanied by parallel changes in the structure of its comparative advantage. Let us assume first that the comparative advantage of a country depends solely on its level or stage of economic development (we ignore size and natural resources). Under such assumptions the trade composition will change continuously as the country's productivity rises, shifting its exports (or net exports) from basic products up the ladder of the technology spectrum to sophisticated goods and shifting the direction of trade from less developed to more industrialized countries. As it moves ahead, each country will lose competitiveness in the lower end of its range of products and gain competitiveness in more advanced products. The leaders will move into brand-new products, based on new technologies. A faster rise of productivity by a "catcher up" may cause a net loss of competitiveness to the more advanced country. The adjustment process will be like that already described: countries losing more at the lower end of their trade assortment than gaining at the upper end will be weak on competitiveness. This is basically Balassa's stages approach to comparative advantage (1981, Essay 6; see also Krugman, 1979).

The technological gaps between leaders and followers and between followers at different stages of development create the advantages of backwardness (Gerschenkron, 1962) or the opportunity of convergence of followers toward leaders (Gomulka, 1986, pp. 51–52; Maddison, 1982). Convergence becomes possible as followers need only to introduce and diffuse fully developed and well-tried technologies, whereas leaders have to keep developing new technologies at much higher costs. The convergence pattern over time may have a logistic shape, with accelerated convergence at earlier stages and a slowing down convergence as a follower approaches the leader. At this later stage the technological opportunities diminish and the follower assumes, to an increasing extent, the role of a leader in developing new technologies on its own.

The actual trade structure of any country will diverge from what is called for by its stage of development for a host of reasons, some with and some without a direct effect on competitiveness. First there are the objective factors of natural endowment, the size of the country, its economic history, and the international trade environment, that is, the other trade partners and the goods being traded. Second, different trade policies produce different trade structures at given levels of economic development. A growth strategy based on import substitution will develop a different trade volume and a different structure than a strategy of export-led growth (Balassa, 1981; Chenery and Syrquin, 1975). The same holds true of any other policy decision to restrict or redirect trade away from its comparative-advantage tendencies. Such different trade policies also have different economic effects on productivity and on competitiveness. Balassa, for example, claims that the strategy of import substitution results in lower growth rates and in a weaker competitive capability when a country shifts to a more open trade policy (1981). Finally, an extreme case is when a country introduces a uniquely different economic system and growth strategy, including particular trade policies, such as in the CPEs. In such a case there are to be expected many divergences from "normal" patterns of productivity growth, industrial structure, trade structure and performance, and interactions between these elements.

Since trade structure can be different between countries for both objective or policy-related reasons, with or without an effect on competitiveness, there is the problem of identifying the sources of the structural difference. A different trade structure at a given level of development cannot in itself serve as conclusive evidence of the degree of competitiveness. To the extent that such policies do affect productivity, as they very likely do, they will have an additional indirect effect on the structure of trade to bring it into line with the new productivity level.

RELATIVE PRODUCTIVITY AND PRODUCTIVITY CHANGES IN CPEs

According to the theoretical framework, the basic or initial measure of competitiveness is the change of productivity of a country over time relative to that of followers and leaders. The main measure of productivity used in this chapter is gross domestic product (GDP) per worker employed. This choice is mainly a pragmatic one—it stems from the great difficulty of locating and calculating comparable data for many countries on capital services, hours, and human capital, in order to estimate changes in total factor productivity (TFP). As is well known, however, there are also substantive arguments in favor of the use of labor productivity rather than the conventional TFP as the proper estimator of productivity. The main argument is that technological change, the main vehicle of productivity growth, is embodied in both human and physical capital, so that part of their conventional measure as inputs should be credited to productivity growth (Maddison, 1982, pp. 22–24). In addition, the ability of a country to set aside enough resources for investment purposes is also considered a contribution to both productivity and competitiveness (Lawrence, 1988). The embodiment argument is of course valid; the only problem is to estimate it correctly, a task that cannot be performed here. In addition, as discussed later, there are sound reasons to question the extent of embodiment in the investments of CPEs. Finally, by measuring productivity on the basis of labor input alone one disregards the possibility that investment may be too large, as in CPEs, or too small from the point of view of long-term maximization of consumption per capita. As a result, both productivity and competitiveness can be higher but still fail to serve their main goal. In view of these problems, and their specific relevance to CPEs, I tend to favor TFP over labor productivity as the most relevant measure when CPEs are involved in the comparisons. Indeed one should go one step further and measure productivity as well as competitiveness in terms of consumption per unit of inputs, thereby taking into account also differences among countries in the number of work hours per capita (or per working-age member). This is also particularly relevant to CPEs where labor participation rates are especially high.

In Table 5-1 comparative data on the rate of change of labor productivity is given for GDP and for manufacturing, and also for GDP per capita for the Soviet Union and the EEs on the one side, and a number of groups of leader and follower countries on the other. The EEs are divided into two groups: the more advanced countries (East Germany, Czechoslovakia, and Hungary), and the less developed ones (Poland, Bulgaria, and Romania). The aggregated figures for the groups and also for all the EEs are weighted averages, the weights

Table 5-1 Income and Productivity Levels, CPEs and Market Economies, 1950–1985 (Annual Rates of Growth)[a]

	GDP Per Employed			GDP Per Capita			GDP Per Employed (Manufacturing)	
	1950–85	1950–70	1970–85	1950–85	1950–70	1970–85	1960–80	1970–80
CPEs								
Soviet Union	2.7	3.5	1.6	3.0	3.9	1.7	2.9[d]	2.6
EEs	2.7	3.2	2.0	3.1	3.7	2.2	3.0	2.3
EEs (developed)	2.5	3.0	1.8	3.2	3.9	2.1	2.7	2.6
EEs (less developed)	2.8	3.3	2.1	3.0	3.6	2.2	3.2	2.2
East Germany	3.0	3.9	1.8	4.0	4.9	2.7	3.2	2.5
Czechoslovakia	2.0	2.2	1.7	2.5	3.0	1.7	2.0	2.3
Hungary	2.5	2.9	1.9	2.8	3.6	1.8	2.7	3.1
Poland	1.8	2.2	1.3	2.3	2.8	1.6	2.7	2.4
Bulgaria	3.8	5.3	1.7	3.7	5.3	1.8	3.4	2.4
Romania	3.9	4.1	3.6	3.8	4.2	3.4	3.9	1.8
Market economies								
United States								
Employed	1.6	2.1	0.9	1.9	1.9	2.0	2.8[b]	1.9
Labor force	1.4	1.8	0.9					
OECD								
Employed	3.5	4.5	2.2	3.0	3.8	1.8	4.0[b]	3.7
Labor force	2.8	3.7	1.7					
UMI	2.9[b]	—[c]	2.1	2.8[b]	—[c]	2.1		
LMI	2.2	—[c]	1.6	1.9[b]	—[c]	1.6		

Sources: Soviet Union, 1950–80, Ofer (1987), Tables 1, 2, pp. 1778, 1780; 1980–85, CIA (1987), Tables 45, 46, p. 70. EEs, 1950–65, Alton (1970), Tables 1, 3, 13, 15; 1965–85, Alton (1988), Tables 18, 19, pp. 27–29, and Alton (1985), Tables 18, 19, pp. 27–29. Labor force data for 1985 are from World Bank (1987), Table 32, pp. 264–65. OECD, United States, 1950–70, Ofer (1987), Table 2, p. 1780; 1970–85; OECD (1987), Tables 1.3, 1.7, 3.1, 3.2, 3.7, 3.9. UMIs, LMIs, World Bank (1983, 1987), world development indicators (tables).

[a]The aggregated figures for EEs and their subgroups are average rates weighted by population size in 1980.

[b]1960–85.

[c]Data not available.

[d]Based on hourly rate.

being proportional to the populations of the individual countries. The table covers the period of 1950–85.

The record of productivity growth of the CPEs is compared in Table 5-1 with those of the United States, with the European members of the Organization for Economic Cooperation and Development (OECD), and with two groups of middle-income economies, lower and upper (LMI and UMI, respectively), according to the World Bank's classification (*World Development Report* [hereafter WDR], 1987). For the purpose of our analysis and in line with the underlying theory and hypothesis, the various country groups have to be ordered by levels of productivity. A comparison of income levels of the groups of countries for 1985 based on the United Nations International Comparison Project (ICP) of purchasing-power parities (Kravis, Heston, and Summers, [ICP II], 1982; UN [ICP III], 1987) and further work done by Marer (1985) for the Eastern European countries provides the following on levels of GDP per capita: the CPE group ranges between half of the U.S. level (East Germany) and around one-third of the U.S. level (Poland, Bulgaria, and Romania). Czechoslovakia, the Soviet Union, and Hungary fall in the middle part of the range— around 40 percent of the U.S. level. Countries of the OECD group occupy the entire range between the United States and East Germany with only a few of its members having lower income levels.[3] The UMI countries include many of the so-called NICs, the newly industrializing countries, such as Brazil, Argentina, and Mexico in Latin America; South Korea, Malaysia, Singapore, and Hong Kong in East Asia; and Israel, Portugal, and Greece (WDR, 1987, pp. 202–3). Although a few have incomes above 50 percent of the American level, most are located at the lower tail of the EEs or below (mostly at 20–30 percent of the U.S. level). Finally, there is the group of LMI countries with an income range of roughly between 10 and 20 percent of U.S. levels. Generally speaking, therefore, in terms of GDP per capita, the CPEs follow the United States and the OECD group but are located ahead of the UMI and LMI groups.

The foregoing order of countries may, however, be somewhat altered when the ordering criterion shifts from GDP per capita to GDP per employed person, the present productivity measure. In particular, rates of labor force participation in the CPEs are significantly higher than those in both the more and less advanced groups of countries. This is mostly due to the CPEs' policy and growth strategy of maximizing labor force participation rates. These rates range in the CPEs between 47 and 52 percent of the population (Alton, 1981, p. 368) at a time when those for the OECD-E group average around 43 percent. The differences between rates of employed are even wider (OECD, 1985, p. 27; see more on this point later). Labor force participation rates for middle-income economies are even lower, due in this case also to their much younger demographic structure. Therefore, on the basis of GDP per employed, the CPEs should be moved further below the OECD group and into the ranks of the UMI group.

Before getting to comparisons, a few observations on the productivity record of the CPEs are warranted (Table 5-1). First, we note the sharp decline in productivity growth in all countries: productivity growth rates have generally declined from 3 percent or more per year in 1950–70 down to 1–2 percent for the more recent period. Second, with the exception of the poor record of Po-land, the less developed EEs, Bulgaria and Romania, have enjoyed faster pro-ductivity advance than the more developed EEs. Even when Poland is included in the former group, that group's average record is somewhat superior to that of the latter throughout. This supports the validity of the theory of catching up by followers for the socialist bloc. The overall productivity record of the Soviet Union is almost identical with that of all the EEs put together; it did slightly better in the early period and somewhat less well lately. Since its position on the productivity scale is right in the middle between the two EE groups, this is yet another backing for the theory. Finally, rates of growth of GDP per capita are consistently higher than those for GDP per worker, due to a much faster growth of employment than of population. Part of this phenomenon results from demographic changes, but to a significant extent this is a dynamic mani-festation of the extensive growth strategy mentioned earlier. Note, however, the convergence of the two series of growth rates, a result of the exhaustion of labor reserves.

Turning to comparisons of productivity growth in Table 5-1, we first observe that while the CPEs have been making advances relative to the United States, their rates of growth have not exceeded those of the OECD countries, even in the early years. As can be seen, the table has two figures for product per worker for the OECD countries—one is per person employed and the other per labor force member—whether employed or not. For the CPEs the two concepts converge into one, as unemployment, even if it exists, is neither recognized nor reported. In any case, unemployment is much more limited in the CPEs than in the West since in the former most redundant labor is kept on the job. When figures for product per employed person are compared, it is found that the record of OECD is superior to that of the CPEs for every subperiod. However, when levels of product per labor force member are compared, the two records look very similar to each other over the entire period. The OECD countries also performed better than the group of the more advanced EEs throughout the period, according to both measures.

There may be arguments going both ways regarding the question of which of the two measures is more appropriate for comparisons. The use of GDP per employed person may better compare actual microlevel production efficiency and the level of technology, but only if one ignores the CPE practice of hoarding labor on the job. On the other hand, comparisons based on labor force are warranted if the overall performance of the economies is considered and the level of unemployment is just another negative aspect of that performance.

Finally, on this score let us note that the figures on labor productivity in manufacturing, as seen in Table 5-1, also indicate a superior performance of the OECD group over the CPEs.

It can therefore be concluded that even on the basis of labor force produc-tivity the CPEs have at least failed to advance relative to the most relevant leader group in front of it. It also may be stated that while both groups of countries have been going through a period of low and declining growth rates, the OECD group is experiencing the slowdown when it is approaching the U.S. level and acquiring a more active technological leadership role, whereas the

CPEs still have a long way to go. There is also some evidence that productivity growth has been resumed to some extent in the West, but not in the East.

A comparison of the productivity growth of the CPEs with the other two groups of countries included in Table 5-1 shows that the UMI group seems to have been doing on average as well or even slightly better than the CPEs, whereas the LMI group performed less well throughout. Among the LMI group are some countries at their initial stages of growth or takeoff as well as some with long histories of wars and internal unrest. The UMI group includes a number of countries (South Korea, Brazil, Malaysia, Hong Kong, Singapore, and Taiwan) with very impressive growth rates.

To shift the basis of comparison from labor productivity to total factor productivity it is necessary to adjust the former to account for rates of change of hours worked per person employed, changes in labor quality (i.e., investment in human capital), and changes in the rate of growth of material capital services per labor unit. The needed adjustments cannot be performed in a precise manner here, but observations on their likely direction may be offered. First, it is difficult to guess what has happened to annual hours worked per worker in the various country groups. Hours definitely declined everywhere, but at least one factor should have contributed to a faster decline in the West—the sharp increase in the participation of women in the labor force, accompanied by a correspondingly sharp rise in employment in services and in part-time work. A similar, more intensive process of increased participation by women took place in the CPEs, but here mostly in full-time jobs. Second, it is highly likely that investment in education, at least in terms of years at school, grew at a faster rate among the CPEs than among the industrialized market economies. The CPEs' initial level in the early 1960s was much lower, and raising the level of education and training had always been a major goal of socialist planners and an acute need for the industrialization drive.[4] Third, the rate of growth of capital per worker was much faster in the CPEs than in the industrialized market economies. The initial levels of capital stocks of the CPEs were clearly lower, and the rates of investment out of national income have been higher all along. Rates of gross investment, as a percentage of GDP, are regularly higher than 25 percent and are reaching 30 percent or more in the CPEs, whereas Western rates range around 20 percent (WDR, 1987, pp. 210–11).[5] If all this is true, then the rates of growth of GDP per unit of combined inputs, adjusted for education, should be lower in the CPEs, compared with the IMEs, than the corresponding rates of labor productivity seen in Table 5-1. The same conclusion is reached if the experience of the Soviet Union with respect to total factor productivity can be extended to the EEs. Total factor productivity in the Soviet Union in 1950–80 is estimated at 0.7 percent per year, and it had been going down from 1.6 percent in 1950–60 to negative figures recently (CIA, 1987, p. 70; Ofer, 1987, p. 15). The record of total factor productivity in industry is even worse (CIA, 1987, p. 70). Recent estimates of total factor productivity in OECD countries (business sector only) come to 2.8 percent per year up to 1973 and 0.6–0.7 percent since then (Englander and Mittelstadt, 1988, pp. 14–15). Without the United States the figures are considerably higher.

It is even more difficult to estimate how the adjustments for hours and human and material capital may affect the comparison of the records of the CPEs with those of the UMIs. We have no comparative data on hours. The available data on education demonstrate a much faster growth among the UMIs, but the investment data indicate faster growth of capital in the CPEs.

Table 5-1 also presents figures comparing rates of change of GNP per capita. Note the higher rates of growth in the CPEs compared to the productivity rates and the similarity between the two sets of rates for the other groups of countries. This is a dynamic manifestation of the CPEs' policy of maximizing labor force participation rates discussed previously. Hence the comparative showing of the CPEs is better when rates of growth of GDP per capita are compared.

The first main conclusion of the discussion thus far is that since around 1950 the CPEs did not advance in terms of labor productivity relative to the leading group of OECD; indeed, the CPEs might even have retreated somewhat. Second, it is very likely that a higher proportion of the advance of labor productivity was achieved for the CPEs by raising the educational level of labor and the amount of capital per worker and less through raising the level of product per unit of combined inputs. Finally, the CPEs are not advancing faster than their peer group of UMIs, and among this last group there are countries with impressive growth rates. On the basis of this record and the naive theoretical model, the conclusion seems to be that the relative competitive level of the CPEs, at least on the world market, has not advanced and may even have been deteriorating.

The low rate of growth of total factor productivity in the CPEs is generally attributed in the literature to a combination of systemic factors and the particular growth strategy chosen and followed by the CPEs. The command, centrally planned, bureaucratically run economy is inhospitable to technological changes and improvements in efficiency. Moreover, a growth strategy that emphasizes haste and fast growth through maximal use of inputs and the application of heavy pressures to achieve quantitative results hardly leaves room for attention to quality or technology. Technological change needs a loose environment, initiative from below, and flexibility in the organization of supply lines and time schedules; it needs quick responses, generous incentives, a competitive environment, and a powerful buyers market; it needs a sound pricing base and correct price signals for cost accounting, and a system that cares about costs and quality. The combination of a sellers market, perennial shortages, soft budget constraints for enterprises, and wrong and inflexible prices can hardly provide any of these, as is extensively documented in the literature. CPEs are generally believed to have a comparative disadvantage in the production and diffusion of technological changes. (See, among many others, Amman and Cooper, 1982; Bergson, 1983; Berliner, 1976; Gomulka, 1986, Chapter 3; Hanson, 1981; Kornai, 1986; and a recent summary survey in Ofer, 1987, pp. 1798–1814). The necessary solution of importing advanced technology, which is also consistent with the follower status of all the CPEs, so far has been less than entirely successful, mainly for two reasons. First, the comparative disadvantage of the CPEs in technology encompasses the introduction and diffusion phases. This has been demonstrated in the recent experience of the Soviet Union, Poland, Romania, Hungary, and other EEs. There are problems of absorption of such technologies into the local supporting environment, such as construction, supplies, and maintenance, as well as aligning them with domestic production patterns. The second difficulty stems from the fact that only in relatively few cases thus far has importation of technology come in the form of foreign investment or even joint ventures. Such a form may be more suitable to overcome some of the previously mentioned problems and to set a pattern that could be emulated later. (See, for example, Bornstein, 1985; Hanson, 1981; Posnanski, 1987; and many others.)

The slow pace of technological change, the long gestation period that precedes introduction of new products, the heavy emphasis on quantity, and the limited variety and assortment of goods produced all contribute to a weaker competitive level, even lower than that called for by the low productivity level. As a result, the CPEs turn out products of mediocre quality for domestic use and very few front-line technology goods that excel in quality and are fit for profitable export. As a technological follower these deficiencies translate into a sluggish response to new developments by leaders at an early stage of the product development cycle, when large profits from exports or import substitution can still be gained (see Krugman, 1979). Furthermore, the strong internal sellers' market environment, the lack of competition, the pressure to meet quantitative results, and relative disregard for costs all make the individual enterprise uninterested in exporting its products into markets with much higher standards in all the areas mentioned. A tendency to shy away from having to export to the West is indeed observed in a number of Eastern European countries, whether there is an alternative of domestic sale or exporting the goods to another CPE (Crane, 1986; Marer, 1987).

The weak technological performance of the CPEs, in conjunction with the pressure for fast growth and haste, also has a retarding effect on the contribution of capital to growth and competitiveness. Under normal conditions a large volume of investment could have provided the vehicle to embody new technologies and accelerate growth. In the CPEs, capital is generally much less technology intensive. Typically a high proportion of all investments is devoted to construction as a result of a system's bias toward new plants and against the modernization of equipment in old ones. Equipment of older technological vintages is continually produced long after innovations have appeared. Due to overextended investment plans and perennial supply bottlenecks, large amounts of capital are constantly being tied up in unfinished construction projects (Hanson, 1981, Chapter 4; Kontorovich, 1985). Large amounts of capital are continuously being invested and tied up in inventories of low-quality non-salable goods. For all these reasons capital productivity in the CPEs has generally been negative and declining over time. As a result, the high rate of investment does not reinforce technological change and productivity, as in the embodied models, such as those put forward by Maddison (1982, pp. 22–24). On the contrary, it substitutes for technological change in the growth process. The contribution of investment to growth may still be very important, but most of it comes at the expense of consumption levels—the ultimate goal of productivity growth and of competitiveness. Therefore, measuring productivity by output per unit of labor is especially unfit for the CPEs. For the same reasons, as long as investment policy is not transformed, high rates of investment per se cannot contribute significantly to competitiveness.

THE SOCIALIST SYSTEM AND COMPETITIVENESS

Thus far the level of competitiveness of the CPEs has been identified almost completely with their productivity level. We look now at other systemic and growth-related aspects of the socialist economies that may have an effect on their trade structure and their level of competitiveness, in addition to their direct effect on productivity.[6]

Industrial Structure and Competitiveness

The socialist growth strategy, developed in the Soviet Union during the late 1920s and early 1930s, prescribed a path of development of the industrial structures that was different in many respects from the development patterns of market and newly developing economies. Growth was to be achieved mainly through a rapid indigenous development of a heavy industrial base consisting mainly of manufacturing of metals and other basic materials and of the production of machinery and equipment. These were designed to become the base for an ambitious investment program, as well as for the military establishment. Agriculture would be collectivized in order to provide the food needs of the industrialization effort with minimal costs. Consumption would be kept at a minimum to allow for maximum investment; hence a relative neglect of consumer industries. The same fate would also apply to services, which, in addition to being mostly consumer oriented, were also considered, according to accepted Marxian doctrine, as "nonproductive." Since capital and investment are the main growth carriers, production in heavy industry and in defense was to be carried out with technologies that were capital intensive and of the highest level. The other sectors of the economy would have to be satisfied with second- or third-rate technologies and labor-intensive input proportions. A corresponding large investment in human capital would follow, with more education and training directed toward the priority sectors, and the best workers would be allotted to them. Heavy industry and defense were to receive high planning and supply priorities, thereby directing every shortfall in plan fulfillment toward the various consumption industries. With relatively minor exceptions, some of which are mentioned later, the same system had been imposed on or emulated by the EEs upon becoming socialist during the second half of the 1940s.

Whatever the intentions were, collectivization of agriculture proved to be disastrous for agricultural production everywhere. Most of the socialist countries (with the exception of East Germany) had been large exporters of grain and other agricultural products before the war. Shortly following collectivization, not only did the exportable surplus dry up but food came into short supply. Since the early 1960s the Soviet Union started to import large amounts of grain and the socialist bloc as a whole became a large net importer of food. In this way the bloc lost the potential to export food at a very early stage of its modernization. Only at a later stage, in the mid-1960s, did Bulgaria and Hungary start to reshift their production and trade structure back in the direction of agriculture, as they and the other CPEs initiated a set of reforms designed to steer their agricultural sectors away from strict collectivization and divert a higher proportion of the investment funds toward agriculture (Ofer, 1980).

The low priority accorded all along by the CPEs to consumer manufacturing industries, including the food industry, has been a permanent source of internal hardships and grievances since the beginning. It has also deprived these countries of one of the most important traditional export bases for newly industrializing countries. Exports of basic manufactures and consumer goods is traditionally an important export starter for such countries. Furthermore, as with respect to agriculture, the more advanced countries among the EEs, mostly Czechoslovakia and East Germany, had been quite important producers and exporters of consumer goods before the war (Ofer, 1980).

The impact of the neglect of services on the trade patterns of the EEs came mostly from another direction, in the form of a severe impairment of know-how, experience, and ability to conduct and support trade. With so little accumulated domestic experience in the provision of business services, in trade, in advertising, packaging, marketing, financing, and servicing, including a perennial shortage in the supply of spare parts, it must take a long time as well as some defeats before a workable world-standard business sector can be established in support of foreign trade. As was mentioned earlier, the CPEs' domestic market is completely dominated by a culture of buying, of struggling to buy, not of selling, and by a lack of competitive experience. To a large degree, these deficiencies apply as well to external trade in services and to tourism, which, even with recent changes in approach, suffers from traditional communist restrictions on entry and free movement.

The strong emphasis and priority treatment accorded in the CPEs to heavy industry, metalworking, and machine building could have created capability, early in the development process, of exporting producers' goods—at least the less sophisticated, capital-intensive kind. Had it happened, it would have made the CPEs highly competitive, in effect ahead of their time or stage. This, however, occurs mostly as intra-CPE trade, trade in arms, and some exports to LDCs, but only little export to industrialized market economies. One reason for this failure is that it is not simple for a follower to vault a number of technological stages and position itself "too early" in direct competition with leaders. To this general explanation one must add the systemic factors affecting productivity discussed earlier, especially the weaknesses in the technological sphere. A third reason is that a substantial proportion of the effort toward heavy industry and machine building, especially in the Soviet Union, but also in a number of other CPEs, is directed toward the development and production of military equipment and arms. This constitutes an additional drain on the technological capability of the civilian sector.[7] Because it is very difficult to sell arms to the developed West, the only outlet for such sales is the Third World. Yet even there, there seems to be a serious problem of competitiveness wherever there is a significant degree of open competition.

Finally, the strong and persistent emphasis of all the CPEs on heavy industry and machine building came at the expense of a number of important new sectors embodying the cutting edge of technological progress and economic growth of both leaders and followers during the last generation or two. One such sector is chemicals, where the Soviet Union and the EEs had been trying to catch up by way of massive technological imports. They are, however, far behind in their full diffusion in a number of industries, as well as in trade (Hanson, 1981; Poznanski, 1987, pp. 104–6). A second leading sector is that of information equipment and electronics, the current mover of the world's technological frontier and the fastest growing industry both in production and in international trade. There are several particular explanations for this serious lag. On the development and production side these technologies require coordination and cooperation of a large number of relatively small institutes and enterprises in a great many industries. Moreover, the exact nature of the products and requirements are elusive and not always well defined in advance. Finally, the human element (the "human factor" according to Soviet parlance) that goes beyond just human capital, which is more or less available, including motivation, initiative, and ambition, is very important here. These are the kinds of tasks that central planning is finding increasingly difficult to coordinate and to manage. Similarly, on the demand side the products of the "informatics" industries (to use Judy's term, 1987, p. 162) should be used by all sectors of the economy, and this creates a very difficult diffusion problem for the CPEs. In all these respects the informatics sector is the extreme opposite of the metallurgical sector, the traditional and original leading sector under socialism, which is concentrated, large scale, and by comparison self-contained, much more suitable for central planning. Also, on the demand side there is the much bigger question of the extent to which the informatic products can be put to use under the current political system (see Judy, 1987; Ofer, 1987, pp. 1823–24).

All these differences in the industrial structure of CPEs affect their respective trade structures, causing them to diverge from "normal" Western patterns. Although some of the differences may be neutral as far as competitiveness is concerned, it seems to follow from the foregoing analysis that most CPEs could have been missing trade opportunities in sectors with potential comparative advantage (like agricultural and food products for the less developed EEs or consumer manufactures for all) and were not able to develop a sufficiently strong comparative advantage in metal and machine production. By using a four-way classification of products of resource-intensive, labor-intensive, capital-intensive routine production, and human capital–intensive high-tech products (Lawrence, 1984, pp. 63–64), it looks as if the particular industrial policy of the CPEs caused the loss of some comparative advantage of the first two categories (but see below), developed some comparative advantage in the third, although not high enough to quality for trade with the West, and failed thus far to advance much on the fourth.

Human Capital and Wages

Under the socialist system and its growth strategy there had always been a strong emphasis on education, so that in the 1960s, as well as today, the educational levels of the CPEs' populations and labor forces were superior to those of the UMIs and in certain aspects the industrialized market economies as well.[8] Educational efforts were also directed to a larger extent than in the West toward actual production needs. There is a much higher concentration on engineering, sciences, and technical skills than on humanities and social sciences. Both as a consequence of this and through ideology, following the initial phase of industrialization and the accompanying expansion of the supply of more educated and skilled workers, wage and income differentials in the CPEs have tended to decline and become more equally distributed compared to other countries at similar levels of development, as well as most industrialized market economies (Bergson, 1984; Morrison, 1984; Vinokur and Ofer, 1987). Put together these two imply a comparative advantage in human capital–intensive products. That such a comparative advantage has not yet materialized has to be credited to the problems listed having to do with difficulties in the technological sector and in the production of high-tech products. That there is a potential for such a comparative advantage to develop can be inferred from the intensive interest in the West in forming joint ventures directly and exclusively with the human capital element of the Soviet labor force. An example of this is the American–Soviet joint venture recently formed directly with the Soviet Academy of Sciences. This venture was set up so that Soviet mathematicians could develop computer software for sale in the West, with the computers and other needed equipment being supplied by the Americans. This is a direct use of less expensive but highly skilled Soviet workers which avoids going through the inhospitable Soviet production environment. This underscores what may be a major source of the technological weakness of CPEs—the embodiment of inexpensive, high human capital capability into the present working arrangements of the socialist system. An important potential source of comparative advantage in advanced products is not being exploited to its full capacity.

The particular industrial structure of CPEs and its near uniformity among them also creates problems for trade among CPEs, that is, excess supply of machines and equipment and other manufactures and shortages in food, materials, and high technology. Each country is trying to sell to the others as much of the first category, "soft" goods, and acquire as much of the other, "hard" goods. But hard goods can be sold on the world market for hard currency (Marer, 1987).

Foreign Trade Policies

It has been traditional to characterize the foreign trade policy of the CPEs as one of almost complete autarky. Judged by foreign trade participation rates (TPR, imports plus exports as a ratio of GDP), this was justified for the Soviet Union during the second half of the 1930s and for a few years after the war.

Since then trade started to develop, first within the newly formed Communist bloc and CMEA (the common market of the CPEs), then with a growing number of LDCs, followed since the early 1960s by an increasing volume of trade with the developed West. Similarly, the volume of trade of the EEs increased rapidly with all the same partners. Today the TPRs of the EEs are anywhere between 30 and 45 percent while those of the Soviet Union are between 11 and 16 percent. The TPRs of all the CPEs have been growing very rapidly until recent years. These figures are within the normal range for market economies of similar size and level of development, although they are possibly somewhat lower than normal for the Soviet Union.[9] Such figures are clearly not consistent with the claim of autarky in the narrow sense of the term. Moreover, starting in the 1960s, most of the EEs as well as the Soviet Union followed a strategy of import-led growth whereby they increased the volume of imports of advanced technology from the West using Western credits while upgrading their industrial sectors and preparing them for export purposes to the West. This strategy was far from a full success and resulted in large debts to the West which the EEs are now struggling to repay. Moreover, they enhanced exports to the West relatively little (Hanson, 1982b). Such policies, as well as the rising volume of trade with noncommunist countries, constitutes a move away from the more autarkic policies of the past.

If, however, the claims about autarkic policies are still made with respect to the CPEs, they stem from an analysis of the directions of trade and from the ways trade and other external economic relations are conducted by the CPEs. First, most of the foreign trade has been conducted by state monopolies that insulate (protect) the domestic sector from any outside influence. In Jerry Hough's words, this is the most protectionistic regime on earth, though without tariffs (Hough, 1988, pp. 106–11). Most importantly, the foreign trade prices with which trade is conducted are completely divorced from the domestic prices the trade monopoly is paying or charging domestic producers and clients. In this way the country is virtually sealed off from the outside world and most domestic producers are completely isolated from the price, efficiency, and quality competition provided by the world market. Second, between one-half (for the Soviet Union) and two-thirds of all CPE trade is conducted within the Communist bloc, almost all of it among the countries included in this study. This in itself would not have been a bad indicator, except that most of this trade is conducted in complete isolation from the world market, mostly on a bilateral barter basis, and with prices which, while aiming at world market levels, very frequently deviate from them. This internal market faces almost no competition from the outside or the inside and therefore can hardly be considered foreign trade. Third, CPEs try to conduct as much of their trade with noncommunist countries in the same manner—through bilateral barter agreements. Fourth, although direct imports of advanced Western technology have been sought since the 1960s (a much improved way of technology transfer than sheer stealing and reverse engineering), the CPEs, with few exceptions, have not been allowing direct foreign investment, and the formation of joint ventures had been used only very selectively until it was sanctioned recently by the Soviet Union.

This restriction proved to be a major obstacle for successful technology transfer. Finally, there have been very severe restrictions on mutual scientific and
industrial exchanges.

In discussing the foreign trade policies of the CPEs and their effects on
competitiveness, a strong distinction must be made between the Soviet Union
on the one hand and the EEs on the other. The Soviet Union is a very large
country, exceptionally rich in natural resources (excepting its inhospitable climate). These two characteristics significantly reduce its dependency on external trade. The large natural endowment base also affects the structure of Soviet
trade, as it creates a natural comparative advantage in raw materials and products produced with them, regardless of the productivity level of the economy.
The EEs, on the other hand, are much smaller and with few exceptions, such
as Poland and Romania, are not generously endowed with natural resources.
This makes the EEs much more dependent on trade in general, and on importation of materials in particular, and thereby forces them to create export capabilities based on manufacturing. Considering the weakness, discussed earlier, of socialist R&D sectors and the general heavy R&D burden on a small
country, the task of developing export sectors is especially heavy for them
(Gomulka, 1986, Chapter 3). Other differences between the Soviet Union and
the EEs stem from the position of the Soviet Union as a world power with
many military and strategic interests and responsibilities and with a dominance
over the other EEs. These imply a large military sector, substantial exports
of arms, and influence over the economic and trade policies of the EEs, as
well as their structure and direction of trade. Finally, the Soviet Union, as a
more mature and conservative socialist system, may find it more difficult to
reform its system compared with the EEs, with a much shorter socialist
tradition.

The sharp contrast in natural endowments, size, and other conditions between the Soviet Union on the one hand and the EEs on the other calls for
different trade strategy and policies for the EEs. However, the shape of the
EEs' socialist system, its growth strategy, and trade policies were largely determined by Soviet conditions and needs. When a system much like the Soviet
Union's was imposed on the EEs, it was done with little or no consideration
or understanding of their different requirements. This applies to the decision to
concentrate on heavy industry and to the entire package of trade policies, including autarky, import substitution, the initial reduction of most relations with
the West, and the monopolistic organization model of foreign trade management. It has been claimed that the imposition of the Soviet socialist model on
the EEs has had negative economic effects, especially for Czechoslovakia and
East Germany, which are the most advanced in the group and for which the
Soviet model is least appropriate. Here it is important to make the more specific point that the trade strategy and policies that came together with, and are
an integral part of, the Soviet model have been and are still much more detrimental to the EEs than to the Soviet Union. The EEs seem to be paying a
higher price in terms of loss of productivity and competitiveness, despite the
partial compensation provided by the Soviet supply of raw materials and energy at somewhat preferential terms.

On the basis of the preceding observations on relative productivity and on the effects of the socialist system on the trade structure and competitiveness of the CPEs, we can turn to a closer examination of their trade patterns and their standing among other groups of countries.

TRADE STRUCTURE AND TRADE DIRECTION

What can we learn from the actual development of the structure and direction of trade of the CPEs? A number of conventional measures of revealed comparative advantage are estimated and presented here in tabular form. Table 5-2 presents data on the development of the structure of merchandise trade of the CPEs by goods category between 1962 and 1985; Table 5-3 presents similar data for two groups of market economies, the entire OECD group, a group of NICs, and the United States. The group of NICs includes, following Balassa (1981, p. 30), Argentina, Brazil, Chile, Mexico, Hong Kong, Singapore, South Korea, Taiwan, and Israel; it also includes Greece, Portugal, Spain, and Turkey, which are the NICs of southern Europe. Unless specified otherwise, countries that belong to the group of NICs are also included in the OECD group or in the group of LDCs in accordance with their usual classification.[10] Tables 5-4 and 5-5 have data on the market shares of the groups listed and a number of goods categories in the trade of the OECD group. Finally, Table 5-6 looks more deeply into the trade patterns of machinery and transportation equipment for the same groups. With few exceptions, trade data come from the United Nations *Yearbook of International Trade Statistics* and from its Trade Data System on tapes. The data usually have been converted in the sources to current U.S. dollars at official exchange rates. In many cases of CPE trade with market economies, the data reflect the reports of the trade partners.

Data on trade among CPEs suffer not only because their currencies are transformed to dollars using overvalued exchange rates, but also due to distorted relative prices that do not conform to world market levels. In particular, prices of manufactured goods are generally inflated, and those for materials of all kinds are too low. As a consequence there are biases in the data with respect to both trade structure and trade directions. There are some attempts in the literature to account for these distortions but they are not systematic over the long run. However, that as long as one is aware of the biases, most of the observations made in this section are not seriously in doubt (see Ellis, 1986, pp. 7–8; Marer, 1978).

As far as one can tell, the trade figures for all countries include trade in arms. Since the first sharp rise in oil prices in 1973, the entire trade picture has been heavily colored by this one factor. Although part of the rise may reflect long-term economic factors, the overshooting in the initial price rises and the long period of adjustments clearly distorted what one may think of as normal long-term conditions. All the above must be taken into account when the figures are examined. Finally, most EEs have developed since the 1970s heavy external debt burdens to the West, which they are struggling to repay mainly with cuts in imports and attempts to increase exports (Marer, 1986).[11]

Table 5-2 Trade Patterns for CPEs, EEs, and the Soviet Union

	Total (Billions of Current Dollars)	Percentage of Trade by SITC Category					
		Food (0,1)	Materials (2,4)	Energy (3)	Chemicals (5)	Manufacturing (6,8)	Machinery (7)
A. CPEs							
Total trade							
Exports							
1962	16.9	12.4	29.6[a]	—[a]	2.4	16.6	27.2
1970	30.5	8.9	9.8	9.5	4.9	25.2	31.8
1975	77.3	7.2	8.8	18.0	5.3	23.8	31.4
1980	155.1	8.1	6.8	27.3	5.0	16.4	29.7
1985	173.9	4.9	5.3	30.9	6.4	14.7	29.0
Net exports							
1962	1.2	−0.7	−1.2[a]	—[a]	−2.5	2.0	−1.9
1970	1.8	−3.1	0.7	4.5	−1.0	0.0	0.7
1975	−5.2	−6.8	−0.4	7.6	−1.7	−5.2	−4.1
1980	11.2	−8.5	0.2	16.3	−1.9	−3.8	1.2
1985	22.9	−7.1	0.1	16.8	0.6	−1.9	1.6
Non CPE Trade							
Exports							
1962	3.4	20.6	14.7	20.6	2.9	20.6	8.8
1970	10.1	11.9	13.9	12.9	5.0	26.7	20.8
1975	30.5	8.2	12.1	23.9	5.9	18.9	17.7
1980	71.5	6.6	8.7	37.6	5.3	15.2	15.1
1985	73.9	6.0	7.3	39.6	7.8	15.3	14.2
Net exports							
1962	0.0	5.9	−8.3	20.6	−5.9	−5.9	−20.6
1970	0.3	−8.2	−1.0	12.2	−4.1	1.0	−3.1
1975	−6.5	−14.3	1.1	14.6	−4.1	−13.0	−11.9
1980	8.6	−19.3	0.8	35.9	−4.9	−8.3	−2.2
1985	18.5	−17.7	0.9	44.2	−0.5	−4.9	−1.4

B. EEs

Total trade

Exports							
1962	8.9	13.1	28.4[a]	—[a]	2.9	17.7	37.9
1970	17.7	12.9	5.7	5.3	6.9	29.5	38.8
1975	44.0	11.7	4.3	7.8	7.4	26.7	41.2
1980	78.7	10.3	4.4	8.1	7.6	25.9	43.0
1985	86.7	8.5	4.0	8.8	9.6	23.6	44.5
Net exports							
1962	−0.3	−2.8	−16.2[a]	—[a]	−4.1	10.7	8.5
1970	0.5	2.8	−7.7	−2.9	1.1	4.6	9.7
1975	−3.2	3.0	−6.1	−6.0	0.2	−0.5	5.8
1980	−3.3	0.4	−5.9	−13.5	0.3	4.6	12.4
1985	5.7	4.1	−2.6	−23.8	3.7	9.8	22.7

Non-CPE trade

Exports							
1962	1.8	27.8	11.1	11.1	5.6	22.2	11.1
1970	4.7	21.1	10.5	7.0	7.0	33.3	19.3
1975	14.7	15.8	7.9	14.5	8.6	30.3	23.0
1980	29.8	12.8	7.5	15.7	9.5	31.5	22.6
1985	32.0	10.6	7.5	19.1	13.4	30.3	18.4
Net exports							
1962	0.0	11.1	−11.1	11.1	−5.6	−5.6	−11.1
1970	−0.5	5.8	−3.9	5.8	−1.9	9.6	−3.8
1975	−2.9	1.1	−4.5	5.1	−4.6	−2.8	−14.1
1980	1.0	−6.2	−3.2	5.5	−2.8	10.4	2.4
1985	11.0	2.4	1.0	9.5	7.1	22.9	7.1

Table 5-2 (cont.)

	Total (Billions of Current Dollars)	Percentage of Trade by SITC Category					
		Food (0,1)	Materials (2,4)	Energy (3)	Chemicals (5)	Manufacturing (6,8)	Machinery (7)
C. Soviet Union							
Total trade							
Exports							
1962	7.0	12.9	18.6	17.1	1.4	17.1	17.1
1970	12.8	3.1	15.6	15.6	2.3	21.9	19.5
1975	33.3	1.5	14.7	31.2	2.7	14.7	19.2
1980	76.4	1.7	9.2	47.0	2.2	6.5	16.0
1985	87.2	1.3	6.7	53.0	3.2	5.8	13.5
Net exports							
1962	0.5	1.6	4.6	15.3	−1.6	−10.8	−10.8
1970	1.3	−12.2	8.7	15.7	−4.3	−7.0	−13.0
1975	−2.0	−19.8	9.1	25.8	−4.0	−13.3	−17.8
1980	14.5	−21.0	7.6	55.7	−5.2	−17.8	−14.2
1985	17.2	−20.0	3.1	63.7	−3.0	−15.3	−22.9
Non-CPE trade							
Exports							
1962	1.6	12.5	25.0	31.3	0.0	18.8	6.3
1970	5.4	1.9	14.8	16.7	1.9	14.8	18.5
1975	15.8	0.6	15.8	32.9	3.2	8.2	13.3
1980	41.7	2.2	9.8	53.7	2.4	3.8	10.1
1985	41.9	2.4	7.2	55.4	3.6	3.8	11.0
Net exports							
1962	0.0	0.0	0.0	31.3	−6.3	−31.2	−6.2
1970	0.8	−21.7	2.2	19.6	−4.3	−10.9	−2.2
1975	−3.4	−28.1	6.3	23.4	−3.6	−21.4	−14.1
1980	7.9	−30.5	4.7	64.8	−6.5	−23.1	−5.9
1985	7.5	−29.9	0.9	65.4	−3.5	−21.8	−6.7

Sources: CPEs, United Nations (1981,1988), Vol. 1, Tables C and B respectively, and Ellis (1986, Tables A,B, pp. 9–10; Tables 1–14, pp. 17–30. Data for 1962: Soviet Union, Marer (1973, pp. 62, 65); EEs, Marer (1973 pp. 52, 61).

[a]Category 3 included in 2 and 4.

Table 5-3 Trade Patterns for NICs, OECD, and the United States, 1962–85

	Total (Billions of Current Dollars)	Percentage of Trade by SITC Category					
		Food (0,1)	Materials (2,4)	Energy (3)	Chemicals (5)	Manufacturing (6,8)	Machinery (7)
A. NICs							
Total trade							
Exports							
1962	7.6	40.9	25.5	3.8	2.9	23.1	3.2
1970	17.8	30.8	15.6	3.3	3.5	37.4	8.8
1975	50.7	23.6	11.1	6.1	3.7	39.9	15.1
1980	147.5	16.8	8.3	11.8	4.9	39.2	18.0
1985	171.4	14.0	7.6	15.5	5.0	34.7	22.2
Net exports							
1962	−3.8	14.6	3.0	−7.6	−7.7	−5.2	−30.2
1970	−8.7	10.7	−1.5	−5.9	−8.4	−0.1	−27.0
1975	−34.0	4.1	−3.1	−15.1	−8.3	2.8	−19.9
1980	−54.4	3.8	−3.2	−17.1	−6.0	9.1	−14.0
1985	−3.5	6.3	−1.1	−7.8	−5.0	13.3	−8.0
B. OECD							
Exports							
1967		12.7	9.4	3.3		41.2	33.3
1975		11.3	6.7	5.1		39.7	37.2
1980		10.3	6.5	7.0		41.1	35.1
1985		8.7	5.5	7.9		38.8	39.0
Net exports							
1967		−3.7	−5.2	−7.6		5.5	10.7
1975		−1.1	−2.7	−17.1		7.0	13.9
1980		0.6	−1.4	−19.5		7.5	12.8
1985		−0.4	−1.0	−12.1		3.5	9.9

Table 5-3 (cont.)

	Total (Billions of Current Dollars)	Percentage of Trade by SITC Category					
		Food (0,1)	Materials (2,4)	Energy (3)	Chemicals (5)	Manufacturing (6,8)	Machinery (7)
C. U.S. Trade							
Exports							
1967		15.1	11.6	3.5		29.4	40.4
1975		15.8	10.1	4.2		26.8	43.1
1980		14.2	11.8	3.7		30.0	40.3
1985		10.7	8.8	4.9		28.1	47.6
Net trade							
1967		−2.4	0.1	−4.9		−11.6	18.8
1975		5.6	3.9	−23.0		−4.5	18.1
1980		6.2	7.4	−29.1		−0.2	15.3
1985		3.9	5.7	−10.6		−8.6	9.8

Sources: OECD ard United States, OECD (1987, Tables 14.1, 14.2, 14.9, 14.10; NICs, U.N. Trade Data System.

The data on the trade patterns of CPEs, presented in Table 5-2, are shown for the CPEs as a group and for the EEs and the Soviet Union separately. There are of course significant differences between the trade patterns of the individual EEs, differences that this chapter cannot accommodate. Shown are the distribution of exports, and for the sake of brevity, the distribution of net exports (expressed as a percentage of total imports). Trade patterns are shown for total trade and for non-CPE trade. As we go along, these data are being compared with the data in Table 5-3 for the other groups of countries.

The structure of exports of all the CPEs put together is somewhat less "advanced" than that of OECD countries or the United States but significantly more advanced than that for the NICs group. The CPEs export only as much agricultural and food products as the OECD group and less than the United States (all quantitative and qualitative statements refer to proportions rather than absolute figures). On the other side the CPEs export nearly as much machinery (including arms) as OECD countries and a great deal more than the NICs. The machinery exports would have definitely been larger without the somewhat artificial role played by oil exports. A proof of sorts for this can be found in the still larger machinery exports of the EEs (and lower for the Soviet Union). However, since most of these exports of machinery are traded among the CPEs, their proportion is somewhat upwardly biased due to inflated prices. The major exception to the statement about the relative position of the CPEs' trade is the relatively low level of exports of manufactures (SITC categories 6 and 8). In this category, both the OECD and NIC groups are doing much better. The Soviet Union has an especially low export proportion of agricultural products and of regular, mostly consumers' manufactures. The socialist bias joins forces with the large Soviet material base and poor climate to produce this result.

The comparative picture of net exports of the CPEs is broadly similar to that of exports, except that a number of tendencies are more pronounced. For example, the CPEs have a negative balance of trade in agricultural products compared with a positive balance for OECD countries. There is also a large gap between the very small machinery deficit in the CPEs and the larger deficit of NICs. Moreover, there is a deficit in the CPEs of manufactures, including chemicals, compared to a large surplus for the OECD group and an emerging surplus (though not in chemicals) for the NICs. Finally, the net trade figures underline the very large Soviet deficits in agricultural products and in manufactures, both "socialist" attributes, but there is a "nonsocialist" deficit in machinery, even when corrected for biases. Here the EEs surpass their mentor by providing a large export of machinery to the Soviet Union in exchange for energy and materials.

This description of the structure of trade of the CPEs conforms with the tendencies of the socialist system as presented in the preceding section of this chapter but tells us very little about the level of their COMP. The main reason for this is that the portion of this trade that actually participates in the world market is just short of 40 percent of exports in 1985 (Table 5-2, column 1), but it was down to only 25 percent of the entire CPEs' trade in 1962. In effect, internal EE trade even harms COMP in many cases. It allows exporters to get away with lower quality products, to charge higher prices, and to be distracted from the main competition (Marer, 1987). As mentioned earlier, most internal CMEA trade is in soft goods, in which there is a surplus and which are generally unsuitable for external trade. Moreover, nearly 40 percent of the external CPE exports are made up of oil and gas, which are not very interesting in this connection. We are thus left with about 25 percent of the total as meaningful external trade. Another part of the external exports consists of arms sales, in which the Soviet Union at least seems to have a comparative advantage but most of which is also not traded in an open-market environment.[12] If oil and arms are included, the proportion of Soviet external trade becomes higher than that of the EEs, and it is difficult to estimate what the picture would be without them. It may, however, point to the difficulties faced by the EEs with no raw materials to export outside of the bloc. Given the previous description of the ways in which most intra-CPE trade is conducted, there is little reason to consider such trade in an evaluation of competitiveness. It is a diametrically opposite environment to the one that prevails in intra-OECD trade, where level of competitiveness is actively being tested. This lends itself to a comparison of the performance of the external trade of the CPEs with the trade of the other groups, which is seen in the lower panels of Table 5-2 and the data in Table 5-3.

For the CPEs as a group we find sharply declining exports of agricultural products over time and similarly sharply rising food deficits. In this aspect the CPEs are the most "advanced" among all the groups, with a very early loss of a proven comparative advantage. Even in the world market the CPEs have a smaller proportion of their trade in basic and consumer manufactures (SITC categories 6 and 8) compared with both NICs and OECD countries. This is even true of the EEs alone, where exports of energy do not blur the picture. The small deficit that the CPEs run in manufactures could and should have been much larger, and the EEs' surplus much smaller, had these countries allowed the importation of consumers' manufactures to satisfy the reasonable needs of their populations. Therefore, one must judge their revealed comparative advantage in this general field as weak. The recent heavy pressure on the EEs to repay their large debts forces them to make exceptional export efforts, hence the large surplus of the EEs in these categories in 1985. But again, if Romania is an example, these exports bear a heavy cost, especially at the expense of the standard of living of the population, and they do not indicate a higher level of competitiveness compared to the fast-growing surpluses in trade in these products by the NICs.

The proportion of external exports of machines is rather low compared to the large intra-CPE trade in machines; during the 1980s it was even lower than that of the NICs. Only the EEs are still exporting the same proportion of machinery as the NICs, although on a much lower absolute scale. The deficits in net exports of machinery with the outside world are declining over time in both the CPEs and the NICs. The reasons for the similar trend, however, are very different: an increase in exports of the NICs on the one hand and a decline of imports, accompanied by a smaller decline of exports of the CPEs on the other. The NICs seem to be joining the suppliers of equipment, following a long period of intensive importation of Western equipment; the CPEs had to reduce their imports of Western machinery due to their accumulated debts and to the not entirely successful experience with the diffusion of such equipment in earlier years. The current decline of such importation may have negative effects on the CPEs' export potential in the future.

The development of the external trade structure of the CPEs has been reflected in the contribution of these countries to world trade. Tables 5-4 and 5-5 present data on the relative shares of total exports and of net exports of a number of merchandise categories into the OECD and the LDC markets between 1962 and 1985. With few exceptions, the data show stagnant overall export shares for the CPEs in both markets. The overall export share of the CPEs in the OECD market is not declining only because of the rise in energy exports (mostly prices) by the Soviet Union. There are declines in the overall EE share as well as in the share of machines and manufacturing goods (only since 1970 for the EEs). On the other side there is a dramatic rise in the export shares of

Table 5-4 Market Shares of Country Groups in Imports of OECD (Percent)

	1962	1970	1975	1980	1985
EEs					
All goods	1.6	1.5	1.6	1.3	1.2
Chemicals (5)	2.0	1.6	1.6	1.5	1.6
Machinery (7)	0.7	0.7	0.8	0.8	0.4
Manufacturing (6,8)	1.3	1.7	2.0	1.9	1.5
Mineral fuels (3)	1.9	1.6	1.4	1.2	1.5
Soviet Union					
All goods	1.4	1.2	1.5	1.8	1.7
Chemicals (5)	0.7	0.5	0.9	1.4	1.0
Machinery (7)	0.2	0.2	0.3	0.2	0.1
Manufacturing (6,8)	1.0	0.8	0.9	0.8	0.4
Mineral fuels (3)	3.9	3.7	3.5	4.7	6.7
NICs					
All goods	6.8	6.7	6.8	8.3	12.0
Chemicals (5)	2.7	2.3	2.7	3.7	5.3
Machinery (7)	0.4	1.8	3.8	5.9	9.0
Manufacturing (6,8)	5.3	8.1	11.2	13.8	18.8
NICs					
All goods	4.8	4.8	4.7	6.1	9.3
Chemicals (5)	1.7	1.0	1.2	1.8	3.0
Machinery (7)	0.2	1.2	2.7	4.2	7.2
Manufacturing (6,8)	3.9	6.1	7.9	10.2	14.7
NICs					
All goods	2.0	1.9	2.1	2.2	2.7
Chemicals (5)	1.0	1.3	1.5	2.1	2.3
Machinery (7)	0.2	0.6	1.1	1.7	1.8
Manufacturing (6,8)	1.4	2.0	3.3	3.6	4.1
LDC–NIC					
All goods	19.9	15.4	22.9	24.6	15.8
Chemicals (5)	3.2	3.3	3.0	3.0	3.3
Machinery (7)	0.5	0.9	0.7	1.6	1.6
Manufacturing (6,8)	6.8	6.7	5.2	6.4	6.4

Sources: 1962, UN Trade Data System; 1970–85, United Nations (1981, 1988, Tables C and B, respectively).

Table 5-5 Market Shares of Country Groups in Imports of LDCs (Percent)

	1962	1970	1975	1980	1985
EEs					
All goods	1.3	2.3	2.0	1.9	2.4
Chemicals (5)	1.2	2.5	2.8	2.9	4.6
Machinery (7)	1.4	3.0	2.3	2.4	2.6
Manufacturing (6,8)	1.9	2.7	2.5	2.2	2.7
Soviet Union					
All goods	1.4	4.7	3.1	3.0	4.4
Chemicals (5)	0.5	0.9	1.2	1.2	1.5
Machinery (7)	1.5	4.7	2.2	2.3	3.1
Manufacturing (6,8)	1.1	1.8	1.0	1.0	1.5
OECD–NICs					
All goods	73.3	75.0	71.0	66.0	66.3
Chemicals (5)	91.5	87.4	85.3	85.0	83.9
Machinery (7)	95.3	92.8	91.2	90.5	84.4
Manufacturing (6,8)	85.3	79.2	79.8	74.7	75.3
NICs					
All goods	5.1	6.8	7.1	10.0	12.6
Chemicals (5)	3.8	4.6	4.8	7.3	10.9
Machinery (7)	1.2	2.9	4.3	6.2	9.3
Manufacturing (6,8)	6.0	8.8	10.0	16.3	18.9
NICs					

Sources: See sources to Table 5-4.

the NICs in the OECD market, both overall and in chemicals, manufacturing, and machinery, the rise in the last category being most dramatic. Table 5-4 also shows that this penetration of the NICs into the market of the developed countries has been shared between the newly industrializing countries in southern Europe, Asia, and Latin America. Finally, the table even registers an *increase* in the share of machinery exports out of the LDCs (excluding the NICs) to OECD countries.

A very similar development has been taking place in the LDCs' market, where the shares of CPEs have stagnated over time in most of the categories presented while those of the NICs have increased dramatically. It is interesting to note that in both markets the dynamic penetration of the NICs came at the expense of the OECD group's own share, which underscores the feasibility of such a penetration.

The final table presents a more detailed breakdown of CPE trade in machinery (SITC category 7). Table 5-6 shows the percentage distribution of EE and Soviet exports and imports of machinery by partner group. It shows again the small proportion of machinery trade conducted outside the CPE group and the large deficits of net trade with the OECD group—deficits that are declining very slowly over time and hardly at all for the Soviet Union.

The record presented here as well as much richer additional evidence collected and analyzed by Posnanski (1987, Chapters 4 and 5) and others (Bornstein, 1985; Marer, 1986; Vanous, 1988) lead to the conclusion that since 1970 or so the CPEs have not forged for themselves the role in the world market expected of them according to their stage of economic development among the

Table 5-6 Trade in Machinery (SITC Category 7) by Partner: EEs, Soviet Union, NICs[a]

		1962	1970	1975	1980	1985
A. EEs						
	EX	3.4	6.9	18.2	33.9	38.6
	IM	2.6	5.2	15.3	23.4	20.2
	R	1.31	1.33	1.19	1.45	1.91
With partner (percent)						
East Europe	EX	43.0	36.2	36.3	31.3	26.1
	IM	56.1	48.0	42.9	44.8	50.0
	R	1.00	1.00	1.00	1.00	1.00
Soviet Union	EX	48.1	45.5	42.9	44.8	53.9
	IM	23.5	27.5	24.2	28.8	27.7
	R	2.68	2.19	2.28	2.28	3.71
OECD	EX	3.8	7.1	9.1	8.6	6.0
	IM	16.2	24.3	32.7	26.2	18.8
	R	0.31	0.39	0.33	0.49	0.61
NICs	EX	1.5	1.6	1.2	1.7	0.8
	IM	0.0	0.1	0.2	0.3	0.7
	R			8.97	9.23	2.30
LDCs	EX	2.7	8.5	9.1	10.3	9.3
	IM	0.1	0.1	0.1	0.1	2.9
	R					6.97
B. Soviet Union						
	EX	1.2	2.8	6.4	12.2	11.8
	IM	2.3	4.3	12.7	21.0	27.8
	R	0.52	0.65	0.50	0.58	0.42
With partners (percent)						
East Europe	EX	49.6	50.0	57.8	55.7	47.5
	IM	71.2	72.1	61.4	70.5	74.8
	R	0.37	0.40	0.47	0.46	0.27
OECD	EX	2.4	5.2	8.6	6.5	3.4
	IM	24.9	25.6	38.2	29.3	18.5
	R	0.05	0.14	0.11	0.13	0.08
NICs	EX	1.0	1.3	1.4	1.7	1.5
	IM				0.1	0.2
	R					9.79
LDC	EX	7.8	32.6	23.9	27.9	35.4
	IM			0.2		6.3
	R				2.38	
C. NICs						
	EX	0.2	1.6	7.6	26.5	38.0
	IM	3.7	8.7	24.5	54.8	52.5
	R	0.06	0.18	0.31	0.48	0.72
With partner (percent)						
OECD	EX	23.4	59.2	56.6	60.2	72.0
	IM	96.4	96.0	94.9	92.2	87.6
	R	0.02	0.11	0.19	0.32	0.60
NICs	EX	15.5	16.7	12.3	14.2	8.7
	IM	0.9	2.7	3.9	6.0	8.2
	R	1.09	1.11	0.98	1.13	0.77
LDC	EX	75.7	40.5	42.9	39.5	27.5
	IM	1.0	2.4	3.8	6.5	11.6
	R	5.03	2.98	3.54	2.93	1.71
CPEs	EX	0.8	0.2	0.4	0.2	0.5
	IM	1.7	1.5	1.3	1.4	0.8
	R	0.03	0.03	0.11	0.11	0.48

Sources: See sources to Table 5-4.

[a]EX = exports (billions of dollars); IM = imports (billions of dollars); R = export–import ratio.

community of nations. Instead, the "next" group of countries in the development ladder (the NICs) is taking the CPEs' "natural" place.

To what extent is the trade peformance of the CPEs as described here an
outcome of a deliberate policy or simply a result of unintended and not clearly
thought-through trade policy? Asking the question twenty-five years ago might
have been legitimate. As of the middle or late 1960s, however, there was no
question that both the EEs and the Soviet Union were following a deliberate
policy of opening up trade relations with the West with a clear goal of achieving
import-led growth, an integral part of which consisted of creating export capabilities into world markets. This was an integral part of the 1968 Hungarian
reform and still is today; an announced policy of Romania as part of its efforts
to achieve independence of the Soviet bloc; a major goal of the Polish investment drive of the early 1970s; part of the economic reform of East Germany;
and a proclaimed goal of all pre-Gorbachev reforms in the Soviet Union (U.S.
Congress, JEC, 1985–86, 1987). It therefore must be concluded with little doubt
that what we witnessed happening to the trade of the CPEs in world markets
since the midsixties occurred despite efforts to improve the record, efforts that
were not very successful mainly due to the systemic features and contradictory
internal policies of the socialist countries. Posnanski makes the point that in
addition to internal obstacles, the CPEs may find themselves—indeed already
have found themselves—facing direct competition with the NICs in all the
world markets with exactly the kind of goods they may be able or prepared to
export (1987, Chapter 5). This is no doubt a consideration to be taken into
account by the new generation of reformers of the socialist system.[13]

CONCLUSION: THE DIRECTION OF REFORMS

The main problem facing the CPEs today is how to reverse the downward trend
in growth. Barred from continuing along the extensive route by resource constraints of both labor and capital, they need to move toward a development
path where growth relies mostly on increasing productivity and efficiency.
Competitiveness is both a tool and a by-product of such a change. CPEs have
to reform their system in a way that will reduce their comparative disadvantage
in the adaptation, absorption, and diffusion of new technologies acquired from
the outside and in the development of their own indigenous new technologies.
The current wave of economic (as well as political, cultural, and social) reforms
in the Soviet Union and in most of the EEs is designed by its initiators to
achieve exactly these goals. These were, however, also the goals of the many
reform attempts in these countries since the early 1960s, most of them too timid
to be successful. This is not the place to survey, let alone analyze the previous
or current reforms.[14] By way of conclusion, I shall concentrate on the functional relationship between the internal and external elements of past and current economic reforms and on the conditions for success.

Many economists and experts, both in the CPEs and outside, emphasize
the key role of the protectionist and isolationist policies of the CPEs in the
failure of these countries to have sustained productivity-led growth. As a re-

sult, when economic reforms became the mode in the 1960s and 1970s, they always included external elements. The first moves were the opening up of trade relations with the West and the Third World in order to receive some gains from international specialization. For example, the CPEs imported food and some raw materials and later, in the sphere of technology transfer, replaced the old methods of "borrowing" and reversed engineering by direct importation of technology in the form of plants (some turnkey), equipment, licenses, and technical assistance. In Hungary and later in other EEs, joint ventures were permitted and even encouraged. There were also various partial steps taken to decentralize the conduct of foreign trade down to the corporation or enterprise level and to open up a vent for some outside competition. In addition, there have been prolonged efforts to create more flexible trade arrangements among the CPEs, to allow multilateral trade and clearing. Some even dreamed about a CMEA internal convertible currency, but so far little has been achieved in this direction. These changes of the 1960s and 1970s were part of an effort to stop the trend of declining growth rates (Marer, 1986, pp. 593–603). The present Soviet reform package includes all these elements, to be installed gradually during the coming years. Some of its main elements are:

1. The abolition of the foreign trade monopoly and the transfer of all trade responsibilities to individual ministries and to large corporations.
2. The sanction, for the first time, of joint ventures between Soviet and Western (and other) corporations, stipulated, among other restrictions, that the Soviet side keeps a majority ownership.[15]
3. The adoption of a set of measures that will eventually liberalize controls on foreign transactions, allow more free movement of goods into the Soviet Union, expose domestic production to foreign competition, and encourage more extensive and free scientific exchanges.

The long-term goal is to reach full convertibility of the ruble, first inside CMEA and later internationally.

Hough quotes a Soviet official responding to arguments in favor of a radical liberalization in the area of foreign trade: "We need a convertible ruble at home before we can have a convertible ruble abroad" (1987, p. 3). This drives home the point that all the expected positive effects of such reforms cannot take hold without parallel complementary internal changes. The experiences of some EEs with joint ventures has demonstrated that although such an approach constitutes a better way of technology transfer than those previously used, joint ventures cannot solve the technological handicaps of the CPEs due to difficulties of diffusion on the one hand and of cooperation with domestic enterprises, suppliers, and bureaucracies on the other (e.g., see Marer, 1987). Even direct, fully owned foreign investments, as some recommend, will be merged into the present system only with extreme difficulty. The form of completely isolated foreign enclaves is possible but will not address the main purpose of the endeavor.

If it is difficult for joint ventures to succeed, most other proposed liberalization steps simply cannot take place without supporting domestic reforms, for example, in the way internal prices are determined. With government-determined prices, output, and procurement plans, and within the environment of the traditional shortage economy, no enterprise manager will willingly work for innovation for exports. Therefore, in order to make the external economic reforms helpful—even a catalyzer of change—the domestic reforms must come first and proceed part of the way. Substantial progress is necessary in the decentralization of decision making as well as reward and risk taking down to the enterprise level, including its supply and sales efforts, and in a parallel sharp decline in government intervention. One needs a much more flexible system of price determination, in addition to more correct prices. And it is necessary to create the needed environment for a fast development of the financial, commercial, and business services sectors that will be able to handle the new foreign economic activities. It may be interesting to note that a substantial proportion of the Western offers for joint ventures concentrate in these service activities.

Most of these requirements are part of the current Soviet domestic reform program, and a few steps are already being implemented. However, the minimum critical distance that must be covered before positive results appear seems to be much longer than many of the reformers, even the radical ones, are willing to permit the reforms to travel. The experience of Hungary, where the most far-reaching reforms were taking place, as well as that of Poland and other EEs, points to the development of an economy made up of a small group of production and trade monopolies, with a very high dose of government intervention remaining, designed mostly to protect and subsidize weak producers. Such an "industrial orgnization" may not be much more efficient than the model it would replace (Kornai, 1986). The problems that actual and potential Western entrepreneurs face when they come to set up joint ventures in the Soviet Union point in the same direction. To sum up, one cannot see the current economic reform of the Soviet Union and the other CPEs succeeding without a radical change in their approach to foreign economic relations. But such changes cannot be implemented and will not be able to contribute significantly to the reforms before a critical minimum of internal changes takes place.

Abram Bergson recently estimated (again) that the (prereform) socialist economic system is less efficient than the market economies at similar levels of development by a margin of 25 to 30 percent (1987). The other side of such a gap is the substantial potential for productivity gains under a reformed system. In addition, the CPEs have a long experience in industrial production, a highly qualified labor force, and a sound system of education. They also possess the institutional tools to formulate and pursue an appropriate industrial organizational policy in the footsteps of Japan or some of the other NICs.[16] These advantages point to a theoretical potential for the CPEs to regain sustained growth and raise their COMP level at some point in the future. The smaller East Europen countries, particularly in contrast to the Soviet Union, can also more easily benefit from a potential influx of capital and of Western managerial skills. However, it is not only the hopeless pessimist who may fail to foresee such developments taking place in the near future.

NOTES

1. CPE is used here to denote all the countries covered in this chapter: the Soviet Union, East Germany, Czechoslovakia, Poland, Hungary, Bulgaria, and Romania; the acronym EE is used for the last six countries. Albania and Yugoslavia are not discussed in this chapter.

2. The discussion on competitiveness and its relation to productivity is based on Bailey and Blair (1988), Lawrence (1984, 1988) and Tyson (1988).

3. These are Ireland (47 percent of the U.S. level in 1985), Greece (42 percent), Portugal (32 percent), and Turkey (19.7 percent).

4. Data on school attendance proportions of the relevant age groups seem to partly support this contention. While college and university attendance rates went up faster in the industrialized market economies in 1964–84 (going up from 16 to 38 percent versus around 10 to 18 percent in the CPEs), high school enrollment went up significantly faster in the CPEs (by a factor of approximately 2 compared with a factor of 1.4 in the industrialized market economies) (WDR, 1983, pp. 196–97; 1987, pp. 262–63). School attendance rates preceded corresponding changes in the educational levels of the labor force.

5. We return later to the connection between investment and technological change and the embodiment issue.

6. A systematic model of the possible effects of the socialist system and of socialist growth strategy and policies is included in Hewett (1980). Though we do not follow the model as formulated, we try to incorporate in this and the previous sections most of its elements.

7. Whereas in the West there is debate on whether there are positive technological spillovers from the military to the civilian sector, it is quite well established that under the shortage conditions prevailing in the CPEs, the impact of the military effort on the civilian economy is negative and there are very few positive spillovers (Campbell, 1986). As part of perestroika in the Soviet Union there is an effort to reduce military spending and to make the military industry produce consumer and other civilian goods.

8. For evidence see WDR (1987), Table 31.

9. It is very difficult to estimate the TPRs of the CPEs because neither their GDP levels nor their trade values can be reliably estimated in a way comparable with the same rates for market economies. The rates cited above are from Marer (1986, pp. 173–76) and Desai (1988). See Desai for a theoretical and empirical discussion of the problems involved. See also Treml (1980).

10. I have excluded Uruguay and Yugoslavia from Balassa's list. Most of these countries belong to the group of UMIs defined earlier, which includes many more countries. Note that the groupings of countries in this section are somewhat different than those discussed earlier. This stems from data availability problems.

11. Previous empirical estimates of the particular trade patterns of CPEs can be found in Van Brabant (1973), Hewett (1980), and Ofer (1980).

12. Soviet arms sales to LDCs are estimated by Vanous (1986, p. 16) at $5.5 billion for 1985.

13. During a recent visit to Romania economists at the Institute of the World Economy, who are studying potential export markets for Romania, made the observation that by the time Romania managed to retool for a new line of export goods, following its crisis of the early 1980s, it found the field congested with competition by the NICs.

14. For an excellent and detailed analysis of the Soviet reforms see Hewett (1988).

15. Since the first draft of this chapter was written, new decrees on foreign eco-

nomic relations (reported December 10, 1988) had further relaxed and liberalized the rules for joint ventures and the conduct of foreign trade (*Izvestiya*, December 10, 1988).

16. At least some economists believe that such a policy can enhance both productivity and competitiveness (see Ethier, 1982; Helpman and Krugman, 1985).

REFERENCES

Alton, T. P. 1970. "Economic Structure and Growth in Eastern Europe." In U.S. Congress, Joint Economics Committee, *Economic Developments in Countries of Eastern Europe*. Washington, D.C.: USGPO, pp. 41–67.

Alton, T. P. 1981. "Production and Resource Allocation in Eastern Europe: Performance, Problems, and Prospects." In U.S. Congress, Joint Economics Committee, *East European Economic Assessment*, Vol. 2. Washington, D.C.: USGPO, pp. 348–408.

Alton, T. P. 1985. "East European GNPs: Origin of Product, Final Uses, Rates of Growth and International Comparisons." In U.S. Congress, Joint Economics Committee, *East European Economics: Slow Growth in the 1980s*, Vol. 1. Washington, D.C.: JEC, pp. 81–132.

Alton, T. P., et al. 1988. *Economic Grwoth in Eastern Europe 1970 and 1975–1987*. Occasional Paper No. 100. New York: L. W. International Financial Research, Inc.

Amann, R., and J. Cooper, eds. 1982. *Industrial Innovation in the Soviet Union*. London: Yale University Press.

Baily, M. N., and M. Blair. 1988. "Productivity and American Management." Washington, D.C.: Brookings Institution. (mimeographed)

Balassa, B. 1981. *The Newly Industrializing Countries in the World Economy*. New York: Pergamon Press.

Bergson, A. 1983. "Technological Change." In A. Bergson and H. S. Levine, Eds., *The Soviet Economy Towards the Year 2000*. London: Allen and Unwin.

Bergson, A. 1984. "Income Inequality Under Soviet Socialism," *Journal of Economics Literature* 22(4), 1052–99.

Bergson, A. 1987. "Comparative Productivity: The USSR, Eastern Europe, and the West," *American Economic Review* 77(3), 342–57.

Berliner, J. S. 1976. *The Innovation Decision in Soviet Industry*. Cambridge: MIT Press.

Bornstein, M. 1985. *The Transfer of Western Technology to the USSR*. Paris: OECD.

Campbell, R. 1986. "Resource Stringency and the Civilian–Military Resource Allocation." (mimeographed)

Chenery, H., and M. Syrquin. 1975. *Patterns of Development, 1950–1970*. London: Oxford University Press and The World Bank.

CIA. 1987. *Handbook of Economic Statistics, 1987*. Washington, D.C.: CIA.

Crane, K. 1986. "Foreign Trade Decisionmaking Under Balance of Payments Pressure: Poland Vs. Hungary." In U.S. Congress, Joint Economics Committee, *East European Economics: Slow Growth in the 1980s*, Vol. 2. Washington, D.C.: USGPO, pp. 434–49.

Desai, P. 1988. Alternative Measures of Import Shares: Theory and Estimate for the Soviet Union." Discussion Paper Series No. 388, Columbia University, New York.

Ellis, J. L. 1986. "Eastern Europe: Changing Trade Patterns and Perspectives." In U.S.

Congress, Joint Economics Committee, *East European Economics: Slow Growth in the 1980s,* Vol. 2. Washington, D.C.: USGPO, pp. 6–30.

Englander, S. A., and A. Mittelstadt. 1988. "Total Factor Productivity: Macroeconomic and Structural Aspects of the Slowdown." *OECD Economic Studies* (Spring), 7–56.

Ethier, W. J. 1982. "National and International Returns to Scale in the Modern Theory of International Trade." *American Economic Review* 76, 177–90.

Eurostat. 1987. *World Comparisons of Purchasing Power and Real Product in 1980.* Luxembourg: Eurostat.

Gerschenkron, A. 1962. *Economic Backwardness in Historical Perspective.* Cambridge, Mass.: Harvard University Press.

Gomulka, S. 1986. *Growth, Innovation and Reform in Eastern Europe.* Madison: University of Wisconsin Press.

Hanson, P. 1981. *Trade and Technology in Soviet–Western Relations.* New York: Columbia University Press.

Hanson, P. 1982a. "The Soviet System as a Recipient of Western Technology." In R. Amann and J. Cooper, Eds., *Industrial Innovation in the Soviet Union.* London: Yale University Press.

Hanson, P. 1982b. "The End of Import-Led Growth? Some Observations on Soviet, Polish, and Hungarian Experience in the 1970s." *Journal of Comparative Economics* 6(2), 130–47.

Helpman, E. 1988. "Growth, Technical Progress, and Trade." NBER Working Paper No. 2592. Cambridge, Mass.

Helpman, E., and P. R. Krugman. 1985. *Market Structure and Foreign Trade.* Cambridge, Mass.: MIT Press.

Hewett, E. A. 1980. "Trade Outcomes in Eastern and Western Economies." In P. Marer and J. M. Montias, Eds., *East European Integration and East–West Trade.* Bloomington: Indiana University Press, pp. 41–69.

Hewett, E. A. 1988. *Reforming the Soviet Economy.* Washington, D.C.: Brookings Institution.

Holzman, F. D. 1987. *The Economics of Soviet Block Trade and Finance.* Boulder, Colo.: Westview Press.

Hough, J. 1988. *Opening Up the Soviet Economy.* Washington, D.C.: Brookings Institution.

Judy, R. W. 1987. "The Soviet Information Revolution: Some Prospects and Comparisons." In U.S. Congress, Joint Economics Committee, *Gorbachev's Economic Plans,* Vol. 2. Washington, D.C.: USGPO, pp. 161–75.

Kontorovich, V. 1985. "The Soviet Investment Process and Capital Labor Substitution." Command Economies Research Inc. (mimeographed)

Kornai, J. 1980. *Economics of Shortage,* Vols. 1, 2. Amsterdam: North-Holland.

Kornai, J. 1986. "The Hungarian Reform Process." *Journal of Economic Literature* 24(4), 1687–1737.

Kravis, I. B., A. Heston, and R. Summers. 1982. *World Product and Income.* Baltimore, Md.: Johns Hopkins University Press.

Krugman, P. 1979. "A Model of Innovation, Technology Transfer, and the World Distribution of Income." *Journal of Political Economy,* 87(2), 253–66.

Kuznets, S. 1966. *Modern Economic Growth: Rate Structure, and Spread.* New Haven, Conn.: Yale University Press.

Lawrence, R. Z. 1984. *Can America Compete?* Washington, D.C.: Brookings Institution.

Lawrence, R. Z. 1988. "American Living Standards: The International Dimension."
    Brookings Institution, Washington, D.C. (mimeographed)
Maddison, A. 1982. *Phases of Capitalist Development*. New York: Oxford University
    Press.
Maddison, A. 1987. "Growth and Slowdown in Advanced Capitalist Economies: Tech-
    niques of Quantitative Assessment." *Journal of Economic Literature* 25 (June),
    649–98.
Marer, P. 1972. *Soviet and East European Foreign Trade, 1946–1969*. Bloomington: In-
    diana University Press.
Marer, P. 1978. "Toward a Solution of the Mirror Statistics Puzzle in East–West Com-
    merce." In F. Levcki, Ed., *International Economics: Comparisons and Inter-
    dependence*. Vienna and New York: Springer.
Marer, P. 1985. *Dollars GNPs of the U.S.S.R. and Eastern Europe*. Baltimore, Md.:
    Johns Hopkins University Press and The World Bank.
Marer, P. 1985b. "Alternative Estimates of the Dollar GNP and Growth Rates of the
    CMEA Countries." In U.S. Congress, Joint Economics Committee, *East Euro-
    pean Economics: Slow Growth in the 1980s*, Vol. 1. Washington, D.C.: USGPO,
    pp. 133–93.
Marer, P. 1986. "Economic Policies and Systems in Eastern Europe and Yugoslavia:
    Commonalities and Differences." In U.S. Congress, Joint Economics Commit-
    tee, *East European Economics: Slow Growth in the 1980s*, Vol. 3. Washington,
    D.C.: USGPO, pp. 595–633.
Marer, P. 1987. "Can Joint Ventures in Hungary Serve as a 'Bridge' to the CMEA
    Market?" European University Institute, Working Paper No. 87/276. Florence.
Marrese, M., and J. Vanous. 1983. *Soviet Subsidization of Trade with Eastern Europe*.
    Berkeley: University of California Press.
Morrison, C. 1984. "Income Distribution in East European and Western Countries."
    Journal of Comparative Economics 8, 121–38.
OECD. 1987. *Historical Statistics 1960–1985* (Economic Outlook). Paris: OECD.
Ofer, G. 1976. "Industrial Structure, Urbanization, and the Socialist Growth Strategy."
    Quarterly Journal of Economics 90(2), 219–44.
Ofer, G. 1980. "Growth Strategy, Specialization in Agriculture, and Trade: Bulgaria and
    Eastern Europe." In P. Marer and J. M. Montias, Eds., *East European Integra-
    tion and East–West Trade*. Bloomington: Indiana University Press.
Ofer, G. 1987. "Soviet Economic Growth: 1928–1985." *Journal of Economic Literature*
    25 (December), 1767–1833.
Poznanski, K. Z. 1987. *Technology, Competition, and the Soviet Block in the World
    Market*. University of California, Berkeley, Institute of International Studies.
Rosefielde, S. 1981. "Factor Proportions and Economic Rationality in Soviet Interna-
    tional Trade 1955–1968." *American Economic Review* 64(4), 670–81.
Treml, V. G. 1980. "Foreign Trade and the Soviet Economy: Changing Parameters and
    Interrelations." In E. Neuberger and L. Tyson, Eds., *The Impact of Interna-
    tional Economic Disturbances on the Soviet Union and Eastern Europe*. New
    York: Pergamon Press, pp. 184–207.
Tyson, L. D. 1988. "Competitiveness: An Analysis of the Problem and a Perspective
    on Future Policy." In M. K. Starr, Ed., *Global Competitiveness: Getting the
    U.S. Back on the Track*. New York: W. W. Norton.
United Nations. 1981. *1980 Yearbook of International Trade Statistics*. New York:
    United Nations.
United Nations. 1988. *1985 Yearbook of International Trade Statistics*. New York:
    United Nations.

World Bank. 1983. *World Development Report 1983.* New York: Oxford University Press.

World Bank. 1987. *World Development Report 1987.* New York: Oxford University Press.

Vanous, J. 1986. "Soviet Foreign Trade Performance During the First Half of 1986, and Final Data on Commodity Composition of Soviet Trade in 1985." *PlanEcon Report* 2 (October 2).

Vanous, J. 1988. "Top Commodities in East–West Trade: What Can Be Bought and What Can Be Sold." *PlanEcon Report 4(12–13).*

U.S. Congress, JEC. 1970. *Economic Developments in Countries of Eastern Europe.* Washington, D.C.: JEC.

U.S. Congress, JEC. 1985–86. *East European Economics: Slow Growth in the 1980s,* Vols. 1–3. Washington, D.C.: JEC.

U.S. Congress, JEC. 1987. *Gorbachev's Economic Plans,* Vols. 1, 2. Washington, D.C.: JEC.

Van Brabant, J. M. P. 1973. *Bilateralism and Structural Bilateralism in Intra-CMEA Trade.* Totterdam: Rotterdam University Press.

Vinokur, A., and G. Ofer. 1987. "Inequality of Earning, Household Income and Wealth in the Soviet Union in the 1970s." In J. .R. Millar, Ed., *Politics, Work, and Daily Life in the USSR.* Cambridge: Cambridge University Press, pp. 171–202.

II

COMPARATIVE STUDIES OF MARKET ECONOMIES

6

An International Comparison of Manufacturing Productivity and Unit Labor Cost Trends

ARTHUR NEEF

This chapter presents comparative trend measures of manufacturing productivity, as measured by output per hour, hourly compensation costs, and unit labor costs in the United States, Canada, Japan, and nine European countries. The U.S. Bureau of Labor Statistics (BLS) has been preparing these annual measures for many years to help assess changes in the U.S. competitive position. This chapter also introduces new research looking into productivity developments in component manufacturing industries, covering the United States, Japan, and Germany. Similar research for a 1984 conference compared productivity developments by manufacturing industry in the United States and three European countries, but the series was not maintained on a current basis (Neef and Dean, 1984). The current manufacturing industry measures, which also include Canada and France, are not expected to be maintained on a regular basis.

Both the total manufacturing and component industry measures are labor productivity measures. The BLS has been engaged in a research effort to develop total manufacturing capital stock measures for Japan and Germany, but this work is still incomplete. The BLS has been publishing capital–labor multifactor measures for the U.S. total private business sector and for total manufacturing since 1983 (Mark and Waldorf, 1983; U.S. Department of Labor, 1983, 1988). In 1987, the BLS also published multifactor productivity measures for twenty manufacturing industries, with productivity defined as gross output per unit of capital, labor, energy, materials, and business service inputs (Gullickson and Harper, 1987).

Comparative multifactor productivity measures would illuminate the productivity growth process better than labor productivity measures. However, labor productivity measures can be produced on a more timely basis and labor inputs can be measured on a more reliable and comparable basis across countries than can capital inputs. In addition, relative changes in labor productivity among countries help explain relative changes in unit labor costs, an important variable in international trade competitiveness.

MANUFACTURING PRODUCTIVITY GROWTH

Since 1960, manufacturing output per hour has risen 2.8 percent per year in the United States. Canada, Japan, and the nine European countries for which the BLS developed comparable measures have all had faster rates of labor productivity growth, ranging from over 3 percent up to about 6 percent in Canada and Europe and nearly 8 percent in Japan (Table 6-1).

It is customary to divide the time period since 1960 into the years preceding and subsequent to 1973. U.S. output peaked in 1973, and the years since 1973 have been characterized by a productivity growth-rate slowdown. The U.S. productivity growth rate for manufacturing slowed from 3.2 percent per year in 1960–73 to 2.5 percent per year in 1973–87. The year 1973 is also a useful breaking point for the other countries. Manufacturing output generally peaked in 1973 or 1974, and all of the other countries also experienced productivity

Table 6-1 Manufacturing Labor Productivity and Hourly Compensation Cost Growth Rates, Twelve Countries, 1960–87

Country	1960–87	1960–73	1973–87	1973–79	1979–87	1979–85	1985–87
Output per hour							
United States	2.8	3.2	2.5	1.4	3.3	3.4	3.3
Canada	3.3	4.5	2.1	2.1	2.1	2.4	1.3
Japan	7.7	10.3	5.3	5.5	5.1	5.8	2.0
Belgium	6.3	6.9	5.7	6.0	5.4	6.0	3.5
Denmark	4.3	6.4	2.3	4.2	1.0	1.7	−1.2
France	5.0	6.4	3.7	4.6	3.0	3.0	3.1
West Germany	4.4	5.8	3.2	4.3	2.3	2.9	0.7
Italy	5.7	7.5	4.0	3.3	4.5	5.4	2.0
Netherlands	5.7	7.4	4.2	5.5	3.3	4.4	0.0
Norway	3.4	4.3	2.6	2.2	2.9	2.8	3.1
Sweden	4.6	6.4	2.9	2.6	3.1	3.5	2.1
United Kingdom	3.7	4.2	3.2	1.2	4.7	4.7	4.8
Hourly compensation							
United States	6.2	5.0	7.4	9.5	5.8	6.8	2.9
Canada	7.9	6.2	9.5	12.0	7.7	8.6	4.9
Japan	11.3	15.1	8.0	12.8	4.5	4.9	3.1
Belgium	10.3	11.0	9.7	14.0	6.5	7.7	2.9
Denmark	11.3	12.2	10.5	14.0	7.9	8.1	7.4
France	11.5	10.0	13.0	16.3	10.5	12.9	3.7
West Germany	8.7	10.3	7.2	9.5	5.5	6.0	4.2
Italy	15.2	13.5	16.7	20.6	13.9	17.1	4.6
Netherlands	10.1	12.9	7.5	11.6	4.5	5.1	2.9
Norway	11.0	10.0	11.9	13.4	10.8	9.9	13.4
Sweden	11.0	10.5	11.4	14.2	9.3	10.0	7.4
United Kingdom	11.6	9.2	13.9	19.4	10.0	10.9	7.2

growth-rate slowdowns. In most of the other countries, the productivity slow-downs have been more substantial than in the United States, although from larger pre-1973 rates of gain. Japan's rate fell from about 10 percent to 5.3 percent and Germany's rate fell from nearly 6 percent to about 3 percent. The U.S. average rate of gain between 1973 and 1987 matched or exceeded the average gains recorded by Canada, Denmark, and Norway but still trailed the other countries.

It is also useful to divide the time period since 1973 at 1979, which was another peak output year for the United States. In addition, the U.S. manufac-turing productivity growth rate appears to have accelerated from 1.4 percent per year in 1973–79 to 3.3 percent per year in 1979–87—almost identical to the 1960–73 average rate of gain—although the total business economy did not have a similar rebound in productivity growth.

The year 1979 has also been used as a breaking point for the other countries, since manufacturing output generally peaked in 1979 or 1980, with the excep-tion of Japan, which has not had a decline in manufacturing output since 1975. Between 1979 and 1987, British labor productivity rose nearly 5 percent per year, greatly exceeding the 1973–79 rate of gain and also exceeding the pre-1973 rate of increase. However, the United States was the only other country to match or exceed its pre-1973 growth rate after 1979. Most, including Japan, France, and Germany, have had slower rates of productivity growth since 1979 than in the 1973–79 period.

Japan still had a higher average rate of productivity growth than the United States in 1979–87, but the differential was less than 2 percentage points, compared with 7 percentage points in the 1960–73 period and 4 percentage points in the 1973–79 period. In addition, the U.S. rate of gain exceeded the average rates recorded in Canada, France, Germany, and the Scandinavian countries.

UNIT LABOR COSTS

While the United States has had the lowest overall manufacturing labor pro-ductivity growth rate since 1960, the United States has also had the smallest average annual increases in hourly compensation costs (Table 6-1) and, along with Japan, the smallest average annual increases in unit labor costs (Table 6-2). Since 1973, however, Japan, Germany, and the Benelux countries have re-corded smaller average annual increases in unit labor costs, as measured in each country's own currency. But currency exchange rates have also changed greatly since about 1973, and these relative changes in currency values need to be taken into account in assessing changes in unit labor costs in competitive terms.

During the manufacturing productivity slowdown of 1973 to 1979, U.S. hourly compensation costs accelerated to 9.5 percent per year and unit labor costs rose 8 percent per year. However, the countries with smaller average rates of increase in unit labor costs—Japan, Germany, and the Benelux coun-

Table 6-2　Manufacturing Unit Labor Cost Growth Rates, Twelve Countries, 1960–87 (Annual Average Percent Change)

Country	1960–87	1960–73	1973–87	1973–79	1979–87	1979–85	1985–87
Unit labor costs: National-currency basis							
United States	3.3	1.8	4.8	8.0	2.4	3.4	−0.4
Canada	4.5	1.6	7.3	9.8	5.4	6.1	3.5
Japan	3.4	4.3	2.6	6.9	−0.6	−0.8	0.3
Belgium	3.8	3.8	3.8	7.5	1.1	1.6	−0.5
Denmark	6.7	5.5	8.0	9.4	6.9	6.3	8.7
France	6.2	3.4	8.9	11.2	7.3	9.6	0.6
West Germany	4.1	4.3	3.9	4.9	3.1	3.0	3.4
Italy	9.0	5.6	12.2	16.7	8.9	11.1	2.5
Netherlands	4.1	5.2	3.1	5.8	1.2	0.6	2.9
Norway	7.3	5.4	9.1	11.0	7.6	6.9	9.9
Sweden	6.1	3.9	8.2	11.2	6.0	6.3	5.1
United Kingdom	7.7	4.8	10.4	18.0	5.1	6.0	2.4
Unit labor costs: U.S. dollar basis							
United States	3.3	1.8	4.8	8.0	2.4	3.4	−0.4
Canada	3.3	1.3	5.1	6.9	3.8	3.4	5.1
Japan	6.9	6.6	7.3	10.8	4.7	−2.3	28.8
Belgium	4.9	5.8	4.1	12.7	−1.9	−9.6	25.3
Denmark	6.8	6.6	7.0	11.9	3.4	−5.4	35.2
France	5.4	4.2	6.6	12.0	2.7	−3.2	23.0
West Germany	7.4	8.0	6.8	11.6	3.4	−4.8	32.3
Italy	6.0	6.1	6.0	10.0	3.0	−3.3	24.4
Netherlands	6.5	7.7	5.5	11.7	1.1	−7.5	31.6
Norway	7.5	7.2	7.8	13.3	3.9	−2.1	24.1
Sweden	5.3	5.3	5.3	11.5	0.9	−5.4	22.4
United Kingdom	5.6	3.7	7.3	15.2	1.7	−2.4	15.1

tries—underwent currency appreciations. Therefore, these four countries, as well as the other European countries, had larger average gains in unit labor costs than the United States when measured on a U.S. dollar basis.

Between 1979 and 1985, the U.S. manufacturing productivity growth rate accelerated, average gains in hourly compensation costs were reduced substantially, and the average annual increase in unit labor costs was reduced to 3.4 percent. This still exceeded the average increases recorded in Germany and the Benelux countries, and Japanese unit labor costs fell nearly 1 percent per year during this time period. In addition, the U.S. dollar rose strongly against all of the European currencies and moderately relative to the Canadian dollar and Japanese yen. Consequently, measured on a U.S. dollar basis, Canadian unit labor costs rose somewhat less than U.S. costs and Japanese and European unit labor costs fell between 2 and 10 percent per year.

U.S. manufacturing unit labor costs declined between 1985 and 1987. In addition, the U.S. dollar began depreciating strongly against the yen and most European currencies in 1985 and continued to depreciate during 1986 and 1987. Between 1985 and 1987, measured on an annual average basis, the value of the U.S. dollar fell about 40 percent relative to the currencies of Japan and Germany and 20–35 percent against the currencies of the other European countries. Measured on a U.S. dollar basis, the average annual 1985–87 increases in unit labor costs in the other countries were about 30 percent or more in Japan, Denmark, Germany, and the Netherlands; 15–25 percent in the other European countries; and 5 percent in Canada.

Measured on a trade-weighted basis relative to the other eleven countries, and taking changes in exchange rates into account, U.S. unit labor costs as of 1985 were over 40 percent above the low point reached in 1978. In 1987, they were several percentage points below the 1978 level.

A Note of Caution

The U.S. manufacturing productivity measures are based on the national accounts measure of gross product originating in manufacturing. Recently, a number of analysts have questioned the accuracy of this measure, suggesting that the real growth in manufacturing output since 1973, and particularly since 1979, may have been less than shown by the published measures (Baily and Gordon, 1988; Denison, 1989; Mishel, 1988; U.S. Congress, 1988). Some of the arguments appear plausible.

The principal criticisms relate to (1) adjustments made by the Bureau of Economic Analysis (BEA) to the industry estimates to eliminate sizable gaps between total gross product originating by industry and gross product estimated as the sum of final expenditures, primarily for the years 1972–74; (2) the new price index for computers BEA introduced in 1986; (3) the price indexes used to deflate materials inputs, which do not reflect prices of imported materials, and the price indexes for service inputs, which may be overstated, both thereby overstating gross product originating in manufacturing; and (4) the lack of current information on the ratio of material and service inputs to gross output. Frank de Leeuw and Robert P. Parker of BEA responded to these criticisms in an article in the July 1988 issue of the *Survey of Current Business,* stating that "these issues are quantitatively important" and "the criticisms warrant careful attention," but "in the light of all evidence, it is not possible to draw firm conclusions about biases in BEA's present estimates of real gross product originating" (1988, pp. 132–33).

Another factor that affects manufacturing measures has nothing to do with possible errors in measurement. The constant price measures are based on 1982 relative prices. BEA's computer price index declined at a rate of about 15 percent per year during the 1980s. Consequently, if current relative prices were used as weights, the relative importance of computers, which are included in nonelectrical machinery, would be greatly reduced. As the BEA article states, "Recent manufacturing growth expressed in 1982 prices substantially exceeds what it would be in 1987 prices, because the relative price of computers was much higher in 1982 than in 1987" (de Leeuw and Parker, 1988, p. 133).

The fact that this note refers only to the U.S. measures does not imply that the other countries' measures are superior and not subject to similar measurement problems. What it does suggest is that the comparative measures are not precise and small differences in measured productivity growth rates should certainly not be considered significant.

PRODUCTIVITY GROWTH IN COMPONENT MANUFACTURING INDUSTRIES

It is useful to look at productivity growth and changes in unit labor costs in component manufacturing industries. Trade, of course, does not take place at the total manufacturing level. In addition, the comparative trends in manufacturing productivity and labor costs may be affected by relative shifts among component industries with different levels of productivity and unit labor costs as well as by movements in productivity and unit labor costs within component industries. In these aggregate manufacturing measures, shifts in industry shares of output and input can affect productivity for manufacturing as a whole even in the absence of productivity growth in the component industries.

As noted earlier, the BLS is currently developing comparative productivity and unit labor cost measures by manufacturing industry for a number of countries—Canada, Japan, France, and Germany. Only the Japanese and German productivity measures are analyzed here, and they should be considered preliminary at this stage of development.

These comparative manufacturing industry measures are not at detailed levels of disaggregation because of data limitations and because of country differences in industrial classification systems; rather they are limited to twenty or fewer manufacturing industry groups. In addition, there are some limitations to labor productivity measures that increase at finer levels of detail. For large aggregates, such as total manufacturing, productivity calculations can appropriately be based on value-added measures of output because most intermediate transactions are between establishments within the sector and cancel out. At finer levels of detail, however, intermediate purchases from outside an industry are more significant.

The Available Measures

The U.S. measures are available for twenty-one component manufacturing industries, the German measures are available for thirty-one component industries, and the Japanese measures are available for thirteen industries. The measures analyzed in this chapter are limited to the thirteen Japanese industry groups, with the exception of the shift analysis, which is based on all available industries. The German measures are available from 1960, but the Japanese measures are not available prior to 1970. The end point for the analysis is 1985, since this is the latest year for which the German data were available when this chapter was prepared.

The thirteen industry groups are largely comparable in industrial coverage across the three countries with one major exception. In the United States, computer and office equipment is included in nonelectrical machinery. In Japan, computer and electronic processing machines are in the electrical machinery industry. Business machine products are a separate industry in Germany; this industry has been combined with nonelectrical machinery for greater conformity with the U.S. classification system. A closer degree of concordance is achieved by combining nonelectrical and electrical machinery. As of 1985, however, this combination accounted for 27 percent of manufacturing output in the United States and Germany and 33 percent of Japanese output. Therefore, the two machinery industries have been analyzed separately, but data for the total have also been included in the tables.

There are some other classification differences. For example, tobacco is grouped with miscellaneous manufactures in Japan; the German stone, clay, and glass products industry includes some quarrying; metal furniture is included in furniture and fixtures in the United States and Japan but in fabricated metal products in Germany; and the German transportation equipment industry includes repair of motor vehicles and excludes railroad equipment, the latter being classified in fabricated metal products.

The Japanese and German labor input measures used in the industry analysis differ somewhat from the total manufacturing measures just discussed. The previous measures relate to employees only, but the industry measures cover all employed persons because there are substantial numbers of self-employed workers in some industries. Self-employed workers are included in the U.S. total manufacturing measures and in the industry measures. The inclusion of self-employed workers raises Germany's labor productivity growth rate for total manufacturing 0.2 percentage point over the full 1960–85 period and 0.3 percentage point in the 1960–73 period, but it does not change the overall 1973–85 growth rate. The inclusion of self-employed workers raises Japan's 1973–85 manufacturing productivity growth rate 0.3 percentage point.

The following analysis looks at (1) the contribution of relative shifts in labor inputs among the component industries to each country's manufacturing productivity growth rate; (2) comparative productivity developments before and after 1973 in the United States and Germany; and (3) comparative developments in all three countries from 1973 to 1985.

Intraindustry and Shift Effects in Productivity Growth

Labor productivity measures for a composite of industries are calculated by direct aggregation, by summing outputs and labor inputs across industries. This aggregate labor productivity measure is affected over time not only by productivity change within the component industries, but by the relative shift of labor hours among industries with different levels of productivity. However, to the extent that component industry measures are available, the total productivity change can be decomposed into (1) the part of aggregate productivity growth that is the result of changes in component industry productivity growth rates with no change in labor input shares (intraindustry effect); (2) the part of aggregate productivity growth that results solely from relative shifts of labor among industries (shift effect); and (3) a third effect which results from the interaction of simultaneous changes in relative productivity levels among industries and relative shifts in labor inputs among industries.

Table 6-3 presents the results of this analysis for the 1960–85 period for the United States and Germany and the 1973–85 period for all three countries. The analysis for Germany was done at two levels of industry detail, the full thirty-one available industries and for twenty-one industries grouped to correspond closely to the U.S. twenty-one–industry breakdown. However, the results for Germany are nearly identical for the thirty-one– and the twenty-one–industry groups.

Over the full 1960–85 period, the intraindustry effect was virtually identical to the total productivity change in both the United States and Germany. That is, the effects of relative shifts in labor hours among industries were almost neutral. The shift effect also had no influence on Germany's productivity growth-rate slowdown. The shift effect did moderate the U.S. productivity slowdown somewhat, since it was negative in the 1960–73 period and slightly positive in the 1973–85 period.

The positive shift effects on U.S. productivity growth occurred in the 1973–79 period—the shift effects were negative after 1979. Consequently, the inter-industry shift effects moderated the substantial improvement in U.S. manufacturing productivity growth after 1979. In Germany, the shift effects were negative between 1973 and 1979 and positive between 1979 and 1985. Consequently, the further slowdown in Germany's productivity growth rate in the latter period was 1.4 percent per year rather than about 1.9 percent per year based on the intraindustry effect alone.

In Japan, the shift effects over the 1973–85 period were a positive 0.2 percentage point. In the 1979–85 period, shift effects raised Japan's productivity growth rate by 0.3 percentage point. In the absence of shift effects, Japan's 1979–85 productivity growth rate would have been 5.9 rather than 6.2 percent.

Productivity Growth by Manufacturing Industry in the United States and Germany, 1960–85

From 1960 to 1985, the U.S. total manufacturing productivity growth rate was 2.8 percent per year. Productivity growth rates in the thirteen industry groups being analyzed ranged between 1 percent in primary metals and 5 percent in textiles (Table 6-4). Germany's productivity growth rate was about 5 percent per year and the differentials across industries were less than in the United States. Germany's productivity growth rate advantage over the United States by industry was generally about 1–3 percent, with the exception of nonelectrical machinery where the two countries had identical growth rates.

As noted earlier, both countries had productivity slowdowns after 1973. Eleven of the thirteen U.S. industry groups experienced productivity slowdowns after 1973. The two exceptions were nonelectrical machinery, in which the productivity growth rate more than doubled, and textiles (Table 6-5). If we look at the period 1973–79, compared with 1960–73, all industries except textiles had productivity growth-rate slowdowns. All thirteen German industry groups had productivity slowdowns in the 1973–85 period. Nonelectrical machinery had the smallest reduction. This was the result of an increase in the productivity growth rate for business machine products, which was combined

Table 6-3 Manufacturing Productivity Growth Rates by Source, United States, Japan, and Germany, 1960–85 (Simple Average of the Year-to-Year Percent Changes)[a]

Country and Item	1960–85	1960–73	1973–85	Difference: 1973–85 vs. 1960–73	1973–79	1979–85	Difference: 1979–85 vs. 1973–79
United States (21 industries)							
Total productivity change	2.81	3.19	2.39	−0.80	1.42	3.37	1.95
Intraindustry effect	2.82	3.27	2.34	−0.93	1.24	3.44	2.20
Shift effect	−0.03	−0.09	0.03	0.12	0.14	−0.09	−0.23
Interaction	0.02	0.01	0.03	0.02	0.03	0.02	−0.01
Germany (31 industries)							
Total productivity change	4.88	6.07	3.58	−2.49	4.29	2.88	−1.41
Intraindustry effect	4.87	6.05	3.58	−2.47	4.53	2.64	−1.89
Shift effect	0.04	0.04	0.03	−0.01	−0.20	0.26	0.46
Interaction	−0.02	−0.02	−0.04	−0.02	−0.05	−0.01	0.04
Germany (21 industries)							
Total productivity change	4.88	6.07	3.60	−2.47	4.29	2.90	−1.39
Intraindustry effect	4.87	6.03	3.61	−2.42	4.52	2.70	−1.82
Shift effect	0.04	0.06	0.02	−0.04	−0.19	0.22	0.41
Interaction	−0.02	−0.02	−0.03	−0.01	−0.04	−0.02	0.02
Japan (13 industries)							
Total productivity change			5.97		5.70	6.24	0.54
Intraindustry effect			5.82		5.71	5.92	0.21
Shift effect			0.21		0.10	0.32	0.22
Interaction			−0.06		−0.11	−0.00	−0.11

[a]Components may not add to totals because of rounding.

Table 6-4 Manufacturing Productivity Growth Rates by Industry, United States and Germany, 1960–85 (Annual Average Percent Change)

Industry	United States			Germany			Germany Minus United States		
	1960–85	1960–73	1973–85	1960–85	1960–73	1973–85	1960–85	1960–73	1973–85
Total	2.8	3.2	2.4	4.9	6.1	3.6	2.1	2.9	1.2
Food and tobacco	2.8	3.8	1.7	3.5	3.9	3.1	0.7	0.1	1.4
Textiles	5.1	4.8	5.4	5.7	6.5	5.0	0.6	1.7	-0.4
Paper	3.0	4.0	1.9	4.9	5.4	4.4	1.9	1.4	2.5
Chemicals	4.0	5.6	2.3	6.5	9.4	3.5	2.5	3.8	1.2
Petroleum	2.2	4.0	0.3	6.7	9.0	4.2	4.5	5.0	3.9
Stone, clay, and glass	2.0	2.3	1.8	4.9	6.5	3.3	2.9	4.2	1.5
Primary metals	0.9	2.2	-0.6	4.3	5.0	3.5	3.4	2.8	4.1
Fabricated metal products	2.0	2.2	1.8	4.2	5.9	2.5	2.2	3.7	0.7
Machinery	4.2	3.4	5.0	4.9	5.4	4.3	0.7	2.0	-0.7
Nonelectrical machinery	4.0	2.5	5.6	4.1	4.4	3.7	0.1	1.9	-1.9
Electrical machinery	4.5	4.9	4.2	6.1	7.2	4.9	1.6	2.3	0.7
Transportation equipment	2.4	3.3	1.4	4.4	5.4	3.4	2.0	2.1	2.0
Instruments	2.7	3.6	1.9	4.2	6.0	2.3	1.5	2.4	0.4
Other manufacturing	2.4	2.9	1.8	4.6	6.3	2.8	2.2	3.4	1.0

Table 6-5 Differences in Manufacturing Productivity Growth Rates by Industry, United States and Germany, 1973–85 vs. 1960–73 (Differences in Average Annual Percent Changes, 1973–85 Minus 1960–73)

Industry	United States	Germany
Total	− 0.8	− 2.5
Food and tobacco	− 2.1	− 0.8
Textiles	0.6	− 1.5
Paper	− 2.1	− 1.0
Chemicals	− 3.3	− 5.9
Petroleum	− 3.7	− 4.8
Stone, clay, and glass	− 0.5	− 3.2
Primary metals	− 2.8	− 1.5
Fabricated metal products	− 0.4	− 3.4
Machinery	1.6	− 1.1
Nonelectrical machinery	3.1	− 0.7
Electrical machinery	− 0.7	− 2.3
Transportation equipment	− 1.9	− 2.0
Instruments	− 1.7	− 3.7
Other manufacturing	− 1.1	− 3.5

with nonelectrical machinery to match the U.S. industry definition. Of the total thirty-one German industry groups available for analysis, only two did not have productivity slowdowns. The productivity slowdown appears to have been quite pervasive across industries in both the United States and Germany.

Productivity Growth by Manufacturing Industry in the United States, Japan, and Germany, 1973–85

Table 6-6 shows productivity growth rates by industry for the three countries from 1973 to 1985 and for the two subperiods, 1973–79 and 1979–85. Over the full period, U.S. total manufacturing productivity advanced by 2.4 percent per year. Three industries had substantially larger productivity growth rates—textiles, nonelectrical machinery, and electrical machinery. All other industries were below the manufacturing average. As seen in Table 6-7, the share of total manufacturing output accounted for by the two machinery industries rose from 18 percent in 1973 to 27 percent in 1985 while their share of manufacturing hours rose only from 20.5 to 22.7 percent. In contrast, the textile share of manufacturing output was about unchanged while the textile share of hours fell more than any other industry except primary metals, which also had the largest decline in output share.

Japan's total manufacturing productivity growth rate over the 1973–85 period was 6 percent, two and a half times the U.S. rate. Four industries had substantially larger productivity growth rates of 9 percent or more—chemicals, the two machinery industries, and instruments. The growth rate for electrical machinery was nearly 18 percent, and the share of manufacturing output accounted for by electrical machinery rose from 4.5 percent in 1973 to 22 percent in 1985 (Table 6-8). Electrical machinery also had the largest increase in labor hours, but the change was much more modest, from 10 to 14 percent. In 1973, the relative level of labor productivity in electrical machinery was less than 50

Table 6-6 Manufacturing Productivity Growth Rates by Industry, United States, Japan, and Germany, 1973–85 (Annual Average Percent Change)

Industry	United States			Japan			Germany		
	1973–85	1973–79	1979–85	1973–85	1973–79	1979–85	1973–85	1973–79	1979–85
Total	2.4	1.4	3.4	6.0	5.7	6.2	3.6	4.3	2.9
Food and tobacco	1.7	0.9	2.7	-1.3	2.6	-5.0	3.1	3.8	2.5
Textiles	5.4	6.6	4.2	6.5	5.3	7.8	5.0	6.1	3.8
Paper	1.9	1.4	2.4	3.9	3.9	3.8	4.4	4.0	4.7
Chemicals	2.3	2.5	2.1	9.5	13.2	6.0	3.5	5.5	1.5
Petroleum	0.3	0.2	0.3	-1.0	-1.4	-0.6	4.2	7.4	1.0
Stone, clay, and glass	1.8	1.3	2.3	0.5	-0.5	1.5	3.3	4.8	1.8
Primary metals	-0.6	-2.1	1.0	5.1	6.2	4.0	3.5	4.1	3.0
Fabricated metal products	1.8	0.6	3.0	2.1	0.2	4.0	2.5	3.8	1.3
Machinery	5.0	2.3	7.7	13.4	13.0	13.8	4.3	4.5	4.0
Nonelectrical machinery	5.6	0.8	10.6	9.1	9.8	8.5	3.7	3.9	3.6
Electrical machinery	4.2	4.4	4.0	17.6	17.7	17.6	4.9	5.3	4.5
Transportation equipment	1.4	0.6	2.1	5.7	6.7	4.8	3.4	4.3	2.5
Instruments	1.9	3.0	0.7	10.4	10.0	10.7	2.3	3.0	1.6
Other manufacturing	1.8	1.5	2.1	4.4	3.4	5.3	2.8	3.5	2.2
Manufacturing less nonelectrical machinery	1.8	1.5	2.2	5.6	5.3	6.0	3.5	4.3	2.8

Table 6-7 Manufacturing Industries Output Shares, Hours Shares, and Relative Productivity Levels, United States, 1973 and 1985

Industry	Output Share		Hours Share		Relative Productivity		1985 Relative to 1973		
	1973	1985	1973	1985	1973	1985	Output Share	Hours Share	Relative Productivity
Total	100.0	100.0	100.0	100.0	1.00	1.00	1.00	1.00	1.00
Food and tobacco	9.9	8.9	8.8	8.5	1.13	1.05	0.90	0.97	0.93
Textiles	2.0	2.1	5.0	3.6	0.41	0.58	1.05	0.72	1.41
Paper	4.0	3.8	3.6	3.6	1.13	1.06	0.95	1.00	0.94
Chemicals	7.2	7.5	5.1	5.4	1.40	1.39	1.04	1.06	0.99
Petroleum	4.1	3.2	1.0	0.9	4.29	3.35	0.78	0.90	0.78
Stone, clay, and glass	3.5	2.9	3.6	3.2	0.97	0.91	0.83	0.89	0.94
Primary metals	9.5	4.3	6.4	4.2	1.46	1.03	0.46	0.66	0.71
Fabricated metal products	8.4	7.2	8.3	7.7	1.01	0.94	0.86	0.93	0.93
Machinery	18.1	27.2	20.5	22.7	0.89	1.20	1.50	1.11	1.35
Nonelectrical machinery	11.1	17.1	10.8	11.5	1.02	1.49	1.54	1.06	1.46
Electrical machinery	7.1	10.1	9.7	11.2	0.73	0.90	1.42	1.15	1.23
Transportation equipment	12.6	12.0	9.8	10.5	1.29	1.14	0.95	1.07	0.88
Instruments	2.5	3.1	2.8	3.7	0.89	0.84	1.24	1.32	0.94
Other manufacturing	18.3	17.7	25.2	25.9	0.73	0.68	0.97	1.03	0.93
Manufacturing less nonelectrical machinery	88.9	82.9	89.2	88.5	1.00	0.94	0.93	0.99	0.94

Table 6-8 Manufacturing Industries Output Shares, Hours Shares, and Relative Productivity Levels, United States, 1973 and 1985

Industry	Output Share		Hours Share		Relative Productivity		1985 Relative to 1973		
	1973	1985	1983	1985	1973	1985	Output Share	Hours Share	Relative Productivity
Total	100.0	100.0	100.0	100.0	1.00	1.00	1.00	1.00	1.00
Food and tobacco	13.1	7.0	9.1	11.4	1.44	0.61	0.53	1.25	0.42
Textiles	4.1	2.8	10.7	6.9	0.39	0.41	0.68	0.64	1.05
Paper	3.5	2.7	2.4	2.3	1.47	1.16	0.77	0.96	0.79
Chemicals	6.5	8.9	3.5	3.2	1.87	2.78	1.37	0.91	1.49
Petroleum	4.8	2.3	0.4	0.4	12.01	5.31	0.48	1.00	0.44
Stone, clay, and glass	6.7	3.2	5.3	4.8	1.26	0.67	0.48	0.91	0.53
Primary metals	14.0	9.8	4.4	3.4	3.15	2.87	0.70	0.77	0.91
Fabricated metal products	7.2	4.4	8.9	8.4	0.81	0.52	0.61	0.94	0.64
Machinery	12.2	33.2	21.2	25.6	0.57	1.29	2.73	1.21	2.25
Nonelectrical machinery	7.7	11.4	10.9	11.3	0.71	1.01	1.48	1.04	1.42
Electrical machinery	4.5	21.8	10.2	14.3	0.43	1.52	4.84	1.40	3.53
Transportation equipment	9.8	10.5	9.7	10.6	1.01	0.98	1.07	1.09	0.97
Instruments	1.3	2.3	2.2	2.4	0.58	0.95	1.77	1.09	1.64
Other manufacturing	16.8	13.0	22.2	20.5	0.76	0.63	0.77	0.92	0.83

percent of the manufacturing average and below all other industries except textiles. In 1985, productivity in the electrical machinery industry was 50 percent above the manufacturing average and above all other industries except chemicals, petroleum, and primary metals.

Germany's manufacturing productivity growth rate was 3.6 percent between 1973 and 1985, some 50 percent above the U.S. rate. All thirteen industries fell within a narrow range. Productivity rose over 2 percent in all industries and the largest average increases were 5 percent in textiles and electrical machinery. However, the category of business machine products, which, as noted, was combined with nonelectrical machinery, had a growth rate of about 12 percent. Output in business machine products more than tripled between 1973 and 1985, rising from 0.9 to 2.6 percent of total manufacturing output. Excluding business machine products, the nonelectrical machinery productivity growth rate was only about 2.5 percent. Plastics and nonferrous metals were the only other industries among the thirty-one available for analysis that had productivity growth rates above 5 percent. Changes in output shares among the thirteen industry groups were substantially less than in the United States or Japan, although the electrical machinery industry's share rose by 25 percent (Table 6-9).

In comparing industry productivity growth rates across countries, Japan had the highest growth rates in eight of the thirteen industries. The Japanese productivity growth rates in chemicals, electrical machinery, and instruments were about triple or more the productivity growth rates recorded by these industries in the United States or Germany. These three industries had rising output shares in all three countries. In the remaining five industries—food, paper, petroleum, stone, clay, and glass products, and fabricated metal products—Germany had the highest productivity growth rates. Output shares in all five of these industries either remained unchanged or fell in all three countries. The United States did have higher rates of productivity growth than Germany in the two industries with the highest U.S. rates of productivity growth, textiles and nonelectrical machinery (Table 6-10).

There appear to be some common industry characteristics across the three countries. Productivity growth rates in the electrical machinery industry are well above the manufacturing average in all three countries. Productivity growth rates in nonelectrical machinery were also well above the manufacturing average in the United States and Japan and in the business machine products component of the German industry. These industries also had the largest increases in output shares in the three countries.

Productivity growth in the textile industry was well above the manufacturing average in the United States and Germany and above the manufacturing average in Japan. In contrast to the machinery industries, however, the higher rates of productivity growth resulted from substantial reductions in labor input shares. The textile industry's share of output remained unchanged in the United States and fell substantially in Japan and Germany.

At the other end, productivity growth rates were well below the manufacturing average or negative in the food industry and in fabricated metal products in all three countries. Fabricated metal products was also among the industries

Table 6-9 Manufacturing Industries Output Shares, Hours Shares, and Relative Productivity Levels, Germany, 1973 and 1985

Industry	Output Share		Hours Share		Relative Productivity		1985 Relative to 1973		
	1973	1985	1973	1985	1973	1985	Output Share	Hours Share	Relative Productivity
Total	100.0	100.0	100.0	100.0	1.00	1.00	1.00	1.00	1.00
Food and tobacco	11.4	11.4	10.5	11.0	1.08	1.03	1.00	1.05	0.95
Textiles	3.0	2.4	4.7	3.1	0.64	0.75	0.80	0.66	1.17
Paper	2.0	2.0	2.3	2.1	0.87	0.95	1.00	0.91	1.09
Chemicals	8.3	9.4	6.3	7.3	1.31	1.29	1.13	1.16	0.98
Petroleum	6.0	5.0	0.5	0.4	11.29	12.13	0.83	0.80	1.08
Stone, clay, and glass	4.7	3.7	5.0	4.0	0.95	0.91	0.79	0.80	0.96
Primary metals	8.3	7.4	9.3	8.3	0.90	0.89	0.89	0.89	1.00
Fabricated metal products	5.8	4.8	6.3	5.9	0.91	0.81	0.83	0.94	0.89
Machinery	23.8	27.0	25.2	26.3	0.95	1.03	1.13	1.04	1.08
Nonelectrical machinery	13.5	14.0	13.5	13.8	1.00	1.02	1.04	1.02	1.02
Electrical machinery	10.4	13.0	11.7	12.5	0.89	1.04	1.25	1.07	1.17
Transportation equipment	10.5	12.8	9.9	12.4	1.05	1.03	1.22	1.25	0.98
Instruments	1.9	2.0	2.1	2.6	0.91	0.78	1.05	1.24	0.87
Other manufacturing	14.2	12.0	17.8	16.3	0.80	0.73	0.85	0.92	0.91

Table 6-10 Differences in Manufacturing Productivity Growth Rates by Industry, Japan and Germany Compared with the United States, 1973–85[a]

Industry	Japan			Germany		
	1973–85	1973–79	1979–85	1973–85	1973–79	1979–85
Total	3.6	4.3	2.8	1.2	2.9	−0.5
Food and tobacco	−3.0	1.7	−7.7	1.4	2.9	−0.2
Textiles	1.1	−1.3	3.6	−0.4	−0.5	−0.4
Paper	2.0	2.5	1.4	2.5	2.6	2.3
Chemicals	7.2	10.7	3.9	1.2	3.0	−0.6
Petroleum	−1.3	−1.6	−0.9	3.9	7.2	0.7
Stone, clay, and glass	−1.3	−1.8	−0.8	1.5	3.5	−0.5
Primary metals	5.7	8.3	3.0	4.1	6.2	2.0
Fabricated metal products	0.3	−0.4	1.0	0.7	3.2	−1.7
Machinery	8.4	10.7	6.1	−0.7	2.2	−3.7
Nonelectrical machinery	3.5	9.0	−2.1	−1.9	3.1	−7.0
Electrical machinery	13.4	13.3	13.6	0.7	0.9	0.5
Transportation equipment	4.3	6.1	2.7	2.0	3.7	0.4
Instruments	8.5	7.0	10.0	0.4	0.0	0.9
Other manufacturing	2.6	1.9	3.2	1.1	2.0	1.0
Manufacturing less nonelectrical machinery	3.8	3.8	3.8	1.7	2.8	0.6

[a]Differences in annual percentage changes: Japan or Germany minus the United States.

with relatively large declines in output in all three countries. Two other industries had below-average productivity gains in all three countries, stone, clay,
and glass products and transportation equipment. However, the transportation
equipment industry was close to the manufacturing average in Japan and both
industries were close to the manufacturing average in Germany.

The 1979–85 Period

As noted earlier, U.S. manufacturing shows a strong rebound in productivity
growth after 1979, whereas productivity growth in Germany slowed further.
Japan also had a lower productivity growth rate in the 1979–87 period than in
the 1973–79 period, but in the period covered by the component industry measures, 1979–85, Japan had a slightly higher rate of productivity growth.

As can be seen in Table 6-11, eight of the thirteen U.S. industry groups had
higher rates of productivity growth in the 1979–85 period. However, one industry accounted for much of the difference in the total. The productivity growth
rate shown for the nonelectrical machinery industry rose from only 0.8 percent
in the 1973–79 period to 10.6 percent in the 1979–85 period. This industry's
output share rose from 12 to 17 percent between 1979 and 1985. According to
a recent study of the Office of Technology Assessment, "More than 100 percent
of that industry's increase was due to the zooming sales, rapidly improving
quality and productivity, and falling real price of computers" (U.S. Congress,
1988, p. 37). The total U.S. manufacturing productivity growth rate went from
1.4 percent in 1973–79 to 3.4 percent in 1979–85. Excluding nonelectrical machinery, the manufacturing productivity growth rate went from 1.5 percent up

Table 6-11 Differences in Manufacturing Productivity Growth
Rates by Industry, United States, Japan, and Germany, 1979–85
Compared with 1973–79[a]

Industry	United States	Japan	Germany
Total	2.0	0.5	−1.4
Food and tobacco	1.8	−7.6	−1.3
Textiles	−2.4	2.5	−2.3
Paper	1.0	−0.1	0.7
Chemicals	−0.4	−7.2	−4.0
Petroleum	0.1	0.8	−6.4
Stone, clay, and glass	1.0	2.0	−3.0
Primary metals	3.1	−2.2	−1.1
Fabricated metal products	2.4	3.8	−2.5
Machinery	5.4	0.8	−0.5
Nonelectrical machinery	9.8	−1.3	−0.3
Electrical machinery	−0.4	−0.1	−0.8
Transportation equipment	1.5	−1.9	−1.8
Instruments	−2.3	0.7	−1.4
Other manufacturing	0.6	1.9	−1.3
Manufacturing less nonelectrical machinery	0.7	0.7	−1.5

[a]Differences in average annual percentage changes: 1979–85 minus 1973–79.

to only 2.2 percent. These figures, excluding nonelectrical machinery, are shown in the bottom row of Table 6-6. Without the computer industry, the 1979–85 productivity growth rate for manufacturing would still be well below the 1960–73 rate of productivity growth, which was 3.2 percent including or excluding nonelectrical machinery. The only other U.S. industries that increased their productivity growth rates in the 1979–85 period more than the total manufacturing average were primary metals and fabricated metal products; however, primary metals had shown negative productivity growth in the 1973–79 period and the fabricated metal products' 1973–79 productivity growth rate was only 0.6 percent. In addition, fabricated metal products is the only industry other than nonelectrical machinery to show a 1979–85 productivity growth rate in excess of the industry's 1960–73 rate. It would appear that the post-1973 productivity slowdown held through 1985 for nearly all manufacturing industries.

Japan's total manufacturing productivity growth rate in the 1979–85 period was 6.2 percent, 0.5 percentage points above the 1973–79 growth rate but well below the 1960–73 productivity growth rate of over 10 percent. Only six of the thirteen industry groups had higher productivity growth rates in the 1979–85 period than in the 1973–79 period. Four industries, including nonelectrical machinery, had lower productivity growth rates than the corresponding U.S. industries. However, the Japanese electrical machinery industry, which includes computer and electronic processing machines in the Japanese classification system, had a productivity growth rate of over 17 percent. If the two machinery industries are combined for greater industrial concordance, the comparative 1979–85 productivity growth rates are 13.8 percent for Japan and 7.7 percent for the United States.

As noted earlier, U.S. manufacturing output growth in the 1980s, and consequently productivity growth, would be lower if measured in current rather than 1982 relative prices because of the sharp decline in BEA's computer price index. The U.S. price index for the total nonelectrical machinery industry fell 27 percent between 1979 and 1985 and 38 percent between 1982 and 1985. The Japanese implicit price deflators are based on 1980 relative prices. The deflator for electrical machinery fell 41 percent between 1979 and 1985, whereas the deflator for all other manufacturing industries fell 4 percent. It appears that the Japanese manufacturing productivity growth rate would also be less if measured in 1985 rather than 1980 relative prices.

Germany's 1979–85 total manufacturing productivity growth rate fell to 2.9 percent and twelve of the thirteen industry groups had lower rates than in the 1973–79 period. The only exception was the paper industry. At the thirty-one–industry level of detail, five industries show improved rates of productivity growth in the 1979–85 period. Business machine products is not among the five, but that industry still had an 11 percent productivity growth rate. Six of the thirteen industry groups as well as total manufacturing had lower 1979–85 productivity growth rates than the corresponding U.S. industries. Excluding the nonelectrical machinery industry from the U.S.–Germany comparison, Germany's 1979–85 productivity growth rate exceeds the U.S. rate, 2.8 percent versus 2.2 percent.

CONCLUSIONS

The first series of major findings concerns total manufacturing labor productivity and unit labor costs in twelve countries:

1. Over the period 1960–87, the United States had the lowest labor productivity growth rate among the twelve countries compared.
2. All twelve countries experienced productivity growth-rate slowdowns in the 1973–87 period. The productivity slowdowns were more substantial in most of the foreign countries than in the United States, but their pre-1973 rates had been higher.
3. The U.S. productivity growth rate appears to have rebounded to the pre-1973 rate in the 1979–87 period. The United Kingdom is the only other country to match or exceed its pre-1973 rate of increase since 1979. Most of the other countries, including Japan, France, and Germany, had even lower productivity growth rates in the 1979–87 period than in 1973–79.
4. Measured in national currency terms, the United States had the smallest average annual increases in unit labor costs over the full 1960–87 period, but Japan, Germany, and the Benelux countries had smaller average increases in the 1973–87 period.
5. Measured in U.S. dollar terms, U.S. unit labor costs rose less than Japanese or European unit labor costs in the 1973–79 period, but Japanese unit labor costs fell in the period 1979–85 and all of the European countries had negative rates of gain because of the strong appreciation of the U.S. dollar.
6. U.S. unit labor costs declined between 1985 and 1987 and the value of the U.S. dollar fell sharply. Consequently, measured on a trade-weighted basis relative to the other eleven countries, U.S. unit labor costs, as of 1987, were below the previous low point reached in 1978.

The next conclusion concerns shift effects for the United States, Japan, and Germany. Relative shifts in labor inputs among component industries moderated the improvement in the U.S. total manufacturing productivity growth rate in the 1979–85 period, compared with 1973–79. Shift effects reduced the further falloff in Germany's productivity growth rate and raised Japan's 1979–85 productivity growth rate.

The final series of conclusions is about labor productivity in thirteen component manufacturing industries in the United States, Japan, and Germany:

1. The post-1973 productivity slowdown was quite pervasive across industries in both the United States and Germany.
2. Japan had the highest 1973–85 productivity growth rates in eight of the thirteen industry groups, and in three industries—chemicals, electrical machinery, and instruments—the Japanese rates were about triple or more than the U.S. and German rates.
3. The apparent rebound in the U.S. manufacturing productivity growth rate after 1979 is largely attributable to the computer industry, which is

classified in nonelectrical machinery. The post-1973 productivity slow-down held through 1985 for nearly all other manufacturing industries.

4. Excluding the nonelectrical machinery industry, Germany had a higher rather than lower 1979–85 productivity growth rate than the United States and the U.S.–Japan differential is wider.

REFERENCES

Baily, M. N., and R. J. Gordon. 1988. "Measurement Issues, the Productivity Slow-down, and the Explosion of Computer Power." *Brookings Papers on Economic Activity*, No. 2.

De Leeuw, F., and R. P. Parker. 1988. "Gross Product by Industry: Comments on Recent Criticisms." *Survey of Current Business* (July), pp. 132–33.

Denison, E. F. 1989. *Estimates of Productivity Change by Industry: An Evaluation and an Alternative*. Washington, D.C.: Brookings Institution.

Gullickson, W., and M. J. Harper. 1987. "Multifactor Productivity in U.S. Manufacturing, 1949–83." *Monthly Labor Review* (October), 18–28.

Mark, J. A., and W. H. Waldorf. 1983. "Multifactor Productivity: A New BLS Measure." *Monthly Labor Review* (December), 3–15.

Mishel, L. 1988. *Manufacturing Numbers: How Inaccurate Statistics Conceal U.S. Industrial Decline*. Washington, D.C.: Economic Policy Institute.

Neef, A., and E. Dean. 1984. "Comparative Changes in Labor Productivity and Unit Labor Costs by Manufacturing Industry: United States and Western Europe." Paper presented at the American Enterprise Institute Conference on Interindustry Differences in Productivity Growth, Washington, D.C., October 11–12.

U.S. Congress, Office of Technology Assessment. 1988. *Paying the Bill: Manufacturing and America's Trade Deficit*. Report No. OTA-ITE-390. Washington, D.C.: U.S. Government Printing Office.

U.S. Department of Labor, Bureau of Labor Statistics. 1983. *Trends in Multifactor Productivity, 1948–81*. Bulletin 2178. Washington, D.C.: U.S. Government Printing Office.

U.S. Department of Labor, Bureau of Labor Statistics. 1988. Productivity Measures, 1987. News Release, September 30.

7

Intercountry Changes in Productivity in the Manufacturing Sector of Five OECD Countries, 1963–86

KLAUS CONRAD

If one measures the economic performance of an individual country, one can find that the economic performance since World War II outstrips any earlier period in the preceding half century. In the case of the United Kingdom, for instance, the postwar record through 1967 was one of success, not failure. But when one compares Britain to other Organization for Economic Cooperation and Development (OECD) countries or to Japan, which accomplished economic miracles, the U.K. performance appears inadequate. The U.K. growth rate of GDP between 1960 and 1980 was only 65 percent of the average rate for member states of the OECD. Several other measures of economic performance indicate that since the midsixties the rank order of economic success has changed drastically. Comparisons of levels of GDP per capita measured at current exchange rates evoke the impression that West Germany moved ahead of the United States, that Britain was overtaken in the early seventies by France, but not by Italy (see Caves and Krause, 1980). From economic theory one would expect that those countries starting at the lowest level of per capita income would make the greatest advance. Japan did, but the performance of both Italy and the United Kingdom was disappointing by this criterion.

In this chapter the United States, the United Kingdom, France, Italy, and West Germany are compared in order to determine whether the relatively good or bad performance of some countries stems largely from their productivity growth or slowdown, or from an adjustment in factor intensities. Such a finding would point to a policy approach to improve industrial relations by increasing individual incentives, by improving the allocation of capital in avoiding, for instance, building large-scale plants (in which labor relations are usually at their worst), by reducing constraints on adaptability, and the like.

The rate of change of differences in productivity between any two countries is calculated as the relative difference in the output level minus the share-weighted sum of the relative difference of input levels (Jorgenson and Nishimizu, 1978). This construction is analogous to the distinction Solow (1957) drew between output growth attributable to movements along a (here joint) production surface (input growth) and output growth attributable to shifts in the production surface when going from one country to another (technology gap). The terms productivity gap and technology gap are frequently used synonymously. This correspondence assumes, however, that production is continuously technically efficient in countries to be compared. If this assumption is relaxed, then the rate of difference in productivity can be decomposed into the rate of difference in technology and the rate of difference in efficiency. If such a decomposition is possible, it enables one to attribute an observed relative difference in output to movements along a path on or beneath the common production surface (difference in inputs), movements toward or away from the production surface (differences in efficiency), and shifts of the production surface (difference in technology). The distinction between them is important because they are fundamentally different phenomena with different sources, and so different policies may be required to address them. We take these issues into account by adjusting differences in productivity by variations in capacity utilization between countries. To accomplish this we will determine the steady-state levels of inputs and outputs for each country and then base our intracountry comparison on these long-run equilibrium levels. Hence we will measure differences in technology from input–output combinations which are located exactly on the production surface. If now a former productivity gap has disappeared, there is no technology gap. The measured gap, based on observed input–output data, has to be attributed to inefficiencies due to underutilization of capacity. The existence of such an output gap between potential and observed output would suggest the need for more stimulative demand management along well-known Keynesian lines. A technology gap, however, is a more serious problem, which cannot easily be solved in the short run.

The first section of this chapter presents the methodology and the theoretical foundation for measuring productivity gaps based on a temporary disequilibrium due to the quasi-fixity of the capital stock. A method to calculate an equilibrium productivity gap based on the steady-state levels of inputs and outputs is presented. The following section deals with the purchasing-power problem and the next presents productivity and technology gaps relative to those of the United States for four main European OECD countries. The econometric model consistent with our choice of Törnqvist index numbers is then introduced, the parameter estimates are interpreted and some hints to the source of the catching-up process of some countries are given. In the final section the results are summarized.

THE METHODOLOGY OF MEASURING PRODUCTIVITY AND TECHNOLOGY GAPS

Let us begin by considering the concept of the primal and dual measurement of productivity gaps.[1] Following Jorgenson and Nishimizu (1978), the methodology used here is based on a constant return to scale (CRTS) joint production function for the output of the manufacturing sector in each of the OECD countries:[2]

$$Y = f(K, L, E, F, D, t) \qquad (7\text{-}1)$$

where Y denotes the level of output and K the capital stock; the variable inputs are labor L, electricity energy E, and nonelecctric fuels F; t is time; and D is a vector of dummy variables equal to one for the corresponding country and zero otherwise. As we express levels of output, inputs, and total factor productivity (TFP) relative to the United States, there is no dummy variable for the United States in the vector D. With P_L, P_E, and P_F as input prices for L, E, and F, respectively, variable costs are $\text{VC} = P_L \cdot L + P_E \cdot E + P_F \cdot F$. Total costs are $\text{TC} = \text{VC} + P_K K$ where P_K is the ex-ante rental or user cost of capital.

Under the assumption of perfect competition and long-run equilibrium, the difference in productivity between any OECD country C and the United States (U) as the base country, say $w_{C,U}$, can be calculated as[3]

$$w_{C,U} = \frac{d \ln Y}{dD_C} - w_K \frac{d \ln K}{dD_C} - \sum w_i \frac{d \ln v_i}{dD_C} \qquad (7\text{-}2)$$

where the weights w_i are output elasticities assumed to be equal to cost shares obtained by logarithmically differentiating Equation 7-1 with respect to the input quantities $(v_1, v_2, v_3) = (L, E, F)$. For capital, for example,

$$w_K = \frac{\partial \ln Y}{\partial \ln K} = \frac{P_K \cdot K}{\text{TC}} \qquad (7\text{-}3)$$

The difference in productivity, or the productivity gap, is the relative difference in output between countries, holding factor input and time constant. The relative output levels produced by the industry at the same input level is a convenient measure of these relative productivity levels. Since we do not observe the industries at the same input level, the following approximate interpretation is useful. The value $w_{C,U}$ is the relative difference in output between country C and the United States that would result if each country were using the geometric mean amounts of inputs.

Given a well-behaved joint production function, we can obtain the corresponding joint cost function:

$$\text{TC} = \text{TC} \, (Y, P_K, P_L, P_E, P_F, D, t) \qquad (7\text{-}4)$$

The difference in cost efficiency (the cost gap $W_{C,U}$) is the relative difference in total cost between countries, holding factor prices, output, and time constant:

$$W_{C,U} \equiv \frac{\partial \ln \text{TC}}{\partial D_C} = \frac{d \ln \text{TC}}{dD_C} - \sum w_i \frac{d \ln P_i}{dD_C}$$

$$- \frac{d \ln Y}{dD_C}, \qquad i = K, L, E, F \quad (7\text{-}5)$$

The cost gap measure is the relative difference in cost if, in a given year, U.S. output Y will be produced in country C with U.S. input remunerations, reflecting marginal productivity of inputs in the U.S. manufacturing sector. Similarly, $W_{C,U}$ is the relative difference in average cost between country C and the United States that would result if producers in the two countries each faced the geometric mean of factor prices. The following relationship holds:

$$-W_{C,U} = w_{C,U} \tag{7-6}$$

(Conrad, 1987). If the productivity gap $w_{C,U}$ is negative, that means that had country C and the United States both been using the geometric mean of inputs, country C would have produced $w_{C,U}$ percent less output. Similarly, if faced with a geometric mean of factor prices, average cost in country C would have been $W_{C,U}$ percent higher; country C has a productivity gap.

We next drop the assumption of immediate adjustment of inputs and incorporate short-run fixity of capital in our measures of productivity gaps. In this approach, we replace the total cost function (Equation 7-4) by the short-run or variable cost function

$$VC = VC\ (Y,K;P_L,P_E,P_F,D,t) \tag{7-7}$$

This function represents short-run demand patterns of the firm. The optimal demand for variable input $i = L,\ E,\ F$ can be determined from Shephard's lemma ($\partial\ VC/\partial\ P_L = L$) and similarly for E and F.

In addition, one can calculate the shadow cost of the quasi-fixed input and compare it to the corresponding ex-ante price P_K:[4]

$$R_K \equiv \frac{\partial\ VC(\cdot)}{\partial K} > 0 \tag{7-8}$$

where R_K is the shadow value, which is endogenous in this context.

The concept of the variable cost function and its shadow value of capital can be used to derive a cost-side productivity gap measure, similar to the derivation of the standard productivity gap measure in Equation 7-5 but consistent with short-run or temporary disequilibrium situations. To see this, recall from Equation 7-6 that, with all inputs variable and CRTS the standard productivity gap, defined from the cost side, can also be measured from the primal (quantity) side by

$$-\frac{\partial\ \ln TC}{\partial D_C} \equiv w_{C,U} = \frac{d\ \ln Y}{dD_C} - \frac{P_K \cdot K}{TC}\frac{d\ \ln K}{dD_C} - \sum \frac{P_i v_i}{TC}\frac{d\ \ln v_i}{dD_C} \tag{7-9}$$

However, with capital as a quasi-fixed input, Equation 7-9 must be modified somewhat. The cost-side productivity gap can be measured again from the quantity side, but this time the formula is

$$-\frac{\partial\ \ln TC}{\partial\ D_C} = w^0_{C,U} = \frac{VC + R_K \cdot K}{TC}\frac{d\ \ln Y}{dD_C}$$

$$-\frac{R_K \cdot K}{TC}\frac{d\ \ln K}{dD_C} - \sum_i \frac{P_i \cdot v_i}{TC}\frac{d\ \ln v_i}{dD_C} \tag{7-10}$$

where $TC = VC\ (Y;K,P_L,P_E,P_F,D,t) + P_K \cdot K$. This is the observed measure of the productivity gap, given short-run disequilibrium in the two countries in question.[5] Compared to Equation 7-9, capital has been weighted by its shadow cost share. To determine this weight, the shadow value R_K can be calculated as an ex-post return to the quasi-fixed factor K. From Euler's theorem,

$$\frac{\partial \text{ VC}}{\partial Y} Y + \frac{\partial \text{ VC}}{\partial K} K = \text{VC}, \quad \text{or} \quad PY - R_K \cdot K = \text{VC} \qquad (7\text{-}11)$$

We next wish to determine a true productivity gap, adjusted for the effect of disequilibrium in different countries. We first note that in case of $R_K = P_K$, the temporary equilibrium is a long-run equilibrium; if $R_K < P_K$, too much capital has been invested (given the observed Y); if $R_K > P_K$, the capital stock has been overutilized.

An obvious procedure would be to apply methods suggested in the literature on productivity measurement. There, a cost-based measure of capacity utilization (CU) in terms of shadow costs (SC) to total costs, that is,

$$\text{CU}_C = \frac{\text{SC}}{\text{TC}} = \frac{\text{VC} + R_K \cdot K}{\text{VC} + P_K \cdot K} \qquad (7\text{-}12)$$

has been used for appropriate adjustment of the standard TFP growth measure from cyclical variations in CU (see Berndt and Fuss, 1986; Morrison, 1985). In our case, the temporary equilibrium gap $w^o_{C.U}$, has to be divided by CU_C:

$$w'_{C.U} = \frac{w^o_{C.U}}{\text{SC/TC}} = \frac{d \ln Y}{dD_C} - \frac{R_K K}{\text{SC}} \frac{d \ln K}{dD_C} - \sum_i \frac{P_i v_i}{\text{SC}} \frac{d \ln v_i}{dD_C} \qquad (7\text{-}13)$$

This adjusted difference in productivity differs from the full equilibrium measure $w_{C.U}$ in Equation 7-9 by its weights, which are now based on the shadow rather than the ex-ante price of capital. This adjusted gap is based on a full equilibrium at shadow prices rather than at market prices of the fixed factors. An excess capacity in country C due to short-run fixity of K is now interpreted as excess capacity due to inefficiency in country C. This so-called adjusted measure w' is nothing but the gap (or TFP) measured by those researchers who define the endogenous ex-post price R_K derived from Equation 7-11 to be the expected ex-ante price P_K (e.g., Jorgenson and Nishimizu, 1978). We conclude that the proposed CU_C adjustment for variations in capacity utilization leads to the same measure (w') as the conventional measure, but the latter is based on the assumption that the temporary equilibrium (i.e., short-run disequilibrium) is a long-run equilibrium that is partly at shadow prices.

A different way to look at the capacity utilization adjustment is to assume that there is no gap and all inputs are quasi-fixed. Now let us assume that there is a shock on the demand side in country C and demand drops 50 percent. Since inputs cannot change in the short run, the relative productivity level in country C compared to the base country is $\exp(w') = \exp(-0.5) = 0.6$. No adjustment of this cyclical variation in capacity utilization can be recognized when measuring the gap by w'. We only recognize that because $w^o = w' \cdot \text{SC/TC}$, the unadjusted gap w^o would be somewhat smaller, so that $0.6 < \exp(w^o) < 1$. In principle, there should be no gap at all, as underutilization of the quasi-fixed inputs is due to their short-run fixity and is not a problem of a technology gap.

A reasonable objective, therefore, is to eliminate the disequilibrium effect from the computed gap.

To measure a pure technology gap, purged from the difference in capacity utilization between the countries, we measure the distance between the surface of the production frontiers of any two countries after adjustment for differences in input levels. For this purpose we need to find the steady-state input–output levels. To get them we note that in the case of a short-run disequilibrium, the desired capital stock K^* to produce the observed output level Y can be determined by replacing the shadow price R_K in Equation 7-8 by the ex-ante capital price P_K (see Berndt and Hesse, 1986; Morrison, 1985):

$$P_K = -\frac{\partial \text{ VC}}{\partial K}(Y,K^*,\cdot) \tag{7-14}$$

This condition is the first-order condition of two minimization problems. It is an envelope condition from minimizing $\text{TC} = \text{VC}(Y, K) + P_K \cdot K$ with respect to K. It is also the first-order condition[6] for the minimization of total average costs TC/Y with respect to Y. Hence Equation 7-14 can also be solved for the potential output Y^*, given the observed capital stock K:[7]

$$P_K = -\frac{\partial \text{VC}}{\partial K}(Y^*,K,\cdot) \tag{7-15}$$

As a measure of capacity utilization, one can choose either the index $\text{CU}_Y = Y/Y^*$ or the index $\text{CU}_K = K^*/K$. Both indexes are less than one in the under-utilization case because in that situation we observe $Y < Y^*$ and $K > K^*$. They coincide, by the way, in the case of CRTS and one quasi-fixed factor.

Next we decompose the productivity gap into the efficiency gap and the technology gap. To obtain the technology gap, we calculate the gap on the base of K^* instead of K with K^* from Equation 7-14.

Thus our intercountry comparison is based on observed output Y, produced from capacity capital K^*. Therefore, the calculations will be based on $\text{VC}^* = \text{VC}(Y,K^*,\cdot)$ and $\text{TC}^* = \text{VC}(Y,K^*,\cdot) + P_K K^*$. The corresponding production function is $Y = f(v^*,K^*,\cdot)$, where $v^* = (L^*, E^*, F^*)$ is the vector of variable inputs consistent with $\Sigma_i P_i v^*_i = \text{VC}(Y,K^*,\cdot)$. The following long-run difference in productivity can be derived, based on fully utilized inputs:

$$-\frac{\partial \ln \text{TC}^*}{\partial D_C} = w^*_{C,U} = \frac{d \ln Y}{dD_C} - \sum_{i=L,F,E} \frac{p_i v^*_i}{\text{TC}^*}\frac{d \ln v^*_i}{dD_C}$$
$$-\frac{P_K \cdot K^*}{\text{TC}^*}\frac{d \ln K^*}{dD_C} \tag{7-16}$$

As $K^* = \text{CU}_K \cdot K$, the magnitude of CU_K will have an impact on $w^*_{C,U}$.

Our method requires the specification and estimation of a restricted cost function.[8] We first have to estimate for each country a standard translog system, based on a translog restricted cost function and necessary conditions for producers' behavior with respect to the variable inputs. We then have to solve Equation 7-14 for K^*, that is,

$$P_K \cdot K^*/VC^* = \frac{\partial \ln VC}{\partial \ln K} (Y, K^*, \cdot)$$

by adding the estimated translog cost function $VC^* = \exp[\ln VC(Y, K^*, \cdot)]$ to this condition. Finally, given the estimated parameters of the variable cost function, we can derive the imputed demand v^* for v in the long run, using the variable cost shares:

$$\frac{p_i v_i^*}{VC^*} = \hat{\alpha}_i + \sum \hat{\gamma}_{ij} \ln P_j + \hat{\zeta}_{Yi} \ln Y/K^* + \hat{\zeta}_{ti} t \qquad (7\text{-}17)$$

With $VC^* = VC(Y, K^*, \cdot)$ calculated from the estimated variable cost function, the quantities v_i^* can be derived from Equation 7-17. This enables us to compute $w_{C.U}^*$. Now we realize that this measure is zero if output and variable inputs do not differ between countries, because in this case capacity capital also does not differ.

To summarize, our measure $w_{C.U}^*$ is based on the argument that productivity gaps should be calculated on the basis of a fully employed capital stock K^* required to produce observed output Y. This procedure avoids an interpretation of disequilibrium due to short-run fixity of capital in the business cycle as a technological inefficiency.

INDEX NUMBERS AND PURCHASING-POWER PARITIES

We approximated the continuous Divisia indexes in Equation 7-10, 7-13, and 7-16 by the discrete Törnqvist index. In a multicountry (multilateral) comparison, however, we cannot use the two-country (bilateral) index as this index is not base-country invariant. Bilateral indexes do not satisfy the circularity condition that all pairs of comparisons should pass the following circularity condition for the differences in productivity relative to the base country the United States:

$$w_{I.U} = w_{I.G} + w_{G.U}$$

for countries I, G, and U. To satisfy the circularity condition, we used the multilateral Törnqvist index, derived by Caves, Christensen, and Diewert (1982).

A crucial point in international comparison studies is the construction of multilaterally comparable data. The simplest technique, the conversion of national currencies to a common currency using market exchange rates, is associated with well-known problems. Our international comparison required purchasing-power parities (PPPs) for manufacturing output and for the four inputs electricity, nonelectric fuel, labor, and capital. All quantities were measured in constant-dollar values, obtained from national data by the definition $Y^C =$

$Y(C)/PPP_Y(C)$, $L^C = L(C)/PPP_L(C)$, . . . , where $L(C)$ and $Y(C)$ are labor input and output quantities in constant national currency units of country C; $PPP_L(C)$ and $PPP_Y(C)$ are the PPPs for labor and output in national currency units per dollar (i.e., francs/\$, lire/\$, £/\$, and DM/\$). As price times quantity on a dollar base should be equal to the nominal value in national currency units, we require, as a factor reversal test, $P_i^C = P_i(C) \cdot PPP_i(C)$, $i = Y, L, E, F, K$, where $P_i(C)$ are price indexes obtained from the national accounts of country C.

As one alternative we used the PPPs for 1975, published by Kravis, Heston, and Summers (1982), and constructed PPP indexes for other years by "chaining" them to the 1975 base-year PPP. PPPs for energy and investment goods can be taken directly from Kravis, Heston, and Summers; a PPP for manufacturing output had to be constructed. As the OECD publishes a PPP for manufacturing output, we employ an arithmetic mean for 1975 based on the PPPs of Kravis and the OECD (see Table 7-1). To obtain PPPs for labor we divide national labor cost per hour in manufacturing in 1975 by the U.S. hourly cost of labor in 1975. To obtain PPPs for capital input in 1975, we take the ratio of the price of capital input (see Jorgenson and Nishimizu, 1978). Rewriting the ratio of the user cost of capital yields

$$PPP_K(C)_{75} = PPP_I(C)_{75} \frac{R_K(C)_{75}}{R_K(U)_{75}} \qquad (7\text{-}18)$$

where PPP_I is the PPP for new investment goods. The ex-post rates of return for OECD's manufacturing industries can be calculated from OECD sources given in Berndt and Hesse (1986). Given base-year PPPs, time series of PPPs have been constructed by

$$PPP_i(C) = PPP_i(C)_{75} [P_i(C)/P_i(U)], \qquad i = Y,L,E,F \qquad (7\text{-}19)$$

The PPP formula has not been employed for all inputs because the change in the PPPs has to obey the following Divisia index formula:

$$\frac{d \ln PPP_Y}{dT} = \sum w_i \frac{d \ln PPP_i}{dT} \qquad (7\text{-}20)$$

(see Conrad, 1985, 1987). If this condition is satisfied, then the calculation data for the change in TFP will be independent of national currency or dollar notation.

For our five-country comparison we used the data set provided by E. Berndt and D. Hesse. This data set ends in 1981 and had to be extended up to 1986. We followed the detailed description given in Berndt and Hesse (1986) for our data extension.

DESCRIPTIVE EMPIRICAL RESULTS

Table 7-2 lists some economic indicators that provide information on the relative economic performance of the manufacturing industry in four OECD countries relative to U.S. industry. For each of the four $C-U$ comparisons, the first

Table 7-1 Purchasing-Power Parities for Output, Labor, Capital, and Aggregated Energy, 1975

	PPP for Output			PPP for Energy[a]	PPP for Labor[c]	PPP for Capital	
	Kravis[a]	OECD	Exchange Rate[b]			Investment[a]	Ex-Post[d] Price of Capital
France (francs/$)	4.69	4.99	4.29	7.71	3.92	5.01	0.12
Italy (lire/$)	582	525	653	802	542	639	0.06
United Kingdom (£/$)	0.406	0.377	0.45	0.542	0.26	0.522	0.053
Germany (DW$)	2.81	3.02	2.46	4.24	2.76	2.86	0.11

[a]Kravis, Heston, and R. Summers (1982), Table 6-3.

[b]OECD National Accounts, 1960–83, Part V, p. 123.

[c]Yearbook of Labor Statistics, Geneva: ILO, 1984, Table 22.

[d]OECD, Flows and Stocks of Fixed Capital, 1955–1980. For U.S. manufacturing it is 0.13.

Table 7-2 Productivity Gap and Relative Marginal Productivities

Year	France—United States				Germany—United States				Italy—United States				United Kingdom—United States			
	Gap	RMPL	RMPK	RMPE	Gap	RMPL	RMPK	RMPE	Gap	RMPL	RMPK	RMPE	Gap	RMPL	RMPK	RMPE
1963	-0.52	0.51	2.41	1.79	-0.35	0.59	2.62	2.03	-0.57	0.58	2.02	2.16	-0.46	0.5	1.1	1.8
1972	-0.25	0.67	1.41	1.95	-0.16	0.79	1.4	1.75	-0.35	0.79	0.86	1.58	-0.36	0.59	0.75	1.7
1980	0.03	0.97	0.67	1.29	0.04	1.04	0.77	1.05	-0.10	0.88	0.66	1.31	-0.30	0.64	0.70	0.98
1986	-0.08	0.91	0.80	1.15	-0.04	0.98	0.98	0.95	-0.16	0.93	0.51	1.47	-0.31	0.64	0.82	0.75

column shows the difference in productivity of country C relative to the United States for four selected years. This gap is $w^o_{C,U}$ under the short-run disequilibrium as assumed in Equation 7-10. If $w^o_{C,U}$ is negative, country C has a productivity disadvantage; if $w^o_{C,U}$ is positive, it has a productivity advantage. To determine the actual gap, one has to calculate $\exp(w^o) - 1$.

Columns 2 to 4 give an economic interpretation of observable changes of PPPs over time in terms of unobservable changes in relative marginal productivities of labor (RMPL), capital (RMPK), and energy (RMPE). To interpret the PPPs in terms of marginal productivities (MP), we employ the necessary conditions for producer equilibrium: $P_i = P_Y \cdot f_{v_i} (v,K,D,t)$. If we divide the necessary condition of country C's industry by the necessary condition of the U.S. industry, we obtain

$$P_i(C)/P_i(U) = P_Y(C)/P_Y(U) \frac{f_{v_{(i)}} (\cdot, D_C = 1)}{f_{v_{(i)}} (\cdot, D_C = 0)} \qquad (7\text{-}21)$$

If we then denote the ratio of MPs in Equation 7-21 by RMP, we can interpret observed changes in PPPs as a result of deviation or equalization in relative MPs in both countries:

$$PPP_i(C)/PPP_Y(C) = RMP_i(C,U), \qquad i = K,L,E,F \qquad (7\text{-}22)$$

For $RMP_i > 1$, the MP of input i is higher in country C's industry than in the U.S. industry; for $RMP_i < 1$, the MP of i is lower in country C. Our four-country–U.S. comparison reveals a productivity disadvantage for all European industries in the sixties and seventies. French and German manufacturing, however, had caught up in 1980 but lost ground again in the early 1980s. In these years of the Reagan administration, our four European countries show again a disadvantage in technology, whereas the United Kingdom has at least held its gap to the United States unchanged.

In 1963, marginal productivity of labor (MPL) was about twice as high in U.S. manufacturing as it was in the European industries. Except for the United Kingdom, we observe an equalization in the MPL over time. Considering capital, we observe a relatively high marginal productivity of capital (MPK) for French, German, and Italian manufacturing in the sixties. Due to rapid capital accumulation in French and German industries, the high difference in MPK vanished over time. This can be explained by the marginal productivity theory. Since 1975, user costs of capital (ex-post rates of return) have been lower in European than in U.S. manufacturing. This influences the PPP of capital downward and increases the capital stock of European countries, in dollar notation. The marginal productivity of energy (MPE) does not differ much between countries. In the early sixties MPE was relatively high in the European countries, but it shows a tendency for equalization.

Table 7-3 lists time series of our three measures of productivity gaps for each country relative to the United States. The first column gives the measure $w'_{C,U}$ for an economy in an equilibrium at (shadow) prices. The measure $w^o_{C,U}$ under a short-run disequilibrium, with capital as a quasi-fixed input, is given in the second column. In the third column, the long-run measure $w^*_{C,U}$ is given,

Table 7-3 Productivity Gaps, Under Short-Run Disequilibrium and Long-Run Equilibrium

Year	France—United States			Germany—United States				Italy—United States				United Kingdom—United States				U.S.
	$\dot{w}_{C,U}$	$w^*_{C,U}$	CU_K^a	$\dot{w}_{C,U}$	$w^{\circ}_{C,U}$	$w^*_{C,U}$	CU_K^a	$\dot{w}_{C,U}$	$w^{\circ}_{C,U}$	$w^*_{C,U}$	CU_K^a	$\dot{w}_{C,U}$	$w^{\circ}_{C,U}$	$w^*_{C,U}$	CU_K^a	CU_K^a
1963	−0.52	−0.45	0.97	−0.34	−0.35	−0.26	1.01	−0.58	−0.57	−0.54	0.72	−0.46	−0.46	−0.40	0.85	1.18
1964	−0.49	−0.41	0.99	−0.30	−0.31	−0.23	1.01	−0.58	−0.57	−0.50	0.66	−0.41	−0.42	−0.38	0.90	1.21
1965	−0.47	−0.38	0.97	−0.29	−0.31	−0.21	0.97	−0.53	−0.53	−0.46	0.66	−0.42	−0.44	−0.37	0.89	1.24
1966	−0.41	−0.34	0.98	−0.28	−0.29	−0.18	0.9	−0.48	−0.48	−0.42	0.67	−0.42	−0.43	−0.36	0.86	1.23
1967	−0.35	−0.31	0.96	−0.21	−0.22	−0.16	0.88	−0.43	−0.42	−0.38	0.70	−0.40	−0.40	−0.35	0.83	1.14
1968	−0.30	−0.28	0.97	−0.17	−0.18	−0.14	0.95	−0.39	−0.38	−0.34	0.72	−0.36	−0.37	−0.34	0.85	1.13
1969	−0.29	−0.25	0.99	−0.12	−0.12	−0.12	1.0	−0.36	−0.35	−0.30	0.71	−0.37	−0.36	−0.34	0.83	1.06
1970	−0.24	−0.22	0.97	−0.11	−0.10	−0.09	0.94	−0.33	−0.30	−0.26	0.68	−0.35	−0.33	−0.35	0.80	0.96
1971	−0.29	−0.18	0.96	−0.15	−0.15	−0.07	0.88	−0.38	−0.35	−0.23	0.65	−0.38	−0.36	−0.34	0.78	0.96
1972	−0.25	−0.16	0.97	−0.16	−0.16	−0.06	0.89	−0.38	−0.35	−0.18	0.66	−0.39	−0.36	−0.33	0.78	1.01
1973	−0.25	−0.14	0.97	−0.16	−0.15	−0.04	0.88	−0.35	−0.33	−0.14	0.68	−0.38	−0.35	−0.33	0.78	1.07
1974	−0.15	−0.10	0.93	−0.08	−0.07	−0.03	0.81	−0.24	−0.21	−0.12	0.61	−0.37	−0.31	−0.33	0.68	0.96
1975	−0.11	−0.09	0.87	−0.04	−0.04	−0.03	0.78	−0.30	−0.25	−0.13	0.53	−0.39	−0.31	−0.34	0.65	0.85
1976	−0.09	−0.07	0.89	−0.02	−0.02	−0.02	0.84	−0.27	−0.23	−0.06	0.51	−0.40	−0.32	−0.35	0.65	0.92
1977	−0.08	−0.07	0.88	−0.03	−0.03	−0.02	0.88	−0.30	−0.25	−0.02	0.48	−0.38	−0.32	−0.30	0.68	0.94
1978	−0.05	−0.07	0.87	−0.03	−0.03	−0.01	0.87	−0.30	−0.25	0.02	0.49	−0.39	−0.33	−0.29	0.66	0.92
1979	−0.01	−0.06	0.87	0.01	0.0	0.01	0.81	−0.22	−0.19	0.05	0.51	−0.41	−0.33	−0.30	0.66	0.88
1980	0.05	−0.07	0.81	0.05	0.04	0.01	0.75	−0.13	−0.10	0.07	0.51	−0.41	−0.30	−0.31	0.59	0.78
1981	0.05	−0.08	0.75	0.02	0.01	0.04	0.66	−0.13	−0.10	0.05	0.5	−0.42	−0.30	−0.30	0.54	0.73
1982	0.03	0.01		−0.02	−0.02			−0.14	−0.11			−0.41	−0.32			
1983	−0.01	−0.01		−0.02	−0.02			−0.17	−0.14			−0.37	−0.29			
1984	−0.04	−0.04		−0.04	−0.04			−0.15	−0.13			−0.39	−0.32			
1985	−0.08	−0.07		−0.04	−0.04			−0.17	−0.15			−0.39	−0.33			
1986	−0.09	−0.08		−0.05	−0.04			−0.18	−0.16			−0.37	−0.31			

[a]CU_K indexes from Berndt and Hesse (1986), Table 2.

whereby the measurement for a technology gap is based on the steady-state levels of output and inputs.

Hence, $w'_{C,U}$ is based on the assumption that the industry is in equilibrium, whereby all observed inputs have been interpreted as an efficient input combination to produce the observed output. On the contrary, $w^o_{C,U}$ is based on a short-run disequilibrium associated with the business cycle. In $w^o_{C,U}$ capital is fixed in the short run, whereas in $w^*_{C,U}$ we employ the capacity capital stock K^*, required to produce the observed output Y, for measuring true technology gaps. This measure ends in 1981, the last year of the observation period in Berndt and Hesse (1986). An extension required either a projection of the steady-state vector (K^*,v^*) based on the fitted translog system or a new estimation of the translog system for each country with a data set running to 1986, neither of which was feasible for this chapter.

We begin by comparing the three alternative measures of productivity gaps over the 1963–70 sample and find hardly any striking differences. Let us take, as an example, the year 1970. If the United States and France had used the geometric mean amounts of inputs, output in France would be 26 percent lower, or, seen from the cost side, average cost would be 26 percent higher. For Germany, the corresponding figure is 11 percent, for Italy 33 percent, and for the United Kingdom 35 percent. Under a temporary disequilibrium, the measure $w^o_{C,U}$ is (-0.24, -0.10, -0.30, -0.33) for (F, G, I, UK); under a long-run equilibrium, the measure $w'_{C,U}$ is (-0.22, -0.09, -0.26, -0.35). The reason for the small differencce between $w'_{C,U}$ and $w^o_{C,U}$ in the sixties is that the cost consequences of disequilibrium were very small (see Berndt and Hesse, 1986, Table 4). For the period 1971–81, however, the difference $(P_K - R_K)$ increased. Since $w^o_{C,U} = w'_{C,U} \cdot$ SC/TC, the temporary disequilibrium measure w^o indicates a smaller disadvantage. Now we realize that France and Germany have caught up in 1980, that Italy has a gap of only 10 percent left, but that the United Kingdom still has a gap of 30 percent in 1981.

Turning finally to our measure w^* for the period 1971–81, we find a significantly lower technology gap. To explain the difference over time between w^* and between w' and w^o, one must focus on the capacity utilization ratio, $CU_K = K^*/K$. For all countries, the CU ratio declined in the late seventies. Under our steady-state measure w^*, which is purged from relative advantages in capacity utilization, we obtain a rather smooth catching-up tendency for France, Germany, and Italy but no improvement for the United Kingdom. This means that if relative differences in output are measured as relative differences from the production surface, Germany has caught up since 1979, France's technology gap remains unchanged since 1976 (7 percent), but Italy has closed its technology gap. Hence Italy's observed gap we^o is mainly an efficiency gap, whereas the U.K. gap w^o is mainly a technology gap. France, on the other hand, still has a technology gap but in terms of efficiency it achieved an advantage relative to the United States in 1980.

The period 1980–86 is characterized by a relatively good economic performance of the United States, which resulted in regaining its former productivity advantage. One reason for that development could be that the productivity slowdown came to a halt in the mideighties, another reason could be the better capacity utilization in the Reagan era, and another a regain of the technology advantage. Since the United Kingdom succeeded in narrowing its gap to the United States somewhat, it is the only European country that has matched the good efficiency performance of the United States since 1981.

AN ECONOMETRIC ANALYSIS OF PRODUCTIVITY GAPS

After the presentation of several measures for differences in productivity it is not obvious which model we should use for carrying out an econometric analysis of the sources of changes in the productivity gaps. Since prices are preferable as explanatory variables of productivity gaps, we will use the approach of a joint cost function dual to our joint production function in Equation 7-1. We further assume that the industry is in a long-run equilibrium at a shadow price for the quasi-fixed input capital. From the previous discussion we know that some researchers would call the resulting gap $w'_{C,U}$ a true gap with the effect of disequilibrium purged.

We use a translog specification of the joint cost function TC $=$ $C(Y,PL,PE,RK,D,t)$. Our simultaneous system of equations consists of the cost-share equations (from Shepherd's lemma)

$$\frac{\partial \ln \text{TC}}{\partial \ln P_i} = \frac{P_i \cdot v_i}{\text{TC}} \equiv w_i, \qquad i = L,E,K, \tag{7-23}$$

the equation for the rate of productivity growth W_t (i.e., the rate of growth of the price diminution $- w_t$):

$$\frac{\partial \ln \text{TC}}{\partial t} = - w_t = W_t \tag{7-24}$$

and the equations for the productivity gap $w_{C,U}$, that is, for the difference in cost efficiency:

$$\frac{\partial \ln \text{TC}}{\partial D_C} \equiv - w_{C,U}, \qquad C = F,I,UK,G \tag{7-25}$$

To express the logarithmic derivations in terms of the parameters of the cost function, we choose the translog approximation of the cost function:

$$\ln \text{TC} = \alpha_U + \sum_{C \neq U} \alpha_{D_C} \cdot D_C + \sum_i \sum_C (\alpha_i + \beta_{i,D_C} \cdot D_C) \cdot \ln P_i$$
$$+ \sum_C (\alpha_T + \beta_{T,D_C} \cdot D_C) \cdot t + \frac{1}{2} \sum_{i,j} \beta_{ij} \ln P_i \cdot \ln P_j \tag{7-26}$$
$$+ \sum \beta_{iT} \cdot t \cdot \ln P_i + \frac{1}{2} \beta_{TT} \cdot t^2$$

with the symmetry restrictions $\beta_{ji} = \beta_{ij}$, and the restrictions $\alpha_K + \alpha_L + \alpha_E = 1$ and $\beta_{iK} + \beta_{iL} + \beta_{iE} = 0$ $(i, j = K,L,E)$, due to the linear homogeneity in prices. Now, for each country C, the cost shares in Equation 7-23 are

$$w_i^C = \alpha_i + \beta_{i,D_C} \cdot D_C$$
$$+ \beta_{iL} \ln (P_L/R_K)^C \qquad\qquad (7\text{-}27)$$
$$+ \beta_{iE} \ln (P_E/R_K)^C$$
$$+ \beta_{iT} \cdot t, \qquad C = U,F,I,UK,G; \quad i = K,L,E$$

After differentiation, Equation 7-24 for the rate of cost diminution is

$$- w_t^C = \alpha_T + \beta_{TD_C} \cdot D_C + \tfrac{1}{2} \beta_{LT} [\ln (P_L/R_K)_t^C$$
$$+ \ln (P_L/R_K)_{t-1}^C] + \tfrac{1}{2} \beta_{ET} [\ln (P_E/R_K)_t^C + \ln (P_E/R_K)_{t-1}^C] \qquad (7\text{-}28)$$
$$+ \tfrac{1}{2} \beta_{TT} (t + (t-1)), \qquad C = U,F,I,UK,G$$

Finally, the differences in cost efficiency (Equation 7-25) have the following form in terms of the parameters of the cost function:

$$W_{C,U} = \alpha_{D_C} + \tfrac{1}{2} \beta_{LD_C} [\ln (P_L/R_K)^C + \ln (P_L/R_K)^U] \qquad (7\text{-}29)$$
$$+ \tfrac{1}{2} \beta_{ED_C} [\ln (P_E/R_K)^C + \ln (P_E/R_K)^U] + \beta_{TD_C} \cdot t, \qquad C = F,I,UK,G$$

Equation 7-29 was obtained by differentiating Equation 7-26 with respect to D_C, ignoring the fact that D is not a vector of continuous variables. The justification for this procedure is the generalization of Diewert's (1976) quadratic lemma to discrete variables by Denny and Fuss (1983a). In order to specify the behavioral equations correctly, that is, averaging variables over time in $-w_t^c$ and over countries in $-w_{C,U}$, we employed the basic efficiency accounting equation by Denny and Fuss (1983a,b). By specifying that all equations of the system have joint normal additive disturbances, the method of maximum likelihood can be used to estimate the unknown parameters. Since the cost shares add to unity, their error terms sum to zero. We remove the energy equation w_E from the system and estimate its parameters from the parameter restrictions.

Due to the circularity condition, for example $W_{G,F} + W_{F,U} = W_{G,U}$, a regression equation for $W_{G,F}$ (and for other non–base country comparisons) can be omitted; their parameters can be obtained from the parameters of the four country equations in Equation 7-29. There is a system of nineteen equations in twenty-five unknown parameters to be estimated (2×5 equations from Equation 7-27, five equations from 7-28, and four equations from 7-29). The model was estimated using the Time Series Processor (TSP) computer program.

The assumed common technology in manufacturing in our five countries shows up in the common β parameters for input prices and time. Therefore, the share elasticities with respect to factor prices (β_{ij}) and time (β_{iT}) do not differ between countries. The α parameters will be corrected, however, in their levels by the dummy parameters. From the equation w_t for TFP, we realize, for instance, that the change in total factor productivity differs by country by the parameters β_{TDC}, $C = I, F, UK, G$. As we have normalized prices to be unity in 1975 and time to be zero in 1975, all α parameters can be interpreted as average cost shares, average change in TFP, or average productivity gaps.

A standard interpretation of the parameters is in terms of price elasticities and elasticities of substitution. The partial elasticity of substitution is $\sigma_{ij}^C = (\beta_{ij} + w_i^C w_j^C)/w_i^C \cdot w_j^C$, $i \neq j$; if $\beta_{ij} > 0$, then $\sigma_{ij}^C > 1$. For the price elasticities, we obtain $\varepsilon_{ij}^C = w_i^C \cdot \sigma_{ij}^C$, $i \neq j$, and $\varepsilon_{ii}^C = (\beta_{ii}/w_i^C) + w_i^C - 1$.

The parameter β_{iT} measures the bias of technical change on the cost shares. By rewriting the cost share regression we obtain as the rate of change of an input with respect to the level of technology

$$\varepsilon_{i,t}^C = \frac{\partial \ln v_i^C}{\partial t} = (\beta_{iT}/w_i^C) - w_t^C, \qquad i = K,L,E \qquad (7\text{-}30)$$

If technical change is input i using, that is, $\beta_{iT} > 0$, then the reduction of input quantities by the average rate w_T^C is reduced for input i by the rate β_{iT}/w_i^C. If technical change is input i saving, that is, $\beta_{iT} < 0$, then the quantity of input i can be reduced additionally by β_{iT}/w_i^C.

In looking at the interpretation of the parameter β_{iT} as $\partial(-w_t^C)/\partial \ln P_i^C = \beta_{iT}$, if technical change is input i saving, an increase in the price P_i enhances the rate of cost reduction. Similarly, if technical change is input i using, an increase in P_i results in a reduced rate of cost reduction (i.e., reduced growth of TFP w_t^C).

A similar interpretation can be given for the parameter $\beta_{i,Dc}$. It measures the difference in the cost share w_i between the United States and country C's industry holding prices and time fixed. For an interpretation as a measure of the country bias of input i, we derive from the cost share equation the measure

$$\beta_{i,Dc} = \frac{\partial \ln v_i^C}{\partial D_C} = (\beta_{iDc}/w_i^C) + W_{C,U} \qquad (7\text{-}31)$$

$\beta_{i,Dc}$ is the rate of change of input i between U.S. industry and industry in country C. If the country bias is input i saving ($\beta_{iDc} < 0$), a cost disadvantage of country C ($W_{C,U} > 0$) is less for input i, by the rate β_{iDc}/w_i^C. The industry of country C requires more of all inputs at a rate $W_{C,U}$, however, differentiated by the bias terms. If the country bias is input i using, country C's industry uses relatively more inputs, especially of input i.

Due to symmetry, the parameter for the country bias permits the derivation of the change in the gap, if in a bilateral comparison the average input price changes (see Equation 7-29):

$$\frac{\partial W_{C,U}}{\partial \ln P_i} = \beta_{i,Dc} \qquad (7\text{-}32)$$

If the country bias is input i saving, that is $\beta_{i,Dc} < 0$, then the difference in cost decreases with the average price of the corresponding input.

Finally, the parameter $\beta_{T,Dc}$ also permits a symmetric interpretation:

$$\frac{\partial(-w_t^C)}{\partial D_C} = \beta_{T,Dc} = \frac{\partial W_{C,U}}{\partial t} \qquad (7\text{-}33)$$

The first derivative describes the implication of the country bias on the rate of cost reduction. If $\beta_{T,Dc} < 0$ the rate of change of cost reduction increases from U to C. Alternatively, the other derivative shows that a cost disadvantage of country C ($W_{C,U} > 0$) will decrease with the level of technology (time t) by the rate $\beta_{T,Dc}$. This shows the contribution of the change in TFP to the catching-up process.

Table 7-4 lists the estimated parameters of our simultaneous system, including the parameters for w_E, derived from the additivity restriction of the cost shares. To save space, the parameters for an inter-European comparison W_{C_1,C_2}, derivable from the circularity condition, are not presented here.

Differences in cost efficiency, calculated from the nonparametric approach, can be compared with the differences in efficiency derived from the parametric approach. In the base year 1975, where variables are normalized to be zero, the parameters α_{DI}, α_{DF}, α_{DUK}, α_{DG} represent the parametric differences in cost efficiency. They can be compared with the nonparametric measures given in Table 7-3 for $W_{C.U} = -w'_{C.U}$ in 1976. We have $(\alpha_{DI}, \alpha_{DF}, \alpha_{DUK}, \alpha_{DG}) = (0.31,$

Table 7-4 Parameter Estimates for the Joint-Cost Model (*T* Ratios in Parentheses)

Parameter	Value	Parameter	Value
α_L	0.71 (174)	α_T	−0.019 (4.)
$\beta_{L.DI}$	0.006 (.9)	$\beta_{T.DI}$	−0.017 (26)
$\beta_{L.DF}$	−0.089 (18)	$\beta_{T.DF}$	−0.014 (20)
$\beta_{L.DUK}$	−0.014 (4.1)	$\beta_{T.DUK}$	−0.002 (6.9)
$\beta_{L.DG}$	−0.037 (11)	$\beta_{T.DG}$	−0.011 (28)
β_{LL}	0.04 (36)	β_{TT}	−0.0019(4.1)
β_{LE}	−0.013	α_{DI}	0.31 (30)
β_{LK}	−0.027 (25)	α_{DF}	0.17 (18)
β_{LT}	−0.0037(16)	α_{DUK}	0.39 (81)
α_K	0.22 (87)	α_{DG}	0.088 (11)
$\beta_{K.DI}$	−0.03 (5.8)	α_E	0.07
$\beta_{K.DF}$	0.083 (18)	$\beta_{E.DI}$	0.024
$\beta_{K.DUK}$	−0.018 (6.5)	$\beta_{E.DF}$	0.006
$\beta_{K.DG}$	0.023 (7.5)	$\beta_{E.DUK}$	0.032
β_{KK}	0.041 (31)	$\beta_{E.DG}$	0.014
β_{EK}	−0.014	β_{EE}	0.027
β_{KT}	0.0001(.5)	β_{ET}	−0.0036

Elasticities of substitution, direct-price elasticities, and input changes with respect to time and country, 1986

	Italy	France	United Kingdom	Germany	United States
σ_{LK}	0.79	0.84	0.82	0.83	0.82
σ_{LE}	0.81	0.71	0.73	0.75	0.73
σ_{KE}	0.43	0.42	0.33	0.14	0.13
ε_{LL}	−0.28	−0.33	−0.28	−0.24	−0.24
ε_{KK}	−0.59	−0.55	−0.57	−0.59	−0.59
ε_{EE}	−0.64	−0.57	−0.56	−0.55	−0.54
ε_{LT}	−0.03	−0.04	−0.04	−0.02	−0.02
ε_{KT}	−0.03	−0.04	−0.03	−0.01	−0.02
ε_{ET}	−0.06	−0.08	−0.08	−0.06	−0.07
$\varepsilon_{L.DC}$	0.15	−0.05	0.31	−0.02	
$\varepsilon_{K.DC}$	0.02	0.35	0.27	0.13	
$\varepsilon_{E.DC}$	0.37	0.18	0.76	0.22	
$W_{C.U}$	0.15	0.1	0.34	0.03	

0.17, 0.39, 0.088), and under the nonparametric approach (0.27, 0.09, 0.40, 0.02). There are some differences, which could be due to the assumption of CRTS or long-run equilibrium at partly shadow prices.

An economic interpretation of the pattern of substitution in terms of some elasticities is also presented in Table 7-4. Although our approach requires that share elasticities be the same for manufacturing industry in the five countries, elasticities of substitution can differ by country. We first observe that the United States has the highest cost share w_L of labor ($\beta_{L,DC} \leq 0$ for all countries). The U.S.-to-country C bias is labor saving, so that the cost advantage of the United States is less with respect to labor (see $\varepsilon_{L,DC}$ in Table 7-4). The negative labor-saving bias term implies that the higher wages worldwide will reduce the cost disadvantage of European manufacturing. With respect to the cost share of capital w_K we observe that the country bias to Italy and the United Kingdom is capital saving ($\beta_{K,DC} < 0$) and to France and Germany it is capital using. An increase in the price of capital (e.g., higher interest rates) would favor the catching-up efforts of Italy and the United Kingdom and hamper the efforts of France and Germany. Finally, the cost share of energy is higher in all four European countries ($\beta_{E,DC} > 0$). Since the country biases for energy are energy using, higher energy prices on the world market are unfavorable for the European countries to reduce their cost efficiency gaps.

We continue with the interpretation of the estimated pattern of technical change on the productivity and cost gaps. Since $\alpha_T = -0.019$, the average rate of cost reduction in the United States is 1.9 percent. This rate is higher in all four European countries because of the negative country biases $\beta_{T,DC}$; hence the cost advantage for the United States will be reduced with the level of technology (time t). If relative factor prices had been constant over time, different growth rates of total factor productivity would be the only source of a catching-up process. As the relative factor prices changed over time, and as the parameters $\beta_{i,DC}$ are significantly different from zero, the observed changes in the technology gaps also reflect changes in input proportions.

Since $\beta_{T,DC} < 0$ for all C, the higher rate of cost diminution in all European countries explains part of the narrowing of their cost disadvantages. Hence the relatively favorable performance of U.S. industry since 1982 is not due to the index t of technology but mainly to modest wages. All country biases are labor saving, which means that U.S. industry has the highest relative advantage from low wages.

CONCLUSION

The widening and closing of productivity gaps between the manufacturing industries of the United States, Italy, France, the United Kingdom, and Germany, were analyzed in two steps. First, performance was described based on the theory of economic indexes. Next the theoretical framework was exploited for an econometric model to explain the sources of the change in productivity gaps. This analysis showed that the observed changes also reflect changes in input proportions.

We found that France and Germany were able to narrow their productivity disadvantages to the United States but lost an advantage in 1982 again during the era of "supply-side economics" in the United States. A similar picture showed up for Italy—a tendency to catch up and unfavorable development since 1982. For the United Kingdom we found no significant tendency to catch up. In the Thatcher era the relative position improved at least with respect to the European countries but not to the United States.

The econometric analysis showed that the European industries reduced their cost disadvantage in periods of worldwide high wages (labor-saving country bias). High interest rates hamper Germany and France in catching up (capital using) but favor Italy and the United Kingdom (capital-saving bias). However, as factor intensities and marginal productivities show a strong tendency to equalize, we can conclude that in the medium run only changes in total factor productivity will affect the differences in technology.

NOTES

1. The primal measure of productivity gaps was introduced by Jorgenson and Nishimizu (1978) for the two-country comparison. This concept has been extended to multilateral comparisons by Caves, Christensen, and Diewert (1982) and has been implemented empirically by Christensen, Cummings, and Jorgenson (1981), Conrad and Jorgenson (1985), and Conrad (1985). The dual measure of productivity gaps in terms of cost gaps based on cost functions instead of production functions has been employed by Denny, Fuss, and May (1981), Denny and Fuss (1983b), and Conrad (1987, 1988).

2. We use the notation and choice of inputs of Berndt and Hesse (1986), who generously provided us the data for the manufacturing sector of nine OECD countries up to 1981.

3. Denny and Fuss (1983a) showed that the discrete variable D can be treated as a continuous variable for the purpose of applying Diewert's (1976) quadratic lemma in the following index procedure.

4. See Berndt and Fuss (1986), Berndt and Hesse (1986), and Morrison (1985). Our measure of the ex-ante capital price P_K was calculated on the basis of the standard formula for the user cost of capital, namely, $P_K = P_I \cdot (r + \delta)$, where r is the interest rate on lowest risk government bonds, P_I is the price of investment goods, and δ is the rate of replacement.

5. See Conrad and Unger (1987). The conceptualization of intercountry productivity gaps is the same as the development for productivity over time. See, for the latter, Berndt and Fuss (1986), Morrison (1985), and Berndt and Hesse (1986).

6. The first-order condition for $\min_Y TC/Y$ is $\partial VC/\partial Y = VC + P_K \cdot K$. Using Equation 7-11 and CRTS we obtain Equation 7-15.

7. This capacity concept was first suggested by Hickman (1964).

8. For further details and parameter estimates see Berndt and Hesse (1986). In addition to their data, we also received their TSP program for carrying out the necessary calculations. Thus we did not base our calculation on others' estimates but were able to repeat and verify their results.

REFERENCES

Berndt, E. R., and M. Fuss. 1986. "Productivity Measurement with Adjustments for Variations in Capacity Utilization and Other Forms of Temporary Equilibrium." *Journal of Econometrics* 33, 7–29.

Berndt, E. R., and D. Hesse. 1986. "Measuring and Assessing Capacity Utilization in the Manufacturing Sectors of Nine OECD Countries." *European Economic Review* 30, 961–89.

Caves, D. W., L. R. Christensen, and W. E. Diewert. 1982. "Multilateral Comparisons of Output, Input and Productivity Using Superlative Index Numbers." *Economic Journal* 92, 73–86.

Caves, R. E., and L. B. Krause, eds. 1980. *Britain's Economic Performance*. Washington, D.C.: Brookings Institution.

Christensen, L. R., D. Cummings, and D. W. Jorgenson. 1981. "Relative Productivity Levels, 1947–1973: An International Comparison." *European Economic Review*, 61–94.

Conrad, K. 1985. *Produktivitätslücken nach Wirtschaftszweigen im internationalen Vergleich; Beschreibung und ökonometrische Ursachenanalyse für die USA, Japan und die Bundesrepublik Deutschland, 1960–1979*. Heidelberg-New York: Springer-Verlag.

Conrad, K. 1987. "Theory and Measurement of Productivity and Cost Gaps in Manufacturing Industries in U.S., Japan and Germany." In W. Eichhorn, ed., *Measurement in Economics*. Heidelberg/New York: Physica Verlag, pp. 725–50.

Conrad, K. 1988. "Productivity and Cost Gaps in Five Manufacturing Industries in U.S., Japan and Germany." *European Economic Review*. (forthcoming)

Conrad, K., and D. W. Jorgenson. 1985. "Sectoral Productivity Gaps between the United States, Japan and Germany 1960–1979." In H. Giersch, ed., *Probleme und Perspektiven der weltwirtschaftlichen Entwicklung*. Berlin: Duncker & Humblot.

Denny, M., and M. Fuss. 1983a. "The Use of Discrete Variables in Superlative Index Number Comparisons." *International Economic Review* 24, 419–21.

Denny, M., and M. Fuss. 1983b. "A General Approach to Intertemporal and Interspatial Productivity Comparisons." *Journal of Econometrics* 23, 315–30.

Denny, M., M. Fuss, and J. D. May. 1981. "Intertemporal Changes in Regional Productivity in Canadian Manufacturing." *Canadian Journal of Economics* 3, 390–408.

Diewert, W. E. 1976. "Exact and Superlative Index Numbers." *Journal of Econometrics* 4, 115–45.

Hickman, B. G. 1964. "On a New Method of Capacity Estimation." *American Statistical Association Journal* 59, 529–49.

Jorgenson, D. W., and M. Nishimizu. 1978. "U.S. and Japanese Economic Growth, 1952–1974: An International Comparison." *Economic Journal* 88, 707–26.

Kravis, I. B., A. Heston, and R. Summers. 1982. *World Product and Income: International Comparisons of Real Gross Product*. Baltimore, Md.: Johns Hopkins University Press.

Lau, L. J. 1979. "On Exact Index Numbers." *Review of Economics and Statistics* 61, 73–82.

Morrison, C. J. 1985. "Primal and Dual Capacity Utilization: An Application to Productivity Measurement in the U.S. Automobile Industry." *Journal of Business and Economic Statistics* 3, 312–24.

Solow, R. 1957. "Technical Change and the Aggregate Production Function." *Review of Economics and Statistics* 39, 312–20.

8

An International Comparison of the Multisectoral Production Structure of the United States, West Germany, and Japan

MITSUO SAITO AND ICHIRO TOKUTSU

The main purpose of this chapter is to make an empirical estimation of the same multisectoral production model for the United States, West Germany, and Japan and to make a comparison of their competitiveness in the world market on the basis of the results.

The basic accounting system of the model is the input–output table, and each industry is assumed to determine the demand for inputs so as to minimize the total cost under the restriction of a two-level CES production function with Hicks-neutral technological progress. The same model is fitted to the time-series data of the three countries. The estimates for the rate of technical progress and for the price elasticity of input demand will reveal the production structure of each country and its implications in market competitiveness: the rate of cost reduction due to technical progress and the flexibility of the input–output relation to the change in input prices.

THE MODEL

Production Scheme of the Whole Economy

The economic activities of individual industries and their interdependence may best be described by the well-known input–output formula of the Leontief type. This is presented in Table 8-1A. The ith column stands for the production activity of the ith industry; that is, the ith industry produces output X_i by using inputs X_{ji} ($j = 1, \ldots, n$), L_i, and K_i.

The production technique between output and inputs of each industry is represented by the production function. To avoid multicollinearity in the esti-

Table 8-1 Input–Output Scheme of the National Economy: Quantity

	(1)	(2)		(n)	Definition
	Industry				

A table follows:

	Industry (1)	Industry (2)		Industry (n)	Definition
A. Individual-industry level					
Input	X_{11}	X_{12}	$\cdots$	X_{1n}	X_{ji} = amount of output j
	X_{21}	X_{22}	$\cdots$	X_{2n}	consumed to produce X_i
	$\vdots$	$\vdots$	$\cdots$	$\vdots$	L_i = labor input of industry i
	X_{n1}	X_{n2}	$\cdots$	X_{nn}	K_i = capital stock of industry i
	L_1	L_2		L_n	
	K_1	K_2		K_n	X_i = output of industry i
	$\downarrow$	$\downarrow$		$\downarrow$	
Output	X_1	X_2	$\cdots$	X_n	
B. First aggregated industry level					
Input	M_1	M_2	$\cdots$	M_n	M_i = aggregated input of nonenergy
	E_1	E_2	$\cdots$	E_n	materials of industry i (X_{ji} for j
	L_1	L_2	$\cdots$	L_n	$\in jm$)
	K_1	K_2	$\cdots$	K_n	
	$\downarrow$	$\downarrow$		$\downarrow$	E_i = aggregated input of energy of
Output	X_1	X_2	$\cdots$	X_n	industry i (X_{ji} for $j \in je$)
C. Second aggregated industry level					
Input	M_1	M_2	$\cdots$	M_n	EK_i = aggregated input of energy
	EK_1	EK_2	$\cdots$	EK_n	and capital of industry i
	L_1	L_2	$\cdots$	L_n	(E_i and K_i)
	$\downarrow$	$\downarrow$		$\downarrow$	
Output	X_1	X_2	$\cdots$	X_n	

mation of the production function, we assume that the nonenergy materials can be aggregated into one input M_i and similarly that energy can be aggregated into one input E_i. The production scheme of the first aggregated industry level is shown in Table 8-1B. Next, E_i and K_i are aggregated into one input EK_i. Thus the number of inputs at athe second aggregated industry level is three, M_i, EK_i, and L_i. This scheme is presented in Table 8-1C.

Table 8-2 and Table 8-3 show the same formula as quantity in terms of value and price, respectively.

Production Technique of Individual Industries

Each industry is assumed to produce output under the following production function of the two-level CES type (see Sato, 1967), which is seen schematically in Table 8-4.

At the individual-industry level the technical relation between material inputs X_{ji} ($j \in jm$) (or $j \in je$) and nonenergy (or energy) material M_i (or E_i) is represented by a Cobb–Douglas function (Equation 8-1 or 8-2). Energy inputs are the products of coal and oil mining, petroleum and coal products manufacturing, and electricity and gas.

At the first aggregated industry level, energy E_i and capital K_i are assumed to produce another composite input EK_i under the technical restriction of the

Table 8-2 Input–Output Scheme of the National Economy: Value

| | Industry | | | |
	(1)	(2)	(n)	Definition
A. Individual-industry level				
Input	VX_{11}	VX_{12}	VX_{1n}	VX_{ji} = value of X_{ji}, i.e., $PI_j X_{ji}$
	VX_{21}	VX_{22}	VX_{2n}	WL_i = labor income of industry i,
	$\vdots$	$\vdots$	$\vdots$	i.e., $W_i L_i$
	VX_{n1}	VX_{n2}	VX_{nn}	WK_i = capital income of industry i,
	WL_1	WL_2	WL_n	i.e., $PK_i K_i$
	WK_1	WK_2	WK_n	VX_i = value of X_i, i.e., $P_i X_i$
	$\downarrow$	$\downarrow$	$\downarrow$	
Output	VX_1	VX_2	VX_n	
B. First aggregated industry level				
Input	VM_1	VM_2	VM_n	VM_i = value of M_i, i.e., $PM_i M_i$, or
	VE_1	VE_2	VE_n	$\sum\limits_{j \in jm} VX_{ji}$
	WL_1	WL_2	WL_n	
	WK_1	WK_2	WK_n	VE_i = value of E_i, i.e., $PE_i E_i$, or
	$\downarrow$	$\downarrow$	$\downarrow$	$\sum\limits_{j \in je} VX_{ji}$
Output	X_1	X_2	X_n	
C. Second aggregated industry level				
Input	VM_1	VM_2	VM_n	VEK_i = value of EK_i, i.e., $PEK_i EK_i$
	VEK_1	VEK_2	VEK_n	
	WL_1	WL_2	WL_n	
	$\downarrow$	$\downarrow$	$\downarrow$	
Output	VX_1	VX_2	VX_n	

Table 8-3 Input–Output Scheme of the National Economy: Price

| | Industry | | | |
	(1)	(2)	(n)	Definition
A. Individual-industry level				
Input	PI_1	PI_1	PI_1	PI_i = price of output i when it is
	PI_2	PI_2	PI_2	used as an input of other
	$\vdots$	$\vdots$	$\vdots$	industries
	PI_n	PI_n	PI_n	W_i = wage rate of industry i
	W_1	W_2	W_k	PK_i = rental price of capital of
	PK_1	PK_2	PK_n	industry i
Output	P_1	P_2	P_n	P_i = the price of output i
B. First aggregated industry level				
Input	PM_1	PM_2	PM_n	PM_i = price of M_i
	PE_1	PE_2	PE_n	
	W_1	W_2	W_n	
	PK_1	PK_2	PK_n	PE_i = price of E_i
Output	P_1	P_2	P_n	
C. Second aggregated industry level				
Input	PM_1	PM_2	PM_n	PEK_i = price of EK_i
	PEK_1	PEK_2	PEK_n	
	W_1	W_2	W_n	
Output	P_1	P_2	P_n	

Table 8-4   Production Function by Industry

A. Individual-industry level

$$M_i = m_i \prod_{j \in jm} X_{ji}^{b_{ji}}, \qquad \sum_{j \in jm} b_{ji} = 1 \tag{8-1}$$

$$E_i = e_i \prod_{j \in je} X_{ji}^{b_{ji}}, \qquad \sum_{j \in je} b_{ji} = 1 \tag{8-2}$$

B. First aggregated industry level

$$EK_i = ek_i(de_iE_i^{-u_i} + dk_iK_i^{-u_i})^{-1/u_i}$$

$$de_i + dk_i = 1 \tag{8-3}$$

$$v_i = \frac{1}{1 + u_i} \qquad \text{(elasticity of substitution between energy and capital)}$$

C. Second aggregated industry level

$$X_i = x_iT_i(dl_iL_i^{-r_i} + dm_iM_i^{-r_i} + dek_iEK_i^{-r_i})^{-1/r_i} \tag{8-4}$$

$$dl_i + dm_i + dek_i = 1$$

$$s_i = \frac{1}{1 + r_i} \qquad \text{(elasticity of substitution between labor,}$$

$$\text{nonenergy materials, and energy capital)}$$

$$T_i = \text{index representing technology level}$$

$$\text{(technical progress of the Hicks-neutral type)}$$

CES function (Equation 8-3). At this level the elasticity of substitution (or simply ES) between energy and capital is given by $v_i = 1/(1\ u_i)$.

At the second aggregated industry level, energy-capital EK_i, labor L_i, and nonenergy materials M_i produce output of industry i, X_i, subject to another CES production function (Equation 8-4). At this level the ES among EK_i, L_i, and M_i is given by $s_i = 1/(1 + r_i)$.

Allen (1938) defined the partial elasticity of substitution (or simply AES) between factors i and j in order to measure the flexibility of factor demand to the change in factor price in a general conceptual formula:

$$\sigma_{ij} = \frac{X}{a_i a_j} \cdot \frac{\partial a_i}{\partial p_j}$$

where

$$\sigma_{ij} = \text{AES between factors } i \text{ and } j$$
$$X = \text{quantity of output}$$
$$a_i = \text{quantity of input } i$$
$$p_j = \text{price of input } j$$

In our production function, AES between energy and capital, σ_{KE}, is computed as

$$\sigma_{KE} = V\left(\frac{1}{S_E + S_K}\right) + S\left(1 - \frac{1}{S_E + S_K}\right)$$

where

$$S_E = \text{the relative share of energy}$$
$$S_K = \text{the relative share of capital}$$
$$V, S = \text{defined in Table 8-4}$$

Here, the industry subscript i is deleted for simplicity.

AES between all other pairs of inputs is equal to s (defined in Table 8-4):

$$\sigma_{KL} = \sigma_{KM} = \sigma_{EL} = \sigma_{EM} = \sigma_{LM} = s$$

THE ESTIMATION METHOD

Production functions are estimated by the time series data for manufacturing industries of the United States, West Germany, and Japan.[1] The estimation procedure is tabulated in Table 8-5. In the estimation firms are assumed to behave so as to minimize the total cost under the restriction of production functions 8-1 to 8-4 of Table 8-4. In our production function, as shown in Table 8-4, each level is separable from each other, and the function of each level is homogeneous of degree 1. It is well known that if one defines a suitable price

Table 8-5 Estimation Method

A. Individual-industry level

$$a_{ji} = VX_{ji}/VX_i, \qquad j,i = 1, 2, \cdots, n \tag{8-5}$$

$$b_{ji} = a_{ji}/\sum_{j \in jm} a_{ji}, \qquad M_i \tag{8-6}$$

$$b_{ji} = a_{ji}/\sum_{j \in je} a_{ji}, \qquad E_i \tag{8-7}$$

The definition of PM_i and PE_i (the dual of Equations 8-1 and 8-2):

$$PM_i = (m_i \prod_{j \in jm} b_{ji}^{b_{ji}})^{-1} \prod_{j \in jm} PI_{ji}^{b_{ji}} \tag{8-8}$$

$$PE_i = (e_i \prod_{j \in je} b_{ji}^{b_{ji}})^{-1} \prod_{j \in je} PI_{ji}^{b_{ji}} \tag{8-9}$$

The units of m_i and e_i are set so that PM_i and PE_i may be unity in the base year. M_i and E_i are calculated as VM_i/PM_i and VE_i/PE_i.

B. First aggregated level

$$\frac{E_i}{K_i} = h_i \left(\frac{PK_i}{PE_i}\right)^{v_i}, \qquad h_i = \left(\frac{de_i}{dk_i}\right)^{v_i} \tag{8-10}$$

The definition of PEK_i (the dual of Equation 8-3):

$$PEK_i = ek_i^{-1}(de_i^{v_i}PE_i^{1-v_i} + dk_i^{v_i}PK^{1-v_i})^{1/(1-v_i)} \tag{8-11}$$

ek_i is computed so that PEK_i may be unity in the base year. EK_i is calculated as VEK_i/PEK_i.

C. Second aggregated level

$$\frac{M_i}{X_i} = g_i \, dm_i^{s_i} \left(\frac{P_i}{PM_i}\right)^{s_i} \tag{8-12}$$

$$\frac{EK_i}{X_i} = g_i dek_i^{s_i} \left(\frac{P_i}{PEK_i}\right)^{s_i} \tag{8-13}$$

$$\frac{L_i}{X_i} = g_i \, dl_i^{s_i} \left(\frac{P_i}{W_i}\right)^{s_i} \tag{8-14}$$

$$g_i = x_i^{s_i-1} T_i^{-1} \tag{8-15}$$

where

$$T_i = \exp (f_i t + f'_i t' + f''_i t'')$$

$t = $ time

$t' = t$ after 1974

$\quad = 0$ before 1973

$t'' = t$ after 1980

$\quad = 0$ before 1979

Equations 8-12 to 8-15 are estimated by one regression.

aggregator for PE_i and PM_i at the individual-industry level and for PEK_i at the first aggregated industry level, the solution of cost minimization with respect to all the inputs is equal to the solution of separate cost minimization of each level. Therefore, we use the conditions of cost minimization at each level in estimating parameters.

At the individual-industry level the value input coefficient a_{ji} is adopted from the value input–output table. Then b_{ji} for M_i is computed as normalized a_{ji}, as described in Equation 8-6. We assume that a change in b_{ji} over time is just compensated by the accompanying change in m_i.[2] As is seen in Equation 8-1, this implies that the change in b_{ji} over time leads to neither increase nor decrease in total factor productivity in the production of M_i. Similarly, b_{ji} and e_i in Equation 8-2 are estimated. The price of aggregated input, PM_i, is defined by the dual of Equation 8-1, as seen in Equation 8-8.[3] Similarly, the price of aggregated input, PE_i, is calculated by Equation 8-9. The quantity of aggregated input, M_i (or E_i), is by definition, calculated as VM_i/PM_i (or VE_i/PE_i), since VM_i (or VE_i) is observable.

At the first aggregated level, the log-linear form of Equation 8-10 is estimated by the Cochrane–Orcutt method. Equation 8-10 is derived by the cost minimization subject to Equation 8-3. Again, the price, PEK_i, is defined by the dual of Equation 8-3, as shown in Equation 8-11, and the quantity of aggregated energy-capital input, EK_i, is calculated as VEK_i/PEK_i.

At the second aggregated level, the log-linear form of Equations 8-12 to 8-14 is estimated by one regression with autoregressive errors to obtain the estimate for a common parameter, s_i. The difference of the three equations is taken into account by introducing two dummy variables for the constant term. We assume that the serial correlation coefficient of errors of each equation is unity; that is, the first difference form of the log-linear equations is estimated. In this case the terms of the two dummy variables disappear from the equation to be estimated. T_i is a time trend with kinks in 1974 and 1980. Further details of the estimation procedure are presented in Appendix 8-2.

THE ESTIMATED RESULTS

The results of the estimation of Equation 8-10 and a combined equation of 8-12 to 8-15 show that the estimates are, in general, fairly stable for all the three countries. The parameter estimates of each industry indicate that they satisfy the concavity conditions of the production function and by and large do not include extremely high or low estimates. The tabulation of obtained statistics, together with further detail of the estimation procedure, is given in Appendix 8-2.

Let us compare the point estimates of the three countries with each other and discuss their implications in the world trade market.[4]

The Rate of Technical Change

Table 8-6 presents a comparison of the rates of technical progress. In the United States before the oil crisis, the range of the estimated rates is 0.0–2.5

Table 8-6 Comparison of the Rate of Technical Progress (Percentage Per Year)

Sector Industry	United States		Germany		Japan		
	1949–73	1974–79	1960–73	1974–79	1953–73	1974–79	1980–86
5. Foods	1.31	1.34	1.63	1.70	0.71	0.66	0.49
6. Textiles	2.45	2.33	2.14	2.25	1.43	2.01	2.75
7. Apparel	0.72	0.66	1.67	1.79			
8. Paper	1.07	1.09	4.18	3.93	2.57	2.53	2.68
9. Printing	0.93	0.81	1.22	0.98			
10. Chemicals	2.03	2.03	3.30	3.32	3.09	3.46	3.68
11. Petroleum and coal	1.81	3.62	2.64	1.18	8.40	5.25	4.30
12. Rubber	1.09	0.78	3.26	2.79			
13. Leather	0.02	0.14	0.63	0.99			
14. Lumber[a]	0.92	0.98	2.12	1.82			
15. Furniture	1.22	1.08					
16. Stone, clay, and glass	0.95	0.93	2.11	2.01	2.15	1.98	1.94
17. Primary metals[b]	0.20	0.52	2.43	2.43	3.16	2.77	2.78
18. Nonferrous metals			2.65	2.49			
19. Fabricated metals	0.99	0.83	1.20	0.91	1.61	1.20	1.27
20. Machinery	0.69	0.94	0.88	1.15	3.47	3.66	4.17
21. Electrical machinery	1.69	1.78	2.42	2.40	5.71	5.26	5.46
22. Transportation machinery[c]	1.90	1.89	–0.23	0.19	3.95	3.87	4.04
23. Motor vehicles	1.58	1.68	2.71	2.33			
24. Precision instruments	0.70	0.66	1.91	2.15	2.52	3.17	3.34
25. Miscellaneous manufacturing[d]	0.07	–0.05	0.73	0.76	2.53	2.25	2.62
Average of total manufacturing	1.24	1.34	2.15	2.09	3.38	3.06	3.16

[a]Including furniture for Germany.

[b]Ferrous metals for Germany.

[c]Including motor vehicles for Japan.

[d]Including apparel, printing, rubber, leather, lumber, and furniture for Japan.

percent. The average of total manufacturing is 1.2 percent. By and large, the difference of the rate between the periods before and after the oil crisis is small. The average of total manufacturing after the oil crisis is 1.3 percent, indicating no practical change between these periods.[5] This differs from the trend in Japan, where the rate of technical change slowed slightly after the oil crisis.

In Germany before the oil crisis the rate of technical progress was higher than that of the United States in most industries. The range of the estimated rates is 0.6–4.2 percent, except for a negative value of transportation equipment (excluding autos), and the average of total manufacturing is 2.2 percent. After the oil crisis the rate slowed in ten industries out of twenty, resulting in a 2.1 percent value for the average of total manufacturing. It is to be noted that, as will be seen in Appendix 8-1, the time-series data of factor inputs of Germany are constructed by the aggregation based on the Divisia index; therefore, the rate of technical progress presented here may be underestimated compared with the estimates by the data based on ordinary aggregation.

For the purpose of comparison, Japan's rate of technical progress is estimated for three periods: 1953–73, 1974–79, and 1980–86. Before the oil crisis the range of estimated rates of Japan was 0.7–8.4 percent, and the average of total manufacturing is 3.4 percent. The rate of technical progress after the oil crisis was observed to fall, although not distinctly. The average of total manufacturing after the oil crisis (1974–79) was 3.1 percent.[6] The rate of technical progress of the heavy industries of Japan was much higher than that of the United States and Germany before the oil crisis. This situation, on the whole, did not change after the oil crisis.

These findings lead us to conclude that (1) before the oil crisis competitive advantage in the rate of cost reduction due to technical progress was highest in Japan and second highest in Germany, (2) after the oil crisis the situation largely did not change, and (3) the estimates for Germany may be too low.

Allen Partial Elasticity Substitution

Table 8-7 presents the estimates for σ_{KE} and σ. In the United States the range of σ_{KE}, -2.5 to 1.4, is fairly wide. A positive value of σ_{KE} implies substitutability between energy and capital, while its negative value means complementarity between them. In the average of total manufacturing, substitutability and complementarity are counterbalanced, resulting in a small negative value, -0.05. In Germany the range of σ_{KE}, -1.2 to 3.3, is also wide. Positive values of σ_{KE}, or substitutability, dominate negative values, or complementarity, giving an average of 1.2. In Japan the range of σ_{KE} is -2.2 to 1.0, except for very large values of -12.8 and -7.2 in textiles and fabricated metals, respectively.[7] The average of total manufacturing is -1.1, implying the dominance of complementarity over substitutability.

As for σ ($= s_i$), in the United States its range is 0.05–0.78 and its average is 0.36. In Germany both the range of σ, 0.01–0.80, and its average, 0.40, are comparable with those of the United States. It is to be noted, however, that in Japan the range of σ, 0.23–0.67, is narrower and its average, 0.49, is higher than those of the other two countries.

Table 8-7 Comparison of the elasticity of substitution[a]

Sector Industry	United States σ_{KE}	σ	Germany σ_{KE}	σ	Japan σ_{KE}	σ
5. Foods	−0.643	0.131	2.346	0.324	0.315	0.590
6. Textiles	1.251	0.254	0.530	0.396	−12.765	0.524
7. Apparel	0.519	0.091	3.303	0.312		
8. Paper	0.778	0.468	−0.881	0.483	0.952	0.381
9. Printing	0.179	0.200	1.150	0.499		
10. Chemicals	−0.191	0.498	0.014	0.660	−0.664	0.538
11. Petroleum and coal	−0.148	0.779	0.560	0.093	0.010	0.400
12. Rubber	−0.283	0.054	0.554	0.205		
13. Leather	−1.086	0.078	2.964	0.304		
14. Lumber[b]	1.361	0.379	2.183	0.237		
15. Furniture	1.429	0.188				
16. Stone, clay, and glass	−0.474	0.465	0.517	0.796	−0.066	0.530
17. Primary metals[c]	0.388	0.695	0.174	0.691	0.868	0.234
18. Nonferrous metals			0.513	0.013		
19. Fabricated metals	1.043	0.300	1.177	0.162	−7.171	0.559
20. Machinery	−0.120	0.522	1.913	0.349	−2.000	0.585
21. Electrical machinery	0.748	0.372	2.215	0.203	0.769	0.447
22. Transportation machinery[d]	−2.506	0.275	−1.234	0.174	−1.182	0.530
23. Motor vehicles	−0.448	0.379	1.426	0.306		
24. Precision instruments	−1.652	0.225	0.648	0.586	0.831	0.647
25. Miscellaneous manufacturing[e]	0.511	0.132	1.742	0.463	−2.171	0.672
Average of total manufacturing	−0.045	0.364	1.249	0.404	−1.066	0.489

[a]σ_{KE} = elasticity of substitution between capital and energy; σ = elasticity of substitution among four inputs (capital, labor, energy, and nonenergy materials) except σ_{KE}.

[b]Including furniture for Germany.

[c]Ferrous metals for Germany.

[d]Including motor vehicles for Japan.

[e]Including apparel, printing, rubber, leather, lumber, and furniture for Japan.

Own-Price Elasticity of Capital, Labor, Energy, and Nonenergy Material

Let us turn to a comparison of own-price elasticities (OPE) of factors, which are presented in Table 8-8. The average of the OPE of capital of the United States, −0.29, is lower (in absolute value) than that of Germany, −0.37, by 0.08,[8] while its U.S. range, −0.62 to −0.06, is almost the same as that of Germany, −0.63 to −0.10. The average of the OPE of capital of Japan, −0.36, is very near to that of Germany.

The average of the OPE of energy in Japan, −0.37, is lower than that of Germany, −0.47, but higher than that of the United States, −0.31. Next, the average of the OPE of labor in Japan, −0.40, is higher than that of Germany, −0.30, and that of the United States, −0.27. Finally, the average of the OPE of nonenergy materials of Japan, Germany, and the United States is −0.19, −0.18, and −0.16, respectively. All of them are very near to each other.

To sum up, there is a tendency for the average of total manufacturing of the OPE to be larger in Japan and Germany than in the United States, although the differences in value among the three countries are not large.

Table 8-8 Comparison of Own-Price Elasticities

Sector Industry	Capital ε_{KK}			Energy ε_{EE}			Labor ε_{LL}			Nonenergy Materials ε_{MM}		
	United States	Germany	Japan	United States	Germany	Japan	United States	Germany	Japan	United States	Germany	Japan
5. Foods	-0.110	-0.357	-0.469	-0.077	-0.515	-0.524	-0.112	-0.277	-0.511	-0.030	-0.090	-0.207
6. Textiles	-0.256	-0.364	-0.120	-0.342	-0.389	-0.459	-0.193	-0.277	-0.374	-0.091	-0.179	-0.167
7. Apparel	-0.091	-0.348		-0.116	-0.621		-0.061	-0.210		-0.037	-0.142	
8. Paper	-0.430	-0.287	-0.379	-0.475	-0.329	-0.422	-0.360	-0.426	-0.334	-0.195	-0.148	-0.126
9. Printing	-0.174	-0.439		-0.195	-0.585		-0.130	-0.314		-0.099	-0.271	
10. Chemicals	-0.382	-0.475	-0.277	-0.377	-0.474	-0.269	-0.405	-0.535	-0.482	-0.192	-0.312	-0.220
11. Petroleum and coal	-0.046	-0.321	-0.043	-0.133	-0.060	-0.037	-0.740	-0.089	-0.393	-0.669	-0.051	-0.372
12. Rubber	-0.038	-0.209		-0.034	-0.215		-0.035	-0.125		-0.023	-0.100	
13. Leather	-0.060	-0.319		-0.041	-0.687		-0.054	-0.190		-0.027	-0.165	
14. Lumber[a]	-0.336	-0.250		-0.539	-0.535		-0.279	-0.156		-0.174	-0.125	
15. Furniture	-0.200			-0.257			-0.132			-0.070		
16. Stone, clay, and glass	-0.335	-0.632	-0.400	-0.323	-0.663	-0.403	-0.318	-0.557	-0.404	-0.236	-0.458	-0.247
17. Primary metals[b]	-0.618	-0.573	-0.267	-0.607	-0.555	-0.307	-0.548	-0.586	-0.220	-0.261	-0.251	-0.076
18. Nonferrous metals	-0.095			-0.033			-0.012			-0.003		
19. Fabricated metals	-0.282	-0.170	-0.210	-0.371	-0.300	-0.421	-0.199	-0.110	-0.357	-0.136	-0.079	-0.235
20. Machinery	-0.459	-0.351	-0.472	-0.449	-0.497	-0.276	-0.336	-0.213	-0.463	-0.246	-0.179	-0.200
21. Electrical machinery	-0.336	-0.222	-0.389	-0.408	-0.426	-0.485	-0.244	-0.124	-0.362	-0.174	-0.107	-0.157
22. Transportation machinery[c]	-0.217	-0.114	-0.445	-0.168	-0.074	-0.337	-0.190	-0.116	-0.426	-0.099	-0.076	-0.169
23. Motor vehicles	-0.348	-0.283		-0.325	-0.457		-0.303	-0.212		-0.104	-0.143	
24. Precision instruments	-0.182	-0.486	-0.573	-0.104	-0.588	-0.658	-0.126	-0.373	-0.454	-0.116	-0.323	-0.281
25. Miscellaneous manufacturing[d]	-0.134	-0.439	-0.567	-0.148	-0.633	-0.478	-0.096	-0.290	-0.480	-0.045	-0.255	-0.249
Average of total manufacturing	-0.294	-0.368	-0.364	-0.308	-0.469	-0.366	-0.273	-0.303	-0.398	-0.158	-0.181	-0.192

[a] Including furniture for Germany.

[b] Ferrous metals for Germany.

[c] Including motor vehicles for Japan.

[d] Including apparel, printing, rubber, leather, lumber, and furniture for Japan.

A large value of the OPE in an industry of a country implies that the industry is more flexible to a change in factor price. This flexibility may include not only the flexibility of existing technology but also a quick and sufficient response of the firm's management to any change in the economic situation, such as the quick adoption of new technology or a proper shift of labor to a new job. In general, one can argue that flexibility of this sort will contribute to a rise in productive efficiency.[9]

COST CHANGE AND COMPETITIVENESS
IN THE WORLD MARKET

The Rate of Technical Progress

Within the framework of our production model the percentage change in cost per unit output, c, is given by

$$\Delta c/c_{-1} = S_L(\Delta W/W_{-1}) + S_E(\Delta PE/PE_{-1}) + S_K(\Delta PK/PK_{-1}) + S_M(\Delta PM/PM_{-1}) - \Delta T/T_{-1} \tag{8-16}$$

Clearly, a larger value in the rate of technical change gives rise to a larger percentage reduction in unit cost, of size $(\Delta T/T_{-1})$. $(\Delta T/T_{-1})$ is the rate of change in total factor productivity.

Other things being equal, a higher rate of technical progress will lead to a higher rate of cost reduction, and thereby to a higher rate of price reduction. The rate of price reduction, when modified by the rate of appreciation in the exchange rate, is regarded as the rate of increase in competitive power in the world market. The rate of increase in competitive power in this sense is tabulated for the average of total manufacturing of 1960–73 and 1974–79 in Tables 8-9 and 8-10, respectively.

The year-to-year movement of exchange rates after 1970 is very volatile, although the tendency of dollar depreciation to mark and yen is distinct. In row 2 of Table 8-9 the average for 1970–85—the period before the G5 agreement in the fall of 1985—is presented. It is seen from row 1 of both tables that, as far as the rate of cost reduction due to technical progress is concerned, the priority in competitiveness is highest in Japan and second highest in Germany for the pre–oil-crisis period. On the contrary, as is seen from row 3, if the rate of change in exchange rates (row 2) is taken into account, the United States gains advantages over both Germany and Japan before the oil crisis, and such advantages are kept after the oil crisis. In addition, by the exchange adjustment Japan loses the advantage over Germany both before and after the oil crisis.

The level of the competitive power at a time point (but not its rate of change) may be best described by the purchasing-power parity (PPP) index. Based on the PPPs given by Kravis, Kenessey, Heston, and Summers (1975), Jorgenson and Kuroda (Chapter 9, this volume) calculated the Japanese price index transformed by the PPP index at 1970 (U.S. price = 1.00) for each industry. Its average for total manufacturing is 0.81; thus Japanese prices in manufacturing are, on average, 19 percent lower than U.S. prices in the trade market of 1970.

Table 8-9 Comparison of the Rate of Change in Competitive Power Due to Technical Progress (1960–73) and Trends in Exchange Rates (1971–85), Total Manufacturing (Percent Per Year)

	United States –Germany	United States –Japan	Germany –Japan
1. Rate of cost reduction due to technical change	−0.91	−2.14	−1.23
2. Rate of change in exchange rates, 1971–85 ($/DM, $/yen, DM/yen)	−1.44	−2.70	−1.29
3. Rate of change in competitive power, 1970–73 = (1) − (2)	0.53	0.56	0.06

Now, as is seen in row 3 of Tables 8-9 and 8-10, the increase in price competitiveness of the United States over Japan is 0.56 percent per year in 1970–73 and 0.98 percent per year in 1974–85.[10] This implies that the total increase in price competitiveness of the United States over Japan in 1970–85 is 13.2 percent, which is not enough to absorb the advantage of 19 percent of Japan in 1970. It is to be noted, however, that the 42 percent depreciation of the dollar to yen in 1985–87 is more than enough to wipe out the remaining advantage of Japan over the United States.

The PPPs between the United States and Germany for output in 1975, which is based on Kravis, Heston, and Summers (1982), is shown in Conrad (Chapter 7, this volume). The German relative price index (U.S. price = 1.00) is 1.14. Therefore, the United States is expanding its advantage over Germany in price competitiveness as far as the effects of technical change and exchange rate are concerned.

The Elasticity of Substitution

As shown in Equation 8-16, an increase in wage rate will yield an increase in unit cost in proportion to the relative share of labor. The relative share of labor

Table 8-10 Comparison of the Rate of Change in Competitive Power Due to Technical Progress (1974–79) and Trends in Exchange Rates (1971–85), Total Manufacturing (Percent Per Year)

	United States –Germany	United States –Japan	Germany –Japan
1. Rate of cost reduction due to technical change	−0.75	−1.72	−0.97
2. Rate of change in exchange rates, 1971–85 ($/DM, $/yen, DM/yen)	−1.44	−2.70	−1.29
3. Rate of change in competitive power, 1974–79 = (1) − (2)	0.69	0.98	0.32

Table 8-11 Change in Unit Cost Induced by a Wage Increase, United States ($s = 0.36$)

	(1) $\Delta W/W_{-1}$	(2) S_L	(3) $\Delta c/c_{-1}$ $= (1)*(2)$	(4) s	(5) $\Delta S_L/S_{L-1}$ $= (1 - s)*[(1) - (3)]$
1. First year	0.10	0.3	0.03	0.36	0.0448
2. Second year	0.10	0.3134	0.03134	0.36	0.0439

is determined by factor price and the elasticity of substitution with respect to labor:

$$\Delta S_L/S_{L-1} = (1 - s)(\Delta W/W_{-1} - \Delta c/c_{-1}) \qquad (8\text{-}17)$$

where s is the elasticity of substitution defined in Table 8-4, or σ presented in Table 8-7.

Now let us show the effect of the elasticity of sbustitution on unit cost by a numerical example. Tables 8-11 and 8-12 present the case of $s = 0.36$ (U.S.) and $s = 0.49$ (Japan), respectively. Suppose that the rate of wage increase is 10 percent and the labor share in the first year is 0.3 in both countries. The rate of increase in unit cost, which is computed by Equation 8-16, is given in column 3. The rate of change in the labor share, which is computed by Equation 8-17, is given in column 5. In the second year the same calculation is done as in the first year. The difference in the labor share induced by the difference in the elasticity of substitution is revealed in the second year. In our example the cost increase in the second year is 0.027 percent lower in the country with a higher elasticity of substitution than in the country with a lower one.

This numerical example will suggest a rough idea of the extent to which a country with a larger elasticity of substitution may get a better position in trade competition than a country with a smaller one.

CONCLUSION

The main findings in this study are as follows:

1. The estimated results of our KLEM function of the two-level CES type indicate that the parameter estimates are very stable, satisfying the concavity conditions in all the industries of the three countries.
2. The estimates for the rate of technical change of the Hicks-neutral type show that before the oil crisis the average of total manufacturing was 1.2, 2.2, and 3.4 percent per year in the United States, Germany, and Japan, respectively, whereas after the oil crisis it was 1.3, 2.1, 3.1 percent, respectively. The results, however, may be subject to qualifications

Table 8-12 Change in Unit Cost Induced by a Wage Increase, Japan ($s = 0.49$)

	(1) $\Delta W/W_{-1}$	(2) S_L	(3) $\Delta c/c_{-1}$ $= (1)*(2)$	(4) s	(5) $\Delta S_L/S_{L-1}$ $= (1 - s)*[(1) - (3)]$
1. First year	0.10	0.3	0.03	0.49	0.0357
2. Second year	0.10	0.3107	0.03107	0.49	0.0352

since the time series of inputs in Germany is aggregated by the Divisia index.

3. The estimates for the AES between energy and capital, σ_{KE}, reveal the fact that the average of total manufacturing is -0.0, 1.3 (substitutability), and -1.1 (complementarity) in the United States, Germany, and Japan, respectively.

4. The estimates for the AES among the four factors (except σ_{KE}), σ, show that the average of total manufacturing is 0.36, 0.40, and 0.49 in the United States, Germany, and Japan, respectively.

5. As for the estimates for the OPE of capital, labor, energy, and nonenergy materials, Japan shows the highest flexibility in the demand for labor and nonenergy materials to the change in factor prices, while Germany shows the highest flexibility in the demand for capital and energy. It is to be noted, however, that the difference of the OPE among the three countries is not very large in each of the four factors.

The implications of our findings concerning the competitiveness in the trade market may be summarized as follows:

1. As far as the combined effects of the *speed* of technical improvement and the *trend* of exchange rates are concerned, the United States had slight advantages over Germany and Japan before and after the oil crisis. However, this tendency was not enough to wipe out the advantage in the *level* of price competitiveness of Japan over the United States in 1970, until the big depreciation of the dollar to yen began in 1985. The United States has kept the advantage over Germany in both the level and the rate of change in competitive power since 1975.

2. A large value for the elasticity of substitution may imply a better position in trade competition, since it will give the firm a more flexible response to changes in the economic situation. The ranking in the AES among the four factors (except σ_{KE}) is highest in Japan and second highest in Germany, although the extent of the difference is not large.

APPENDIX 8-1
SOURCES OF STATISTICAL DATA

United States

The time-series data, 1948–79, are compiled from Appendix B (labor input), C (capital input), and D (output and intermediate input) in Jorgenson, Gollop, and Fraumeni (1987).

The series of input (or input price) based on the Divisia index is converted into that based on the simple index, using the quality index presented in the same source.

The input–output table for 1977 is used in calculating a_{ji} in Equation 8-5. The disaggregation of the value of intermediate input into the value of input VE_i and that of nonenergy material input VM_i is also made by using the input coefficient of the 1977 table.

West Germany

Time-series data, 1960–79, compiled by Klaus Conrad at Mannheim University, are available to us through Shinichiro Nakamura. This is based on the aggregation of the Divisia index. Since the series of the quality index is not available to us, we use the original series. This will lead to an underestimation of the rate of technical progress compared with the results for the United States and Japan. The input–output table of 1980 is used to estimate a_{ji}, VE_i, and VM_i.

Japan

The time-series data of 1955–86 in *Annual Report on National Accounts* (Economic Planning Agency) are used; before this period the series is extended to 1953 by the National Income Accounts (the old version of the official data). The time series of capital stock is adopted from *Gross Capital Stock of Private Enterprises* (Economic Planning Agency). The input–output tables of 1960, 1965, 1970, 1975, 1980, and 1985 and the linearly interpolated tables are used to estimate a_{ji}, VE_i, and VM_i.

APPENDIX 8-2
STATISTICAL RESULTS

Equation 8-10 in Table 8-5

The estimated results are presented in Table 8-13. In order to get stabler estimates the following adjustments are made. For the United States, a dummy
variable representing a shift in the constant term in 1975–79 is introduced in
foods. In apparel the Cochrane–Orcutt method does not work; the coefficient
of serial correlation errors is set to unity. For Germany, the observation of 1979
is dropped in fabricated metal products. For Japan, the observations of years
during the oil crisis are dropped in textile, petroleum and coal products, and
fabricated metal products.

On the whole the estimated results are stable and the t value for v_i is high.
The t value of v_i is more than 2.0 in twelve industries out of twenty in the
United States; it is over 2.0 in all industries, except one, in both Germany and
Japan.

Equations 8-12 to 8-15 in Table 8-5

The estimated results are presented in Table 8-14. By and large the estimated
results are stable and the t value for s_i is high. The t value of s_i is more than
2.0, except for 1.39 for rubber in the United States; it is more than 2.0, except
for 0.89 for petroleum and coal products and 0.66 for nonferrous metals in Germany; and it is more than 2.0 in all the industries in Japan.

Since the equations are estimated for the first difference form, $\bar{R}^2$ tends to
be low. However, the standard error of estimate of the equation (SSE) is rather
low. Since the equations are log linear, the magnitude of SSE represents the
percentage error. The range of the SSEs is 0.026–0.073 in the United States; it
is 0.025–0.074 in Germany, excluding 0.123 of the petroleum and coal products;
and it is 0.038–0.089) in Japan, excluding 0.108 of the petroleum and coal products.

Table 8-13 Estimated Result at the First Aggregated Level[a]

Sector Industry	United States v_i	$\bar{R}^2$/SSE	ρ	Germany v_i	$\bar{R}^2$/SSE	ρ	Japan v_i	$\bar{R}^2$/SSE	ρ
5. Foods	0.066	0.805	0.84	0.591	0.882	0.57	0.531	0.944	0.86
	(0.78)	0.054		(7.04)	0.061		(7.92)	0.059	
6. Textiles	0.375	0.744	0.63	0.416	0.914	0.78	0.073	0.791	0.52
	(4.78)	0.085		(6.43)	0.051		(4.71)	0.088	
7. Apparel	0.122	−0.123	1.00	0.697	0.928	0.20			
	(1.40)	0.092		(13.0)	0.069				
8. Paper	0.525	0.915	0.69	0.224	0.651	0.74	0.500	0.885	0.88
	(10.5)	0.042		(2.76)	0.073		(5.57)	0.080	
9. Printing	0.197	0.904	0.83	0.611	0.858	0.75			
	(2.33)	0.059		(4.96)	0.067				
10. Chemicals	0.361	0.821	0.66	0.477	0.779	0.77	0.172	0.039	1.00
	(5.67)	0.060		(4.92)	0.080		(2.44)	0.083	
11. Petroleum and coal	0.030	0.778	0.91	0.337	0.666	0.86	0.045	0.938	0.94
	(0.50)	0.099		(3.69)	0.083		(0.38)	0.104	
12. Rubber	0.023	0.689	0.84	0.240	0.775	0.78			
	(0.79)	0.142		(3.27)	0.093				
13. Leather	0.027	0.698	0.83	0.754	0.906	0.34			
	(0.55)	0.105		(9.82)	0.075				
14. Lumber[b]	0.570	0.855	0.41	0.591	0.916	0.87			
	(10.3)	0.071		(6.79)	0.074				
15. Furniture	0.284	0.642	0.57						
	(3.20)	0.105							
16. Stone, clay, and glass	0.284	0.764	0.64	0.719	0.944	0.97	0.394	0.969	0.92
	(4.22)	0.066		(11.6)	0.042		(7.84)	0.072	
17. Primary metals[c]	0.644	0.539	0.83	0.582	0.869	0.75	0.401	0.774	1.00

Table 8-13 (cont.)

Sector Industry	United States			Germany			Japan		
	v_i	$\bar{R}^2$/SSE	ρ	v_i	$\bar{R}^2$/SSE	ρ	v_i	$\bar{R}^2$/SSE	ρ
	(5.05)	0.147		(6.68)	0.075		(10.5)	0.075	
18. Nonferrous metals				0.119 (2.26)	0.870 / 0.192	0.89			
19. Fabricated metals	0.389 (3.31)	0.675 / 0.098	0.63	0.335 (4.66)	0.827 / 0.067	0.91	0.104 (3.85)	0.942 / 0.120	0.97
20. Machinery	0.447 (4.50)	0.663 / 0.100	0.58	0.542 (6.60)	0.898 / 0.063	0.78	0.241 (2.41)	0.818 / 0.163	0.85
21. Electrical machinery	0.419 (4.75)	0.674 / 0.126	0.47	0.472 (4.56)	0.846 / 0.106	0.70	0.499 (5.60)	0.880 / 0.114	0.80
22. Transportation machinery[d]	0.125 (1.24)	0.796 / 0.136	0.70	0.032 (0.66)	0.599 / 0.130	0.89	0.318 (3.90)	0.919 / 0.105	0.90
23. Motor vehicles	0.321 (7.67)	0.701 / 0.098	0.53	0.488 (5.70)	0.772 / 0.093	0.77			
24. Precision instruments	0.079 (0.76)	0.625 / 0.137	0.74	0.598 (6.05)	0.883 / 0.065	0.94	0.672 (21.2)	0.966 / 0.107	0.31
25. Miscellaneous manufacturing[e]	0.160 (1.55)	0.651 / 0.125	0.73	0.692 (7.62)	0.907 / 0.071	0.60	0.430 (5.29)	0.937 / 0.091	0.83

[a] The figures in parentheses are the t statistics of the coefficients; $\bar{R}^2$ is the coefficient of determination adjusted for degrees of freedom; SSE is the standard error of the equation; and ρ is the autocorrelation coefficient of errors.

[b] Including furniture for Germany.

[c] Ferrous metals for Germany.

[d] Including motor vehicles for Japan.

[e] Including apparel, printing, rubber, leather, lumber, and furniture for Japan.

Table 8-14 Estimated Results at the Second Aggregated Level[a]

Sector Industry	United States s_i	$(s_{i-1})f_i$	$(s_{i-1})f'_i$	$\bar{R}^2$/SSE	Germany s_i	$(s_{i-1})f_i$	$(s_{i-1})f'_i$	$\bar{R}^2$/SSE	Japan s_i	$(s_{i-1})f_i$	$(s_{i-1})f'_i$	$(s_{i-1})f'_i$	$\bar{R}^2$/SSE
5. Foods	0.131 (3.61)	−0.011 (4.05)	−0.002 (0.33)	0.111 / 0.026	0.324 (4.86)	−0.011 (2.77)	−0.001 (0.47)	0.300 / 0.027	0.590 (8.93)	−0.003 (0.68)	0.000 (0.19)	0.001 (0.86)	0.471 / 0.038
6. Textiles	0.254 (5.97)	−0.018 (5.17)	0.001 (1.26)	0.285 / 0.032	0.396 (5.22)	−0.013 (2.33)	−0.001 (0.44)	0.326 / 0.038	0.524 (7.27)	−0.007 (1.24)	−0.003 (2.06)	−0.004 (3.36)	0.432 / 0.048
7. Apparel	0.091 (2.18)	−0.007 (1.79)	0.001 (0.70)	0.038 / 0.033	0.312 (5.31)	−0.012 (2.66)	−0.001 (0.61)	0.343 / 0.025					
8. Paper	0.468 (8.35)	−0.006 (1.75)	−0.000 (0.20)	0.442 / 0.029	0.483 (5.57)	−0.022 (2.81)	0.001 (0.57)	0.358 / 0.053	0.381 (5.16)	−0.016 (2.92)	0.000 (0.11)	−0.001 (0.78)	0.275 / 0.046
9. Printing	0.200 (4.05)	−0.007 (2.34)	0.001 (1.28)	0.192 / 0.029	0.499 (5.82)	−0.006 (1.16)	0.001 (0.78)	0.389 / 0.036					
10. Chemicals	0.498 (5.87)	−0.010 (2.39)	0.000 (0.04)	0.312 / 0.037	0.660 (7.81)	−0.011 (1.63)	−0.000 (0.05)	0.527 / 0.046	0.538 (6.27)	−0.014 (2.16)	−0.002 (1.04)	−0.001 (0.77)	0.304 / 0.054
11. Petroleum and coal	0.779 (12.1)	−0.004 (0.63)	−0.004 (2.83)	0.620 / 0.059	0.093 (0.89)	−0.024 (1.34)	0.013 (2.17)	0.131 / 0.123	0.400 (3.95)	−0.050 (4.06)	0.019 (4.98)	0.006 (2.03)	0.559 / 0.108
12. Rubber	0.054 (1.39)	−0.010 (1.67)	0.003 (2.16)	0.064 / 0.057	0.205 (3.04)	−0.026 (3.30)	0.004 (1.58)	0.171 / 0.054					
13. Leather	0.078 (3.32)	−0.000 (0.04)	−0.001 (1.20)	0.104 / 0.041	0.304 (4.53)	−0.004 (0.87)	−0.003 (1.63)	0.289 / 0.035					
14. Lumber[b]	0.379 (6.92)	−0.006 (1.14)	−0.000 (0.41)	0.341 / 0.046	0.237 (2.86)	−0.016 (2.14)	0.002 (1.04)	0.131 / 0.051					
15. Furniture	0.188 (3.11)	−0.010 (2.04)	0.001 (1.06)	0.102 / 0.045									
16. Stone, clay, and glass	0.465 (7.72)	−0.005 (1.39)	0.000 (0.15)	0.102 / 0.033	0.796 (8.59)	−0.004 (0.87)	0.000 (0.12)	0.575 / 0.033	0.530 (5.59)	−0.010 (1.55)	0.001 (0.48)	0.000 (0.13)	0.299 / 0.057
17. Primary metals[c]	0.695	−0.001	−0.001	0.438	0.691	−0.008	0.000	0.477	0.234	0.024	0.003	−0.000	0.073

Table 8-14 (cont.)

Sector Industry	United States				Germany				Japan				
	s_i	$(s_{i-1})f_i$	$(s_{i-1})f'_i$	$\bar{R}^2$/SSE	s_i	$(s_{i-1})f_i$	$(s_{i-1})f'_i$	$\bar{R}^2$/SSE	s_i	$(s_{i-1})f_i$	$(s_{i-1})f'_i$	$(s_{i-1})f'_i$	$\bar{R}^2$/SSE
18. Nonferrous metals	(8.35)	(0.08)	(0.61)	0.069	(7.08)	(1.26)	(0.02)	0.040	(2.06)	(2.93)	(1.26)	(0.09)	0.068
					0.013 (0.66)	−0.026 (2.48)	0.002 (0.50)	−0.024 / 0.074					
19. Fabricated metals	0.300 (4.84)	−0.007 (1.44)	0.001 (1.08)	0.245 / 0.044	0.162 (2.27)	−0.010 (1.63)	0.003 (1.36)	0.116 / 0.043	0.559 (4.76)	−0.007 (0.83)	0.002 (0.78)	−0.000 (0.19)	0.296 / 0.074
20. Machinery	0.522 (7.78)	−0.003 (0.63)	−0.001 (1.08)	0.399 / 0.048	0.343 (4.29)	−0.006 (1.07)	−0.002 (1.13)	0.249 / 0.037	0.585 (4.20)	−0.014 (1.38)	−0.001 (0.31)	−0.002 (1.06)	0.142 / 0.089
21. Electrical machinery	0.372 (6.96)	−0.011 (1.60)	−0.001 (0.44)	0.358 / 0.060	0.203 (2.99)	−0.019 (2.57)	0.000 (0.09)	0.116 / 0.052	0.447 (2.86)	−0.032 (2.77)	0.003 (0.99)	−0.001 (0.59)	0.073 / 0.088
22. Transportation machinery[d]	0.275 (4.53)	−0.014 (1.75)	0.000 (0.06)	0.174 / 0.073	0.174 (4.65)	0.002 (0.20)	−0.004 (1.25)	0.282 / 0.065	0.530 (5.51)	−0.019 (3.00)	0.000 (0.29)	−0.001 (0.72)	0.228 / 0.053
23. Motor vehicles	0.379 (12.1)	−0.010 (1.28)	−0.001 (0.35)	0.630 / 0.071	0.305 (4.74)	−0.019 (2.50)	0.003 (1.13)	0.335 / 0.045					
24. Precision instruments	0.225 (2.95)	−0.005 (0.71)	0.000 (0.16)	0.075 / 0.071	0.585 (6.05)	−0.008 (1.23)	−0.001 (0.53)	0.402 / 0.044	0.647 (6.40)	−0.009 (1.18)	−0.002 (1.41)	−0.001 (0.49)	0.503 / 0.057
25. Miscellaneous manufacturing[e]	0.132 (2.27)	−0.001 (0.11)	0.001 (0.78)	0.053 / 0.053	0.463 (5.72)	−0.004 (0.74)	−0.000 (0.13)	0.368 / 0.037	0.672 (11.5)	−0.008 (1.62)	0.001 (1.65)	−0.001 (1.14)	0.588 / 0.046

[a] The figures in parentheses are the t statistics of the coefficients; $\bar{R}^2$ is the coefficient of determination adjusted for degrees of freedom; and SSE is the standard error of the equation.

[b] Including furniture for Germany.

[c] Ferrous metals for Germany.

[d] Including motor vehicles for Japan.

[e] Including apparel, printing, rubber, leather, lumber, and furniture for Japan.

APPENDIX 8-3
COMPARISONS OF OUR ESTIMATES WITH THOSE BY OTHER
RESEARCHERS

Total Factor Productivity

Let us represent the production function of the general form as

$$X = F(Q_i, \text{TFP}) \tag{8A-1}$$

where

$$X = \text{quantity of output}$$
$$Q_i = \text{quantity of input}$$
$$\text{TFP} = \text{total factor productivity}$$

Then, on the assumption of the marginal productivity relationship, the rate of change in TFP is calculated by Denison's method as follows:

$$\Delta\text{TFP}/\text{TFP}_{-1} = \Delta X/X_{-1} - \sum_{i=1}^{n} W_i(\Delta Q_i/Q_{i,-1}) \tag{8A-2}$$

where

$$W_i = \text{relative share of input } i$$
$$T = \text{level of total factor productivity}$$

The estimate for TFP by this formula may be denoted by DTFP. In terms of our production function the rate of change in TFP corresponds to the growth rate of T, or the rate of technical progress in Table 8-5.

Table 8-15 presents the growth rate of DTFP, or the simple average of the figures calculated by Equation 8A-2 for the relevant period. This computation is made using our time-series data. A comparison of the figures in Tables 8-6 and 8-15 reveals the following facts. In general, the growth rate of DTFP is lower than our estimates of the rate of technical change. In the United States the growth rate of DTFP on the average of total manufacturing before the oil crisis is smaller by 0.31 percent than our estimate for the rate of technical progress, whereas after the oil crisis the former is smaller by 1.35 percent than the latter. After the oil crisis, the growth rate of DTFP of thirteen industries out of twenty is negative, and the average of total manufacturing is −0.01 percent. In Germany, the growth rates of DTFP of the average of total manufacturing before and after the oil crisis are smaller by 1.06 and 1.80 percent, respectively, than our estimates for the rate of technical progress. In Japan the growth rate of DTFP of the average of total manufacturing in 1953–73, 1974–79, and 1980–86 is smaller by 0.93, 3.13, and 2.38 percent, respectively, than our estimates.

The yearly rates of change in TFP computed from Equation 8A-2 reveals unstable movement in many industries, since it includes the errors in marginal productivity for all the inputs as well as the rate of change in TFP. This means that the simple average of the rates of change is likely to be subject to errors. To obtain stabler estimates for the average rate of change in TFP we first cal-

Table 8-15 Growth Rate of Total Factor Productivity (Percent Per Year)[a]

Sector Industry	United States		Germany		Japan		
	1949–73	1974–79	1960–73	1974–79	1953–73	1974–79	1980–86
5. Foods	0.75	0.64	0.31	0.87	0.77	0.22	-1.50
6. Textiles	1.18	2.84	0.91	2.69	2.71	2.41	1.79
7. Apparel	0.97	1.58	1.20	1.55			
8. Paper	0.94	-0.66	1.42	1.19	2.13	0.02	0.33
9. Printing	0.76	-0.24	0.84	0.32			
10. Chemicals	2.09	-1.76	1.42	1.54	2.47	0.83	1.79
11. Petroleum and coal	-0.27	-0.31	0.74	-6.63	2.17	-15.55	-1.81
12. Rubber	0.52	-1.48	2.50	1.24			
13. Leather	0.31	-0.97	0.58	1.52			
14. Lumber[b]	0.56	-0.20	2.35	0.65			
15. Furniture	0.81	0.77					
16. Stone, clay, and glass	0.65	-0.83	1.01	1.10	3.23	-1.61	-0.79
17. Primary metals[c]	-0.20	-1.29	0.41	1.06	1.66	0.72	0.79
18. Nonferrous metals			0.30	0.49			
19. Fabricated metals	0.86	-0.27	1.04	0.72	3.44	-0.28	1.04
20. Machinery	0.63	0.22	1.09	0.61	2.41	2.03	1.07
21. Electrical machinery	1.72	2.01	2.43	2.39	3.32	3.80	4.22
22. Transportation machinery[d]	0.68	-0.57	0.96	-0.16	3.34	1.18	0.26
23. Motor vehicles	1.70	0.36	0.98	2.12			
24. Precision instruments	1.36	-0.92	1.54	1.63	4.48	3.16	2.03
25. Miscellaneous	0.43	-3.60	0.18	1.06	2.88	0.56	1.04
Average of total manufacturing[e]	0.93	-0.01	1.09	1.29	2.45	-0.07	0.78

[a]Computed by the Denison method. simple average.

[b]Including furniture for Germany.

[c]Ferrous metals for Germany.

[d]Including motor vehicles for Japan.

[e]Including apparel, printing, rubber, leather, lumber, and furniture for Japan.

Table 8-16 Growth Rate of Total Factor Productivity (Percent Per Year)[a]

Sector Industry	United States		Germany		Japan		
	1949–73	1974–79	1960–73	1974–79	1953–73	1974–79	1980–86
5. Foods	1.00	0.57	0.37	0.33	0.88	0.63	0.37
6. Textiles	1.90	1.94	1.15	1.41	4.12	4.15	3.89
7. Apparel	1.01	1.14	1.31	1.48			
8. Paper	0.82	0.74	1.55	1.41	2.71	1.97	1.74
9. Printing	0.77	0.62	0.95	0.73			
10. Chemicals	2.31	1.66	1.52	1.76	3.52	2.77	2.62
11. Petroleum and coal	0.69	0.21	-0.45	-3.03	4.28	-4.12	-3.23
12. Rubber	0.81	0.54	2.52	2.26			
13. Leather	0.42	0.28	0.67	0.88			
14. Lumber[b]	1.31	0.70	2.65	2.22			
15. Furniture	0.83	0.82					
16. Stone, clay, and glass	0.69	0.58	1.25	1.26	4.79	3.22	2.28
17. Primary metals[c]	-0.27	-0.34	0.54	0.53	1.87	1.63	1.60
18. Nonferrous metals			0.02	0.31			
19. Fabricated metals	0.98	0.78	1.11	0.79	4.99	4.23	3.76
20. Machinery	0.60	0.60	1.12	1.05	3.67	3.33	3.43
21. Electrical machinery	2.20	2.23	2.78	2.95	4.12	5.01	6.42
22. Transportation machinery[d]	0.74	0.70	0.41	1.02	4.86	4.43	3.73
23. Motor vehicles	1.96	1.78	1.14	1.46			
24. Precision instruments	1.27	1.14	1.57	1.74	5.78	6.44	6.95
25. Miscellaneous manufacturing[e]	0.43	0.17	0.32	0.40	3.22	2.35	2.02
Average of total manufacturing	1.13	0.93	1.19	1.20	3.33	2.41	2.40

[a]Computed by the Denison method, time-trend regression.
[b]Including furniture for Germany.
[c]Ferrous metals for Germany.
[d]Including motor vehicles for Japan.
[e]Including apparel, printing, rubber, leather, lumber, and furniture for Japan.

culate an index of TFP by successively multiplying the level of TFP of the last
year by the rate of change of this year, and then estimate the average rate of
change in TFP by the time-trend regression of this index. This is shown in Table
8-16. In general, the estimates for the growth rate of DTFP becomes higher
than the figures of Table 8-15, particularly in 1949–73 of the United States and
all the subperiods of Japan. It is to be noted, however, that even in the time-
trend regression, the growth rate of DTFP is lower than our estimates in Table
8-6 by 0.1–0.4, 0.9–1.0, and 0.1–0.8 percent in the United States, Germany, and
Japan, respectively.

One can argue that the Denison method does not assume any particular
form of the production function, except for the marginal productivity relationship, and thus the estimate for TFP by this method is basic and reliable. However, this is not necessarily so. The estimate for TFP by the Denison method
includes not only the total factor productivity but also the errors in marginal
productivity relation of all the inputs.

Our method allocates the errors of marginal productivity relation to each
factor by Equations 8-6 to 8-9, and it may serve for the purpose of finding a
stabler estimate for the rate of technical progress.

Nemoto's Cross-Sectional Study for Japan

Nemoto (1984) estimated a KLEM function of a two-level CES function for
foods, paper and pulp, and stone, clay, and glasses on the basis of Japanese
cross-sectional data (1965, 1970, 1975, 1977, and 1978 input–output tables). His
estimates are listed in Table 8-17. The estimates of ES, σ_{KE}, for the three industries are different from those in our Table 8-7; the estimates of ES, σ, by
Neomoto are about twice as much as ours in the same table. It is interesting to
note, however, that the estimates of the OPE by Nemoto are fairly comparable
with ours in Table 8-8 for all the factors and all the industries, although Nemoto's estimates tend to be higher than ours by about one-third on average.

Others' Findings

Table 8-18 presents findings by Berndt and Wood (1979), Griffin and Gregory
(1976), and Pindyck (1979). For σ_{KE}, their estimates for the United States are
large in absolute values and are different from our estimate of the average of
total manufacturing in Table 8-7, −0.045. Their estimates for Germany are
more comparable with ours for total manufacturing average, whereas that for
Japan is not.

Table 8-17   Nemoto's ES Estimates for Japan[a]

Industry	σ_{KE}	σ	ε_{KK}	ε_{EE}	ε_{LL}	ε_{MM}
Foods	0.05	0.94	−0.75	−0.76	−0.70	−0.25
Paper and pulp	−0.48	0.89	−0.62	−0.54	−0.46	−0.29
Stone, clay, and glass	−0.63	1.19	−0.72	−0.56	−0.50	−0.46

Source: Nemoto (1984).
[a]$\sigma = \sigma_{KL} = \sigma_{KM} = \sigma_{EM} = \sigma_{LM}$.

Table 8-18 Other Findings

	σ_{KE}	σ_{KL}	σ_{LE}
Berndt and Wood (1979)			
United States	-3.22	1.01	0.65
1947–71			
Griffin and Gregory (1976)			
United States	1.07	0.06	0.87
Germany	1.03	0.50	0.78
Pindyck (1979)			
United States	0.61	0.82	0.93
Germany	0.82	0.81	0.94
Japan	0.86	0.81	0.96

As for σ_{KL} and σ_{LE}, their estimates are about twice as high as ours for all three countries, except for σ_{KL} by Griffin and Gregory.

NOTES

We thank Mashiro Kuroda, Shinichiro Nakamura, and Kazuhisa Matsuda for allowing us to use their statistical data bank and Lawrence R. Klein, Bert Hickman, Pierre Lassere, Jiro Nemoto, and participants of the conference for helpful comments and advice. We are also indebted to Takuyuki Oono for his cooperative work with us at the early stages of this research. Needless to say, remaining errors are ours.

1. The sources of statistical data are given in Appendix 8-1.
2. In other words, the estimate for the rate of change in M_i is represented as

$$\Delta m_i/m_{i,-1} = \sum_{j \in jm} \Delta b_{ji} \ln X_{ji}$$

3. The unit of m_i is set so that PM_i may be unity in the base year.
4. Our estimates are compared with those by other researchers in Appendix 8-3.
5. The rate of technical progress of petroleum and coal products in 1974–79 is 3.62 percent. If one takes into account the effort of these industries to increase productivity in this period, this estimate is not unreasonably high. The average of total manufacturing, excluding petroleum and coal products, is 1.25 percent instead of 1.34 percent.
6. As is seen from Table 8-6, the rate of technical progress in 1980–86 was almost unchanged from that in 1974–79. In fact, the estimated results of the equation with one kink in 1974 show that the average rate of total manufacturing was 3.6 and 3.2 percent in 1953–73 and 1974–86, respectively. This finding is fairly consistent with the figures of Table 8-6.
7. The average of total manufacturing, excluding textiles and fabricated metals, is -0.37. This means that complementarity is still dominant in manufacturing.
8. In the following discussion the estimates for the OPE are compared in absolute values, since the OPEs presented here are all negative.
9. More specifically, see a numerical example in the next section, where it is shown that a higher value of the ES defined in Table 8-4, or σ presented in Table 8-7, leads to a greater cost reduction in case of a fall in factor price. Within the framework of our

production function a higher value of σ, ceteris paribus, brings about a higher value of the OPEs.

10. In this calculation the rate of change in competitiveness between the United States and Japan in 1974–79 is extended for 1979–85.

REFERENCES

Allen, R. G. D. 1938. *Mathematical Analysis for Economics*. London: Macmillan.

Berndt, E. R., and D. O. Wood. 1975. "Technology, Prices, and Derived Demand for Energy." *Review of Economics and Statistics* 56 (August), 259–68.

Griffin, J. M., and P. R. Gregory. 1976. "An Intercountry Translog Model of Energy Substitution Responses." *American Economic Review* 66 (December), 845–57.

Jorgenson, D. W., F. M. Gollop, and B. M. Fraumeni. 1987. *Productivity and U.S. Economic Growth*. Cambridge, Mass.: Harvard University Press.

Kravis, I. B., A. Heston, and R. Summers. 1982. *World Product and Income: International Comparisons of Real Gross Product*. Baltimore, Md.: Johns Hopkins University Press.

Kravis, I. B., Z. Kenessey, A. Heston, and R. Summers. 1975. *A System of International Comparisons of Gross Product and Purchasing Power*. Baltimore, Md.: Johns Hopkins University Press.

Nemoto, J. 1984. "On Substitution Possibilities between Energy and Nonenergy Inputs: A Nested CES Production Function Analysis." *Economic Studies Quarterly* 35 (August), 139–58. (in Japanese)

Pindyck, R. S. 1979. *The Structure of World Energy Demand*. Cambridge: MIT Press.

Sato, K. 1967. "A Two-Level Constant-Elasticity-of-Substitution Production Function." *Review of Economic Studies* 34 (April), 201–18.

9

Productivity and International Competitiveness in Japan and the United States, 1960–85

DALE W. JORGENSON AND MASAHIRO KURODA

The political relationship between Japan and the United States has become increasingly preoccupied with "trade frictions." These disputes over trade issues have accompanied the massive expansion of Japanese exports to the United States. Explanations for the resulting trade imbalance must include variations in the yen–dollar exchange rate, changes in the relative prices of capital and labor in the two countries, and the relative growth of productivity in Japanese and U.S. industries. We analyze the role of each of these factors in explaining the rise in competitiveness of Japanese industries relative to their U.S. counterparts.

At the outset of our discussion it is essential to define a measure of international competitiveness. Our measure of international competitiveness is the price of an industry's output in Japan relative to the price in the United States. Japanese exports are generated by U.S. purchases from Japanese industries, while U.S. exports result from Japanese purchases from U.S. industries. The relative price of an industry's output enters the decisions of purchasers in both countries and the rest of the world. In order to explain changes in international competitiveness we must account for changes in the determinants of this relative price.

The starting point for our analysis of the competitiveness of Japanese and U.S. industries in the yen–dollar exchange rate. This is simply the number of yen required to purchase one U.S. dollar in the market for foreign exchange. Variations in the yen–dollar exchange rate are easy to document and are often used to characterize movements in relative prices in the two countries. However, movements in relative prices of goods and services do not coincide with variations in the exchange rate. To account for changes in international competitiveness a measure of the relative prices of specific goods and services is required.

To assess the international competitiveness of Japanese and U.S. industries it is necessary to carry out price comparisons for industry outputs in the two countries. These comparisons are hampered by the fact that the makeup of a given industry may differ substantially between Japan and the United States. For example, the steel industry produces an enormous range of different steel products. The relative importance of different types of steel differs between the two countries. The composition of the output of the steel industry in each country also changes over time. These differences must be taken into account in comparing the relative prices of steel between Japan and the United States.

Relative prices between Japanese and U.S. industries can be summarized by means of purchasing-power parities (PPPs). The PPP for a specific industry's output is the number of yen required to purchase an amount of the industry's output in Japan costing one dollar in the United States. The dimensions of PPPs are the same as the yen–dollar exchange rate, namely, yen per dollar. However, the PPPs reflect the relative prices of the goods and services that make up the industry's output in both countries.

The most familiar application of the notion of purchasing-power parity is to the relative prices of such aggregates as the gross domestic product (GDP). This application has been the focus of the landmark studies of Kravis, Heston, and Summers (1978). As a consequence of their research, it is now possible to compare the relative prices of GDP for a wide range of countries, including Japan and the United States. Kravis, Heston, and Summers based their PPPs for GDP on relative prices for 153 commodity groups.

In this study we estimate PPPs for twenty-nine industries in Japan and the United States for the period 1960–85. These are relative prices of the outputs of each industry in the two countries in terms of yen per dollar. We divide the relative price of each industry's output by the yen–dollar exchange rate to translate PPPs into relative prices in terms of dollars.[1] We find it convenient to employ relative prices in dollars as measures of international competitiveness. Variations in the exchange rate are reflected in the relative prices of outputs for all twenty-nine industries.

To account for changes in international competitiveness between Japanese and U.S. industries we have compiled PPPs for the inputs into each industry. By analogy with outputs, the PPPs for inputs are based on the relative prices of the goods and services that make up the inputs of each industry. We have disaggregated inputs among capital and labor services, which are primary factors of production, and energy and other intermediate goods, which are produced by one industry and consumed by other industries. We can translate PPPs for inputs into relative prices in dollars by dividing by the yen–dollar exchange rate. We describe PPPs for output and inputs in twenty-nine industries of the U.S. and Japan in the following section.

Our final step in accounting for international competitiveness between Japanese and U.S. industries is to measure the relative levels of productivity for all twenty-nine industries. For this purpose we employ a model of production for each industry. This model enables us to express the price of output in each country as a function of the prices of inputs and the level of productivity in that country. We can account for the relative prices of output between Japan and the United States by allowing input prices and levels of productivity to differ between countries. We have compiled data on relative productivity levels in Japan and the United States for the period 1960–85. For this purpose we revised and extended the estimates for 1960–79 reported by Jorgenson, Kuroda, and Nishimizu (1987).

The methodology for our study was originated by Jorgenson and Nishimizu (1978). They provided a theoretical framework for productivity comparisons based on a bilateral production function at the aggregate level. They employed this framework in comparing aggregate output, input, and productivity for Japan and the United States.[2] This methodology was extended to the industry level by Jorgenson and Nishimizu (1981) and employed in international comparisons between Japanese and U.S. industries. The industry-level methodology introduced models of production for individual industries based on bilateral production functions for each industry. This methodology was used in our earlier study with Nishimizu, involving Japan–U.S. comparisons at the industry level for the period 1960–79.[3] We discuss the theoretical framework for international comparisons briefly in the appendix to this chapter.

We present comparisons of productivity levels between the U.S. and Japan by industry in a later section. Jorgenson, Kuroda, and Nishimizu (1987) presented a taxonomy of Japanese and U.S. industries, based on the development of relative productivity levels over the period 1960–79. They used this taxonomy to project the likely development of relative productivity levels for each industry. We can now assess the validity of these projections on the basis of developments during the period 1960–85. We find that the taxonomy has been very useful in forming expectations about future developments in productivity. Finally, we employ changes in relative productivity levels and relative prices of inputs in accounting for changes in international competitiveness between Japanese and U.S. industries over the period 1960–85. The last section provides a summary and conclusion.

PURCHASING-POWER PARITIES

We treat data on production patterns in Japan and the United States as separate sets of observations. We assume that these observations are generated by bilateral models of production for each industrial sector presented in detail in the appendix. We can describe the implications of the theory of production in terms of production functions for each industry. These production functions give industry outputs as functions of capital, labor, energy, and other intermediate inputs, a dummy variable equal to one for Japan and zero for the United States, and time as an index of technology.

In our bilateral models of production the capital, labor, energy, and other intermediate input prices are aggregates that depend on the prices of individual capital inputs, labor inputs, energy inputs, and other intermediate inputs in Japan and the United States. The product of price and quantity indexes must equal the value of all the components of each aggregate. We define price indexes corresponding to each aggregate as ratios of the value of the components of the aggregate to the corresponding quantity index. In international comparisons the price indexes represent PPPs between the yen and the dollar. For example, the price index for labor input represents the Japanese price in yen for labor input costing one dollar in the United States.

Our methodology for estimating PPPs is based on linking time-series data sets on prices in Japan and the United States. Suppose that we observe the price of the output of the ith industry in Japan and the United States, say $q_i(J)$ and $q_i(U)$, in the base period, where these prices are evaluated in terms of yen and dollars, respectively. We can define the purchasing-power parity for the output of the ith industry, that is, PPP_i, as

$$PPP_i = \frac{q_i(J)}{q_i(U)}, \qquad i = 1, 2, \ldots, I) \qquad (9\text{-}1)$$

The PPP gives the number of yen required in Japan to purchase an amount of the output of the ith industry costing one dollar in the United States in the base period.

To estimate PPPs for outputs of all industries in Japan and the United States we first construct a time series of prices for the output of each industry in both countries in domestic currency. To obtain price indexes for industry outputs in the United States, we normalize the price index for each industry, that is, $q_i(U,T)$, at unity in the base period. We normalize the corresponding price index for Japan, $q_i(J,T)$, at the PPP in the base period. We obtain estimates of purchasing-power parities for all years, $PPP_i(T)$, from these price indexes and the purchasing-power parity for the base period from the equation

$$PPP_i(T) = PPP_i(0) \frac{q_i(J,T)}{q_i(J,0)} \frac{q_i(U,0)}{q_i(U,T)}, \qquad i = 1, 2, \ldots, I \qquad (9\text{-}2)$$

where $PPP_i(0)$ is the purchasing-power parity in the base period and $q_i(J,0)$ and $q_i(U,0)$ are the prices of outputs of the ith industry in Japan and the United States in the base period.

Finally, we define the relative price of the output of the ith industry in Japan and the United States in dollars, $p_i(J,U)$, as the ratio of the purchasing-power parity for that industry to the yen–dollar exchange rate, E.

$$p_i(J,U) = \frac{PPP_i}{E}, \qquad i = 1, 2, \ldots, I \qquad (9\text{-}3)$$

The relative price of the output of the ith industry in Japan and the United States is the ratio of the number of dollars required in Japan to purchase an amount of the industry's output costing one dollar in the United States. This index is our measure of international competitiveness between the Japanese industry and its U.S. counterpart.

To construct PPPs and the corresponding relative prices between Japanese and U.S. industries, we require an estimate of the PPP for each industry in the base period. For this purpose we have developed PPPs for industry outputs based on the results of Kravis, Heston, and Summers (1978). They provided PPPs between the yen and the dollar for 153 commodity groups for the year

1970. These commodity groups are components of the gross domestic product of each country, corresponding to deliveries to final demand at purchasers' prices.

We construct PPPs for industry outputs, energy inputs, and other intermediate inputs by mapping the 153 commodity groups employed by Kravis, Heston, and Summers (1978) into the industry classification system shown in Table 9-1. Unfortunately, a complete correspondence between the two systems is impossible, since not all intermediate goods delivered by the different industrial sectors are included among the 153 commodity groups delivered to final demand. We eliminated the gap between the two systems by utilizing the PPPs of close substitutes for a given industry's deliveries to intermediate demand.

To obtain PPPs for industry outputs from the producer's point of view, we adjust the price indexes for commodity groups in Japan and the United States by "peeling off" the indirect taxes paid and trade and transportation margins for each industry. We estimate these margins from the interindustry transactions table for 1970 for each country. To obtain the PPPs for industry outputs, we aggregate the results for commodity groups, using as weights the relative shares of each commodity in the value of industry output from the 1970 interindustry transactions tables. Similarly, to obtain PPPs for components of inter-

Table 9-1   List of industries commonly classified

Sector Industry	Abbreviation
1. Agriculture, forestry, and fisheries	Agric.
2. Mining	Mining
3. Construction	Construct.
4. Food and kindred products	Foods
5. Textile mill products	Textiles
6. Apparel and other fabricated textile	Apparel
7. Lumber and wood products except furniture	Lumber
8. Furniture and fixtures	Furniture
9. Paper and allied products	Paper
10. Printing, publishing, and allied products	Printing
11. Chemical and allied products	Chemical
12. Petroleum refining and coal products	Petroleum
13. Rubber and miscellaneous plastic products	Rubber
14. Leather and leather products	Leather
15. Stone, clay, and glass products	Stone
16. Primary metal products	Prim. metal
17. Fabricated metal products	Fab. metal
18. Machinery	Machinery
19. Electric machinery	Elec. mach.
20. Motor vehicles and equipment	Mot. veh.
21. Transportation equipment except motor vehicles	Trsp. eqpt.
22. Precision instruments	Prec. inst.
23. Miscellaneous manufacturing	Mfg. misc.
24. Transportation and communication	Trsp. comm.
25. Electric utility and gas supply	Utilities
26. Wholesale and retail trade	Trade
27. Finance, insurance, and real estate	Finance
28. Other service	Service
29. Government services	Gov. serv.

mediate input in each industry, we aggregate PPPs for goods and services delivered by that industry to other industries. We employ relative shares in the value of deliveries of intermediate input from other industries from the 1970 interindustry transactions tables as weights.

For both Japan and the United States capital stocks are divided among seven types of depreciable assets and two types of nondepreciable assets for each industry. These assets are further subdivided among legal forms of organization. We employ the equality between the price of an asset and the discounted flow of future capital services to derive service prices for capital input. Although we estimate the decline in efficiency of capital goods for each component of capital input separately for Japan and the United States, we assume that the relative efficiency of new capital goods in a given industry is the same in both countries. The appropriate PPP for new capital goods is the PPP for the corresponding component of investment goods output. To obtain the PPP for capital input, we multiply the PPP for investment goods by the ratio of the price of capital services to the price of capital goods for Japan relative to the United States. The resulting price index represents the PPP for capital input.

For both Japan and the United States labor inputs are cross-classified by employment status, sex, age, education, and occupation. Given the detailed classification of labor input for each industry in our data base, we construct PPPs for labor input on the basis of relative wage levels for each component of labor input in each industry. Finally, we convert the PPPs to relative prices using the 1970 exchange rate. The relative prices for industry, output, capital, labor, energy, and other intermediate inputs in 1970 are listed in Table 9-2.

According to our relative price indexes for industry output in 1970, prices in Japan were higher than those in the United States in only six sectors—agriculture-forestry-fisheries, construction, food and kindred products, petroleum refinery and coal products, rubber products, and electricity and gas. The relative prices for labor input in 1970 represent substantially lower costs of labor input in Japan relative to the United States. In that year hourly wages in Japan were 30 percent or less of U.S. hourly wages. By contrast, the cost of capital in Japan averaged about 80 percent of the U.S. cost in 1970. The relative prices for intermediate inputs are calculated as a weighted average of the relative prices of industry outputs. The cost of intermediate inputs in Japan, other than energy, is between 60 and 90 percent of the cost in the United States in 1970. On the other hand, the relative prices for energy inputs in 1970 are greater than unity, implying that the cost of energy in Japan was higher than that in the United States.

We estimated PPPs between the yen and the dollar in 1970 for the twenty-nine industries listed in Table 9-1. We also compiled price indexes for industry outputs and inputs in both countries for the period 1960–85. We obtain indexes of prices of outputs and inputs for each industry in Japan relative to those in the United States for each year from Equation 9-2. Table 9-3 presents time series for price indexes of value added and capital and labor inputs for 1960–85 in Japan and the United States. Column 1 in each part of the table represents the yen–dollar exchange rate. Columns 2 and 3 represent price indexes for Japan. Column 2 gives the domestic price index with base equal to the PPP, ad-

Table 9-2   The Japanese Relative Price Indexes in the 1970 Base Year (U.S. Price = 1.000)[a]

Industry	Output Price	Capital Price	Labor Price	Energy Price	Material Price
Agric.	1.04556	0.90835	0.21352	1.48236	0.91204
Mining	0.72125	0.88095	0.21263	1.44013	0.70573
Construct.	1.03487	0.92127	0.18607	1.42641	0.72203
Foods	1.03569	0.9219	0.21894	1.26554	0.88483
Textiles	0.77898	0.90871	0.24099	1.18329	0.76975
Apparel	0.76952	0.86037	0.18975	1.24298	0.74821
Lumber	0.79154	0.84363	0.22805	1.2268	0.90165
Furniture	0.67945	0.84214	0.22952	1.22178	0.74429
Paper	0.58858	0.89567	0.2217	1.18606	0.65664
Printing	0.78107	0.86742	0.21251	1.12482	0.65975
Chemical	0.6621	0.91711	0.25039	1.3363	0.712
Petroleum	1.59952	0.89588	0.21846	1.31298	0.88291
Rubber	1.06186	0.86013	0.24042	1.22499	0.76731
Leather	0.71273	0.82076	0.23569	1.31561	0.81086
Stone	0.69603	0.89998	0.23083	1.31627	0.72567
Prim. metal	0.81706	0.91205	0.252	1.37079	0.80318
Fab. metal	0.81514	0.90205	0.21072	1.32346	0.77507
Machinery	0.61327	0.9202	0.22564	1.28346	0.71093
Elec. mach.	0.68127	0.92036	0.22308	1.24327	0.71054
Mot. veh.	0.78627	0.91647	0.18581	1.1729	0.76428
Trsp. eqpt.	0.94794	0.87722	0.21944	1.24063	0.76549
Prec. inst.	0.71912	0.86402	0.2315	1.22607	0.71774
Mfg. misc.	0.69473	0.88034	0.22549	1.27395	0.71238
Trsp. comm.	0.47247	0.91027	0.22713	1.43624	0.68624
Utilities	1.02936	0.90389	0.26605	1.4949	0.78528
Trade	0.66155	0.93094	0.26889	1.35118	0.73683
Finance	0.86176	0.833	0.30796	1.1449	0.77297
Service	0.56751	0.91719	0.25592	1.22718	0.73724
Gov. serv.	0.30797	0	0.19482	1.35489	0.68436

[a]Relative prices in 1970 as defined in Equation 9-3.

justed by the exchange rate, in 1970. Column 3 gives this price index divided by an index of the yen–dollar exchange rate (1970 = 1). Column 4 gives the corresponding price index in the United States (1970 = 1).

According to the results presented in Table 9-3, the dollar-denominated price deflator for aggregate value added in Japan was 0.49401 in 1960, while that in the United States was 0.78454 in that year. This implies that the Japanese aggregate price index in 1960 was only 63 percent of that in the United States. Under the fixed yen–dollar exchange rate of 360 yen to the dollar that prevailed until 1970, the ratio of the Japanese price index to the U.S. price index rose to 76 percent in 1970. With the collapse of the fixed exchange rate regime in 1970 and the beginning of the energy crisis in 1973 the price index in Japan, denominated in dollars, exceeded the corresponding U.S. price index. This was a consequence of more rapid inflation in Japan and a substantial appreciation of the yen through 1973. The competitiveness of U.S. industries relative to their Japanese counterparts reached a temporary peak in that year.

Table 9-3 Comparisons of Trends Between Japan and the United States[a]

Year	(1) Exchange Rate	(2) Value-Added, Japan (1)	(3) Value-Added, Japan (2)	(4) Value-Added, United States
A. Value-added price indexes
1960	360	0.49401	0.49401	0.78454
1961	360	0.53183	0.53183	0.79409
1962	360	0.55298	0.55298	0.80279
1963	360	0.57685	0.57685	0.80636
1964	360	0.59492	0.59492	0.81536
1965	360	0.61978	0.61978	0.83047
1966	360	0.64779	0.64779	0.86174
1967	360	0.67604	0.67604	0.88078
1968	360	0.69657	0.69657	0.91007
1969	360	0.72318	0.72318	0.95491
1970	360	0.75878	0.75878	1
1971	348	0.77834	0.80517	1.0476
1972	303.1	0.80947	0.96143	1.09325
1973	271.7	0.92428	1.22466	1.16623
1974	292.1	0.8719	1.0746	1.29731
1975	296.8	0.99093	1.20194	1.42734
1976	296.5	1.05665	1.28294	1.49954
1977	268.3	1.10367	1.48088	1.60448
1978	210.1	1.18892	2.03717	1.73642
1979	219.5	1.21565	1.99378	1.89859
1980	203	1.27198	2.25578	2.09651
1981	219.9	1.30588	1.13787	2.29653
1982	235	1.34193	1.05572	2.43595
1983	232.2	1.36365	2.11418	2.51156
1984	251.1	1.37795	1.97556	2.59771
1985	224.05	1.38862	2.23121	2.66754
B. Capital input price indexes
1960	360	0.62499	0.62499	0.79723
1961	360	0.7001	0.7001	0.80034
1962	360	0.64268	0.64268	0.87577
1963	360	0.62544	0.62544	0.9131
1964	360	0.68795	0.68795	0.96814
1965	360	0.68865	0.68865	1.05671
1966	360	0.71741	0.71741	1.08764
1967	360	0.7829	0.7829	1.06235
1968	360	0.86281	0.86281	1.07711
1969	360	0.88634	0.88634	1.09371
1970	360	0.89842	0.89842	1
1971	348	0.81956	0.8478206	1.07581
1972	303.1	0.83773	0.9949943	1.16855
1973	271.7	0.9224	1.2221715	1.22005
1974	292.1	0.99464	1.2258486	1.12504
1975	296.8	0.9234	1.1200269	1.29908
1976	296.5	0.94393	1.1460870	1.42287
1977	268.3	0.96151	1.2901364	1.63368
1978	210.1	1.15219	1.9742427	1.78198
1979	219.5	1.21611	1.9945312	1.82541
1980	203	1.00809	1.7877458	1.85044

Table 9-3   (cont.)

Year	(1) Exchange Rate	(2) Value-Added, Japan (1)	(3) Value-Added, Japan (2)	(4) Value-Added, United States
1981	219.9	0.98245	1.6083765	2.00438
1982	235	1.04394	1.5992272	1.96229
1983	232.2	1.06156	1.6458294	2.13968
1984	251.1	1.10386	1.5825949	2.43909
1985	224.05	1.1502	1.8481231	2.46379
C. Labor input price indexes				
1960	360	0.06759	0.06759	0.60926
1961	360	0.07795	0.07795	0.64391
1962	360	0.08871	0.08871	0.65408
1963	360	0.10203	0.10203	0.66726
1964	360	0.10864	0.10864	0.68739
1965	360	0.12425	0.12425	0.70308
1966	360	0.13732	0.13732	0.74533
1967	360	0.15215	0.15215	0.79066
1968	360	0.17714	0.17714	0.8549
1969	360	0.20104	0.20104	0.90917
1970	360	0.23211	0.23211	1
1971	348	0.26643	0.2756172	1.07431
1972	303.1	0.30113	0.3576601	1.14898
1973	271.7	0.38076	0.5045034	1.24142
1974	292.1	0.46834	0.5772078	1.36978
1975	296.8	0.55019	0.6673463	1.49983
1976	296.5	0.59518	0.7226468	1.62713
1977	268.3	0.6492	0.8710846	1.73529
1978	210.1	0.67337	1.1537991	1.84918
1979	219.5	0.70365	1.1540501	2.00071
1980	203	0.75423	1.3375507	2.21758
1981	219.9	0.79732	1.3052987	2.39774
1982	235	0.8339	1.2774638	2.54319
1983	232.2	0.83456	1.2938914	2.64133
1984	251.1	0.85129	1.2204874	2.73005
1985	224.05	0.89202	1.4332836	2.864

ᵃColumn 1, market exchange rate (yen/dollar); column 2, Japanese PPP-based price index; column 3, Japanese PPP-based price index denominated by the market exchange rate; column 4, corresponding U.S. price index.

After 1973 the U.S. inflation rate continued at a high level, whereas Japan underwent a severe deflation accompanied by depreciation of the yen. This had the short-run effect of restoring the competitiveness of Japanese industries. Inflation resumed in Japan after 1974 and the yen was allowed to appreciate again, reaching an exchange rate of 210 yen to the dollar in 1978. Once again Japanese prices, denominated in terms of dollars, exceeded U.S. prices. This situation continued until 1980 as inflation in the United States continued at high rates. In the 1980s U.S. prices rose to well above the level of Japanese prices in dollars due to the rapid appreciation of the U.S. dollar relative to the Japanese yen. By 1985 the Japanese price level in dollars was only 83 percent of the U.S. price, which implies that Japanese industries had a substantial competitive advantage relative to their U.S. counterparts.

According to the international comparison of capital input prices seen in Table 9-3, the cost of capital in Japan was almost 78 percent of that in the United States in 1960 and gradually rose to within 89 percent of the U.S. level by 1970. After the energy crisis in 1973 the cost of capital in Japan increased relative to that of the United States, exceeding the U.S. level by almost 11 percent in 1978. The appreciation of the U.S. dollar reversed this trend. By 1985 the relative cost of capital in Japan had fallen to only 75 percent of the U.S. level, which is below the level prevailing almost a quarter century earlier in 1960. The rise in the cost of capital in Japan relative to that in the United States after the energy crisis was a consequence of the appreciation of the yen. The fall of this relative price in the 1980s resulted from the appreciation of the dollar.

Finally, a comparison of labor input prices in Table 9-3 shows that the Japanese wage rate in 1960 was only 11 percent of the U.S. wage rate. By 1970 the Japanese wage rate had reached 23 percent of the U.S. level. Rapid wage increases in Japan during the 1970s and the sharp appreciation of the yen raised wage rates in Japan to 60 percent of the U.S. level in 1980. The subsequent appreciation of the dollar and rapid wage increases in the United States resulted in a decline in Japanese wage rates relative to the United States. The relative price of labor input in Japan was only 50 percent of the U.S. level in 1985.

Our international comparisons of relative prices of aggregate output and inputs show, first, that the Japanese economy has been more competitive than the U.S. economy throughout the period 1960–85, except for 1973 and 1978–79. Second, lower wage rates contributed to Japan's international competitiveness throughout the period, especially before the energy crisis in 1973. Lower costs of capital have also contributed to Japan's international competitiveness for most of the same period with important exceptions in 1973 and 1978–80.

We turn next to international competitiveness of Japanese and U.S. industries. Exchange rates play the same role in relative price comparisons at the industry level as at the aggregate level. However, industry inputs include energy and other intermediate goods as well as the primary factors of production—capital and labor inputs. The price of energy inputs in each industrial sector is an aggregate of inputs of petroleum and coal products and electricity and gas products. The relative prices of the outputs of these two industries in Japan and the U.S. are seen in Table 9-4. The energy crisis of 1973 had an enormous impact on the prices of energy in both Japan and the United States. Prices of petroleum and coal products in Japan were almost double those in the United States, while prices of electricity and gas were about 1.3 times those in the United States in 1985. By comparison, petroleum and coal products in Japan were only 1.6 times as expensive as those in the United States in 1970, while electricity and gas were only slightly more expensive in Japan than in the United States in that year.

Table 9-5 lists average annual growth rates of input prices in Japan and the United States in the 1960s, 1970s, and 1980s at the industry level. Differences in the growth rates of the cost of capital between Japan and the United States were negligible in the 1960s. Since 1970 average rates of growth in the United States have been considerably higher. The rates of growth of wage rates in

Table 9-4 Relative Prices of Outputs for Two Industries

Year	12. Petroleum and Coal		25. Electricity and Gas	
	Japan	United States	Japan	United States
1960	1.71118	0.97477	0.83247	0.94299
1965	1.51919	0.94523	1.00311	0.96430
1970	1.59952	1.00000	1.02936	1.00000
1975	5.34666	2.51780	2.26813	1.78555
1980	14.75987	6.46713	5.99713	3.45804
1985	13.28313	5.98764	6.25211	5.04334

Japan were substantially higher than those in the United States throughout in the 1960s and 1970s. During the 1980s, however, annual rates of growth of wages in the United States exceeded those in Japan by about 1.5 percent per year.

The movements of energy input prices were similar in the two countries in the 1960s. We have already described these movements during the energy crisis of the 1970s. Rates of growth of energy prices in the United States in the 1980s were about 3 percent per year higher than those in Japan. This implies that differences between energy prices in the two countries have been decreasing

Table 9-5 Annual Rates of Price Increase[a]

Year	Country	Price Increase (%)
Capital service		
1960–70	Japan	2.8435
	United States	2.2153
1970–80	Japan	−0.5899
	United States	6.3782
1980–85	Japan	0.0777
	United States	5.9044
Labor service		
1960–70	Japan	12.2062
	United States	4.5325
1970–80	Japan	11.6868
	United States	8.0232
1980–85	Japan	3.8273
	United States	5.2741
Energy input		
1960–70	Japan	0.5881
	United States	0.4518
1970–80	Japan	13.8936
	United States	15.1777
1980–85	Japan	1.2662
	United States	4.3062
Material input		
1960–70	Japan	2.1515
	United States	2.0432
1970–80	Japan	7.7005
	United States	8.1342
1980–85	Japan	0.5704
	United States	3.2437

[a]Annual rates of price increases are estimated in terms of a simple average of an annual rates by industry in each category.

since 1980, in spite of the relatively high level of energy prices in Japan. The growth rates of other intermediate input prices in the United States were also higher than that in Japan after 1980. The higher growth rates of input prices in the United States since 1980—including capital, labor, energy, and other intermediate inputs—have resulted in a substantial deterioration of international competitiveness of U.S. industries relative to their Japanese counterparts.

RELATIVE PRODUCTIVITY LEVELS

In this section we estimate relative levels of productivity in Japan and the United States for each of the twenty-nine industries included in our study. Jorgenson, Kuroda, and Nishimizu (1987) reported relative productivity levels for the two countries for 1960–79. All Japanese industries had lower levels of productivity than their U.S. counterparts in 1960. However, there were nine industries in which productivity gaps between the two countries closed in 1960–79. In nineteen industries differences in productivity levels between Japan and the United States remained in 1979.

Jorgenson, Kuroda, and Nishimizu (1987) divided Japanese and U.S. industries into seven categories. Type I includes four industries in which productivity gaps between Japan and the United States were expected to increase in the future: agriculture-forestry-fisheries, textiles, printing and publishing, and trade. Type II includes industries in which the productivity gaps were decreasing before 1973 but increasing after 1973: food and kindred products, apparel, furniture, rubber, stone and clay, other transportation equipment, utilities, and other services. Type III includes investment goods industries such as nonelectrical machinery, electrical machinery, and motor vehicles, in which the United States had an advantage in productivity in 1979, but productivity gaps were expected to close in the near future.

Paper and allied products comprise type IV; in this industry U.S. productivity levels increased relative to those in Japan before 1973, but the productivity gap was decreasing afterward due to deterioration of productivity in the U.S. industry. Petroleum and coal products, with a constant productivity gap favoring the United States, and construction, with negative growth rates of productivity in both countries, are classified as type V and type VI, respectively. Finally, type VII includes the nine industries in which Japan had a productivity advantage in 1979. The Japanese advantage was expected to increase in the future. These include mining, lumber, chemicals, primary metals, fabricated metals, precision instruments, miscellaneous manufacturing, transportation and communication, and finance and insurance.

To assess the validity of this taxonomy in projecting future patterns of relative productivity growth in Japan and the United States we consider additional observations for 1979–85. However, we must take note of the following revisions in our data base. First, we revised U.S. intermediate input measures by constructing a time series of interindustry transactions tables for 1947–85. The methodology is consistent with the approach used for constructing a time series of Japanese interindustry transactions tables for 1960–85.[4] Second, we were able to obtain more detailed information on wage differentials between full-time employees and other employees in Japan. We used this information to improve our estimates of labor compensation for temporary employees, day laborers, and unpaid family workers in Japan.

Our earlier estimates of PPPs for labor input were based on relative wage levels for full-time workers in Japan and the United States. In the agricultural sector in Japan, however, there are substantial numbers of irregular and part-time workers, especially unpaid family workers. Taking the labor compensation of these workers into account, we find that we overestimated the PPP of labor input in the agricultural sector in our earlier work. We revised the PPP index of labor input in the agriculture-forestry-fisheries industry in 1970 from 0.60588 to 0.21352, as shown in Table 9-2. This is much closer to results for other industries, where we take account only of ordinary full-time employees in estimating the PPP index for labor input.

The three revisions in our data base resulted in two substantial changes in the taxonomy of industries we presented for the period 1960–79 in our earlier paper with Nishimizu. The fabricated metal products industry was moved to type I from type VII in our previous paper. Second, the trade sector was classified in type I and is now classified in type VII in the revised version. The remaining twenty-six industries were classified in the same way as in the industrial taxonomy of our earlier paper.

A new industrial taxonomy, based on our revised data base for 1960–85, is given in Table 9-6. Industries in which the United States has a substantial advantage in productivity in 1980 and productivity gaps between Japan and the United States are expected to persist into the future include agriculture-forestry-fisheries, textile products, and printing and publishing industries. These industries coincide with type I in our previous paper. Productivity growth since 1980 has added three industries to this category—petroleum and coal products, construction, and food and kindred products. These industries were classified in types II, V, and VI in our previous paper.

Type II includes those industries in which the United States had a productivity advantage in 1980 after productivity gaps had been closing during the 1960s and 1970s, but the U.S. productivity advantage was expected to grow in the future. The industries in this category in our previous paper included furniture and fixtures, rubber products, stone, clay and glass, and other transportation equipment. Motor vehicles was added to this category in the 1980s. In our previous paper we had classified this industry in type III, where the technology gaps were expected to close in the near future.

According to new evidence on the productivity gap in the motor vehicle industry during 1980–85, the gap between Japan and the United States had closed by 1982, as we expected from our earlier observations. After 1983, however, the gap increased again due to rapid productivity growth in the U.S. industry. Table 9-7 gives the index of productivity in motor vehicles in Japan and the United States during 1979–85.

Type III includes industries in which productivity gaps are expected to close in the near future, even though the United States had a productivity advantage in 1980. Three industries included in this category in our previous paper—

Table 9-6 An Industrial Taxonomy in Terms of Technology Gaps

Type of Technology	Industry	Technical Gaps, 1980	Average Annual Growth Rate of Productivity						Technical Gaps, 1985
			1960–70		1970–80		1980–85		
			Japan	United States	Japan	United States	Japan	United States	
Type I[a]	1. Agric.	U > J	0.452	1.178	-1.641	0.673	-0.274	4.431	U > J
	3. Construct.	U > J	0.854	0.228	0.717	-1.07	-1.707	0.516	U > J
	4. Foods	U > J	-0.155	0.556	0.37	0.208	-0.917	0.8	U > J
	5. Textile	U > J	0.526	1.437	-1.22	0.187	0.188	0.309	U > J
	10. Printing	U > J	0.858	0.647	-1.469	0.218	0.02	0.979	U > J
	12. Petroleum	U > J	-1.358	1.616	-3.889	-4.56	-1.29	3.422	U > J
	17. Fab. metal	U > J	2.668	0.295	0.837	0.618	0.009	0.376	U > J
Type II[b]	8. Furniture	U > J	1.405	0.03	1.364	0.792	1.02	1.475	U > J
	13. Rubber	U > J	1.499	0.868	0.55	0.981	2.623	3.502	U > J
	15. Stone	U > J	2.794	0.339	-1.248	0.555	0.414	2.443	U > J
	20. Mot. veh.	J > U	0.086	0.155	0.512	0.282	-1.286	2.553	U > J
	21. Trsp. eqpt.	U > J	6.649	1.395	0.706	-4.26	2.107	3.456	U > J
Type III[c]	6. Apparel	U > J	2.294	0.625	1.414	1.16	0.42	0.203	U > J
	28. Service	U > J	1.378	0.7	-3.033	0.018	0.502	-1.179	U > J
	27. Finance	U > J	1.81	0.535	0.15	0.181	3.311	-1.179	U > J
Type V[d]	25. Utilities	U > J	3.222	2.111	-2.991	-1.497	0.603	-1.668	U > J

Type VII[e]

2. Mining	$J > U$	1.662	1.084	1.722	−5.584	0.301	0.045	$J > U$
7. Lumber	$J > U$	2.781	0.965	2.032	0.738	3.522	1.211	$J > U$
9. Paper	$J > U$	1.616	0.338	0.505	0.233	1.982	1.207	$J > U$
11. Chemical	$J > U$	3.343	1.501	0.731	−1.517	2.671	1.63	$J > U$
14. Leather	$U > J$	0.926	0.452	0.713	1.066	0.552	−4.352	$J > U$
16. Prim. metal	$J > U$	0.915	0.088	0.781	0.534	0.624	−2.294	$J > U$
18. Machinery	$J > U$	2.212	0.809	0.377	0.693	−1.073	0.785	$J = U$
19. Elec. mach.	$J > U$	3.304	0.093	3.663	0.693	3.222	0.5	$J > U$
22. Prec. inst.	$J > U$	1.943	0.729	3.626	0.13	1.513	3.105	$J > U$
23. Mfg. misc.	$J > U$	1.741	0.647	1.257	0.795	0.252	0.23	$J > U$
24. Trsp. comm.	$J > U$	3.056	1.085	0.49	0.995	1.186	0.251	$J > U$
26. Trade	$J > U$	2.507	0.077	0.838	0.316	0.607	2.6	$J = U$

[a]The United States had an advantage in the 1980 technology. The technology gaps are expected to continue to expand in the future.

[b]The United States had an advantage in the 1980 technology. Before 1980, the technology gaps were partly closing, but they were expanding in the 1980s and are expected to expand in the future.

[c]The United States had an advantage in the 1980 technology. The technology gaps are expected to close in the near future.

[d]The United States had an advantage in the 1980 technology. The technology gaps were mostly constant in 1960–85.

[e]Japan had an advantage in the 1980 technology. The technology gaps are expected to continue to expand in the future.

Table 9-7   Index of Productivity, Motor Vehicles

Year	Japan	United States
1979	0.91639	0.97490
1980	0.91050	0.53853
1981	0.89246	0.88842
1982	0.86165	0.84402
1983	0.85502	0.95674
1984	0.85545	1.02915
1985	0.85379	0.98393

leather, nonelectrical machinery, and electrical machinery—had already attained U.S. levels of productivity by 1980, as we expected. In Table 9-6 we reclassified these industries in type VII. Industries added to type III in the 1980s are apparel, miscellaneous manufacturing, and finance, insurance, and real estate, previously classified as type II and type VII. These are three industries in which we were unable to project relative trends in productivity during the 1980s. Finally, type VII includes industries in which Japan had a productivity advantage that we expected to increase in the future. Three industries previously classified in type III were added to this category in the 1980s, so that twelve industries of the twenty-nine are included in type VII.

In evaluating the usefulness of the industrial taxonomy presented in our previous paper, we find only four industries in which we were unable to project the trend of technology gaps. We expected the U.S. productivity advantage to increase in apparel and miscellaneous manufacturing. We expected the Japanese advantage to increase in motor vehicles and finance. We conclude that the predictive power of our taxonomy is substantial. We can also draw attention to the findings from new observations during 1980–85. According to Table 9-6 industries with a clear advantage in productivity in Japan or the United States fall into two groups: type I includes seven industries with a U.S. advantage, while type VII includes twelve industries with a Japanese advantage.

To analyze the trend of productivity differences between Japan and the United States, we estimated the mean and variance of relative productivity by industry during 1960–85. The results are shown in Figures 9-1 and 9-2. The mean of relative productivity levels between the two countries remained fairly stable until 1973 and then rose through the 1970s. This movement peaked in 1980. Since that time the trend has reversed with gains in productivity levels for the United States during the 1980s. The variance of the relative productivity levels seen in Figure 9-2 was stable until the oil crisis in 1973 and expanded rapidly thereafter.

We conclude that the energy crisis had a very substantial impact on patterns of productivity growth by industry. Both the mean and the variance of relative productivity levels between Japan and the United States expanded during 1974–80. In the 1980s the mean of the relative productivity levels fell while the variance increased rapidly. This implies that the relative productivity levels in the two countries tended to differ substantially among industries, as shown in Table 9-6.

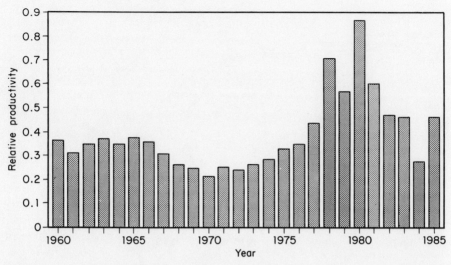

Figure 9-1 Average of proportional gap in technology between the United States and Japan.

Finally, we turn to international competitiveness between Japan and the United States. We can account for movements in the relative prices of industry outputs in the two countries by changes in relative input prices and changes in relative productivity levels. Figures 9-3 to 9-10 show the relative prices of industry outputs between Japan and the United States in terms of dollars. We express these prices in logarithmic form so that a negative difference implies that the U.S. output price is below the Japanese price, whereas a positive difference implies the Japanese price is below the U.S. price.

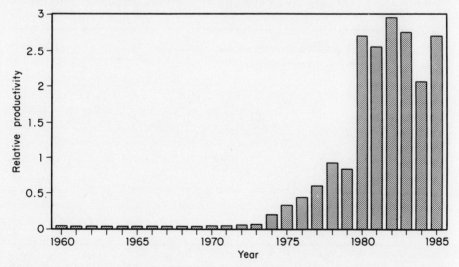

Figure 9-2 Variance of proportional gap in technology between the United States and Japan.

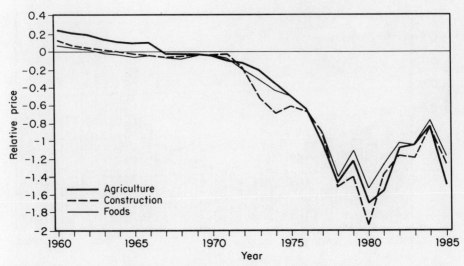

Figure 9-3 Relative prices for agriculture, construction, and foods in the United States and Japan.

Figures 9-3 to 9-6 include plots of the relative prices of industries in which the United States had a higher level of productivity in 1985. In the 1960s the Japanese output prices were relatively low, due primarily to lower labor costs. Although lower relative wage rates in Japan helped to reduce relative prices of output, they were almost totally offset by the lower levels of productivity in Japan during the 1960s.

After the energy crisis of 1973 U.S. output prices in the industries plotted in Figures 9-3 to 9-6 fell relative to Japanese prices until 1980 due to a much greater increase in energy prices in Japan and appreciation of the yen relative

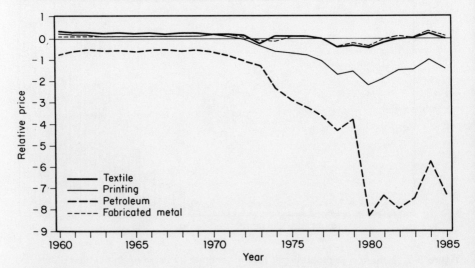

Figure 9-4 Relative prices for textiles, printing, petroleum, and fabricated metal in the United States and Japan.

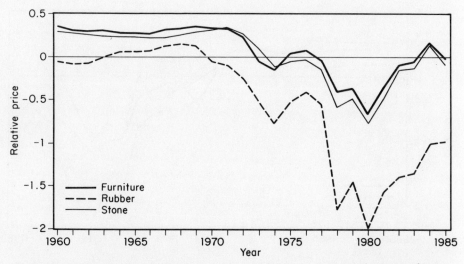

Figure 9-5   Relative prices for furniture, rubber, and stone in the United States and Japan.

to the dollar. During the 1980s the international competitiveness of Japanese industries increased in spite of the productivity gains in the United States. This is due to the more rapid increase in U.S. wage rates and costs of capital and the appreciation of the dollar. It is especially interesting that output prices in textile products, motor vehicles, and fabricated metals industries have been almost the same in Japan and the United States since 1980, notwithstanding the increasing U.S. productivity advantage in these industries.

In Figures 9-7 to 9-10 we present plots of the relative output prices of industries in which Japan had a productivity advantage in 1985. The time trends of relative prices in these industries during 1960–85 are very similar to those of

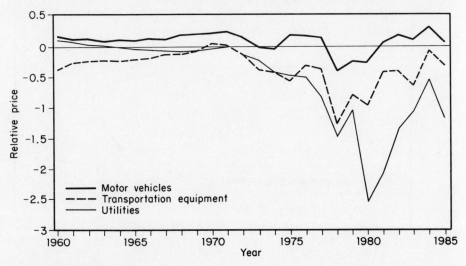

Figure 9-6   Relative prices for motor vehicles, transportation equipment, and utilities in the United States and Japan.

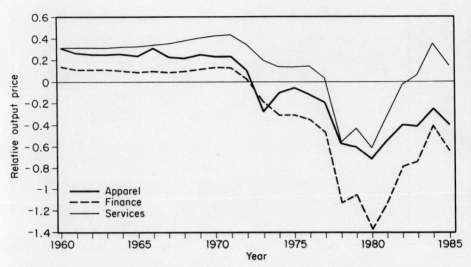

Figure 9-7 Relative prices for apparel, finance, and services in the United States and Japan.

industries in which the United States had a productivity advantage. However, the price levels are lower in Japan, so that Japan has a clear advantage in international competitiveness. These features are especially evident in industries classifed as type VII in our industrial taxonomy.

CONCLUSION

Jorgenson (1988) recently summarized the results of international comparisons between Japan and the United States. The period 1960–73 was characterized

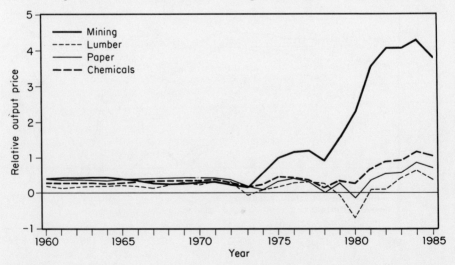

Figure 9-8 Relative prices for mining, lumber, paper, and chemicals in the United States and Japan.

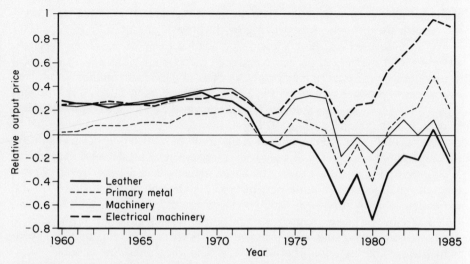

Figure 9-9   Relative prices for leather, primary metal, machinery, and electrical machinery in the United States and Japan.

by substantial economic growth in the United States and very rapid economic growth in Japan. Capital input was by far the most important source of growth in both countries, accounting for about 40 percent of U.S. economic growth and 60 percent of Japanese growth. The period 1973–79 was dominated by the energy crisis, which began with drastic increases in petroleum prices in 1973. Growth slowed significantly in the United States and declined dramatically in Japan during this period. The growth of capital input remained the most important source of economic growth in both countries, but productivity growth at the sectoral level essentially disappeared.

During 1960–73 productivity growth in Japan exceeded that in the United

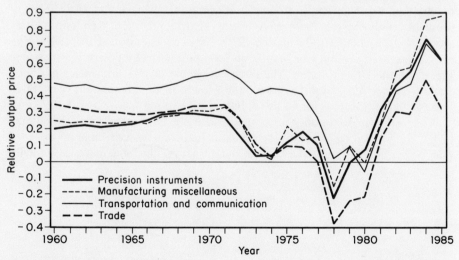

Figure 9-10   Relative prices for precision instruments, manufacturing miscellaneous, transportation and communication, and trade in the United States and Japan.

States for almost all industries. After the energy crisis in 1973, there were very few significant differences between growth rates of productivity in Japanese and U.S. industries. In this chapter we extended these observations through 1985. An important focus for our work is the assessment of longer term trends in productivity growth. In particular, we tried to establish whether or not the slowdown in productivity growth in Japan and the United States after the energy crisis has become permanent. For this purpose we focused on productivity growth in both countries since 1979.

The second issue we considered is the trend of industry-level productivity differences between the two countries. Jorgenson, Kuroda, and Nishimizu (1987) showed that almost every Japanese industry had a lower level of productivity than its U.S. counterpart in 1960. By the end of the period 1960–79 there were nine industries in which productivity gaps between the two countries had closed. These industries were primarily concentrated in producer's goods manufacturing and were oriented to exports. In the remaining nineteen industries productivity gaps between Japan and the United States remained in 1979. In this chapter we reexamined these findings in light of the experience accumulated during the period 1979–85.

We can summarize our conclusions as follows. After 1970 productivity growth deteriorated substantially in both Japan and the United States. An important issue is whether the productivity slowdown is a permanent feature of both economies. To resolve this issue, in Table 9-8 we consider average productivity growth rates in Japanese and U.S. industries over the period 1960–85. We conclude that productivity growth in Japan and the United States has revived somewhat since 1980. However, the growth rates for 1980–85 are well below those for 1960–73, especially in Japan.

A second issue is whether productivity levels in Japan and the United States have tended to converge. Whereas the mean of relative productivity levels between Japan and the United States has fallen since 1980, the variance has expanded rapidly. This implies that convergence of Japanese and U.S. levels of productivity during the 1960s gave way to sharply divergent trends in relative productivity by industry during the 1970s and especially during the 1980s. Figures 9-3 to 9-10 present our results on international competitiveness between Japan and the United States. The competitiveness of U.S. industries has been declining since 1980, due to more rapid growth of input prices in the United States and the appreciation of the dollar relative to the yen.

The industrial taxonomy presented by Jorgenson, Kuroda, and Nishimizu (1987) has proved to be relatively robust. The productivity trends by industry that we projected here on the basis of our earlier results have materialized with

Table 9-8 Average Productivity Growth Rates

Period	Japan (%)	United States (%)
1960–65	1.478	1.993
1965–70	1.946	−0.985
1970–73	0.686	0.941
1973–75	−1.481	−3.064
1975–80	0.178	−1.058
1980–85	0.760	0.448

only a few exceptions. Although the United States retains an overall advantage in relative productivity levels, Japan has gained an advantage in a substantial number of industries and seems likely to increase it. Perhaps equally important, the increase in the variance of relative productivity levels among industries has created opportunities for both countries to benefit from the great expansion in Japanese–U.S. trade that has already taken place. However, this increase is also an important source of "trade frictions," so that continuing efforts at coordination of trade policies in the two countries is needed.

APPENDIX 9-1

The industries in our data base for Japan are classified into thirty-one industrial sectors. For the United States the industries are classified into thirty-five industrial sectors. (This classification is a consolidation of that used by Jorgenson, Gollop, and Fraumeni, 1987.) For international comparisons we have aggregated these industries to the twenty-nine sectors given in Table 9-1. To represent our bilateral models of production we require the following notation:

q_i—price of the output of the ith industry.

$p_{Ki}, p_{Li}, p_{Ei}, p_{Mi}$—prices of capital, labor, energy, and other intermediate inputs in the ith industry.

$v_{Ki}, v_{Li}, v_{Ei}, v_{Mi}$—value shares of capital, labor, energy, and other intermediate inputs in the ith industry.

We represent the vector of value shares of the ith industry by v_i. Similarly, we represent the vector of logarithms of input prices of the ith industry by $\ln p_i$. We employ a time trend T as an index of technology and a dummy variable D, equal to one for Japan and zero for the United States, to represent differences in technology between the two countries. Under competitive conditions we can represent technology by a price function that is dual to the production function relating each industry's output to the corresponding inputs, the level of technology, and differences in technology between the two countries:

$$\ln q_i = \ln p_i' \, \alpha^i + \alpha_t^i \, T + \alpha_d^i \, D + \tfrac{1}{2} \ln p_i' \, B^i \ln p_i + \ln p_i' \, \beta_t^i \, T$$
$$+ \ln p_i' \, \beta_d^i \, D + \tfrac{1}{2} \beta_{tt}^i \, T^2 + \beta_{td}^i TD + \tfrac{1}{2} \beta_{dd}^i D^2, \qquad i = 1, 2, \ldots, I \qquad \text{(9A-1)}$$

For each industry the price of output is a transcendental or, more specifically an exponential function of the logarithms of the input prices. We refer to these functions as translog price functions. (The translog price function was introduced by Christensen, Jorgenson, and Lau, 1971, 1973.) In this representation the scalars—α_t^i, α_d^i, β_{tt}^i, β_{dd}^i—the vectors—α^i, β_t^i, β_d^i—and the matrices—B^i—are constant parameters that differ among industries. These parameters reflect differences in technology among industries. Within each industry differences in technology among time periods are represented by time as an index of technology. Differences in technology between Japan and the United States are represented by a dummy variable, equal to one for Japan and zero for the United States.

In analyzing differences in each industry's production patterns between Japan and the United States, we combine the price function with demand functions for inputs. We can express these functions as equalities between the shares of each input in the value of the output of the industry and the elasticity of the output price with respect to the price of that input. These elasticities depend on input prices, dummy variables for each country, and time as an index of technology. The sum of the elasticities with respect to all inputs is equal to unity, so that the value shares also sum to unity.

For each industry the value shares are equal to the logarithmic derivatives of the price function with respect to logarithms of the input prices:

$$v_i = \alpha^i + \beta^i \ln p_i + \beta^i_t T + \beta^i_d D, \qquad i = 1, 2, \ldots, I \qquad (9A\text{-}2)$$

We can define rates of productivity growth, v_{Ti}, as the negative of rates of growth of the price of output with respect to time, holding the input prices constant:

$$-v_{Ti} = \alpha^i_t + \beta^{i\prime}_t \ln p_i + \beta^i_{tt} T + \beta^i_{td} D, \qquad i = 1, 2, \ldots, I \qquad (9A\text{-}3)$$

Similarly, we can define differences in technology between Japan and the United States, v_{Di}, as the negative of rates of growth of the price of output with respect to the dummy variable, holding the input prices constant:

$$-v_{Di} = \alpha^i_d + \beta^i_d \ln p_i + \beta^i_{td} T + \beta^i_{dd} D, \qquad i = 1, 2, \ldots, I \qquad (9A\text{-}4)$$

The price of output, the prices of inputs, and the value shares for all four inputs are observable for each industry in 1960–85 in both countries. The rates of productivity growth are not directly observable, but average rates of productivity growth between two points of time, say T and $T - 1$, can be expressed as the difference between a weighted average of growth rates of input prices and the growth rates of the price of output for each industry:

$$-\bar{v}_{Ti} = \ln q_i(T) - \ln q_i(T - 1) - \bar{v}'_i [\ln p_i(T)$$
$$- \ln p_i(T - 1)], \qquad i = 1, 2, \ldots, I \qquad (9A\text{-}5)$$

where the average rates of technical change are

$$\bar{v}_{Ti} = \frac{1}{2}[v_{Ti}(T) + v_{Ti}(T - 1)]$$

and the weights are given by the average value shares:

$$\bar{v}_i = \frac{1}{2}[v_i(T) + v_i(T - 1)]$$

We refer to the index numbers (Equation 9A-5) as translog price indexes of the rates of productivity growth. (Diewert, 1976, showed that the index numbers employed, e.g., by Christensen and Jorgenson, 1973, were exact for the translog price function of Christensen, Jorgenson, and Lau, 1971, 1973.)

Similarly, differences in productivity v_{Di} are not directly observable. However, the average of these differences for Japan and the United States can be expressed as a weighted average of differences between the logarithms of the input prices, less the difference between logarithms of the output price:

$$-\bar{v}_{Di} = \ln q_i(J) - \ln q_i(U) - \hat{v}'_i[\ln p_i(J)$$
$$- \ln p_i(U)], \qquad i = 1, 2, \ldots, I \qquad (9A\text{-}6)$$

where the average differences in productivity are:

$$\hat{v}_{Di} = \frac{1}{2}[v_{Di}(J) + v_{Di}(U)]$$

and the weights are given by the average value shares:

$$\hat{v}_i = \frac{1}{2}[v_i(J) + v_i(U)]$$

We refer to the index numbers (Equation 9A-6) as translog price indexes of differences in productivity.

NOTES

We are grateful to Paul David and Bert Hickman for their comments on an earlier draft of this chapter and advice about preparation of the final manuscript. Obviously, they do not share our responsibility for any remaining deficiencies in the paper. We are also indebted to Mieko Nishimizu for her collaboration on earlier phases of the research reported. Financial support for this research has been provided by the Harvard–MITI World Oil Project and the Program on Technology and Economic Policy of Harvard University.

1. Equivalently, these prices could be expressed in terms of yen.
2. Christensen, Cummings, and Jorgenson (1980, 1981) compared aggregate outputs, inputs, and productivity levels for nine countries, including Japan and the United States. Their estimates of relative productivity levels are based on the methodology for multilateral comparisons developed by Caves, Christensen, and Diewert (1982a,b). An alternative approach is presented by Denny and Fuss (1983).
3. See Jorgenson, Kuroda, and Nishimizu (1987). A similar approach is employed by Conrad and Jorgenson (1985) in comparisons for 1960–79 among West Germany, Japan, and the United States. This methodology is also used by Nishimizu and Robinson (1986) in comparisons among manufacturing industries in Japan, Korea, Turkey, and Yugoslavia.
4. The methodology was originated by Kuroda (1981).

REFERENCES

Caves, D. W., L. R. Christensen, and W. E. Diewert. 1982a. "Multilateral Comparisons of Output, Input, and Productivity Using Superlative Index Numbers." *Economic Journal* 92(365), 73–86.

Caves, D. W., L. R. Christensen, and W. E. Diewert. 1982b. "The Economic Theory of Index Numbers, and the Measurement of Input, Output, and Productivity." *Econometrica* 50(6), 1393–1414.

Christensen, L. R., D. Cummings, and D. W. Jorgenson. 1980. "Economic Growth, 1947–1973: An International Comparison." In J. W. Kendrick and B. Vaccara, eds., *New Developments in Productivity Measurement*. Chicago: University of Chicago Press, pp. 595–698.

Christensen, L. R., D. Cummings, and D. W. Jorgenson. 1981. "Relative Productivity Levels, 1947–1973." *European Economic Review* 16(1), 61–94.

Christensen, L. R., and D. W. Jorgenson. 1973. "Measurement of Economic Performance in the Private Sector." In M. Moss, ed., *The Measurement of Economic and Social Performance*. New York: Columbia University Press, pp. 233–351.

Christensen, L. R., D. W. Jorgenson, and L. J. Lau. 1971. "Conjugate Duality and the Transcendental Logarithmic Production Function." *Econometrica* 39(4), 255–56.
———. 1973. "Transcendental Logarithmic Production Frontiers." *Review of Economics and Statistics* 55(1), 28–45.
Conrad, K., and D. W. Jorgenson. 1985. "Sectoral Productivity Gaps between the United States, Japan and Germany 1960–1979." In H. Giersh, ed., *Probleme und Perspektiven der weltwirtschaflichen Entwicklung*. Berlin: Duncker and Humblot.
Denny, M., and M. Fuss. 1983. "A General Approach to Intertemporal and Interspatial Productivity Comparisons." *Journal of Econometrics* 23(3), 315–30.
Diewert, W. E. 1976. "Exact and Superlative Index Numbers." *Journal of Econometrics* 4(4), 115–46.
Jorgenson, D. W. 1988. "Productivity and Economic Growth in Japan and the United States." *American Economic Review* 78(2), 217–22.
Jorgenson, D. W., F. M. Gollop, and B. M. Fraumeni. 1987. *Productivity and U.S. Economic Growth*. Cambridge, Mass.: Harvard University Press.
Jorgenson, D. W., M. Kuroda, and M. Nishimizu. 1987. "Japan–U.S. Industry-Level Productivity Comparisons, 1960–1979." *Journal of the Japanese and International Economies* 1(1), 1–30.
Jorgenson, D. W., and M. Nishimizu. 1978. "U.S. and Japanese Economic Growth, 1952–1974: An International Comparison." *Economic Journal* 88(352), 707–26.
Jorgenson, D. W., and M. Nishimizu. 1981. "International Differences in Levels of Technology: A Comparison Between U.S. and Japanese Industries." In Institute of Statistical Mathematics, *International Roundtable Congress Proceedings*. Tokyo: Institute of Statistical Mathematics.
Kravis, I. B., A. Heston, and R. Summers. 1978. *International Comparisons of Real Product and Purchasing Power*. Baltimore, Md.: Johns Hopkins University Press.
Kuroda, M. 1981. "Method of Estimation for Updating the Transactions Matrix in Input–Output Relationships." Keio Economic Observatory, Discussion Paper No. 1, Keio University, Tokyo.
Kuroda, M., K. Yoshioka, and D. W. Jorgenson. 1984. "Relative Price Change and Biases of Technical Change in Japan." *Economic Studies Quarterly* 35(2).
Nishimizu, M., and C. R. Hulten. 1978. "The Sources of Japanese Economic Growth: 1955–1971." *Review of Economics and Statistics* 60(3), 351–61.
Nishimizu, M., and S. Robinson. 1986. "Productivity Growth in Manufacturing." In H. Chenery, S. Robinson, and M. Syrquin, eds., *Industrialization and Growth*. Oxford University Press, pp. 283–308.

10

International Competitiveness of U.S. and Japanese Manufacturing Industries

TOSHIKO TANGE

Steady increases in Japan's trade surpluses and U.S. trade deficits in recent years indicate that Japan has been continuously gaining position in competitiveness while the United States has been losing position. There are several measures of competitiveness of a country relative to other countries: market shares, trade balances, productivity, and unit costs of production. This chapter focuses on cost competitiveness of the two countries, since a continuous increase in a country's unit costs relative to those of other countries must be reflected in the country's higher export prices, especially in the long run, which are followed by a weakening of its competitive strength.

In determining cost competitiveness of U.S. and Japanese manufacturing industries, unit costs are estimated by industry within a cost-minimization Cobb–Douglas framework. In this respect unit costs are measured both in a country's own currency and in U.S. dollars. Given the estimates of unit costs, we hypothesize that a country is revealed to be competitive in its trade with other countries for a product if its estimated unit cost of a product is considerably below that of other countries. The periods covered in the study are 1973–85 for the United States and 1973–86 for Japan. A previous study for 1957–74 is also presented for comparison. Unit cost changes of each country are then decomposed into their determinants. A source analysis of intercountry differences in unit cost changes is also performed.

The first section discusses the framework for analysis and methodology. The following section presents results, and the final section suggests some conclusions.

FRAMEWORK FOR ANALYSIS AND METHODOLOGY[1]

The theory underlying the analysis is conventional. To examine export competitiveness of Japan and the United States, we assume that their relative exports are related to their relative prices by the following equation:[2]

$$(E_{jt}^J/E_{jt}^U) = a(P_{jt}^J/P_{jt}^U)^b \tag{10-1}$$

where E is for exports, P is price, b is the elasticity of substitution, and a is a constant. Superscripts J and U indicate Japan and the United States. Subscripts j and t denote an industry and time, respectively. We assume that prices in each country are determined by a markup on unit costs and that export products and domestic products have similar costs while costs differ across industries:

$$P_{jt}^J = (1 + m_j^J)\text{UC}_{jt}^J \tag{10-2}$$

and

$$P_{jt}^U = (1 + m_j^U)\text{UC}_{jt}^U \tag{10-3}$$

where m is a constant markup factor over years and UC is unit cost. We substitute Equations 10-2 and 10-3 into 10-1. Then, taking logarithms and differentiating with respect to time, we obtain the following relationship in terms of intercountry differences in growth rates:

$$\dot{E}_j^J/E_j^J - \dot{E}_j^U/E_j^U = b(\dot{P}_j^J/P_j^J - \dot{P}_j^U/P_j^U) = b(\dot{\text{UC}}_j^J/\text{UC}_j^J - \dot{\text{UC}}_j^U/\text{UC}_j^U) \tag{10-1}$$

Thus differences in export growth between two countries are a function of intercountry differences in the rates of changes in unit costs. A steady rise in a country's unit cost relative to that of foreign countries indicates a deteriorating position in its competitiveness. An increase in unit costs and the resulting decline in competitiveness can be absorbed by reducing profit margins, or possibly can be offset by changes in exchange rates toward depreciation of the currency of the country concerned. However, intercountry cost differences would still play an important role in determining the competitive position of a country, particularly in the long run.

Unit cost is estimated on the basis of a cost-minimization Cobb–Douglas framework, since it is difficult to obtain a direct measure. The Cobb–Douglas production function is written as

$$X_t = Ae^{\lambda t}L_t^\alpha K_t^\beta \Pi X_{it}^{\gamma_i} \tag{10-5}$$

where X is gross output, L is labor input, K is gross capital input, and X_i is the ith intermediate input used in the production of the industry. λ is the rate of Hicks-neutral technical progress or total factor productivity. α, β, and γ_i are output elasticities with respect to labor, capital, and the ith intermediate input, respectively. An industry subscript j is excluded for simplification.

With inputs priced competitively, we define total costs as

$$C_t = w_t L_t + r_t K_t + \sum p_{it} X_{it} \tag{10-6}$$

where C is total costs and w, r, and P_i are prices of labor, capital, and the ith intermediate input, respectively.

Assuming cost minimization subject to the production function, we have

$$\beta/\alpha = r_t K_t / w_t L_t \qquad (10\text{-}7)$$

and

$$\gamma_i/\alpha = p_{it} X_{it} / w_t L_t \qquad (10\text{-}8)$$

Substituting Equations 10-7 and 10-8 into 10-6 and dividing by X, we obtain unit costs. A subscript t is excluded for simplification:

$$UC = SX^{(1-s)/s} (Ae^{\lambda t} \alpha^{\alpha} \beta^{\beta} \Pi \gamma_i^{\gamma_i})^{-1/s} (w^{\alpha} r^{\beta} \Pi P_i^{\gamma_i})^{1/s} \qquad (10\text{-}9)$$

where $S = \alpha + \beta + \Sigma\gamma_i$. Taking logarithms and differentiating with respect to time, we have

$$\frac{\dot{UC}}{UC} = \frac{\alpha}{S} \cdot \frac{\dot{w}}{w} + \frac{\beta}{S} \cdot \frac{\dot{r}}{r} \Sigma\left(\frac{\gamma_i}{S} \cdot \frac{\dot{P_i}}{P_i}\right) + \frac{(1-S)}{S} \cdot \frac{\dot{X}}{X} - \frac{1}{S} \cdot \lambda \qquad (10\text{-}10)$$

Thus the rate of change in unit costs is determined by the rates of change in factor prices, output growth (due to economies of scale), and productivity growth. As indicated, a higher rate of productivity growth leads to a lower rate of change in unit costs.

To calculate the rates of change in unit cost by industry for the two countries, we begin with a time series estimation of Equation 10-5. To avoid difficulties involved in a direct estimation of the Cobb–Douglas production function in log-linear form, an indirect estimation method using factor shares is adopted.[3]

The marginal conditions of cost minimization, Equations 10-7 and 10-8, when written in logarithms, become

$$\log(r_t K_t / w_t L_t) = \log(\beta/\alpha) + \log u_t \qquad (10\text{-}11)$$

and

$$\log(p_{it} X_t / w_t L_t) = \log(\gamma_i/\alpha) + \log v_t \qquad (10\text{-}12)$$

where $\log u_t$ and $\log v_t$ are random disturbances. If we assume random disturbances have zero expected values, we obtain the estimates of β/α and γ_i/α as the sample geometric means of $r_t K_t / w_t L_t$ and $p_{it} X_{it} / w_t L_t$, respectively.

Written in logarithms, Equation 10-5 with a newly constructed variable on the basis of the estimates of β/α and $\gamma/_i$ becomes

$$\log X_t = \log A + \lambda t + \alpha[\log L_t + (\widehat{\beta/\alpha})\log K_t + \Sigma(\widehat{\gamma_i/\alpha})\log X_{it}] + \log e_t \qquad (10\text{-}13)$$

where $\log e_t$ is a random error term and $\odot$ denotes an estimate. From Equation 10-13 we have estimates of α and λ. Now we can estimate β and γ_i as $\textcircled{a}$ multiplied by $\widehat{(\beta/\alpha)}$ and $\widehat{(\gamma_i/\alpha)}$ respectively.

Given these estimates of the Cobb–Douglas production functions, we calculate average annual rates of change in unit costs according to Equation 10-10.

EMPIRICAL RESULTS

Table 10-1 summarizes the annual rates of total factor productivity growth (or the rates of technical progress) of Japan and the United States at the two-digit manufacturing industry level, estimated on the basis of a cost-minimization Cobb–Douglas framework.[4] The gross output concept is used since the study at the industry level requires all inputs, labor, capital, and intermediate inputs. Labor input is measured in worker-hours and capital is defined by gross capital concept. Gross output, gross capital stock, and intermediate inputs are measured in constant prices. The period covered in the study is 1973–86, together with the two subperiods 1973–79 and 1980–86. For the United States, however, the year 1986 is excluded because some data are not available. The previous study for 1957–74 also is considered for comparison. The choice of industries depends on availability of data, in particular, availability of Japan's capital stock data.

The productivity growth rates vary considerably among industries. Table 10-1 indicates that all Japanese industries experienced sharp slowdowns in productivity growth in the 1973–86 period. During the post-1973 period, productivity slowdowns became more substantial after 1980: five out of the eight industries had a relative decline in their productivity growth in 1980–86. The productivity growth of U.S. industries was not always in the same direction as that of Japanese industries. In the 1973–85 period, only four out of the eight U.S. industries slowed down their productivity growth below the 1957–74 level and the remaining four industries accelerated their productivity growth. Furthermore, in most of the U.S. industries (the only exceptions being fabricated metal products and transportation equipment), productivity growth was stepped up after 1980.

Over the period of 1957–74 all Japanese industries attained much higher rates of productivitiy growth than those of the corresponding U.S. industries, on a case-by-case basis. Japan's superior position in productivity growth relative to that of the United States was maintained in the 1970s; however, the positions were reversed in the 1980s in all industries except paper products and chemicals. That is, U.S. productivity progress tended to exceed that of Japan.

Compared with the rates of total factor productivity growth in this study, Table 10-2 presents the average annual growth rates of labor productivity of Japanese and U.S. industries, which were estimated from labor productivity indexes (Japan Productivity Center, 1988), over the period 1973–84 along with the two subperiods, 1973–79 and 1980–84. Total factor productivity in this study is based on gross output framework, whereas labor productivity indexes are based on value-added data taken from the Census of Manufactures. Therefore, data sources for the two studies of productivity are different. The industry classification is also somewhat different. To obtain similar industry classification, we aggregated the industries in the study of labor productivity by using either value-added or industrial production as weights. Growth rates of labor productivity then were estimated by industry.

As seen in Table 10-2, the rates of labor productivity growth for five of the eight Japanese industries declined in 1980–84 more than in 1973–79. On the

Table 10-1 Growth Rates of Total Factor Productivity (Estimation Based on the Cobb–Douglas Production Functions)

Industry[a]	Japan				United States			
	1957–74	1973–79	1973–86	1980–86	1957–74	1973–79	1973–85	1980–85
Textiles	0.025	0.009	0.012	0.015	0.016	0.012	0.012	0.022
Paper products	0.026	0.007	0.007	0.011	0.016	−0.026	0.022	0.0005
Chemicals	0.030	0.017	0.021	0.035	0.027	0.012	0.020	0.026
Primary metals	0.015	0.008	0.002	0.004	−0.005	−0.003	0.011	0.059
Fabricated metal products	0.019	0.015	0.008	0.003	0.007	0.008	0.001	0.005
Machinery	0.033	0.017	0.017	0.010	0.014	0.016	0.034	0.069
Electrical machinery	0.055	0.020	0.021	0.016	0.026	0.016	0.033	0.047
Transportation equipment	0.055	0.016	0.010	0.004	0.016	0.012	0.012	0.007
Total manufacturing		0.003	0.004	0.007		0.010	0.022	0.033

Source: Estimates of total factor productivity growth for 1957–74 from Tange (1987). For estimates for the other periods, see Tables 10-7 and 10-8.

[a]Different estimation periods are used for some industries.

Table 10-2 Growth Rates of Labor Productivity

Industry	Japan			United States		
	1973–84	1973–79	1980–84	1973–84	1973–79	1980–84
Textiles	0.057	0.055	0.039	0.069	0.080	0.053
Paper products	0.045	0.039	0.060	0.024	0.022	0.070
Chemicals	0.106	0.111	0.130	0.034	0.048	0.057
Primary metals	0.055	0.039	0.023	−0.008	−0.021	0.020
Fabricated metal products	0.055	0.043	0.037	0.012	0.010	0.027
Machinery	0.083	0.078	0.061	0.034	0.012	0.099
Electrical machinery	0.208	0.178	0.180	0.052	0.057	0.050
Transportation equipment	0.063	0.066	0.043	0.011	0.026	0.027
Total manufacturing	0.061	0.051	0.056	0.024	0.024	0.042

Source: Growth rates estimated from Japan Productivity Center (1988).

contrary, six U.S. industries increased the pace of labor productivity growth in 1980–84, although five U.S. industries still lagged behind the corresponding Japanese industries in labor productivity growth. The findings on labor productivity growth presented in Table 10-2 support the results on total factor productivity in this study. To repeat, Japan's total factor productivity growth declined after 1973 and in five industries decreased even more substantially after 1980. By contrast, after also declining in the 1970s, total factor productivity growth in six of the eight U.S. industries increased again in the 1980s.

Given the estimates of the rates of total factor productivity growth as well as other parameter estimates of the Cobb–Douglas production functions, the average annual rates of change in unit costs were calculated at the industry level on the basis of Equation 10-10. The periods are 1973–86, 1973–79, and 1980–86 for Japan and 1973–85, 1973–79, and 1980–85 for the United States.

Table 10-3 presents the rates of unit cost changes measured on the basis of both yen and U.S. dollars. The growth rates of unit costs increased in six Japanese industries and eight U.S. industries after 1973. Unit costs actually fell in Japan during 1980–86, however, despite the concurrent slowdown of productivity growth in five of the eight industries.

Measured on an own-country currency basis, unit cost changes in every period were generally smaller in Japan than in the United States: five Japanese industries in 1957–74, eight industries in 1973–79, and eight industries in 1980–86 had smaller unit cost changes than the corresponding U.S. industries. As far as productivity growth in the 1980s is concerned, the United States showed a distinct recovery. However, with respect to relative cost competitiveness measured on an own-currency basis, the United States still lost position in the 1980s. It is of particular interest that in the 1980s the U.S. machinery industry attained a much smaller rate of increase in unit costs than Japan's machinery industry. That is, the U.S. machinery industry tended to have a relative cost advantage over its Japanese counterpart.

If we look at unit cost changes measured on a U.S. dollar basis, we see the different competitive position of the two countries. In comparing unit costs measured on a yen basis and on a U.S. dollar basis, the number of Japanese industries gaining position in competitiveness relative to U.S. industries decreased in every period: from eight (in the case of unit costs in yen) to six (in the case of unit costs in U.S. dollars) in 1973–86, from eight to zero in 1973–79, and from seven to five in the 1980s. Put differently, on the basis of the unit cost changes adjusted by exchange-rate changes, all U.S. industries had definite advantages in their cost competitiveness in 1973–79 and three U.S. industries maintained their competitive power in the 1980s.

Growth rates of unit costs next are decomposed into their components. Use of Equation 10-10 permits us to decompose average annual rates of change in unit costs into factors attributable to changes in wages, capital costs, intermediate input costs (material costs), and output and productivity growth. The results for Japan are presented in Table 10-4.

In six of the eight Japanese industries, the rates of unit cost changes were higher in 1973–86 than in 1957–74. In most industries, a major portion of higher

Table 10-3 Rates of Changes in Unit Costs for Japanese and U.S.
Manufacturing Industries

Industry	Japan		United States
	In yen	In U.S. dollars	
	1957–74		1957–74
Textiles	0.0168		0.0105
Paper products	0.0274		0.0180
Chemicals	− 0.0011		0.0078
Primary metals	0.0095		0.0319
Fabricated metal products	0.0231		0.0207
Machinery	0.0150		0.0187
Electrical machinery	− 0.0057		0.0056
Transportation equipment	0.0025		0.0151
Total manufacturing			
	1973–86		1973–85
Textiles	0.0130	0.0395	0.0389
Paper products	0.0327	0.0592	0.0655
Chemicals	0.0336	0.0600	0.0545
Primary metals	0.0251	0.0515	0.0654
Fabricated metal products	0.0233	0.0498	0.0644
Machinery	0.0172	0.0437	0.0447
Electrical machinery	− 0.0296	− 0.0031	0.0394
Transportation equipment	0.0158	0.0422	0.0667
Total manufacturing	0.0223	0.0488	0.0539
	1973–79		1973–79
Textiles	0.0284	0.0772	0.0472
Paper products	0.0383	0.0871	0.0810
Chemicals	0.0628	0.1117	0.0702
Primary metals	0.0561	0.1049	0.1024
Fabricated metal products	0.0407	0.0896	0.0822
Machinery	0.0397	0.0886	0.0759
Electrical machinery	0.0189	0.0677	0.0547
Transportation equipment	0.0434	0.0923	0.0738
Total manufacturing	0.0536	0.1025	0.0713
	1980–86		1980–85
Textiles	− 0.0075	0.0200	0.0056
Paper products	− 0.0124	0.0152	0.0714
Chemicals	− 0.0321	− 0.0046	0.0101
Primary metals	− 0.0278	− 0.0003	− 0.0058
Fabricated metal products	− 0.0173	0.0102	0.0289
Machinery	− 0.0030	0.0245	− 0.0273
Electrical machinery	− 0.0598	− 0.0323	− 0.0036
Transportation equipment	− 0.0033	0.0242	0.0407
Total manufacturing	− 0.0194	0.0081	0.0044

Source: Results for 1957–74 from Tange (1987).

unit cost changes for 1973–86 was attributed to the material cost effect. In all industries the productivity effect became less favorable.

Over the period of 1973–79 all of the Japanese industries had large positive rates of change in unit costs, due mostly to the large positive material cost effect. By contrast, in 1980–86 all industries had negative rates of change in unit costs, ascribable largely to the negative material cost effect and to a lesser degree to the output effects. In five industries the productivity effect became less favorable in the 1980s than it had been in the 1970s. These results show that material costs were more important than productivity in determining the behavior of Japanese unit costs after 1973, with productivity growth becoming less favorable to cost reduction especially after 1980.

The results for the United States are shown in Table 10-5. In all industries unit cost increases were higher in 1973–85 than in 1957–74. The higher rates of increase in 1973–85 were due mostly to more rapid rises in wages and material costs, although these unfavorable effects weakened in all industries in the 1980s. The productivity effect was favorable in most industries in the post-1973 years and especially after 1980. These findings contrast sharply with those of Japan: in Japan the wage effect became more favorable while the productivity effects became less favorable in 1973–86 than in 1957–74.

Intercountry differences in the rates of changes in unit costs, summarized in Table 10-6, are also decomposed into sources attributable to wage rates, capital costs, material costs, and output and productivity growth. Since the differences between countries in this study refer to the rates of change in unit costs of Japanese industries minus those of the corresponding U.S. industries, all negative values show effects relatively favorable to Japan and positive values are favorable to the United States.

As can be seen in Table 10-6, for 1957–74 five Japanese industries (chemicals, primary metals, machinery, electrical machinery, and transportation equipment) became more competitive relative to the corresponding U.S. industries. In this period the dominant contribution to Japan's increased cost competitiveness was made by the productivity effect. The wage effects were unfavorable sources for cost competitiveness of all Japanese industries relative to U.S. industries.

The story differs after 1973. All Japanese industries increased cost competitiveness against the comparable U.S. industries after 1973, except for U.S. machinery after 1980. The largest source of favorable unit cost changes in Japanese industries in the post-1973 period was the reduction in material costs and, to a lesser degree, the wage and output effects. Productivity growth itself was generally faster in our sample of U.S. industries in 1973–85. These tendencies became even more pronounced in the 1980s.

Japan is more dependent on imports of oil than is the United States. Since 1973 Japanese industries have tried to restrict oil consumption and have developed energy-saving technology. As a result, Japan's oil consumption per gross domestic product in 1986 sharply decreased to half the 1973 level. The comparable figure for the United States is 68 percent of the 1973 level.[5] It is thus considered that these efforts of Japanese industries led to the promising material cost effect and the resulting cost advantage over U.S. industries.

Table 10-4 Decomposition of Unit Cost Changes of Japanese Manufacturing Industries

Industry	Rates of Change in Unit Costs	Wage Effect	Capital Cost Effect	Material Cost Effect	Output Effect	Productivity Effect
1957–74						
Textiles	0.0168	0.0204	0.0026	0.0147	0.0056	−0.0265
Paper products	0.0274	0.0186	0.0051	0.0223	0.0087	−0.0273
Chemicals	−0.0011	0.0240	0.0052	0.0109	−0.0141	−0.0271
Primary metals	0.0095	0.0152	0.0006	0.0108	−0.0028	−0.0144
Fabricated metal products	0.0231	0.0298	−0.0042	0.0105	0.0069	−0.0200
Machinery	0.0150	0.0231	−0.0045	0.0102	0.0233	−0.0371
Electrical machinery	−0.0057	0.0229	0.0015	0.0078	0.0239	−0.0617
Transportation equipment	0.0025	0.0201	−0.0026	0.0078	0.0458	−0.0686
Total manufacturing						
1973–86						
Textiles	0.0130	0.0071	−0.0019	0.0159	0.0165	−0.0246
Paper products	0.0327	0.0077	0.0035	0.0272	0.0027	−0.0084
Chemicals	0.0336	0.0087	0.0060	0.0407	−0.0021	−0.0199
Primary metals	0.0251	0.0047	0.0002	0.0244	−0.0024	−0.0018
Fabricated metal products	0.0233	0.0184	−0.0047	0.0257	−0.0108	−0.0054
Machinery	0.0172	0.0191	0.0027	0.0198	−0.0103	−0.0140
Electrical machinery	−0.0296	0.0215	−0.0036	0.0074	−0.0391	−0.0158
Transportation equipment	0.0158	0.0165	−0.0066	0.0171	−0.0014	−0.0097
Total manufacturing	0.0223	0.0133	−0.0012	0.0256	−0.0121	−0.0032

1973–79

Textiles	0.0284	0.0091	0.0055	0.0204	0.0041	−0.0108
Paper products	0.0383	0.0127	−0.0066	0.0372	0.0024	−0.0074
Chemicals	0.0628	0.0136	0.0087	0.0644	−0.0127	−0.0113
Primary metals	0.0561	0.0065	0.0038	0.0543	−0.0011	−0.0075
Fabricated metal products	0.0407	0.0253	−0.0090	0.0434	−0.0100	−0.0090
Machinery	0.0397	0.0243	−0.0030	0.0360	−0.0028	−0.0148
Electrical machinery	0.0189	0.0230	0.0129	0.0228	−0.0262	−0.0137
Transportation equipment	0.0434	0.0211	0.0061	0.0326	0.0000	−0.0164
Total manufacturing	0.0536	0.0177	0.0034	0.0441	−0.0093	−0.0023

1980–86

Textiles	−0.0075	0.0059	−0.0036	−0.0095	0.0572	−0.0574
Paper products	−0.0124	0.0040	0.0036	−0.0129	0.0079	−0.0151
Chemicals	−0.0321	0.0061	0.0070	−0.0165	0.0405	−0.0691
Primary metals	−0.0278	0.0036	−0.0032	−0.0192	−0.0069	−0.0021
Fabricated metal products	−0.0173	0.0138	−0.0050	−0.0049	−0.0195	−0.0017
Machinery	−0.0030	0.0161	−0.0058	0.0054	−0.0108	−0.0079
Electrical machinery	−0.0598	0.0183	−0.0046	−0.0200	−0.0411	−0.0123
Transportation equipment	−0.0033	0.0148	−0.0065	−0.0034	−0.0048	−0.0033
Total manufacturing	−0.0194	0.0103	−0.0017	−0.0126	−0.0101	−0.0053

Table 10-5 Decomposition of Unit Cost Changes of U.S. Manufacturing Industries

Industry	Rates of Change in Unit Costs	Wage Effect	Capital Cost Effect	Material Cost Effect	Output Effect	Productivity Effect
1957–74						
Textiles	0.0105	0.0142	−0.0011	0.0074	0.0093	−0.0192
Paper products	0.0180	0.0154	−0.0017	0.0112	0.0138	−0.0206
Chemicals	0.0078	0.0131	−0.0040	0.0073	0.0342	−0.0429
Primary metals	0.0319	0.0140	0.0034	0.0152	0.0013	0.0048
Fabricated metal products	0.0207	0.0152	−0.0006	0.0148	−0.0026	−0.0061
Machinery	0.0187	0.0185	−0.0031	0.0108	0.0086	−0.0161
Electrical machinery	0.0056	0.0183	−0.0084	0.0070	0.0221	−0.0335
Transportation equipment	0.0151	0.0201	−0.0012	0.0110	0.0011	−0.0160
Total manufacturing						
1973–85						
Textiles	0.0389	0.0269	−0.0013	0.0301	0.0050	−0.0217
Paper products	0.0655	0.0239	−0.0042	0.0548	0.0609	−0.0699
Chemicals	0.0545	0.0226	−0.0064	0.0542	0.0099	−0.0259
Primary metals	0.0654	0.0257	−0.0004	0.0499	0.0013	−0.0110
Fabricated metal products	0.0644	0.0261	−0.0017	0.0431	−0.0020	−0.0012
Machinery	0.0447	0.0342	−0.0042	0.0433	0.0375	−0.0661
Electrical machinery	0.0394	0.0378	−0.0018	0.0382	−0.0046	−0.0301
Transportation equipment	0.0667	0.0247	−0.0000	0.0533	0.0017	−0.0130
Total manufacturing	0.0539	0.0239	−0.0031	0.0545	0.0043	−0.0256

1973–79

Textiles	0.0472	0.0244	−0.0015	0.0322	0.0115	−0.0194
Paper products	0.0810	0.0262	−0.0063	0.0571	−0.0103	0.0143
Chemicals	0.0702	0.0241	−0.0086	0.0678	−0.0008	−0.0122
Primary metals	0.1024	0.0308	−0.0041	0.0680	0.0057	0.0021
Fabricated metal products	0.0822	0.0290	0.0004	0.0613	−0.0003	−0.0081
Machinery	0.0759	0.0356	−0.0009	0.0504	0.0112	−0.0204
Electrical machinery	0.0547	0.0354	0.0002	0.0397	−0.0068	−0.0140
Transportation equipment	0.0738	0.0245	−0.0002	0.0555	0.0074	−0.0134
Total manufacturing	0.0713	0.0261	−0.0038	0.0640	−0.0064	−0.0086

1980–85

Textiles	0.0056	0.0215	−0.0014	0.0142	0.0033	−0.0322
Paper products	0.0714	0.0119	0.0024	0.0421	0.0157	−0.0007
Chemicals	0.0101	0.0170	−0.0026	0.0213	−0.0004	−0.0252
Primary metals	−0.0058	0.0101	−0.0000	0.0131	0.0139	−0.0429
Fabricated metal products	0.0289	0.0182	−0.0019	0.0154	0.0006	−0.0033
Machinery	−0.0273	0.0245	−0.0057	0.0236	0.0032	−0.0729
Electrical machinery	−0.0036	0.0297	0.0003	0.0240	−0.0248	−0.0328
Transportation equipment	0.0407	0.0170	0.0000	0.0335	−0.0033	−0.0064
Total manufacturing	0.0044	0.0158	0.0038	0.0195	−0.0126	−0.0221

Table 10-6 Decomposition of Intercountry Differences in Unit Cost Changes[a]

Industry	Rates of Change in Unit Costs			Decomposition of Unit Cost Differences				
	Japan	United States	Differences	Wage Effect	Capital Cost Effect	Material Cost Effect	Output Effect	Productivity Effect
	1957–74	1957–74						
Textiles	0.0168	0.0105	0.0063	0.0062	0.0037	0.0073	−0.0037	−0.0073
Paper products	0.0274	0.0180	0.0094	0.0032	0.0068	0.0111	−0.0051	−0.0067
Chemicals	−0.0011	0.0078	−0.0089	0.0109	0.0092	0.0036	−0.0483	0.0158
Primary metals	0.0095	0.0319	−0.0224	0.0012	0.0040	−0.0044	−0.0041	−0.0192
Fabricated metal products	0.0231	0.0207	0.0024	0.0146	−0.0036	−0.0043	0.0095	−0.0139
Machinery	0.0150	0.0187	−0.0037	0.0046	−0.0014	−0.0006	0.0146	−0.0532
Electrical machinery	−0.0057	0.0056	−0.0113	0.0046	0.0099	0.0008	0.0018	−0.0282
Transportation equipment	0.0025	0.0151	−0.0126	0.0000	−0.0014	−0.0032	0.0447	−0.0526
Total manufacturing								
	1973–86	1973–85						
Textiles	0.0130	0.0389	−0.0259	−0.0198	−0.0006	−0.0142	0.0115	−0.0029
Paper products	0.0327	0.0655	−0.0328	−0.0161	0.0078	−0.0276	−0.0582	0.0615
Chemicals	0.0336	0.0545	−0.0209	−0.0139	0.0124	−0.0135	−0.0120	0.0060
Primary metals	0.0251	0.0654	−0.0403	−0.0209	0.0006	−0.0255	−0.0036	0.0091
Fabricated metal products	0.0233	0.0644	−0.0411	−0.0077	−0.0030	−0.0174	−0.0088	−0.0042
Machinery	0.0172	0.0447	−0.0275	−0.0151	0.0069	−0.0235	−0.0478	0.0521
Electrical machinery	−0.0296	0.0394	−0.0690	−0.0163	−0.0018	−0.0307	−0.0345	0.0143
Transportation equipment	0.0158	0.0667	−0.0510	−0.0083	−0.0066	−0.0362	−0.0031	0.0033
Total manufacturing	0.0223	0.0539	−0.0316	−0.0106	0.0019	−0.0289	−0.0164	0.0225

	1973–79	1973–79						
Textiles	0.0284	0.0472	−0.0188	−0.0152	0.0070	−0.0119	−0.0074	0.0087
Paper products	0.0383	0.0810	−0.0427	−0.0135	−0.0003	−0.0199	0.0127	−0.0217
Chemicals	0.0628	0.0702	−0.0074	−0.0105	0.0173	−0.0034	−0.0118	0.0009
Primary metals	0.0561	0.1024	−0.0464	−0.0243	0.0080	−0.0137	−0.0067	−0.0097
Fabricated metal products	0.0407	0.0822	−0.0414	−0.0036	−0.0094	−0.0179	−0.0096	−0.0009
Machinery	0.0397	0.0759	−0.0362	−0.0113	−0.0022	−0.0144	−0.0140	0.0056
Electrical machinery	0.0189	0.0547	−0.0358	−0.0124	0.0126	−0.0169	−0.0194	0.0003
Transportation equipment	0.0434	0.0738	−0.0304	−0.0034	0.0063	−0.0230	−0.0074	−0.0030
Total manufacturing	0.0536	0.0713	−0.0177	−0.0084	0.0072	−0.0199	−0.0028	0.0062
	1980–86	1980–85						
Textiles	−0.0075	0.0056	−0.0130	−0.0157	−0.0022	−0.0238	0.0538	−0.0252
Paper products	−0.0124	0.0714	−0.0838	−0.0079	0.0012	−0.0550	−0.0077	−0.0144
Chemicals	−0.0321	0.0101	−0.0421	−0.0109	0.0096	−0.0378	0.0409	−0.0439
Primary metals	−0.0278	−0.0058	−0.0220	−0.0065	−0.0031	−0.0322	−0.0208	0.0407
Fabricated metal products	−0.0173	0.0289	−0.0462	−0.0044	−0.0031	−0.0204	−0.0201	0.0017
Machinery	−0.0030	−0.0273	0.0244	−0.0084	−0.0001	−0.0181	−0.0140	0.0650
Electrical machinery	−0.0598	−0.0036	−0.0562	−0.0114	−0.0049	−0.0440	−0.0163	0.0204
Transportation equipment	−0.0033	0.0407	−0.0440	−0.0022	−0.0065	−0.0369	−0.0015	0.0031
Total manufacturing	−0.0194	0.0044	−0.0238	−0.0055	−0.0055	−0.0321	0.0025	0.0168

Source: Results for 1957–74 from Tange (1987).

[a]The entries in the last six columns are the differences between the corresponding columns of Tables 10-4 and 10-5.

To examine the relationship between unit cost changes and price changes, the following cross-sectional regressions across industries over the period 1973–86 for Japan and 1973–85 for the United States were performed:

Japan:
$$\dot{P}_w/P_w = 0.563^a(\dot{UC}/UC) + \qquad\qquad \bar{R}^2 = 0.634$$
$$0.015^a$$
$$(4.07) \qquad\qquad (4.25)$$

Japan:
$$\dot{P}_e/P_e = 0.816^a(\dot{UC}/UC) + \qquad\qquad \bar{R}^2 = 0.763$$
$$0.0003$$
$$(5.47) \qquad\qquad (0.08)$$

United States:
$$\dot{P}_w/P_w = 0.446(\dot{UC}/UC) + 0.050^a \qquad \bar{R}^2 = 0.115$$
$$(1.43) \qquad\qquad (2.83)$$

where P_w stands for wholesale prices, P_e for export prices, UC for unit costs, and $\bar{R}^2$ for the coefficient of determination adjusted for degrees of freedom. The figures in parentheses are t values. A superscript a indicates that the estimate is significant at the 5 percent (or better) level.

The results indicate that in Japan changes in wholesale prices and in export prices are largely associated with unit cost changes, whereas in the United States no definite relationship between wholesale prices and unit costs can be noticed. Since U.S. export price data are not readily available, the analysis with regard to its export prices is excluded.

In this context the rates of change in Japan's wholesale prices were higher than those of unit costs in four industries out of nine in 1973–79 and in eight industries in 1980–86 (not shown). On the contrary, Japan's export price changes (in yen) were lower than its unit cost changes in all nine industries in 1973–79 and in six industries in 1980–86. Moreover, in both periods wholesale prices grew faster than export prices (in yen) in most sectors. As generally expected, export price changes lag behind unit cost changes and wholesale price changes. This seems likely to contribute to Japan's competitive position in terms of prices. However, there exists ambiguity, since Japan's competitiveness depends on how actual export prices (in U.S. dollars) move with changes in foreign exchange rates.

Finally, we examine the relationship between relative export performance and relative cost competitiveness in the two countries. We regress intercountry differences in export growth on intercountry differences in unit cost growth. In measuring export growth rates, export quantity data are preferable; however, U.S. export quantity or export price data by industry are not available. We use export value data expressed in U.S. dollars. Unit cost data are expressed in own-currency units.[6] The results of the cross-sectional regressions across industries as well as the previous results for 1957–74 (Tange, 1987) are

1957–74:
$$\dot{E}^J/E^J - \dot{E}^U/E^U = -3.031^a(\dot{UC}^J/UC^J - \dot{UC}^U/UC^U) + 0.107^a \qquad \bar{R}^2 = 0.521$$
$$(-2.94) \qquad\qquad\qquad (9.21)$$

1973–86:
$$\dot{E}^J/E^J - \dot{E}^U/E^U = -1.628^b(\dot{UC}^J/UC^J - \dot{UC}^U/UC^U) - 0.034 \qquad \bar{R}^2 = 0.315$$
$$(-2.17) \qquad\qquad\qquad\qquad (-1.13)$$

The coefficient estimate for 1957–74 is significant at the 5 percent level (indicated by a superscript a) and the estimate for 1973–86 is significant at the 10 percent level (indicated by a superscript b). Both estimates have negative signs. This means that the relatively high export growth of Japanese industries compared to their U.S. counterparts is associated with the relatively slow growth in unit costs of Japanese industries. Although $\bar{R}^2$ is not so high, this gives at least some support for the hypothesis that relative export performance between the two countries can be related to their relative cost competitiveness. However, the explanatory power of relative cost competitiveness is weaker in the post-1973 period.

Besides the preceding regressions, separate Japanese and U.S. cases were also considered. Cross-sectional regressions of export growth on unit cost growth of each country in the post-1973 period yielded the following results:

Japan:
$$\dot{EQ}/EQ = -2.561^a(\dot{UC}/UC) + 0.148^a \qquad \bar{R}^2 = 0.576$$
$$(-3.64) \qquad\qquad (8.19)$$

United States:
$$\dot{E}/E = -0.367(\dot{UC}/UC) + 0.106^b \qquad \bar{R}^2 = -0.109$$
$$(-0.46) \qquad\qquad (2.40)$$

where EQ is export quantity. Japan's coefficient estimate is highly significant and has a negative sign as expected, whereas the U.S. estimate is not significant. Japan's cost competitiveness accounts considerably for its export (quantity) growth. In the U.S. case, however, the explanatory power of its unit cost change for its export performance is negligible. The poor results for the United States may be due partly to the use of U.S. export values instead of export quantities. As shown, however, there is little relationship between wholesale price changes and unit cost changes in the U.S. data. These pieces of evidence, taken together, suggest problems for the United States because of weak relationships among unit costs, prices, and resulting export growth.

CONCLUSION

We have examined the relative cost competitiveness of Japanese and U.S. industries. A slowdown in productivity growth after the 1973 period was observed in both countries, but the pace of productivity of U.S. industries recovered substantially in the 1980s relative to the 1970s. Unit cost trends (in local currency units) were universally favorable to Japan relative to the United States in this sample of manufacturing industries. This tendency was even more pronounced in the 1980s, since most Japanese industries experienced negative rates of change in unit costs. The main sources of relative cost advantage for Japanese industries were the material cost effect and, to a lesser extent, the output and wage effects. After 1973 productivity growth effects on balance favored the United States over Japan.

In conclusion, some limitations of this study should be noted. First, the study focuses only on cost competitiveness among a number of measures of competitiveness. Second, the effects of dollar depreciation since 1985 on U.S. competitiveness are not measured in this chapter because recent data are not available.

Considering the recovery of productivity growth in U.S. industries in the 1980s and the recent trend toward depreciation of the U.S. dollar, however, it can be said that there are hopeful prospects for the competitive ability of U.S. manufacturing industries.

Table 10-7 Cobb–Douglas Production Functions, Japan[a]

$\log X_i = \log A + \lambda t + \alpha [\log L_i + (\beta'/\alpha)\log K_i + \Sigma(\gamma_i'/\alpha)\log X_{it}] + \log e_i$

Industry	λ	α	β	$\Sigma\gamma_i$	Constant	$\bar{R}^2$	Durbin–Watson
1973–86							
Textiles	0.013[b] (6.189)	0.097[b] (2.538)	0.039	0.374	5.672[b] (4.379)	0.956	1.883
Paper	0.007[b] (2.927)	0.118[b] (6.137)	0.099	0.664	3.023[b] (3.186)	0.936	1.193
Chemicals	0.021[b] (4.956)	0.144[b] (4.748)	0.127	0.784	1.962 (1.217)	0.976	1.314
Primary metals	0.002[b] (2.011)	0.102[b] (9.898)	0.125	1.097	−0.895 (−0.779)	0.938	1.606
Fabricated metal products	0.008[b] (6.622)	0.491[b] (30.410)	0.089	0.967	−0.570[c] (−1.835)	0.992	2.735
Machinery	0.017[b] (9.420)	0.287[b] (23.455)	0.092	0.840	1.318 (3.734)[b]	0.997	1.820
Electrical machinery	0.021[b] (4.090)	0.288[b] (23.002)	0.150	0.921	0.296 (0.784)	0.998	1.110
Transportation equipment	0.010[c] (1.867)	0.207[b] (10.575)	0.086	0.729	2.758[b] (4.270)	0.998	2.286
Total manufacturing	0.004[b] (2.039)	0.240[b] (19.053)	0.122	1.007	0.651 (1.090)	0.998	0.915
1973–79							
Textiles	0.009 (1.459)	0.148[c] (1.944)	0.067	0.595	3.665 (1.346)	0.779	2.476
Paper	0.007 (1.525)	0.119[b] (5.988)	0.096	0.666	2.981[b] (3.058)	0.952	2.800[d]
Chemicals	0.017[b] (2.797)	0.211[b] (5.814)	0.172	1.089	−0.946 (−0.521)	0.945	2.291
Primary metals	0.008[c] (1.846)	0.079[b] (5.272)	0.104	0.895	1.241 (0.713)	0.951	1.974[c]
Fabricated metal products	0.015[b] (3.386)	0.530[b] (17.242)	0.126	1.007	−1.363[b] (−2.253)	0.981	3.414
Machinery	0.017[b] (12.967)	0.282[b] (26.790)	0.077	0.768	2.007[b] (6.984)	0.994	3.489
Electrical machinery	0.020[b] (3.682)	0.329[b] (14.373)	0.190	0.967	−0.498 (−0.737)	0.990	1.399

Table 10-7 (cont.)

Industry	λ	α	β	$\Sigma\gamma_i$	Constant	$\bar{R}^2$	Durbin–Watson
Transportation equipment	0.016[c]	0.192[b]	0.117	0.691	2.819[b]	0.991	2.864
	(1.833)	(5.680)			(2.369)		
Total manufacturing	0.003[c]	0.235[b]	0.132	0.992	0.684	0.994	1.756
	(1.560)	(19.296)			(1.159)		
1980–86							
Textiles	0.015[b]	0.052	0.018	0.193	7.388[b]	0.968	2.709
	(2.452)	(0.850)			(3.749)		
Paper	0.011[b]	0.096[b]	0.084	0.557	4.010[b]	0.950	1.169
	(2.681)	(3.019)			(2.439)		
Chemicals	0.035[b]	0.065[b]	0.063	0.382	6.064[b]	0.991	2.582
	(15.210)	(3.522)			(5.601)		
Primary metals	0.004[b]	0.146[b]	0.165	1.499	−5.002[c]	0.958	1.912
	(2.299)	(11.651)			(−3.473)		
Fabricated metal products	0.003	0.469[b]	0.064	0.984	−0.271	0.989	2.346
	(0.283)	(6.216)			(−0.182)		
Machinery	0.010[b]	0.272[b]	0.102	0.862	1.287	0.997	1.602
	(2.269)	(11.039)			(1.628)		
Electrical machinery	0.016	0.254[b]	0.119	0.927	0.884	0.998	2.122[f]
	(0.631)	(6.450)			(0.636)		
Transportation equipment	0.004	0.223[b]	0.063	0.810	2.454[b]	0.993	2.249[g]
	(0.411)	(6.398)			(2.045)		
Total manufacturing	0.007[c]	0.221[b]	0.102	0.936	1.400	0.998	1.937[h]
	(1.845)	(11.004)			(1.214)		

[a] t ratios appear in parentheses below coefficients.

[b] Significant at better than the 5 percent level.

[c] Significant at better than the 10 percent level.

[d] Estimation period is 1974–81.

[e] Estimation period is 1974–79.

[f] Estimation period is 1980–85.

[g] Estimation period is 1981–86.

[h] Estimation period is 1979–86.

Table 10.6 Co. J-Douglas Production Functions, United States

$$\log X_t = \log A + \lambda t + \alpha\,[\log L_t + (\hat{\beta}/\alpha)\log K_t + \Sigma(\hat{\gamma}_i/\alpha)\log X_{it}] + \log e_t$$

Industry	λ	α	β	$\Sigma\gamma_i$	Constant	$\bar{R}^2$	Durbin–Watson
1973–85							
Textiles	0.013[b] (3.447)	0.001 (0.039)	0.0001	0.001	10.389[b] (48.401)	0.419	1.156[d]
Paper	0.022[b] (3.482)	0.084[c] (1.754)	0.018	0.208	9.366[b] (12.067)	0.872	2.018[c]
Chemicals	0.020[b] (6.538)	0.196[b] (6.620)	0.063	0.522	7.448[b] (12.361)	0.962	1.379
Primary metals	0.011[c] (1.496)	0.307[b] (6.927)	0.005	0.731	6.408[b] (8.471)	0.887	0.868[f]
Fabricated metal products	0.001 (0.829)	0.439[b] (11.869)	0.069	0.728	4.537[b] (8.036)	0.924	1.496[g]
Machinery	0.034[b] (6.716)	0.202[b] (2.231)	0.028	0.280	8.518[b] (6.388)	0.860	1.246
Electrical machinery	0.033[b] (4.555)	0.463[b] (3.854)	0.053	0.572	5.061[b] (3.195)	0.935	1.153
Transportation equipment	0.012[b] (6.555)	0.289[b] (13.582)	0.0001	0.629	7.102[b] (20.228)	0.962	1.883
Total manufacturing	0.022[b] (7.623)	0.243[b] (4.302)	0.055	0.561	7.754[b] (5.359)	0.898	0.956
1973–79							
Textiles	0.012[c] (1.971)	0.182[b] (2.173)	0.027	0.424	7.454[b] (5.435)	0.736	3.045
Paper	−0.026[b] (−3.110)	0.494[b] (6.819)	0.136	1.176	2.493 (2.059)	0.925	1.794
Chemicals	0.012 (1.222)	0.252[b] (5.020)	0.103	0.659	6.124[b] (5.885)	0.974	1.861
Primary metals	−0.003 (−0.561)	0.400[b] (7.899)	0.066	0.972	4.057[b] (4.232)	0.910	2.601
Fabricated metal products	0.008[b] (2.544)	0.358[b] (2.495)	0.059	0.594	5.709[b] (13.029)	0.978	2.567
Machinery	0.016[b] (2.294)	0.305[b] (4.601)	0.056	0.426	6.895[b] (6.900)	0.943	2.918
Electrical machinery	0.016 (1.509)	0.479[b] (4.692)	0.069	0.608	4.710[b] (3.407)	0.904	2.654

Table 10-8 (cont.)

Industry	λ	α	β	$\Sigma\gamma_i$	Constant	$\bar{R}^2$	Durbin–Watson
Transportation equipment	0.012 (1.379)	0.255[b] (5.320)	0.036	0.571	7.193[b] (8.318)	0.940	2.358
Total manufacturing	0.010[b] (2.526)	0.341[b] (8.621)	0.085	0.783	5.194[b] (5.116)	0.977	2.953
1980–85							
Textiles	0.022[b] (6.048)	0.243[b] (7.194)	0.035	0.397	6.464[b] (11.613)	0.956	1.680[h]
Paper	0.0005 (0.021)	0.131 (1.512)	0.023	0.535	7.991[b] (4.164)	0.847	1.571
Chemicals	0.026[b] (2.516)	0.253[c] (1.863)	0.063	0.709	6.432[b] (2.262)	0.507	1.419
Primary metals	0.059[b] (6.131)	0.409[b] (11.711)	0.0004	0.966	4.769[b] (8.301)	0.972	1.999
Fabricated metal products	0.005 (1.301)	0.554[b] (11.294)	0.083	0.923	2.741[b] (3.589)	0.957	2.094[i]
Machinery	0.069[b] (4.738)	0.381[b] (2.766)	0.038	0.528	6.142[b] (3.062)	0.816	2.533
Electrical machinery	0.047[b] (3.081)	0.620[b] (3.032)	0.055	0.759	3.292 (1.222)	0.920	2.461
Transportation equipment	0.007 (1.464)	0.340[b] (12.889)	0.0000001	0.728	6.430[b] (15.272)	0.988	2.288
Total manufacturing	0.033[b] (11.610)	0.0416[c] (10.378)	0.084	1.002	3.297[b] (3.164)	0.982	3.156

[a] t ratios appear in parentheses below coefficients.

[b] Significant at better than the 5 percent level.

[c] Significant at better than the 10 percent level.

[d] Estimation period is 1971–85.

[e] Estimation period is 1974–85.

[f] Estimation period is 1975–85.

[g] Estimation period is 1972–85.

[h] Estimation period is 1981–85.

APPENDIX 10-2 Data

		Sources	
Variables		Japan	United States
X	Gross output in constant prices	2	7
L	Worker-hours	5	7
K	Gross capital stock in constant prices	3	7
X_i	The ith intermediate inputs in constant prices	2,4	7–10
wL	Wage income	2	7
w	Wage rates $= wL/L$	2	7
rK	Non wage income	2	7
r	Price of capital $= rK/K$		
P_i	Deflators of intermediate inputs	2	8
P_w	Wholesale price indexes	1	8
P_e	Export price indexes	1	
E	Export values	6	6
EQ	Export quantity $= E/Pe$		

Notes. A brief description of the data is provided. U.S. gross output by industry in 1977 prices is measured as the industry's total output in the 1977 input–output table, which are multiplied by industrial production indexes with base year 1977. Since U.S. deflators of intermediate inputs are not available, producer's prices are used instead.

The time series of interindustry flows of intermediate inputs are estimated as follows. The composition coefficients of intermediate inputs calculated in each industry of input–output tables for the three benchmark years are interpolated or extrapolated for non–benchmark years. The time series of the composition coefficients then are multiplied by the corresponding industry's total values of material costs.

Sources. (1) Bank of Japan, *Price Indexes Annual;* (2) Japan's Economic Planning Agency (EPA), *Annual Report on National Accounts;* (3) EPA, *Capital Stock of Private Enterprises, 1965–86;* (4) EPA, *The 1970–1975–1980 Link Input–Output Tables;* (5) Japan's Ministry of Labor, *Monthly Labor Statistics;* (6) Organization for Economic Cooperation and Development, *Trade by Commodities;* (7) U.S. Bureau of Economic Analysis, *Survey of Current Business;* (8) U.S. Bureau of Labor Statistics, *Producer Prices and Price Indexes;* (9) U.S. Bureau of the Census, *Annual Survey of Manufactures;* (10) U.S. Bureau of the Census, *United States Census of Manufactures.*

NOTES

I am indebted to Professors Lawrence R. Klein, Bert G. Hickman, and Hidekazu Eguchi for their helpful comments and to Taizo Ujiie and Shuichi Araki for their competent assistance in finding and processing the data.

1. The same method of estimation is used in my earlier article (Tange, 1987). To some extent, descriptions in the two papers overlap.

2. This is the elasticity of substitution model in international trade, which has been subject to theoretical criticism because of the rigid assumptions required for its validity. However, there exists some support for the use of the elasticity of substitution. See Leamer and Stern (1970) and Richardson (1973).

3. The following discussion rests on Klein's (1974) substitution theorem.

4. For the estimates of the Cobb–Douglas production functions, see Tables 10-7 and 10-8.

5. See the Bank of Japan, *Comparative Economic and Financial Statistics: Japan and Other Major Countries 1986*, p. 195, Table 83.

6. In a cross-sectional regression across industries, changes in exchange rates affect all industries equally. Accordingly, were unit costs measured in U.S. dollars used in the cross-sectional regression, only the estimate of the constant term would be affected. Professor H. Eguchi provided valuable comments on this point.

REFERENCES

Baily, M. N. 1982. "The Productivity Growth Slowdown by Industry." *Brookings Papers on Economic Activity* 2, 423–54.

Bodkin, R. G., and L. R. Klein. 1967. "Nonlinear Estimation of Aggregate Production Functions." *Review of Economics and Statistics* 49, 28–44.

Denison, E. F. 1984. "Accounting for Slower Economic Growth: An Update." In J. W. Kendrick, ed., *International Comparisons of Productivity and Causes of the Slowdown*. Cambridge, Mass.: Ballinger.

Gollop, F. M., and D. W. Jorgenson. 1980. "U.S. Productivity Growth by Industry." In J. W. Kendrick and B. N. Vaccara, eds., *New Developments in Productivity Measurement and Analysis*. Chicago: University of Chicago Press.

Japan Productivity Center (Nihon Seisansei Honbu). 1988. *Report on International Comparison of Labor Productivity*. Tokyo: Nihon Seisansei Honbu.

Kendrick, J. W., and E. S. Grossman. 1980. *Productivity in the United States*. Baltimore, Md.: Johns Hopkins University Press.

Klein, L. R. 1974. *A Textbook of Econometrics*. Englewood Cliffs, N.J.: Prentice-Hall.

Lawrence, R. Z. 1979. "Toward a Better Understanding of Trade Balance Trends: The Cost–Price Puzzle." *Brookings Papers on Economic Activity* 1, 191–211.

Leamer, E. E., and R. M. Stern. 1970. *Quantitative International Economics*. Chicago: Allyn and Bacon.

Nadiri, M. I. 1980. "Sectoral Productivity Slowdown." *American Economic Review* 70 (May), 349–52.

Richardson, J. D. 1973. "Beyond (But Back to?) the Elasticity of Substitution in International Trade." *European Economic Review* 4, 381–92.

Tange, T. 1987. "United States–Japan Trade Frictions and Competitiveness." In D. Salvatore, ed., *The New Protectionist Threat to World Welfare*. New York: Elsevier Science Publishing Co.

III

U.S. INTERNATIONAL COMPETITIVENESS

11

Macroeconomic Policies, Competitiveness, and U.S. External Adjustment

PETER HOOPER

The sharp decline in the U.S. external balance during the 1980s represents the acceleration of a downward trend that began three decades earlier. After being comfortably in surplus during the 1960s, the U.S. current account was about in balance, on average, during the 1970s, and fell steeply into deficit during the 1980s. Some analysts have suggested that this downward trend reflects a secular decline in U.S. international competitiveness, due in good measure to a deterioration in the relative performance of U.S. labor productivity in manufacturing. These trends in competitiveness and relative labor productivity, in turn, are viewed as having decidedly negative implications for the dollar's exchange rate in the longer run. With the dollar now back to where it was at the end of the 1970s and the current account still substantially in deficit, many observers feel that significant further depreciation is inevitable.

This chapter comes to a somewhat less negative conclusion about the prospects for U.S. external adjustment and the dollar, based on an analysis of past movements in the external balance, competitiveness, productivity, and macroeconomic policies. Much of the earlier downtrend in the U.S. nominal external balance was the result of adverse movements in the U.S. terms of trade, as oil prices soared and the dollar fell. In real terms, the external balance actually showed a significant uptrend during the 1970s. Changes in price and cost competitiveness, as well as swings in relative aggregate demand, are shown to have had major impacts on the real external balance over the past two decades. During the 1970s, the effects of shifts in competitiveness were largely positive, despite a substantially lower rate of growth for labor productivity in manufacturing in the United States than abroad. The decline in U.S. relative productivity was more than offset by a decline in U.S. relative nominal wages. As a result, U.S. international competitiveness in terms of relative unit labor costs in manufacturing rose strongly and contributed to the rise in real net exports during that period.

These positive trends were reversed in the first half of the 1980s, as U.S. price competitiveness and the external balance turned sharply downward. This decline in U.S. competitiveness occurred despite an improvement (or at least a leveling off of the downward trend) in U.S. relative productivity in manufacturing. Over most of the floating exchange-rate period, movements in U.S. price and cost competitiveness have been influenced predominantly by swings in nominal exchange rates, which, in turn, largely reflect the effects of shifts in macroeconomic policies at home and abroad.

Looking ahead, this analysis has mixed implications for the dollar and external adjustment. On the one hand, the effectiveness of macroeconomic policies designed to reduce the external deficit in the short to medium term will be enhanced to the extent that they increase U.S. price competitiveness by lowering the dollar. On the other hand, a lower dollar would be counterproductive unless domestic demand is restrained enough or output capacity is expanded enough to accommodate a further expansion of net exports.

In any case, exchange rates may already be at a level that could contribute to an eventual upturn in U.S. manufacturing productivity relative to that in other industrial countries. By some estimates, labor costs are now far enough below those in many other countries to make the United States a relatively attractive place to invest in manufacturing capacity, ceteris paribus. Such a shift in output capacity would tend to raise U.S. relative productivity. In the longer run this development would tend to ease downward pressure on the dollar while contributing to a further narrowing of the external deficit. Of course, the effectiveness of adjustment through such shifts in output capacity will be enhanced to the extent that U.S. macroeconomic policies restrain government and private consumption and facilitate investment, particularly in the manufacturing sector.

The chapter begins with a review of longer term trends in the U.S. external position, competitiveness, and the relationship between the two. The next section analyzes trends in relative labor costs in manufacturing in the United States and other major countries as a fundamental indicator of U.S. competitiveness, focusing on the contributions of underlying movements in productivity and exchange rates. The linkage between exchange rates and macroeconomic policies is discussed in the next section, followed by an assessment of the implications of swings in exchange rates for longer term trends in productivity and external adjustment.

TRENDS IN THE U.S. EXTERNAL BALANCE AND ITS DETERMINANTS

The sharp decline in the U.S. external balance during the 1980s was preceded by lesser declines over the preceding two decades. As indicated by the solid curve in Figure 11-1a, the current-account balance expressed as a percentage of nominal GNP was consistently positive during the 1960s (averaging +0.5 percent). The ratio fluctuated during the 1970s but fell to an average of 0.0 percent for the decade. During the first eight and a half years of the 1980s, the ratio plunged to an average of −1.7 percent. The decline in the external balance between the 1960s and the 1970s occurred despite a substantial deprecia-

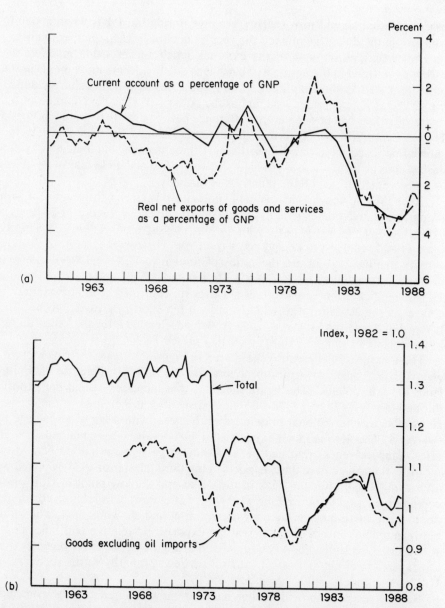

Figure 11-1 (a) U.S. external balances. (b) U.S. terms of trade, where total represents the GNP deflator for exports of goods and services divided by the GNP deflator for imports of goods and services. *Source:* Department of Commerce, Bureau of Economic Analysis.

tion of the dollar over that period. This development has been interpreted by Krugman and Baldwin, among others, as indicative of an underlying secular decline in the competitiveness of the U.S. manufacturing sector associated with a significant shortfall in the growth of U.S. labor productivity relative to that abroad (1987, pp. 34–36). In this view it was not at all surprising that the external deficit should turn sharply negative during the 1980s when a significant rise in the dollar augmented the secular decline in U.S. competitiveness.

However, a closer look at the external deficit suggests that much of the earlier downtrend in the nominal balance was due to adverse movements in the terms of trade. As shown in Figure 11-1b, the terms of trade fell sharply during the 1970s, as import prices rose and as the dollar fell. (The contribution of the rise in oil prices can be seen in the difference between the two curves in Figure 11-1b.) Expressed in real terms, the external balance fluctuated widely but showed no discernible trend over the past three decades (as indicated by the dashed line in Figure 11-1a). Indeed, between 1970 and 1980 real net exports as a percentage of real GNP actually rose strongly.[1]

Since 1969 movements in real net exports have been closely associated with swings in relative domestic activity and competitiveness. Figure 11-2 shows a comparison of real net exports with various measures of relative real activity (part a) and relative prices and costs (part b).[2] The two measures of relative activity in Figure 11-2a are the ratios of foreign to U.S. real GNP and real domestic expenditures $(C + I + G)$.[3] In the early 1970s and again in the late 1970s, significant increases in real net exports coincided with substantial increases in the activity ratios as U.S. growth fell short of growth abroad. The reversal of the activity ratios as U.S. growth accelerated after 1982 contributed to the decline in real net exports over that period.[4]

The measures of competitiveness seen in Figure 11-2b are the ratios of foreign to U.S. consumer prices in dollars and the ratio of foreign to U.S. unit labor costs in dollars.[5] The figure indicates that increases in real net exports during both 1972–75 and 1978–80 followed significant increases in these measures of U.S. international price competitiveness, with a lag of about one to two years. The decline in net exports after 1980 followed a dramatic decline in price competitiveness that had peaked about a year and a half earlier. More recently, the trough in real net exports in the third quarter of 1986 occurred by a year and a half after the peak in the dollar and the low point in U.S. price competitiveness. (The correlation between net exports and relative consumer prices with a five-quarter lag over the entire period shown is 0.83, while that between annual observations of real net exports and relative unit labor costs with a one-year lag is 0.64.) A comparison of Figure 11-2a and b suggests that the expansion of net exports in 1987–88 was due primarily to the recovery of U.S. competitiveness that began in 1985.

Several recent empirical studies have attempted to quantify the contributions of movements in activity and relative prices to the widening of the U.S. real net export deficit between 1980 and 1986, based on simulations with partial-equilibrium models of the U.S. current account (see Helkie and Hooper, 1988; Hooper and Mann, 1989a,b; Krugman and Baldwin, 1987). The consensus seems to be that the more rapid expansion of income and domestic demand in the United States than abroad accounted for between one-quarter and one-third of the total widening of the deficit, while the decline in U.S. price competitiveness associated with the rise in the dollar accounted for between one-half and three-fourths of the total.

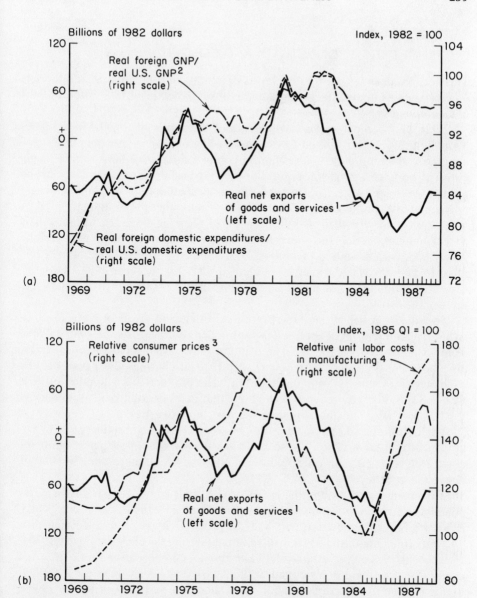

Figure 11-2 Determinants of U.S. real net exports of goods and services. *Source:* Federal Reserve Board USIT Model database.

[1]Adjusted for trend growth in U.S. trade volume between 1969 and 1987.

[2]Foreign GNP includes all OECD countries, OPEC and non-OPEC developing countries.

[3]Ratio of consumer prices in ten industrial countries and eight developing countries (in dollars) to U.S. consumer prices. Foreign prices are weighted by multilateral trade shares.

[4]Ratio of manufacturing until labor costs in dollars in eight industrial countries (weighted by shares in world GNP) to U.S. manufacturing unit labor costs.

EXCHANGE RATES, PRODUCTIVITY, AND COMPETITIVENESS

This section analyzes the relative levels of and movements in U.S. and foreign unit labor costs in manufacturing, an important indicator of U.S. international competitiveness.[6]

Table 11-1 compares the components of the levels of unit labor costs in manufacturing in the United States and in a group of eight other industrial countries.[7] The top panel shows hourly compensation in dollars, where local-currency compensation for foreign countries is translated into dollars at current nominal exchange rates.[8] In 1980, hourly compensation in U.S. manufacturing, at roughly $10 per hour, was slightly above that in other major industrial countries on average. By 1985, the difference had risen significantly, to more than $5 per hour, reflecting the sharp appreciation of the dollar over that period. After 1985, with the fall in the dollar, U.S. compensation fell substantially relative to that abroad. At average exchange rates for the year 1988, the U.S. level was estimated to be about the same as that in other industrial countries, on average.

The middle panel of the table presents estimates of levels of labor productivity in manufacturing, expressed as output per hour measured in 1980 dollars. Foreign productivity data, measured in constant (1980) local-currency units, have been translated into 1980 dollars with 1980 purchasing-power parity (PPP) exchange rates specific to manufacturing.[9] The productivity estimates suggest that U.S. productivity remains well above that in other countries, although the gap has narrowed substantially over the past three decades.

The bottom panel shows the ratios of compensation to productivity, or estimates of unit labor costs. These estimates suggest that in 1988 average manufacturing labor costs in other industrial countries were more than 30 percent above the U.S. level.

Movements over time in the ratios of U.S. unit labor costs and their components relative to those in other industrial countries can be seen more clearly in Figure 11-3. As shown in part *a*, U.S. productivity relative to foreign productivity (the long-dash line) fell substantially during the 1960s and early 1970s. However, U.S. compensation relative to foreign compensation (in dollars) fell even faster, resulting in a net gain in U.S. cost competitiveness (as indicated by the decline in relative unit labor costs shown in part *b*). During the 1960s, most of this gain in U.S. cost competitiveness was due to relatively faster domestic wage inflation abroad (in local currencies), as the dollar's average nominal exchange rate was fairly stable (part *b*). From the early 1970s on, however, most of the variance in relative unit labor costs was attributed to movements in nominal (and real) exchange rates, as domestic inflation rates in the United States and other industrial countries, on average, have converged.[10]

Table 11-1 Comparative Levels of Hourly Compensation, Productivity, and Unit Labor Costs in Manufacturing

	1960	1965	1970	1975	1980	1985	1987	1988[a]
Total compensation per hour (current dollars)								
United States	2.6	3.1	4.2	6.4	9.8	13.0	13.5	14.2
Foreign industrial countries[b]	0.6	1.0	1.6	4.5	8.4	7.7	12.8	14.3
Output per hour (1980 dollars)								
United States	9.2	11.3	11.9	13.7	15.0	18.4	19.5	20.2
Foreign industrial countries[b]	3.4	4.6	6.8	8.8	11.0	13.9	14.3	14.9
Unit labor costs (ratio of compensation per hour to output per hour)								
United States	29	28	35	46	66	71	69	70
Foreign industrial countries[b]	18	21	24	51	76	55	88	95

Sources: Bureau of Labor Statistics and Hooper and Lavin (1989).

[a]Projections based on average exchange rates for 1988, and extrapolation of recent trends in compensation and productivity.

[b]Canada, Japan, Germany, France, the United Kingdom, Italy, Belgium, the Netherlands, Denmark, and Norway; weighted by shares in world GNP.

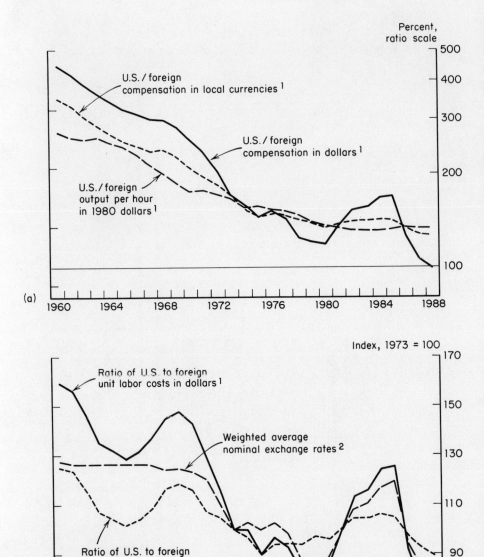

Figure 11-3 (a) Relative unit labor costs in manufacturing and their components. (b) Relative unit labor costs and the nominal exchange rate. *Source:* Federal Reserve Board and Bureau of Labor Statistics.
[1]Foreign includes average of Japan, Germany, France, Canada, the United Kingdom, Italy, the Netherlands, and Belgium, in dollars, weighted by manufacturing output.
[2]Weighted by shares in world GNP.

MACROECONOMIC POLICIES AND EXCHANGE RATES

In this section we first review a key component of the link between macroeconomic policies and the exchange rate—real interest parity. We then review empirical evidence on the effects of shifts in macro policies on real interest rates and exchange rates.

Real Interest Parity

Long-term real open interest parity has held up as well as any empirical relationship in explaining movements in the dollar over the floating-rate period. In essence, this model equates the long-run expected change in the real exchange rate with the long-term real interest rate differential.[11] The basic assumptions of the model are, first, that assets denominated in different currencies are highly substitutable, and second, that expectations about the equilibrium level of the real exchange rate in the long run remain unchanged. Under the first assumption, exchange risk premia are unimportant, so that open interest parity holds:

$$s_t^e - s_t = \gamma(i_t^* - i_t) \tag{11-1}$$

where

$\quad s_t$ = log of the nominal spot exchange rate (foreign
$\qquad$ currency/home currency) in period t
$\quad s_t^e$ = expected value of s γ years ahead
$\quad i_t$ = log of 1 plus the annual rate of interest on home-currency
$\qquad$ bonds with a term of γ years

and the asterisk (*) denotes a foreign variable and e denotes expectations.

Under the second assumption, the expected value of the nominal spot exchange rate (s_t^e) in the long run (γ years ahead) is defined as

$$s_t^e = p_t^{*e} - p_t^e + q_t^e \tag{11-2}$$

where p_t^{*e} and p_t^e are log values of expectations in the current period about the levels of foreign prices and home prices, respectively, γ years ahead, and q_t^e is the constant expected long-run equilibrium value of the real exchange rate. Substituting current price levels and expected average annual rates of inflation (π) for expected future price levels in Equation 11-2, we have

$$s_t^e = p_t^* + \gamma\pi_t^{*e} - (p_t + \gamma\pi_t^e) + q_t^e \tag{11-3}$$

Substituting the right-hand side of Equation 11-3 for s_t^e in Equation 11-1 and rearranging yields

$$s_t - p_t^* + p_t = q_t^e + \gamma(i_t - \pi_t^e - i_t^* + \pi_t^{*e}) \tag{11-4}$$

which expresses the log of the real exchange rate as a function of the expected real exchange rate in the long run and the real interest rate differential. The horizon γ is defined as being long enough for q_t^e to be considered constant.

Figure 11-4 is an empirical representation of the relationship in Equation 11-4. Figure 11-4a shows the real dollar against G-10 currencies and a measure of the difference between U.S. and foreign (G-10) long-term real government bond yields. Part b shows the U.S. and foreign components of the real interest differential. In calculating the real bond yields, a three-year centered moving average of CPI inflation rates (i.e., ranging from six quarters in the past to six quarters in the future) was used as a proxy for inflation expectations. (The countries and weights in the foreign interest rate index are the same as in the exchange rate index.)

Movements in the dollar's real exchange rate have been at least roughly correlated with the long-term real interest rate differential over much of the floating-rate period.[12] The decline in the dollar during the 1970s followed a general downtrend in the interest differential. The rise in U.S. real interest rates in the early 1980s then accounted for much of the rise in the dollar, at least through early 1984. And in 1985–86, the dollar fell as U.S. real interest rates declined.

During 1984, however, the dollar continued to rise after U.S. real interest rates had turned sharply downward relative to those abroad. Although the relationship is far from perfect, movements in real interest rates nevertheless do appear to have been a major factor underlying longer term swings in the dollar's real exchange rate over the floating-rate period. Movements in the dollar's real exchange rate have also been a good indicator of movements in the nominal exchange rate, as changes in relative domestic consumer prices have been small in comparison.

Macroeconomic Policies

The influence of macroeconomic policies on real interest rates and exchange rates has received considerable attention in the literature. The rise in U.S. real interest rates in the early 1980s has been attributed to a combination of monetary tightening beginning with the shift in the Federal Reserve's operating procedures in November 1979 and fiscal expansion following the passage of the federal tax cuts in 1981.[13] Similarly, the decline in U.S. real rates in 1984–86 has been linked both to the adoption of a more accommodative monetary policy stance by the Federal Reserve and to improved prospects for a significant reduction of the federal budget deficit following the passage of the Gramm-Rudman Act in 1985 (see Johnson, 1986).

Quantitative estimates of the impacts of shifts in U.S. and foreign macroeconomic policies during the early 1980s (on real interest rates, the dollar, and the U.S. real external deficit) are provided by Hooper and Mann (1989b). Their estimates are based on a combination of OECD and IMF estimates of shifts in structural budget deficits and the results of policy simulations reported by a group of twelve multicountry models in a March 1986 Brookings conference.[14] The models that took part in the Brookings exercise simulated the effects of sustained exogenous shifts in government spending in the United States and in other OECD countries while holding the growth of monetary aggregates exog-

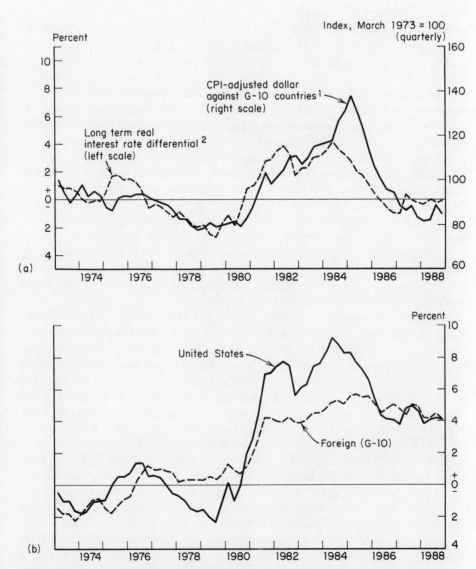

Figure 11-4 (a) The dollar and real interest rates (quarterly data). (b) Real long-term interest rates, where long-term government or public authority bond rates are adjusted for expected inflation estimated by a thirty-six-month centered calculation of actual inflation. Foreign index uses the trade weights described in note 1. *Source:* Federal Reserve Board macro database.

[1] The CPI-adjusted dollar is a weighted average index of the exchange value of the dollar against the currencies of the foreign Group-of-Ten countries plus Switzerland, where nominal exchange rates are multiplied by relative levels of consumer price indexes. Weights are proportional to each foreign country's share in world exports plus imports during 1978–83.

[2] Long-term real U.S. interest rate minus weighted average of long-term real foreign-country interest rates.

enous. They also simulated the effects of an exogenous change in the U.S. money stock. The theoretical structure that most of these models conform to is the "expectations-augmented" Mundell–Fleming model, as described, for example, by Frankel (1988).

The average model simulation results suggested that a U.S. fiscal expansion equivalent to 1 percent of GNP during the early 1980s would have raised U.S. GNP for several years, eventually leading to a 0.5 percentage point increase in U.S. long-term real interest rates relative to foreign rates, a 2–2.5 percent appreciation of the dollar in real terms against OECD currencies on average, and a $15 billion to $20 billion decline in the current-account balance. A fiscal contraction abroad would also have induced an appreciation of the dollar and a decline in the U.S. current-account balance, though by smaller amounts than a comparable U.S. fiscal shock. A U.S. monetary contraction would have raised the real interest rate differential and the dollar's exchange rate, but it also would have reduced U.S. real income. With the fall in income tending to reduce imports and the rise in the dollar working in the opposite direction to depress net exports, the U.S. monetary contraction by itself would have had a *negligible* impact on the current-account balance.

Using these simulation results, Hooper and Mann estimate that the combined effects of the U.S. fiscal expansion and the foreign fiscal contraction in the early 1980s accounted for only about one-third of the increase in the long-term real interest rate differential between late 1979 and early 1984 and about one-fifth of the rise in the dollar to its peak in early 1985. At the same time, the fiscal shifts accounted for between half and two-thirds of the widening of the current-account deficit. Much of this impact on the current account resulted from the strong effects that the shifts in fiscal policy are estimated to have had on relative GNP growth. (However, the actual level of U.S. GNP relative to foreign [OECD] GNP rose much less over the first half of the 1980s than the effects of the fiscal shifts alone would have suggested. This is because other factors tended to depress U.S. relative GNP growth, as discussed later.)

Hooper and Mann also conclude that much of the remaining rise in the real interest differential (and hence the dollar) can be explained by a significant tightening of U.S. monetary policy relative to monetary policy abroad, beginning in late 1979. However, the U.S. monetary tightening by itself does not explain any of the widening of the current-account deficit. This is because the U.S. monetary tightening, in the face of double-digit inflation, significantly reduced U.S. real GNP growth. The positive current-account effects of the reduced growth in output were large enough to offset the negative effects of the rise in the dollar caused by the same monetary tightening.

Quantitative estimates by Hooper and Mann suggest that, taken separately, neither the shift in monetary policy alone nor the shift in fiscal policies alone can adequately explain the changes in the U.S. external sector that took place during the first half of the 1980s. Taken *together*, however, the combined effects of these policy changes can explain something approaching two-thirds of the increases in both the dollar and the current-account deficit. They suggest that explanations for the remaining rise in the dollar and the widening of the current-account deficit may be found in exchange market bubbles and the international debt crisis, among other factors.

This analysis implies that in the period ahead, a significant reduction of the U.S. external deficit could be achieved through some combination of U.S. fiscal contraction and foreign fiscal expansion. In the absence of further fiscal expansion abroad, achieving the adjustment without a substantial reduction in U.S. growth would require some monetary easing. In this case more of the adjustment would depend on the expenditure-switching effects of a decline in the dollar induced by lower U.S. interest rates. Some observers have suggested that the announcement of a credible and substantial planned reduction in the budget deficit would cause the dollar to appreciate, because of the favorable implications of that announcement for the external deficit. (In terms of the exchange-rate model described earlier, expectations about the long-run equilibrium real exchange rate would be revised up.) In this case, however, significant external adjustment would have to depend on a substantial reduction in domestic expenditures. Such a reduction in expenditures would result in significantly lower interest rates, which, in turn, would tend to weaken the dollar.

At the same time, the effectiveness of dollar depreciation by itself, as a means of reducing the deficit, is diminished by the current high level of resource utilization in the U.S. economy. Some slowing of growth in U.S. domestic expenditures, ideally through either a fiscal contraction or an increase in private savings (or, less ideally, through a reduction in domestic investment) would be needed to accommodate a significant further expansion of U.S. net exports. If such accommodation were not forthcoming, the increase in aggregate demand and resulting upward pressure on domestic prices and interest rates would tend to reverse both the decline in the dollar in real terms and the improvement in the external balance.[15]

EXCHANGE RATES AND PRODUCTIVITY IN THE LONGER RUN

To this point the analysis has considered primarily the shorter run effects of macroeconomic policies on external adjustment through their impacts on real interest rates, competitiveness, and relative domestic demand. This section addresses the possible effects of large (and sustained) shifts in exchange rates on relative productivity and external adjustment in the longer run.

Exchange rates are related causally to relative (U.S./foreign) labor productivity, through their impact on relative capital formation. Relative capital formation, in turn, is influenced by exchange rates through their impacts on relative labor costs. Fixed investment decisions are based on a number of factors that influence the expected return on the investment. One important factor is the cost of variable inputs, of which labor is a major component. Figure 11-5 illustrates the relationship between movements in the ratio of foreign to U.S. manufacturing capital stocks (part *b*) and relative levels of unit labor costs in manufacturing (part *a*) since 1963.[16] The figure indicates that the ratio of U.S. to foreign capital fell sharply during the 1960s and early 1970s when U.S. labor

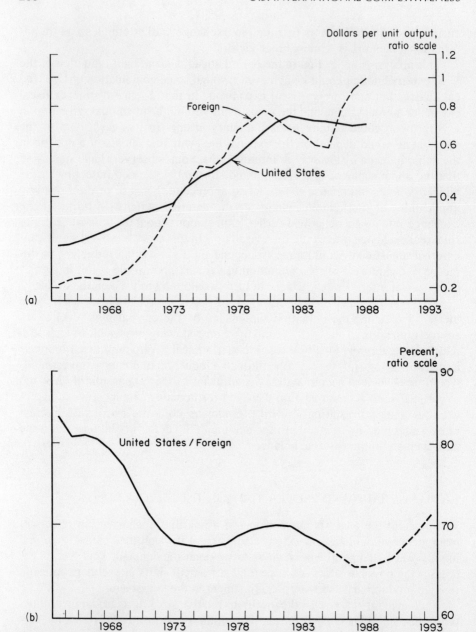

Figure 11-5 (a) Unit labor costs and (b) relative capital stocks in manufacturing. Foreign includes average of Japan, Germany, France, Canada, and the United Kingdom, in dollars, weighted by manufacturing output. Relative capital stocks are calculated from OECD estimates of U.S. and foreign real capital stocks in manufacturing, measured in 1980 dollars. *Source:* Bureau of Labor Statistics and OECD.

costs were well above those abroad, on average. The downtrend in the capital stock ratio was then reversed in the late 1970s when foreign labor costs rose above the U.S. level as a result of the decline in the dollar during that period. The capital stock ratio turned down again in the early 1980s when the rise in the dollar pushed U.S. labor costs back above the foreign level.

Causation runs in both directions between the top and bottom panels of the chart. During the 1960s, the direction of causation probably ran chiefly from relative capital stocks to relative unit labor costs. Unit labor costs abroad were held down by rapid increases in productivity that resulted in part from the rapid rate of capital formation abroad during that period. During the 1970s and 1980s, causation probably ran the other direction, since most of the variation in relative unit labor costs was due to swings in nominal exchange rates rather than movements in relative productivity, as we saw earlier. The correlation between movements in the capital stock ratio and movements in the ratio of foreign to U.S. unit labor costs over the floating-rate period (1973–85) is 0.45. Movements in the ratio of U.S. to foreign capital stocks in manufacturing evidently were significantly influenced by factors other than relative unit labor costs.

Other factors that might well have influenced relative capital formation include relative growth of output (leading to differential accelerator effects at home and abroad) and the relative cost of capital. To the extent that the cost of borrowing funds represents a significant portion of the cost of capital, and to the extent that firms borrow in the country in which they are investing, the long-term real interest rate differential could represent a significant element of the relative cost of capital across countries. It is quite possible, therefore, that some of the correlation between relative capital stocks and relative labor costs represents the effects of shifts in the real interest rate differential underlying the swings in real exchange rates and relative labor costs. As U.S. real interest rates rose during the early 1980s, for example, this would have depressed U.S. investment relative to that abroad by raising the relative cost of capital in the United States as well as by raising the dollar and the relative cost of labor in the United States.

In any event, shifts in relative labor costs appear to have had at least some impact on relative rates of capital formation over the period of floating rates. Should the recent differential between U.S. and foreign unit labor costs persist, it could help to induce another upturn in the capital stock ratio. For illustrative purposes, the path of the capital stock ratio has been extended through 1993 in Figure 11-5 under the optimistic assumptions that (1) the growth of foreign real gross investment in manufacturing slows to about 3 percent per year, (2) U.S. real gross manufacturing investment continues to grow at the rapid pace (nearly 11 percent) recorded in 1988, and (3) both U.S. and foreign replacement investment continues to grow at 5 percent per year (see Hooper, 1988). Of course, the realization of such a shift in capital stocks would depend heavily on whether U.S. macroeconomic policies were conducive to a significant expansion of U.S. capital formation in manufacturing.[17]

The data in Figure 11-5 suggest the possibility of a causal link from exchange rates to relative capital stocks. To complete the connection between exchange rates and relative productivity, a link between relative capital stocks and relative productivity must also be established. In a production function or growth-accounting framework, labor productivity depends on the ratio of capital to labor, as well as on total factor productivity, or Hicks-neutral technical progress. Relative (U.S./foreign) capital–labor ratios can be constructed using available Bureau of Labor Statistics data on hours worked in manufacturing in the United States and major foreign industrial countries. These data are shown in Figure 11-6, where the dashed lines are actual hours and the solid lines are the underlying trends (which were obtained in regressions of actual hours against a constant and time over the historical period shown). The actual hours series show significant cyclical fluctuations—witness the large drop in U.S. hours worked during both the 1975 and 1982 recessions. The underlying trend in the U.S. case has been flat since 1970, and that in other major countries, on average, has been distinctly negative.

Figure 11-7a shows the ratios of U.S. to foreign hours worked in manufacturing, using both actual data and underlying trends. The trend ratio has been extrapolated through 1993 at its historical growth rate. Figure 11-7b compares movements in U.S. relative to foreign productivity in manufacturing with those in (1) relative (U.S./foreign) capital stocks, (2) relative capital–labor ratios based on actual hours worked, and (3) relative capital–labor ratios based on the trends in hours worked. The relative productivity series is the same as that shown in Figure 11-3a. The relative capital–labor ratios were computed by dividing the U.S./foreign capital stock ratio by the U.S./foreign hours ratios shown in Figure 11-7a. As might be expected, the correlation between relative productivity and either of the relative capital/labor ratios is quite high (0.90 in the case of actual hours; 0.92 in the case of trend hours).

These data and extrapolations suggest that if labor inputs and technical progress at home and abroad continue to grow at their recent historical trend rates, and if relative capital stocks turn around as strongly as shown in this illustration, the improving performance of U.S. relative labor productivity in recent years would continue, and could even strengthen further. This improvement would lessen the need for significant further depreciation of the dollar in order to achieve external balance in the longer run.[18]

CONCLUSION

This chapter makes essentially four points. First, movements in U.S. international price and cost competitiveness have been major factors underlying swings in the U.S. external balance, particularly those in real net exports, over the past two decades.

Second, since the early 1970s, movements in U.S. international price and cost competitiveness have been dominated by swings in nominal exchange rates. In the aggregate, movements in relative productivity between the United States and other countries have had only minor impacts on U.S. international competitiveness in comparison to the influence of changes in exchange rates.

Third, movements in exchange rates, and therefore in price and cost competitiveness and the external balance, have been determined to a large extent

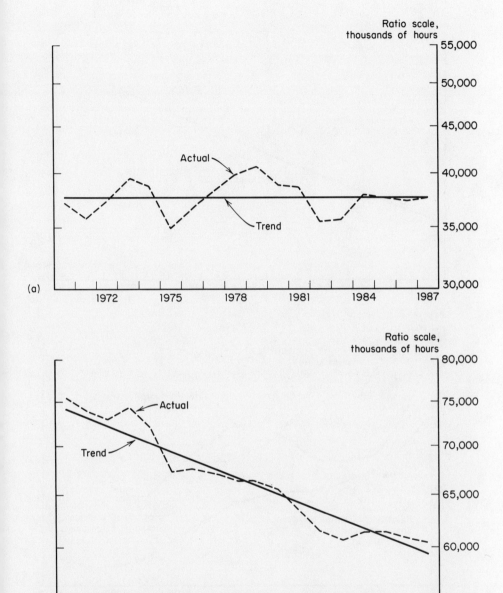

Figure 11-6 Hours worked in manufacturing in (a) the United States and (b) Japan, Germany, the United Kingdom, France, and Canada. *Source:* Bureau of Labor Statistics.

by shifts in U.S. and foreign macroeconomic policies, through their impacts on relative real rates of return on assets.

Foruth, the recent labor cost differential in favor of the United States, if sustained, could induce a shift in relative capital stocks in manufacturing that would result in significant gains in U.S. relative to foreign labor productivity in manufacturing. Such gains could reverse the longstanding downward trend in

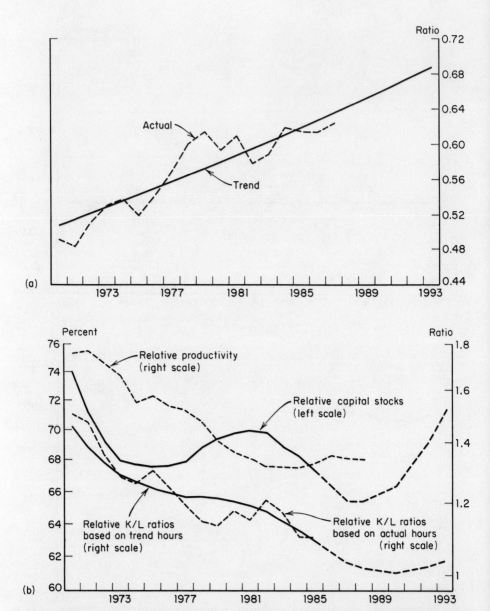

Figure 11-7 Ratio of (a) U.S. to foreign hours worked and (b) U.S. to foreign capital stocks, capital–labor ratios, and productivity in manufacturing. Foreign includes Japan, Germany, the United Kingdom, France, and Canada. *Source:* Bureau of Labor Statistics and OECD.

U.S. relative productivity and would lessen further depreciation of the dollar, which might be needed to achieve U.S. external balance.

NOTES

I wish to thank Bert G. Hickman, Ronald I. McKinnon, and Sean Craig for their comments on an earlier draft and Kathryn A. Larin for her research assistance. The views expressed in this chapter are my own, and do not necessarily reflect the views of the Federal Reserve Board, the Brookings Institution, or other members of their staffs.

1. Most of the rise in real net exports of goods and services during this period reflected an increase in the volume of nonagricultural exports relative to the volume of non-oil imports.

2. Net exports have been normalized by trend growth in total U.S. real trade over the period 1969–87 in order to make them more comparable with the other series shown over the entire period covered. Between 1969 and 1987, total U.S. trade increased about 250 percent in real terms. Without scaling for this trend growth, a given percentage change in relative activity or relative prices would be associated with a substantially greater change in net exports at the end of the period shown than it would be at the beginning.

3. Foreign domestic expenditures were not measured directly but were approximated by adding U.S. net exports to aggregate rest-of-world GNP.

4. The simple correlation between the GNP ratio and net exports over the period shown is 0.35; that between the domestic expenditure ratio and net exports is 0.70. A higher correlation can be expected in the second case because net exports are included in domestic expenditures but not in GNP. In econometric tests with both GNP and domestic expenditures in separate behavioral equations for imports and exports, Hooper and Mann (1989a,b) found relatively little difference in the "explanatory power" of these two activity variables.

5. The ratio of unit labor costs used is described more fully later.

6. The data presented in this section are described more fully in Hooper and Larin (1989).

7. A more complete assessment of changes in U.S. international cost competitiveness would also have to take into account data for a number of important developing countries. Data on these countries are much less readily available, however.

8. These data are compiled by the Bureau of Labor Statistics.

9. The PPP exchange rates are constructed from purchasing power parities for individual expenditure categories, compiled by the U.N. International Comparison Project. The movements in relative productivity over time are based on BLS estimates. See Hooper and Larin (1989).

10. The simple correlation between quarterly movements in the exchange rate and the unit labor cost ratio between 1972 and 1988 is 0.95.

11. The following discussion draws on Hooper and Mann (1989a,b).

12. The simple correlation between the two series shown in Figure 11-4a is 0.85 for the period 1973–83 and 0.78 for the entire period shown.

13. See Blanchard and Summers (1984) for an analysis of factors underlying the rise in real interest rates in the early 1980s. Analyses by Branson (1988), Branson, Fraga, and Johnson (1985), Feldstein (1986), and Hooper (1985) all link the rise in the dollar to the 1981 tax cut through its impact on real interest rates.

14. The results of the conference are documented in Bryant, Henderson, Holtham, Hooper, and Symansky (1988).

15. In addition to the negative effect of a higher real dollar exchange rate on net exports, the increase in aggregate demand would raise demand for imports, and the increase in U.S. interest rates would depress net exports through its impact on net investment income payments to foreigners (given the large and growing U.S. net international debt position).

16. The capital stock ratio shown here was constructed from OECD data, as described by Hooper (1988); the unit labor cost shown are the same data that were discussed earlier but limited to the five foreign countries—Japan, Germany, France, the United Kingdom, and Canada—for which capital stock data are available.

17. Maintaining a rapid rate of growth of manufacturing investment would not require substantial cutbacks in other expenditure categories, however. In recent years, investment in manufacturing has accounted for only about 13 percent of total private fixed investment and 2.5 percent of real GNP.

18. Hooper (1988) analyzes the implications for the current account of the shift in capital stocks considered here, based on simulations with conventional models of the U.S. current account.

REFERENCES

Blanchard, O. J., and L. Summers. 1984. "Perspectives on High World Interest Rates." *Brookings Papers on Economic Activity* 2, pp. 273–324.

Branson, W. H. 1988. "Sources of Misalignment in the 1980s." In R. C. Marston, ed., *Misalignment of Exchange Rates*. Chicago: University of Chicago Press, pp. 9–38.

Branson, W. H., A. Fraga, and R. A. Johnson. 1985. "Expected Fiscal Policy and the Recession of 1982." International Finance Discussion Paper 272. Washington: Board of Governors of the Federal Reserve System.

Bryant, R. C. 1988. "The U.S. External Deficit: An Update." Brookings Discussion Papers in International Finance, No. 63 (January).

Bryant, R. C., D. W. Henderson, G. Holtham, P. Hooper, and S. A. Symansky, eds. 1988. *Empirical Macroeconomics for Interdependent Economies*. Washington, D.C.: Brookings Institution.

Bryant, R. C., G. Holtham, and P. Hooper. 1988. *External Deficits and the Dollar: The Pit and the Pendulum*. Washington, D.C.: Brookings Institution.

Feldstein, M. 1986. "The Budget Deficit and the Dollar." In Stanley Fischer, ed., *NBER Macroeconmics Annual*, Vol. 1. Cambridge: MIT Press, pp. 355–92.

Frankel, J. A. 1988. "Ambiguous Policy Multipliers in Theory and in Empirical Models." In R. C. Bryant, D. W. Henderson, G. Holtham, P. Hooper, and S. A. Symansky, eds., *Empirical Macroeconomics for Interdependent Economies*. Washington, D.C.: Brookings Institution, pp. 17–26.

Helkie, W. H., and P. Hooper. 1988. "The U.S. External Deficit in the 1980s: An Empirical Analysis." In R. Bryant, G. Holtham, and P. Hooper, eds., *External Deficits and the Dollar: The Pit and the Pendulum*. Washington, D.C.: Brookings Institution, pp. 10–56.

Hooper, P. 1985. "International Repercussions of the U.S. Budget Deficit." Brookings Discussion Papers in International Economics, No. 27 (February).

Hooper, P. 1988. "Exchange Rates and U.S. External Adjustment in the Short Run and the Long Run." Brookings Discussion Paper in International Economics.

Hooper, P., and K. A. Larin. 1989. "International Comparisons of Labor Costs in Manufacturing." *Review of Income and Wealth,* Series 35, No. 4, 3–123.

Hooper, P., and C. L. Mann. 1989a. "The U.S. External Deficit: Its Causes and Persistence." In A. E. Burger, ed., *U.S. Trade Deficit: Causes, Consequences and Cures.* Boston: Kluwer Academic Publishers.

Hooper, P., and C. L. Mann. 1989b. "The Emergence and Persistence of the U.S. External Imbalance." *Princeton Studies in International Finance,* No. 65, October.

Johnson, R. A. 1986. "Anticipated Fiscal Contraction: The Economic Consequences of the Announcement of Gramm-Rudman-Hollings." International Finance Discussion Paper 291. Washington, D.C.: Board of Governors of the Federal Reserve System.

Krugman, P. 1987. "Adjustment in the World Economy." NBER Working Paper 2424. Cambridge, Mass.: National Bureau of Economic Research (October), pp. 1–43.

Krugman, P., and R. Baldwin. 1987. "The Persistence of the U.S. Trade Deficit." *Brookings Papers on Economic Activity* 1.

OECD. 1987. *Flows and Stocks of Fixed Capital 1960–1985.* Paris: OECD, Department of Economics and Statistics.

12

U.S. Competitiveness and the Exchange Rate: A General Equilibrium Analysis of the U.S. Economy, 1982–86

IRMA ADELMAN AND
SHERMAN ROBINSON

Dramatic changes in the position of the United States in the world economy began to unfold in 1981. There has been a substantial acceleration in the loss of international competitiveness[1] of the United States, resulting in a massive deterioration in the deficit in the U.S. balance of trade. By 1986, the U.S. trade deficit had quintupled relative to 1980, becoming the largest trade deficit ever run by the United States or any other nation. The loss in international competitiveness has been broad based, occurring in all sectors and with all trading partners. At the same time, the degree of openness of the U.S. economy has increased very substantially, making the economy much more sensistive to fluctuations in international trade. Trade became 11 percent of GNP, more than double the percentage in 1980. At least 20 percent of manufacturing employment and 55 percent of agricultural employment are now in trade-related industries.

The mix of macroeconomic policies adopted during the Reagan administration turned the small budget surplus inherited from the Carter years into a deficit that now stands at a threatening 5 percent of GDP. The deficit imparted a Keynesian fiscal stimulus to the economy. But together with the tight monetary policies of the Federal Reserve aimed at reducing inflation, it also generated the unprecedentedly large capital inflows that, in turn, gave rise to the large trade deficit. From the world's largest creditor, the United States turned into the world's largest debtor. The net effect was a set of macro "shocks" to the economy. In this chapter, we are concerned only with the effects of these

shocks on the structure of the economy. We are not concerned with the links
between specific macro policies and the resulting shocks. For a discussion of
such links, see Hooper (Chapter 11, this volume) and the literature cited
therein.

The macro policy mix of the Reagan years led to a large effective revaluation of the dollar[2] and to high U.S. interest rates. These twin developments, in
turn, had major consequences for the decline in international competitiveness
of U.S. exports in industry and agriculture. The revaluation led to a significant
decrease in the average relative price of tradables to nontradables (the real
exchange rate), which shifted incentive away from exporting toward importing
and the production of nontradables.

In effect, the changes in relative prices induced by the swings in macro
balances constituted an industrial policy, shifting resources away from sectors
producing tradables (exports and import substitutes) toward nontradables. Industry and agriculture were affected, both by the shifts in relative prices and
by the unprecedentedly high real interest rates.[3] The revaluation hurt exports
and increased imports. The high interest rates led to lower investment and innovation. They were also capitalized in declining agricultural land prices, leading to severe financial problems for farmers in debt.

There are two different schools of thought concerning the loss of competitiveness of U.S. industry. Some see it as a result of slow productivity growth
due to fundamental choices concerning U.S. innovation and technology policy,
investment in human capital, the crowding out of private investment, and the
absence of a coherent industrial policy. Others see the loss of competitiveness
as due primarily to the overvaluation in exchange rate. This chapter analyzes
the explanatory power of the second view in the short run.[4] In particular, we
first develop a quantitative model that replicates the changes in U.S. trade,
GNP, and exchange rate between 1982 and 1986. We then impose on the model
the more conservative budget deficit and tax policy of the last Carter year and
track the consequences of these counterfactual policies for relative prices, exports, and imports.

We use a computable general equilibrium (CGE) model of the U.S. economy to analyze the impact of the swings in macro balances on the structure of
relative prices, production, trade, income, and demand. We use the model as
a counterfactual laboratory to isolate the impact of the observed swings the
trade and federal deficits have on the equilibrium real exchange rate, relative
prices, and the structure of output, employment, demand, and trade. In our
analysis, we impose the two deficits as exogenous magnitudes in our model.
Aggregate employment and sectoral capital stocks are also maintained fixed
across the counterfactual experiments, so we are not attempting to analyze any
business cycle effects. The model is designed to focus on foreign trade issues,
incorporating sectoral demand elasticities for imports and supply elasticities
for exports. In the next section, we present a summary of the CGE model. We
next discuss calibration of the model for 1982 and a base solution for 1986. We
then analyze experiments in which we consider the impact of alternative macro
scenarios. Finally, we present some sensitivity analyses on the elasticities relevant to the study of U.S. competitiveness.

A CGE MODEL OF THE U.S. ECONOMY

Our CGE model is in the tradition of models developed for the analysis of issues of trade policy in developing countries.[5] The model equations describe the supply and demand behavior of the various economic actors across markets for factors and commodities, including exports and imports. The model is neo-classical and Walrasian in spirit, solving for a set of relative prices (including the exchange rate) that achieve flow equilibria in the various markets. The model assumes (1) full employment, (2) sectorally fixed capital stocks, (3) an exogenously set aggregate price level, (4) exogenously set world prices (in foreign currency) of export and import commodities, (5) an exogenously set balance of trade, and (6) an exogenously set government deficit. The model determines flow equilibria in product and factor markets, with no assets, financial instruments, or interest rate variables. The model is used for doing comparative static experiments relative to a 1986 base—no dynamics, no lags, no expectation variables.[6]

The model contains ten sectors, including three agricultural sectors, five industrial sectors (including construction), and two service sectors. Sectoral production functions are all Cobb–Douglas in labor and capital. In two sectors, grains and other agriculture, cultivated land is also included as a factor. The total supply of cultivated land is fixed but is assumed to be freely allocable to either crop. The model thus solves for a single equilibrium land rental rate. Sectoral capital stocks are assumed to be immobile so that model solutions generate differential rental rates across sectors. Labor is assumed to be completely mobile across sectors, and the model solves for a single equilibrium wage. The demand for intermediate inputs is given by fixed input–output coefficients.

On the demand side, the model includes the following actors who receive income and demand goods: households, government, capital account, and the rest of the world. There are three categories of households classified by income level who receive income from wages, profits, rents, and transfers. They in turn save (according to fixed average savings rates) and then allocate their consumption expenditure across goods according to a simple linear expenditure system. Aggregate government expenditure on goods is specified exogenously (in real terms) and is allocated across sectors according to fixed shares. The government receives income from taxes (direct and indirect), which it then spends on goods and transfers to households. Government saving (the deficit) is determined residually as receipts minus expenditures. The capital account deals only in flows from current income, collecting savings from all sources (private, government, and foreign) and spending it on investment goods. The model is static in that the sectoral and aggregate capital stocks are fixed, and the investment flow is not "installed" or incorporated into sectoral capital stocks as part of an experiment.[7]

On the import side, the model specifies product differentiation between imports and domestically produced goods in the same sector. Demanders purchase a "composite" commodity in each sector, which is a constant elasticity of substitution (CES) aggregation of domestically produced and imported goods.[8] The effect is that import demand is a function of the ratio of the price in domestic currency of the import (PM) to that of the domestic good in the same sector (PD). On the export side, suppliers are assumed to have different production functions for goods sold on the domestic and export markets. Using factor inputs, they produce a "composite" commodity which can then be transformed into goods intended for exporting versus those for the domestic market according to a constant elasticity of transformation (CET) function. Given the assumption of profit maximization, the ratio of export goods to goods for the domestic market in each sector is a function of the relative price in domestic currency of exports (PE) and domestic sales (PD). In effect, each sector is a two-product firm with a separable production function. The determination of the level of aggregate production is based on the producer price of the composite commodity (PX), while the composition of supply to the export and domestic markets depends only on the relative prices in the two markets (PE/PD).

Sectoral world prices of exports and imports (PWE and PWM) are assumed to be fixed exogenously and to be independent of the volume of U.S. exports and imports. While such a specification would not be adequate if we were focusing on, say, export incentive policies, it is acceptable given that we are concerned in the experiments with the structural impact of swings in macroeconomic balances and exchange rates.[9]

The effect of this trade specification is potentially to insulate the domestic price system from world prices. In a model in which all goods are tradable and are perfect substitutes with foreign goods, domestic relative prices are completely determined by world prices. By contrast, in this model, all domestically produced goods sold on the domestic market are only imperfectly substitutable with goods either bought from or sold to the rest of the world. As a result, domestic prices are only partly determined by world prices. This specification has proven to yield much more realistic behavior than a model incorporating perfect substitutability and is widely used in CGE models focusing on international trade.[10]

The model incorporates a number of different prices in each sector. On the demand side, the price of the composite good (P) corresponds to a retail sales price and is a weighted average of the domestic currency prices of imports (PM) and domestic goods sold on the domestic market (PD). On the supply side, the producer price (PX) represents an average of the prices in domestic currency of goods sold on the domestic market (PD) and exports (PE). The domestic prices of imports and exports are related to world prices by the equations

$$PE = (1 + TE)EXR*PWE$$

and

$$PM = (1 + TM)EXR*PWM$$

where TE and TM are export subsidies and import tariffs, EXR is the exchange rate, and PWE and PWM are the world prices of exports and imports.[11]

Since the model determines relative prices only, some price must be chosen as numeraire. We chose an aggregate index of domestic prices (*PD*) as numeraire, using base-year output weights. In effect, we are fixing the average price of nontradables in the model. Thus when we solve for the equilibrium exchange rate (*EXR*), we are effectively solving for the relative prices of tradables to nontradables in the domestic economy, or the real exchange rate. We chose this index as numeraire to facilitate interpretation of the equilibrium exchange rate solved in the model. The important point to note is that the model does not incorporate inflation, so all results are effectively measured against 1982 base prices.

The model focuses on flow equilibria and does not include any asset markets or money. It does, however, incorporate the major macroeconomic aggregate balances:

$$Z = SH + SG + F$$
$$SG = T - G$$
$$F = M - E$$

where *Z* is aggregate investment, *SH* is total private savings, *SG* is government savings, *F* is foreign savings (the balance on current account), *T* is total government revenue, *G* is government expenditure, *M* is aggregate imports, and *E* is aggregate exports. How a CGE model achieves balance among these macro aggregates in equilibrium defines the model's "macro closure." Issues of macro closure have been much discussed in the literature on CGE models.[12] For our analysis, however, the issue is straightforward.

Given our assumption of full employment, there can be no significant feedback from macro disequilibrium to employment and aggregate output. The model is Walrasian, not Keynesian. We are focusing on the impact of changes in the composition of these macro aggregates and so essentially set them exogenously.

We assume that aggregate government expenditure on goods is fixed exogenously in real terms. Government revenue is determined by a variety of taxes, given fixed average tax rates. Government saving (the deficit) is thus determined endogenously as a residual. Given the assumption of full employment, the tax base changes very little across experiments. With fixed tax rates and exogenous government expenditures, the government deficit is thus largely exogenous.

Foreign saving (the balance on current account, or the balance of trade in goods and services, including factor services) is set exogenously in world market prices. Its value in domestic currency depends on the equilibrium exchange rate. Private savings are generated by using fixed average savings rates for corporate and household income. Aggregate investment is determined by summing all savings. There is no independent investment function and no interest rate variable, so investment is essentially "savings driven."

Our neoclassical CGE model incorporates a stable relationship between the real exchange rate and the balance of trade. This relationship implies that a macro model (or macro economist) can set two, but only two, of the following three variables: (1) the nominal exchange rate, (2) the aggregate price level, and (3) the balance of trade. Given any two of these variables, the CGE model will determine the third. We chose to fix the domestic price level and the balance of trade, with the real exchange rate determined endogenously. In addition, of course, the CGE model determines the sectoral structure of domestic relative prices, demand, output, factor employment, exports, and imports.

In the experiments reported later, we vary foreign savings by changing the exogenously specified balance on current account. In this case, the real exchange rate (EXR) must adjust to generate the new equilibrium levels of imports and exports. We also vary the government deficit by changing the exogenously specified average tax rates on corporate and household income. In both cases, there are major changes in aggregate savings and hence investment. Since the model does not include interest rates or asset markets, we are effectively specifying experiments with complete "crowding out" of investment. This treatment is adequate given our focus on examining the structural implications for international trade of swings in macro aggregates. We are not seeking to explain the process of macro adjustment.

1982 DATA AND 1986 BASE SOLUTION

Table 12-1 is a social accounting matrix, or SAM, for the U.S. economy in 1982.[13] This SAM shows the macro aggregates and the flows among the various actors in the model, grouping the income and expenditure accounts of each actor into a square matrix. The sectoral and household accounts are aggregated for presentation; the full SAM includes the input–output accounts and different types of households. A SAM provides the underlying data framework for a CGE model in much the same way that the national income and product accounts underlie macro models.[14]

The model disaggregates households into three groups ranked by income: the bottom 40 percent of households, the middle 40 percent, and the top 20 percent. The model includes ten sectors (or "activities" in the SAM), and Table 12-2 provides sectoral detail on the structure of production, value added, and trade. The choice of sector aggregation partly reflects an attempt to group sectors with similar trade characteristics. For example, the agricultural sectors were grouped into one with a low trade share (dairy and meat), one with high exports (grains), and one with significant imports (other agriculture). Table 12-2 also gives the assumed elasticities of import substitution and export transformation by sector. These data indicate the importance of trade in different sectors and their responsiveness to changes in relative prices.

The parameters of the model are calibrated so that the base-year data for 1982 represent an equilibrium solution. Most of the parameters are computed using base-year shares from the SAM. The various trade elasticities are estimates based on a literature survey of scattered econometric work. No original econometric estimation has been done for this model. Units are chosen so that all product prices (including imports, exports, and domestic sales) and the exchange rate equal one in the base year.

Given the 1982 solution, we then generate a solution for 1986 by specifying

Table 12-1 Social Accounting Matrix for the United States, 1982

Expenditures (Billions of Dollars)

Receipts	(1) Commodities	(2) Activities	(3) Factors	(4) Indirect Taxes	(5) Employee Compensation	(6) Proprietors' Income	(7) Other Property Income	(8) Enterprises	(9) Households	(10) Capital Accounts	(11) Government	(12) Rest of the World	Total
1. Commodities		2892.4							1984.9	414.9	650.5	348.4	6291.1
2. Activities	5961.7												5961.7
3. Factors (value added)		2810.5											2810.5
4. Indirect taxes		258.8											258.8
Sum (GNP)		3069.3											
5. Employee compensation			1864.2										1864.2
6. Proprietors' income			111.5										111.5
7. Other property income			470.7										470.7
Sum (national income)			2446.4										
8. Enterprises			14.1				470.7				44.4		529.2
9. Households			358.8		1612.9	111.5		439.3			362.0	−1.2	2524.5
10. Capital account								29.2	135.5		−115.2	6.6	414.9
11. Government			−8.8	258.8	251.3			60.7	404.1			−24.4	941.7
12. Rest of the world	329.4												329.4
Total	6291.1	5961.7	2810.5	258.8	1864.2	111.5	470.7	529.2	2524.5	414.9	941.7	329.4	

Source: Robinson and Roland-Holst (1987).

247

Table 12-2 Sectoral Composition, Trade Shares, and Elasticities[a]

Sector	Sectoral Composition (%)				Trade Shares (%)		Elasticities	
	(1) Value Added	(2) Gross Output	(3) Exports	(4) Imports	(5) Exports/XD	(6) Imports/X	(7) Import Substitution	(8) Export Transformation
1. Dairy	0.3	1.3	0.1	0.2	0.3	0.8	4.0	1.5
2. Grains	1.3	1.2	5.0	0.0	24.3	0.2	4.0	4.0
3. Other agriculture	1.0	0.8	0.5	1.4	3.7	9.5	4.0	1.5
Sum/average	2.6	3.3	5.6	1.6	9.4	3.5	4.0	1.5
4. Light consumer	6.6	10.9	7.9	12.9	4.3	6.6	2.0	3.0
5. Basic intermediate	9.7	14.8	16.1	34.3	6.4	12.9	3.0	3.0
6. Capital goods	6.1	8.5	23.0	18.0	15.9	11.8	1.2	3.0
7. Construction	5.4	6.7	0.0	0.0	0.0	0.0	0.9	1.5
8. Electronics	1.9	2.0	4.4	9.0	13.1	25.3	1.1	3.0
Sum/average	29.7	42.9	51.4	74.2	7.9	11.3	2.5	3.0
9. Trade and finance	75.8	13.8	5.5	0.0	2.35	0.0	0.2	0.6
10. Other service	51.9	40.0	37.5	24.2	5.48	3.3	0.2	0.6
Sum/average	67.7	53.8	43.0	24.2	3.92	1.7	0.2	0.6
Overall sum/average	100.0	100.0	100.0	100.0	7.6	7.1	1.7	1.8

[a]Columns 1–6: data for 1982; XD is gross production and X is domestic supply (production plus imports minus exports). Columns 7 and 8: model parameters.

1986 values for the exogenous variables in the model, including total labor force, sectoral capital stocks, total acreage planted, real government expenditure (including its sectoral composition), average tax rates, the current account balance, and world prices of exports and imports. Most of the parameters in the model were assumed unchanged, including those for the production functions, import aggregation functions, export transformation functions, and household expenditure functions. In the production functions, both the input–output coefficients and the level of total factor productivity were assumed constant (i.e., no total factor productivity growth).[15] We also held the numeraire price index for domestic goods constant, so all exogenous variables were projected in terms of constant 1982 prices. World prices of exports and imports for 1986 were projected to move together, except for basic intermediates (which includes oil), in which there was a significant relative decline in the import price (an improvement in the international terms of trade).

The model solution for 1986 is given in Tables 12-3 to 12-8. In general, the various macro aggregates are within 1–2 percent of the 1986 data. Most of the numbers are not directly comparable to published data because we held constant a price index of goods sold on the domestic markets. This is a fixed-weight gross-output index that is conceptually unlike the GNP deflator used in deriving constant-price GNP accounts. Also, the calibration of the model was to preliminary 1986 data, and we have not made revisions as new data became available. Nevertheless, rough calculations, deflating published GNP data by a fixed-weight price index approximating ours, indicate that our macro aggregates are close to the actual data. GNP, for example, is within 1 percent of the actual value. Real exports and imports given in Table 12-3 are within 2 percent of the published data. The projected 15.3 percent appreciation in the real exchange rate between 1982 and 1986 is consistent with the evidence.

The model is used for counterfactual comparative statics experiments. Sensitivity analyses with the model indicate that the basic results from macro experiments reported in the next section are very robust to variations in the 1986 base solution. Given this robustness, we have not felt it necessary to recalibrate our 1986 calculations to the finally revised 1986 data here.

MACRO SHOCKS AND FULL-EMPLOYMENT INCOME

Between 1982 and 1986, the economy recovered from a recession. Real annual growth rates were 3.8 percent for GNP, 2.4 percent for civilian employment, and 5.1 percent for aggregate absorption (GNP + imports − exports).[16] During this period, however, imports rose dramatically and exports stagnated. Net exports of goods and services (the balance on current account in the national income and product accounts) moved from a surplus of $26.3 billion in 1982 deficit to a deficit of $105.7 billion in 1986 (in current prices). During the period, the United States also benefited from a significant improvement in its international terms of trade, largely through the collapse of the world price of oil. Real imports thus grew faster than nominal imports, and the real net export

Table 12-3 Gross National Products Accounts, Base Run and Experiments[a]

	Base Runs (Billions of Dollars)		Experiments[b]		
	(1) 1982	(2) 1986	(3) Foreign Savings	(4) Government Savings	(5) Combination
Gross national product, 1986 relative prices, and 1982 average price level			Ratio to 1986 (%)		
GNP	3078.6	3578.9	99.7	100.6	100.3
Consumption	1994.0	2276.2	99.6	96.1	95.5
Investment	415.1	619.8	77.5	117.5	96.1
Government	650.5	763.9	100.2	99.9	100.2
Exports	348.4	314.3	140.5	102.6	143.6
Imports	329.4	395.4	98.0	102.2	100.3
			Billions of dollars		
Balance of trade	19.0	−81.1	54.4	−81.6	43.8
Government deficit	−115.0	−134.9	−143.2	0.2	0.3
Real trade (1982 prices)			Ratio to 1986 (%)		
Exports	348.4	370.0	120.8	101.9	123.0
Imports	329.4	519.1	84.1	101.6	85.9
Absorption and employment (1982 prices)					
Absorption	3059.6	3666.3	95.7	100.5	96.3
Employment	96.6	106.4	99.5	100.2	99.8

[a]Column 1: social accounting matrix; column 2: base solution of CGE model; column 3: balance of trade set to 1982 level; column 4: government deficit set to 1980 level; column 5: combination of foreign savings and government savings experiments.

[b]In the experiments the average domestic price level is kept at the 1982 level. World prices of exports and imports were set reflecting 1986 international terms of trade. Exports and imports in the first part of the table are valued at the equilibrium exchange rate times the world price.

Table 12-4 Composition of Gross National Product and Savings, Base Run and Experiments[a]

	Base Runs		Experiments[b]		
	(1) 1982	(2) 1986	(3) Foreign Savings	(4) Government Savings	(5) Combination
Gross national product shares					
Consumption	64.8	63.7	63.5	60.9	60.6
Investment	13.5	17.3	13.5	20.2	16.6
Government	21.1	21.3	21.5	21.2	21.3
Balance of trade	0.6	-2.3	1.5	-2.3	1.5
Total	100.0	100.0	100.0	100.0	100.0
Investment shares					
Foreign savings	1.6	19.5	-6.1	16.6	-4.9
Private savings	126.1	102.3	135.9	83.4	104.9
Government savings	-27.7	-21.8	-29.8	0.0	0.0
Total	100.0	100.0	100.0	100.0	100.0

[a]Column 1: social accounting matrix; column 2: base solution of CGE model; column 3: balance of trade set to 1980 level; column 4: government deficit set to 1980 level; column 5: combination of foreign savings and government savings experiments.

[b]In the experiments the average domestic price level is kept at the 1982 level. World prices of exports and imports were set reflecting 1986 international terms of trade. Exports and imports in the first part of the table are valued at the equilibrium exchange rate times the world price.

Table 12-5   Price and Income Indices, Base Run and Experiments[a]

	Base Runs		Experiments[b]		
Indexes (1982 = 100)	(1) 1982	(2) 1986	(3) Foreign Savings	(4) Government Savings	(5) Combination
Agricultural terms of trade	100.0	101.9	108.9	101.4	108.2
Exchange rate	100.0	84.9	98.8	85.5	99.1
Domestic import price (PM)	100.0	79.8	92.8	80.3	93.1
Domestic export price (PE)	100.0	84.9	98.8	85.5	99.1
Producer price (PX)	100.0	99.1	99.9	99.1	100.0
Domestic market price (PD)	100.0	100.0	100.0	100.0	100.0
Composite good price (P)	100.0	98.5	99.4	98.5	99.4
Cost of living	100.0	99.8	100.2	99.7	100.0
Wage	100.0	106.7	106.4	106.9	106.6
Land rent	100.0	102.3	120.7	101.0	118.8
Household income					
Poorest 40 percent	100.0	111.2	111.0	108.0	107.8
Middle 40 percent	100.0	114.0	113.4	111.9	111.4
Richest 20 percent	100.0	113.7	113.3	110.2	109.8

[a]Column 1: social accounting matrix; column 2: base solution of CGE model; column 3: balance of trade set to 1980 level; column 4: government deficit set to 1980 level; column 5: combination of foreign savings and government savings experiments.

[b]In the experiments the average domestic price level is kept at the 1982 level. World prices of exports and imports were set reflecting 1986 international terms of trade. Exports and imports in the first part of the table are valued at the equilibrium exchange rate times the world price.

Table 12-6   Sectoral Gross Output, Base Run and Experiments[a]

	Base Runs (Billions of Dollars, 1982)		Experiments (Ratio to 1986, %)[b]		
Sector	(1) 1982	(2) 1986	(3) Foreign Savings	(4) Government Savings	(5) Combination
Dairy	77.3	85.4	100.7	98.8	100.0
Grains	72.0	70.7	103.0	99.6	102.8
Other agriculture	46.8	47.2	105.0	99.6	103.8
Light consumer	647.4	725.9	100.5	99.0	99.5
Basic intermediate	877.9	929.5	104.0	101.8	106.0
Capital goods	504.0	597.3	99.4	107.0	107.3
Construction	399.0	531.8	86.8	110.0	97.5
Electronics	117.1	131.7	100.7	102.4	103.4
Trade and finance	820.0	938.0	98.7	99.5	98.1
Service	2381.7	2759.6	100.2	98.9	99.1

[a]Column 1: social accounting matrix; column 2: base solution of CGE model; column 3: balance of trade set to 1980 level; column 4: government deficit set to 1980 level; column 5: combination of foreign savings and government savings experiments.

[b]In the experiments the average domestic price level is kept at the 1982 level. World prices of exports and imports were set reflecting 1986 international terms of trade. Exports and imports in the first part of the table are valued at the equilibrium exchange rate times the world price.

Table 12-7 Index of Producer Prices, Base Run and Experiments[a]

Indexes (1982 = 100)	Base Runs		Experiments[b]		
	(1) 1982	(2) 1986	(3) Foreign Savings	(4) Government Savings	(5) Combination
Dairy	100.0	102.6	107.5	102.1	106.9
Grains	100.0	97.8	109.7	97.3	108.8
Other agriculture	100.0	103.0	108.5	102.6	107.9
Light consumer	100.0	99.4	101.2	99.2	101.0
Basic intermediates	100.0	92.8	95.0	93.6	95.7
Capital goods	100.0	100.4	100.9	100.8	101.4
Construction	100.0	100.1	100.1	100.8	100.9
Electronics	100.0	100.4	101.0	100.7	101.4
Trade and finance	100.0	102.1	101.7	102.1	101.7
Other service	100.0	99.6	99.8	99.3	99.4

[a]Column 1: social accounting matrix; column 2: base solution of CGE model; column 3: balance of trade set to 1980 level; column 4: government deficit set to 1980 level; column 5: combination of foreign savings and government savings experiments.

[b]In the experiments the average domestic price level is kept at the 1982 level. World prices of exports and imports were set reflecting 1986 international terms of trade. Exports and imports in the first part of the table are valued at the equilibrium exchange rate times the world price.

balance in 1986 was −149.7 billion in 1982 dollars. In the same period, the total government deficit (including federal, state, and local government) rose from $111 billion to $143 billion. In 1980, at the beginning of the Reagan administration, the total government deficit was $34.5 billion; in 1979, it had been zero.

In this section, we analyze the economic impact of the macroeconomic shocks observed in the 1980s on the structural characteristics of production, employment, international trade, and the size distribution of income among households. In analyzing the impact of these macro shocks, we consider a set of counterfactual questions which we simulate with the CGE model. The first question we ask is: "Ceteris paribus, had we achieved the same balance-of-trade surplus as in 1980 (the last Carter year), what would the effects have been?" This "foreign savings" experiment assumes no reliance on foreign borrowing to finance the deficit and is modeled by changing the exogenous balance of trade in goods and services to achieve the same trade balance in 1986 as obtained in 1980. The second question is: "Ceteris paribus, had the increase in government expenditures been financed by increasing taxes without generating a budget deficit, what would the effects have been?" This "government savings" experiment is modeled by increasing the exogenous tax rates on corporate income and the income of the richest households to achieve approximately the same total government deficit in 1986 as obtained in 1980. In a third "combination" experiment, we combine the first two questions and ask: "Ceteris paribus, had both foreign borrowing and the budget deficit been at 1980 levels, what would the full-employment U.S. economy have looked like in 1986?"

The results of these experiments are given in Tables 12-3 to 12-8. The foreign borrowing increased absorption 4.3 percent and went mostly into investment, which was 22.5 percent higher than it would have been without the borrowing, thus avoiding a crowding-out effect due to the government deficit. Foreign borrowing also reduced the budget deficit about $8 billion, since em-

Table 12-8 Sectoral Exports and Imports, Base Run and Experiments[a]

| | Base Runs (Billions of Dollars, 1982) | | | | Experiments (Ratio to 1986, %)[b] | | | | | | Elasticities with Regard to Exchange Rate | |
| | 1982 | | 1986 | | Foreign Savings | | Government Savings | | Combination | | | |
Sector	(1) Exports	(2) Imports	(3) Exports	(4) Imports	(5) Exports	(6) Exports	(7) Exports	(8) Imports	(9) Exports	(10) Imports	(11) Exports	(12) Imports
Dairy	0.20	0.65	0.17	1.53	117.6	59.5	100.0	84.8	117.6	56.6	1.05	2.60
Grains	17.46	0.12	9.75	0.26	119.3	84.6	104.9	92.3	124.4	76.9	1.46	1.38
Other agriculture	1.75	4.45	1.30	10.02	123.8	69.3	103.1	95.4	123.8	66.4	1.43	2.01
Light consumer	27.62	42.52	22.63	61.51	131.2	81.0	100.6	97.8	131.1	79.5	1.86	1.23
Basic intermediate	55.95	112.99	54.06	214.61	134.5	83.2	101.5	102.1	135.6	85.5	2.13	0.87
Capital goods	80.21	59.41	80.87	92.60	133.1	78.4	107.5	106.6	143.3	84.9	2.59	0.90
Construction	0.04	—[c]	0.04	—[c]	120.0	—[c]	120.0	—[c]	132.5	—[c]	1.95	
Electronics	15.39	29.59	12.39	42.47	134.5	81.6	103.1	101.9	138.1	83.9	2.28	0.97
Trade and finance	19.27	—[c]	19.75	—[c]	108.2	—[c]	99.9	—[c]	107.8	—[c]	0.47	
Service	130.53	79.67	169.02	96.07	109.7	96.6	99.5	98.7	108.8	95.2	0.53	0.29

[a]Columns 1 and 2: social accounting matrix; columns 3 and 4: base solution of CGE model; columns 5 and 6: balance of trade set to 1980 level; columns 7 and 8: government deficit set to 1980 level; columns 9 and 10: combination of foreign savings and government savings experiments; columns 11 and 12: computed from combination of foreign savings and government savings experiments relative to 1986.

[b]In the experiments, the average domestic price level is kept at the 1982 level. World prices of exports and imports were set reflecting 1986 international terms of trade. Exports and imports in the first part of the table are valued at the equilibrium exchange rate times the world price.

[c]Imports less than $10 million.

ployment was 0.5 percent higher than without the borrowing, and hence social security taxes and household income taxes were about $4 billion more.[17] But the major effect of restricted foreign capital inflows is on the exchange rate: the 15 percent revaluation in exchange rate relative to 1982 which occurred in 1986 would not have taken place had we not borrowed from abroad. Exporters would not have suffered a loss in competitiveness, and imports would have been $83 billion less than they were in 1986.

The "foreign savings" experiment indicates that the revaluation of the dollar induced by foreign borrowing had a major effect on decreasing the competitiveness of U.S. exports. Had foreign borrowing not occurred, the exchange rate would have been within one percentage point of that in 1982. Exports would then have been significantly higher than in 1982 and imports substantially lower than in 1986. In light consumer goods, exports would have been 31 percent higher than with the actual 1986 value of the dollar, which was 15 percent higher; in basic intermediates, capital goods, and electronics, they would have been about one-third higher; and in services exports would have been 8–10 percent higher. Thus the experiment indicates that the revaluation of the dollar which occurred between 1982 and 1986 more than accounts for the loss of international competitiveness of nonagricultural exports experienced by U.S. firms between those two dates.

On the import side, the effect of the revaluation of the dollar is to decrease imports dramatically relative to 1986 but not enough to get them back to 1982 levels, partly due to changes in GDP between 1982 and 1986. Industrial imports would have been about 20 percent lower than in 1986 but between 17 percent (for light consumer goods and electronics) and 57 percent (for intermediates) higher than in 1982. Had the import shares in each sector remained at their 1982, pre–dollar-appreciation levels, imports would have been 17 percent lower than they were in our combined experiment. In our 1986 combined experiment, which restored the exchange rate to its 1982 level, import shares in all sectors were (between 1 and 44 percent) higher than in 1982. There was thus negative import substitution in all sectors between 1982 and 1986. The bulk of the increase in imports (86 percent) was in basic intermediates, suggesting that there was a substantial increase in the globalization of U.S. production. Had the price of oil not dropped between the two dates, the increase in imports of basic intermediates would probably have been even higher. It is possible to decompose the sources of the change in imports between 1982 and 1986. Of the total import increase of $188 billion, the increase in income accounts for $50.6 billion, the increase in constant-exchange rate import share accounts for $65.4 billion, and the change in exchange rate accounts for $72 billion. Thus one can attribute only 38 percent of the overall increase in imports between 1982 and 1986 to the appreciation of the dollar; negative import substitution accounts for 35 percent of the increase.

The revaluation of the real exchange rate had major effects on agricultural trade as well. The experiment indicates that agricultural exports would have been about 20 percent higher if the real exchange rate had not risen. The exchange rate appreciation induced by the foreign finance of the budget deficit also increased agricultural imports dramatically: 40 percent in dairy production, 15 percent in grains, and 30 percent in other agriculture. The revaluation of the real exchange rate had a major effect on the agricultural terms of trade, partly as a result of its dramatic effect on agricultural exports. Clearly, farmers were hurt by the increased foreign borrowing; the experiment indicates that their incomes were about $12 billion lower than they would have been had foreign savings not been used to finance the investment recovery.[18]

Our second counterfactual experiment, the "government savings" experiment, in which the government deficit is set to zero and government expenditures are financed by corporate tax increases and by raising the tax rate on the richest households, essentially restores the exchange rate and the agricultural terms of trade and agricultural incomes to their 1986 values.

The short-run effects of the government savings experiment on international competitiveness were much smaller than the effects of the foreign savings experiment, in large part because the impact of a smaller deficit per se on the real exchange rate was quite small. The exchange rate would have been within one percentage point of the 1986 exchange rate. Except for capital goods, manufacturing exports would have been about one percentage point higher and manufacturing imports would have been about two percentage points lower than in 1986. In capital goods, the effect of the government savings experiment was more pronounced: an 8 percent increase in exports and a 6 percent decrease in imports.

The experiment has only minor effects on absorption, employment, wages, imports, and exports compared to their actual 1986 value. The major effect of the budget deficit on full-employment income appears to be that consumption is lower, in both absolute and relative terms, and investment is considerably higher than with the 1986 deficit. This experiment makes it clear that the major effect of the budget deficit per se is on crowding out of investment. With a more conservative budget policy, investment would have been 17.5 percent higher and consumption 4 percent lower than in 1986. As a result, while the short-run effects of the government savings experiment on competitiveness are small, the long-run effects on competitiveness of the crowding out of investment by the government deficit are likely to be significant.

The final macro experiment combines both counterfactuals, setting both the trade deficit and the budget deficit to their pre-Reagan values. The results are close to those of the foreign savings experiment in aggregate terms and in their incidence on farmers and farm production and to the government savings experiment in composition of GNP between consumption and investment and in investment-related production.

One can calculate the implicit "total" trade price elasticities of sectoral exports and imports with respect to the exchange rate, given full general equilibrium adjustment. The last two columns of Table 12-8 present the results of these calculations for the "combined" experiment relative to 1986. We see that in manufacturing, all exports are elastic, with elasticities around 2, and most imports are inelastic, with elasticities somewhat below unity. These elasticities suggest that whereas a decline in exchange rate will go far toward increasing exports, imports will decline more slowly. There will be a decline in the trade deficit with a devaluation of the dollar, but this decline will be due more to an increase in exports than to a decline in imports. In basic grains, the relationship between export and import elasticities is reversed, with imports being more elastic than exports, indicating the reasons for the very substantial impact of exchange-rate movements on net grain exports and farmer incomes.

The experiments suggest that, ignoring cyclical effects, the short-run impact of the macro shocks during the Reagan years has been dominated by the import of capital from abroad and the concomitant major revaluation of the real exchange rate, which imposed a heavy burden on exporters and farmers. The revaluation of the dollar more than accounts for the decrease in competitiveness of U.S. exports. But it accounts only partially for the decrease in competitiveness of import substitutes. Something more than relative price or income effects appears to have been at work on the import side.

The effects of Reagan macroeconomics on the rest of the world have been more mixed. On the one hand, we have siphoned savings out of the rest of the world, reducing their investment rate. On the other hand, by vastly increasing our imports over what they would have been with more conservative macro policies, we have generated export-led growth in our supplier countries.

SENSITIVITY TO TRADE ELASTICITIES

The ability of the economy to adjust to trade-related macro shocks depends on its ability to substitute domestic for foreign goods in demand and to shift between domestic and world markets in production. Our model assumes moderately elastic import substitution and export transformation elasticities (see Table 12-2), which are reasonable for the five-year time horizon of our experiments. One would expect these elasticities to be less in the short run. In any case, it is important to explore the sensitivity of the results to variations in these parameters.

Tables 12-9 and 12-10 report the results of an experiment in which we replicated the exogenous changes underlying the 1986 base run but cut all the sectoral import substitution and export transformation elasticities in half. On average, the elasticities on both the export and import sides become less than unity, indicating a major change in the economy's ability to adjust to a shock through changes in trade. Intuitively, restricting the ability of the economy to make a quantity adjustment should increase the observed price adjustment, and this is the case. The real revaluation in the half-elasticity experiment is 29 percent compared to 15 percent in the 1986 base run.

Intuition is less clear about what should happen to the aggregate volume of imports and exports and to their sectoral composition. Several different forces are at work. At the sectoral level, the elasticity of demand for the composite good, the dependence on imported intermediate inputs, and the trade shares in both exports and imports are at least as important as the trade elasticities.[19] In addition, overall trade is affected by changes in the sectoral composition of aggregate production and demand. At the aggregate level, the result from this experiment is to increase the volume of foreign trade. The sum of exports and imports goes up by $44 billion (or 5 percent) relative to the 1986 base-run total.

Table 12-9 Trade Elasticity Experiment, Sectoral Results (1986 Ratios to 1982 Base Run, Percent)

Sector	Output		Imports		Exports		Producer Price		Retail Price	
	Base	Half Elasticity	Base	Half Elasticity	Base	Half Elasticity	Base	Half Elasticity	Base	Half Elasticity
Dairy and meat	110.5	111.1	235.4	203.1	83.1	88.6	102.6	105.5	102.4	105.2
Grains	98.2	99.6	216.7	217.8	55.9	57.0	97.8	103.3	100.8	109.1
Other agriculture	100.9	104.1	225.2	193.3	76.0	82.9	103.0	105.8	101.1	103.2
Light consumer	112.1	112.7	144.7	137.6	81.9	88.4	99.4	99.7	98.8	99.0
Basic intermediate	105.9	101.7	190.1	224.0	96.8	95.5	92.8	90.6	88.6	85.7
Capital goods	118.5	121.3	155.9	148.5	100.8	112.8	100.4	99.8	100.7	100.6
Construction	133.0	131.6			104.8	109.5	100.1	99.2	100.1	99.2
Electronics	112.5	115.5	143.6	138.2	80.5	90.3	100.4	99.9	98.0	96.7
Trade	114.4	114.3			102.1	105.2	102.1	101.9	102.5	102.4
Services	115.9	115.9	120.6	119.3	129.5	132.6	99.6	99.3	100.1	100.0
Total	114.7	115.5	157.6	165.7	106.8	111.1	99.9	98.6	99.4	98.0

Table 12-10 Trade Elasticity Experiment, Aggregate Results (1986
Ratios to 1982 Base Run, Percent)

Index	1986 Base Run	Half Elasticity
GNP	116.3	116.3
Consumption	114.2	113.9
Investment	149.3	146.1
Agricultural terms of trade	101.9	106.4
Exchange rate	84.9	78.1
Real wage	106.9	100.0
Land rent	102.3	112.5

But even though trade elasticities are cut, the economy retains enough substitution possibilities in production and demand so that total real GNP is identical in the two runs.

In the case of agriculture, farmers would gain in a situation in which all trade elasticities are lower. After the change, their import substitution elasticities and the export transformation elasticity in grains remain above one. However, agricultural supply elasticities are lower than those in most other sectors since the agricultural sectors have two specific factors (land and capital) while other sectors have only capital as a specific factor. In all three agricultural sectors, in the new equilibrium, imports are lower and exports are higher than in the 1986 base run. With the higher relative demand and low supply elasticities, the agricultural terms of trade improve substantially (106.4 in the low-elasticity experiment compared to 101.9 in the 1986 base).

We did a number of experiments replicating the macro shock experiments but with lower trade elasticities. In general, the results are consistent with the experiments reported: the real exchange rate varied more, but the macro aggregates were unchanged. Also, the basic results with regard to the effects of exchange rate on competitiveness remained. Exporters would have gained substantially from alternative macro policies in the 1982–86 period, which would have lowered the trade deficit even with much lower trade substitution elasticities.

CONCLUSION

The experiments we performed with our CGE model yield a number of interesting conclusions. With respect to competitiveness, our macro experiments indicate that a major part of the loss in international competitiveness of U.S. exports between 1982 and 1986 can be accounted for by the revaluation of the dollar. This, however, is not the entire story, even in the short run, since the rise in the real exchange rate accounts for only between 83 and 42 percent of the increase in sectoral imports experienced between 1982 and 1986.

Our experiments suggest two propositions. First, import elasticities are generally low, except in agriculture. Second, sectoral import shares have increased between 1982 and 1986, especially in manufacturing, by more than can be explained by changes in relative prices and income. The "residual" is sizable and must reflect changes in consumer tastes, sectoral technology, and foreign sourcing of intermediate inputs. Our CGE model does not incorporate these effects. It is suggestive, however, that the change in the equilibrium exchange rate in the model is least successful in accounting for the rise in imports of basic intermediates, where internationaliztion of production has become an increasingly important phenomenon.

In the introduction, we mentioned two schools of thought seeking to explain the change in U.S. trade over the 1980s. Our results indicate a major role, especially on the export side, for changes in the real exchange rate. However, especially on the import side, other factors have been at work. Although we cannot sort out the other forces at work, analysis with the CGE model delineates the magnitudes of the effects that need to be explained by the "productivity" school.

Our macro experiments suggest that the short-run welfare effects of "Reaganomics" have been mixed. Producers of tradables suffered substantially from the macro policies followed in the 1981–86 period. However, through increased foreign borrowing, the economy as a whole had a higher growth rate and a higher investment rate, while maintaining consumption growth, than would have been possible if the increasing government deficit had been financed domestically. It also underwent a substantially larger adjustment in the structure of production and trade than would have otherwise occurred. The mechanism through which this adjustment was induced was a major revaluation in the real exchange rate, leading to major changes in domestic relative prices and international competitiveness.

It is arguable whether the long-run effects of the overvalued real exchange rate have been good or bad. In essence, what the high real exchange rate has accomplished is the equivalent of policies of structural adjustment through import liberalization, policies that have been advocated by many economists for developing countries. To the extent that the United States is incapable of implementing good industrial policies, the very high real exchange rate provided an alternative that has had an across-the-board effect of forcing U.S. producers in manufacturing to cut costs and become more competitive and to reduce output in sectors in which it has no comparative advantage (although the damage to exporters was clearly excessive). Like many developing countries, the United States has borrowed in order to achieve this structural adjustment in a relatively painless way. As a result of the restructuring which has taken place, U.S. manufacturing and agriculture are more competitive. They are poised to take advantage of the decline in the real exchange rate that is now occurring.

The dangers of the policy of financing the restructuring of the U.S. economy by foreign borrowing are a debt overhang, the potential for greater macroeconomic instability, and less scope for independent adjustment of U.S. macro policies in the future. We recently had a "soft landing" for the exchange-rate devaluation accompanied by only moderate inflationary pressures so far. By borrowing, we bought ourselves some time and an easier adjustment but it is not clear how much longer we can continue to increase our foreign debt.

It is important to understand that the current trade deficit was brought about by U.S. macro policy choices and not by the policies of our trading partners. Indeed, it is difficult to see what they could have done about it, since they could not singly do anything to change our macro policies. However, the recent exchange-rate devaluations signal a change. It will be increasingly difficult for the United States to finance its deficit through foreign borrowing, and there will be increasing pressure on the United States to change macro policy. The change also signals a major opportunity for the U.S. producers of tradable goods, both exports and import substitutes. It would be a great pity, for both the United States and the world economy, if this opportunity were to be missed by a round of protectionist legislation, perhaps setting loose a full-scale trade war.

NOTES

1. There are numerous definitions of competitiveness. The one we use focuses on changes in the structure and volume of trade arising from changes in relative prices, especially the real exchange rate.

2. According to Benjamin Friedman (1988), there was a 60 percent appreciation in the real exchange rate between 1981 and 1985.

3. In 1986 the real interest rate was about 6.4 percent, around triple the "normal" long-term real rate. The real interest rate, defined as the annual prime rate minus the actual inflation rate, jumped in 1981 from 2 to about 8 percent and declined slowly thereafter.

4. Our notion of "short run" is Marshallian. It is a period short enough so that sectoral capital stocks and productivity do not change, but prices and variable inputs (labor and intermediates) do adjust.

5. The model is like that used in Adelman and Robinson (1987).

6. The 1986 base updates exogenous variables from 1982, so that a trend is imposed on the model solutions. All comparisons, however, are made against the 1986 solution.

7. In fact, the model identifies investment by sector of destination and then converts it into demand for investment goods by sector of origin using fixed capital composition coefficients. Dynamically, this is a "putty-clay" formulation. In the comparative statics experiments in this chapter it is more like "concrete."

8. This formulation follows Armington. The implications of this specification within neoclassical trade theory and the effect on the behavior of CGE models are explored in de Melo and Robinson (1981, 1985, 1989).

9. In later variants of this model, used to analyze the impact of liberalizing agricultural trade, downward-sloping world demand curves are specified. See Kilkenny and Robinson (1988).

10. The model can be seen as a multisectoral generalization of the Salter–Swan two-sector real trade model. See de Melo and Robinson (1981, 1985, 1989).

11. In the 1982 base data, there are no export subsidies, so TE is set to zero in every sector. The tariffs are very low, averaging 2–3 percent.

12. For a survey of these issues in models of developing countries, see Robinson (1989) and Adelman and Robinson (1988).

13. The table is taken from Robinson and Roland-Holst (1987). There are some minor inconsistencies between the SAM and the base data used in the model arising from some simplifications in the model, including the treatment of tariffs and the consolidation of some transfers. The SAM is based on data for 1982, including an input–output table at the 528-sector level, provided by Engineering Economics Associates, Berkeley,

California; it reconciles exactly with the published national income and product accounts for 1982. See U.S. Department of Commerce (1984). Recent revisions to the macro data have not been taken into account.

14. A SAM can also provide a framework for multiplier analysis similar to input–output models. See Adelman and Robinson (1986) and Robinson and Roland-Holst (1987), who analyze various kinds of multiplier linkages with the same 1982 U.S. data set.

15. Many of the chapters in this volume address the issue of whether and/or how much TFP growth occurred in the 1970s and 1980s. Assuming some exogenous sectoral TFP growth would change our base solution for 1986, but would have little effect on our comparative statics experiments.

16. All data reported in this paragraph, and in any discussion of actual data below, come from the U.S. Government (1987). There are some minor discrepancies between these data and 1982 data used in the model because of later revisions not taken into account in the input-output accounts used in the model.

17. The rest of the change in the deficit is due to the fact that official capital outflows (which appear as an exogenous government expenditure in the model) are fixed in foreign currency, and their value in domestic dollars increased with the devaluation.

18. The actual payment to farmers in 1982 dollars under the government commodity programs was $13.8 billion—a nominal payment of $11.9 billion times the change in the GNP deflator (1.154) (see U.S. Government, 1987, p. 157). In the aggregate, farmers were thus compensated by just about the right amount for the income losses they incurred as a result of the declines in their terms of trade. This, of course, does not mean that the distribution of the compensation matched the distribution of losses. The empirical evidence suggests it did not (see U.S. Government, 1987).

19. See de Melo and Robinson (1985) and Dervis, de Melo, and Robinson (1981) for discussions of these effects in empirical models.

REFERENCES

Adelman, I., and S. Robinson. 1986. "U.S. Agriculture in a General Equilibrium Framework: Analysis with a Social Accounting Matrix." *American Journal of Agricultural Economics* 68, 1196–207.

Adelman, I., and S. Robinson. 1987. "Macroeconomic Shocks, Foreign Trade, and Structural Adjustment: A General Equilibrium Analysis of the U.S. Economy, 1982–1986." University of California, Department of Agricultural and Resource Economics, Working Paper No. 453, Berkeley.

Adelman, I., and S. Robinson. 1988. "Macroeconomic Adjustment and Income Distribution: Alternative Models Applied to Two Economies." *Journal of Development Economies* 29, 1–22.

de Melo, J., and S. Robinson. 1981. "Trade Policy and Resource Allocation in the Presence of Product Differentiation." *Review of Economics and Statistics* 63(2), 169–77.

de Melo, J., and S. Robinson. 1985. "Product Differentiation and Trade Dependence of the Domestic Price System in Computable General Equilibrium Trade Models." In T. Peeters, P. Praet, and P. Reding, eds., *International Trade and Exchange Rates in the Late Eighties*. Amsterdam: North-Holland.

de Melo, J., and S. Robinson. 1989. "Product Differentiation and the Treatment of Foreign Trade in Computable General Equilibrium Models of Small Economies." *Journal of International Economics* 27, 47–67.

Friedman, B. M. 1988. "Lessons on Monetary Policy from the 1980s." *Journal of Economic Perspectives* 2(3), 51–72.

Robinson, S. 1989. "Multisectoral Models." In H. Chenery and T. N. Srinivasan, eds., *Handbook of Development Economics*. Amsterdam: North-Holland, Chap. 18.

Robinson, S., and D. W. Roland-Holst. 1987. "Modelling Structural Adjustment in the U.S. Economy: Macroeconomics in a Social Accounting Framework." University of California, Department of Agricultural and Resource Economics, Working Paper No. 440, Berkeley.

U.S. Department of Commerce. 1984. *The Detailed Input-Output Structure of the U.S. Economy, 1977*. U.S. Department of Commerce, Bureau of Economic Analysis.

U.S. Government. 1987. *Economic Report of the President, 1987*.

13

Technology, Capital Formation, and U.S. Competitiveness

RALPH LANDAU

We hear much about the lack of competitiveness of the United States, but seldom is this term defined. It is obvious that this country could improve its trade balance by reducing the wages and living standards of the American working population to those of Korea or Brazil, but this would not make the United States more competitive. What we should mean by competitiveness, and thus the principal goal of our economic policy, is the ability to sustain, in a global economy, an acceptable *growth* in the real standard of living of the population with an acceptably fair distribution, while efficiently providing employment for substantially all who can and wish to work, and doing so without reducing the growth potential in the standard of living of future generations. This latter condition constrains borrowing from abroad, or incurring excessive future tax or spending obligations, to pay for the present generation's higher living standard. As discussed in this chapter, such criteria for competitiveness have historically been best realized in industrial countries by a healthy annual increase in productivity, in which the United States has been the leader for most of the past century.

If the U.S. economy could be isolated, so that international trade balances were not significant, and domestic capital needs were met by domestic savings, these growth criteria for the economy would remain, but policy could be adjusted more easily to reflect domestic political choices, such as tariffs, interest rates, and the value of the dollar. Now, with trade in goods and services constituting almost 20 percent of gross national product, and the country importing approximately $120 billion per year of capital, this independence in policy making is no longer possible, and the country must be able to pay for its essential imports (of goods, services, and capital) by exports, and thus international competitiveness and growth in living standards cannot be independent of each other. It is important to examine briefly the changes in the international economy since World War II to understand this growing economic interdependence among nations.

For twenty or twenty-five years following the war, the United States enjoyed an essentially unlimited economic horizon. From this launch, real U.S. gross domestic product since 1950 tripled and income per capita almost doubled; meanwhile, real GDP of the world, aided by the United States to recover from the war, quadrupled. World trade grew sevenfold and enhanced this remarkable economic growth. Despite this impressive record, it is clear that the arena of U.S. firms and farmers has irrevocably changed, and not only because other nations have caught up and become strong competitors. International capital and technology flows have become global and in many cases virtually instantaneous. On the other hand, fiscal and monetary policies, as well as those dealing with trade, legal, tax, financial, and other matters, vary widely among countries. Such domestic freedom to control national destinies, formerly taken for granted, is increasingly constrained by the disciplines of the international capital markets, as well as by the trade in goods and services.

At the same time, the world now sees the availability of extraordinary new technologies that promise to substantially raise global living standards. The age of the computer has just started, but it has already penetrated widely (Figure 13-1). Telecommunications via satellite and fiber optics are binding the world together at an ever-increasing rate. The biotechnology revolution has hardly begun, but already its potential to affect human health and improve productivity in farm and factory is immense. Superconductivity is certain to play a major role in the twenty-first century; new materials are penetrating realms as diverse as medicine and aerospace; new catalysts and pharmaceuticals are improving the efficiency of industry and the human body. Many of these developments are American. Scientists and technologists are at the frontier of human explorations and aspirations, but we must be cognizant of the economic and social limitations on such exciting prospects. What about these makes us worry?

From 1870 to 1984, the country's average real growth rate in GDP was about 3.39 percent per year; from 1948 until recently it exceeded this level. This growth was accomplished mainly by a growth rate in real income per person in the United States of almost 2 percent per year and an approximately 1 percent per year average growth rate in population. Standards of living nearly doubled between generations. The United States surpassed the United Kingdom, the one-time leading industrial power, whose per capita real income grew at only 1 percent per year. The United Kingdom now is not even the leading member of the Common Market. On the other hand, since the Meiji restoration of 1868, Japan has exceeded even the high U.S. growth rate. With an annual real GDP growth rate of over 5 percent since 1930, it has become the second largest economy in the world.

Such is the power of compounding over long periods of time. Differences of a few tenths of a percentage point, which may not appear very significant in the short term, are an enormous economic and social achievement when viewed in the long term. Thus it is of concern that since 1979 the U.S. real annual GDP growth rate has averaged only about 2.2 percent with an almost static per capita real income, despite a six-year economic recovery, although in the late 1980s it rose above 3 percent. Will the United States follow the fate of the United Kingdom, while Japan and other countries in the Far East even-

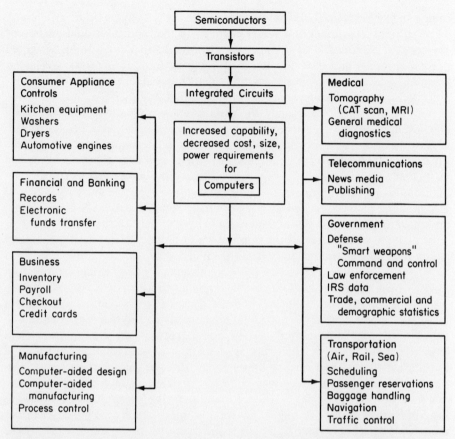

Figure 13-1 The impact of technology on economic development: new processes, products, and services. *Source: The Technological Dimensions of International Competitiveness.* Prepared by the Committee on Technology Issues that Impact International Competitiveness, National Academy of Engineering, Washington, D.C., 1988, p. 14.

tually outdistance it? Or can it maintain a prominent position of economic and strategic leadership, which its unique position of belonging to *both* the economic and military superpowers demands of it?

To achieve this goal, the promise of the new technologies must be realized, but this cannot be accomplished without taking into account the historical realities under which new technology is applied.

THE ROLE OF TECHNOLOGICAL CHANGE

The United States could have achieved its growth in per capita real income by (1) using more resources or (2) getting more output from each unit of resources (increasing productivity). How much of the long-term rise in per capita incomes is attributable to each? The surprising answers that emerged early in the 1950s indicated that long-term economic growth (since the Civil War) had not come from simply using more and more resources, that is, capital and labor, but rather overwhelmingly (85 percent) from using resources *more efficiently.* Many attached the label "technical change" to that entire residual portion of the growth in output which cannot be attributed to the measured, weighted growth in inputs and thus equated it to the growth in productivity. Certainly, however, many social, educational, and organizational factors, as well as economies of scale and resource allocation, also affect productivity.

Out of this early work came the growth-accounting studies of the sixties and seventies, based on the neoclassical growth theory of Robert Solow (1956, 1957) at MIT. But recently other economists, including colleagues at Stanford's Program in Technology and Economic Growth as well as at Harvard's Program in Technology and Economic Policy, have begun to examine more critically the limitations inherent in this theory. My colleagues in the National Academy of Engineering, also concerned with the practical significance of these questions, approved an important White Paper dealing with many of these issues in November 1988, which stresses the importance of linking science and technology policy tightly to economic and regulatory policy.

In particular, we perceive that there are in actuality two key departures from Solow's neoclassical growth theory: (1) it applies to long-run steady-state equilibrium of the economy and not necessarily for periods less than perhaps a quarter or a half century, because the economy is in a dynamic transition disequilibrium stage almost continuously; and (2) technology in a mature society like the United States is largely endogenous (i.e., new technology is generated by internal forces) and not, as assumed, exogenous (imposed or given from outside the economy). Moreover, the U.S. economy is not operating everywhere at the technological frontier. It may well take twenty to thirty years to fully utilize currently existing or potentially important new technologies, but meanwhile GDP may double, as happened in Japan from 1960 to 1980. These key departures from neoclassical theory underlie the observations made in this chapter. Other deficiencies of the neoclassical theory lie in the omission of public, environmental, and R&D capital stocks; the growing openness of the economy and trade; premature technological obsolescence from external shocks; the different vintages of capital stock, which are not perfectly substitutable for one another; and the fact that returns to scale in production are not constant. Markets are not always perfectly competitive; rather, the competition is more often Schumpeterian (innovative, entrepreneurial), and this is a much more powerful force for growth than standard classical price competition. Because of these theoretical limitations, comprehension of changing trends in growth from decade to decade requires comparative empirical studies among nations over shorter periods of time, as a guide to national policies.

Since the mid-1960s productivity increases in the U.S. economy have greatly diminished from previous levels. For the period 1964–73, the labor productivity growth of the U.S. economy was 1.6 percent per year; but in 1973–78, it fell to − 0.2 percent, and in 1979–86 it revived to only 0.6 percent (Crafts, 1988). (The Japanese labor productivity growth rates for the same periods were 8.4, 2.9, and 2.8 percent per year, respectively.) In much of the later part of this period, the growth of total output was brought about almost entirely by increases in capital and labor, especially (in the 1970s) the latter, as the baby boom peaked. Although explanations for the collapse in U.S. productivity vary, it seems clear from extensive recent studies of the two economies by Dale Jorgenson of Harvard and his colleagues that the comparative performance of the U.S. and Japanese labor productivity growth rates has been heavily influenced by *the much higher (often doubled) rate of Japanese capital investment* in a number of their industrial sectors, made possible by the very high Japanese savings rates (Jorgenson, 1988; Jorgenson, Gollop, and Fraumeni, 1987; Jorgenson, Kuroda, and Nishimizu, 1987). This helped fuel the rapid adoption by most Japanese industries of the latest available technologies from abroad. Many U.S. industries were not incorporating new technology with the same urgency.

Other data also suggest a very high correlation between national investment and economic growth rates; for example, Germany and France, with investment rates roughly twice those of the United States, also had about twice the productivity growth rate. These higher investments were due in part to lower capital costs relative to labor costs. In the United States, the capital–labor ratio grew by 3 percent per year between 1948 and 1973, when it slowed to under 2 percent.

Jorgenson also found that capital formation contributed far more significantly to long-term economic growth than earlier estimates had suggested—that it accounts for about 40 percent of economic growth in the postwar era. And technological change constitutes less than 30 percent, rather than the earlier 85 percent estimates; labor factors were the remainder. Angus Maddison's (1987) comprehensive review of growth economics generally agrees with these figures. Assar Lindbeck (1983) also surveyed these issues. The important point of these new findings is that there is a priority list for improving growth rates over the medium term of twenty to thirty years: physical capital investment, R&D and technology, and improvement in labor quality. There is a further complication in understanding the causes of growth, however: quantitative measures of productivity do not fully describe the performance of any economy. Quality is also of great importance, as the Japanese have shown us, but is very difficult to measure. For example, one dollar's worth of transistor has a million times the capability a dollar's worth had as recently as 1960. In 1989, a small box containing the new Intel microprocessor (486) costing perhaps $25,000 had about two-thirds of the performace capability of a Cray-1 Supercomputer costing many millions of dollars. But because of such steady cost reductions, and therefore pricing, the value of production in dollar terms understates the quality improvement, and productivity improvement is understated. The same is true in other industries, such as chemicals.

HOW GROWTH RATES CAN BE INCREASED

According to Michael Boskin of Stanford University (1986, 1988), who cites Solow's work, the fundamental variables that increase the rate of real per capita growth of a country in the long term are the rate of technical change and the increase in quality of the labor force. Increasing just the capital–labor ratio will lead only to a *temporary* increase in the rate of growth (moving from growth path 1 to growth path 2 in Figure 13-2), but to a higher level of living standards—a desirable goal in itself. As mentioned, such an increase in physical capital formation occurred during the 1960–79 period in Japan. These large growth rates have proved difficult to sustain, but permanent advantages for many industries and for the population have been created.

Measurements of productivity growth alone are not, however, a complete expression of the role of technology in economic growth. In the original formulations, and in much of the work that followed, the inputs of labor, capital, and productivity were deemed essentially independent of one another. However, in my experience, R&D and creative design are seldom performed by themselves—but rather only when they are expected to be employed in new or improved facilities and/or in superior operating modes. So technological change is not only embodied in physical capital investment, it is itself capital—intangible capital—and also a powerful inducement to it, since the availability of superior technology is a major incentive to invest. Investment in turn stimulates more R&D and creative learning. Similarly, improvements in labor quality (human knowledge, skill, and training) are both a requirement of and a spur to technological change and are another form of investment—human capital. Capital investment creates a favorable emotional and intellectual commitment to people and evokes individual creativity. Thus technology now often takes an embodied and reinforcing form within each of the basic factors of production—labor and capital—to a far greater extent than thought before. And when workers, managers, and technologists utilize such capital investment, particularly

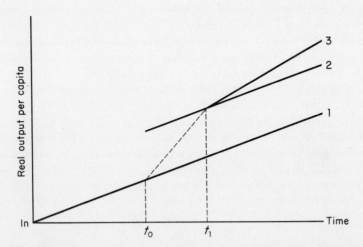

Figure 13-2 Alternative growth paths: technical change and capital formation. At t_0, proinvestment policy leads to higher capital formation and transition to higher level of income. At t_1, economy resumes long-run growth rate or, through interaction of investment and technical change, moves to a more rapid growth path. *Source:* Boskin (1988, Figure 1).

when they feel a sense of participation, they are also learning from and drawing on an expanded store of human knowledge, which yields continuing improvements in efficiency and output. (This is further discussed in Landau, 1989.)

Boskin's growth path curve 3 in Figure 13-2 illustrates that if these interactions between technological change, physical capital, and labor quality are in fact occurring, then a higher rate of capital investment *can* move the economy to a higher rate of medium-term economic growth as well as an upward shift in the level at any given time. He believes, therefore, that the rate of investment and technical change are positively linked. This is especially true when it comes to exploiting results of "breakthrough" R&D which require large new investments. This increased growth path may be viewed as a series of transitions in a dynamic economy never really at equilibrium because of continuing unpredictable, endogenous technical changes. If technical change is not exogenous, embodiment and learning by doing (phenomena which the neoclassical growth economists did recognize) *interact* with capital investment to improve growth rates, and capital investment is critical in reaching a higher equilibrium and approaching the technological frontier throughout the economy at a faster rate. Hence, in view of the substantial number of really novel technologies now available and the effects of continuing R&D and design efforts, the need for totally new facilities and closing down of obsolete units is becoming much greater—a version of "catch up" for the United States.

The current revival of interest in growth economics has been further aided by the award of the 1987 Nobel Prize in Economics to Solow, who recently expressed his own reconsideration of the role of capital formation in long-term growth. He stated that he feared the implication of his theory, as reflected in much of the subsequent economic literature and in government policies—which downplayed the importance of capital by making his long-term growth equation independent of savings—might have been carried too far, resulting in a severe underinvestment in the nation's physical infrastructure. "You can't take an old plant and teach it new tricks," he said (Solow, 1987). It is therefore incorrect to focus on increasing R&D efforts, important though these are, because the physical capital required to realize the R&D is usually much greater than the cost of the R&D involved. Such growing recognition of the critical role of capital investment leads to closer study of its availability and cost relative to other countries.

Although professional opinion is not yet conclusive, I believe that earlier distinctions between technology, capital, and labor as inputs to economic growth need to be modified in favor of a view that sees them as intertwined parts of the *same process*—they form a three-legged stool of physical, intangible, and human capital. It is only in this broad sense that it is correct to say that technological change has been responsible for perhaps 70–80 percent of U.S. economic growth in recent decades. Thus, directly and through its stimulus to and interaction with the other factors of production, it has been and is central to U.S. economic growth. And in the past, *the successful entrepreneurial exploitation of new technologies in the private sector to create new and improved products, processes, and businesses has been a distinctive U.S. char-*

acteristic and comparative advantage, requiring a favorable economic climate for longer term steady growth and a proper balance between current consumption and investment for more future consumption. Do we have such a climate today?

THE CLIMATES FOR PRODUCTIVITY AND GROWTH

Postwar experience has confirmed that long-term growth is established in the microeconomy—the world of firms and individuals (and to a limited degree governments in some of their longer range investment and research activities) who do the investing, the learning, the researching, and the conducting of the numerous businesses. Solow termed the study of these activities the true supply-side economics. On the other hand, short-term cyclical effects are stabilized by the macroeconomic policies of national governments (primarily fiscal and monetary), and these relate to the demand side of economics.

Nevertheless, the microeconomy may also be adversely or benignly affected by short-term macropolicies, including second-tier macropolicies relating to taxes, regulations, trade, labor, and finances. These effects may sometimes be long lasting, although often they are inadvertent:

1. The tight monetary policy of the 1979–82 era to subdue inflation led to the hard dollar and a huge trade deficit, permanently closing many businesses that lost comparative advantage and injuring the competitiveness of many more. On the other hand, some not only survived but also improved their competitiveness, as the Japanese did in their turn, later in the decade, as the yen appreciated.
2. The high inflation of the seventies left a residue of high long-term interest rates because of the negative expectations of investors and reduced spending by firms and individuals for capital investments by raising the cost of capital. This has had a long-term depressing effect on the productivity and hence competitiveness of U.S. firms.
3. The rapid succession of tax bills in the eighties has made long-term business planning more hazardous than ever, although the low marginal rate trend may eventually be beneficial if left alone for some years.
4. The high government budget deficits of the eighties reduced total social saving and investment in the United States and compelled the import of capital for consumption as well as for investment (Paulus, 1988). These deficits, along with the increasing indebtedness of firms and individuals, led to an extraordinary expansion in credit growth, which increases future uncertainty and contributes to high interest rates. The effects are now spilling over into the real economy, for example, in company takeovers and leveraged buyouts, leading to higher debt–equity ratios, which further increase the economy's financial vulnerability, and reduced R&D and long-range strategy of managements. These debts in part have bought time to restructure the economy to one that is more competitive

internationally, but time is no longer on our side in this process. To illustrate, the net interest payments of nonfinancial corporations rose from 8.6 percent of cash flow in late 1959 to 24.2 percent by the late 1970s; by the first quarter of 1988, this figure had reached 31.5 percent (and 44.9 percent of profits).

5. The ad hoc mix of all these policies has, however, provided a large number of the jobs required to meet the demographic increase in the work force, despite the oil price rises of the seventies. Table 13-1 shows how well the U.S. did relative to Europe in job formation. But this extraordinary U.S. "job machine," based in substantial measure on a unique ability to generate many new small and medium-size companies, has perforce lowered our productivity increase compared with our competitors. Thus Europe, with a lower growth rate in job seekers, has indeed had a higher productivity growth, but at the cost of unemployment rates over 10 percent (vs. the U.S. rate of 5.3 percent) that would be unacceptable in the United States. Since our criterion of true competitiveness includes adequate job formation, with declining demographics the United States can have *both* if it adopts the policies advocated in this chapter. Thus a change in direction is now justified, but recriminations about past policies are unjustified, when all the problems facing political leaders of the world since the midsixties are viewed in perspective.

In addition to this domestic climate (set largely by the federal government), there is now an international climate encompassing trade in goods and services, in capital, and in technology. Gross capital flows, however, dwarf gross trade flows. Even though net flows for direct investment abroad do not move so rapidly, exchange and interest rates are set by the much larger sums of "hot" money that flow around the world. Thus it seems clear from the realities of today's international climate that the larger driving force in determining exchange rates is in capital flows, rather than trade in goods and services. So I lay special emphasis on capital considerations in this chapter.

Table 13-1 Job Formation

Year	Civilian Employment (Millions)		
	EEC[a]	United States	Japan
1955	101.4[b]	62.2	41.9
1965	104.8[b]	71.1	47.3
1975	105.5	85.8	52.2
1985	106.7	107.2	58.1
1986	107.5	109.6	58.5
1987	108.3	112.4	59.1
1988	110.8	115.0	60.1
Net increase	9.4	52.8	18.2

Source: OECD, EEC, Bank of Japan, IFO. Courtesy of *The Economist.*

[a]The Group-of-Ten countries.

[b]Estimate.

THE CAPITAL FORMATION PROBLEM

The international accounting systems provide a basic identity that illuminates the problem underlying U.S. noncompetitiveness in capital flows: the current-account balance (the net of international trade and factor income) is equal to domestic savings minus domestic investment. For the past few years, this balance is approximately -3.5 percent of our GDP. Either domestic investment is too high, or domestic savings too low, to be sustainable in the long run. The data in Table 13-2 show that business fixed investment has been stagnant, although it must be borne in mind that much of recent investment has been in information technology, whose prices have been declining rapidly; also, useful life is shorter, so that these figures do not have quite the same meaning as when more traditional investments were made. For greater accuracy, debt should be corrected for inflation to assess its impact on the real economy. Thus it is certainly true that the exact magnitudes of savings and investments are subject to various unavoidable measurement and interpretation errors. This emphasizes all the more the need to look across national boundaries to see how we are doing relative to others, and why the differences exist.

Nevertheless, in view of the aging of American plants and the new technologies available, and because of a reasonably constant gross investment rate over several decades, U.S. domestic investment cannot be too high. The only rational explanation is that savings are too low and that the cost of physical and intangible capital must have been too high (Hatsopoulos and Brooks, 1987). Intangible capital encompasses not only R&D, but also engineering, experimental production, worker training, construction costs, market development, sustained operating losses, and legal precautions. These and many other expenses can frequently be deducted by the firm, but they are equity capital costs all the same, yielding a return only after some years have passed. It is equity, not debt, that finances technological development. The higher cost of equity defines the rate at which future benefits from technology are discounted. The high present current account deficit reflects the saving investment imbalance; it is primarily a fiscal problem. Another way of stating this identity is that the country spends more than it earns, implying an excess of credit over available savings.

Since it is obvious that changing the private savings rates is not easy (Summers and Carroll, 1987), the United States has become dependent on foreign savings. This has happened to the United States before, and to other countries at certain stages of development, but not to fund consumption, which seems to be the current U.S. pattern. Global investors are necessarily wary of committing capital to a nation with an overconsumption problem, and interest rates must rise to tempt them to finance our deficits, which, of course, also raises the cost of capital. As a result, control over U.S. macroeconomic and other policies is no longer firmly in U.S. hands, and the cost of the borrowing and investing from abroad will become an increasing burden on future generations, impeding satisfactory long-term growth. The quickest and most manageable step toward putting the destiny of the United States much more into its own

Table 13-2 U.S. Net Saving and Investment, 1951–87[a]

	1951-60	1961-70	1971-80	1981	1982	1983	1984	1985	1986	1987
Total net saving	6.9%	7.5%	6.1%	5.2%	1.6%	1.8%	4.0%	3.1%	1.9%	1.9%
Net private saving	7.2	8.0	7.1	6.1	5.4	5.9	7.4	6.5	5.4	4.3
Personal saving	4.7	4.7	4.9	4.6	4.4	3.6	4.3	3.2	2.8	2.7
Corporate saving	2.5	3.3	2.2	1.4	1.0	2.3	3.2	3.3	2.6	1.6
State–local government surplus	-0.2	0.1	0.9	1.3	1.1	1.3	1.4	1.5	1.4	1.0
Federal government surplus	-0.2	-0.5	-1.9	-2.2	-4.8	-5.4	-4.8	-4.9	-4.9	-3.4
Total net investment	7.0%	7.5%	6.3%	5.4%	1.6%	1.8%	3.8%	3.0%	2.1%	1.8%
Net foreign investment	0.3	0.5	0.1	0.2	-0.2	-1.0	-2.6	-2.8	-3.4	-3.5
Private domestic investment	6.7	7.0	6.2	5.2	1.8	2.9	6.4	5.1	5.1	5.3
Plant and equipment	2.7	3.5	3.0	3.1	2.0	1.5	2.4	2.5	1.9	
Residential construction	3.2	2.5	2.5	1.3	0.6	1.8	2.4	2.3	2.8	
Inventory accumulation	0.8	1.1	0.7	0.9	-0.9	-0.4	1.6	0.2	0.4	1.0
Memoranda: capital consumption	8.9%	8.5%	9.9%	11.2%	11.7%	11.4%	11.0%	11.0%	10.8%	10.7%
Gross private saving	16.1	16.4	17.0	17.2	17.1	17.3	18.4	17.5	16.2	15.0

Source: U.S. Department of Commerce.

[a]Data are averages (except for 1981–87) of annual flows, as percentages of gross national product. Total net saving and total net investment differ by statistical discrepancy. Detail may not add to totals because of rounding; 1987 figures are preliminary.

hands is to reduce the dissaving of government: the net budget deficits of federal, state, and municipal governments combined. By so doing, savings available for investment may rise (the exact amount depending in part, of course, on whether the level of other savings remains constant) and reduce the need for foreign capital inflow.

Unfortunately, there is another major obstacle to improving long-term growth: the *extreme volatility* in the seventies and eighties of government policies, resulting in wide swings in inflation and interest rates, dollar exchange rates, tax liabilities, and so on. There is a continuing threat of volatility of the dollar exchange rate staring every investor in the face, and there are increasing prospects of excessive protectionism. These threats have also pushed up interest rates, because expectations of sudden unhedgeable and unpredictable changes (for which forward currency hedging markets beyond even five years are thin or nonexistent) add a real risk premium to interest rates, particularly for longer term assured financing, raising the cost of debt. This limits investment rates. Risk (plus the nondeductibility of dividends) also adds to the cost of equity, making it more expensive than debt ("What Does Equity Finance Really Cost?" 1988). In a recent conference at Harvard University on the cost of capital, three experts from the United States and Japan confirmed that hurdle rates to justify a proposed industrial investment for investors in the United States are 15 percent at a minimum, whereas in Japan they are 8–10 percent. A prominent American high-technology executive stated that 20 percent is his company's minimum. More recently, the chief executive of a major Japanese company, in a seminar at Harvard, pointed out that the cost of funds in Japan is now less than 1 percent, due to the soaring, little-regulated stock market and the extraordinary boom in land prices. Japanese financial and social institutions also spread risk widely, so that Japanese risk premiums are relatively low. Nevertheless, he fears that the high leverage in Japan could react sharply to abrupt changes in world or domestic conditions. In global capital markets, there is no Federal Reserve of last resort. A collapse in a major creditor could trigger a worldwide depression. Is it possible that Japan in the nineties could be like the United States in the late twenties?

Figures 13-3 and 13-4 present a summary of what these capital obstacles have done to reduce U.S. competitiveness. Both in savings rates and investment rates, we are near the bottom. There is, however, an important element inherent in these international comparisons: the technology level of our principal competitors in 1960 was well below ours. For the investment curve in Figure 13-4, the 1979–84 data show the declining slope due to a more nearly uniform level of technology among the nations.

Nevertheless, the truly significant fact is that for these five mature economies, the effect of physical capital investment per worker on productivity is substantially higher than neoclassical theory would indicate, for some of the reasons indicated here. The 1979–84 data shown in Figure 13-4 suggest an output elasticity of physical capital of about 0.5: for every 1 percent increase in the rate of growth of physical capital per worker there is a 0.5 percent increase in the rate of growth of output per worker. Preliminary unpublished research

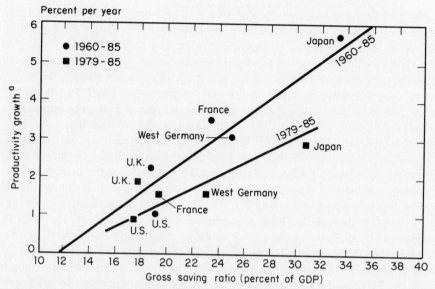

Figure 13-3 Comparison of saving and productivity growth rates, 1960–85 and 1979–85. *Source:* OECD. Courtesy U.S. Department of the Treasury.
[a]Growth rate of real gross private domestic product per person employed.

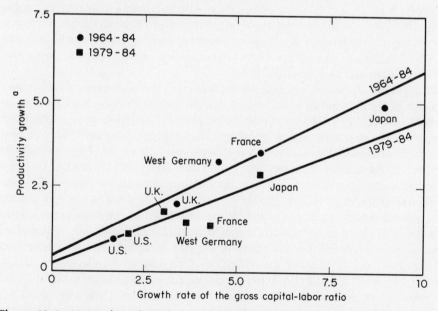

Figure 13-4 National productivity vs. the capital–labor ratio (average annual growth rates). *Source:* OECD. Courtesy of Stephen Brooks.
[a]Growth rate of real gross private domestic product per person employed.

results by Michael Boskin and Lawrence Lau of Stanford indicate that technological change is capital augmenting, implying that the benefit of technological change is higher the higher the capital stock. For the United States, Boskin and Lau find that the augmentation rate of capital is approximately 8 percent per annum and the elasticity of output with respect to augmented capital is 0.2. However, a 5 percent increase in the rate of growth of physical capital per worker translates into a 13 percent increase in the rate of growth of augmented capital per worker, which provides an explanation for the high measured elasticity of output with respect to *physical* capital in Figure 13-4. Hatsopoulos, Krugman, and Summers (1988), who give data for manufacturing only, similar to Figures 13-3 and 13-4, have deduced that the causation does run from capital to growth. Of course, the reverse can also occur, as previously mentioned: good technology can induce new investment, even in maintenance spending, and both can be induced by favorable macroeconomic conditions. However, if the cost and availability of capital are too high, few such projects will qualify. These authors show that managements have actually invested more than purely financial considerations would indicate; they have had a longer term perspective than the financial world considered justified. Increasingly, though, their financial pessimism is affecting the economy.

The findings of Figure 13-4 thus relate directly to studies of the cost of capital. In the United States it has been and continues to be from two to three times as high as it is in Japan. Combined with the high availability of capital (Japan, unlike the United States, is a net exporter of capital), this permits a much longer investment horizon—a patient money approach—which is the hallmark of the Japanese company (Hatsopoulos, Krugman, and Summers, 1988; Landau and Hatsopoulos, 1986).

Inevitably, therefore, one keeps returning to the problems of inadequate domestic savings and investments. A budget deficit that declines to zero or close to it over perhaps a four-year period must be the primary tool within our control for a short-term policy to increase the savings rate of the United States. This, in turn, would reduce the current-account balance to at least a modest and manageable level. Accompanying this fiscal constraint should be monetary easing, resulting in lower short-term interest rates, which the Federal Reserve can control. Policies should be *steady*, predictable, and not subject to sudden change. Simultaneously, and aided by these reduced interest rates, consideration must be given to increasing the incentives to invest in productive facilities, including in particular the reduction in the risk premiums and their effect on the cost of equity. Risk and uncertainty include long-term inflationary expectations, which the Federal Reserve cannot effectively influence except by perception of its determination to act whenever necessary, without causing a recession. The current 4 percent per year is too high, and it is a form of tax on earnings and savings, thereby greatly reducing incentives to save and invest. Only by the proper balancing of fiscal and monetary policy can inflation be restrained, as the experience of the late sixties and seventies teaches us. It is no longer possible to fool investors with easy fiscal and monetary policies combined—that well known path leads only to inflation. The financial markets will not permit our inflating our way out of our ever-mounting debt.

As suggested later, the possibility of accomplishing the necessary goals is really much better than one might suppose—small relative changes (mostly in growth rates) per year in income and expenditures, perhaps about $25 billion to 30 billion per year, should be enough to cut the deficit sufficiently by 1992, or more or less what is required under the Gramm-Rudman-Hollings Act. These are small effects in a trillion-dollar budget.

THE SOCIAL CLIMATE

Another stream of economic research, initiated by Moses Abramovitz (1956) of Stanford, deals with the social capabilities or climate for a nation to grow over the long term—including such factors as education, labor relations, and the legal system. For optimum growth, a cooperative social climate is required, and this has lagged behind the pace of technical change (Blumenthal, 1987/88; Wei-Ming, 1988).

The preeminent example of a favorable social climate is in Japan. This is not an inherent cultural characteristic. The Japanese specifically built their institutions after the war to catch up by rapid growth. As a result, the Japanese have developed many unique advantages not now open to the United States: a high savings rate; friendly stock ownership with no takeover threats; close relations among companies, suppliers, and governments, all of whom get their returns by continuing business from growing corporations; one-party government; cooperative, company-oriented trade unions; tight discipline; better secondary education; less litigiousness; and so on. The United States has a different culture and must adopt its own set of solutions, taking advantage of the unique risk-taking entrepreneurial nature of its private sector, its extraordinary research university system, its huge domestic market, its extremely broad range in size and composition of manufacturing and service industries, and its many natural resources. Yet if the problems of high cost and inadequate capital persist in the United States, the engineer as CEO and the reliance on long-term strategy will give way to the concepts of the MBA and the myopic horizons that American corporations have been forced to adapt to by the scarcity and high cost of capital, with fatal results for our own competitiveness in an increasingly technological era.

POLICY RECOMMENDATIONS

In view of the problems just cited, priorities for policy actions must be set. The United States cannot solve all of its problems at once. I would divide them into the three "R's"—recession, reinvestment, and redistribution.

Recession: The Short Term—Two to Four Years

As this is written in 1988, the present six-year recovery is often deemed to be approaching its end; the next president must be prepared to deal with a recession. It *should not paralyze decisive action to plan for long-term growth, which should start at his inauguration.* However, as the J.P. Morgan Financial Markets Letter (May 1988) indicates, there is no inevitability of a recession if actions like those described here are taken in a timely manner.

A sudden constriction of demand by sharp budget deficit reduction is undesirable. It might even deepen and accelerate the recession and could possibly pull the rest of the world down with us. There is still a world demand shortage, and the United States was the world locomotive of growth in the eighties. It is the other side of our merchandise trade deficit. Too rapid a policy of budget deficit reduction could therefore damage many countries' economies and prevent smooth domestic readjustment. This is why I advocate a definitive four-year program for deficit reduction. Indeed, the growing social security surpluses appear to offer assistance to this problem by about the midnineties, but they could also be considered as desirable additional savings (up to about 2 percent of GNP) if the general budget is made the goal of deficit reduction (but only after 1992 when the tax system can be reexamined). Thus if a favorable climate for long-term investment is created at the very beginning of the new term, an investment-cum-export boom could cushion the reduction in domestic demand arising from the deliberate elimination of the fiscal deficit. Japan experienced such rapid supply-led growth with robust exports while the yen was stable or rising.

This policy and the lower interest rates from the parallel easing of monetary policies could ultimately also contribute to a world investment boom, during which world growth incorporating the new technologies could accelerate because of the greater role expectations have come to play, particularly on long-term interest rates and on the price/earnings multiples of equities. Increased government deficits expand real output only if they are expected to be temporary. Thus we cannot run deficits for longer periods of time without raising interest rates, and expectations of such policies would negate any stimulus from the deficit even before it actually occurs. On the other hand, if the expectations are that budget deficits really are being reduced, then lowered interest rates from the *start* of such a policy will counteract the depressing effects of the lower deficits to come by encouraging investment.

Thus economic policy of the nineties must be to shrink imports relative to exports, to make investment and saving a high priority, and to increase exports to a world that must not be thrown into recession either. Unfortunately, our ability to increase exports may soon bump up against domestic capacity constraints, as well as the ability of other nations to absorb more. This is why we need an investment boom, which has already been occurring in basic industries such as paper, chemicals, and light metals, although its current level is by no means what could ultimately develop. But for U.S. companies to expand capacity, primarily to serve export markets, is an unaccustomed undertaking that requires precisely the steadiness of economic policy which, as this chapter contends, has been conspicuously lacking. If properly managed, with understanding of other nations' interests, the foreign capital now coming to the United States will tend to stay home instead, adding to domestic demand there, including demand for our exports. This process might well be aided by the growth impulse expected from the 1992 market integration of the European economic community.

If the budget deficit is thus gradually but definitively reduced to zero, the ultimate value of the dollar is not predictable when the exchange rate is left free to float. If the reduced interest rates cause foreigners to lose their appetite for U.S. investments, then a side effect could be a lower dollar (but, if gradual enough, this is not necessarily a threat to the financial markets, since a bottom to this decline could be foreseen). This is the mechanism through which the trade deficit would be reduced. Alternatively, despite the reduction in interest rates, the United States could still be a desirable place in which to invest because the (long-term) fiscal improvement greatly reduces the risk of holding dollar assets and still may offer a better return. Then, from this safe-haven effect, the dollar could actually rise. GNP growth would be less than GDP growth, but employment might be quite satisfactory. These considerations derive from the basic fact that, in the short term, there really are two equilibrium values for the dollar, one set by capital flows, the other by trade flows. Because international capital flows today are over fourteen times greater than trade flows in goods and services, the capital flow considerations must dominate.

Once a credible program for reducing the budget deficit was announced, therefore, investors in the foreign exchange markets would have no idea which effect would control. Hence if the Federal Reserve System had no announced or well-understood targets for the dollar exchange rate, a substantial source of financial risk would remain. Consequently, the announcement of a fiscal improvement would be somewhat less effective in reducing U.S. interest rates—particularly for longer term maturities—if U.S. monetary policy was not also openly geared to stabilizing the foreign exchange value of the dollar, within a narrow band, adjustable from time to time, as in the European Monetary System (EMS), and using this as a method for price level control. There will be a necessary transition period from current practices before this goal can be achieved, and American businesses must use such a period when the dollar may be significantly undervalued to further improve their competitiveness. The degree of their success will influence the proper level for a more stable value for the dollar. Macroeconomic policy can influence the nominal exchange rate for a relatively short period; nevertheless, that rate must depend on relative inflation and interest rates between the major political powers. However, the real (inflation-adjusted) exchange rate, which determines the longer level of exchange rates, depends on relative productivity increases and on the quality of a nation's goods and services, as well as on relative real rates of return on investments. The markets will determine these in the long run, but because of short-term lags, it is difficult to predict the currency bands until the trends are clear.

Such policies for macroeconomic price control are certainly difficult to apply to large economies, such as the United States and Japan. Some have even suggested a monetary association with Japan (a yen/dollar bloc) similar to the reasonably successful EMS, and maybe the same association with Europe. If such measures do not contribute a greater degree of international stability of capital flows and domestic prices, there is always the possibility that frustrated governments may turn to anti-Americanism (Abegglen, 1988; Kuroda, 1988; Nakamae, 1988) and antiforeign sentiments (Hale, 1988) as means to insulate their economies from excessive volatility, even though these too can no longer be effective in the global economy.

A successful reduction in the fiscal deficit and U.S. interest rates will naturally reduce the trade deficit but, as stated, the U.S. economy could still depend on foreign capital inflows to finance any significant increase in investment. The trade deficit would continue, albeit at a lower level. Nevertheless, because foreign capital would now be used to augment the American capital stock along with the by now increased U.S. savings rate (by up to the 3.5 percent GDP represented by the disappearing budget deficit), and thus increase productivity, it would be self-liquidating—and not a real cause for future concern. There are actually genuine benefits to the United States from foreign direct investments, such as organization and technology, and the stimulus of competition, although there are other legitimate fears of its becoming excessive (Roach, 1988; Tolchin and Tolchin, 1988). We don't want to sell America's crown jewels to finance our deficits.

If the budget deficit is not clearly headed toward a manageable level, the financial markets may impose a solution of their own, perhaps in the form of a more severe "crash" (Paulus, 1988). A president should be under no delusion that he can meet domestic demands for more spending, already picking up, before the program for reducing the budget (and trade) deficit has been put in place. The temptation to force the dollar sharply lower, as a substitute for fiscal inaction to reduce the trade deficit, will be persistent. But not only will actual devaluation ultimately fail to improve the trade balance; threatened devaluation will greatly increase the likelihood of some sort of financial panic as foreigners withdraw their financial support. Because of the fear of future inflation and of continuing devaluation, long-term U.S. interest rates would increase. Recession becomes even more probable.

A successful fiscal and monetary policy, as described, requires at least some awareness of and provision for other countries' changing economic policies—not necessarily real coordination. Indeed, there are American observers who feel that any such linkage cannot or should not be put in place, particularly *before* the trade deficit disappears (Feldstein, 1987; Krugman, 1988a). But, in fact, it already exists, to some extent, and in view of the genuine international effects abroad, as described earlier, it is unrealistic to ignore other nation's interests (Krugman, 1988b; Reynolds, 1988). If we address the budget deficit problem along the lines supported herein, accompanied by adequate stabilization of the dollar by monetary policy, we can largely control U.S. destinies by ourselves.

Foreign governments are willing to cooperate, up to a point, as the Louvre and G-7 agreements have shown, because it is in their interest to sustain their exports by not allowing their currencies to appreciate excessively, which contributes to growth. It is also in their interest to keep the value of their dollar assets abroad from shrinking too much. Furthermore, it helps resist pressure from the United States to share more of the common defense burden. However, absent effective U.S. policies, these governments can resist too high a currency only by large-scale intervention in the exchange markets. This tends to create more domestic money supplies and raise inflation, so that there is a limit to such intervention. From the American perspective, as pointed out earlier, a depreciating currency raises inflation and interest rates and leads to the buying out of our assets both here and abroad to finance our current account deficits. Though these foreign assets may appear to be more valuable in dollar terms, it may be attractive in foreign-currency terms for foreigners to buy American parents. This is equivalent to selling our bodies for the gratification of over-consumption! Thus there would seem to be a relatively narrow band in which currencies should be maintained to provide the greater international stability while still permitting each country to make individual economic decisions. Any changes in these bands need to be gradual, to permit appropriate adjustments by investors and companies.

U.S. monetary policy should, therefore, continue to seek reasonable stability for the dollar so that no great number of holders of the large stock of dollar assets held in international-currency portfolios panic and "dump" their dollars into the currency markets or by sales to others. These markets could not sustain such a sudden influx, and thus the dollar exchange rate would rapidly decline—and worse, increase the incentives for the "buying out" or "selling" of America. Even if no such panic occurs, foreigners will become increasingly reluctant to finance continuing future deficits, so interest rates must rise as foreigners see a bottomless pit for the exchange rate and prefer to move to other countries. There needs to be a balance between favoring trade conditions and the buying out of U.S. assets at bargain prices. A falling dollar raises the cost of capital in the United States, especially if a "free fall" occurs, and probably leads to attempts at capital controls, trade wars, and world depression. But unless the budget deficit reduction plan is clearly implemented, and the requirement for continuing foreign financing eliminated, attempts to stabilize the value of the dollar by government interventions will fail as market forces push it even lower. Devaluation of the dollar cannot cure the fundamental saving–investment imbalance in the economy (*The Economist*, 1988b; Turner, 1988) unless we accept a much lower investment rate. The country would be facing the danger of rising inflation and relative impoverishment in living standards.

Although many economists find some features of the 1986 tax reform act to be anti-investment and antigrowth, I nevertheless insist that for the best growth policy, the government should leave the basic income tax structure alone. Business needs five to ten years with no new laws to adjust its activity and grow. After that period, the country can review the results and determine, for example, among other options, whether the income tax system should be replaced in whole or in part by a value-added tax, which could further domestic savings. There is still a tax-favored bias toward housing and against productive investment. We have already shifted incentives away from overbuilding commercial real estate and tax shelters, from household borrowing for consumption, and have built some obstacles toward the most destructive of company takeovers in the present tax code. However, the 1986 tax code eliminated certain provisions—such as the investment tax credit, the capital gains differential,

and accelerated depreciation—which had compensated U.S. firms and investors for ongoing price inflation in the 1970s and early 1980s. Without these
provisions, the real value of ordinary depreciation allowances would have
fallen even further below the replacement cost of capital, and risk-taking capital for longer term investment would have faltered. Thus it is doubly important
to avoid exchange depreciation and price inflation in the future when these
compensatory provisions are no longer in the tax code.

Ways of Reducing the Fiscal Deficit

Even in the event of a recession or growth slowdown, then, we must start the
process of reducing the *structural* full-employment deficit. This can be feasible
politically only by adherence to the Gramm-Rudman-Hollings Act.

First, the government should reduce all unnecessary budget expenditures
that do not affect long-term growth favorably. These include removing subsidies to large farmers (much of the $20 billion spent on agriculture), also bene-
fiting consumers; carefully continuing the gradual reversal of defense spending
increases by better management, rethinking our strategy and need for bases in
light of recent Soviet moves, and sharing some costs with our allies (the 1989
budget showed a real decrease for the first time); eliminating, delaying, or sharing the costs with other nations of the big-ticket "show" items of big science,
such as the superconducting supercollider, the space station, and sequencing
the human genome (but using a portion of the savings for more basic scientific
and engineering research such as more engineering and technology centers);
applying means tests to many entitlement programs by bringing all transfer
payments within the income tax system (and raising the basic exemption a bit
to ensure that poor people, with income still low even under this definition,
stay off the tax rolls); and considering a one-year freeze of indexations on entitlements (this is especially justified in light of overindexing of cost-of-living
provisions established in the 1970s; the older portion of the population has
generally raised its living standards more than other segments, especially
young people struggling to bring up their children). Medicare's faltering reserves call for a restudy of the whole system, as was done for Social Security.
Selective "freezes" that on average restrict increases to inflation rates, coupled
with larger reductions in spending increases to compensate for necessary increases that exceed this level, could make serious inroads on the deficit. The
real gain in long-term growth would come from government spending reductions for consumption, thus freeing more resources for private investment, although additional government appropriations for infrastructure investment are
needed. Ideally, more than half the burden of budget deficit reduction must and
can be drawn from such measures. Because investors are justifiably skeptical
of promises to cut the deficit, a tax increase may be viewed as being offset by
more consumption-type expenditures. Therefore, the most effective policy may
well be to avoid any tax increase proposals.

Second, firmly reject a value-added-tax system, because it adds complica-
tions and uncertainties; it is an engine to fuel new spending programs that may
be economically undesirable but politically attractive; it preempts state sales
taxes; and it adds to inflation.

Third, add a special gasoline user fee for environmental and energy conservation of 25 cents per gallon at once, perhaps rising to 50 cents or $1.00 in four years. As a beneficial side effect, this excise or consumption fee is the most likely *not* to transfer dissaving from the public to the private sector—a self-defeating process. The price of oil will inevitably rise in the 1990s and everyone will be paying more for gasoline in due course. In 1988 crude oil imports are expected to be 7 million barrels per day, up from 4.9 million in 1985. Such imports account for 37–40 percent of the total U.S. trade deficit. As we become bigger importers, the price of oil will rise. Americans pay no more than a third to a half of the European price of gasoline. The United States does not require such low prices—in real terms gasoline now costs barely half as much as it did in 1980. By biting the bullet now, we can start reducing energy consumption (by encouraging more fuel-efficient cars), the greenhouse effect, pollution, and highway congestion. The president of General Motors stated recently that gasoline consumption is most influenced by changes in prices (Stempel, 1988). As the price of gasoline rises, the fee can be reduced, but its greatest value in lowering the budget deficit by the early nineties will have been achieved. Some of these user fees can also be applied to improving the growing garbage and waste effluent problems, as well as the infrastructure (Matthews, 1988). In addition, incentives to utilize more domestic natural gas in place of imported oil could be devised. This would also reduce carbon dioxide emissions into the atmosphere.

Fourth, raise tobacco and alcohol taxes.

By some such combination of these four measures, with increased consumption levies contributing a minor portion but certainly not more than half of the money needed to resolve the budget deficit, it is feasible that by 1992 the structural deficit will have been reduced to a manageable percentage of GNP.

No new major spending programs which have consumption characteristics should be undertaken in this period, or the discipline of the budget will be lost, long-term interest rates will go through the roof, and inflation will come back. The time for new spending programs should come only when recovery is firmly in place, and always to allow a zero or slightly positive budget balance. Any new consumption-type spending programs should be balanced against elimination or reduction of others—a continuation of the revenue-neutral philosophy of the 1986 tax reform.

Reinvestment: The Middle Term—A Decade

Incentives for productive physical, intangible, and human investment must be strengthened. The capital–labor ratio must go up as the growth of the work force diminishes, so that while job loss is minimized, productivity rises. *With improved productivity, we can finance our debts, hardly notice the decline in living standards, and grow our way out of the present impasse.*

Increasing corporate cash flow is the major priority for investment. To accomplish this, suggestions have been made that the corporate and related-entity marginal tax rate of 34 percent be replaced by a much lower business transfer tax across the board, based on revenue minus raw material and energy costs, with no other deductions. Such a rate could be as low as 5 percent, and this one step would substantially lower the cost of capital. It is more efficient than restoring investment credits and the like, which would otherwise be needed to stimulate investment. It also would limit takeovers, many of which raise enough uncertainties that long-range and risk-taking planning is suppressed. Despite the non–tax deductibility of dividends, highly leveraged buyouts, by higher stock values, in effect permit corporations to pay dividends to shareholders. In essence, the company pays tax-free dividends to shareholders through higher equity prices. This plan should be studied, along with a change in the capital gains tax system to encourage longer term investment. At such a time, it may also be politically feasible to put a reasonably low cap on home mortgage interest deductibility, which has been much used recently to permit otherwise limited deductibility of interest for consumption loans.

Thus with a neutral tax system, the other key to encouragement of investment lies in reducing the cost of capital by getting the interest rates down. Interest rates will move down with greater stability of policy and reduction of the need for borrowing abroad. Although lower interest rates reduce incentives for foreign investors to send capital to the United States, they increase the incentive for domestic investors to invest. *This is equivalent to a tax cut.*

We must eschew protectionism, which is a negative-sum game. There are those who still advocate "fair" or managed trade, but it benefits only the companies affected, injures the consumer, and slows growth. Who in the government can resist the pressure of the "losers" for favored treatment, and who will speak for the "winners" yet unborn or for the consumer? Trade policy should be directed at opening other nations' markets instead.

The same considerations apply to direct government intervention in the private economy (industrial policy). In an era of worldwide rapid technical change, only firms and individuals closest to the market can make the judgments that ultimately spell genuine competitiveness. Government can foster innovation, not force it, and such intervention always will eventually be based of clout instead of merit. Sematech is no panacea; it is an experiment and remains to be proved ("Sematech," 1988). Lowering the cost of capital and raising its availability is the most neutral way to encourage investment.

These essentially economic policies are the basic requirements for making the United States more competitive and prosperous. There are other less specifically economic issues also fundamental to better growth, such as the growing deficiency of the legal system in dealing with intellectual property rights, tort litigation, and excessive regulation. Technology does have a dark side, and it must be dealt with, but our methods are not competitive. Social problems such as inadequate public education, the increasing drug abuse, and the adversarial nature of business, government, and labor relations all need to be addressed, but this is not the place for a discussion of methods (U.S. Congress, 1988). Neither is the matter of LDC debts or their fragile politics, the solution of which would improve markets for our products and services.

Redistribution: The Long Term—A Generation

The underclass—those who have essentially dropped out of the economy altogether—needs to be brought into the mainstream. This is the principal area where redistribution may be feasible. In a recent article in the *New York Times*, Solow (1988) said, *"Redistribution is not something that Americans are good at."* His remedy, greater growth, seems appropriate.

WHAT MUST BE DONE?

The influence that the federal government has on the climate for innovation and long-term growth has been discussed. Capital formation and its costs have been pinpointed as the major problems facing U.S. industry in its efforts to improve its competitiveness in a vastly different world economy than that of the midseventies. The opportunities available in new science and technology are breathtaking, but the horizons for exploring them are long, and they require cheap and abundant capital investments per worker—of both physical and intangible capital.

But even if this fundamental capital problem is ameliorated, there is much that firms and individuals must do for themselves, particularly in the manufacturing sector, which performs 95 percent of commercial R&D (Table 13-3). This sector constitutes two-thirds of the nation's tradable goods, nourishes the service sector, provides for defense needs, and boosts the overall productivity of the economy. The task of management and technologists must be to create wealth by steady cost reductions and incremental improvements in large-scale

Table 13-3　Major R&D Investment Industries, 1988 Estimates (More than $1 Billion)[a]

Industry	R&D Expenditures (Billions of Dollars)	Financing
Aerospace	24.0	80% government
Electrical machinery and communications	20.0	60% industry
Machinery	11.9	87.5% industry
Chemicals	9.4	97% industry
Autos, trucks, transportation equipment	9.2	77% industry
Professional and scientific instruments	6.8	84.8% industry
Petroleum products	2.5	Nearly all industry
Rubber products	1.5	84% industry
Food and beverages	1.07	Practically all industry
Total	86.37	

Source: Battelle Memorial Institute.

[a]Total U.S. R&D estimated at $132 billion, of which all industrial R&D is $96 billion (70% comes from companies and the rest from government) so that this table indicates the bulk of the investors in R&D.

production, which will be needed for the innovative activity involved in utilization of the new technologies. This will, as is already happening in Japan, lead to a concentration on higher value-added products with advanced technology, in which labor costs are small and high wages can be justified. This type of strategy fits the U.S. entrepreneurial spirit, which is hospitable to the new. It is what has taken the United States to the highest actual productivity levels among industrial nations. In effect, however, today's comparative advantages are dynamic and ever-changing. Managements and governments must accept that firms need to become increasingly multinational and move closer to their markets (this reduces trade barriers and also permits some hedging of currency risks, by reinvestment of profits, which is a favorite strategy for U.S. firms overseas). In fact, multinationals account for 75 percent of U.S. exports and 45 percent of imports. Only a global market allows a company to afford the large development costs required to keep up with advancing technology. Managers must thus become more technically sophisticated and more internationally minded. This will aid in spreading growth prospects in the world as a whole. The force of international competition will eventually drive out the bad managements and firms; government should not prop them up but provide for reasonable retraining and adjustment costs for their employees. The United States cannot be walled in any more. Such isolation is a recipe for progressive impoverishment and technological sterility. In the long run, other nations prefer not to rely too heavily on imported products. Manufacturing and marketing need to be performed in the home of the customer wherever feasible, and innovation must be linked with the marketplace.

THE NATIONAL GOAL

We should aim, within several years, at the 3.5 percent real GNP growth, which was the rate during most of the postwar years (Landau, 1988). In the 1990s, the work force should increase only 1 percent. In addition, a probable drag of up to 1 percent of GNP per year should be required to service the foreign capital we have borrowed (by increasing exports; Friedman, 1988), even though the market value of our holdings abroad exceeds that of foreigners in the United States by perhaps $400 billion.[1] But it is the steady *growth* in foreign debt that requires financing from abroad, preferably by not selling these assets to foreigners. Thus even a 3.5 percent growth rate translates into perhaps only a 1.5 percent per capita growth, slightly below our historic figure of nearly 2 percent. A 3 percent GNP growth rate would be a minimum goal.

If we are to achieve even this desirable aim, great structural changes in national and international economic policies are inevitable, and technology must be woven into the national fabric as never before. Without it, the best that economists now see is a noninflationary GNP growth rate potential of 2.5 percent, which means a virtually static standard of living (Gay, 1987, 1988; Mann and Schultze, 1988/89). This would be dangerous to social stability, as noted in *The Economist* (1988a), and would not encourage the needed capacity expansions in tradable goods. The way to escape this trap is illustrated in Figure 13-2—the interaction of investment, technology, and education. A higher productivity growth will permit a higher stable rate of real growth of the economy. Even though gross investment rates have recently increased, this is still insufficient to meet the available and potential technological opportunities. We must achieve in a decade the double-digit net investment rates of our principal international competitors and a corresponding savings rate. New capacities in plant and equipment grew only 0.7 percent annually during the late 1980s, well below others' and our own previous history. Highly leveraged companies do not invest in R&D or new facilities. Net investment relates to new facilities and younger, more modern technologies. A strategy of retrofitting existing plants may reduce the capital required for modernization but is insufficient by itself. To obtain results from this process, greater freedom and incentive to innovate, to invest in productive facilities, to save, and to risk must be the fundamental elements of government policy.

NOTES

I am grateful for the advice and valuable comments of Martin Neil Baily, George N. Hatsopoulos, Michael Boskin, Lawrence Lau, John Taylor, Ronald McKinnon, Dale Jorgenson, Nathan Rosenberg, and Robert Eisner, but the opinions and errors are my sole responsibility.

1. To see this, recall that in 1988, income from U.S. investments abroad just about equaled payments to foreign nationals for their investments in the United States; also, the current-account balance and the merchandise trade balance were almost equal. But if, in each of the next four years, the merchandise trade balance continues at the same level while U.S. income from abroad merely rises with inflation, then new obligations totaling about $560 billion will have accumulated by the end of 1992. Only a minor part of this would reflect inflation from 1989 on. Assuming a 5 percent real interest rate (high by historical standards), the service charge to finance this obligation (which will still be largely in financial assets) would rise to about $28 billion per year in 1993. With about a $5 trillion GNP, this is approximately 0.6 percent of real GNP. This calculation makes no provision for repayment of any principal, which could easily raise the overall burden close to 1 percent of GNP. Although very elementary and approximate, such a simple calculation demonstrates how rapidly foreign debt can mount from now on, to a very burdensome level, even though the annual effect may seem small.

REFERENCES

Abeglen, J. 1988. "Black Monday's Bottom Line—Japan Is No. 1." *International Economy* 2(1), 64.
Abramovitz, M. 1956. "Resource and Output Trends in the United States Since 1870." *American Economic Review* 46 (May), 5–23.
Blumenthal, W. M. 1987/88. "The World Economy and Technological Change." *Foreign Affairs, American and the World* 66(3), 529–50.
Boskin, M. 1986. "The Positive Sum Strategy." In R. Landau and N. Rosenberg, eds.,

Macroeconomics, Technology and Growth: An Introduction to Some Important Issues. Washington, D.C.: National Academy Press, pp. 35–56.

Boskin, M. 1988. "Tax Policy and Economic Growth: Lessons from the 1980s." *Journal of Economic Perspectives* 2(4), 71–97.

Crafts, N. 1988. "The Assessment: British Economic Growth Over the Long Run." *Oxford Review of Economic Policy* 4(1), xv.

The Economist. 1988a. June 18, "Toronto Summit: A Route for the Seven Summiteers," p. 1719.

The Economist. 1988b. September 24, special section on the world economy.

Feldstein, M. 1987. Introduction to Summary Report, NBER Conference on International Economic Cooperation, p. 6.

Feldstein, M. 1988. "Let the Market Decide." *The Economist,* December 3, pp. 21–24.

Friedman, B. 1988. *Day of Reckoning.* New York: Random House.

Gay, R. S. 1987. "Learning to Live with Slow Growth." Morgan Stanley, August 12.

Gay, R. S. 1988. "Wage–Price Spirals and the End-Phase of Expansion." Morgan Stanley, April 7.

Hale, D. 1988. "Will We Hate Japan as We Hated Britain?" *International Economy* 2(1), 84.

Hatsopoulos, G. N., and S. H. Brooks. 1987. "The Cost of Capital in the United States and Japan." International Conference on the Cost of Capital, Kennedy School of Government, Harvard University, Cambridge, Mass., November 19–21.

Hatsopoulos, G. N., P. R. Krugman, and L. H. Summers. 1988. "U.S. Competitiveness: Beyond the Trade Deficit." *Science* 241 (July 15), 299–307.

Jorgenson, D. W. 1988. "Productivity and Postwar U.S. Economic Growth." *Journal of Economic Perspectives* 2(4), 23–41.

Jorgenson, D. W., F. Gollop, and B. Fraumeni. 1987. *Productivity and U.S. Economic Growth.* Cambridge, Mass.: Harvard University Press.

Jorgenson, D. W., M. Kuroda, and M. Nishimizu. 1987. "Japan–U.S. Industry-level Productivity Comparisons, 1960–1979." *Journal of the Japanese and International Economies* 1, no. 1 (March):1–30.

Krugman, P. 1988a. "Louvre's Lesson—Let the Dollar Fall." *International Economy* 2(1), 76.

Krugman, P. 1988b. Robbins Lecture, London School of Economics, January.

Kuroda, M. 1988. "Japan Is Getting a Bum Rap on Trade." *International Economy* 2(1), 48.

Landau, R. 1988. "U.S. Economic Growth." *Scientific American* 258(6), 44–52.

Landau, R. 1989. "Technology and Capital Formation." In D. Jorgenson and R. Landau, eds., *Technology and Capital Formation.* Cambridge: MIT Press, pp. 485–505.

Landau, R., and G. N. Hatsopoulos. 1986. "Capital Formation in the United States and Japan." In R. Landau and N. Rosenberg, eds., *The Positive Sum Strategy.* Washington, D.C.: National Academy Press, pp. 583–606.

Lindbeck, A. 1983. "The Recent Slowdown in Productivity Growth." *Economics Journal* 93 (March), 13–34.

Maddison, A. 1987. "Growth and Slowdown in Advanced Capitalist Economies: Techniques of Quantitative Assessment." *Journal of Economics Literature* 25 (June), 649–98.

Mann, T. E., and C. L. Schultze. 1988/89. "Getting Rid of the Budget Deficit." *Brookings Review* 7(1), 3–17.

Matthews, J. T. 1988. "A $1 Per Gallon Gasoline Tax, Without Tears." *New York Times,* June 28, p. A19.

Nakamae, T. 1988. "America's Coming Manufacturing Renaissance." *International Economy* 2(1), 56.

Paulus, J. D. 1988. "Global Economic Paralysis: Letting the Dollar Solve America's Overconsumption Problem." *World Economic Outlook 1988* (Morgan Stanley), pp. 4–11.

Reynolds, A. 1988. "How Not to Lower the Trade Deficit." *International Economy* 2(1), 108.

Roach, S. S. 1988. "Hooked on Foreign Investment." Morgan Stanley, April 13.

"Sematech's Weary Hunt for a Chief." 1988. *New York Times,* April 1, p. D1. ("Sematech," 1988.)

Solow, R. 1956. "A Contribution to the Theory of Economic Growth." *Quarterly of Economics* 70 (February), 65–94.

Solow, R. 1957. "Technical Change and the Aggregate Production Function." *Review of Economics and Statistics* 39 (August), 312–20.

Solow, R. 1987a. "Interview: Nobel Laureate, MIT Economist Robert Solow." *Challenges* 1(2).

Solow, R. 1988a. *New York Times,* January 24, Section 4, p. 1.

Solow, R. 1988b. "Growth Theory and After." *American Economic Review* 78 (June), 307–17.

Stempel, R. C. 1988. *New York Times,* September 11, p. F2.

Summers, L. H., and C. Carroll. 1987. "Why Is the U.S. National Saving Rate So Low?" Harvard Institute of Economic Research, Cambridge, Mass., Discussion Paper 1351, November.

Tolchin, M., and S. Tolchin. 1988. *Buying into America.* New York: Times Books.

Turner, P. 1988. "Saving and Investment, Exchange Rates, and International Imbalances: A Comparison of the U.S., Japan, and Germany." *Journal of Japanese and International Economy* 2(3), 259–85.

U.S. Congress, Office of Technological Assessment. 1988. "Technology and the American Economic Transition." Washington, D.C.

Wei-Ming, T. 1988. "A Confucian Perspective on the Rise of Industrial East Asia." *Bulletin of the American Academy of Arts and Sciences,* October, pp. 32–50.

"What Does Equity Financing Really Cost?" *Business Week,* November 7, 1988, pp. 146–48.

IV

COUNTRY STUDIES

14

Price and Output Adjustment in Japanese Manufacturing

WILLIAM H. BRANSON AND
RICHARD C. MARSTON

Since the mid-1970s, manufacturing firms in the United States and Japan have had to cope with large fluctuations in real exchange rates. Firms in the two countries are said to have responded quite differently to these fluctuations. As shown in Branson and Love (1988), output and employment in U.S. manufacturing varied sharply in response to changes in the real value of the dollar. But Japanese manufacturers are said to have varied prices, particularly the yen prices of exports, to limit the effects of changes in the real exchange rate of the yen on Japanese output and employment. This chapter studies price adjustment in Japanese manufacturing to determine the extent to which price behavior shielded Japanese output from fluctuations in the yen.

When there are variations in real exchange rates, manufacturers can respond in two different ways. They can vary production in the home country, perhaps shifting between home and offshore plants. Or they can vary the markups of prices over marginal costs in order to stabilize the foreign-currency prices of exports. In that case, profit margins rather than output and employment absorb the impact of the variations in real exchange rates.

If the yen appreciates, for example, Japanese firms can hold down the foreign-currency prices of their exports by squeezing profit margins at home. The markups of the yen prices of their products over marginal costs are reduced to keep them competitive in foreign markets. As a result, only a fraction of the yen appreciation is "passed through" into Japanese export prices expressed in dollars and other foreign currencies. Manufacturing firms may even follow a differential pricing policy where they reduce the yen prices of their exports more than they reduce domestic prices. Such differential pricing, which involves varying markups for the export market more than domestic markups, is called "pricing to market" by Krugman (1987) and others.[1]

This chapter examines price and output behavior in nine sectors of Japanese manufacturing which rely substantially on export markets. For each industry, separate equations are used to estimate Japanese wholesale prices and export prices in order to measure the sensitivity of markups to changes in foreign prices. And for each of these industries, demand equations are used to estimate the sensitivity of output to changes in real exchange rates.

The first section derives reduced-form equations for prices in an individual industry. The key departure from earlier studies is the introduction of markup behavior, which alters the relative response of prices and output to changes in real exchange rates. The second section presents equations for domestic and export prices by industry, and the third section presents demand equations. The final section of the chapter discusses the overall pattern of price and output adjustment found in Japanese manufacturing.

A MODEL OF MARKUP BEHAVIOR

When markups are variable, firms may respond to a rise in foreign prices by raising their markups rather than by increasing output and employment. In general, the more responsive markups are to foreign prices, the less effect foreign prices have on output. Because markups are central, we develop a model of demand and cost behavior that focuses specifically on markup behavior.

The Markup Function

Consider the behavior of a firm producing a good i for both the domestic and export markets. This firm has a short-run marginal cost function of the form

$$C_1 (Z_{it}, W_t, R_t, t) \qquad C_{11}, C_{12}, C_{13} > 0, \quad C_{14} < 0^2 \qquad \text{14-1}$$

where

$$Z_{it} = \text{output of good i}$$
$$W_t = \text{nominal wage}$$
$$R_t = \text{raw materials price}$$
$$t = \text{time}$$

Marginal cost is assumed to increase as output or factor prices increase but to decline over time in response to productivity growth. Marginal cost is also assumed to be homogeneous of degree 1 in wages and raw materials prices, so that Euler's law holds: $C_{12}W_t + C_{13}R_t = C_1$.[3] The firm faces a demand curve of the form

$$Z_{it} = h [P_{it}/(S_t Q_{it}), Z_t, Y_t], \qquad h_1 < 0; \quad h_2, h_3 > 0 \qquad (14\text{-}2)$$

where

$$P_{it} = \text{price of good } i$$
$$Q_{it} = \text{price of a competing good in foreign currency}$$

S_t = exchange rate (domestic currency price of foreign currency

Z_t = total domestic output

Y_t = total foreign output

Demand is negatively related to its own relative price and positively related to output in either country.

The firm is assumed to set P_{it} to maximize profits according to the first-order condition:

$$h_1 \frac{P_{it}}{S_t Q_{it}} + h(\cdot) - h_1 \frac{C_1}{S_t Q_{it}} = 0 \qquad (14\text{-}3)$$

The *markup* (*M*) of price over marginal cost can be obtained by rearranging this first-order condition as follows:

$$\frac{P_{it}}{C_1} = 1 / \left[1 + \frac{h(\cdot) S_t Q_{it}}{h_1 P_{it}} \right]$$

$$= M \left(\frac{P_{it}}{S_t Q_{it}}, Z_t, Y_t \right)$$

Notice that the markup is a function of the same variables as the demand function on which it is based. The markup can also be written in terms of the price elasticity of demand, $\varepsilon = -(h_1 P_{it})/(Z_{it} S_t Q_{it}) > 0$ as follows:

$$M(\cdot) = \varepsilon/(\varepsilon - 1)$$

If the demand elasticity is constant (case 1 below), then the markup is also constant. For many demand curves, however, the elasticity increases and the markup falls as prices rise (case 2 below).

To determine how demand and cost functions interact to determine prices, we totally differentiate the first-order conditions and solve for the domestic price. In the next section, the elasticities of the price with respect to each of the independent variables are described in detail.

Price Behavior

The price of good i can be expressed in terms of the factors influencing both demand and cost behavior. The reduced-form equation for P_{it} is expressed in terms of percentage changes, so the coefficients represent elasticities of price with respect to the demand and cost variables. In Equation 14-4, all prices are deflated by the wage in order to reduce collinearity between the independent variables in the estimation to follow:[4]

$$\frac{dP_{it}}{P_{it}} - \frac{dW_t}{W_t} = \alpha_{i1} \left[\frac{dS_t Q_{it}}{S_t Q_{it}} - \frac{dW_t}{W_t} \right] + \alpha_{i2} \left[\frac{dR_t}{R_t} \right.$$

$$\left. - \frac{dW_t}{W_t} \right] + \alpha_{i3} \frac{dZ_t}{Z_t} + \alpha_{i4} \frac{dY_t}{Y_t} + \alpha_{i5} dt \qquad (14\text{-}4)$$

where

$$\alpha_{i1} = 1 - (S_t Q_{it})/H$$
$$\alpha_{i2} = (S_t Q_{it} R_t C_{13})/(HC_1)$$
$$\alpha_{i3} = [Z_t S_t \ Q_{it}(C_1 M_2 + M(\cdot)C_{11}h_2)]/(HP_{it})$$
$$\alpha_{i4} = [Y_t S_t Q_{it}(C_1 M_3 + M(\cdot)C_{11}h_3)]/(HP_{it})$$
$$\alpha_{i5} = [S_t Q_{it} C_{14}]/(HC_1)$$
$$H = [S_t Q_{it} - C_1 M_1 - M(\cdot)C_{11}h_1] > 0$$

Among the independent variables is one which measures the relative competitiveness of industry i: $S_t Q_{it}/W_t$. The coefficient of this relative price, called the *sectoral real exchange rate*, measures the influence of foreign prices on domestic prices in the same industry. The size of this real exchange rate coefficient depends on two different factors, the price elasticity of demand (ε) and the elasticity of the markup with respect to prices (which we label δ). To investigate the influence of these two elasticities, we consider two special cases.

Case 1: Constant Markups with Increasing Marginal Cost

If the elasticity of demand is constant, which would be the case if the demand curve is log linear, then the markup is also constant ($M_1 = M_2 = M_3 = 0$). Thus the coefficient of the real exchange rate reduces to

$$\alpha_{i1} = 1 - \frac{1}{[1 + \varepsilon (C_{11} Z_{it}/C_1)]}$$

As long as marginal cost increases with output ($C_{11} > 0$), this coefficient lies between zero and one. An appreciation of the yen, by raising export prices in *foreign currency*, reduces output demanded. Thus marginal costs fall, as do prices in yen. But since there is no change in the markup of prices over marginal costs, the fall in prices is accomplished only through variations in output leading to reductions in marginal cost. So this case cannot explain the lack of output adjustment in Japan; with constant demand elasticities, there is no tradeoff between price adjustment and output adjustment.

A higher demand elasticity increases the real exchange rate coefficient. And as this elasticity approaches infinity, α_{i1} approaches unity, while all other coefficients in Equation 14-4 approach zero. Thus in this polar case where domestic and foreign goods are perfect substitutes, the price equation collapses to the law of one price (in percentage changes): $d(P_{it})/P_{it} = d(S_t Q_{it})/(S_t Q_{it})$. Short of this polar case, higher demand elasticities result in *greater* output variation, since any movement in relative prices leads to changes in output proportional to this elasticity.

Case 2: Variable Markups with Constant Marginal Cost

A second special case focuses specifically on markup behavior. We assume that markups *decline* with increases in prices (i.e., $M_1 < 0$). Such markup behavior is characteristic of any demand curve less convex (more linear) than the log-linear curve, including the linear case itself.[5] To isolate the role of markups, assume that marginal cost is constant ($C_{11} = 0$) so that the last term in the denominator of α_{i1} involving the elasticity of demand is zero. Then the coefficient of the real exchange rate is given by

$$\alpha_{i1} = 1 - \frac{1}{[1 - \delta]}$$

where δ is the elasticity of the markup with respect to price:

$$\delta = \frac{M_1 P_{it}}{M(\cdot)\ S_t Q_{it}} < 0$$

As δ increases in absolute value, α_{i1} also increases. So as the demand curve becomes more linear, the effect of higher foreign prices is enhanced.

Consider the effects of an appreciation of the yen once again. This appreciation raises the foreign currency price of exports. But the exporting firm reduces the markup to limit the rise in that price. The firm's price in *domestic* currency thus falls. If the firm "prices to market," it may reduce the domestic currency price of its exports more than the price of its domestic goods. A greater sensitivity of the markup to prices (i.e., a higher δ in absolute value) increases the response of the firm's prices to the appreciation. And it reduces the impact of the appreciation on output. In this case of a variable markup, there *is* a *tradeoff* between price variations and output variations.

In the case of a linear demand curve, we can also relate the size of δ to the elasticity of demand through the equation

$$\delta = -(1 + \varepsilon)/(\varepsilon - 1) < 0$$

Since an increase in the elasticity of demand reduces the absolute value of δ, it also reduces α_{i1}. In contrast to case 1, the *lower* the demand elasticity, the *higher* is α_{i1}, the coefficient of the real exchange rate. Consider the implications for the behavior of output. If markup behavior is responsible for a high coefficient for the real exchange rate, then output may be relatively unresponsive to the real exchange rate because of low demand elasticities *even though* domestic prices are highly responsive to the real exchange rate.

General Case: Variable Markups and Increasing Marginal Cost

We now consider the more general case where markups are allowed to fall as prices rise and where marginal costs may increase with output: $M_1 \leq 0$, $C_{11} \geq 0$.[6] The coefficient of the real exchange rate can be written as follows:

$$\alpha_{i1} = 1 - \frac{1}{[1 - \delta + \varepsilon(C_{11}\ Z_{it}/C_1)]}$$

The denominator of the fraction must be positive,[7] so α_{i1} must lie between zero and one. As in case 1, moreover, an increase in ε, given δ, increases α_{i1}, while as in case 2 an increase in the absolute value of δ, given ε, also increases α_{i1}. Thus if we find that α_{i1} is large in the equations estimated later, we can attribute the response of domestic prices to the real exchange rate to one of two influences: high demand elasticities or variable markup elasticities. Only by examining output behavior will we be able to distinguish between these two influences.

To round out the analysis of the price equation, we note that α_{i2} can be written as

$$\alpha_{i2} = \frac{R_i C_{13}}{C_1} (1 - \alpha_{i1})$$

Thus $0 \leq \alpha_{i2} < 1$. An increase in ε or in the absolute value of δ, moreover, reduces the size of this coefficient. The coefficients of domestic and foreign output, α_{i3} and α_{i4}, are positive as long as the markup derivatives, M_2 and M_3, are positive or zero.[8] Finally, the coefficient of time, α_{i5}, is negative, since increasing productivity reduces marginal costs.

EMPIRICAL PRICE EQUATIONS

In this section, we report equations explaining price changes in Japanese manufcturing as a function of changes in foreign prices as well as other variables. We focus on those sectors of manufacturing with significant reliance on exports for which there are series for export prices as well as domestic prices available. Nine sectors in all are studied: textiles, chemicals, three metal sectors, and four machinery sectors. The machinery sectors alone (general machinery, electrical machinery, transport equipment, and precision instruments) account for over half of Japanese exports.

Description of the Data

The data appendix describes the series used in the estimation and reports the source of each series. This section briefly describes these series and outlines the specification of the price equations.

For the nine sectors studied, the Bank of Japan reports prices for the export market separate from prices for the domestic market. The domestic prices are those reported at the primary wholesale level for sale in Japan, while the export prices are FOB export prices expressed in yen. The product categories are listed in Table 14-1. The price equations to be estimated have as a dependent variable the domestic or export price for that sector relative to the wage in Japanese manufacturing. (The relative domestic price is denoted PW_{it}; the relative export price is denoted PXW_{it}). To reduce spurious correlation between the price series, all variables are expressed as first differences (of their log values).

The independent variables include a sectoral real exchange rate (RW_{it}) defined as the U.S. producer price for that sector, converted into yen, deflated by the Japanese manufacturing wage. It would have been preferable to use a

Table 14-1 Price Equations, 1974.01–1986[a].12

Sector	Σ RW	Σ RM	Σ CIP	Constant	$\bar{R}^2$ SEE	ρ Durbin–Watson
Textiles						
Domestic	0.240 (4.05)	0.068 (1.10)	0.784 (3.52)	−0.042 (−1.98)	0.583 0.017	0.220 1.96
Export	0.628 (11.2)	0.101 (1.70)	0.416 (1.96)	−0.037 (−1.35)	0.773 0.015	0.468 1.95
Chemicals						
Domestic	0.245 (4.51)	0.230 (3.89)	0.720 (3.43)	−0.036 (−1.70)	0.676 0.016	0.287 2.17
Export	0.890 (15.8)	0.121 (1.94)	0.496 (2.27)	−0.047 (−1.62)	0.873 0.016	0.489 2.16
Iron and steel						
Domestic	0.169 (3.32)	0.109 (2.07)	0.677 (3.45)	−0.031 (−1.90)	0.618 0.017	1.75
Export	0.774 (10.6)	0.261 (3.25)	0.263 (.924)	−0.040 (−1.39)	0.721 0.021	0.280 1.86
Nonferrous metals						
Domestic	0.647 (6.79)	0.268 (2.40)	1.34 (3.38)	−0.097 (−2.58)	0.702 0.031	0.211 1.93
Export	0.740 (9.23)	0.036 (.386)	0.201 (.597)	−0.008 (−.226)	0.629 0.025	0.321 1.78
Metallic products						
Domestic	0.309 (4.26)	0.248 (3.20)	0.439 (1.59)	−0.018 (−.619)	0.561 0.021	0.301 1.67

Table 14-1 (cont.)

Sector	ΣRW	ΣRM	ΣCIP	Constant	$\bar{R}^2$ / SEE	ρ / Durbin–Watson
Export	0.438	0.220	0.247	−0.051	0.602	0.179
	(6.53)	(3.21)	(.972)	(−2.17)	0.020	1.93
General machinery						
Domestic	0.270	0.161	0.332	−0.033	0.559	0.209
	(4.25)	(2.52)	(1.42)	(−1.50)	0.018	1.74
Export	0.496	0.080	0.227	−0.039	0.802	0.140
	(11.3)	(1.82)	(1.41)	(−2.78)	0.013	1.74
Electrical machinery						
Domestic	0.227	0.108	0.210	−0.048	0.552	
	(4.21)	(2.03)	(1.03)	(−2.88)	0.017	1.61
Export	0.650	−0.039	0.106	−0.065	0.830	−0.204
	(16.8)	(−1.03)	(.737)	(−5.49)	0.012	1.98
Transport equipment						
Domestic	0.266	0.131	0.321	−0.039	0.569	0.233
	(4.61)	(2.15)	(1.43)	(−1.81)	0.017	1.84
Export	0.494	0.037	0.206	−0.021	0.826	
	(13.4)	(.989)	(1.44)	(−1.75)	0.012	1.85
Precision instruments						
Domestic	0.252	0.119	0.269	−0.043	0.525	
	(4.14)	(1.97)	(1.21)	(−2.25)	0.018	1.68
Export	0.255	0.130	0.360	−0.060	0.533	0.143
	(4.11)	(2.07)	(1.57)	(−2.95)	0.018	1.73

[a]The figures below the coefficients are t statistics. Seasonal dummy variables are included in each equation, but their coefficients are not reported. Most equations are corrected for serial correlation in which case the serial correlation coefficient (ρ) is reported.

weighted average of many countries' prices in forming this sectoral real exchange rate, but it is difficult to obtain disaggregated prices defined on a consistent basis across countries. The coefficient of this sectoral real exchange rate measures the elasticity of the domestic or export price with respect to a 1 percent change in the foreign price or exchange rate. This coefficient should be larger in the export price equation than in the domestic price equation if Japanese firms price to market, varying export price markups more than domestic markups as foreign prices change.[9]

The second independent variable is the relative price of imported raw materials (RM_{it}) defined as the import price of petroleum, coal, and natural gas expressed in yen relative to the wage.[10] Japanese output (Y_t) also enters as an independent variable. To reduce collinearity between output and the time trend, this variable is expressed as the cyclical deviation from a time trend, formed by fitting a time trend to the log of Japanese industrial production.[11] A variable representing cyclical movements in U.S. industrial production was also included in the equation but proved to be statistically insignificant throughout the estimation. Cyclical output should have a positive coefficient, since this variable reflects the influence of higher demand on prices and higher markups due to that increased demand. With cyclical output replacing actual output, the time trend (t) now reflects two influences, productivity growth and the trend growth in demand. Since the price equation is expressed in first differences, the constant in this equation measures any trend influence on prices.

The equation estimated for sector i has the following form:

$$PW_{it} = \sum_j a_{i1j} RW_{i,t-j} + \sum_j a_{i2j} RM_{i,t-j} + \sum_j a_{i3j} CIP_{t-j} + a_{i0} + U_{it} \quad (14\text{-}5)$$

where the dependent variable is either

PW_{it} = change in the log of the Japanese domestic wholesale price for sector i less the wage in manufacturing

or

PXW_{it} = change in the log of the Japanese wholesale price for exports (in yen) for sector i less the wage in manufacturing

and where

RW_{it} = change in the log of the U.S. wholesale price for sector i converted into yen at the current spot rate less the wage in manufacturing

RM_{it} = change in the log of the price of imported petroleum, coal, and natural gas less the wage in manufacturing

CIP_t = change in the log of Japanese cyclical production (measured as the deviation from the log trend of industrial production)

The period of estimation begins in January 1974, following the start of generalized floating, and ends in December 1986, so there are 156 monthly observations. Since the data are not seasonally adjusted,[12] we include seasonal dummy variables in each equation.[13]

Estimation Results

Table 14-1 reports the price equations for the nine sectors of Japanese manufacturing with significant export activity. The table reports the coefficients for the relative price terms, output terms, and constant as well as four summary statistics: the adjusted R^2, the standard error of the equation, the serial correlation coefficient (ρ) when it is statistically significant, and the Durbin–Watson statistic.

Since the estimation employs monthly data, we fit polynominal distributed lags to each independent variable. The lags proved to be quite short, however, particularly for the relative price terms. A linear lag of only two months was found for the sectoral real exchange rates and the relative price of imported materials. This suggests that price changes in Japan occur quite rapidly following changes in exchange rates or foreign prices. In the case of cyclical output, the lag was four months long. In the table, we report the sum of the coefficients for each lag distrubtion and the t statistic for their sum.

The sectoral real exchange rate enters significantly in all eighteen regressions. Recall that the coefficient of this term measures the elasticity of the domestic or import price with respect to changes in the foreign price or exchange rate. In only one equation, the export price equation for chemicals, is the foreign price coefficient insignificantly different from one (at the 5 percent level), but in many sectors it is much larger than zero. The elasticity varies between 0.169 for domestic iron and steel prices to 0.890 for export prices in the chemical sector.

In all sectors, the foreign price coefficient in the export equation exceeds that in the domestic equation. In many sectors, such as chemicals, iron and steel, and electrical machinery, the price sensitivity of export prices is much larger than that of domestic prices, which suggests that there is substantial pricing to market in these sectors.[14]

In seventeen of the eighteen equations, the coefficient of the imported materials price has the expected positive sign, although in only twelve of these equations is the coefficient statistically significant at the 5 percent level. The coefficients are generally much smaller than those of the foreign price term, which suggests a relatively low dependence on imported materials in these sectors.

Cyclical movements in Japanese output are statistically significant in six of the eighteen equations and have the correct positive sign in all equations.[15] The coefficients represent elasticities of domestic or export prices with respect to changes in output. In the textile sector, for example, a 1 percent increase in output above trend leads to a rise in the price by 0.784 percent.

The constant term in each regression measures the influence of trends on the price *level,* since the regressions relate *changes* in price to other variables. The theoretical model suggests an ambiguous sign for the trend term, since higher output raises demand and therefore raises prices, whereas higher productivity lowers prices. The influence of productivity growth appears to be dominant, since the constant is negative in all eighteen equations, although in only eight equations is the coefficient statistically significant at the 5 percent level. Most of the statistically significant trends occur in the four machinery sectors where productivity growth has been especially rapid.[16]

The fit of these equations is excellent considering that they are estimated in first-difference form. Overall, the results indicate that changes in foreign prices are the most important determinant of price changes in Japan, at least in the export-oriented sectors of manufacturing that are studied here. Other influences are also important, including cyclical movements in output, but domestic and export prices appear to be more systematically related to foreign prices than any other variable.

DEMAND BEHAVIOR

The results reported in Table 14-1 suggest that for many sectors of Japanese manufacturing, foreign prices and exchange rates have a strong influence on Japanese prices. But as explained earlier, there are two competing explanations for these results corresponding to the two ways in which foreign prices affect domestic prices. The first involves price elasticities. If demand has a high price elasticity, then Japanese prices will be relatively sensitive to foreign prices. In this case, output should also be relatively sensitive to foreign prices. The second way involves markup behavior. If markups are relatively responsive to price changes, then Japanese prices will once again be relatively sensitive to foreign prices. But in this case, output should be relatively *insensitive* to price changes.

To help distinguish between these two cases, we now investigate the price elasticity of demand (ε) by estimating demand equations for each sector. The demand equation (14-2) is written in terms of percentage changes as follows:

$$\frac{dZ_{it}}{Z_{it}} = -\varepsilon \left[\frac{dP_{it}}{P_{it}} - \frac{dS_t Q_{it}}{S_t Q_{it}} \right] + \mu \frac{dZ_t}{Z_t} \qquad (14\text{-}6)$$

The last coefficient represents the income elasticity of demand, $\mu = (h_2 Z_t)/Z_{it}$.

The empirical counterpart of Equation 14-6 relates (the percentage change in) industrial production in sector i to distributed lags of relative price changes and income changes:

$$IP_{it} = -\Sigma_j b_{i1j} PQ_{i,t-j} + \Sigma_j b_{i2j} CIP_{t-j} + b_{i0} + V_{it} \qquad (14\text{-}7)$$

where

IP_{it} = change in the log of industrial
production in industry i
PQ_{it} = change in the log of the Japanese export
price for sector i relative to the corresponding
U.S. wholesale price expressed in yen
CIP_t = change in the log of Japanese cyclical industrial
production (measured as the deviation of the log of industrial
production from its trend)

The series for industrial production represent monthly data disaggregated according to the same nine industry classification as are the wholesale price series. The export price rather than domestic price is employed as an independent variable since it is the export component of demand that is likely to be the most price-sensitive. Because the current export price is likely to be correlated with the error term in this equation, *only lagged* values of PQ_{it} are included in the equation. The period of estimation extends from January 1974 to December 1986. Since the industrial production series are not seasonally adjusted, we include seasonal dummy variables in each equation. As in the price equation, the constant term reflects the combined influence of productivity growth and the trend growth of demand.

Table 14-2 reports demand equations for the nine sectors of Japanese manufacturing with significant export activity. The table reports the coefficients for the relative price and output terms as well as summary statistics. We fit a ten-month second-degree polynominal lag to the price and output terms; the coefficients reported are for the sum of these lags.

Unlike the corresponding price equations in Table 14-1, these demand equations exhibit little sensitivity to foreign prices. In all nine equations, the relative price terms are statistically insignificant, and they are positive rather than negative in seven of these equations.[17] The cyclical income terms, in contrast, are all of the correct sign and are statistically significant in seven of the nine equations. The constant terms, moreover, are positive in all but one equation, although they are statistically significant in only two equations. Thus income— particularly cyclical income—seems to play a major role in the demand equations, but relative prices do not.

Because demand does not appear to be significantly affected by relative prices, one of the two explanations for the results reported in Table 14-1 must

Table 14-2 Demand Equations, 1974.01–1986[a].12

Sector	Σ PO	Σ CIP	Constant	$\bar{R}^2$ SEE	ρ Durbin–Watson
Textiles	0.007	0.811	−0.005	0.949	
	(.090)	(3.78)	(−.474)	.011	2.06
Chemicals	.267	.810	.036	.560	
	(1.71)	(1.85)	(1.65)	.022	2.31
Iron and steel	.110	1.40	.007	.757	
	(.986)	(4.34)	(.429)	.016	1.84
Nonferrous metals	.197	1.60	.016	.881	
	(1.37)	(4.53)	(.912)	.018	2.14
Metallic products	.058	1.91	.008	.860	−2.55
	(.428)	(4.80)	(.404)	.025	2.06
General machinery	.146	2.22	.033	.915	−.331
	(.920)	(5.83)	(1.73)	.026	2.10
Electrical machinery	.301	2.10	.128	.695	−.559
	(.652)	(2.22)	(2.41)	.075	2.29
Transport equipment	−.176	.716	.023	.881	−.467
	(−.800)	(1.54)	(.982)	.035	2.28
Precision instruments	−.104	1.90	.104	.761	−.302
	(−.629)	(3.50)	(3.70)	.037	2.06

[a]See Table 14-1.

be rejected. High demand elasticities can hardly account for the price responsiveness reported in that table. Instead, the explanation seems to be that markups are sufficiently variable to account for the high correlation between foreign and domestic prices. As explained earlier, if markups are sufficiently variable, domestic prices will respond to foreign prices even though demand elasticities are low. And with demand elasticities low, Japanese output will not be very sensitive to relative price changes.

AN AGENDA FOR FUTURE RESEARCH

This chapter has suggested that markup behavior may be the key to understanding the patterns of price and output adjustment found in Japanese manufacturing. We have provided evidence that Japanese firms have varied markups systematically in order to limit the effects of exchange-rate changes on output. This behavior is quite different from that found in U.S. manufacturing where output and employment have borne the main impact of exchange-rate changes.

We hope to extend this analysis by examining Japanese demand behavior in more detail. In the model outlined here, we have not distinguished between domestic and foreign demand for Japanese goods. It is possible that the output behavior we observe is due to different markup behavior in the two markets, a possibility consistent with higher coefficients for foreign prices in the export price equations. Consider a model of pricing to market in which the markups of export prices in domestic currency over marginal costs are varied systematically to limit changes in export prices in *foreign* currency. The markups of export prices will vary widely, while those in the domestic market may not vary much at all. To investigate this possibility, we hope to estimate separate demand equations for export and domestic markets if we can obtain quantity data disaggregated by market.

APPENDIX 14-1

Japanese Sectoral Prices

Domestic and export price indexes for the following sectors: textile products, chemicals, iron and steel, nonferrous metals, metal products, general machinery, electrical machinery, transport equipment, and precision instruments. Note that the domestic price indexes are for domestic goods only. (A separate set of "overall" wholesale price indexes is also available.) The indexes are calculated using the Laspeyres formula. *Source: Bank of Japan, Price Indexes Annual,* various issues.

Japanese Import Price for Fuel

Import price index for petroleum, coal, and natural gas. *Source:* Bank of Japan, *Price Indexes Annual,* various issues.

U.S. Sectoral Prices

Producer price indexes for the following sectors: apparel, chemicals and allied products, iron and steel, nonferrous metals, fabricated structural metal products, general-purpose machinery and equipment, electrical machinery and equipment, motor vehicles and equipment. Note that the series for general-purpose machinery and equipment was used as an explanatory variable in both the general machinery and precision instruments price equations. *Source:* Department of Commerce, *Business Conditions Digest.*

U.S. (Aggregate) Wholesale Price

Producer price index for U.S. manufacturing: *Source:* Department of Commerce, *Business Conditions Digest.*

Japanese Wages

Monthly earnings in Japanese manufacturing, regular workers, seasonally adjusted. *Source:* OECD, *Main Economic Indicators.*

Exchange Rate

Yen price of the dollar, monthly average. *Source:* International Monetary Fund, *International Financial Statistics.*

Japanese Sectoral Industrial Production

Industrial production by sector of manufacturing, available for the same nine sectors listed for the price series. *Source:* Economic Planning Agency, unpublished data.

Japanese (Aggregate) Industrial Production

Industrial production in Japanese manufacturing. *Source:* OECD, *Main Economic Indicators*.

U.S. Industrial Production

Industrial production in U.S. manufacturing. *Source:* OECD, *Main Economic Indicators*.

NOTES

We would like to thank Orazio Attanasio, Bert Hickman, and other participants at the conference for their helpful comments on an earlier draft.

1. Other recent studies of pricing to market and the related phenomena of currency pass-through include Feenstra (1987), Froot and Klemperer (1988), Giovannini (1988), Ohno (1988), and Schembri (1988).
2. The subscripts refer to the arguments of the function; C_1, for example, is marginal cost, or the derivative of total cost with respect to output, while C_{12} is the derivative of marginal cost with respect to the second argument, wages.
3. In the case of a Cobb–Douglas production function, for example, the short-run marginal cost function is homogeneous of degree 1 in the prices of the variable factors, W_t and R_t.
4. Note that the second-order conditions in Equation 14-4 require $H > 0$.
5. Krugman (1987) and Feenstra (1987) also focus on the role of demand-curve convexity in determining the influence of exchange rates on domestic prices, although they focus on the pass-through of foreign costs into export prices. Krugman points out that in the literature on trade policy under imperfect competition, the effect of tariffs is shown to depend on the convexity of the demand curve.
6. We cannot rule out other cases a priori. For example, markups would be positively related to prices if the demand curve were more convex than the log-linear case. And marginal costs may decline rather than increase with output. We focus on the more normal case described here because it is consistent with the empirical results that follow.
7. Note that as long as $M_1 \leq 0$, then $\delta \leq 0$.
8. These coefficients may be positive even if M_2 and M_3 are negative since the second terms in the expressions for α_{i3} and α_{i4} are positive.
9. If export prices expressed in yen vary more than domestic prices, this in itself is evidence of pricing to market and variable markups. If demand elasticities are constant, on the other hand, markups are constant and export prices in yen vary just as much as domestic prices of the same product (i.e., as much as marginal costs vary).
10. This component of raw materials, representing 48 percent of the total import price index, performed better than the price series for imported raw materials and fuels (representing 61 percent of the import index).
11. The trend equation is estimated over the period January 1973 to December 1986. Because Japanese growth appears to have slowed after the first oil shock, we estimated a separate trend for the period prior to July 1974 and a separate intercept term for the period through the end of 1974 when the economy reached its lowest point.

12. The Japanese wage in manufacturing is seasonally adjusted, since the unadjusted wage has a strong seasonal component corresponding to year-end bonuses.

13. The seasonal dummy variables are defined as $V_i = S_i - S_1$ for $i \neq 1$, and $V_1 = S_1$, where S_i is a normal seasonal variable (with 1 in the ith month and 0 elsewhere). The coefficient of the V_1 term provides an estimate of the constant independent of any seasonal effect.

14. As explained previously, if export prices expressed in yen vary more than domestic prices, this in itself is evidence of pricing to market and of variable markups.

15. Cyclical movements in U.S. industrial production proved to be statistically insignificant in the equations.

16. Since a reduced-form equation is being estimated, it is difficult to interpret the magnitude of the coefficients in terms of productivity growth rates. Even the relative magnitude of the trend terms across equations will depend on structural coefficients rather than just on the productivity growth rates.

17. The price terms are statistically insignificant regardless of the length of the lag or the degree of the polynomial being fitted.

REFERENCES

Branson, W. H., and J. P. Love. 1988. "U.S. Manufacturing and the Real Exchange Rate." In R. C. Marston, ed. *The Misalignment of Exchange Rates: Effects on Trade and Industry*. Chicago: University of Chicago Press.

Feenstra, R. C. 1987. "Symmetric Pass-Through on Tariffs and Exchange Rates under Imperfect Competition: An Empirical Test." NBER Working Paper No. 2453 (December).

Froot, K. A., and P. Klemperer. 1988. "Exchange Rate Pass-Through When Market Share Matters." NBER Working Paper No. 2542 (March).

Giovannini, A. 1988. "Exchange Rates and Traded Goods Prices." *Journal of International Economics*, February, pp. 45–68.

Krugman, P. 1987. "Pricing to Market When the Exchange Rate Changes." In S. W. Arndt and J. D. Richardson, eds., *Real-Financial Linkages Among Open Economies*. Cambridge: MIT Press, pp. 49–70.

Ohno, K. 1988. "Export Pricing Behavior in Manufacturing: A U.S.–Japan Comparison," June.

Schembri, L. 1988. "Export Prices and Exchange Rates: An Industry Approach." Universities Research Conference on Trade Policies for International Competitiveness (April).

15

The Trade and Industrial Policies of Postwar Japan: A Theoretical Perspective

MOTOSHIGE ITOH AND KAZUHARU KIYONO

Potwar economic growth has been stimulated worldwide by the remarkable development of capital- or technology-intensive industries that produce such goods as steel, automobiles, machinery, chemicals, semiconductors, and computers. These industries are often characterized as exhibiting various types of large economies of scale, both static and dynamic. Their growth, often entailing a vast amount of capital or R&D investment, reduces production costs and induces demand expansion, which in turn yields greater incentives for investment.

However, this mechanism of accelerated economic development is set in motion only after industries with economies of scale have been established. Countries trying to catch up with the advanced economies are seriously disadvantaged in this respect, since industries in the advanced economies have already gained substantial cost advantages compared with the potential newcomers. The presence of economies of scale, as often pointed out in industrial organization theory, results in entry barriers. And even should they successfully enter the market, newcomers will find it very difficult to expand their market share due to the cost disadvantage, which also hinders a more rapid growth of the national economy.

The postwar history of resource-poor Japan has been one in which it has overcome those entry barriers in the leading industries of the time and equipped itself with an advanced trade and industrial structure. From Figure 15-1, which traces this development, it is clear that the heavy and chemical industries and, subsequently, machinery industries have increased their shares at a remarkable speed. Without such changes in its trade and industrial structure, Japan, which had to reconstruct an economy devastated by the war, would have been unable to achieve such a high growth rate during the postwar period.

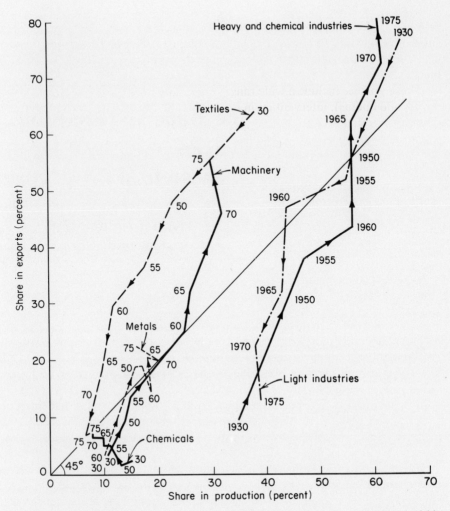

Figure 15-1 Shifts in industrial structure and pattern of trade. *Source:* Nenji Keizai Ho-kokusho (Annual Economic Report), Fiscal 1978.

Many factors have contributed to Japan's rapid industrial growth: a high saving propensity and rapid capital accumulation, efficient use of technology borrowed from the advanced countries, diligent and industrious workers, and various policy measures introduced by the government, to mention a few. There are a number of different views regarding the relationship between Japan's industrial policies and its rapid industrial growth. There is, on the one hand, the view that Japan's industrial policies did not contribute to its growth at all and, moreover, these policies were actually detrimental to a healthy functioning of the economy. There is the opposite view, however; namely, that Japan's rapid economic growth was derived from its industrial policies.

Our view differs from these two extremes. There can be no doubt that Japan's industrial policies had enormous effects, both positive and negative, on its economic performance. It is impossible to disregard these effects when one discusses Japan's rapid postwar growth. However, since numerous policy measures were introduced by government, and their effects were even more varied, it is almost impossible to provide an overall evaluation of Japan's industrial policies.

These policies include a wide range of measures, such as border restrictions (tariffs and quotas), intervention in production activities (e.g., through production subsidies), R&D promotion such as the formation of a government-led R&D cooperation group, adjustment assistance toward declining industries, and so-called industry rationalization such as government-supported cartel and merger measures.

It would prove impossible, even meaningless, to attempt to cover this wide range of policy measures in the limited space of this chapter. We have therefore restricted our discussion to trade-related policy measures, particularly infant-industry protection policy, since we believe that infant-industry protection policy was the core of Japan's industrial policies in the postwar period until the mid-1970s.

Many countries have attempted to implement an infant-industry protection policy, but in most cases these have been unsuccessful in promoting industrial growth. The Japanese experience in the postwar era is exceptional in this respect. If Japan's infant-industry protection policy effectively promoted industrial growth, what kind of mechanism lay behind that growth? An answer to this, in terms of the Japanese experience, is important not only for evaluating Japan's industrial policies but also for a better understanding of infant-industry protection policy in general.

A recent increase of interest in trade and industrial policies in general invites an evaluation of those implemented by Japan.[1] In this chapter, we explore from a theoretical perspective how Japan's trade and industrial policies in the postwar era contributed to and affected its economic welfare and industrial growth pattern.[2]

The first section provides a brief overview of the policy measures that were introduced by the Japanese government to protect its infant industries. The following section discusses the economic implications of so-called selective protection policy (sometimes called industrial targeting). We next deal with the issue of increasing returns and Marshallian externalities. The following section explains how the temporary nature of Japan's protection policy accelerated investment by domestic firms. A discussion of some aspects of oligopoly precedes our brief concluding remarks.

OVERVIEW OF INFANT-INDUSTRY PROTECTION POLICY

Soon after World War II, the government had to confront the challenge of reconstructing and reinforcing the economy in order to survive international competition. For this purpose, it first had to overcome two great obstacles: a shortage of domestic resources, physical as well as nonphysical, and a lack of foreign currency reserves to finance a rapid expansion of import demand for goods necessary for industrialization, such as raw materials, machinery, and

new technology. These two obstacles made for a vicious circle of foreign exchange shortage: the lack of domestic resources means that Japan had to import raw materials from abroad; while these could be purchased with foreign
exchange obtained by export, this was impossible when any increase in production demanded the availability of sufficient raw materials. This vicious circle continually threatened the Japanese economy as it moved toward industrialization, and it was faced with an adverse international balance-of-payments
situation for a long time after the war. The situation was more serious immediately after the war than in any other period in the history of Japan's modernization, because the devastation of its production facilities jeopardized its economy, producing a great shortage of necessities and massive unemployment.

This critical situation impelled the government to formulate a comprehensive policy program to reinforce and refine Japan's trade and industrial structure. Its policy program consisted of:

1. Trade restrictions to secure the home market for domestic industries
   through (a) quantitative import restrictions, (b) import tariffs, and (c)
   regulation of inward direct investment.
2. Subsidization to promote market expansion for domestic industries
   through (a) export promotion by export tax credit, special depreciation
   allowances, and preferential loans, and (b) production and investment
   subsidization by tax credit, special depreciation allowances, and preferential loans.

Employing several well-known criteria for choosing industries that would
receive special protection, such as "income elasticity" and "productivity
growth," the government applied these policies to a specified group of industries producing such goods as steel; nonferrous metals; petroleum; chemicals;
machine tools; electric, transport, and electronic machinery; and, later, semiconductors and computers.

It should be mentioned that the focal point of industrial policy was gradually
shifted to the more selective infant-industry protection policy. However, the
foregoing policy measures continued to be used, although in a more selective
and less comprehensive manner than before.

The first group of policy measures prevented established foreign firms from
exercising strategic entry deterrence against potential new entrants from Japan
and capturing the Japanese market. As Figures 15-2 and 15-3 indicate, the leading industries at that time were protected initially by quantitative restrictions
up to 1965 (up to the 1970s in the case of some high-tech goods), but later by
high tariffs up to the first half of the 1970s. With regard to specific industries,
Figure 15-4 shows that the import tariffs on major machinery industries, which
received special attention for promotion of indigenous industries, were relaxed
only after this sector became internationally competitive enough and its export–production ratio had risen.

Japan's border protection policy was quite comprehensive, covering a large
portion of import goods industries up to the mid-1960s; since then, it has become more selective. It is interesting to note also that the level of tariff protection in Japan is not significantly higher than in the United States and the EC.[3]

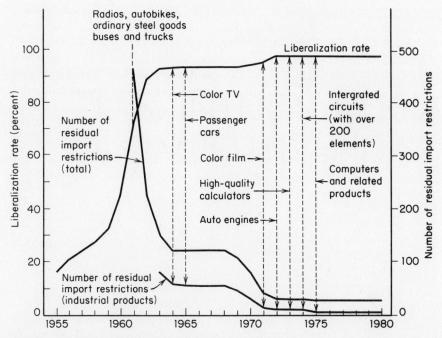

Figure 15-2 Trade liberalization in Japan. Key historical events: Japan joins the International Monetary Fund and World Bank (1952) and the General Agreement on Tariffs and Trade (1955); Trade and Exchange Liberalization Guidelines (1960); Inclusion into Article 8 Countries of the IMF (1964); Kennedy Round (1967).
Figures for 1961 for number of residual import restrictions are those for April 1962. Calculation for liberalization rate now discontinued. *Source:* Tsusansho (1980), p. 55; Naikai (1961), p. 37.

The second group of policy measures helped domestic industries to secure a market for their growth, especially when it appeared that the domestic market would be too small for them to make the best of economies of scale. As regards the magnitude of sectoral disbursement of subsidies in the postwar era, agriculture, forestry, and fisheries accounted for more than 80 percent of the total subsidies provided for private industry, while the high-technology, transport machinery, medical equipment, and other such industries, comprise a rather small portion of that amount (Ogura and Yoshino, 1988, p. 123).

Table 15-1 indicates government involvement in export promotion through the figures showing the reduction in gross tax receipts, which measure the size of the incentives that were provided by four major tax schemes designed to promote exports. Even though the policy authorities were actively involved in export promotion, the figures reveal that the incentives actually resulted in less than 2 percent of the total value of exports.

Our review of Japan's trade and industrial policies reveals the following features:

1. The Japanese government provided little direct subsidization to indigenous manufacturing industries through the postwar era.

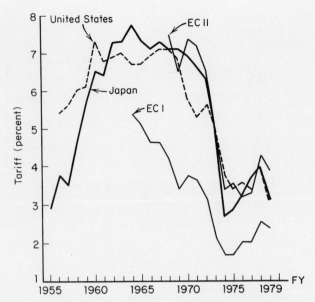

Figure 15-3 Tariff burden in major countries. The EC figures through to 1977 include six old EC member countries, West Germany, France, Italy, Netherlands, Belgium, and Luxembourg. For 1978 and 1979, the United Kingdom, Denmark, and Ireland are also included. Tariff burden in the case of EC includes agricultural surcharges. EC I represents the tariff burden on total imports including intraregional imports. EC II gives the tariff burden on imports from outside the EC. *Source:* Nihon Keizai Kenkya Senta (1979); Tsusansho (1982).

2. A crucial role during the establishment of Japan's major industries—that is, up to the 1970s—was played by the protection of the domestic market against foreign competition through restrictions on imports from, and inward direct investment by, foreign competitors.

We next consider what kind of economic mechanism was working behind the policy measures already described.

SELECTIVE PROTECTION AND THE CHANGE IN JAPAN'S TRADE AND INDUSTRIAL STRUCTURE

Infant-industry protection by the Japanese government has relied heavily on border restriction policies. Under the slogan "the sophistication of industrial structure," the government nurtured the heavy and chemical industries, such as the steel, shipbuilding, and petrochemical industries, but gradually moved its attention to the machinery and high-tech industries.

The government selected a particular group of industries based on several specific criteria and directed its protection to them. Most of these have successfully become the country's leading industries: textiles in the 1950s, steel in the late 1960s, electronic goods and automobiles in the 1970s, and other high-tech industries since the mid-1970s. The development of each of these indus-

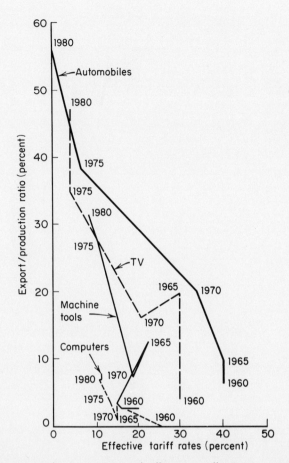

Figure 15-4 Export–production ratios and effective tariffs. Export–production ratio = amount of exports/production × 100. For automobiles, number of units is used. Automobiles include passenger cars, buses, trucks, and three wheelers. Television includes black-and-white and color TVs; effective tariffs refer to color TVs only. Machine tools include NC and others. Effective tariff rate pertains to NC machine tools only after 1970. Computers include analog type; effective rate of tariff is for digital type only. Computers include not only the mainframe but accessories and other related equipment as well. Tariffs are applied in the following order: (1) preferential tariffs, (2) GATT rates, (3) temporary rates, and (4) basic rates. The one that is actually applied is called effective tariff rate; (2) is used only if it is lower than (3) or (4). Since we are concerned with effective tariffs on trade with developed countries only, (1) has been ignored.

tries resulted in serious trade friction in each of these decades with other advanced countries, such as the United States. Like the success stories of other late-developing countries, the postwar history of Japan is characterized by its assimilation of the least competitive industries of the advanced countries. We now inquire into the mechanism of advanced-industry assimilation from the viewpoint of trade and industrial structure.

Figure 15-5 categorizes three kinds of goods traded between advanced and late-developing countries.[4] The first category is "basic technology goods,"

Table 15-1 Effect of Export-Promoting Tax System

Year	Revenues Lost Due to Export-Promoting Tax System (A) (Millions of Dollars)[a]	Revenues Lost Due to Special Tax Measures (B) (Millions of Dollars)	A/B	Amount of Exports (C) (Millions of Dollars)	A/C	Rate of Export Subsidies in Korea (%)[b]
1953	13.1	162.5	8.0	1,275	1.0	
1954	11.1	191.7	5.8	1,629	0.7	
1955	9.7	259.4	3.7	2,011	0.5	
1956	12.5	264.7	4.7	2,501	0.5	
1957	20.8	204.2	10.2	2,858	0.7	
1958	34.7	197.5	17.6	2,877	1.2	2.3
1959	27.8	229.7	12.1	3,456	0.8	2.5
1960	31.9	280.8	11.4	4,055	0.8	1.9
1961	30.6	284.7	10.4	4,236	0.7	6.6
1962	59.7	349.4	17.1	4,916	1.2	16.5
1963	65.3	471.1	13.9	5,452	1.2	15.1
1964	66.1	596.7	11.1	6,673	1.0	12.8
1965	68.3	613.3	11.1	8,452	0.8	14.8
1966	72.5	650.3	11.1	9,776	0.7	19.0
1967	71.6	635.8	11.3	10,442	0.7	23.0
1968	104.2	720.8	14.5	12,972	0.8	28.1
1969	139.7	879.2	15.6	15,990	0.9	26.1
1970	210.8	1,040.8	20.3	19,318	1.1	27.8

Sources: Zeisei Chosakai (Tax System Council), 1963, 1972; Keizai Kikakucho (Economic Planning Agency), various years; Frank et al., 1975.

[a]Includes accelerated depreciation for exports, special deductions on overseas incomes, and reserves for opening up of overseas markets.

[b]Total export subsidies/total exports. Export subsidies include direct subsidies, domestic tax concessions, tax rebates on exports, and interest subsidies.

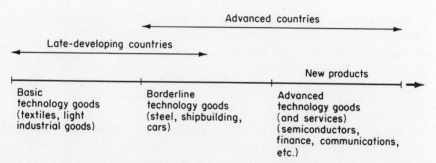

Figure 15-5   Types of goods traded between advanced and late-developing countries.

such as textiles and other light industrial products, in which the late-developing countries have a strong comparative advantage. The second is "borderline technology goods," in which the international competitiveness of the late-developing countries is quite close to that of the advanced countries. Steel, shipbuilding, and perhaps mass-produced automobiles fall into this category. The third category is "advanced technology goods," goods that only the advanced industrial countries can produce competitively. An example of these is high-technology goods, such as semiconductors, aircraft, and services like finance and communication.

When the advanced and late-develping countries trade with each other, the advanced countries export advanced technology goods, the late-developing countries export basic technology goods, and both compete in the area of borderline goods. What happens then if the late-developing countries protect any of their industries?

A question that inevitably arises in the industrialization process is whether effort should be put into making preexisting export industry more competitive or whether the industrial base should be broadened by establishing new export industries. In Japan, there was serious policy debate in the 1950s over whether it should protect industries that were not internationally competitive at the time, such as the automobile and steel industries. If the pattern of industrial development can be changed by government policy, then this question is a legitimate one for industrial policy.

If industrial policy protects the basic technology goods industries to reduce their production costs, then insofar as the economy is under perfect competition, the late-developing countries will gain little from such a policy. They may even lose from the policy as a result of it. This is because protection—subsidization, say—leads only to a deterioration in the late-developing countries' terms of trade as well as the protection cost incurred by them.

However, if industrial policy protects borderline goods industries, the result is somewhat different, for by the protection of these industries, the late-developing countries can capture the foreign market, which expands the world demand for their primary factors of production and thus raises their prices. The rise in the factor prices unfavorably affects the basic technology goods industries and causes their prices to rise. However, this price increase amounts to an improvement in the terms of trade for the late-developing countries.

As already mentioned, the pattern in Japan's postwar development was to shift the industrial structure toward borderline technology goods. Industrial development that moves the late-developing countries into borderline technology goods serves to raise their relative income position vis-à-vis advanced countries through the change in the factor prices mentioned. Since the welfare gains from the establishment of borderline technology goods spread to the entire economy, the national gains from the establishment of the borderline goods industry are much larger than the private gains for the industry itself. Thus there is a reason for government to protect borderline technology goods. This kind of general equilibrium impact resulting from infant-industry protection policy has received little attention in the traditional literature. It is, however, one of the most important features of Japan's postwar industrial policy.

It is quite clear that the industrial development of late-developing countries toward borderline technology goods may have adverse effects on the welfare of the advanced countries, since the terms of trade are changing against the advanced countries. This may explain why there has often been trade friction related to borderline technology goods between Japan and the United States in the postwar period.

SETUP COSTS OF INDUSTRY AND MARSHALLIAN EXTERNALITIES

In this review of postwar trade and industrial policies, one element runs contrary to the widespread view on Japanese industrial policies, and that is the success of economic development when backed up with a deep involvement in industry protection. However, even a small subsidy on production or exports, if concentrated on a suitably chosen group of industries, can have a significant protection effect in the presence of certain industry-wide economies of scale. This also accords with the argument of infant-industry protection and thus is welfare enhancing in national economic terms, even if it is not in international terms.

There are several factors through which industry expansion leads to its cost reduction; these can be classified roughly into the following three types. The first is industry-wide externalities in which the overall expansion of the industry yields an improvement in the technology conditions of each firm, often associated with development of a parts–suppliers network, as in the automobile and the household electrical goods industries. These industries require numerous parts, and their productivity depends greatly on the efficiency of parts production, which can be improved by promoting a division of labor among parts suppliers.

But as Adam Smith once argued, such division of labor is often limited by the extent of the market. It is sometimes possible to coordinate such division of labor internationally, and in that case the size of each national market does not matter. However, it is often difficult to achieve this, for complicated and frequent information exchanges are necessary to coordinate such division of labor effectively.

With market growth, a trained labor force or workers with higher technological knowledge move actively in the parts sector seeking higher rewards. This movement of human capital promotes a dissemination of higher technological knowledge throughout the sector and thus raises the production efficiency of parts production. In addition, demand growth will be helpful for each parts supplier in overcoming the barriers of fixed costs for specializing in the production of more specialized parts. It will also be conducive to enhancing the productivity of final goods production.

The second type of factor through which industry expansion leads to cost reductions is related to more dynamic sources of increasing returns to scale, such as learning by doing or the accumulation of experience and improved production know-how, which are typically observed in the integrated circuit, computer, and other high-technology industries. In these industries, output expansion leads a firm to much lower unit production costs, with a downward movement along the so-called learning curve. The semiconductor industry is prominent among those industries that exhibit a substantial learning-curve effect: its unit production cost is observed to have been halved within a couple of years. These gains from learning effects are limited by the size of the market which a firm can secure. Put another way, unless firms are able to obtain a sufficient market, they do not have an incentive to enter the market, for the massive production and the already reduced cost level entertained by foreign incumbents become high barriers to entry and growth.

The last type of factor involves more intricate effects of information externalities in the presence of firm- or plant-specific internal economies of scale, which, coupled with oligopolistic interaction among firms, leads to coordination failures in production and investment.[5] Typical examples are steel and petrochemicals. These industries are directly or indirectly related to other industries through transactions of goods and services. This interrelation is particularly close among vertically related industries.

Suppose that some of the interrelated industries exhibit internal scale economies and that the markets therefore are oligopolistic. Since each firm in an oligopolistic market can exercise its market power, one cannot rely on divine guidance or a price mechanism to achieve efficient resource allocation. Price does not convey all the information on the scarcity of the goods and services in question. Oligopolistic firms decide what price they will quote and what amount they will produce and sell by taking into account the shapes of their demand functions.

However, the production level of other industries affects their own productivity. But a lack of coordination among the industries tends to trap them in low productivity. For example, in the case of the steel and shipbuilding industries, an expansion of steel production reduces the unit cost of steel through economies of scale, but output expansion incentive hinges critically on the demand for steel by the shipbuilding industry, which is one of the biggest buyers of steel. On the other hand, the cost for the shipbuilding industry depends on the price of steel, which in turn depends on the amount of steel production.

If the two industries look ahead, understand the situation, and coordinate their production, they both expand their output and realize cost reduction, along with a great increase in profits. However, since they cannot coordinate their production, such cost reduction gains from simultaneous mutual output expansion are unlikely to eventuate. And the social gains from economies of scale in each industry are again limited by the extent of the market.

These three types of increasing returns to scale share the property that the average cost of the industries or the sector consisting of closely related industries is decreasing in total output. This is why these phenomena are often attributed to Marshallian externalities. Let us use Figure 15-6 to consider the role played by temporary domestic industry protection in the presence of such Marshallian externalities.

In the figure, curve AC is the long-run industry supply curve, which also designates the average cost curve of the individual firm.[6] P^* is the international price of the good which the industry faces in free trade, the horizontal line p^*F is the foreign export supply curve, and the curve DD' represents the domestic demand curve for the goods in question.

Let us first assume that free trade initially prevails. Then the domestic output is zero and all the domestic demand of x_2 is supplied by imports from abroad. The domestic industry cannot produce any positive output, for its marginal cost, which is higher than the international price, does not induce each firm to engage in production. If each firm could understand the global nature

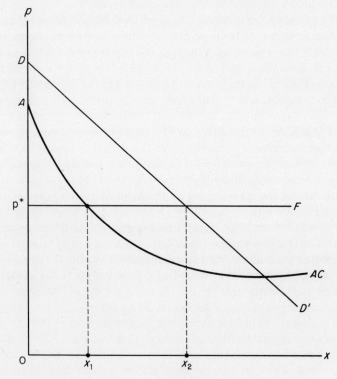

Figure 15-6 Marshallian externalities and domestic industry protection.

of the long-run industry supply curve and most producers could coordinate to expand the overall output up to x_1, then they could take off and gain sufficient profits. However, individual producers can neither see that far ahead nor attain an output greater than x_1 in cooperation.

To a government facing this situation, several altnerative policies are available for establishing the industry in question, such as temporary measures involving production subsidies and import restrictions. In the case of production subsidies, the government is required to provide the industry with an amount of unit production subsidy slightly exceeding Ap^*. With this subsidy an individual firm finds an incentive for positive production, which initiates a cumulative process of Marshallian externalities and soon expands the industry output beyond the critical level x_1. Note that along with development of the industry the government can reduce the required unit production subsidy rate, so that the total subsidy expenses can be limited to a certain low level. And once the industry overcomes the threshold of establishment, it can achieve self-sustained development and consolidate its international competitiveness. The imposition of tariffs, though entailing an additional cost on consumers, has protection effects similar to constantly adjusting tariff rates.

TEMPORARY NATURE OF THE PROTECTION POLICY AND THE MODE OF OLIGOPOLISTIC COMPETITION[7]

Generally, when the domestic market is cut off from competition from abroad, domestic firms base their structures and business procedures on protection. As a result, they often lack an aggressive interest in investment and growth. After all, when protection to some degree is expected to continue, there is no merit in sharply increasing capital investment. That a domestic industry protected from overseas competition never adopts a policy of redoubling capital investment and expanding its R&D program at a rapid rate is a fact observed in many countries. Under certain conditions, the policy of protecting domestic industry may discourage domestic firms from investing.

A salient feature in Japan's postwar protection policy was the awareness of industries of the fact that the import and direct investment restriction policies would never in effect be permanent. Japan joined the GATT in 1955 and gradually lifted one trade restriction after another. Although the Japanese government at that time did not consider lifting of trade restrictions the most desirable policy, it had to do so if Japan was to be accepted as a full member of the GATT and the IMF by the "Club of Advanced Industrial Nations."

External and internal pressures for liberalization also contributed greatly to the view that Japanese protection of manufacturing industries would not last long. At the start of the 1960s, pressure on Japan from the United States and other countries to open its market began mounting, and the magnitude of such pressure became a critical factor in determining the pace at which Japan opened its market.

Once liberalization became an established fact, corporate behavior, especially incentives for investment, was subject to government influence in a substantial way. Many of the indigenous industries, such as the automobile, computer, and other machinery industries, were considerably less competitive than their U.S. and European counterparts. Each firm was quite aware of sustaining a possible defeat in the event of the liberalization of the Japanese market. Consequently, the major concern of each firm, under a temporary protection policy certain to be lifted in the future, must have been how to gain a sufficiently competitive edge prior to liberalization.

The policy of temporary protection is particularly important when the industry is oligopolistic. As made clear by Spence (1979), the behavior pattern of firms in an oligopolistic market varies depending on whether the market is in a growth phase or a stable phase. When the market is growing rapidly, as in the case of many industries in Japan during the high-growth era, the short-term profit is not as significant as it appears. The primary target of each firm should be to obtain as much competitive strength as possible and as stable a share of the market as possible can be secured in the long run.

The share ranking of firms in an industry established during a growth phase in the industry tends to be stable in the later stages. This is because capital equipment and technology accumulated in each firm during the growth stage become a commitment, weakening the incentives to invest by other firms. The levels of capital equipment and technology of rival firms affect the incentive to invest by each firm, for if the rivals have strong competitiveness provided by a large amount of capital equipment and a high technology level, the return on investment will be low. In this situation an early commitment to investment is important in order to gain a larger profit in the later stages. Competition under these conditions bears a strong resemblance to an investment race.

In Japan, this investment race was strengthened by the threat of foreign firms entering the Japanese market. The existence of overseas manufacturers was regarded as a major threat even in the protected market.

The foregoing argument brings to mind the question of the dynamic inconsistency of temporary protection policy. In most countries, once protection measures are introduced, they have a tendency to become permanent, even if they were initially intended to be temporary. Temporary protection policy can be dynamically inconsistent in that, if domestic firms simply ignore an announcement to remove protection measures in the future, the government would observe that the domestic firms have not accumulated enough capital by the end of the protection period and would be tempted to postpone liberalization. Unless the government finds a way of making a credible commitment to temporary protection, there is no way it can avoid extending the protection period.

Many countries face this inherent inconsistency in temporary protection policies. Japan's experience has been unique in this respect. As already mentioned, Japan could not avoid opening its markets, not because of a voluntary commitment to do so on the part of the Japanese government, but rather from pressure imposed by the international environment.

INDUSTRY PROMOTION UNDER
OLIGOPOLISTIC INTERACTIONS

With a serious lack of physical and financial capital, private industries found it very difficult to raise capital to establish new plants. The problem was acute in the capital-intensive industries, such as the steel, chemical, and automobile industries, for these industries had already been established in the United States and Europe, and their large economies of scale constituted high entry barriers to new entrants. Since such capital investment generally entails sunk costs, the incumbent firms have a great incentive to strategically deter new entrants by agreeing to a large investment for the purpose of securing their monopoly position. Under these circumstances, the government of an under-developed country is expected to restrain the incumbent's entry deterrence in order to promote entry and raise the country's economic welfare.

To see how this is possible, let us suppose, for the sake of simplicity, that the industry in question is initially monopolized by a foreign firm and that a potential new entrant in the home country is considering entry into the industry. The production technology is assumed to be identical for the two firms and characterized by economies of scale. The economies of scale work owing to the investment on specific capital in advance of entry, which, once invested, becomes sunk costs. When the two firms operate simultaneously, they play Cournot quantity competition in the market. Here, to highlight the foreign firm's first-mover advantage as an incumbent, we simply assume that the domestic entrant, once it enters, acts as a Stackelberg follower (in other words, it chooses its output based on the foreign firm's output so as to maximize its profit), whereas the foreign incumbent acts as a Stackelberg leader (in other words, it maximizes its profit with respect to its own output by fully predicting the domestic firm's reaction curve).[8]

The equilibrium of the present duopoly market is described by a well-known reaction-curve diagram seen in Figure 15-7. The horizontal axis measures the output of the foreign firm X, while the vertical axis measures that of the domestic firm x. The kinked curves rr_0X_0X and RR_0x_0x represent the reaction curves of the domestic and foreign firms, respectively.

Two remarks are in order here. First, the reaction curves have a kink because a sufficiently large output by the rival (e.g., for the domestic firm, more output than X_0 by the foreign firm) sufficiently lowers the market price, and neither firm is able to raise a positive profit due to large fixed costs. Second, the reaction curve of each firm, when producing a positive amount of output, is assumed to be downward sloping with respect to the rival's output. This is because the marginal revenue of each firm is assumed to be decreasing along with the rival's output.

Since the foreign firm has the first-mover's advantage as an incumbent, it will strategically choose its output level. Roughly speaking, there are two alternatives for the foreign firm: one is to accommodate the entry, the other is to deter it. When the foreign firm chooses to accommodate the entry, the best point for it is the Stackelberg leader point S, realized by producing X_L units of

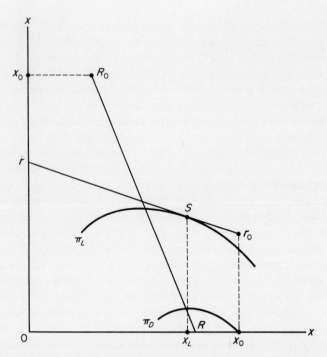

Figure 15-7 Duopoly analysis of entrance deterrence strategy of foreign supplier.

output to gain profit Π_L. In the figure, the corresponding isoprofit curve is described by the curve Π_L. When the foreign firm chooses to deter entry, it must produce up to the level X_0 and obtain the profit Π_D, the isoprofit curve of which is represented by the curve Π_D. Since the profit of the foreign firm increases as the isoprofit curves approach the horizontal axis along the reaction curve, in the situation described by Figure 15-7 the foreign firm finds it more advantageous to deter entry. Hereafter, we assume $X_0 > X_L$.

Let us first consider the welfare effect of quantitative import restriction. This policy has a remarkable effect on the entry deterrence strategy of the foreign incumbent. Even when the quantitative restriction is slightly less than the initial limit output X_0, the foreign incumbent is dissuaded from strategically deterring entry. The equilibrium switches from X_0 to the Stackelberg equilibrium: the foreign incumbent's threat of producing X_0 for entry deterrence becomes empty or not credible, and the domestic firm produces x_L and the foreign firm X_L.

The domestic firm, by capturing some portion of the market, obtains some positive profit; the foreign firm, losing some portion of the market, loses profit. The change in the total output is usually ambiguous, but it is generally the case that the total output becomes greater after the entry of the domestic firm, as illustrated in the figure. Not only does the price then decline to enhance the consumers' welfare, but the domestic industry also entertains an increase in profit. As a result, even slight quantitative import restriction, along with an extraction of the foreign firm's monopoly rent, improves the domestic country's economic welfare in this case.

One remark is in order here. As far as the foreign country's producer is concerned, the present quantitative import restriction policy amounts to a "beggar-thy-neighbor" policy. However, in the presence of foreign consumers, it does not necessarily have the same implication, for the foreign consumers also benefit from the price reduction. In fact, unless the cost condition of the domestic firm is sufficiently inferior to that of the foreign firm, such an import restriction will reduce the world's oligopolistic distortion and improve world economic welfare.

It is worthwhile comparing this result with the effects of import tariffs and production subsidies. The imposition of import tariffs or the provision of production subsidies affects the location of the firms' reaction curves: tariffs, by raising the effective cost of exports by the foreign firm, shift its reaction curve inward, while the production subsidy to the domestic firm, by reducing the marginal cost of the domestic firm, shifts its reaction curve outward.

It is quite clear that slight pecuniary incentives toward the domestic firm's potential entry, either direct (production subsidy) or indirect (import tariffs), never remove the foreign firm's entry deterrence threat. Sufficiently high rates of pecuniary incentives are needed to promote the domestic firm's entry.

CONCLUSION

We have seen that there are various features of infant-industry protection policy which can be explained through a discussion of postwar Japan's experience in industrial policy. The features that we have observed may be summarized as follows.

The changes in industrial structure and trade pattern and their impact on the gains from trade are critical to an evaluation of the infant-industry protection policy. One of the salient features of Japan's postwar infant-industry protection policy was the rapid expansion of its industrial base to borderline technology goods. This kind of broadening of the industrial base has considerable impact on the distribution of gains from trade among countries.

We can think of several different types of increasing returns to scale which are relevant for infant-industry protection policy. The underlying mechanism varies somewhat depending on the type of scale economies, and a careful analysis of each case is necessary to obtain any concrete policy implications.

A considerable number of infant industries have some oligopolistic character. Competition within an oligopolistic world has many fascinating facets which do not exist in a world of perfect competition. The forms of competition are extremely varied and not limited to price. Competition can take place in the area of R&D investment, plant investment, marketing, and so on. How much competition matters and how much influence government policy has on it depend greatly on the type of competition that prevails in a given industry. We have seen how temporary protection policy accelerated the investment race. We have also seen that temporary protection policy may prevent foreign incumbent firms from deterring the entry of domestic firms.

We are not, by any means, advocating postwar Japan's infant-industry protection policy. An overall evaluation of Japanese policy is extremely difficult, since so many different types of economic players are affected by the policy— and affected quite differently depending on their positions. Furthermore, the effects of the policy are far more complicated than indicated by the static and partial equilibrium theory of infant-industry protection.

NOTES

This chapter is heavily dependent on a recently published book by M. Itoh, K. Kiyono, M. Okuno, and K. Suzumura. *Sangyo-Seisaku no Keizai Bunseki (Economic Analysis of Industrial Policy)* (1988). We owe many of our ideas and insights to Professors Okuno and Suzumura.

1. For instance, see Krugman (1984) and Komiya, Okuno, and Suzumura (1988).
2. We have undertaken a more empirical and descriptive evaluation of postwar Japan's trade and industrial policy in other works. See Komiya and Itoh (1988) and Itoh and Kiyono (1988).
3. It should, however, be noted that the tariff burden ratio presents many difficulties as a measure of the level of tariff barriers.
4. The following argument is a simplified discussion of the analysis in Itoh and Kiyono (1987). See the original article for a more detailed and rigorous analysis.
5. For more detail, see Okuno-Fujiwara (1988).
6. The average cost curve of the individual firm is assumed to be increasing, but due to Marshallian external economies the curve shifts downward along with the overall output expansion of the industry.
7. See Matsuyama and Itoh (1985) for a more detailed discussion of this section.
8. See Dixit (1979) for a more complete analysis of entry deterrence using this type of model.

REFERENCES

Dixit, A. K. 1979. "A Model of Duopoly Suggesting a Theory of Entry Barriers." *Bell Journal of Economics* 10, 20–32.
Frank, C. R., Jr., K. S. Kim, and L. E. Westphal. 1975. South Korea (National Bureau of Economic Research). New York: Columbia University Press, pp. 70–71.
Itoh, M., and K. Kiyono. 1987. "Welfare Enhancing Export Subsidies." *Journal of Political Economy* 95(1), 115–37.
Itoh, M., and K. Kiyono. 1988. "Trade and Direct Investment." In R. Komiya, M. Okuno, and K. Suzumura, eds., *Industrial Policy of Japan*. New York: Academic Press.
Itoh, M., K. Kiyono, M. Okuno, and K. Suzumura. 1988. *Sangyo-Seisaku no Keizai Bunseki (Economic Theory of Industrial Policy)*. Tokyo: University of Tokyo Press. (in Japanese)
Keizai Kikakucho (Economic Planning Agency). Keizai Yoran (Basic Economic Data).
Komiya, R., and M. Itoh. 1988. "International Trade and Trade Policy of Japan: 1955–1984." In T. Inoguchi, and D. Okimoto, eds., *The Political Economy of Japan*,

Vol. 2: The Changing International Context. Stanford, Calif.: Stanford University Press.

Komiya, R., M. Okuno, and K. Suzumura, eds. 1988. *Industrial Policy of Japan.* New York: Academic Press.

Krugman, P. R. 1984. "The U.S. Response to Foreign Industrial Targeting." *Brookings Papers on Economic Activity* 1, 77–131.

Matsuyama, K., and M. Itoh. 1985. "Protection Policy in a Dynamic Oligopoly Market." Discussion Paper Series, Faculty of Economics, University of Tokyo.

Ogura, M., and N. Yoshino. 1988. "Zeisei to Zaiseitoyushi" (Tax System and Government Loan Program). In R. Komiya, M. Okuno, and K. Suzumura, eds., *Industrial Policy of Japan.* New York: Academic Press.

Okuno-Fujiwara, M. 1988. "Interdependence of Industries, Coordination and Strategic Promotion of an Industry." *Journal of International Economics* 25, 25–43.

Spence, A. M. 1979. "Investment Strategy and Growth in a New Market." *Bell Journal of Economics* 10, 1–19.

Zeisei Chosakai (Tax System Council). 1963. Zeisei Chosakai Kankei Siryo-shu (Data Set of Tax System Council). Government of Japan, pp. 422–23. (in Japanese)

Zeisei Chosakai (Tax System Council). 1972. Zeisei Chosakai Kankei Siryo-shu (Data Set of Tax System Council). Government of Japan, p. 187. (in Japanese)

16

Protection and International Competitiveness: A View from West Germany

GERNOT KLEPPER AND
FRANK D. WEISS

For some years now, theoretical and policy interest in the determinants of countries' international competitiveness has been increasing, probably because of the apparent imbalance in the U.S. current account. Although this may be considered a problem for macroeconomic analysis, international competitiveness means different things to different people. Because this macro phenomenon is translated into micro price changes, it has been tempting for some to treat the issue of international competitiveness from a micro point of view. Thus international competitiveness has been associated with changing levels of productivity across industries and countries, with the presence or absence of an industrial policy, and with a host of other microeconomic phenomena. The purpose of this chapter is to explore the impact of the overall pattern of protection observed in one country—West Germany—on the commodity composition of that country's international trade and on its factor content of trade, and hence on its international competitiveness in the sense of comparative advantage.

A new comprehensive data set on German trade and industrial policy measures is explored with the help of some older and newer developments in the theory of international trade. Until about a decade ago one could have, in analogy to the 2×2 Heckscher–Ohlin framework, tried to identify key factors of production, factors with whose endowments countries differed measurably, and then predict the interindustry pattern of competitiveness. Even then, however, one would have been explaining only a small and dwindling portion of an advanced country's international trade. Intra-industry trade already loomed large. Poorer countries had on average been catching up to the richer countries, implying an international equalization of factor proportions and dwindling of the share of interindustry trade, much as Heckscher–Ohlin would have predicted.

Two strands of recent developments in trade theory throw more cold water on the feasibility of predicting the commodity composition of trade. One is the modernization of the Heckscher–Ohlin to a multifactor, multicommodity world (Ethier, 1984). It turns out that in the uneven case (more commodities than factors) almost nothing can be said about commodity trade any more. This is not as bad as it sounds, because it turns out that something fairly rigorous can be said about the factor content of trade. At least equally appalling prospects for predicting commodity composition are generated by theories of trade relying on imperfect competition. In its competitive versions (perfect monopolistic competition or contestable markets) and in the absence of international differences in factor endowments—the case relevant for interindustrial country trade—it turns out which country produces which good is random (see especially Helpman and Krugman, 1985). In its noncompetitive versions, usually involving duopoly (Brander and Spencer, 1983), much can be said about market share, but not much can be said about why the particular duopolists who are in the market actually are in the market, unless it had been due to some kind of initial policy measure. But these theories, too, offer positive predictions about phenomena aside from the commodity composition of trade, such as scale of operations, which can be confronted with the evidence.

TRADE AND INDUSTRIAL POLICY
IN WEST GERMANY

West Germany has a reputation as a liberal trading nation; that reputation is partly deserved. Of course there is no centrally determined industrial policy, but a few ad hoc government initiatives and many ad hoc government responses to economic problems can be documented. They are quantitatively weighty, as will be shown. It bears emphasis that even for a member country of the European Communities (EC) trade and industrial policy is overwhelmingly a national prerogative. What is definitively in centralized EC hands is tariff policy and antidumping measures; these are quantitatively small and the first component changes only slowly subject to yet wider international agreement. Everything else—including quantitative restrictions and subsidies—is a national matter. The only function of the EC here is to see to it that one member country's trade policy does not hurt another member country, at least not without the victim's permission.

Trade and industrial policy measures are conveniently grouped into border measures and subsidies. Among the border measures, price undertakings, antidumping duties, voluntary export restraints, and quotas can be identified aside from tariffs. A catalogue of all such measures was compiled for the year 1982 on a tariff line by tariff line basis (Weiss, Heitger, Jüttemeier, Kirkpatrick, and Klepper, 1988); noteworthy is their extraordinary sectoral concentration. Estimates of tariff equivalents of these measures in the affected sectors were compiled and extrapolated to 1978 and 1985, the year before and the year after the Tokyo Round cuts in tariffs (Table 16-1).

Table 16-1 Estimates of Ad Valorem Tariff Equivalent of Border
Trade Barriers (Including Tariff) in West Germany (Percent)

Sector	Industry	Source Values (Year)	Extrapolated Values 1978	1985
1, 2	Agriculture	54.0 (1980–82)	66.0	50.0
38, 39	Food and beverages	26.7 (1972)	27.3	20.3
6	Coal mining		27.0	47.4
16	Iron and steel	20.0 (1982)	17.0	25.0
36	Textiles		28.9	26.4
37	Clothing	32.0 (1980–84)	35.0	32.0

Source: Calculated from Tyers and Anderson, (1986); Dicke (1977); Roningen and
Yeats (1976); Hamilton (1986); Bundesministerium für Ernährung, Landwirtschaft
und Forsten (various issues); Statistisches Bundesamt (various issues).

This selection of industries does not at first glance correspond well with other widely publicized measures to restrict international trade. Thus in 1981 a bilateral voluntary export restraint was negotiated limiting Japanese automobile exports to the German market to 110 percent of the 1980 level (Bronckers, 1983). In addition, since 1983 voluntary restraints on Japanese exports to the EC were negotiated for nine addition product groups: videocassette recorders, color television sets, cathode ray tubes, numerically controlled machine tools, radio receiving and transmission equipment, and quartz watches (Anjaria, Kirmani, and Petersen, 1985). These voluntary export restraints were later lifted (*Financial Times*, 1985). At the same time the EC unilaterally raised the tariff rate on videocassette recorders from 8 to 14 percent, effective January 1, 1986. In fact, new registrations of Japanese cars in Germany in 1986 amounted to about 25 percent of the market. Aside from the automobile case for a short period of time, only the voluntary export restraint on videocassette recorders seems to have been particularly effective at the outset (Hindley, 1986). Japanese exports of videocassette recorders to the EC dropped from 5 million units in 1982 to about 1.8 million units in 1985, less than the 2.3 million allowed.

As tariffs, and even some quotas, have become subject to international agreement, the preferred national policy instrument has become the subsidy. These have been compiled for Germany and include current and capital transfers as shown in the national accounts, as well as the subsidy equivalent of government-guaranteed loans to business.[1] In addition, discriminatory direct and indirect tax rates are accounted for. The data are presented in Appendix 16-1, Table 16-8. Together with nominal tariffs, presented in Table 16-9, and the information in Table 16-1, Corden's (1971) concept of effective protection was implemented using the 1980 German input–output table. The results of the calculations are seen in Table 16-2.

The pattern of assistance to industries in West Germany is clearly biased toward old industries lacking competitiveness, although these are not the exclusive beneficiaries. Agriculture and coal mining clearly profit most. Coal mining and steel have seen their protection shoot up since the mid-1970s. Shipbuilding also is among the heavily promoted industries. Of the modern industries only aircraft (Airbus) stands out; support programs of the late sev-

enties for elecronic data processing and nuclear energy industry are not notice-
able in the data. They are dwarfed by support for old industries, including
railways. All in all, the data show that although West Germany may have no
centralized industrial policy, the importance to individual industries of industrial policy measures, including subsidies, can be very great indeed.[2] The pattern of subsidization reduces the selectivity of border measures only slightly.

COMPETITIVENESS AND PROTECTION IN WEST GERMANY

Commodity Composition—Ad Hoc Approaches

The interindustry structure of industries' competitiveness needs to be measured in such a way that the effect of macroeconomic variables that impinge
on the trade balance is allowed for. One such measure is Liesner's (1958) and
Balassa's (1967) concept of revealed comparative advantage (RCA). The version chosen here is

$$RCA = \ln \left[\frac{(x_i/m_i)}{\Sigma_k x_k / \Sigma_k m_k)} \right]$$

where x and m refer to exports and imports, respectively, and the indices run
over industries at a point in time.

These values were calculated for West German industries' trade with the
total world and for selected regions in the mid-1970s and the mid-1980s. The
results are presented in Table 16-3. It is immediately apparent that the interindustry structure of competitiveness changed very little overall. This even applies to the industries identified as objects of pronounced trade or industrial
policy—coal mining, iron and steel, aircraft, data processing equipment, and
textiles and clothing—which changed but little in RCA values. Indeed, some
gained and some lost in competitivness. Traditionally strong German export
industries, such as mechanical engineering and road vehicles, declined slightly,
but precision mechanics and electrical engineering declined more noticeably.
The relative changes in each industry's position is much more pronounced in
trade with Japan and trade with the LDCs than in trade with the total world.
In general, moreover, there is a decline in the variation of competitiveness
across industries, which is consistent with declining international differences
in factor endowments.

As Leamer (1984) has not tired of pointing out, such commodity patterns
cannot be rationalized by Heckscher–Ohlin in a more than two-factor world.
Yet the econometric evidence accumulated to date seems remarkably robust,
and deserves to be taken seriously.[3] This suggests that the observed stability is
due to something else. Perhaps cross-industry regressions merely test partial
equilibrium response by different industries to changes in relative factor prices.
Be that as it may, the results of regressions to explain the interindustry pattern

Table 16-2 Effective Rates of Assistance in West Germany (Corden Method)

Sector	Industry	Mid-1970s[a]			Mid-1980s[a]		
		EIT (1978) +	ES (1974) =	ERA	EIT (1985) +	ES (1984) =	ERA
	Traded goods						
1, 2	Agriculture, forestry, and fisheries[b]	295.8	201.1	497.9	149.0	198.6	347.6
6–8	Mining						
6	Coal mining	70.3	38.7	109.0	200.2	116.5	316.7
7, 8	Other mining	–4.1	16.7	12.6	–4.0	6.0	2.0
	Manufacturing						
	Intermediate goods						
9	Chemicals	15.1	2.0	17.1	8.6	2.4	11.0
10	Petroleum refining	10.7	5.7	16.4	10.7	5.0	15.7
12	Rubber goods	11.7	2.9	14.6	7.0	3.8	10.8
13	Stone goods	7.8	0.3	8.1	4.9	0.3	5.2
16	Iron and steel	–3.1	1.0	–2.1	40.8	24.4	65.2
17	Nonferrous metals	10.8	3.6	14.4	9.4	2.8	12.2
18	Foundries	10.6	1.3	11.9	4.4	1.0	5.4
19	Drawing mills, cold rolling mills	7.7	0.4	8.1	–2.0	0.6	–1.4
30	Wood	21.5	1.8	23.3	15.7	2.9	18.6
32	Pulp, paper, and paperboard	18.4	2.1	20.5	13.1	1.2	14.3
	Investment goods						
20	Structural engineering, rolling stock	4.8	2.1	6.9	–1.3	1.7	0.4
21	Mechanical engineering	2.6	2.2	4.8	0.6	3.1	3.7
22	Electronic data processing equipment[c]	8.0	5.8	13.8	9.1	2.1	11.2
23	Road vehicles	10.0	1.3	11.3	10.7	1.8	12.5
24	Shipbuilding	–7.2	9.8	2.6	–4.7	24.6	19.9
25	Aircraft, aerospace[d]	15.6	45.0	60.6	14.1	20.8	34.9
26	Electrical engineering	8.6	3.7	12.3	4.8	3.4	8.2
27	Precision mechanics, optics, watches	7.2	1.6	8.8	5.1	2.3	7.4
28	Metal products	7.8	1.5	9.3	2.7	1.7	4.4
	Consumer goods						
	Plastic products	15.2	1.8	17.0	6.5	1.9	8.4
	Precision ceramics	7.2	1.7	8.9	5.5	2.8	8.3

15	Glass and glass products	10.4	1.4	7.8	17.8	2.4	10.0
29	Musical instruments, toys, sporting goods, jewelry	8.1	1.0	8.5	9.1	1.3	9.8
31	Wood products	11.9	0.9	5.7	12.8	1.3	7.0
33	Paper and paperboard products	27.4	1.9	19.5	29.3	3.7	23.2
34	Printing	2.0	3.9	0.8	5.9	4.5	5.3
35	Leather, leather goods, shoes	8.7	0.5	6.8	9.2	0.9	7.7
36	Textiles[c]	55.5	1.9	48.0	57.4	2.4	50.4
37	Clothing	84.0	2.5	71.0	86.5	2.8	73.8
38, 39	Food and beverages	47.6	3.6	31.2	51.2	3.1	34.3
40	Tobacco	124.0	26.2	124.0	150.2	37.1	161.0
	Nontraded goods						
3, 4, 5	Electricity, gas, water	−40.6	2.0	−46.4	−38.6	1.9	−44.5
41, 42	Construction	−5.5	0.4	−4.5	−5.1	0.8	−3.7
43, 44	Retail and wholesale trade	−2.4	0.7	−2.1	−1.7	0.8	−1.3
45, 46, 48	Transportation						
45	Railways	−5.9	64.5	−6.1	58.6	100.0	93.9
46	Water transport	−7.4	20.3	−6.6	12.9	23.3	16.7
48	Other transport	−4.8	14.8	−4.3	10.0	10.3	6.0
47	Communication (Federal Post Office)	−1.9	2.7	−1.8	0.8	7.1	5.3
49, 50	Banking and insurance						
49	Banking[f]						
50	Insurance	−2.5	4.8	−2.1	2.3	10.2	8.1
52–55	Other private services						
52	Hotels and restaurants	−23.5	2.2	−20.6	−21.3	1.6	−19.0
53	Education, research, publishing	−7.1	10.3	−5.5	3.2	8.5	3.0
54	Health and veterinary services	−3.1	11.7	−2.4	8.6	20.1	17.7
55	Miscellaneous private services	−3.0	1.8	−2.4	−1.2	2.4	0.0
	Coefficient of variation	2.8	2.7	2.6	2.6	2.4	2.3

Source: Weiss, Heitger, Jüttemeier, Kirkpatrick, and Klepper, 1988, p. 26.

[a] EIT = effective implicit tariff protection; ES = effective subsidization; ERA = effective rate of assistance.

[b] Inputs at world prices approximately equal value added at world prices. Implicit nominal protection rates just above actual rates yield negative effective protection.

[c] Own-input tariffs set at zero.

[d] All input tariffs set at zero.

[e] Agricultural input implicit tariff set at zero.

[f] Due to writeoffs, banks' intermediate inputs approximately equal gross output. Effective rate estimate unstable.

Table 16-3 Revealed Comparative Advantage of West German Industries, 1978 and 1985

Sector	Industry	World		Japan		LDCs	
		1978	1985	1978	1985	1978	1985
6–8	Mining						
6	Coal mining	−2.56	−2.44	3.86	5.18	−4.09	−5.42
	Manufacturing						
	Intermediate goods						
9	Chemicals	0.35	0.14	1.26	1.32	1.74	1.37
10	Petroleum refining	−1.65	−2.19	1.57	0.89	−1.44	−3.29
12	Rubber goods	−0.04	−0.20	−0.31	−0.09	1.40	0.32
13	Stone goods	−0.85	−0.19	−0.35	−0.26	−0.14	0.51
16	Iron and steel	−0.14	0.13	−3.59	−0.96	1.29	0.98
17	Nonferrous metals	−1.28	−0.76	1.33	2.13	−2.76	−1.37
18	Foundries	0.15	0.30	−2.21	−0.72	1.78	1.96
19	Drawing mills, cold rolling mills	0.56	0.37	−0.98	−0.40	3.36	1.36
30	Wood	−1.58	−0.98	−1.20	2.21	−3.72	−2.88
32	Pulp, paper, and paperboard	−1.46	−0.88	1.72	1.29	1.76	−0.19
	Investment goods						
20	Structural engineering, rolling stock	0.32	0.81	1.81	2.21	2.22	2.75
21	Mechanical engineering	1.16	0.95	1.44	0.74	4.22	2.87
22	Electronic data processing equipment	0.17	−0.23	0.57	−1.68	1.55	−0.95

23	Road vehicles	1.06	0.89	1.11	−1.10	3.61	2.19
24	Shipbuilding	0.50	0.29	−4.59	−3.80	3.80	0.39
25	Aircraft, aerospace	−1.16	−0.44	−3.33	1.73	0.62	0.02
26	Electrical engineering	0.54	0.10	−1.14	−1.27	1.71	0.37
27	Precision mechanics, optics, watches	0.53	0.04	−0.74	−0.84	1.41	0.36
28	Metal products	0.81	0.41	−0.42	0.20	2.11	0.76
	Consumer goods						
11	Plastic products	0.33	0.19	−0.58	−0.21	0.15	0.20
14	Precision ceramics	0.33	−0.23	−2.34	−0.22	2.10	−0.44
15	Glass and glass products	−0.25	−0.06	−0.04	1.74	1.35	0.31
29	Musical instruments, toys, sporting goods, jewelry	−0.77	−0.24	−1.71	−0.14	−2.30	−1.55
31	Wood products	−0.38	−0.23	−1.19	1.93	−1.54	0.56
33	Paper and paperboard products	0.04	0.32	−1.03	0.59	1.80	1.18
34	Printing	0.70	0.69	1.76	0.93	1.69	1.38
35	Leather, leather goods, shoes	−1.32	−1.35	−0.23	1.08	−2.66	−2.71
36	Textiles	−0.90	−0.55	−0.43	0.28	−2.16	−1.86
37	Clothing	−1.25	−1.06	−1.97	1.08	−3.87	−3.50

Source: Calculated from Statistisches Bundesamt, Fachserie 7, Reihe 7, various issues.

of competitiveness by human and physical capital intensity are shown in Table 16-4. They are—not without reason—only partly convincing. The evidence is certainly consistent with the observation that Germany is still a relatively capital-rich country, but in trade with the world as a whole the explained variation is low. Factor proportions alone explain nothing about German–Japanese bilateral trade. Only in trade with the LDCs do the hypotheses have any explanatory power worth noting, a result now seen frequently. This outcome should not be too surprising given the relatively small difference in per capita incomes and hence relative resource endowments between Germany and its larger trading partners.

Another cause of this problem may be that other countries' structures of protection are codetermining trade outcomes in a systematic way, and if these could be included in the analysis, the statistical results would be more convincing. For the case of Germany's bilateral trade with Japan this was made possible by the availability of Shouda's (1982) effective tariff protection calculation for the pre–Tokyo Round and the post–Tokyo Round periods. The statistical analysis was undertaken not because relative bilateral trade balances have any welfare significance, but because it seems like a conceivable way to isolate the effect of trade policy on trade flows. These rates, insofar as they could reasonably be assigned to the German industrial classification, are seen in Table 16-10.

The interindustry structure of effective tariff protection in Japan is not so different from that of other mature industrial countries. Raw material–intensive goods, including food and beverages, are protected more than most industries. The usefulness of the tariff protection estimates for further analysis might seem to be limited by the widely discussed apparent prevalance in Japan of other border measures and financial assistance. This is not the place to enter that discussion.[4] Suffice it to say that industrial policy measures in Japan appear to be uncorrelated with tariff protection across industries (Heitger and Stehn, 1988).[5] The results of the new regressions are presented in Table 16-5. First, for the early period, factor proportions cum human capital, are confirmed. Second, the respective levels of effective protection exhibit the correct sign. Protection does keep out imports, and it restricts imports more than it hinders exports. For the later period, factor proportions break down, but this is entirely consistent with Japan's rapid catching-up process relative to Germany and other countries. Nevertheless, the German effective protection structure hinders exports from Japan. Finally, the change in Germany's interindustry competitiveness is consistent with the change in Germany's trade and industrial policy.[6] The significant negative sign on human capital is—once again—consistent with Japan's relatively rapid growth.

The technology-based hypotheses of Vernon and others fared uniformly poorly in explaining the interindustry pattern of competitiveness. Statistical tests of the influence of R&D intensity of industries were unsuccessful. Vernon (1979) suggested that rapid dissemination of innovations from one country to the next through the channel of the multinational corporation would tend to produce this result for international flows of manufactured goods.

Table 16-4 Regression Results[a]: Revealed Comparative Advantage[b] as a Function of Human and Physical Capital Intensity,[c] 1978 and 1985

Equation	Region/Country	Constant	Exogenous Variables		$\bar{R}^2$	F
			1978			
1	World	−7.23 (−1.71)	+0.80 HUM CAP (2.12)[d]	−0.14 PHYS CAP (−0.50)	0.09	2.29
2	Japan	−8.75 (−1.96)	+0.28 HUM CAP (0.34)	+0.46 PHYS CAP (−0.72)	−0.04	0.47
3	LDCs	−36.62 (−3.78)[d]	+3.40 HUM CAP (3.87)[d]	+0.08 PHYS CAP (0.11)	0.37	8.82[d]
			1985			
4	World	−6.97 (−1.96)	+0.71 HUM CAP (2.46)[d]	−0.12 PHYS CAP (−0.54)	0.13	3.06[d]
5	Japan	8.44 (0.94)	−0.63 HUM CAP (−0.87)	−0.06 PHYS CAP (−0.10)	−0.04	0.46
6	LDCs	−27.15 (−3.00)[d]	+2.26 HUM CAP (3.10)[d]	+0.06 PHYS CAP (0.10)	0.25	5.46[d]

Source: Statistisches Bundesamt (c) and (e); Baumgart, Boehme, and Schintke, various issues.

[a]Cross-sectional analysis; manufacturing industries, oil refining exluded ($N = 28$). All variables in natural logarithms.

[b]Revealed comparative advantage (RCA), see text.

[c]Human capital intensity is the difference between average and unskilled worker earnings per unit labor in each industry; physical capital intensity is measured as the net value of equipment and plant (current prices) per unit labor in each industry. t values in parentheses.

[d]Significant at the 5 percent level.

Table 16-5 Protection and Human Capital as Determinants of West German–Japanese Trade, 1978–85[a]

Endogenous variable		Constant	Exogenous Variables[c]			R^2	F
RCA[b]	=	−25.28 (−4.88)[d]	+2.16 HUM CAP (4.84)[d]	1978 +0.93 ERA G (4.94)[d]	−0.35 EFF PROT J (−2.17)[d]	0.70	19.67[d]
RCA	=	2.02 (0.25)	−0.21 HUM CAP (−0.32)	1985 +0.71 ERA G (2.43)[d]	−0.39 EFF PROT J (−1.52)	0.20	3.01
ΔRCA	=	24.16 (4.56)[d]	−2.17 HUM CAP (−4.40)[d]	+0.61 ΔERA G (2.89)[d]	+0.15 ΔEFF PROT J (0.36)	0.47	8.00[d]

Source: Weiss 1988, p. 121.

[a]Cross-sectional analysis (N = 25). Observations are for those industries for which Japanese tariffs are available. All variables in natural logarithms.

[b]revealed comparative advantage;

[c]HUM CAP, human capital (1978); ERA G, total effective assistance in West Germany; EFF PROT J, effective tariff protection in Japan; Δ, change from 1978 to 1985. *t* values in parentheses.

[d]Significant at the 5 percent level.

JPACK6 8324$$1602
Comp "A"   Oxford

JPACK6 8324$$T30
Comp "C"   Oxford

The newer theories of international trade are difficult to test across industries on trade data. In the competitive versions a domestic industrial policy may improve welfare by getting domestic producers to move down their average cost curves, that is, to expand output, attaining a more efficient scale of production. Specific predictions about which country produces which commodity or which product variant, on the other hand, are scarce (Krugman, 1980). The oligopolistic versions of the newer theories, in turn, do not make predictions about trade flows in all industries, but only in industries that are characterized by few producers and, of necessity, limited entry.

Instead of correlating changes in trade and industrial policy with trade flows, they can be correlated with changes in average firm size across industries. It has been argued that a rise in protection favors inefficient entry by new firms (Horstmann and Markusen, 1986); that is, these firms move up the average cost curve. The same may be true if competitive pressures from abroad force distinct industries to reduce capacities and discharge employees. If in such a situation policymakers raise protection, the process of shrinkage is held up and firms—perhaps especially those of small scale—which otherwise would have to stop producing now operate in a less economical range of production. Thus in analogy to Horstmann and Markusen, one might conceivably speak of "insufficient exit."

That such tendencies—less efficient scale of production in highly protected industries—have been at work in West German manufacturing industries is illustrated in Table 16-6. As can be seen (equation 1), the change in average firm size, measured in percentage changes in real sales per firm, has been lowest in those industries which since the late seventies received the highest additional effective assistance. In addition, another observation is in line with the foregoing hypothesis of inefficient entry (or exit). If one compares labor productivity changes in small and large firms by industries, the relative productivity growth of small firms in an industry turns out to be smaller the greater the increase in protection. Both empirical results lend support to the foregoing hypotheses, according to which increases of protection lead to an inefficient scale of production, be it because of entry of new firms or the insufficient exit of redundant firms. Similar results for Canadian manufacturing industries support this view.

Completely independent data further harden the view that, on average, trade policy encourages inefficient producers to remain in the market. For years the Ifo-Institute in Munich has surveyed German manufacturing firms about the intentions of their investment, much as McGraw-Hill does for U.S. firms. Three motives are distinguished: capacity expansion, replacement, and rationalization.

Capacity expansion is not quite what Baldwin and Gorecki (1985) call the rationalization effect, but it comes close. Presumably investment aimed at capacity expansion will lead to larger optimum scale, that is, push the cost curve down and out. A rank correlation between the share of firms in an industry reporting capacity expansion as their prime motive and the change in effective assistance equals -0.35, easily significant at the 5 percent level.

Table 16-6 Firm Size, Efficiency, and Effective Rates of Assistance, 1978–85[a]

Equation	Endogenous variables[b]		Constant	Exogenous Variable[c]		$\bar{R}^2$	F	N
1	ΔFS	=	15.71	−0.63	ΔERA	0.14	5.40[d]	28
			(3.89)[d]	(−2.32)[d]				
2	Δ REL PROD	=	0.77	−0.003	ΔERA	0.17	6.18[d]	27
			(28.22)[d]	(−2.49)[d]				

Source: Weiss, Heitger, Jüttemeier, Kirkpatrick, and Klepper, 1988, p. 122.

[a]Cross-sectional regression analysis.

[b]ΔFS, percent change in real sales per firm, 1978–85; ΔREL PROD, relative growth of labor productivity of small to large firms, 1978–85.

[c]ΔERA, change in total effective protection, 1978–82/85 (%). *t* values in parentheses.

[d]Significant at the 5 percent level.

Factor Content of Trade

Measuring interindustry comparative advantage and competitiveness on the commodity structure of trade has no theoretical justification on Heckscher–Ohlin grounds, in a world with many factors and more goods than factors. Factor proportion theory cannot predict the commodity composition of trade, since the factor endowment vector leaves indeterminate the commodity structure of production (Leamer, 1984; Travis, 1964). Comparative advantage measured in relative resource endowments can therefore be reflected only in the factor content of exports and imports.

The factor content version of the Heckscher–Ohlin theorem can be used to analyze comparative advantage in a multicommodity, multifactor framework. Empirical tests of the Heckscher–Ohlin–Vanek theorem, however, come out with cautious support (Bowen, Leamer, and Sveikauskas, 1987; Leamer, 1984). Yet, as long as there is no superior alternative, Heckscher–Ohlin–Vanek is taken as the correct theory.

Of course, factor proportion theory is based on factor price equalization. Protection, on the other hand, undermines equalization of prices. In a simple model distortions due to protection are incorporated and the factor content of trade in this price-distorted world is computed. Whereas in Bowen and colleagues (1987) a direct computation of the factor content of net exports is possible because of the assumed factor price equalization, in our case computation of factor services embodied in net exports would require computation of factor content of imports via the factor requirement matrices of the countries in the rest of the world (see Helpman, 1984), an infeasible approach. Here we rely on predicting trade in factor services from the differences between factors embodied in production and factors embodied in consumption, thus getting a prediction of protection-distorted trade in factors.

The Model

Net exports of factors of some country can be expressed as the difference between factors absorbed in production and factors absorbed in consumption (see Bowen, Leamer, and Sveikauskas, 1987):

$$\mathbf{AT} = \mathbf{AQ} - \mathbf{AC} \qquad (16\text{-}1)$$

where

$\mathbf{A} = K \times N$ matrix of factor input requirements (direct and indirect input of each of K factors needed to produce one unit of output in one of N industries)

$\mathbf{T} = N \times 1$ vector of net trade flows

$\mathbf{Q} = N \times 1$ vector of final output

$\mathbf{C} = N \times 1$ vector of final consumption

Bowen and co-workers (1987) show that under the assumptions of

identical commodity prices worldwide,
identical and homothetic tastes of consumers,
identical technologies, that is, $\mathbf{A}_\ell = \mathbf{A} \, \forall \, \ell$ countries, and
full employment of factors,

the relationship between net trade in factor services and factor endowments of the domestic country is defined by

$$\mathbf{AT} = \mathbf{V} - s\mathbf{V_W} \qquad (16\text{-}2)$$

where

$\mathbf{V} = K \times 1$ vector of resource endowments of the country

$\mathbf{V_W} = K \times 1$ vector of world resource endowments

$s = (Y - B)/Y_W =$ the country's consumption share

$B =$ trade balance

$Y, Y_W =$ respectively, GNP of domestic country and world GNP

Hence each country is a net exporter of factor services with which it is relatively well endowed and a net importer of its relatively scarce factors.

Under tariff protection, factor as well as commodity prices are no longer equalized. Still, an equivalent relation for the factor content of net exports can be derived. The production side of the model is determined by fixed and equal input coefficients in all countries. Consumers have identical tastes. Consumer demand is derived from a log-linear (Cobb–Douglas) utility function.

If all trade barriers consist of ad valorem tariffs, τ_i, the internal price of commodity i is p_i, and its world market price is π_i, then

$$p_i = \pi_i (1 + \tau_i) \qquad (16\text{-}3)$$

The consumption decision of domestic consumers with log-linear utility functions is

$$p_i C_i^* = \alpha_i \bar{Y}^*, \qquad \forall_i = 1, \dots, N \qquad (16\text{-}4)$$

where

$\alpha_i =$ expenditure share of commodity i

$Y^* =$ internal absorption at domestic prices

and an asterisk (*) denotes variables depending on domestic prices.

For the rest of the world we have

$$p_i C_i^* + \pi_i C_i^W = \alpha_i (\bar{Y}^W + \bar{Y}^*), \qquad \forall_i = 1, \ldots, N \qquad (16\text{-}5)$$

where

C_i^W = consumption of commodity i in the rest of the world

$\bar{Y}^W$ = internal absorption in the rest of the world

Consumption of each commodity in the rest of the world equals production plus net exports of the home country:

$$\mathbf{C}^W = \mathbf{Q}^W + \mathbf{T}^* \qquad (16\text{-}6)$$

By combining Equations 16-4 to 16-6, the vector of domestic consumption can be expressed as

$$\mathbf{C}^* = s [1 + \mathbf{r}]^{-1} (\mathbf{Q}^W + \mathbf{T}^*) \qquad (16\text{-}7)$$

where

$$s = \bar{Y}^* / Y_W$$

and $[1 + \tau]$ is an $N \times N$ diagonal matrix with $(1 + \tau_i)$, $i = 1, \ldots, N$, on the diagonal.

Since domestic and world market prices of traded goods are not equalized nontraded goods prices diverge as well. This effect of changes in the real exchange rate due to protection can be incorporated in the model. Suppose that of the N commodities m are traded and $N - m$ are nontraded goods, that is, $i = 1, \ldots, m, m + 1, \ldots, N$. Then the difference between domestic and world market prices for $i = 1, \ldots, m$ is determined by equation 16-3, whereas for the nontraded goods, $i = m + 1, \ldots, N$, the difference between p_i and π_i depends on the domestic and rest of the world factor price vectors $\mathbf{W}^*$ and $\mathbf{W}$.

Premultiplying the net trade equation

$$\mathbf{T}^* = \mathbf{Q} - \mathbf{C}^* \qquad (16\text{-}8)$$

by the matrix of factor input requirements A and using Equation 16-7 yields

$$A\mathbf{T}^* = A\mathbf{Q} - sA [1 + \tau]^{-1} (\mathbf{Q}^W + \mathbf{T}^*) \qquad (16\text{-}9)$$

Full employment implies $\mathbf{V} = A\mathbf{Q}$, hence

$$A\mathbf{T}^* = \mathbf{V} - sA [1 + \tau]^{-1} (\mathbf{Q}^W + \mathbf{T}^*) \qquad (16\text{-}10)$$

Equation 16-10 has a form similar to the free trade equation (16-2). The protection-induced distortions in consumption and trade change the second term on the right-hand side of Equation 16-10. Under free trade the vector of domestic consumption is proportional to world consumption. In the case of protection, domestic consumption that is protection distorted is proportional to consumption in the rest of the world after adjusting to protection. In other words, the quantity version of the Heckscher–Ohlin–Vanek theorem could be reproduced, if the rest of the world had the same protection-distorted consumption pattern.

Another interpretation makes an analogy between the consumption losses of protection and efficiency losses in production. Postmultiplying the factor requirement matrix $\mathbf{A}$ with the tariff matrix $[1 + \tau]^{-1}$ results in protection-adjusted coefficients

$$a_{ji}^* = a_{ji}/(1 + \tau_i), \qquad i = 1, \ldots, N; \quad j = 1, \ldots, K$$

that is, each column vector of $\mathbf{A}$ is multiplied by $1 + \tau_i$. The factor content of the world consumption vector is then proportional to the domestic, if the protection-distorted production technology $\mathbf{A}[1 + \tau]^{-1}$ is used.

The classical Heckscher–Ohlin–Vanek equation (16-2) is based on commodity price and factor price equalization. Computing $\mathbf{V} - s\mathbf{V_w}$ therefore yields a prediction of the factor content of trade according to the country's relative resource endowment when *free trade* prevails. Computing the right-hand side of Equation 16-10, however, results in the prediction of the factor content of trade with free trade replaced by protection.

Equations 16-2 and 16-10 then allow a comparison of the factor content of net trade under free trade and under protection, provided the factor proportions theory adequately predicts net trade in factor services. An empirical computation of Equation 16-2 is straightforward. Equation 16-10, however, can be determined only by directly computing the second term on the right-hand side. To do this, Equation 16-10 must be expressed in slightly different form, as shown in the next section.

Computation of Factor Content of Trade

The production side of the model under identical technologies and Leontief technology can be expressed as

$$\mathbf{A} = \mathbf{W}^{-1}\boldsymbol{\theta}\boldsymbol{\Pi} = \mathbf{W}^{*-1}\boldsymbol{\theta}^*\mathbf{P} \tag{16-11}$$

where

$\boldsymbol{\theta} = K \times N$ matrix of factor shares $\theta_{ji} = W_j V_j/\Pi_i Q_i$
$\boldsymbol{\theta}^* = K \times N$ matrix of factor shares $\theta_{ji}^* = W_j^* V_j^*/P_i Q_i$
$\mathbf{P},\boldsymbol{\Pi} = $ diagonal matrices of domestic and world market prices

$\boldsymbol{\theta}$ can be thought of as the world input–output matrix, whereas $\boldsymbol{\theta}^*$ is derived from the domestic matrix. Equation 16-10 then becomes

$$\mathbf{A}\mathbf{T}^* = \mathbf{V} - s\mathbf{W}^{*-1}\boldsymbol{\theta}^*\mathbf{P}[1 + \tau]^{-1}(\mathbf{Q}^\mathrm{W} + \mathbf{T}^*) \tag{16-10'}$$

Premultiplying by the matrix $\mathbf{W}^*$ yields

$$\begin{aligned}\mathbf{W}^*\mathbf{A}\mathbf{T}^* &= \mathbf{W}^*\mathbf{V} - s\boldsymbol{\theta}^*\boldsymbol{\Pi}(\mathbf{Q}^\mathrm{W} + \mathbf{T}^*) \\ &= \mathbf{W}^*\mathbf{V} - s\mathbf{V}_\mathrm{W}^* - s\boldsymbol{\theta}^*\boldsymbol{\Pi}\mathbf{T}^*\end{aligned} \tag{16-12}$$

Equation 16-12 is very similar to 16-2, except that domestic and foreign factor endowments are valued in domestic factor prices and $\mathbf{V}_\mathrm{W}^*$ denotes a fictitious value of factor endowments in the rest of the world. It can be interpreted as the value of factors necessary to product rest of the world output with domestic factor shares.

With this approach the protection-distorted value of factor content of net exports can be computed by using the right-hand side of Equaton 16-12. The computation requires data on output by commodity groups from many countries. Availability of comparable statistical information has restricted the commodity vector to twenty-two commodity groups. The rest of the world had to be reduced to thirty countries, and presumed Heckscher–Ohlin trade with Africa and nonmarket economies could not be included. The included countries cover about 70 percent of German exports and imports. If Belgium, Luxembourg, and Switzerland—countries with resource endowments very similar to Germany's—were also included, this ratio would increase to well over 80 percent (see Appendix 16-2 for details).

Six factors were identified: land, high-quality labor (labor 1), low-quality labor (labor 2), energy, minerals, and capital. Again, the choice was dictated more by the statistical sources than by theoretical considerations. The endowment categories labor 1 and labor 2 in particular do not fit the division into the three groups—professional, craftsperson, and low-skill—which presumably better represent German relative labor endowments. It is generally believed that Germany has a comparative advantage in the quality of craftspersons (see Weiss, 1983, and the literature cited there). This specific group cannot be extracted from international statistics. Craftspersons are included in less-skilled labor.

Table 16-7 summarizes computation of Equations 16-2 and 16-12. The original Heckscher–Ohlin–Vanek equation (16-2) predicts the free trade factor content of net exports. For one sample of thirty countries Germany would import more than ten times its own endowment in land. Labor 2, energy, and minerals would also be imported in large amounts. Imports of skill labor amounted to only 37 percent of endowments. Germany's relatively abundant capital is the only factor it would export. These findings are very similar to Leamer's (1984) relative abundance profile of Germany, which is based on a sixty country data set.

Surprisingly, computation of the protection-distorted factor content of production and consumption results in very low levels of trade in factors. Except for 8 percent of net imports of energy, all other factors are zero or close to it (see Table 16-7). For minerals no value is reported, since imputing a rent on minerals from German value added yields a negative or at most zero value. The results for land are questionable for the same reason. Imputing a reasonable

Table 16-7 Predicted Factor Content of German Net Exports
(Percentage of Factor Content of Production)

Sector	Free Trade[a]	Protection[b]
Land	− 1076	0.0
Capital	+ 7	− 0.5
Labor 1	− 37	4.0
Labor 2	− 99	3.4
Energy	− 86	− 8.1
Minerals	− 160	

[a]$AT/V = (V - sV_W)/V.$

[b]$W*AT*/\Theta*PQ = (\Theta*PQ - s\Theta*\Pi Q^W - s\Theta*\Pi T*)/\Theta*PQ.$

rent on land would drive capital and labor prices in agriculture down to unrealistic values.

The main result is that protection substantially reduces the measure of implicit trade in factors of production through actual trade in goods. This is what one should expect: protection probably protects those industries that use intensively the factors of production that the country does not have in abundance. Thus protection moves trade from free trade closer to autarky with zero net implicit trade in the factors of production.

Table 16-2 reveals that agriculture and coal mining, which use intensively some of the resources that are relatively scarce in Germany (i.e., land and minerals), are also highly protected sectors. Since the protective structure is concentrated in these sectors, the trade in factor services of land can be expected to be much lower than under a free-trade regime. Similar arguments explain the reduction in the net imports of labor. Labor-intensive industries like clothing experience considerable protection. In all, the results indicate that Germany's protective system distorts the structure of production away from comparative advantage and thus wastes the benefits from the international division of labor.

CONCLUSION

Macro problems such as the U.S. current-account deficit or the catching up of developing countries, most notably the NICs in the Pacific rim, have attracted the attention of policymakers, the public, and the scientific community alike. International competitiveness is the catchword in this regard. In this chapter international competitiveness is associated with comparative advantage. The empirical evidence on industrial and trade policy is summarized and its likely implication for West Germany's international competitiveness is investigated.

West Germany's trade and industrial policy measures can be characterized as highly sectorally selective. A relatively low average level of effective assistance comes with a high variance across industries. Especially old industries together with agriculture get the lion's share of assistance. Of modern industries only aerospace stands out with high protection, though it is not exceptional in an international perspective.

In terms of revealed comparative advantage West Germany is competitive in the so-called medium-technology areas. Compared to other industrial countries its lack in competitiveness in high-tech industries and low variation in RCAs is noteworthy. In addition, a decline in variation can be observed. This could be the result of declining differences in relative factor endowments of countries; it also could be the result of industrial and trade policy measures supporting industries with declining comparative advantage.

Indeed, effective rates of assistance reveal that old industries such as the iron–steel complex, shipbuilding, textiles, and agriculture receive most of the assistance. It is generally believed that West Germany's comparative advantage has more or less disappeared in these industries. A regression on bilateral trade and protection with Japan confirms that RCAs are positively affected by protection.

In a multicountry, multifactor world, an analysis of the commodity structure of trade is difficult to justify theoretically. In fact, it is factor services embodied in commodities which are exchanged according to comparative advantage. Comparative advantage is therefore revealed only in the factor content of trade. A computation of West Germany's hypothetical free-trade factor content of trade according to the quantity version of the Heckscher–Ohlin theorem predicts net imports of factor services of all factors but capital.

This result contrasts sharply with the predicted factor content of trade if protection is introduced in the model. Except for energy, there is very little net trade in factors compared to West Germany's factor endowment. Like the low variation in the commodity structure of trade, this suggests that protection reduces the exploitation of West Germany's comparative advantage and reduces international competitiveness.

West Germany's intra-industry trade has also been affected by trade and industrial policies. Regression analyses confirm that protected industries have a structure with inefficient firm size and low productivity growth. By combining this with the other evidence, it is fair to conclude that structural change has been retarded. West Germany has slowed down its adjustment to global changes in international factor endowments and comparative advantage. Its trade and industrial policy has resulted in a loss of international competitiveness.

Table 16-8 Nominal Subsidization in West Germany, 1974 and 1984

Sector	Industry	Absolute Amount (Millions of DM)		Producer Subsidy Equivalent, s (%)[a]	
		1974	1984	1974	1984
	Traded goods				
1, 2	Agriculture, forestry, fisheries	10,769	20,216	22.2	28.0
6–8	Mining	2,094	5,676	10.0	16.3
6	Coal mining	1,913	5,528	10.7	18.2
7, 8	Other mining	181	148	5.8	3.2
	Manufacturing	6,476	13,482	0.7	0.9
	Intermediate goods				
9	Chemicals	562	1,081	0.5	0.6
10	Petroleum refining	154	193	0.3	0.2
12	Rubber goods	96	217	0.2	0.2
13	Stone goods	25	32	0.4	0.5
16	Iron and steel	129	2,009	0.3	3.9
17	Nonferrous metals	97	136	0.6	0.5
18	Foundries	43	51	0.5	0.4
19	Drawing mills, cold rolling mills	40	73	0.2	0.2
30	Wood	26	61	0.3	0.6
32	Pulp, paper, and paperboard	43	38	0.5	0.2
	Investment goods				
20	Structural engineering, rolling stock	114	163	0.7	0.7
21	Mechanical engineering	747	1,819	0.8	1.2
22	Electronic data processing equipment	240	154	2.6	0.6
23	Road vehicles	275	899	0.4	0.5
24	Shipbuilding	242	614	3.9	8.4
25	Aircraft, aerospace	643	727	17.9	8.6
26	Electrical engineering	1,203	1,971	1.3	1.3
27	Precision mechanics, optics, watches	91	214	0.7	1.0
28	Metal products	145	276	0.5	0.6
	Consumer goods				
11	Plastic products	96	217	0.6	0.6
14	Precision ceramics	24	57	0.9	1.3
15	Glass and glass products	35	78	0.5	0.7

Table 16-8 (cont.)

Sector	Industry	Absolute Amount (Millions of DM)		Producer Subsidy Equivalent, s (%)[a]	
		1974	1984	1974	1984
29	Musical instruments, toys, sporting goods, jewelry	18	39	0.4	0.5
31	Wood products	78	157	0.3	0.4
33	Paper and paperboard products	63	186	0.5	1.0
34	Printing	282	511	1.9	2.0
35	Leather, leather goods, shoes	12	26	0.2	0.3
36	Textiles	123	175	0.4	0.5
37	Clothing	94	137	0.5	0.6
38, 39	Food and beverages	601	962	0.5	0.5
40	Tobacco	116	242	0.9	1.3
	Nontraded goods				
3, 4, 5	Electricity, gas, water	513	1,072	1.0	0.7
41, 42	Construction	252	741	0.2	0.4
43, 44	Retail and wholesale trade	616	1,343	0.1	0.1
45, 46, 48	Transportation	13,234	19,053	17.0	13.4
45	Railways	10,055	14,325	56.2	66.9
46	Water transport	638	776	6.0	5.5
48	Other transport	2,541	3,952	5.1	3.7
47	Communication (Federal Post Office)	497	2,283	2.0	4.8
49, 50	Banking and insurance	1,081	2,202	1.7	1.5
49	Banking	736	580	1.7	0.6
50	Insurance	345	1,622	2.0	4.1
52–55	Other private services	4,232	12,311	2.6	3.1
52	Hotels and restaurants	283	407	0.9	0.7
53	Education, research, publishing	836	1,802	3.7	3.2
54	Health and veterinary services	2,164	6,906	8.3	12.4
55	Miscellaneous private services	949	3,196	1.2	1.4
1–55, except 51	Business sector	39,764	78,379	1.8	2.0
	Coefficient of variation			2.498	2.558

Source: Calculated from Statistisches Bundesamt (a); see also Table 16-5.

[a]Subsidy divided by gross output, in percent.

Table 16-9 MFN Nominal Tariff Protection, 1978 and 1985
(Percent ad valorem)[a]

Sector	Industry	1978	1985
	Manufacturing		
	Intermediate goods		
9	Chemicals	10.7	6.5
10	Petroleum refining	3.4	2.8
12	Rubber goods	9.6	6.3
13	Stone goods	5.6	4.2
16	Iron and steel	6.5	4.7
17	Nonferrous metals	6.4	5.3
18	Foundries	7.5	5.2
19	Drawing mills, cold rolling mills	7.4	5.2
30	Wood	6.7	5.1
32	Pulp, paper, and paperboard	8.0	5.9
	Investment goods		
20	Structural engineering, rolling stock	5.5	4.1
21	Mechanical engineering	6.2	4.1
22	Electronic data processing equipment	8.1	5.9
23	Road vehicles	11.0	10.0
24	Shipbuilding	2.8	2.4
25	Aircraft, aerospace	8.0	6.5
26	Electrical engineering	8.4	5.5
27	Precision mechanics, optics, watches	9.4	5.6
28	Metal products	7.8	5.6
	Consumer goods		
11	Plastic products	11.7	6.1
14	Precision ceramics	7.2	5.1
15	Glass and glass products	8.5	5.9
29	Musical instruments, toys, sporting goods, jewelry	8.3	7.2
31	Wood products	9.0	5.4
33	Paper and paperboard products	12.2	8.9
34	Printing	4.2	2.7
35	Leather, leather goods, shoes	7.7	6.1
36	Textiles	13.0	9.7
37	Clothing	16.1	12.5
	Average	8.8	6.3
	Coefficient of variation	0.355	0.365

Source: Werner and Willms (1984), supplemented by Bundesministerium der Finanzen, Deutscher Gebrauchszolltarif.

[a]Mining, except coal mining, is duty free. The tariff on cigarettes amounts to 90 percent, and that on cured tobacco 52 percent.

Table 16-10 Effective Tariff Protection in Japan, 1972–87[a]

Sector	Industry	1972	1975	1987
1, 2	Agriculture, forestry, fisheries	2.8	4.9	6.7
6–8	Mining	−0.7	−0.7	−0.5
	Manufacturing	14.4	25.3	22.0
9	Chemicals	8.8	15.4	11.6
10	Petroleum refining	7.1	12.6	19.2
12, pt. 35	Rubber goods, leather goods	12.3	16.9	14.1
13	Stone goods	8.1	11.6	8.4
16, 19	Iron and steel, rolling mills	17.1	57.3	19.5
17	Nonferrous metals	22.1	30.3	20.8
32	Pulp, paper, and paperboard	11.0	17.3	9.4
21	Mechanical engineering	8.7	8.7	6.2
23, 24	Road vehicles, shipbuilding	9.2	7.1	2.8
26	Electrical engineering	5.4	10.2	7.4
27	Precision mechanics, optics, watches	10.4	8.6	6.2
28	Metal products	9.9	10.3	6.5
31	Wood products	16.1	22.2	18.1
34	Printing	−0.9	−8.3	−0.6
36	Textiles	18.6	38.6	38.3
38, 39	Food and beverages	42.8	67.5	103.9

Source: Shouda (1982).

[a]Based on unweighted nominal tariffs. Allocated to German industry classification where reasonable.

APPENDIX 16-2

Factor content computations were made using the following countries:

Europe	Asia/Oceania	America
Austria	Australia	Canada
Denmark	Hong Kong	Chile
Finland	India	Columbia
France	Japan	Costa Rica
Greece	Korea	Ecuador
Ireland	New Zealand	Mexico
Italy	Philippines	United States
Netherlands	Saudi Arabia	
Norway	Sri Lanka	
Portugal	Turkey	
Spain		
Sweden		
United Kingdom		International standard industrial classification (ISIC) of all economic activities

Commodity classification	
1. Agriculture	
2. Forestry	
3. Electricity, gas, etc.	4
4. Coal mining	210
5. Other mining	290
6. Chemicals	351–56
7. Pottery, glass, nonmetal not elsewhere classified	361, 362, 369
8. Metals	371, 372
9. Metal products	381
10. Machinery not elsewhere classified	382
11. Transport equipment	384
12. Electrical machinery	383
13. Professional goods	385
14. Other industries	390
15. Wood products, furniture	331, 332
16. Paper and paper products	341
17. Printing, publishing	342
18. Leather and leather products, including footwear	323, 324
19. Textiles	321
20. Wearing apparel	322
21. Food, beverages, tobacco	311–14
22. Nontradables	

NOTES

1. This work was carried out by the late Karl-Heinz Jüttemeier.
2. It has been suggested that industrial policy toward the aircraft industry might have been motivated on grounds put forth by Brander and Spencer (1983), namely, that a legitimate case for rent shifting could be made in this industry. At the time that subsidies to the aircraft industry were implemented, during the 1960s, there were in fact notions afloat of maintaining one's position in the international technology race, though nothing as precise as the rent-shifting function of an industrial policy was argued. Our interpretation of the data is somewhat different: although there may indeed be a rationale for industrial policy on these grounds for one industry or another, the overall pattern of industrial policy is best explained by considerations of political economy (see Weiss, Heitger, Jüttemeier, Kirkpatrick, and Klepper, 1988). Later in this chapter the evidence for the overall pattern of assistance to industry is related to the evidence for changes in firm size, for which the rent-shifting hypothesis does make predictions. Whether subsidization of aircraft in Europe can in fact be justified on antimonopoly grounds is subjected to scrutiny by Klepper (1988). The evidence suggests it can be. A noteworthy feature of industrial policy toward the two modern industries which are prominent in the data—aircraft and computers—is that it meets at least some of the criteria of Japanese industrial policy success set forth by Itoh and Kiyono (Chapter 15, this volume). Although the policy has not been strictly temporary, it has been scaled down absolutely for computers and relative to value added in aircraft. Yet success in international competition free of subsidies has not materialized by any means.
3. See the surveys of work on the United States by Deardorff (1985) and on West Germany by Weiss (1983). Work along these lines was carried out initially by Fels (1972) and later by Stern (1975).
4. See, for example, Balassa (1986) and Saxonhouse (1983) for opposing views.
5. Staiger, Deardorff, and Stern (1987) present some tariff equivalents of NTBs in Japan. A comparison of their Table 2 with Table 16-10 of this Chapter confirms this impression.
6. The change in Japanese tariffs has no discernible effect, perhaps because of the increase in the relative importance of NTBs in that country.
7. This is not encouraging many small firms along infant-industry lines. The lines of activity supported are clearly not infants but quite the reverse: they belong in nursing homes, not nurseries.

REFERENCES

Anjaria, S., N. Kirmani, and A. B. Petersen. 1985. "Trade Policy Issues and Developments." IMF Occasional Paper 38. Washington, D.C.

Balassa, B. 1967. *Trade Liberalization among Industrial Countries: Objectives and Alternatives.* New York: McGraw-Hill.

Balassa, B. 1986. "Japan's Trade Policies." In H. Giersch, ed., *Free Trade in the World Economy: Towards an Opening of Markets.* Tübingen: Mohr, pp. 111–70.

Baldwin, J. R., and P. K. Gorecki. 1985. "The Determinants of Small Plant Market Share in Canadian Manufacuring Industries in the 1970s." *Review of Economics and Statistics* 67, 156–61.

Baumgart, E., S. Boehme, and J. Schintke. Produktionsvolumen und -potential, Produktionsfaktoren des Bergbaus und des Verarbeitenden Gewerbes in der Bundesrepublik Deutschland. Deutsches Institut für Wirtschaftsforschung, Berlin, various years.

Bowen, H. P., E. E. Leamer, and L. Sveikauskas. 1987. "Multicountry, Multifactor Tests of the Factor Abundance Theory." *American Economic Review* 77, 791–809.

Brander, J., and B. J. Spencer. 1983. "International R&D Rivalry and Industrial Strategy." *Review of Economic Studies* 50, 707–22.

Bronckers, M. C. E. J. 1983. "A Legal Anslysis of Protectionist Measures Affecting Japanese Imports into the European Community." In J. H. J. Bourgeois and E. Völker, eds., *Protectionism and the European Community*. Boston: Kluwer Academic Publishers.

Bundesministerium für Ernährung, Landwirtschaft und Forsten. 1985, 1986, 1987. *Statistisches Jahrbuch über Ernährung, Landwirtschaft und Forsten der Bundesrepublik Deutschland.*

Bundesministerium der Finanzen (BMF). 1982. Deutscher Gebrauchszolltarif.

Corden, W. M. 1971. *The Theory of Protection*. Oxford: Clarendon Press.

Deardorff, A. V. 1985. "Major Recent Developments in International Trade Theory." Research Seminar in International Economics, Seminar Discussion Paper No. 150, University of Michigan.

Dicke, H. 1977. *Die Wirkungen strukturpolitischer Massnahmen in der Ernährungsindustrie*. Kieler Studie, No. 144. Tübingen.

Ethier, W. 1977. "The Theory of Effective Protection in General Equilibrium: Effective-Rate Analogues of Nominal Rates." *Canadian Journal of Economics* 10(2), 233–45.

Fels, G. 1972. "The Choice of Industry Mix in the Division of Labor between Developed and Developing Countries." *Weltwirtschaftliches Archiv* 108, 71–121.

Financial Times. 1985. "Japan Keeps VCR Export Curbs." December 16.

Hamilton, C. 1986. "An Assessment of Voluntary Restraints on Hongkong Exports to Europe and the USA." *Economica* 53 (August), 339–50.

Heitger, B., and J. Stehn. 1988. "Protektion in Japan: Interessendruck oder gezielte Industriepolitik?" *Die Weltwirtschaft* 1, 123–37.

Helpman, E. 1984. "The Factor Content of Foreign Trade." *Econmic Journal* 94 (March), 84–94.

Helpman, E., and P. R. Krugman. 1985. *—arket Structure and Foreign Trade*. Cambridge: MIT Press.

Hindley, B. 1986. "European Community Imports of VCR's from Japan." *Journal of World Trade Law* 20, 168–84.

Hayami, Y., and V. W. Ruttan. 1985. *Agricultural Development: An International Perspective*. Baltimore: Johns Hopkins Press.

Horstmann, I., and J. R. Markusen. 1986. "Up the Average Cost Curve: Inefficient Entry and the New Protectionism." *Journal of International Economics* 30, 225–47.

International Labour Office. 1985. *Yearbook of Labour Statistics*. Geneva: ILO.

Klepper, G. 1988. "Simulating Competition in the Market for Large Transport Aircraft." Paper presented at the NBER/CEFR Workshop on Emprical Studies of Strategic Trade Policies, Sussex, July.

Krugman, P. 1980. "Scale Economies, Product Differentiation, and the Pattern of Trade." *American Economic Review* 70, 950–59.

Krugman, P. R. 1987. "Is Free Trade Passé?" *Journal of Economic Perspectives* 1(2), 131–44.

Leamer, E. E. 1984. *Sources of International Comparative Advantage: Theory and Evidence*. Cambridge, Mass.: MIT Press.

Liesner, H. H. 1958. "The European Common Market and British Industry." *Economic Journal* 68, 302–16.

Roningen, V., and A. Yeats. 1976. "Nontariff Distortions of International Trade: Some Preliminary Empirical Evidence." *Weltwirtschaftliches Archiv* 112, 615–25.

Saxonhouse, G. 1983. "What Is All This About Industrial Targetting in Japan?" *World Economy* 6, 253–74.

Shouda, Y. 1982. "Effective Rates of Protection in Japan." *Japan Economic Studies*, No. 11, pp. 68–70.

Staiger, R. W., A. V. Deardorff, and R. M. Stern. 1987. "Employment Effects of Japanese and American Protectionism." In D. Salvatore, ed., *The New Protectionist Threat to World Welfare*. Amsterdam: North-Holland.

Statistisches Bundesamt (Wiesbaden). (a) Fachserie 18: Volkswirtschaftliche Gesamtrechnungen, Reihe 1: *Konten und Standardtabellen*, various annual issues.

Statistisches Bundesamt (Wiesbaden). (b) Fachserie 18: Volkswirtschaftliche Gesamtrechnungen, Reihe 2, *Input–Output Tabellen*, 1980.

Statistisches Bundesamt (Wiesbaden). (c) Fachserie 7: Aussenhandel, Reihe 7: *Aussenhandel nach Ländern und Warengruppen der Industriestatistik*, various issues.

Statistisches Bundesamt (Wiesbaden). (d) Fachserie 4: Bergbau und Verarbeitendes Gewerbe, Reihe 4.1.1: *Beschäftigung, Umsatz und Energieversorgung der Unternehmen und Betriebe im Bergbau und im Verarbeitenden Gewerbe*, various annual issues.

Statistisches Bundesamt (Wiesbaden). (e) Fachserie 16: Löhne und Gehälter, Reihe 2.1: *Arbeiterverdienste in der Industrie*, various annual issues.

Statistisches Bundesamt (Wiesbaden). (f) Fachserie 4: Bergbau und Verarbeitendes Gewerbe, Reihe 4.1.2: *Betriebe, Beschftigte und Umsatz im Bergbau und im Verarbeitenden Gewerbe nach Beschäftigtengrössenklassen*, various annual issues.

Statistisches Bundesamt (Wiesbaden). (g) Fachserie 17: Preise, Reihe 2: *Erzeugerpreise*, various annual issues.

Statistisches Bundesamt (Wiesbaden). (h) *Statistisches Jahrbuch fṙ die Bundesrepublik Deutschland*. 1984.

Stern, R. M. 1975. "Testing Trade Theories." In P. B. Kenen, ed., *International Trade and Finance: Frontiers for Research*. Cambridge: Cambridge University Press, pp. 3–49.

Travis, W. P. 1964. *The Theory of Trade and Protection*. Cambridge, Mass.: Harvard University Press.

Tyers, R., and K. Anderson. 1986. "Restrictions in World Food Markets: A Quantitative Assessment," Background Paper for the World Development Report, The World Bank, Washington, D.C.

United Nations, Commission of the European Communities. 1987. *World Comparisons of Purchasing Power and Real Product for 1980*, Parts 1 and 2. New York: United Nations.

United Nations, Department of International Economic and Social Affairs. 1987. *Energy Statistics Yearbook 1985*. New York: United Nations.

United Nations, Department of International Economic and Social Affairs. 0000. *World Energy Supplies 1950–1974, 1973–1978*. New York: United Nations.

United Nations, Food and Agriculture Organisation. 1977. *Fao Production Yearbook 1976*, Vol. 30. Rome: FAO.

U.S. Department of the Interior. 1987. *Minerals Yearbook 1985*. Vol. 3. Washington, D.C.:

Vernon, R. 1979. "The Product Cycle Hypothesis in a New International Environment." *Oxford Bulletin of Economics and Statistics* 41, 255–67.

Weiss, F. D. 1983. "The Structure of International Competitiveness in the Federal Republic of Germany. An Appraisal." World Bank Staff Working Paper No. 571, World Bank, Washington, D.C.

Weiss, F. D., B. Heitger, K. H. Jttemeier, G. Kirkpatrick, and G. Klepper. 1988. *Trade Policy in West Germany.* Kieler Studie, No. 217. Tübingen.

Werner, H., and D. Willms. 1984. "Zollstruktur und Effektivzölle nach der Tokio-Runde, Die Auswirkungen der Tokio-Runde auf die Tarifeskalation und die Effektivzölle der Bundesrepublik Deutschland und der EG." Cologne: Institut fur Wirtschaftspolitik an de Universitat Köln.

Zeitschrift für Zölle und Verbrauchssteuern. Siegburg, various issues.

Index

Adams, F. Gerard, "Productivity, Competitiveness, And Export Growth in Developing Countries," 80–96

Adelman, Irma, "U.S. Competitiveness and the Exchange Rate: A General Equilibrium Analysis of the U.S. Economy, 1982–86," 276–98

Adult literacy, economic growth and, 85

Advanced technology goods, 353

African countries, economic growth rate (1974–86), 80

Aggregate absorption, U.S. (1982–86), 284, 288

Aggregate productivity
international comparisons, 49–79
multisectoral, U.S./Germany/Japan, 177–90

"Aggregate Productivity and Growth in an International Comparative Setting" (Helliwell & Chung), 49–79

Agricultural trade, U.S.
revaluation of real exchange rate (1982–86), 290–91
surplus, 41

Agriculture industry
decline in employment, 34
postwar subsidization in Japan, 349
U.S./Japan relative prices (1960–85), 220
West German subsidies, 366

Agriculture collectivization, 109–10

Airline industry
deregulation and, 47
West German subsidies, 366

Alcohol tax, for reducing U.S. budget deficit, 319

Allen partial elasticity of substitution (AES)
formula, 180
comparisons for manufacturing sectors, U.S./Japan/Germany, 184–85

Apparel industry, U.S./Japan relative prices (1960–85), 222

Argentina
annual output per worker, 81
economic growth rate (1974–86), 80

Arms trade, 115, 122

Australia, 41

Automobile industry
Japan:
EC export restraints (1980s), 366
protection policy, 350
postwar development, 345
U.S./Japan:
productivity gap (1980–85), 215, 221
relative prices (1960–85), 221

Balassa's & Liesner's revealed camparative advantage (RCA) measure, 367, 370–71

Barter agreements, bilateral, 113

Basic technology goods, 351–53

Behrman, Jere R., "Productivity, Competitiveness, and Export Growth in Developing Countries," 80–96

Benelux countries, 41
manufacturing unit labor costs, 139–41

Bilateral barter agreements, 113

Biotechnology, 300

Boldin, Michael, "Productivity, Competitiveness, and Export Growth in Developing Countries," 80–96

393

Border restriction measures/policies, 365
    infant-industry protection and, 350
Borderline technology goods, 353–54
Boskin, Michael, growth theory, 303–05
Branson, William H., "Price and Output
    Adjustment in Japanese
    Manufacturing," 329–44
Brazil, annual productivity growth rate,
    81
Budget deficit, U.S. *See* U.S. budget
    deficit
Bulgaria, productivity growth (1950–85),
    105
Business machine products. *See also*
    Computer industry
    productivity growth rates:
        U.S./Germany, 144, 147
        U.S./Japan/Germany, 151, 155

Canada, productivity/cost trends in
    manufacturing (1960–87), 137–57
Capacity expansion, investment and,
    West Germany, 375–76
Capacity utilization, 162
Capital. *See also* Capital formation; Cost
    of capital
    intangible, 308
    OECD countries:
        marginal productivities (1963–86),
            166, 167
        PPPs for (1975), 166
    OPE comparisons, U.S./Japan/
        Germany, 185–87
    shadow value, 161
    U.S./Japan inputs, relative price
        indexes, 208–12
Capital deepening, 4
Capital expansion. *See* Capital formation
Capital formation
    CPEs, 106, 108
    economic growth and, 303
    economic restructuring and, 44–45
    from foreign sources, economic growth
        and, 11, 50–53
    growth rates in U.S. manufacturing, 38
    relative labor costs, exchange rates
        and, 267–70
    technical change and, 299–325
Capital-intensive industries, 345
Capital-labor ratios, national productivity
    and, U.S./Japan/OECD (1964–84),
    310, 311
Catch-up model, 25. *See also*
    Convergence
    productivity growth, OECD countries,
    55, 56–57

Centrally-planned economies (CPEs), 13–
    14
    convergence, 98–99
    economic growth strategy, 109–11
    economic reforms, 99–100, 126–
        28
    joint ventures, 127
    productivity and competitiveness in,
        13–14, 97–133
        1950–85, 102–09
    trade patterns & policies, 99, 112–26
CES production functions
    aggregate productivity of OECD, 54
    manufacturing productivity, U.S./
        Japan/Germany, 16, 178, 180–
        82
CGE model, of U.S. economy, 277, 278–
    96
Chemicals industry
    increasing U.S. exports, 314
    Japan:
        postwar protection policy, 348
        price changes (1974–86), 334–39
    postwar development, 345
    U.S./Japan:
        productivity growth rates (1973–85),
            147, 151
        relative prices (1960–85), 222
China, People's Republic of, 42
    participation in world economy, 46
Chung, Alan, "Aggregate Productivity
    and Growth in an International
    Comparative Setting," 49–79
Clothes. *See* Apparel industry
Coal. *See* Petroleum & coal
Cobb-Douglas production functions, 4,
    230, 231–32
    developing countries, 83–86
    export competitiveness, U.S./Japan,
        234, 247–51
Competitive power, estimating, 187, 188
Competitiveness, international. *See also*
    Cost competitiveness; Price
    competitiveness; U.S.
    competitiveness
    capital formation and, 45
    China, 46
    criteria for measuring, 98–99
    export growth and, in developing
        countries, 12, 80–96
    measures of, 6–8
    microeconomic view, 364
    policies for achieving, 46–48
    productivity and, 60–63
        comparisons for U.S./Japan (1960–
            85), 17–18, 203–29

multisectoral production model,
U.S./Japan/Germany, 16–17, 177–
202
socialist countries, 13–14, 97–133
Schumpeterian competition, 302
Soviet Union, 46
trade structures/policies and, 99, 101–02
trade protection and, West Germany,
364–91
Computable general equilibrium (CGE)
model, of U.S. economy, 277,
278–96
Computer industry
postwar development, 345
Japan's protection policy, 348
U.S./Japan/Germany productivity
growth rates (1973–85), 154–55
Conrad, Klaus, "Intercountry Changes in
Productivity in the Manufacturing
Sector of Five OECD Countries,
1963–86," 158–76
Constant return to scale (CRTS)
production function, for measuring
OECD manufacturing productivity
gaps, 159–60
Construction industry, U.S./Japan
relative prices (1960–85), 220
Convergence, 25–26, 52, 101
"follower" countries, 98, 101
international trade and, 59–64
OECD countries, 54–57
slowdown, socialist countries, 13, 97
U.S./Japan industry productivity levels
(1960–85), 224
Corporate tax reduction, 319–20
Cost change
due to technical progress, international
comparisons, 187–89
formula, 187
Cost competitiveness
U.S. wage compensation and (1960–
present), 260
U.S./Japan manufacturing industries
(1957–86), 18, 230–52
worldwide (1960–present), 43
Cost gap measure, 160–61
Cost of capital
investment and, 310
U.S. interest rates and, 320
CPEs. See Centrally-planned economies
Currency convertibility, ruble, 127
Current-account balance, U.S., 308, 312

Defense spending
economic growth and, 90
U.S., gradual reduction, 318

Demand elasticities, Japanese, price
markup and, 331, 332–34, 339–41
Demand-side economics, 306
Denison's method, for calculating TFP,
197–99, 200
Deregulation, international
competitiveness and, 47
Developing countries. See also Less
developed countries
after World War II, 33
convergence hypothesis and, 52–53
debt, import restriction and, 39–40
growth of trade and, 40
productivity and export growth in, 12,
80–96
production function estimates (1974–
86), 83–86
reduced-form equations, 91–92
Dollar, CPI-adjusted, 264, 265
Dollar appreciation/depreciation
foreign investors and, 316–17
U.S. budget deficit and, 267, 315
U.S. external trade balance and, 255–
75, 316
U.S. real interest rates and, 264–67
Dollar revaluation, U.S. competitiveness,
exports and (1982–86), 288–89
Duopoly market, 359–60, 365

East Asian countries, convergence
slowdown, 97
Eastern European countries
convergence, 98–99
economic growth strategy, 109–11
economic reforms, 98, 99–100, 126–
28
joint ventures, 127
productivity and competitiveness in,
13–14, 97–133
1950–85, 102–09
trade patterns & policies, 99, 112–26
Economic Analysis, U.S. Bureau of,
141
Economic growth/development
aggregate productivity and, 49–79
convergence hypothesis, 52
export growth and (1974–86), 80–96
export-led, 11, 51–52
government spending and, 90
increasing, 303–06
investment, savings and, 11, 50–53,
303
reduced-form equations for middle-
income countries, 91–92
social climate and, 313
socialist strategy, 109–11

Economic growth/development
(*Continued*)
technological change and, in U.S.,
301–03
trade structure/policies and, 101
Economic interdependence, among
nations, 299–300
Economic policies, U.S., 313–21. *See
also* Macroeconomic policies
Economic reforms, socialist countries,
98, 99–100, 126–28
Economic restructuring, 10, 33–48
capital formation and, 44–45
developing countries debt and, 39–40
employment opportunities and, 34–35
international competitiveness and,
policy considerations, 46–48
international trade flows and, 39–42
manufacturing productivity and, 35–38
process of, 42–46
profit margin factor, 43–44
trade imbalances and, 42
trade in international finance and, 41–
42
United Kingdom, 38–39
Economics
demand-side, 306
supply-side, 306
Economies of scale, 345
Education & research
economic growth and, 85
importance, trade competitiveness and,
45
levels in CPEs, 112
Elasticity of demand, Japan, 331, 332–33,
339–41
Elasticity of substitution (ES)
AES formula, 180
large values, international
competitiveness and, 188–89
manufacturing sectors of U.S./Japan/
Germany:
AES estimates, 184–85
OPEs, 185–87
Nemoto's estimates for Japan, 200
Electricity & gas, U.S./Japan relative
prices of outputs, 213, 221
Electronics industry, Japan's protection
policy, 348
Employment. *See also* Labor force
economic restructuring and, 34–35
U.S.:
trade-related industries and, 276
U.S./EEC/Japan job formation
(1955–88), 307

Endogenous technology, 302
Energy industry. *See also* Petroleum &
gas
OECD countries:
marginal productivities (1963–86),
166, 167
PPPs (1975), 166
OPE comparisons of U.S./Japan/
Germany, 185–87
U.S./Japan inputs, relative price
indexes, 208–12
Energy consumption, U.S., reducing, 319
Energy crisis (1973), 10, 48
international trade and, 40
U.S./Japan:
efforts to restrict oil consumption
after, 237
impact on productivity industrial
growth, 218, 220
price indexes and, 209
technical change comparisons for,
182–84
world productivity slowdown and, 10,
24–25, 43
Energy policy, international
competitiveness and, 48
Entitlements freeze, 318
Euler's law, 330
Europe. *See also* Eastern European
countries; European Communities;
OECD countries
capital formation, 45
employment levels, 35
productivity and cost trends in
manufacturing, 137–57
European Communities (EC)
international trade and, 365
restraints on Japanese exports (1980s),
366
European Monetary System (EMS),
315
Exchange rates, 9–10. *See also*
Purchasing-power parities; U.S.
exchange rates
competitiveness, productivity and, 26,
60–63
estimating competitive power using,
187, 188
macroeconomic policies and, 263–67
profit margin factor and, 44
relative prices and, 203
variations, manufacturing sector and,
329
world trade imbalances and, 42
yen-dollar, 203

Exogenous technology, 302
Export growth
  Feder model, 86–90
  productivity and, in developing
    countries, 12, 86–92
  reduced-form equations for middle-
    income countries, 91–92
Exports. *See also* U.S. exports
  CPEs and Soviet Union (1962–85),
    115–26
  economic growth and, 11, 51–52
  factor content, West Germany, 376–
    81
  Japan:
    price changes (1974–86), 334–
      39
    prices of, yen fluctuations and, 329–
      44
    promotion by tax incentives, 349,
      352
  price indexes, 44
  worldwide, growth rate estimates
    (1965–85), 33–34

Factor content of trade, 365, 376
  model for, 376–81
"Factor utilization" approach, 54
Farm subsidies, U.S. budget deficit
  reduction and, 318
Feder model, for measuring export and
  productivity growth, 86–90
Federal Reserve Board, U.S. real interest
  rates and, 264
Finance industry, U.S./Japan relative
  prices (1960–85), 222
Financial innovation, 41
Financial services, trade in, 41–42
Fiscal policies, international
  competitiveness and, 46–47
"Follower" countries, 98, 101
Food industry
  productivity growth rates, 151
  U.S./Japan relative prices (1960–85),
    220
Foreign borrowing, U.S.
  competitiveness, exchange rates
    and (1982–86), 288–91, 295
Foreign trade. *See* Trade
France
  economic growth and national
    investment in, 303
  OECD productivity gap comparisons,
    166–70
Furniture industry, U.S./Japan relative
  prices (1960–85), 221

Garganas, N., 35
Gas. *See* Electricity & gas
Gasoline user fee, U.S. budget deficit
  reduction and, 319
GATT, 357
GDP. *See also* Per capita GDP income
  growth
  global (since 1950), 300
  relative prices of, PPPs and, 204
Germany, West
  economic growth and national
    investment in, 303
  economic status after World War II,
    33
  growth in manufacturing component
    industries (1960–85), 142–55
  industrial subsidies, 366–67, 368–69
  multisectoral production model,
    international comparisons, 16–17,
    177–202
  OECD productivity gap comparisons,
    166–70
  protection and international
    competitiveness in, 364–91
  RCA estimates (1978, 1985), 370–71,
    373
  technical change/progress comparisons
    (1949–86), 182–84
  trade surplus, 42
  trade tariffs (1978, 1985), 365–66
  unit labor costs (1960–present), 43
Globalization, aggregate productivity
  and, 57–60
GNP. *See also* U.S. GNP
  per capita income growth and
    investment, 11, 50–53
Government deficit, U.S. (1982–86), 288.
  See also U.S. budget deficit; U.S.
  trade deficit
Government service, 35
Government spending, economic growth
  and, 90
Gramm-Rudman-Hollings Act, 318
Gross domestic product. *See* GDP; Per
  capita GDP income growth
Gross national product. *See* GNP; U.S.
  GNP
Gross product originating in
  manufacturing, value of measure,
  141
Growth theories
  Boskin, 303–05
  Solow, 302, 305
Guatamala, annual productivity growth
  rate, 81

Harrod-neutral technical change/
progress, 25
OECD measures, 56
Heckscher-Ohlin framework, 364,
365
Heckscher-Ohlin-Vanek theorem, 376
Helliwell, John F., "Aggregate
Productivity and Growth in an
International Comparative
Setting," 49–79
Hickman, Bert G., "International
Productivity and Competitiveness:
An Overview," 3–30
Hicks-neutral technical change, 5, 182–84
formula, 4
High-tech industries, in Japan, 348, 349,
350. *See also* Computer industry
Hong Kong, 41
economic growth rate (1974–86), 80
Hooper, Peter, "Macroeconomic
Policies, Competitiveness, and
U.S. External Adjustment," 255–
75
Hourly compensation
costs in manufacturing sector, market
economies (since 1960), 138
relative U.S. rates (1960–88), 260,
261

Imports
price indexes, 44
percentages by sector (1982), 283
restriction:
industrial promotion and, 360–61
Japanese tariffs, 348, 350, 351
national debt of developing countries
and, 39–40
U.S.:
elasticities of substitution by sector
(1982), 283
growth rate (1982–86), 284
Income growth, CPEs (1950–85), 103,
104. *See also* Per capita GDP
income growth
Income indexes, U.S., CGE model
estimates (1982, 1986), 287
Increasing returns to scale, 355–56
Industrial assistance. *See also* Subsidies
rates in West Germany (mid-70s, mid-
80s), 366, 368–69
Industrial development, socialist
countries, 109–11
Industrial economies of scale, 345
Industrial policies
and postwar growth of Japan, 22–23,
345–61

international competitiveness and, 47
West Germany, 365–67
Industrial targeting, 22, 347
Industrialized countries. *See also*
France; Germany, West; Japan;
OECD countries; Soviet Union;
United Kingdom; United States
economic growth rate (1974–86), 80
export performance (1974–86), 82
Feder model, 86–90
production function estimates (1974–
86), 83–86
Industries
common sector classifications, 207
expansion of, cost reduction and, 354–
57
Inefficient exit or entry, 375
Infant-industry protection policies,
postwar Japan, 347–54, 357–58
Inflation/deflation
capital formation and, 45
U.S., 312
U.S./Japan, energy crisis and, 209, 211
"Intercountry Changes in Productivity in
the Manufacturing Sector of Five
OECD Countries, 1963–86"
(Conrad), 158–76
Interest rates. *See also* Real interest rates
capital formation and, 45
reducing budget deficit and, 314
U.S., cost of capital and, 320
"International Comparison of
Manufacturing Productivity and
Unit Labor Cost Trends, An"
(Neef), 137–57
"International Comparison of the
Multisectoral Production Structure
of the United States, West
Germany, and Japan, An" (Saito
& Tokutsu), 177–202
International Comparison Project (ICP),
9, 12
"International Competitiveness of U.S.
and Japanese Manufacturing
Industries" (Tange), 230–52
International competitiveness. *See*
Competitiveness, international
International finance, trade in, 41–42
International policy coordination,
competitiveness and, 47
International Price Indexes, and real
GDP per capita relative to U.S.
(1980, 1985), 61–63
"International Productivity and
Competitiveness: An Overview"
(Hickman), 3–30

Investment. *See* Savings & investment
Italy, OECD productivity gap
   comparisons, 166–70
Itoh, Motoshige, "The Trade and
   Industrial Policies of Postwar
   Japan: A Theoretical Perspective,"
   345–61
Ivory Coast, annual productivity growth
   rate, 81

Japan
   bilateral trade with Germany (1978–85),
      372, 374
   capital formation, 44, 45
   cost of capital and investment, 310
   EC export restraints (1980s), 366
   economic growth and national
      investment in, 303
   economic status after World War II,
      33
   import tariffs, 348, 350, 351
   job formation (1955–88), 307
   labor productivity growth rates:
      1960–present, 43
      1964–86, 302–03
   manufacturing sector:
      cost competitiveness comparison
         with U.S. (1957–86), 18, 230–52
      growth in component industries
         (1960–85), 142–55
      price and output adjustment in, 329–
         44
      productivity and cost trends in, 137–
         57
   multisectoral production model of
      competitiveness levels,
      international comparisons, 16–17,
      177–202
   Nemoto's cross-sectional study, 200
   postwar, trade and industrial policies,
      22–23, 345–61
   product quality, 45
   productivity and international
      competitiveness, U.S. and (1960–
      85), 17–18, 203–29
   real income growth rate, 300
   savings and productivity growth rates
      (1960–85), 310, 311
   social climate & economic growth in,
      313
   tariff protection in, 372, 374
   technical change/progress comparisons
      (1949–86), 182–84
   trade imbalance with U.S., 203
   trade surplus, 42
   unit labor costs (1960–present), 43

Job formation, U.S./EEC/Japan (1955–
   88), 307
Job satisfaction, productivity and, 45
Joint cost function, 160, 170, 171
Joint ventures, socialist/non-socialist, 127
Jordan, 53
Jorgenson, Dale W., "Productivity and
   International Competitiveness in
   Japan and the United States, 1960–
   85," 203–29

Kenessey, Zoltan, 35
Kiyono, Kazuharu, "The Trade and
   Industrial Policies of Postwar
   Japan: A Theoretical Perspective,"
   345–61
Klein, Lawrence R., "Restructuring of
   the World Economy," 33–48
KLEM production functions, 48
   U.S./Japan/Germany, 16, 180–82
Klepper, Gernot, "Protection and
   International Competitiveness: A
   View from West Germany," 364–
   91
Korea, South
   annual productivity growth rate, 81
   cost competitiveness, 43
   trade surplus, 42
Kuroda, Masahiro, "Productivity and
   International Competitiveness in
   Japan and the United States, 1960–
   85," 203–29

Labor
   marginal productivities, OECD
      countries (1963–86), 166, 167
   OPE comparisons of U.S./Japan/
      Germany, 185–87
   PPPs for, OECD countries (1975), 166
   U.S./Japan inputs, relative price
      indexes, 208–12
Labor costs. *See* Unit labor costs
Labor force
   distribution worldwide (1965, 1980), 34
   improvements in quality, economic
      growth and, 303–04
   job formation, U.S./EEC/Japan (1955–
      88), 307
   self-employed, 143
   rates of participation of CPEs (1950–
      85), 103, 104, 106
Labor productivity, 5. *See also* U.S.
      labor productivity
   aggregate measure, 143
   CPEs, 103, 105, 107
   developing countries (1974–86), 80–81

Labor productivity (*Continued*)
  formula, 4
  growth rates (1960–79), 43
  Japanese rates (1964–86), 302–03
  protection policies in West Germany
    and, 375
  unit labor costs and, in manufacturing
    sector of market economies, 137–
    57
  vs total factor productivity, 102
Labor Statistics, U.S. Bureau of, 137
Landau, Ralph, "Technology, Capital
    Formation and U.S.
    Competitiveness," 299–325
Latin America, convergence slowdown,
    97
LDCs. *See* Less developed countries
Leather industry, U.S./Japan relative
    prices (1960–85), 223
Leontief-type input-output formula, 177–
    79
Less developed countries (LDCs)
  debt, import restriction and, 39–40
  machine exports (1962–85), 124, 125
Liesner's & Balassa's revealed
    camparative advantage (RCA)
    measure, 367, 370–71
Literacy, economic growth and, 85
Low-income countries
  economic growth rate (1974–86), 80
  export performance (1974–86), 82
  Feder model, 86–90
  production function estimates (1974–
    86), 83–86
Lumber industry, U.S./Japan relative
    prices (1960–85), 222

Machine tools industry, postwar Japan's
    protection policy, 348
Machinery industry
  electrical, productivity growth rates,
    145, 151, 155
  exports, socialist countries, 124–26
  Japanese price changes (1974–86), 334–
    36
  nonelectrical, productivity growth
    rates, 144, 145, 147, 151, 154, 155,
    157
  postwar development, 345
  postwar Japan's protection policy, 348,
    349
  U.S./Japan relative prices (1960–85),
    223
Macroeconomic policies
  effects on microeconomy, 306–07

exchange rates and, 263–67
for price control, 315
in Reagan era, 276–77, 284–96
U.S. real estate rates and, 264–67
"Macroeconomic Policies,
    Competitiveness, and U.S.
    External Adjustment" (Hooper),
    255–75
Manufactures exports, 89
  socialist countries, 122
Manufacturing sector. *See also* U.S.
    manufacturing
  economic restructuring and, 35–38
  major R&D investment industries
    (1988), 321
  price and output adjustment in
    Japanese industries, 329–44
  productivity and cost trends in market
    economies, 137–57
  productivity gaps in OECD countries,
    15–16, 158–76
  productivity measures, 7
  motives for investment in, West
    German industries, 375
Marginal costs, markup and, 330, 332–
    34
Marginal productivities, for labor/capital/
    energy, OECD countries (1963–
    86), 166, 167
Market economies, 15. *See also*
    Germany, West; Japan; United
    Kingdom; United States
  comparative studies, 15–18
  multisectoral production model for
    measuring competitiveness of
    U.S./Japan/Germany, 16–17, 177–
    202
  productivity gaps, OECD countries,
    15–16, 158–76
  productivity and cost trends in
    manufacturing, 137–57
  productivity and international
    competitiveness, U.S./Japan
    (1960–85), 17–18, 203–29
  productivity levels (1950–85), 102–
    09
Market exchange rates, *vs* PPPs, 8–10
Markup behavior, Japanese, model, 330–
    34
Marshallian externalities, 354–57
Marston, Richard C., "Price and Output
    Adjustment in Japanese
    Manufacturing," 329–44
Medical equipment industry, postwar
    subsidization in Japan, 349

Metals industry
  increasing U.S. exports, 314
  Japanese price changes (1974–86), 334–36
  postwar Japan's protection policy, 348
  productivity growth rates, 144, 151, 154, 155
  U.S./Japan relative prices (1960–85), 220, 223
Microeconomy
  long-term economic growth and, 306
  macroeconomic policies and, 306–07
Middle Eastern countries
  OPEC countries, international trade and, 40
  savings and investment in, 52–53
Middle-income countries
  economic growth rate (1974–86), 80
  export performance (1974–86), 82
  Feder model, 86–90
  production function estimates (1974–86), 83–86
  productivity levels (1950–85), 102–09
  reduced-form equations for measuring economic growth in, 91–92
  "sources of growth" allocation for, 90
Mining industry, U.S./Japan relative prices (1960–85), 222
Monetary policies, international competitiveness and, 46–47
Motor vehicles. *See* Automobile industry
Mozambique, economic growth rate (1974–86), 80
Multinational corporations, 322

Neef, Arthur, "An International Comparison of Manufacturing Productivity and Unit Labor Cost Trends," 137–57
Nemoto's cross-sectional study of Japan, 200
Netherlands, unit labor costs (1960–present), 43
New technology
  advanced/late-developing countries' trade, 353
  CPEs, 108
  global standards of living and, 300
Newly industrialized economies/countries (NIEs/NICs), 10
  machine exports (1962–85), 124, 125
  product quality, 45
  productivity levels (1950–85), 104
  trade patterns, 115, 119, 121

OECD countries
  machine exports (1962–85), 124, 125
  productivity and income levels (1950–85), 103, 104, 105
  productivity gaps, 15–16, 158–76
  productivity growth, 53–57
  savings and (1960–85), 310, 311
  trade in international finance and, 41
  trade patterns, 115, 119, 121
  unit labor costs (1960–present), 43
Ofer, Gur, "Productivity, Competitiveness, and the Socialist System," 97–133
Oil crisis. *See* Energy crisis
Oligopolistic competition, 357–61
Oman, 53
OPEC countries. *See also* Energy crisis
  international trade and, 40
Output
  measures, 4–5
  per hour, manufacturing sector of market economies (since 1960), 138
  PPPs for, OECD countries (1975), 166
  U.S./Japan industries, relative prices (1970), 208, 209
Output conversions, for purpose of international comparison, 8–10
Own-price elasticities (OPE)
  estimates for manufacturing sectors of U.S./Japan/Germany, 185–87
  large values, flexibility to change and, 187

Paper industry
  increasing U.S. exports, 314
  productivity growth rates, 151, 155
  U.S./Japan relative prices (1960–85), 222
Per capita GDP income growth
  as measure of economic performance, OECD countries, 158
  CPEs (1950–85), 102–09
  increasing, 303–06
  international differences in prices and (1980, 1985), 61–63
  reduced-form equations, middle-income countries, 91–92
  U.S./United Kingdom/Japan, 300
Per capita GNP income growth, investment and, 11, 50–53
Petrochemical industry, 355
Petroleum & coal industry. *See also* Energy *headings*
  postwar Japan's protection policy, 348

Petroleum & coal industry (*Continued*)
   productivity growth rates, 151
   relative prices of outputs, U.S./Japan,
      213, 220
   West German subsidies, 366
Plastics industry, productivity growth
      rates, 151
Policy coordination, worldwide,
      international competitiveness and,
      47
Population growth, income levels and, 80
Precision instruments
   Japanese price changes (1974–86), 334–
      36
   U.S./Japan relative prices (1960–85),
      223
Price adjustments/changes
   in Japanese manufacturing, 329–44
   markups and, 331, 332–34, 339–41
   OPE values and, 185–87
"Price and Output Adjustment in
      Japanese Manufacturing"
      (Branson & Marston), 329–44
Price competitiveness, 7
   productivity and, 66
   U.S., 43
      factors in measuring, 42
      net exports and (1969–87), 258–
         59
      technical change and, comparisons
         for U.S./Japan/Germany, 187–
         89
      unit cost changes and, U.S./Japan
         comparisons (1957–86), 230–52
   U.S./Japan industries (1960–85),
      219–25
Price control, macroeconomic policies
      for, 315
Price conversions, for international
      comparison, 8–10
Price equalization, trade protection and,
      376
Price indexes
   imports and exports, 44
   real GDP per capita relative to U.S.
      (1980, 1985) and, 61–63
   U.S., CGE model estimates (1982,
      1986), 287
Price markup behavior, model, 330–34
Prices, relative. *See* Purchasing-power
      parities; Relative prices
Pricing to market, 22, 329
Printing industry, U.S./Japan relative
      prices (1960–85), 220
Producer prices, U.S., CGE model
      estimates (1982, 1986), 288

Production functions. *See also* CES
      production functions; Cobb-
      Douglas production functions
   constant return to scale (CRTS), 159–
      60
   developing countries (1974–86), 83–86
   formula, 4
   KLEM, 48
   U.S./Japan/Germany, 16, 180–82
   value-added, 48
Productivity. *See also* Labor
      productivity; Productivity gaps;
      Productivity growth; Productivity
      slowdown; Total factor
      productivity
   aggregate:
      economic growth and, 49–79
      international trade and, 57–60
   capital formation and, 44, 45
   concepts & measures, 4–6
   exchange rates and, 26
   growth rates for centrally-planned
      economies (1950–85), 102–09
   international competitiveness and, 60–
      63
   overview, 3–30
   socialist countries, 13–14, 97–133
   U.S./Japan comparisons (1960–85),
      17–18, 203–29
   U.S./Japan/Germany comparisons,
      16–17, 177–202
   manufacturing, measures, 7
   policies for enhancing, 48
   trade performance and, 100–01
   U.S., capital formation and, 308–13
"Productivity and International
      Competitiveness in Japan and the
      United States, 1960–85"
      (Jorgenson & Kuroda), 203–29
Productivity convergence. *See*
      Convergence
Productivity gaps, 25–26
   econometric analysis, 170–74
   equations for measuring, 159–70
   OECD countries, 15–16, 158–76
   technical change and, 174
   U.S./Japan industries, 214, 216–25
Productivity growth
   Cobb-Douglas production function
      estimates, 83–86
   export growth and, in developing
      countries, 12, 86–92
   Feder model, 86–90
   OECD countries, 53–57
   savings and, in U.S./OECD (1960–85),
      310, 311

shift effects, 143, 144, 156
U.S. *vs* EEC (1955–88) job formation
     and, 307
U.S./Japan industries (1960–85), 216–
     17, 224
Productivity slowdown, 10, 24–25
after energy crisis (1973), 43
in manufacturing, since 1973, 138–39,
     144
"Productivity, Competitiveness, and
     Export Growth in Developing
     Countries" (Adams, Behrman &
     Boldin), 80–96
"Productivity, Competitiveness, and the
     Socialist System" (Ofer), 97–
     133
Profit margin, world economic
     restructuring and, 43–44
Project LINK, 35
"Protection and International
     Competitiveness: A View from
     West Germany" (Klepper &
     Weiss), 364–91
Protection policies
postwar Japan, 347–54, 357–58
West Germany, 364–91
Protectionism, in trade, avoiding, 320
Purchasing-power parities (PPPs), 8–10
base-year, 9
estimating competitive power using,
     187, 188
input/output measures, OECD
     countries, 164–67
productivity, competitiveness and, 61
U.S./Japan industries, 204, 205–14

Quaternary sector, 35

Rationalization effect, 375
Reagan administration
international competitiveness and
     exchange rates during (1982–86),
     276–98
U.S. budget deficit and, 276
Real exchange rates, 9–10
overvaluation, U.S. loss of
     international competitiveness and
     (1982–86), 276–98
variations, manufacturing sector and,
     329
Real interest parity, 263–64, 265
Real interest rates, U.S., 264–67
Recession, in U.S., avoiding, 313–19
Relative cost of capital, U.S., 269
Relative price indexes, U.S./Japan
     industries (1960–85), 208–14

Relative prices. *See also* Purchasing-
     power parities (PPPs)
exchange rates and, 203
imported raw material, 337
in international comparisons, 9–10
U.S./Japan industries (1960–85), 220–
     25
Relative productivity. *See* Productivity
"Restructuring of the World Economy"
     (Klein), 33–48
Revealed comparative advantage (RCA)
     measure, West Germany (1978,
     1985), 367, 370–71
Romania, productivity growth (1950–85),
     105
Rubber industry, U.S./Japan relative
     prices (1960–85), 221
Ruble convertibility, 127

Saito, Mitsuo, "An International
     Comparison of the Multisectoral
     Production Structure of the United
     States, West Germany, and
     Japan," 177–202
SAM, for U.S. economy (1982), 281, 282
Saudi Arabia, 53
Savings & investment. *See also* Capital
     formation; U.S. savings &
     investment
as factor in measuring productivity
     growth, 102
CPEs, 106, 108
economic growth and, 11, 50–53, 303
reduced-form equations to measure,
     91–92
economic restructuring and, 44–45
industrial protection policies and, 357–
     58
motives for in German manufacturing
     firms, 375
Scandinavia, 41
Schumpeterian competition, 302
Sectoral real exchange rate, 332, 334,
     337, 338
Selective protection policies, postwar
     Japan, 347–54, 357–58
Self-employed workers, 143
Semiconductor industry
cost reductions in, 355
Japanese industrial protection policy,
     348
postwar industrial development in,
     345
Service sector
growth in U.S. & worldwide
     employment levels, 34–35

Service sector (*Continued*)
 U.S./Japan relative prices (1960–85), 222
Shadow value of capital, 161
Shift effects, in productivity growth, 143, 144, 156
Shipbuilding industry, 355–56
 West German subsidies, 366
Shouda's effective tariff protection calculation, 372
Singapore, 41
Social accounting matrix (SAM), for U.S. economy (1982), 281, 282
Social climate, economic growth and, 313
Socialist countries. *See also* China, People's Republic of; Soviet Union
 collectivization of agriculture, 109–10
 convergence, 98–99
 economic growth strategy, 109–11
 economic reforms, 98, 99–100, 126–28
 industrial development, 109–11
 joint ventures, 127
 participation in world economy, 45–46
 productivity and competitiveness in, 13–14, 97–133 (1950–85), 102–09
 trade patterns & policies, 99, 112–26
Solow, Robert, growth theory of, 302
"Sources of growth" allocation, for middle-income countries, 90
South Korea. *See* Korea, South
Southeast Asian countries, economic growth rate (1974–86), 80
Soviet Union, 42
 economic reforms, 126–28
 joint ventures, 127
 new technology and, 108
 participation in world economy, 46
 productivity and competitiveness in, 97–133
  1950–85, 103, 105
 total factor productivity (1950–80), 103, 106
 trade patterns & policies, 112–26
Stackelberg-leadership theory, 359
Standard of living, U.S., international competitiveness and, 299
Steel industry, 355
 factors affecting production, 355–56
 postwar development, 345
 postwar Japan's protection policy, 348
 West German subsidies, 366
Stone, clay & glass products
 productivity growth rates, 151, 154
 U.S./Japan relative prices (1960–85), 221

Subsidies
 industrial, West Germany, 366–67, 368–69
 industry start-up and, 357
 postwar Japan's manufacturing industries, 348, 349, 351
Substitution, elasticity of. *See* Elasticity of substitution
Superconductivity, 300
Supply-side economics, 306
Switzerland, 41

Taiwan
 economic growth rate (1974–86), 80
 trade surplus, 42
Tange, Toshiko, "International Competitiveness of U.S. and Japanese Manufacturing Industries," 230–52
Tariffs
 industry start-up and, 357
 West Germany (1978, 1985), 365–66
 Japan (1955–79), 348, 350, 351
Tax incentives, postwar, for Japanese exports, 349, 352
Tax reform act, U.S. (1986), 317–18
Tax system, value-added, 318
Taxes, tobacco and alcohol, U.S. budget deficit and, 319
Technical change/progress, 24. *See also* New technology; *and* Technology *headings*
 aggregate productivity and, industrialized countries, 53–57
 capital formation, economic growth and, 303–06
 CPEs, 107–08
 economic development and, 300, 310
 international trade flows and, 39
 measuring, 4, 5
 OECD countries, 11–12, 54–57
 productivity gaps and, 174
 U.S.:
  competitiveness, capital formation and, 299–325
  economic growth and, 301–03
  international competitiveness and, comparisons for U.S./Japan/Germany, 182–84, 187–88
  U.S./Japan manufacturing sector (1957–86), 233, 234
Technology, endogenous *vs* exogenous, 302
Technology gaps
 between leader and follower countries, 101

equations for measuring, 159–70
U.S./Japan industries, 214, 216–25
Technology transfer
CPEs, 113–14
Soviet Union, 113–14
"Technology, Capital Formation and
U.S. Competitiveness" (Landau),
299–325
Technology-intensive industries, 345
Telecommunications industry, 300
Terms of trade, U.S., 257, 258
(1982–86), 284–85
Tertiary sector, 35
Textiles industry
Japanese price changes (1974–86), 334–
36
postwar Japan's protection policy, 348
productivity growth rates, 144, 145,
147, 151
U.S./Japan relative prices (1960–85),
220
Tobacco tax, U.S. budget deficit and, 319
Togo, economic growth rate (1974–86), 80
Tokutsu, Ichiro, "An International
Comparison of the Multisectoral
Production Structure of the United
States, West Germany, and
Japan," 177–202
Tornqvist indexes, for productivity gaps
(1963–86), 164–70
Total cost function, 160
Total factor productivity (TFP), 4–5, 10,
24
CPEs, 106, 107
Denison's method for calculating, 197–
99, 200
for measuring productivity growth, 81–
82
international competitiveness and, 48
slowdown, 24
U.S./Japan manufacturing sector
(1957–86), 233, 234
vs labor productivity, as measure of
productivity, 102
Total government deficit, U.S. (1982–86),
288
Trade. *See also* U.S. external balance;
U.S. trade
advanced technology goods, 352
basic technology goods, 351–52
between advanced and late-developing
countries, 351–53
borderline technology goods, 352
commodity composition of, 365
cost competitiveness and, U.S./Japan,
230, 244

economic restructuring and, 39–42
factor content of, 365, 376–81
factors affecting performance, 100
global:
growth rates (1965–85), 40
restructuring, 33–48
since 1950, 300
international finance, 41–42
productivity and, 57–60, 100–01
socialist countries, 97–133
protectionism in, avoiding, 320
"Trade and Industrial Policies of Postwar
Japan: A Theoretical Perspective,
The" (Itoh & Kiyono), 345–61
Trade deficits/surpluses, 39. *See also*
U.S. trade deficit
foreign exchange rates and, 42
Trade in arms, 115, 122
Trade liberalization, Japan (1955–80),
349, 357–58
Trade participation rates (TPR), CPEs,
113–15
Trade policies & patterns
competitiveness and, 101–02
CPEs, 112–26
Eastern European countries, 99
Soviet Union, 126
economic growth and, 101
industrial growth of postwar Japan, 22–
23, 345–61
West Germany, 365–67
Trade-related industries, U.S.
employment and, 276
Transport industry
Japanese price changes (1974–86), 334–
36
postwar Japan's protection policy, 348
postwar subsidization in Japan, 349
U.S./Japan relative prices (1960–85),
223
Transportation equipment industry
productivity growth rates, 154
U.S./Japan relative prices (1960–85),
221

Uganda, economic growth rate (1974–86),
80
Underclass, U.S., 321
Unit costs
export prices and, 230
U.S./Japan manufacturing sector
(1973–85), 235–43
wholesale prices, export prices and,
Japan, 244
Unit labor costs
in dollars (ULC), 7

Unit labor costs (*Continued*)
   in national currency units (ULCN), 7
   manufacturing sector, market
      economies (since 1960), 139–57
   U.S./foreign manufacturing industries:
      (1960–88), 260–62
      since 1963, 267–70
   worldwide (1960–present), 43
Unit value estimates, 44
United Kingdom
   economic growth, 300
      postwar to 1980, 158
   economic restructuring, 38–39
   labor productivity growth rate (1960–
      present), 43
   OECD productivity gap comparisons,
      166–70
United States. *See also following* U.S.
      headings
   agricultural trade surplus, 41
   avoiding recession in, 313–19
   capital formation, 45
   change in sector employment, 34–35
   computable general equilibrium (CGE)
      economic model, 277, 278–81
   cost of capital and investment, 310
   current-account balance, 308, 312
   dollar and real interest rates, 264–67
   domestic demand and external balance,
      267
   economic growth (1870–1984), 300
      technical change and, 301–02
   economic policies, 313–21
   economic status after World War II,
      33
   employment and trade-related
      industries, 276
   energy problems:
      importance of interventionist policy,
         48
      reducing consumption, 319
   external deficit, reducing, 266–67
   fluctuations in international trade and,
      276
   gradual reduction of defense spending,
      318
   interest rates and cost of capital, 320
   labor productivity growth rates:
      1960–present, 43
      (1964–86), 302–03
   OECD productivity gap comparisons,
      166–70
   price competitiveness, 43
   productivity and international
      competitiveness, U.S./Japan
      (1960–85), 17–18, 203–29

   productivity levels (1950–85), 103
   social climate and economic growth,
      313
   standard of living and international
      competitiveness, 299
   tax reform act (1986), 317–18
   technical change comparisons (1949–
      86), 182–84
   trade imbalance with Japan, 203
   trade in international finance, 41–42
   trade patterns (1962–85), 120
   unit labor costs (1960–present), 43
U.S. budget deficit
   in Reagan administration, 276
   reducing, dollar depreciation and, 267
   reducing it gradually, 314–15
   savings rates and, 312
U.S. Bureau of Economic Analysis, 141
U.S. Bureau of Labor Statistics, 137
U.S. competitiveness, 19, 27–29
   defense budget and, 46
   exchange rates and (1982–86), 276–
      98
   external adjustment and, 255–75
   fiscal/monetary policies and, 46–47
   multisectoral production model, U.S./
      Japan comparisons, 16–17, 177–
      202
   prices, factors in measuring, 42
   productivity and, comparisons (1960–
      85), 17–18, 203–29
   relative unit labor costs (1960–88) and,
      260–62
   savings/investment rates and (1960–85),
      310, 311
   technical change, capital formation
      and, 299–325
U.S. Competitiveness and the Exchange
      Rate: A General Equilibrium
      Analysis of the U.S. Economy,
      1982–86" (Adelman & Robinson),
      276–98
U.S. employment
   trade-related industries and, 276
   U.S./EEC/Japan job formation (1955–
      88), 307
U.S. exchange rates. *See also*
      Purchasing-power parities
   competitiveness and, 42, 43, 44
   labor productivity, external adjustment
      and, 267–70
   macroeconomic policy, real interest
      rates and, 264–67
   overvaluation, loss of international
      competitiveness and (1982–86),
      276–98

productivity, external adjustment and, 255–75
reducing budget deficit and, 315
relative productivity and, 269–70
yen-dollar, 203
U.S. exports
by sector, CGE model estimates (1982, 1986), 283, 289
cost competitiveness and, comparisons, 230, 244
competitiveness, dollar revaluation and (1982–86), 288
elasticities of transformation by sector (1982), 283
increasing in 90s, 314–15
price competitiveness and (1969–87), 258–59
U.S. external balance. *See also* U.S. trade; U.S. trade deficit
productivity, macroeconomic policy and, 255–75
trends (1960s–present), 255–59
U.S. GDP
since 1950, 300
CGE model estimates (1982, 1986), 285, 286
U.S. GNP
manufacturing share (1979–86), 35, 38
real annual growth rate (1982–86), 284
U.S. imports
percentages by sector (1982), 283
U.S. labor productivity
1960–present rates, 43
1964–86 rates, 302–03
exchange rates, external adjustment and, 267–70
manufacturing sector (1973–84), comparisons with Japan, 233–35
vs foreign manufacturing industries (1960–88), 260–61
U.S. manufacturing
change in share of GNP (1979–86), 35, 38
cost competitiveness of Japanese and (1957–86), 18, 230–52
economic restructuring in, 35–38
growth in component industries (1960–85), 142–55
growth of capital stock (1970s, 1980s), 38
hours worked (1970–87), 270, 271
productivity and cost trends in, 137–57

productivity and international competitiveness in:
comparisons (1960–85), 17–18, 203–29
multisectoral production model, 16–17, 177–202
relative unit labor costs (1960–88), 260–62
trade flows, 39
U.S. savings & investment (1951–87), 308, 309
budget deficit reduction and, 314
increasing, 319–20
increasing exports and, 314
productivity growth rates and (1960–85), 311
U.S. trade
cost competitiveness and, U.S./Japan comparison, 230, 244
fluctuations in, the economy and, 276
relative prices (1960–85), 223
shares by sector (1982), 283
terms of trade, 257, 258
U.S. trade deficit, 39, 40, 42
(1986), 276
budget reduction and, 316
U.S./Japan, 203
Uruguay, economic growth rate (1974–86), 80
Utilities. *See* Electricity & gas

Value added factor
measuring, in manufacturing sector, 37
tax system, 318
Variable cost function, 161

Weiss, Frank D., "Protection and International Competitiveness: A View From West Germany," 364–91
West Germany. *See* Germany, West
Women in labor force, CPEs, 106
Work ethic, productivity and, 45
World Bank, world exports growth rates, 33–34

Yemen, 53
Yen appreciation/depreciation
Japanese export prices and, 329–44
Yen/dollar exchange rate, 203
Yen/dollar price indexes, 208–14

Zaire, economic growth rate (1974–86), 80
Zambia, economic growth rate (1974–86), 80